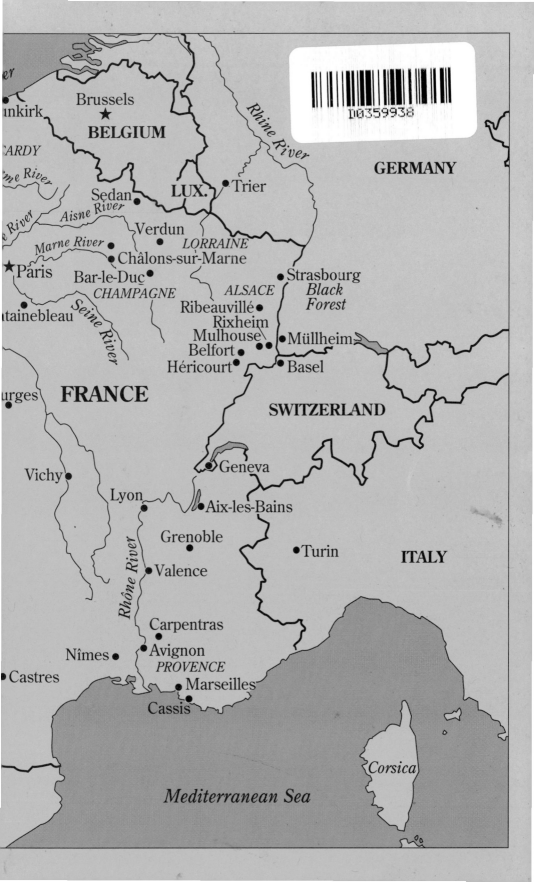

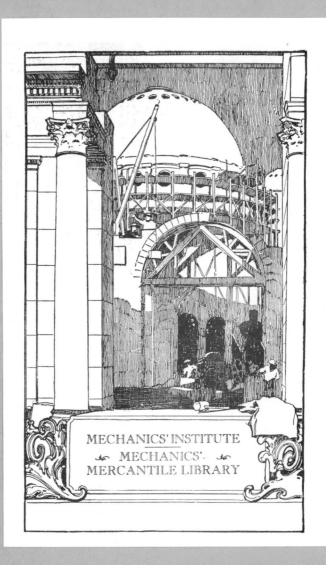

DREYFUS
A FAMILY AFFAIR
1789–1945

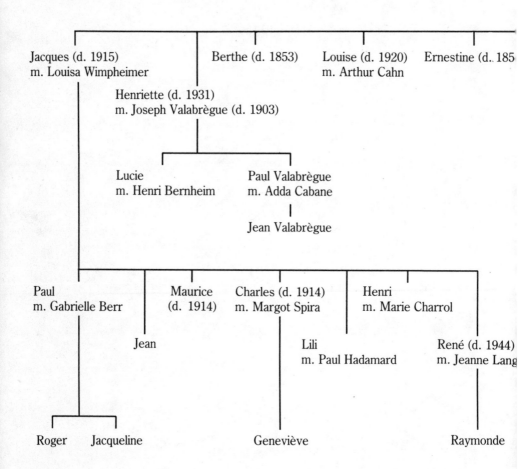

Rösslein (d. 1789?)

Jacques (d. 1915)
m. Louisa Wimpheimer

Berthe (d. 1853)

Louise (d. 1920)
m. Arthur Cahn

Ernestine (d. 185

Henriette (d. 1931)
m. Joseph Valabrègue (d. 1903)

Lucie
m. Henri Bernheim

Paul Valabrègue
m. Adda Cabane

Jean Valabrègue

Paul
m. Gabrielle Berr

Maurice
(d. 1914)

Charles (d. 1914)
m. Margot Spira

Henri
m. Marie Charrol

Jean

Lili
m. Paul Hadamard

René (d. 1944)
m. Jeanne Lang

Roger   Jacqueline

Geneviève

Raymonde

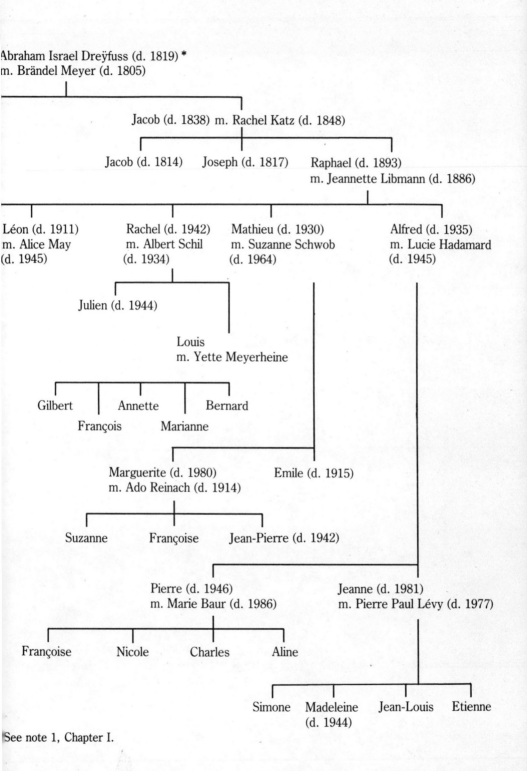

Abraham Israel Dreÿfuss (d. 1819) *
m. Brändel Meyer (d. 1805)

Jacob (d. 1838) m. Rachel Katz (d. 1848)

Jacob (d. 1814)   Joseph (d. 1817)   Raphael (d. 1893)
                                       m. Jeannette Libmann (d. 1886)

Léon (d. 1911)   Rachel (d. 1942)   Mathieu (d. 1930)   Alfred (d. 1935)
m. Alice May   m. Albert Schil   m. Suzanne Schwob   m. Lucie Hadamard
(d. 1945)   (d. 1934)   (d. 1964)   (d. 1945)

Julien (d. 1944)

Louis
m. Yette Meyerheine

Gilbert   Annette   Bernard
    François   Marianne

Marguerite (d. 1980)   Emile (d. 1915)
m. Ado Reinach (d. 1914)

Suzanne   Françoise   Jean-Pierre (d. 1942)

Pierre (d. 1946)   Jeanne (d. 1981)
m. Marie Baur (d. 1986)   m. Pierre Paul Lévy (d. 1977)

Françoise   Nicole   Charles   Aline

Simone   Madeleine   Jean-Louis   Etienne
          (d. 1944)

See note 1, Chapter I.

DREYFUS

A FAMILY AFFAIR

1789–1945

Michael Burns

MECHANICS' INSTITUTE

HarperCollins*Publishers*

FIRST EDITION

Designed by Cassandra J. Pappas

Photo insert designed by Barbara DuPree Knowles

Maps drawn by Paul Pugliese

Library of Congress Cataloging-in-Publication Data

Burns, Michael.
    Dreyfus: a family affair, 1789–1945/Michael Burns.—1st ed.
       p.   cm.
    Includes bibliographical references.
    ISBN 0-06-016366-6
    1. Dreyfus family. 2. Dreyfus, Alfred, 1859–1935—Family.
3. Jews—France—Biography. 4. Jews—France—Cultural
assimilation. 5. Antisemitism—France. 6. France—Ethnic
relations.   7. France—Politics and government—1870–1940.
I. Title.
DC354.B87   1991
944'.004924022—dc20
[B]   90-56350

91 92 93 94 95 AC/RRD 10 9 8 7 6 5 4 3 2 1

For Liz

Contents

x * Contents

ILLUSTRATIONS FOLLOW PAGE 240.

Acknowledgments

In Paris and the French provinces, in England and the United States, research for this book was supported by the Rockefeller Foundation, the American Philosophical Society, the National Endowment for the Humanities, and, through its generous sabbatical and faculty grant programs, Mount Holyoke College. I am grateful to those institutions and to the archivists and librarians on both sides of the Atlantic who guided me through their collections with patience and skill. Daniel Latapie allowed me to consult his superb private archives on the Resistance in the Haute-Garonne; the Camargo Foundation gave me a room—with a view—in which to write; and the staff of the Interlibrary Loan Department at Mount Holyoke College, called on often and at short notice, searched out obscure titles like academic Maigrets.

Among those present with encouragement and faith when I embarked on this book—and through its later stages as well—were Wendy Weil, Aaron Asher, Susanna Barrows, Peter and Ruth Gay, William and Mary McFeely, Jacqueline Weber, Carol Rossen, and Ingeborg Day. I am indebted to them all, as I am to Terry Karten, for being the consummate editor, at once persevering and patient; to copy editor Sue Llewellyn, for a sense of literary style that matches her sense of history; to John Merriman, for his excellent comments and good humor, even in towns like La-Roche-sur-Yon; and to Mavis Gallant, for helping confirm my suspicion that while the affair was the central drama in the

Dreyfus family's history, there were other significant stories to tell. I have also received invaluable insights, and, in some cases, documentation, from Vicki Caron, Mark Peterson, Frances Malino, Eugene Black, Daniel Czitrom, Robert Schwartz, Robert Rothstein, George Whyte, Yvette Baumann Farnoux, Françoise and Raymond Naville, Irma Rabbino, Carol Merriman, Norman L. Kleeblatt, Dr. Michael Levine, and Rabbi Carolyn Braun. I thank again, and always, Sandy Dennis for introducing me to the literature that became my transatlantic passport; and I thank Eugen Weber for having taught me that the historian can be a respectful traveler through the social sciences while maintaining a primary residence in the humanities.

Across more than a half decade, many members of the Dreyfus family have shared with me their documents and their memories. I owe them an enormous debt, and I apologize that I have space to name only a few among them. Dr. Jean-Louis Lévy's splendid epilogue to the 1982 edition of his grandfather Alfred Dreyfus's memoirs prompted my interest in the family; and my first interview with Dr. Lévy in Paris inspired me to press on. My thanks go to him, and to his sister Simone Perl, who was so consistently generous with her time and her family papers and photographs. I also learned a great deal from correspondence and conversations with Charles Dreyfus, Françoise Kullmann, Nicole Bernheim, Gilbert Schil, Naomi and Bertrand Goldschmidt, Geneviève Stirn, Jacqueline Amar, Germaine Franck, Robert Duteil, Jean Valabrègue, Madame Jacques Kayser, and Madame Pierre Dreyfus.

The towering scholar of the Dreyfus affair was Joseph Reinach, and two generations later no complete history of the case or of the Dreyfus family can be written without calling on the expertise of Joseph Reinach and Mathieu Dreyfus's granddaughter, France Reinach Beck. It has been a pleasure to meet with Madame Beck on many occasions in Paris and Séguret, and to receive her intelligent and meticulously researched letters. I thank her for her kindness, her unflagging interest, and her respect for the historian's craft, in which she is a colleague.

Introduction

HISTORIANS, like landscape architects replenishing an old garden, often revisit familiar ground from a new angle. Some scholars are more revisionist than others, more eager to explode the received ideas of traditionalist colleagues; but most historians, unlike most people, thrive on going home again. According to those who count such things (and the data are far from scientific), more books and articles have been written on the subject of Napoleon Bonaparte, for example, than days have passed since the ex-emperor's death on the island of Saint Helena in 1821. That would make something in the neighborhood of sixty thousand titles, an arsenal of literature surpassed in modern European historiography only by accounts, perhaps, of World War I. With just enough exaggeration to make the point, we are told that it would be nearly impossible to digest even the titles of the histories of the "Great War for Civilization" in a lifetime.

The Dreyfus case—the most celebrated affair of the Belle Epoque and the conflict that helped shape the political landscape of modern France—figures lower on the bibliographic list than do Napoleon and World War I. Still, more than one thousand works now in print have described, analyzed, quantified, and deconstructed almost every aspect of the affair, from the military and political intrigues that led to Captain Alfred Dreyfus's arrest for the crime of high treason in 1894, to the anti-Semitism unleashed against the Jewish "traitor," to the novels, manifestos, and memoirs of Marcel Proust, Emile Zola, Anatole France, and legions of lesser literary lights. There is, as one observer put it, a "Himalaya of texts" on the affair, and scores of them have been translated into dozens of languages, from Czech to Japanese. There are other renditions as well; theater pieces (almost all bad) and motion pictures (some of them classics) depict the Dreyfus case, as do paintings, lithographs, posters, card games, and political cartoons. Nor is there a shortage of historical overviews to guide the uninitiated through the maze of frame-ups, forgeries, double agents, and suicides that marked the scandal.

L'Affaire sans Dreyfus (The Affair Without Dreyfus) is what Marcel Thomas called his important history published thirty years ago, and he kept the promise: The captain played a bit part in his own drama. More recently, lawyer and historian Jean-Denis Bredin—in a masterful work of synthesis that builds on the volumes by Dreyfus's friend, Joseph Reinach—described the fate of the prisoner during his affair. But the judicial case and the familiar personalities remained, as always, at center stage. Like the allies and enemies of the epoch, who insisted that Dreyfus served only as a symbol of more cosmic struggles, most historians have preserved the abstraction. With their focus on the major issues and ideologies of anti-Semitism, socialism, militant nationalism, Zionism, and the separation of church and state, they have left to peripheral vision the family that gave its name to the most significant conflict in France since the great Revolution. Charles Péguy, poet and Dreyfusard, insisted that the name Dreyfus, "repeated throughout the world," had become "the most celebrated name since the death of our ruler Napoléon." But the mountain of texts on the affair contains no history of the man or of the family that helped save the prisoner from certain death in exile. If "human beings are too important to be treated as mere symptoms of the past," as Lytton Strachey had it, Alfred Dreyfus and his wife, children, siblings, and in-laws are too important to be left in the shadows of the affair.

But their uniqueness is only part of the story, and not, in many ways, the most telling part. Before and after the affair, the family's history, in its broad outlines, was typical of the history of Jews in France. Through the crisis of the 1890s and its revival in the ideological battles that culminated in the collaborationist Vichy regime of World War II, the Dreyfus family articulated and rearticulated the principles of citizenship and equality on which their successful assimilation into France had been based. The allegiance that sustained Dreyfus on Devil's Island and his family at home had its origins in the revolutionary edict of 1791 that emancipated French Jews and that, over time and with the added ingredients of education and economic prosperity, converted them to the belief that France was a new promised land. A young witness to the Franco-Prussian War of 1870, which severed his Alsatian homeland from his French fatherland, Alfred Dreyfus felt honor bound to serve the nation through its military. And in the same spirit, and out of the same sense of duty, members of his family entered the trenches of 1914–18 and the Resistance movements of World War II.

Their story is a chronicle of two faiths—religious and national— that were often, but not always, in conflict. While some members of the family departed from the Judaism of their ancestors and others observed it, they all held firm to the belief that *Justice* (a word they almost always capitalized) found its deepest roots in French soil. They were not alone. Listen to the testament of a Dreyfusard whose personal history followed a similar path: "I was brought up in the traditions of patriotism which found no more fervent champions than the Jews of the Alsatian exodus," wrote historian Marc Bloch in his 1940 "statement of evidence," *Strange Defeat,* going on to say: "France . . . will remain . . . the one country with which my deepest emotions are inextricably bound up." In his testamentary instructions to his family, Bloch repeated the pledge: "I have loved [France] greatly, and served her with all my strength. I have never found that the fact of being a Jew has at all hindered these sentiments. Though I have fought in two wars, it has not fallen to my lot to die for France. But I can . . . declare that I die now, as I have lived, a good Frenchman." Four summers after he completed his "statement of evidence," the Resistance fighter Marc Bloch fell victim to a Nazi firing squad in a meadow near Lyon. At the same time, across France, members of the Dreyfus family engaged in the same struggle for the same ideals.

Anti-Semitism took its modern form in the crucible of the affair. Religious intolerance and old accusations of Jewish "huckstering" (rekindled by the rapid industrial changes of the nineteenth century) were joined to pseudoscientific notions of race, and most important (because most likely to push the conflict from angry words to calculated public actions), they were exploited in the mass politics of the modern age. Alfred Dreyfus's affair signaled an assault on the entire civil state, on the ideals of·justice and community for which the French Revolution stood. And his affair served as a training ground (Hannah Arendt called it a "dress rehearsal") for twentieth-century leaders who would launch a new, more deadly assault on the French republic—and on Dreyfus's descendants. Through all its trials, that family never wavered in its allegiance to a nation that often wavered in the fulfillment of its promises. The story of how the family's faith evolved begins on the eve of the Revolution in a village far from Paris, close to the Rhine.

PART 1

Out of Alsace

CHAPTER I

Promised Lands

ABRAHAM ISRAEL DREŸFUSS, born in the eastern French village of Rixheim in 1749, grew up a close neighbor of the Teutonic Knights. A few hundred yards from the stone-and-wood Dreÿfuss home, down roads cut by wagon wheels and peddlers' carts, the knights' regional headquarters rose above the central square like the baroque chateau of a minor aristocrat: 150 feet long and three stories high, its two wings enveloped a carefully tended garden. Founded in the twelfth century to convert the heathen by force, the Teutonic Order had turned its crusading attentions from Palestine to the Baltic and into the heart of the Rhineland, and by the late Middle Ages it had established headquarters in Mülhausen near the Swiss border. Protestants won control of that town, however, and the knights decamped again, to nearby Rixheim, where they had owned property for three hundred years, and where, during Abraham Dreÿfuss's youth, fifteen hundred Christians shared the village with two hundred Jews.[1]

Stronghold of a militant Catholic order, Rixheim was also part of a "veritable human and spiritual reservoir" of Judaism in the southern Rhine Valley. Some Jewish families traced their origins in the region to the Roman era or to migration from Italy in the ninth and tenth centuries; others had taken refuge there in the wake of persecutions surrounding the Black Death and expulsion from France in the fourteenth century; and still others were recent arrivals. Rixheim's rocky soil held

3

traces of that history. Under fields of rye, oats, barley, and potatoes, and beneath the stone and gypsum quarries that built the village, lay an elaborate Merovingian city of the dead; deeper still, with civilizations superimposed one upon the other, were the shards of Roman artifacts, the pottery and coins of first-century settlers. Abraham's ancestors seem to have been among the earliest travelers from the Mediterranean: Treveris (later called Trèves, and then Trier) the great Roman encampment north of Rixheim on the Moselle River, provided the linguistic skeleton for his family name. After Germanic tribes pushed Romans from the region in the fifth century, Jewish families who stayed on borrowed the language of the new colonizers and used the words *drei* (three) and *füss* (foot) to approximate the original Latin sound of "Treveris." By the eighteenth century, the name Dreÿfuss, in all its variations, was common among the fifteen thousand Jews who lived in nearly two hundred villages and *bourgs* southeast of the Moselle in the province of Alsace. Bordered on the west by the Vosges Mountains and on the east by the Rhine, the area had passed from Hapsburg rule to French control in the wake of the Thirty Years War.[2]

Unlike the *shtetl* of Eastern Europe, Abraham Dreÿfuss's Rixheim had no clearly marked area of Jewish quarantine. Its tight labyrinth of roads made it a face-to-face village, and the interplay of Jews and Gentiles at market fairs generally prevented rigid barriers of division. On the well-traveled route from Basel, Switzerland, to the Vosges Mountains and on to Paris, and at the juncture of three natural regions—the Hardt Forest, the Sundgau, and the alluvial plain of the Ill River, a tributary of the Rhine—Rixheim attracted peddlers, livestock dealers, roving bandits, itinerant barbers (doubling as doctors or dentists), and other travelers who, welcome or not, followed the seasonal circuits of rural trade. Pigs, cattle, horses, and the brokers who sold them filled the market square with their sounds and smells, and on special days in April and late July more peddlers came from the hinterlands to hawk farm tools, fabrics, and cheap engravings of saints, sinners, folk heroes, and kings. Jewish cantors, assistant cantors, circumcisers, and sellers of Hebrew Bibles traveled the same roads as Christian peddlers until they entered Rixheim to serve their own clientele.[3]

Starting a butcher trade in the 1770s, Abraham provided kosher meat to some of the forty families who observed the dietary laws of *kashrut,* and then, under the strict royal regulations governing commercial dealings between Jews and Gentiles, sold the hindquarters and other "unclean" parts to Gentile villagers who came to the dark, low-ceilinged shop and stable on the ground level of the Dreÿfuss house. Working near leather tanners and close to gutters that washed away the blood and refuse of slaughtered animals, Abraham needed a strong stomach to tolerate the "detestable stench" described by travelers, the "foul odors" that attracted black swarms of "flies and fleas." And he needed the muscle to heft, chop, carve, and dress carcasses, as he must have done from dawn till dusk. No portrait of Abraham Dreÿfuss exists—no sketch, woodcut, engraving, or prose description to confirm that he sported a long beard like other Alsatian Jewish men or that, like his grandsons and great-grandsons, he had steel blue eyes and light brown hair sprinkled prematurely with gray. The details of his appearance are lost, but he must have been a worker of formidable strength and enterprise.[4]

His community, large enough to support its own synagogue and rabbi, also had a *Schulé-klopfer,* a special village crier who tapped shutters three times with a wooden hammer to call families to services. Dressed in their finest clothes, they gathered along Rixheim's synagogue road. Abraham, when he could afford it, would replace his butcher's garb with coarse black trousers, a short blue frock coat, and a shirt with a high collar that touched the back of his narrow-brimmed hat; village women, also in dark garments, added shawls adorned with green palm designs and tulle bonnets laced with red ribbons. Prohibited from lighting fires on the Sabbath, those women prepared Friday evening and Saturday meals in advance, and some left other household duties to a *Schabbés-goié,* a "Sabbath Gentile." Though royal officials condemned the custom of Christians working in Jewish homes, even the most modest rural families had part-time domestics, and the habit persisted throughout Alsace. On Saturdays, Rixheim's Jews worshiped and refrained from labor while other villagers, in muslin smocks and hay-filled wooden clogs, continued chores in fields and shops; on Sundays, the schedules of prayer and labor were reversed.[5]

Changing seasons also brought separate festivities. Farmers gathered for firebrand feasts and May festivals, which fit with planting and harvesting rituals (the calendar of the field blending with the calendar of the church), while Abraham, prohibited by royal decree and local custom from owning land, would join other Jews to commemorate their history. Following the High Holy Days of autumn, and after the raucous feast of Purim and then Passover in early spring, they observed the "great season of the Jewish peddler." Villagers paraded down roads pushing wooden carts filled with new pots and pans—practical reminders of change and regeneration—and with the coming of warmer weather, they placed benches in front of their homes. Day and night they heard the village crier mark the hour in local dialect: *"Horiché vos i eich vel soyé: Die Glock het zvelfi gschoyé"* ("Listen to what I tell you: The clock has struck twelve").[6]

Thirty years old in 1779, Abraham Dreÿfuss met Brändel Meyer, daughter of Jacob, from the Black Forest village of Müllheim ten kilometers across the Rhine. Their introduction may have been arranged by a *shadchan,* a Jewish marriage broker, who, for a small percentage of a bride's dowry, searched for suitable mates in communities throughout the region. Married in Rixheim in February 1780, Abraham and Brändel probably chose a Tuesday, the "lucky day" for Alsatian Jewish weddings.[7]

Brändel Meyer's short journey west from the Black Forest confirmed that the Rhine was not always or for everyone a river of division. It had marked a "shock line" between French Alsace and the Germanic duchy of Baden since the Thirty Years War,[8] but boundaries drawn by kings and generals had nothing to do with the frontiers of peddlers and marriage brokers. One a German subject, the other French, Brändel and Abraham had been raised in strikingly similar worlds—and they spoke the same language, a Judeo-Alsatian dialect that mixed Hebrew-Aramaic, German, and a smattering of French. Close enough to other dialects to facilitate Abraham's butcher trade, it was also the language of "a life apart." A local ballad, referring to German, French, and provincial customs, captured the regional mix: "Three castles on one mountain . . . three churches in one churchyard, three cities in one valley— such is Alsace everywhere."[9] And everywhere there was dialect. For strangers exposed to the sounds of Rixheim's marketplace—with its cacophony of German words, French phrases, Hebrew expressions, and local patois—the village must have seemed like a modern Babel. One British tourist, the indefatigable traveler and writer Arthur Young, visited the area shortly after Abraham and Brändel were married, and found only a handful of locals who knew French (barely one in three hundred), a good number who spoke German, and a vast majority who communicated in bizarre "jargons" incomprehensible to outsiders. Not much had changed in the century since Louis XIV had corrected an ambassador who called Alsatians "more French than the Parisians themselves." Louis knew better; on a visit to the university at Strasbourg he had searched in vain for a single professor who understood the language of Paris. However apocryphal, the story contained a grain of truth, and its lessons applied through the reigns of the Sun King's successors. If Louis XVI had crossed the Vosges on a royal visit to Rixheim in 1780 he would have needed an interpreter. Barely a half dozen villagers could read or write the king's French.[10]

Jacob Dreÿfuss, born in 1781 and named after Brändel's father in keeping with Jewish custom,[11] could learn Hebrew and the basic lessons of rural trade in Rixheim's Jewish elementary school (*heder*). But he would have to travel far and wide to learn French, a language that was in the same lamentable state in Alsace as it was throughout the French interior. As late as 1812 officials complained that barely 20 percent of the teachers in the eastern provinces could give lessons in French, and not even 10 percent could do it effectively. The language had little relevance for families who continued to tell tales, sing ballads, and trade merchandise in the local dialect. Furthermore, royal authorities—most of them strangers and some of them tax collectors— spoke French, and that was enough to queer the language for many villagers.[12]

Country roads and market fairs, rather than school benches, became the most important sites of young Jacob Dreÿfuss's education. Noting the routines of traders and travelers, he set out at an early age to peddle secondhand goods and help with the family budget. The family remained small; Abraham and Brändel had one other child, a daughter they named Rösslein, but she died in infancy, perhaps a victim of a fever epidemic that swept through the region, along with other troubles, in 1789.[13]

The previous fall's harvest had been disastrous, and when hard weather hit in December and the temperature plummeted to below zero, peasants looked ahead to an even more miserable spring and summer. In the best of times Rixheim's soil gave up decent harvests, but the area had never been as fertile as other parts of the Rhine Valley, and the patchwork of vineyards that surrounded the village never produced crops like those from Ribeauvillé or Riquewihr. At least five major agricultural crises had struck in the past four decades, pushing death rates up with the price of grain, and driving down the number of marriages and births. And one of the worst came in 1788–89. The winter freeze gave way to a wet and muddy spring; grain stocks fell and prices rose; and country people not yet stricken by fever or immobilized by famine searched for ways to survive the coming months.[14]

For the Dreÿfuss family the crisis would bring opportunity and danger, both sudden and violent. Engaged in a trade that involved cash income as well as barter, Abraham joined other merchants who doubled as bankers and lent money at interest for the purchase of seeds, livestock, farm tools, and small plots of land. As the only sources of credit in a world in which banking institutions were unknown, local lenders helped neighbors who always had a seasonal need for cash. "Happy the man who far from schemes of business," wrote Horace eighteen centuries before, "works his ancestral acres . . . from all usury free." Never happy by Horace's definition, Rixheim's peasants negotiated with lenders like Abraham. As the foundation of the village economy, the system helped farmers get seeds in and crops out, and it also served artisans, day laborers, and widows who had fallen on hard times. Well-made loans, well invested and paid off annually, benefited lenders and clients alike; but when hard weather, fire, flood, or vermin ravaged crops, the repayment of a loan was jeopardized, and the interest rate agreed on by private contract the season before began to look like usury exacted under pressure.[15]

Contrary to popular belief, or to definitions of "usury" crafted by the Académie Française, moneylending had never been a Jewish monopoly.[16] Christian lenders (innkeepers, well-heeled peasants, priests, and free-lancing government functionaries) were as numerous as Jewish ones and, according to local reports, frequently more stubborn in their negotiations. Still, if the reality was complex, the myth was not, and for centuries it had focused on the Jews. "You shall not lend upon interest to your brother," the Bible instructed, "interest on money, interest on victuals, interest on anything that is lent for interest. To a foreigner you may lend upon interest, but to your brother you shall not."[17] In the palaces and village squares of Christian Europe, popes, kings, feudal lords, and peasants had called on Jews to serve as bankers, and since Jews had been prevented from owning anything but money, they had to live (as one sensible official put it) by making that money valuable. In Parisian dictionaries and in Alsatian legend, however, "Jews" had long been synonymous with "usury" and exploitation.[18]

Early in 1789 "grievance reports" (*cahiers de doléances*) requested by royal officials repeated familiar complaints that southern Alsace had become a center of usury. "Every day, Jews offer pernicious examples of their vexations, graft and duplicitous greed," went one account that spoke for others. "They are the first and principal cause of the people's misery . . . and moral depravation." Some reports called for tighter restrictions on Jewish migration and marriage, and others insisted on "mass expulsion" of the Jews as the only solution. But while local notables and town dwellers drafted official grievances, country people vented their anger in customary ways. In late July peasant gangs gathered in a valley north of Rixheim demanding an end to their debts and threatening the lives and property of their lenders. In the same sweep they attacked priests and seigneurs, the privileged orders who levied taxes and controlled forest rights, and then turned on the Jews. Three to four thousand peasants marched through the village of Uffoltz, where they pillaged Jewish homes until royal troops pushed them back into the hinterlands. Worse rebellions took place closer to the town of Huningue near the Swiss border; and in Durmenach, where Jews outnumbered Gentiles, troubles were constant. In Sierentz and Blotzheim peasants chased Jews into the countryside, and soon the uprising reached Rixheim.[19]

Hearing reports of violence nearby, village families searched for an avenue of escape. Word had it that hundreds of Jews had taken refuge in the Swiss town of Basel or in the small republic of Mülhausen to the west, and as rebels plundered the village and forced moneylenders to cancel all debts, Rixheim's Jews fled to those centers of sanctuary. In their absence the doors, shutters, and floorboards of their homes were torn away, their ovens and stoves destroyed. Some families kept their distance until early fall and then returned to the village to find ransacked houses open to the cold wind blowing off the Jura Mountains; they would "thank God," said one observer, "for a mild winter."[20]

Whichever choice Abraham and Brändel made—if they escaped with their son or took shelter behind the bolted doors of their village home—they were victims of the first large-scale rebellion in Rixheim in living memory. As the headquarters of a militant Catholic order, the village had been the scene of troubles in the past, and Abraham must have witnessed the private feuds that spiraled into public conflict; but through his lifetime none of those incidents had triggered widespread violence, and none had led to the massive flight of Jewish families. Though royal troops stationed along the eastern frontier tried to maintain order, the uprisings of the early summer of 1789 were part of a larger rebellion the king's men could not control. A "great fear" spread across much of the French countryside as peasants seized tax records, burned the châteaus of noble lords, and pillaged the homes of moneylenders, including Christian moneylenders well beyond Alsace.[21]

In the months to come rabbis and peddlers, the carriers of news into Rixheim, described a revolution unfolding in Paris and a gathering of provincial representatives at Versailles. Most immediately the Dreÿ-fuss family would feel the impact of a state decree: "In response to violence perpetrated against Alsatian Jews," went the announcement, the National Assembly informed public authorities that "Jews are under the safeguard of the law" and are assured of the "protection that they need." Through the fall and winter, Alsatian Jews gathered in their communities to hear other reports from Paris and Versailles, accounts that chronicled distant debates over promises of permanent protection. Translating official edicts into the local language that all could comprehend, Rixheim's rabbi would help his 250 coreligionists define new notions—French notions—of justice, citizenship, and the rights of man.[22]

Those debates—like many others—had moved from Parisian clubs to the baroque halls of Versailles and on to a royal tennis court in the early summer of 1789. The defiant guests of an anxious king aimed to replace the arbitrary privileges of their Bourbon host with uniform rights articulated by enlightened leaders. Lawyers, liberal theorists, prosperous merchants, and other members of the Third Estate joined a radical cadre of priests and noblemen to destroy the divisions of the Old Regime. As architects of a new nation, their quest, more passionate than practical in those early and optimistic months, was to design a single community and to make Frenchmen of Bretons, Basques, Flemings, Provençaux, and Alsatians. They struggled with a blueprint for cultural unity.

Most members of the National Assembly treated the Jewish question as a minor subplot to the greater drama of national unification and placed it low on the list of revolutionary priorities. Other issues took precedence, from rebellion in the countryside and on the streets of Paris to debates about the gift of citizenship to actors, public executioners, and Protestants. As for the forty thousand Jews in French territory, less than 1 percent of the population, if they agreed to be patriots of France, their present land, and not Palestine, their Promised Land, they too might enjoy the benefits of liberation and the protection of French law. Choosing integration over separation, they might be invited, with other subjects, to celebrate 1789 as "the birth date, the year zero of a new world founded on equality."[23]

Southwest of Versailles, in the port cities of Bordeaux and Bayonne, Sephardic Jews—those of Spanish and Portuguese origin—had enjoyed special privileges (rewards for their commercial acumen) under the Old Regime, and they knew the benefits of assimilation. By January 1790 revolutionary leaders were prepared to grant those highly acculturated Sephardim the full rights of citizenship; and they would do the same for another small community of Avignon Jews living in Bordeaux. Far to the east, however, toward the Rhine, the vast majority of French Jews—distinguished by Germanic customs, traditional rituals, moneylending practices, and systems of communal autonomy—seemed unlikely candidates for assimilation. Enlightened theories confronted entrenched prejudices, and the debate over full Jewish emancipation stretched on. Fearing that it would spark another "enormous fire" among Alsatian peasants, some deputies in the National Assembly argued against citizenship for Ashkenazic ("Germanic") Jews, while others insisted that if they ceased their "rapacious" usury, if they freed themselves from the "dark phantoms of the Talmudists," and if they abandoned their "judesco-hebraico-rabbinical jargon" they could be incorporated into "universal society."[24] "Let us begin by destroying all the humiliating signs which designate them as Jews," noted one observer, "so that their garb, their outward appearance, shows us that they are fellow citizens." "Let us restore them to happiness," added Maximilien de Robespierre, a provincial lawyer who would make a career of telling citizens how to behave, "by restoring to them the dignity of human beings and of citizens." Deny them "everything as a nation," proclaimed still another advocate of emancipation, Count Clermont-Tonnerre, and grant them "everything as individuals," and they would become useful citizens of the new French nation. If they resisted, he added, "expel them. The existence of a nation within a nation is unacceptable to our country."[25]

Not surprisingly, a deputy from Alsace, a product of his provincial prejudices, emerged as the last holdout on the question of Jewish emancipation. Echoing diatribes that had resonated across the Rhine Valley for centuries, Jean-François Rewbell pleaded with the assembly to understand the plight of his non-Jewish compatriots, that "numerous, industrious and honest class . . . ground down by cruel hordes of Africans who have infested my region."[26] Conjuring up every collective memory of fear and bigotry to condemn "Africans" for their foreign and predatory nature, Rewbell warned that the Jews' chosen separateness would forever keep them a nation of aliens within France. But the president of the assembly, rejecting Rewbell's appeals, announced that an attack on complete emancipation was an attack on the Constitution itself and moved toward a vote.

By the time final debates took place in the late summer of 1791, the promise of assimilation had emerged as part of an unwritten but powerful covenant of freedom. Troubled by issues of cultural and juridical autonomy, deputies were assured by Jewish leaders that citizenship would elicit concessions; one Jewish notable called for his coreligionists to divest themselves "entirely of that narrow spirit, of corporation and congregation, in all civil and political matters, not immediately connected with our spiritual laws . . . we must appear simply as individuals, as Frenchmen." Honoring the Declaration of the Rights of Man and Citizen, Jews would respect the laws of the state and work to overcome the "bondage and abasement" of their poverty-stricken past; and while maintaining freedom of worship, they would dismantle much of their ancient communal structure. A legally separate nation of Jews would become an integrated community of "French Israelites."[27]

On September 27, 1791, deputies voted by an overwhelming margin for the emancipation of the Jews of Alsace and the neighboring province of Lorraine. Formally approving the edict, Louis XVI announced that all previous restrictions on Jews would be abolished, and that every French Jew who "swears the oath of citizenship and fulfills all the duties that the Constitution imposes will have the right to all of its benefits." Nearly two millennia after the destruction of the Second Temple in Jerusalem and the exodus that had brought the first families of the Diaspora to Gaul—families like Abraham Dreÿfuss's, who had pitched camp with Romans at settlements from Provence to the Rhine— the basic rights of civil equality were extended to all Jews in French territory. In Britain, Spain, and Russia, in German and Italian states and beyond, they remained a nation apart—tolerated by some, persecuted by others, denied citizenship by all—while revolutionary France embraced them as compatriots with the force of law. The "Promised Land of the Jews will be the place where they finally secure peace and tranquillity," an advocate of emancipation announced on the eve of the Revolution, and a leading Jewish periodical later proclaimed that the "ancient messianic idea had been realized . . . with the Declaration of the Rights of Man." Another witness praised "these generous French to whom we owe the first example of justice that the world has given to our unfortunate Nation. Yes, my children, this is your fatherland, your Jerusalem, the land that God promised to our ancestors." And in a letter published a few months after the assembly's vote, one French Jew captured the language of gratitude and the celebration of freedom that would be repeated over coming generations: "France, who first wiped out the disgrace of Judah," he wrote, "and broke the shackles of all the captives, she is our land of Israel; her mountains—our Zion; her rivers—our Jordan."[28]

Near the western bank of the Rhine, the river most familiar to the majority of French Jews, the Dreÿfusses faced the local consequences of the Versailles debates. Promised protection in the wake of the "great fear," they had the autumn months of 1789 to repair the damages of July before reports of the emancipation of Sephardic Jews triggered new uprisings. Convinced that full Jewish citizenship would lead to tyranny in Alsace, peasants retraced their steps through Rhine Valley villages in the spring of 1790, and in the following year, on the eve of the September edict, they again forced Rixheim's Jews to fill satchels with what few possessions they could carry and take refuge in Mülhausen or Basel. "How glorious it is for that [French] nation," proclaimed one Jew from the eastern provinces on the morning of emancipation, "which has, in so short a time, made so many people happy!" But only in a few cities, and only for a handful of Jewish leaders, had that dawn been clear or happy.[29]

The oath of citizenship that Jews took *en masse* in the countryside did nothing to spare them the effects of the impending wide conflict. Living along a principal route linking the Rhine to the Vosges Mountains and the French interior, Abraham Dreÿfuss's family would watch that passageway for Alsatian peddlers become a thoroughfare for European armies after 1792. Part of the eastern battleground on which the revolutionary soldiers of the new French regime confronted the troops of Austria and Prussia, Rixheim and its environs attracted the attention of officials who worried about the allegiance of all Alsatian subjects. As the enemy approached, the warnings issued by French authorities ranged from quaint suggestions that women "give up their German fashions because their hearts are French," to more serious attempts to suppress Germanic dialects and purge potential traitors.[30] The Dreÿfuss family would have been uniquely exposed to the ambiguities that war brought to Rixheim; Brändel's Black Forest origins confirmed their ties beyond the Rhine, and Abraham's moneylending conjured up memories—and tall tales—of other wars, in which Jews had provided livestock and cash to enemy troops. The dialect, garb, "Mosaic" beards of Jewish men, and special wigs worn by married women like Brändel Dreÿfuss, along with their separate religious rituals, had always contributed to their image as members of a nation within a nation; and when Alsatian Jews did not shed those customs instantaneously on emancipation, new problems arose. At the same time, Central and Eastern European Jews, pulled by the hope of the 1791 decree and pushed by persecution in their own homelands, began to enter Alsace. They came from villages and towns beyond the Rhine, and their presence added to the suspicions of a population that, in times of trouble, made few distinctions between "French" and "foreign" Jews.[31]

Fears of strangers and of native Jews who were now citizens intensified after the summer of 1793, when Paris representatives of the Committee of Public Safety exported their mission to Alsace. Censoring Hebrew prayers and Latin masses, plundering synagogues and churches, and vilifying the Old Testament with the New, those crusaders in the name of reason railed against all superstitions and called for the destruction of Catholic icons along with an "auto-da-fé in the name of Truth of all Hebrew books." Hebrew had become an idiom of conspiracy, they said, and Jews were potential spies. Seizing the opportunity to unleash personal prejudices, some officials warned that a constant watch must be kept on "dangerous" Jews . . . the devouring bloodsuckers of the citizenry."[32]

But the Reign of Terror did not become a pogrom. The Committee's "mission" was too broad for that, and Jews were only a minor part of a larger problem. Robespierre's emissaries aimed to secure every French province for the Revolution while championing a new nationalism that, from its birth, had little tolerance for particularisms of any kind. Dialects were only the most obvious "primitivisms" that "extended the infancy of reason and prolonged obsolescent prejudices," and Judeo-Alsatian was only one of many "jargons" that must give way to the language of the Declaration of the Rights of Man and Citizen. Revolutionary officials launched a full-scale assault on all the tenacious faithful by attempting, like ferrets in search of prey, to hunt down all adherents to provincialism and revealed religion. If necessary, they would "open the eyes" of reluctant citizens through the "regeneration of the guillotine," though that new instrument of humane removal was used far less frequently in Alsace than in other French regions. There, by dint of their large numbers and distinct customs, Jews, like Catholic priests and nuns holed up in monasteries and convents, would be among the easiest targets for the missionaries of revolution to identify.[33]

In the end, however, they were victims less of official acts designed in Paris than of local rumors acted on in Alsace, and they felt the worst impact of the Terror when peasants turned on Jewish families in the winter of 1793–94. It mattered little that Jewish loans had enabled some of those country people to purchase national lands and become proprietors for the first time; memories were selective, and when debts came due gratitude gave way to resentment. In a reenactment of the "great fear," the same villages that had been plundered in 1789 had their synagogues and cemeteries vandalized and their tombstones stolen. At the height of the rebellion, for the third time in five years, Jews fled to Mülhausen and Basel.[34]

Designed to destroy the inequities of the Old Regime and secure "peace and tranquillity" in the eastern provinces, emancipation, in its early stages, had aggravated the prejudices of country people who insisted that Jews embraced no cause but self-interest and belonged to no community but their own. Before the Revolution, when the divisions were clearer, Rixheim's Jews and Gentiles worked together, not in harmony, but in a system of customary inequality; that system had kept many Jews miserably poor by keeping them overtaxed and overregulated, but it had also kept peasants confident that moneylenders could be controlled by official restrictions and unofficial threats. Now, however, the revolutionary regime faced a critical choice: It could join the local population by punishing—or banishing—the Jews, or it could honor its own promises by protecting its new citizens from the crowd.[35] The regime's choice became clear when it sent a detachment of troops from the garrison at Huningue, close by Rixheim, "to intervene and put an end" to the violence. By late 1794 the "Thermidorian reaction" that followed the Terror in Paris reached into Alsace, where—along with other recent memories of soldiers mobilized for their safety—Jews would welcome the state's protection as the first fulfillment of a revolutionary promise.[36]

By the time Jacob Dreÿfuss began his peddling trade, French troops had secured much of the "natural frontier" along the Rhine. After Napoleon's coup d'état in 1799, and throughout the brief life of his Consulate, England struck a temporary peace with France, and, a short time later, Russia withdrew from the war, but not for long. Meanwhile, Austrian troops continued to roam the Rhine's eastern bank; French battalions pushed deep into Central Europe by way of Alsace, and the entire region remained on a war footing. Armies requisitioned crops, cattle, pigs, and horses and billeted troops in village homes, and the rumors never ended. Legend had it that satchels carried by peddlers like Jacob contained counterrevolutionary tracts, and that moneylenders profited from the spoils of war. Brigands kept those rumors circulating as they preyed on the countryside, and their popularity increased with the intensity of their anti-Jewish attacks.[37]

One celebrated bandit, Schinderhannes, who treated Jews no better than the horses he slaughtered as a sideline, prompted one witness to confirm that "not only the uncouth peasant but the enlightened town dweller laughs and rejoices at every coup he carries out against the Jews." Schinderhannes's exploits were legendary, and one story, which reached south toward Rixheim, described him raiding the shop of one Moses Löb; after running to the verger for help (only to be told that church bells were rung for peasants in distress and not for Jews), Löb returned to find his brother in a pool of blood. And that family was only one of many on Schinderhannes's route. Sheltered by Austrians and pursued by the French, the brigand was finally captured in 1803 and guillotined in front of a "mass of people who had swarmed in from a radius of twelve hours' traveling distance by water and by land, on horseback and on foot." The story provided an important lesson for Jews west of the Rhine: The crowd had encouraged the brigand's attacks, Austrians had protected him, and the French had brought him to justice.[38]

At the same time French officials made good on yet another promise, no less revolutionary in its implications. As a longtime resident of Alsace, Abraham Dreÿfuss had been permitted to own his house and butcher trade, but the same royal decrees had also reconfirmed ancient prohibitions on Jewish landholding.[39] In 1791, however, the emancipation edict granted Jews the right to own land, and though it would take time for Abraham's family to afford parcels of property, there could be no more concrete expression of citizenship. "Land attaches people to the soil and makes them citizens," said one spokesman, and another early advocate of emancipation had asked how Jews could "not love a state that permitted them to own property . . . their locality [pays] would become their fatherland [patrie]."[40] In addition the revolutionary edict threw city gates open to Jews; moving beyond the limited reforms of royal lettres patentes, the emancipation decrees abolished "body tolls" levied on Jews and livestock entering towns (the taxes of the "cloven hoof"), and did away with the "tickets" of protection that Abraham Dreÿfuss would have paid officials of the Old Regime. His son could now travel to the commercial centers of Alsace to sell his wares, and he would not be chased into the hinterlands when church bells tolled at sundown.[41]

But the Dreÿfuss family could realize none of those changes until peace returned to their region, and only Abraham and Jacob would reap the early benefits of emancipation. On July 31, 1805, Brändel Meyer Dreÿfuss died in Rixheim of unknown causes at an unrecorded age, though she was probably in her early fifties. Her life had spanned both banks of a river and an old and new regime, and if the men of her family would be the primary beneficiaries of citizenship, Brändel had faced with her husband and son its first impact in Rixheim. Sixteen years after the Revolution and a quarter of a century after her journey from Müllheim, she died in a house in a Jewish quarter that, despite all the promises from Paris, still resembled the Black Forest village of her childhood across the Rhine.[42]

Twenty-four years old when his mother died, Jacob stayed with Abraham and worked as a *revendeur,* an all-purpose dealer, a trade that often included week-long trips to sell secondhand goods in outlying farmsteads and towns. On Sunday mornings, after spending the Sabbath with his father, he would set off with other peddlers, walking sticks in hand, bent under the weight of sacks and boxes strapped to their backs. Living on black bread and water or, in good times, on potatoes and eggs, they bought and sold old clothes, small pieces of furniture, Bibles, tools, and trinkets, and they slept along roads or in the homes of other Jewish families. Their daily call, *"Nix zu handel?"* ("Nothing to sell?") had echoed across the Rhine Valley and Vosges Mountains for centuries.[43]

Far from bucolic, Jacob's country labors at least helped him contribute to Abraham's savings, and the mobility that came with emancipation taught him more about the world beyond Rixheim. Visiting the towns of Mülhausen, Huningue, or Altkirch, peddlers traded used merchandise and products crafted by Rixheim's cottage workers and then filled satchels with the leather and woolen goods that merchants sold to their rural contacts. On trips home, depending on the season and the state of the local economy, Jacob would travel through villages where children looked forward to the visits of colorful Jewish hawkers (youngsters called one peddler "sugar water"—Tsoukerwässerle—his midday meal being a slice of bread and two lumps of sugar dipped in the village fountain), or, as on Good Friday in the area around Rixheim, Jacob would dodge youths burning a figure of Judas and chanting *"Havele! Havele! for de ewig Jude verbrane!"* ("Sticks! sticks! to burn the everlasting Jew!"). One peddler in the region clenched his fists "with rage" each time he heard the shouts of country gangs, and each time he felt their stones. Though not always trusted, peddlers known for their "frugality and endurance" remained "indispensable intermediaries" between country and town in the years before railroads came to Rixheim.[44]

Jacob soon added part-time moneylending to his secondhand trade and invested in small parcels of land. Only a few years after his father had been forced to pay for the right to pass through city gates, Jacob paid property taxes on plots near the family home and, later, on other holdings in Rixheim. Rented to farmers or sold for a profit, those properties, along with earnings from peddling and his father's butcher trade, enabled Jacob to start a family of his own. At the age of thirty-two, he married his Rixheim neighbor, Rachel Katz, four years his junior, and brought her to live in the same house with Abraham. No document describes the details of their wedding ceremony, but it must have been presided over by the family's fifty-three-year-old rabbi, Moses Munius; born in Alsace, trained in Prague, and celebrated for his rabbinic scholarship, Munius had served Rixheim's Jews since 1794.[45]

When peddlers left villages on Sunday mornings, their wives accompanied them down the road reciting prayers for their safe travel—far from bandits and bad weather—and for their return in good health. Those prayers must have taken on added urgency in the winter of 1813, when Russian and Austrian soldiers returned to the Rhine Valley on their march toward Mülhausen and the French interior. Revolutionary wars had given way to Napoleonic campaigns, and after a decade of victories that pushed the emperor's troops deep into Central and Eastern Europe, the states allied against France pushed back across the Rhine. Six hundred Cossacks invaded the Dreÿfuss village in December 1813, followed by a "great passage" of Austrians; they billeted troops in Rixheim, destroyed neighboring Riedisheim, and after losing the region and taking it again, they settled in as an occupying force. But the crisis did not trigger new peasant uprisings; Russian and Austrian troops would not tolerate rebellion, nor would Napoleon, who kept a close eye on the problematic "German Jews" of French Alsace.[46]

Since stopping in the region on his return from Austerlitz in 1806, flushed with victory and ready to set things right on his troubled eastern border, Napoleon had been hearing accounts of "shameful Jewish speculation," warnings that unbridled usury would lead to new uprisings. He considered Jews "perfectible" and believed that they should "participate in their [own] regeneration," but he also shared prejudices shaped by memories of Jewish army contractors. "It would be dangerous," he warned, "to let the keys of France . . . fall into the hands of a population of spies who are not attached to the country"; they must not "take possession" of Alsace. Responding to unfounded but unquestioned rumors that "vile" and "degraded" Jews languished in a "state of abasement" and that they charged interest rates of 75 percent, he set out to punish usurers and hasten the assimilation of all Jews into the French nation. What revolutionary leaders had hoped to achieve through an enlightened edict of equality, the emperor wanted to order by fiat. Ignoring suggestions for gradual reform outlined by Jewish notables in Paris, he designed his own laws for moneylenders like Jacob Dreÿfuss in villages like Rixheim. After bringing the governing boards of all Jewish congregations under firm state control, he canceled or reduced all debts, restricted new Jewish residences in Alsace, and limited migration to the French interior. As one Alsatian Jew put it, many of the rights granted by the Revolution had vanished "with the sweep of a despot's pen." "I am a Frenchman," exclaimed another citizen in response to the decrees. "Why am I expelled from the temple of justice? . . . I am an Israelite, that is the reason for my condemnation."[47]

He was right. Napoleon aimed to instruct French Jews in the lessons of citizenship and teach them the perils of obstinate separation. In that quest he had the support of many Jewish leaders, who agreed that village families had done too little to shed their atavistic ways and prove their allegiance to France. "Do not forget," Jewish notables in Paris told their Alsatian coreligionists in 1808, "that it was the detestable conduct of some of you that armed the persecution. . . . It was on your horizon that the storm took shape, and the lightning that first struck you spread to other Israelites."[48] The dress, dietary laws, and dialects still used by most Alsatian Jews were unsettling reminders of an "abased past" for many Jewish leaders west of the Vosges, and signs of uncivilized defiance for Napoleon.

The emperor's double assault on usury and cultural separatism in Alsace had uneven results. With banking institutions still unknown, the end of moneylending would mean the collapse of the rural economy, and neither clients nor lenders would allow the state to undermine that system of survival. Napoleon's bureaucracy could not police every loan, and later, when enemy troops occupied Rixheim, Parisian decrees would have even less effect: Jacob Dreÿfuss would have little difficulty negotiating clandestine deals with neighbors eager for funds. Napoleon's cultural crusade met with similar problems. State officials and Jewish leaders had been insisting that "French ought to be the Jews' mother tongue, since they are reared with and among Frenchmen," but Abraham and Brändel had reared Jacob with and among very few Frenchmen at all (or at least very few who spoke French), and into the second decade of the nineteenth century most citizens in Rixheim were like most citizens in Brittany or Provence: They had neither the means, nor the opportunity, nor any practical reason to learn the language of Paris. Functionaries tried to hasten the change by Gallicizing names on census lists and village records, but the "Jacques Dreyfus" who appeared on imperial documents charting Jewish moneylending and land-holding remained "Jacob Dreÿfuss" in Rixheim.[49]

After 1815, with allied powers gathered in Vienna to save Europe from future Napoleons, and with Austrian troops still in Alsace, a fragile peace held through the years when Rachel and Jacob began to raise a family. Their first child died in infancy, and three years later a son they named Joseph also died days after birth. Only their third child, born on May 12, 1818, survived. They named him Raphael, after the angel of Jewish legend who visited the biblical Abraham and whose name implied "God's healing." But young Raphael Dreÿfuss had barely a year with his Abraham. His grandfather died in Rixheim on July 24, 1819, at the age of sixty-nine.[50]

When the last Austrians left the region in 1818 and Bonaparte's decrees expired (three years after his empire), country people suffering the "catastrophe" of recent crop failures renewed their threats against Jewish lenders. Witnesses warned that if the decrees were not renewed Alsace would fall "in servitude" to the "political lepers of France" and that rebellion would surely follow.[51] Louis XVIII, installed on the French throne by victorious European powers, refused to comply, however, and with moneylending unregulated, Jewish loans in Jacob's region nearly doubled in the five years following 1818, from 4.7 million to 7 million francs; and those numbers did not reflect many unrecorded transactions. A few localities reported no alarming incidents (because "the Judaic leprosy of moneylending" had not "devoured" their areas), but in the legendary center of usury, south toward the Swiss border, the expiration of the decrees served as a catalyst for new troubles.[52] Loans granted by Rixheim's moneylenders ranged from a few francs to 2,000 (sums that paled in comparison to 10,000-franc transactions involving other Alsatian lenders), but the amount mattered less than the resurgence of private credit and the readiness of the local population to trace every abuse to the doorsteps of the Jews: "We now see the mistake [of granting them citizenship]," said one observer. "Why did we forget at that moment [of emancipation] the Jewish evils that had existed since before the Christian era?" And he posed another question that was on the minds of others when he asked if France "should continue to extend the law to those who do not fulfill the duties that it imposes. . . . We do not wish to burn them," he concluded, "only put an end to their abuses." A petition circulating in 1818 demanded "the massive deportation of the Jews as the solution to the problem of usury."[53]

Along country roads where Jacob sold his wares, a chant imported from across the Rhine joined local shouts of "Sticks! sticks! to burn the everlasting Jew!" in the fall of 1819. Police reported that Jews sought protection after being attacked by gangs yelling "hep-hep," a marching chant of medieval Crusaders that had taken a circuitous route to the Dreÿfuss region. In Germany the murder of a poet sympathetic to the Jews had sparked demonstrations among students sympathetic to the assassin in the town of Würzburg. Pillaging homes and fatally wounding some Jewish residents, rioters had taken up the chant, and within days it had moved southwest to the Black Forest, where peasants expressed their own grievances by turning on Jews, shouting "hep-hep." By October 1819 the slogan had crossed the river and reached the Alsatian countryside. From Paris, the minister of the interior instructed the mayor and the police of Ribeauvillé, a town north of Rixheim, to protect Jews and restore order. But subsequent seasons brought more reports of conflict, and by 1822, according to one observer, the situation had become intolerable. Referring to the massacre of Protestants in the sixteenth century, another account warned that peasants were in the mood for a "Saint Bartholomew's Day for the Jews."[54]

On a festival day in 1823 in the environs of Rixheim, peasants "inflamed by wine" marched to the homes of their moneylenders, pushed through doorways, demanded an end to their debts, and warned Jews that they would "exterminate them all."[55] Gangs in Zillisheim, barely ten kilometers from the Dreÿfuss village, plundered the synagogue and pushed Jews into the river, and during wine harvests through the 1820s, seasonal conflicts included battles with Jewish lenders. One story had it that at times of drought, when peasants were unable to pay debts, Jews worried about the consequences and "prayed for rain."

Later, when the Rhine froze in the winter of 1829, blocking an essential transport route and adding to the crisis, issues surrounding a new revolution in Paris were grafted on to local troubles, and officials reported yet another "explosion" of violence. Aware that anti-Jewish propaganda attracted popular support in Alsace, opponents of the Bourbon regime played on the issue of moneylending and accused royal officials of protecting Jews more than their victims. The Bourbons fell in 1830, but the campaign continued. A few months after the Orleanist Louis Philippe became king of the French, new taxes levied on livestock fueled suspicions that Jews had conspired with the new regime to exploit the local population. Catholics shattered windows and in one town pillaged a meeting hall, where Jewish families made the mistake of organizing a dance too close to the church. In the summer of 1832, the Jews of Bergheim, a village on Jacob's route of country peddling, fled to the town of Selestat, north of Colmar, in the hope that government officials would protect them. They did, but barely. A report warned that all Jews in the vicinity would be the targets of another uprising: "We lack neither gunpowder nor bullets," went one note to local authorities. "We will burn these devil Jews, this scourge of the country, in their own homes." Another report insisted that Jews, four decades after emancipation, remained "a veritable plague on Alsace."[56]

The principal road out of Rixheim led west to Mülhausen. On trips with his father, young Raphael Dreÿfuss skirted the banks of the Ill River, a tributary of the Rhine, and passed millhouses that had given the town its name centuries before. "I have traveled through this place on at least ten occasions," wrote a seventeenth-century visitor, "without finding a single thing worth noting. All I can say is that it's a pretty little town located on a plain bordered by rolling hills and vineyards."[57] By the 1830s, however, there was much worth noting, as rural laborers abandoned fields and vineyards and moved to the city, and as millhouses became quaint artifacts of a slower, artisanal age. Cotton spinning and weaving enterprises and the region's first *maison textile* had been established in Mülhausen by 1760, and over the next two generations mechanized factories with families working to the rhythms of a new industrial discipline eclipsed the small-scale production of leather and woolen goods and printed calico cloth. Cottage workers migrated to new steam-powered textile factories (the first steam-driven mill had been constructed in 1812), and the road from Rixheim expanded with the industrializing landscape of Alsace. On their short journeys to the city, Jacob and Raphael would make way for long convoys of up to fifty wagons with seven-horse teams hauling massive balls of raw cotton and piles of charcoal from port cities to Mülhausen factories.[58]

In a few years that city's commerce had reached out to envelop Rixheim and threaten Jacob's livelihood as an intermediary between country and town—a service that Jews had provided since the Roman era and that Jacob had taught his son. But the changes in Mülhausen, which destroyed many rural enterprises,[59] had an uneven impact on Rixheim's economy, and not all residents shared the Dreÿfuss family's dilemma. One enterprising Alsatian industrialist, Jean Zuber, had come to their village from Mülhausen in 1802 to take over a small factory specializing in paints and paper for the salon walls of the European bourgeoisie. The factory enjoyed a thriving business in the years following the Napoleonic Wars; a laboratory was installed for the development of new chemical techniques, and the enterprise attracted workers from other areas of Alsace. Improved European trade led to further expansion, and when Rixheim's population approached three thousand in the late 1820s, one enthusiastic official attributed most of that growth to Zuber's "beautiful *papiers peints* industry"[60]—"beautiful" because the Protestant Jean Zuber had taken over the abandoned baroque headquarters of the Catholic Teutonic Knights. Expropriated by the state in the early years of the Revolution, those buildings had been transformed into a prison and then into a hospital, until they were put up for sale with other "national properties" taken from religious orders and purchased by one of Zuber's associates in 1797. Eager to establish factory branches beyond customs barriers that limited access to French markets, Mülhausen industrialists chose Rixheim, only five kilometers to the east, as a prime center for development.[61]

Like the religious order it replaced, the Zuber factory became the dominant local enterprise, and though small tile and plaster industries remained and Jews still peddled livestock and loans, the village of Jacob Dreÿfuss's youth, now a small town, had changed dramatically. Entering its most prosperous period in the 1830s, Zuber's factory employed scores of Rixheim residents and supported many more, but the enterprise had a particular profile; when company officials recorded the religious affiliations of their workers, they listed 232 Catholics, 9 Protestants, and no Jews.[62] Once linked by the elaborate fairs of April and late July when Jews and Gentiles gathered to sell horses, cattle, old clothes, and Bibles, Rixheim's two communities had been driven apart by years of conflict and by a radical transformation of the local economy that had left little room for the Jews.

Watching Rixheim change and Mülhausen grow, Jacob learned that city commerce also promised opportunities for peddlers who could put country work to urban use. On trips to Mülhausen with Raphael he saw rural scrap iron dealers working as hardware salesmen; livestock brokers setting up stables, tanneries, and shoe trade shops; and peddlers selling fabrics and furniture or becoming commission agents for textile manufacturers and their clients.[63] With barely 6,000 residents at the time of the Revolution, Mülhausen's population had more than doubled, and its Jewish community, nonexistent four decades earlier, numbered more than 1,000, some of them Jacob's former Rixheim neighbors. In the early 1830s, with no need to provide for a daughter's dowry, and every reason to plan a better future for his son, Jacob took the savings he had accumulated from peddling, moneylending, and renting parcels of land and purchased a small apartment on a Mülhausen street with a French name. The rue de la Justice was a promising place for a new beginning.[64]

Like Colmar and Strasbourg, Mülhausen had for centuries prohibited the establishment of permanent Jewish residences. It had granted temporary refuge to families in times of crisis, however, and Jews had honored it with a "prayer of gratitude" for its "hospitality"; moreover, in sheltering Jews from peasants "in the mood for a new Saint Bartholomew's Day," Protestants followed the precedent set by their ancestors, who had sent troops to aid Huguenot victims of the sixteenth-century massacre.[65] The city's location near the Rhine had opened it to the influence of Martin Luther, Huldrych Zwingli, and John Calvin, and by the early seventeenth century, with no Catholics remaining within town limits, the reformed faith had drawn Mülhausen and Basel into a close, if not always friendly, alliance. The region became a sanctuary not only for Jews but for Huguenots on the run from the Sun King. Stripped of privileges by Louis XIV and expelled from France, they learned that "reversals" invariably followed periods of tolerance, and that separation, whether chosen or imposed, could have violent consequences.[66] The term "refugee" was first applied to French Protestants, and the revocation of their rights in the late seventeenth century was, in some ways, a modern counterpart to the destruction of the Jews' Second Temple. Both groups had been pushed from their homelands, and both had been treated as pariahs. Barred from guilds, liberal professions, and state offices and forced into the "commerce of money," the ancestors of many Mülhausen residents had also lived as "foreigners within."[67] While Lutherans in northern Alsatian towns showed little sympathy for Jews ("such a poisonous and devilish lot," Luther had written, "we are at fault in not slaying them"),[68] Calvinists to the south recognized the similarities of suffering experienced by "the people of two diasporas." They also shared a common gratitude for the liberties granted by French edicts of emancipation.

A place of refuge remembered by Rixheim's Jews, Mülhausen had also become an enclave of French culture in an overwhelmingly Germanic and Catholic Alsace. "Spreading Calvin's language along with his heresy," as their counterparts had done in other regions, the town's Protestant leaders had established French schools in the seventeenth century, and into the nineteenth they shielded their children from the coarse Germanic dialects of mill workers and servants, making certain that French "reigned exclusively in their homes." Voltaire's earlier comment on the mix of cultures in Colmar ("half-German, half-French, and completely Iroquois") could still apply to Mülhausen's general population, but it could not apply to the families who controlled the town's high and official culture. They knew that to speak French—and to speak it without an accent—was one of the "essential and distinctive signs of belonging to a good family"; and as they developed French markets as the source of their wealth, they cultivated the French language as a source of their pride.[69]

The Dreÿfuss family chose a new home in "the most French city in Alsace." Now legally part of French territory and subject to its laws, Mülhausen attracted many Jews who had been there before, though only in flight and only for a few nights of protection. When Jacob, Rachel, and Raphael took the western road out of Rixheim in 1835, they followed the lesson of an old adage that Abraham and Brändel would have understood but whose truth only their son's family would realize: *"Meschané môkem, meschané massel,"* went that Judeo-Alsatian proverb, "Change of place, change of luck."[70]

CHAPTER II

Exodus

PUSHING CARTS or hiring a wagon to move their belongings five kilometers along the road to Mülhausen, the Dreÿfuss family traveled past neighboring Riedisheim, across the wide route leading south to Switzerland, and onto a bridge near Mülhausen's Porte de Bâle, the location of a synagogue when a small Jewish community was permitted in the town in the fourteenth century. Fortress walls had been dismantled shortly after the Treaty of Union with France in 1798, and moats had given way to canals that circled the city to carry charcoal in and fabrics out. To the south a "new quarter" of gardens and mansions for the manufacturing elite had been constructed over recent years ("new" had become the modifier of preference for local developers), but the core of the medieval town—with its churches, marketplaces, municipal offices, and the Dreÿfusses' new home—had changed little over the centuries. Textile factories and workers' settlements grew up near pasturelands to the west and north, while merchants, artisans, functionaries, and factory owners who had not yet moved to houses overlooking southern quais still resided along the winding streets of the town center.[1]

Moving north from the Porte de Bâle, Jacob, Rachel, and Raphael entered the rue de la Justice, one of the narrow streets leading out toward the city's eastern limits. A woolen works owned by Pierre Schlumberger, whose family enterprises would expand dramatically over the decades to come, had recently moved from the rue de la

26

Justice to larger quarters; but with new lithography studios and other shops, the street maintained a commercial character. Formerly called Schindergasse, after the knacker who lived and worked there in the sixteenth century, it became the rue de la Justice when many of Mül-hausen's squares, monuments, and streets took on new names in cele-bration of union with France.[2]

In 1798 town notables had proclaimed the marriage of their six-hundred-year-old republic to the French nation, and they had mixed provincial color with smart politics. Conveniently forgetting the ten-sions that marked the wedding (France had blockaded Mülhausen with eleven tax offices supported by nine brigades of troops in an attempt to secure a "customs conquest"), local officials mounted a pageant of allegiance—for manufacturers eager to convert to French citizenship and for immigrant workers, many of them of German origin, who would have to be taught the reasons for conversion. Fifty cannon blasts, echoing to Rixheim, opened the festivities at dawn on March 15, 1798, and after children presented French officials with a key to the town on a silver platter, they handed laurel branches to soldiers who would soon be needed to battle Austrians regrouping across the Rhine. Moving on to the city gates, they planted Liberty Trees, sym-bols of the Revolution, and heard one French dignitary announce, "France adopts you as her children." Crowds gathered to hear the Treaty of Union proclaimed in French and German, and near the end of the ceremony officials planted Mülhausen's ancient seal and sword of justice under another Liberty Tree. Finally, to drive the lessons of allegiance home, they placed the town flag in a tricolor box wrapped with a ribbon reading: "The Republic of Mülhausen rests in the bosom of the Republic of France." With its historic ties to Swiss cantons now severed, Mülhausen became part of the Haut-Rhin department re-cently shaped from the Old Regime province of Haute Alsace. Drink-ing, dancing, and more cannon blasts followed, along with the singing of a special version of the "Marseillaise" translated into German for the crowd (though the majority, who knew only dialect, would have trouble with the words of any official version): *"Auf, o Mülhausen Bürger, stimmet Heut neue Jubellieder an!"* ("Awake, oh citizens of Mülhausen, and sing today new songs of joy!"). The celebration cost the town nearly seventy thousand francs—a small price to pay for the dismantling of customs barriers and for the chance to share in the promises of the French Revolution.[3]

Forty years after that celebration, Jacob, Rachel, and Raphael Dreÿfuss came to the rue de la Justice, a street that remained French in name alone. Like other recent migrants, the family brought their dialect and village customs to town. One Alsatian Jew, looking back across the decades since the Revolution, noted a profound transformation in the "moral and social state of the Israelites of Alsace. . . . Traditions have been obliterated," he said, "or have lost their influence. . . . In a word, Jews involved in the same institutions and activities as the general population have become French in name and in their hearts."[4] But the observer, too eager to celebrate change, was wrong on many counts; like Bretons and Provençaux settling in Paris and Marseille, the Dreÿfusses were not immediately "crushed into the mold" of a French culture that, in Mülhausen, remained the rarified domain of city functionaries and a Protestant manufacturing "patriciate."[5]

The Jewish community now approached twelve hundred, or 7 percent of the town's residents at a time when the Jewish population of Paris stood at less than .5 percent. A new synagogue had been built on the site of an old hospital in 1822, and nine years later Mülhausen's rabbi, David Bernheim, was the first Jew to be buried within city limits (an uncommon sign of acceptance in Alsatian towns).[6] In the family's central neighborhood, Jacob befriended Wolf Salomon, a tailor; David Franck, a police agent assigned to the synagogue; and M. Guggenheim and Lazare Weil, both tradesmen. Now living in a town where commission agents, pawnbrokers, and café owners doubled as informal bankers, Jacob abandoned his moneylending practice and focused instead on adapting his other country trades to what his French-speaking neighbors called *affaires commerciales*. He and Raphael became *marchands* (merchants), though local records never specified the products they sold.[7]

Part of the first generation of Alsatian Jews to seize the benefits of emancipation and break with centuries of settlement in the countryside, Jacob had moved from a troubled village to a town that promised peace and opportunity. Only his son, however, would see the promise fulfilled. On the evening of May 27, 1838, less than three years after settling in Mülhausen, Jacob died in the apartment on the rue de la Justice. He was fifty-seven years old, and the cause of his death was not recorded. The first member of his family to buried in a city as a French citizen, his simple marker in the "Israélite" section of Mülhausen's cemetery confirmed the year of his death—5598, according to the Jewish calendar— and the traditions that had traveled with him from country to town.[8]

* * *

Lazare Weil, a friend of Raphael's, was related to the Libmann family in the Rhine Valley *bourg* of Ribeauvillé, fifty kilometers north of Mülhausen.[9] Simon Libmann worked as a butcher on the rue des Tanneurs close to the town synagogue, and, as Abraham Dreÿfuss had done a half century before in Rixheim, he sold kosher meat from the house he shared with his wife, Ehlen-Judas, and their daughter Jeannette, a seamstress. Down the road, past the town gates, the Strengbach River irrigated a fertile valley, and the vineyards lining nearby hills provided the town's main source of income. But the solid stone-and-beam houses of local winegrowers, like Ribeauvillé's medieval castle on the promontory above, stood in striking contrast to the Jewish quarter, where deep ditches carried away the refuse from butcher and tanner shops.[10]

Raphael met Jeannette Libmann in 1840. Sharing the customary sweets and small glasses of liqueur that Jewish parents offered future sons-in-law, Simon and Ehlen-Judas would discuss the financial details of their daughter's marriage. Her training as a seamstress promised opportunities in the leading textile center of Alsace, as well as a few francs to send home,[11] and she would start a new life in a town known as a place of refuge. (No less important, Jeannette and Raphael's later years together suggest that affection figured as prominently in their union as did the negotiated conveniences of marriage.) Having worked to contribute to her own dowry, Jeannette, at the age of twenty-four, traveled south to Mülhausen in the spring of 1841 to marry Raphael, one year her junior.[12]

Joining Rachel Dreÿfuss in the apartment on the rue de la Justice, Jeannette worked as a seamstress while Raphael continued his merchant trade. The young couple named their first son, born at home in 1844, after his deceased grandfather (as if taking his grandfather's "place on earth"), but a simple difference signaled a profound change. In defiance of French bureaucrats, Jacob Dreÿfuss had kept the biblical form of his name in country and town and had never relented. His son and daughter-in-law, however, blended Jewish tradition with a language they barely understood and named their boy Jacques.[13]

He grew up in a city that changed more during his childhood years than it had in its six centuries as an independent republic. The evidence was everywhere: in new cotton, wool, chemical, and machine factories; in city parks and shops; in new street signs and the consistent numbering of buildings, which began in the early 1840s; in the network of wider and deeper canals; and in the new railroads that linked Mülhausen to nearly industrial centers (including Rixheim), and on to the major cities of Switzerland, Alsace, and the French interior. The journey to Strasbourg, which had taken six days in 1600 and nearly two days in 1800, could be done in two hours in 1841, and in relative comfort. The most important rail line, to be completed in 1858, stretched west to Paris.[14] More people entered Mülhausen on those trains than departed, and even more came along the expanded provincial roads leading from villages and *bourgs* on both sides of the Rhine. Census takers, overwhelmed by the deluge of newcomers, complained about the enormity of their task. While Jacob Dreÿfuss had come to a town of thirteen thousand inhabitants living in a few hundred houses, his grandson Jacques was born in a city of thirty thousand living in more than two thousand residences. A few years later, when Mülhausen became an administrative district, an *arrondissement,* the population approached one hundred thousand.[15]

The Jewish community had grown even more rapidly since 1800 when only thirty Jewish merchants had worked in the town; it numbered more than fifteen hundred in the year that Raphael and Jeannette were married, and five years later the community constructed a new synagogue.[16] Supported by a fifteen-thousand-franc subsidy from the municipal council, and designed by the same architect who would build Protestant churches in Mülhausen and Ribeauvillé, its four stories of rose brick, Romanesque windows, and attached classical columns secured its reputation as "one of the most beautiful synagogues of Alsace." Located west of the Dreÿfuss's quarter, across the central Place de la Réunion, its rabbi, Samuel Dreyfus—no relation to Raphael—became widely known as a progressive Jewish leader "open to reform."[17]

Relative calm marked the family's early years in the town, but in late June 1847, grain shortages and a potato blight led to looting and massive urban revolt. "Five thousand men will open fire in every corner of Mülhausen," warned striking workers, and when local officials refused demands for lower bread prices, crowds shattered windows and smashed furniture in sixty shops; they came away with bread, tobacco, wine, clothes, umbrellas, shoes, and cash. Bakers and innkeepers were among the hardest hit, some of them recording from one to eight thousand francs in damages, and the uprising spread to the town periphery. A summer rainstorm and the arrival of troop reinforcements finally put an end to the revolt, but four men were dead, twenty injured, and sixty arrested.[18]

For Raphael and Jeannette, however, with memories of Rixheim and Ribeauvillé, it was an uprising with a difference. Known ironically as the "bakers' festival" (*Bäckefest*), it did not focus on Mülhausen's Jewish population.[19] Only in the countryside, beyond the town's canals, did troubles take a more familiar turn when crop shortages set peasants against their Jewish neighbors. In Durmenach crowds broke into the synagogue to lacerate Torah scrolls, and in the nearby Altkirch region gangs chased families into the hinterlands and gave their uprising the same name they gave their Jews—*Judenrumpel*, "Jewish rubbish." Police tried to intervene "with diligence" to stem the violence, and the minister of the interior ordered authorities to protect "Israelites who, like others, are French citizens." But the troubles that ended in Mülhausen in the summer of 1847 continued in the countryside through the following year—a year marked by yet another Paris-based revolution.[20]

Mülhausen's town council had taken "energetic measures" to limit the local impact of the revolution, from calling in troops to granting concessions to mill workers. An infusion of credit from Swiss banks helped revitalize the textile economy, and work on a major sewage canal defused tensions by reducing unemployment. In 1848, when even more Alsatian Jews fled the countryside for refuge in Mülhausen, they encountered not a revolution but a birthday celebration. On the fiftieth anniversary of the Treaty of Union, town leaders reconfirmed their ties to the land across the Vosges by officially abandoning the Germanic spelling of their former republic for the French variation, Mulhouse.[21]

Raphael Dreÿfuss would remember 1848 less for its local celebration or Parisian revolution than as the year his mother died in the apartment on the rue de la Justice. A short time later, he moved the family a few steps away to a new home on the rue de la Porte de Bâle, where Jeannette's second child, Henriette, was born, followed by three more daughters— Berthe, Louise, and Ernestine—in three years. With Raphael's merchant trade expanding along with the town's commerce, Jeannette left her seamstress job to care for the five children; and, soon after, she helped manage yet another move, to a larger apartment in the same neighborhood at the corner of the rue du Sauvage and the Place des Victoires. The early months in that new home could not have been happy ones; a cholera epidemic claimed Berthe and Ernestine. But in October 1854, when Jeannette gave birth to a second son, Léon, the family numbered six.[22]

The dramatic changes of the 1850s, including Jeannette's decision to stop working away from home, were related to Raphael's increasing involvement in the textile industry. After a brief setback in the late

1840s, Mulhouse entered a period of industrial expansion that secured its reputation as the principal textile center of the eastern region. For the first time Alsatian enterprises seriously challenged their English counterparts, and Mulhouse became the Manchester of the Continent—a place, said its proud fathers of industry, where "cotton is king."[23] Cloth printing, the original source of the local textile revolution, was done manually through the 1820s, until hydraulic rollers increased both production and quality. The first 10-horsepower steam engine for cotton spinning, introduced in 1812, had been replaced by 40-horsepower machines from England a few years later; and that equipment would be eclipsed in turn by 250-horsepower engines manufactured by André Koechlin and other Mulhouse companies. With the invention of the circular and continuous carding machine in 1854—another Mulhouse contribution—production quadrupled. Six thousand mechanized looms were installed in factories throughout Alsace when Jacob Dreÿfuss moved from Rixheim, but by 1850 there were more than fifteen thousand (a number that would nearly double in the next decade), and Mulhouse had the largest share. Trade barriers limiting cloth imports helped save French markets for local manufacturers, and chemical factories in nearby Thann, like the paint and wallpaper enterprise in Rixheim, shared in the city's prosperity. If a "dynamic" entrepreneurial spirit had been lacking in some industrial centers of the French interior, technological innovations and the marketing of cheap cotton and luxury fabrics made Mulhouse an exemplar of modern manufacturing. The Société Industrielle, the organization of local captains of industry, had good reason to praise those years as a time of boundless expansion and progress.[24]

In 1850, at the age of thirty-two, Raphael began work as a commission agent dealing in printed and embroidered fabrics, a job as important to city commerce as Jacob Dreÿfuss's peddling had been essential to the Rixheim marketplace. In special rooms reserved by mill owners to present fabrics to wholesale dealers, and on trips in search of clients in Mulhouse, Colmar, Altkirch, and Basel, Raphael acted as an intermediary between manufacturers and buyers; well situated to learn all aspects of the textile trade—fashion trends, labor costs, production techniques, and distribution networks—he kept clients informed of what products were in demand and helped serve as a "regulator of production." He specialized in the colorful, elegant fabrics that, since the eighteenth century, had draped the furniture, covered the salon walls, and made up the wardrobes of the European aristocracy and *haute bourgeoisie*—a clientele, from Vienna to St. Petersburg, whose tastes in language, diplomacy, dress, and decor were distinctly French. In response to competition from cheap cotton producers, the town's early industrialists had turned to luxury fabrics, and Madame de Pompadour had helped secure their fortunes by creating a demand for their cloth. By the time Raphael launched his commission trade, those printed fabrics were less expensive and more widely distributed, and young village women used local dialect to name their special Sunday dresses after the mistress of a king; fashioned from Mulhouse materials, "Pomppaturs" were among the many products that Raphael had a hand in marketing.[25]

He dealt in fabrics and in fortune, in a trade of chance. Commission agents, their work highly sensitive to market fluctuations and clients' ability to pay fees, added loans to the services they offered; they provided the funds needed to purchase land, building materials, and machinery for cotton mills and chemical factories. With no salaries to pay or elaborate shop or office to maintain, Raphael began to invest indirectly in the city's textile economy. As the manufacturers for whom he worked enjoyed their most prosperous years, his negotiations multiplied, and his loans, at interest rates of 5 or 6 percent, were made good.[26]

Four decades after his father purchased his first parcels of land in Rixheim, Raphael began to buy property in Mulhouse. He purchased the family apartment on the rue du Sauvage and then bought and sold small lots and buildings in the western and northern quarters. The pasturelands that once surrounded the town's medieval walls became prime properties for the development of new houses, mills, and roadways, and Raphael sold his first two holdings to the municipality in 1855 and 1859—one for the construction of a road and small park, the other to create a second entrance to a primary school and "assure the complete separation of the sexes." Those transactions earned the Dreÿfuss family nearly one thousand francs—more than the annual salary of a Mulhouse mill worker—and helped provide the capital for larger and more lucrative ventures.[27]

Fierce competition in the town led to failure as well as fortune during those years, and the pages of a local newspaper, the *Industriel Alsacien,* ran announcements of bankruptcies and foreclosures. On at least two occasions Raphael made his way to the courthouse to bid for real estate at auction, and on both he bought the land and sold it at a profit. For his largest purchase, however, a series of northern parcels, he needed help. On a trip to nearby Basel or during his work in Mulhouse, he had met a Swiss banker, Jean Forçat, who had a keen interest in the future of Alsatian industries. In 1858 the two men raised more than twenty-five thousand francs to purchase land north of the rue Koechlin. A few years later they sold off a small section to the municipality—again, at a profit—and held on to the rest.[28]

But Raphael's most formidable income was still to be made, and the source of his good fortune lay in London, Paris, and the American South. In 1860 an Anglo-French free-trade agreement, marking a turn toward lower tariffs, forced Alsatian mill owners into new competition with their Lancashire counterparts. With the closing of American ports during the Civil War, a "cotton famine" hit textile centers in Lancashire and Normandy and then spread across Europe. Mulhouse had more reserve stock than did most port cities, but after 1861 the *Industriel Alsacien* became an obituary sheet of failed enterprises. Major industries—the Koechlin, Dollfus, Mieg, Schlumberger, and other factories—could weather the troubles, but many smaller businesses succumbed to the double pressure of cotton shortages and stiff competition from elsewhere in Europe.[29]

Hard times were the best times for Raphael Dreÿfuss. As prices rose so did the profits of commission agents who had no raw materials to buy, no equipment to maintain, no mortgages to meet, and no workers to pay—or to lose. "This period so fatal for industry," concluded one report, "has been a flourishing time for intermediaries . . . who, directly or indirectly, have gotten involved in businesses and have enjoyed extreme good fortune and considerable profits."[30] Some wholesale merchants provided raw materials to manufacturers and took back finished goods at a profit, while others advanced capital at interest. One of Raphael's colleagues in Mulhouse, J. J. Eberhardt, lent one cotton enterprise sixty thousand francs in 1862 with a clause stipulating that the factory's equipment serve as collateral; that company failed at the height of the crisis and then reopened under Eberhardt's ownership.[31]

In 1861 Raphael, now a keen student of the Alsatian economy, made a short trip northwest from the rue du Sauvage to the vast symmetrical blocks of small houses that made up Mulhouse's "workers' city." Members of the Société Industrielle, inspired by model dwellings displayed at London's Crystal Palace exhibition, had fashioned their own plans to improve the conditions of mill workers by settling them in new quarters close to their factories. By the early 1860s hundreds of back-to-back houses, with garden plots and narrow pathways between, had been completed in pasturelands north of the town center. Beyond those houses, however, and reaching out to the hills surrounding Mulhouse, more open land was available, and Raphael arranged to purchase one large triangular section at 20,500 francs.[32] Creating a limited partnership with his Basel colleague, Jean Forçat, he then approached André Koechlin—owner of a mammoth factory that would turn out five thousand steam locomotives in the nineteenth century—about financing heavy machinery over eleven years at a fixed rate of 5 percent. Koechlin agreed, and in 1862, at the height of the cotton crisis and with a flood of workers in search of employment, Raphael launched his own cotton mill on the rue Lavoisier.[33]

Grandson of a kosher butcher whose few francs at interest helped peasants get through bad harvests, and son of a peddler who sold secondhand goods along country roads so his family could move to town, Raphael matched Forçat's investment of three hundred thousand francs and began construction of a major Alsatian factory the year he turned forty-four. Gambling a broker's profits on the promise of a fixed place in Mulhouse, he joined the ranks of a few dozen Protestant and Jewish industrialists and gave his enterprise the same new French name, stripped of its Germanic form, he had recently chosen for his family—Dreyfus.[34]

Intensely private men, known for their sobriety, discipline, and disdain for ostentation, the Koechlins, Dollfuses, Schlumbergers, and Miegs did not rush to embrace that Jewish broker turned mill owner; the town's powerful *grandes familles* rushed at few things outside the competitive arena of business. But they had worked with Raphael in his role as a commission agent, accepted him as a client for their equipment, and now recognized the owner of Raphael Dreyfus et Compagnie as a new Alsatian industrialist. Mulhouse Protestants made room for "self-made" men. "There exists among old and new enterprises within the same industrial center," observed one leading manufacturer, "a solidarity as undeniable as that which reigns among residents of the same commune."[35]

Raphael shared with his colleagues the industrial ground of the northwestern quarters and the commercial ground of the cotton exchange near the train station. The town's frock-coated businessmen gathered there for the latest quotes of prices in the Levant and the Antilles and for news of competitors in Lille, Rouen, and Manchester. Like the Jews and Gentiles, who traded together and worshiped apart in Rixheim, the Jews of Mulhouse had been joining Protestants as brokers and factory owners for more than four decades. The Katz and Lantz families opened agencies as early as 1818, and shortly after Raphael launched his mill another Jewish-owned enterprise, Dreyfus-Lantz (no relation to Raphael's family), began construction across the rue Lavoisier. Others had been established in previous years. Lantz, Lang, Blum, and Rosenstiehl appeared on the membership lists of the Société Industrielle, the inner circle of the manufacturing elite, and Lazare Lantz began a thirty-one-year tenure on the town council in 1860.[36] Protestant notables subsidized the education of Jewish youngsters like Léon Bloch, a promising chemistry student whose family had come to the city the same year as Raphael; and Rabbi Samuel Dreyfus applauded the Protestant mayor as that "honorable and much loved" man who made a special effort to procure land for the new synagogue— a synagogue designed by a Protestant architect. The textile world town leaders kept closed to Catholics (not one major Catholic enterprise would be established in Mulhouse in the nineteenth century) they opened, if only part way, to Jews.[37]

Unable to penetrate that industrial establishment, Catholic immigrants still came by the thousands from Alsatian villages and Baden and Bavaria to work in cotton, wool, chemical, and machine factories. During Raphael's early years in Mulhouse, Catholics and Protestants had been almost equal in number, but by the 1860s, nearly 45,000 Catholics lived among 15,000 Protestants and fewer than 2,000 Jews. Many of them poor and barely literate, and nearly all clinging to Germanic dialects, those men, women, and children provided the labor for the local industrial revolution. After 1863, with raw materials scarce, bread prices nearly doubling, and many industries closing, scores came to work at Raphael Dreyfus et Compagnie on the rue Lavoisier.[38]

A solid, unornamented factory of wood beams and white plaster, running nearly 100 yards along the main facade and 120 yards deep, the new mill grew to four stories, with combing machines on the first floor and three large spinning halls located above. Amid the clatter of cotton spools and the heat and dust generated by Koechlin's massive steam engines and steel boilers, mill hands worked from dawn till dusk and then returned to small houses across the road, to one-room apartments along dark streets of the town center, or to semirural villages on the western periphery. On the journey from the Place des Victoires, Raphael passed workers' quarters described by one contemporary— with some exaggeration to make his point— as "slums with infected and

foul alleyways, hovels without light or air that speculators rent at inflated prices, and where honest folks are piled on top of the dregs of
society and forced by lack of space to live in a degrading promiscuity."
Wages had risen since the 1840s, but thousands of mill hands still
earned barely enough to afford cramped lodgings and meals of bread
dipped in coffee or chicory, potatoes, thin soup, and, on a Sunday or
festival day, meat. Poor diets and tenements covered with grime from
smokestacks contributed to the high infant mortality rate among workers as well as to the protests of labor groups. The Dreyfuses' Mulhouse
and Dickens's Manchester had more than cotton in common.[39]

Trips through those quarters must have put Raphael in mind of the
roads of Rixheim, where his grandfather had worked amid the foul odors
of slaughtered animals, and where his Jewish community looked after its
poor. Local officials had tried to outlaw Jewish "beggars and vagabonds"
in Alsatian villages, only to be told by community leaders that the
indigent would always be cared for "because nature and religion demand
it."[40] In his village *heder* Raphael would have learned that the Hebrew
word *tzedakah* meant both charity and justice, and he knew from his
father that peddlers were given food and lodging in Jewish homes. The
hungry and homeless took a prominent place at Rixheim's Sabbath meals
and wedding tables, and children heard of the "chariot of cares" that
traveled at night with rations for the needy. Charity was a *mitzvah,* a
good deed commanded by the Talmud as a form of justice, not as a
casual gift, and Raphael set out to extend, within limits, those lessons
to his new community of mill workers.[41]

Reared on the same biblical teachings—"You shall open wide your
hand to your brother, to the needy and to the poor, in the land"—many
Protestant and Jewish factory owners had learned similar notions of
social responsibilty. And if not all of them acted on those teachings,
Raphael, at least, shared the sentiments of his colleague Engel-Dollfus,
who insisted that "manufacturers owe their workers something more
than a wage."[42] By the 1860s legislation had reduced work hours in
Mulhouse factories and allotted more time for rest and food, but at the
Koechlin-Dollfus mill, the Trapp woolen works, the Dreyfus-Lantz enterprise, and elsewhere, owners aimed to "advance the moral and material civilization" of their community and assert their "civic pride."
They worked with labor groups to devise retirement plans, death benefits, and other aid programs, and in keeping with their belief that the
progress of industry leads to the progress of "human society," they
penalized laborers who, hung over from Sunday drinking or exhausted

from a week of backbreaking work, took "Saint Monday" off. Serious men in a serious business, Mulhouse industrialists had little sympathy for injuries suffered as a result of "brawls, an excess of wine or other debaucheries." Still, they invested in schemes to improve their workers' plight. By establishing nurseries, old age homes, workers' savings banks, and shelters for the poor, they acted as the enlightened patrons and disciplined taskmasters of their industrial society.[43] When Raphael joined their ranks, he followed their lead and implemented a progressive program of accident insurance for his employees on the rue Lavoisier. In a world where parents and children still worked fifteen hours a day with little support in case of accident or hope of relief in times of sickness, Raphael's programs, however limited and paternalistic, were appreciated by mill hands, who later presented him with an ornate bronze medal as a gift of gratitude.[44]

The Dreyfus apartment on the rue du Sauvage was becoming a crowded home for a family of nine. After Jacques, Henriette, Louise, and Léon came Rachel, in 1856, and Mathieu, born the following year. Jeannette's last childbirth, on October 9, 1859, when she was forty-two years old, was the most difficult, and she fell seriously ill in the days and months that followed. She turned to her midwife, the widow Marie Dantzeisen, and to her eldest daughter, Henriette, for help with the new child they named Alfred.[45]

Studying the industrial arts of carding equipment and cotton prices on the rue Lavoisier, Jacques and Léon followed a path similar to another son of a Mulhouse industrialist whose "practical life" began the "day he left his mother's side: at five years old he knew the price of coal, at eight he understood steam engines, and at fifteen he was a foreman earning 3,000 francs a year."[46] While less privileged Jewish youngsters apprenticed at the local vocational school, the Ecole Israélite des Arts et Métiers à Mulhouse, Jacques and Léon worked with Raphael amid the sharp clatter of spinning machines and the guttural dialects of Alsatian, Swiss, and German workers. They learned the lessons they would need to be partners in their father's mill. Meanwhile, Mathieu and Alfred explored with their sisters the busy squares and streets near the rue du Sauvage. Their apartment looked out on the cobblestoned Place des Victoires, and shared the square with linen and bedding shops. At the end of arcades leading up from the Porte de Bâle, the flat was situated only steps from the colorful Renaissance town hall where the republic of Mülhausen had been laid to rest by French officials seventy years before. Across the Place de la Réunion and towering over the family's apartment only a few dozen yards away, the Protestant church of Saint Etienne was in the midst of massive reconstruction. Rebuilt through the 1860s, its ornate neo-Gothic windows, niches, and spires decorated with thousands of small arabesque sculptures must have fascinated the children who watched it take shape; for years, it was the central event in their neighborhood, and when masons, carpenters, and glaziers completed their work, the church stood in striking contrast to the city's more modest temple on the rue de la Synagogue.[47]

The High Holy Days and rites of passage observed in that synagogue, like the Hebrew inscriptions chiseled on Dreyfus grave markers in the Mulhouse cemetery, or the wig that Jeannette seems to have worn in keeping with Jewish custom, had not hindered Raphael's entry into the textile trade. In fact, Rabbi Samuel Dreyfus, while working to maintain the integrity of his community of nearly two thousand Jews, encouraged their integration into the larger society. In contrast to the grand rabbi of Colmar, his orthodox superior to the north, Samuel Dreyfus was known for his liberal reforms—for the daily visits he made to public schools for the religious instruction of Jewish students, for the publications he issued in French, and for his close ties to Protestant leaders. The rabbi called Mulhouse one of the first cities in France, "where the spirit of equality and veneration for our religion has become deeply rooted," and his civic activism aimed to improve the lives of local Jews by hastening their inclusion into what contemporaries called *la grande famille française*. Even the *initiation réligieuse* of thirteen-year-old Jewish youngsters included a statement on the union of French patriotism and Jewish tradition. The Dreyfus family left no record of the children's religious instruction in Mulhouse; nor did the synagogue hold documentation of their formal schooling, if any. But if they learned the Hebrew required for the confirmation ceremony—a ceremony of special significance for their observant parents—the children also had to learn the "sacred declaration of patriotic loyalty" to France that accompanied the religious rite.[48]

Religion did not stand in the way of Raphael Dreyfus's economic success, as it did for Mulhouse Catholics, but, having been reared in a village where French was a foreign tongue, the question of culture threatened to slow his entry into the upper reaches of the town's manufacturing society. By the 1860s the men who had directed the local textile revolution had conceived and financed an equally dramatic French cultural and social revolution. From libraries, schools, and adult night courses in chemistry and literature, to museums of natural history, industrial design, and fine arts, those men had worked to shape Mulhouse in their own image. Most were Protestants, some were Jews, but all were self-confident architects of the town's future who knew from experience that civilization was synonymous with France and that French, not German or Alsatian, was the language of progress. By the middle decades of the century, French had become the dominant language of the *haute bourgeoisie* throughout Alsace, the language that connected them to the markets and politics of the interior and set them off from their workers and rivals across the Rhine. In Mulhouse, where Gallic roots went even deeper, French—along with an unwavering faith in science, reason, and free enterprise—became a prerequisite for full membership in the town's industrial society.[49]

If Raphael Dreyfus did not appear in the Société Industrielle's ornate leather volumes containing the photographic portraits of its members and the litany of their accomplishments, his absence had less to do with his Jewish faith than with the French culture he never quite mastered. Only the early signs of change were there: The children had been given French names, and by the late 1850s Raphael had abandoned the Germanic spelling of his family name; also, along with other members of the Jewish community, he had rejected some of the constraints of Orthodoxy and had adopted French customs of dress and more. His photograph shows him clean shaven and with short side-whiskers—a striking contrast to the long, full beards of his forefathers. His dark suit, silk tie, and starched wing collar were those of a town businessman, far removed from the garb that Abraham and Jacob Dreÿfuss would have worn in Rixheim. The picture, so similar to that of Auguste Dollfus and other prosperous, high-collared, and confident Mulhouse manufacturers, would not have looked out of place in the publications of the Société Industrielle.

Entering the textile economy at a moment of extraordinary expansion, Raphael had amassed the capital needed to start his own enterprise. But his loan documents and building permits also recorded the survival of his country ways; in the decade between 1854 and 1864, notaries drafted his contracts in French, and then translated them for his signature into German, the one official language he understood. He could not have survived in the Mulhouse marketplace without a rudimentary knowledge of French; he had to make his way through the pages of the town's most important paper, the *Industriel Alsacien* (though raw cotton prices and bankruptcy statistics were part of a universal language), and he had to negotiate with French-speaking brokers at the cotton exchange. But those conversations were punctuated with German words and a thick Alsatian accent—an accent that often met with ridicule. Raphael, now in his mid-forties, could not break all the habits of Rixheim.[50]

He could, however, follow the lead of colleagues who insisted that French "reign exclusively" in their homes, and, with Jeannette, he could make certain that the children master that language and perfect its pronunciation, the subtle sounds of belonging. The Dreyfuses were not alone. In the 1860s efforts to ensure the ascendancy of French over German reached their peak, with town leaders mobilizing to sever ties to German and Germanic dialects among children of all classes; they aimed to radically restructure a school system notorious for its indifference to anything unrelated to industry. A youngster in Mulhouse "has no idea that speech is good for anything other than discussing budgets or explaining new ways of dying cloth," one journalist had noted, and contemporaries in Colmar had exaggerated only a little when they called their affluent neighbor to the south "an ignorant and dullwitted town." Literature and the arts were in a "savage" state in Mulhouse (just like "America before Columbus," said locals), and in schools, homes, or workplaces nearly all teaching was geared to the practical needs of a textile society. An inspector had called the Collège de Mulhouse nothing more than a huge industrial training center where "the teaching of Greek and Latin is a joke"— and French fared only slightly better. In most of France educators worried about the poor scientific preparation of their students and feared that too great an emphasis on the classics would put them behind the more scientifically sophisticated Germans; but across the Vosges in Mulhouse hard facts and the sums of industry, like Gradgrind's curriculum in Dickens's "Coketown," had always been more important, because they were more relevant, than Plato, Virgil, or the language of Montaigne.[51]

All that was changing when the youngest Dreyfus children were growing up, and at every level of schooling. While technological innovations in the cotton industry led to new schools specializing in mechanical weaving, spinning, chemistry, and commerce, other projects concentrated on the cultivation of French language and literature. Acknowledging that fully one-third of the children in Mulhouse were illiterate, officials confirmed that "serious efforts" were being made to ensure that "the generation now growing up will almost all speak French"; from industrial centers to back mountain villages, all youngsters "will soon be able to express themselves in the language of their country" (and many youngsters would have to be taught that the country in question was France). Mulhouse had a long history of taking language seriously, and one reminder hung from the town hall in the form of a twenty-five-pound "blabber's stone"; from the sixteenth through the eighteenth century, as punishment for intemperate language, rumormongering, and slander ("especially among women"), delinquents were seated backwards on a donkey and paraded through the streets with the stone attached to a chain around their neck. The rules had changed, but the passion for good speech had not.[52] Plans inspired by Engel-Dollfus, and later by Jean Macé (an Alsatian schoolmaster whose *Ligue de l'enseignement* received the support of the Société Industrielle), called for the free and compulsory primary education of all Mulhouse youngsters. On the secondary level, the offspring of factory owners, functionaries, leading merchants, and highly skilled artisans would enter schools in which history, the classics, and, above all, French would complement industrial arts, mathematics, and science. German, necessary for future Alsatian leaders, would still be a part of the curriculum, but French, the idiom of industry and emancipation, would have pride of place; and those requirements would apply in both the Jewish and non-Jewish schools of Mulhouse.[53]

By 1865 Raphael, Jeannette, and their seven children, from six-year-old Alfred to twenty-one-year-old Jacques, made up a family universe of many accents and languages. With the parents' German and Judeo-Alsatian and the youngsters' French, life in the apartment on the rue du Sauvage must have sounded like a market day in eighteenth-century Rixheim. Working to soften the hard edges of their Alsatian accents, all the children would eventually perfect their French. But only the last two boys, Mathieu and Alfred, were young enough and had time enough to make it their mother tongue. Helped along by their eldest sister Henriette and, perhaps, by other tutors, they began their studies at home while their parents prepared for the next step and considered schools in Mulhouse, Basel, Strasbourg, or Paris. With Jacques and Léon in line to manage the factory, and with the sisters in line to be married, Raphael and Jeannette Dreyfus could afford to provide their youngest boys with the French skills they would need to lead the family business into the twentieth century and to do so as cultivated members of the Mulhouse "patriciate."

*　　*　　*

An ideal spot for a commission agent, the rue du Sauvage was in the wrong quarter for a captain of industry. From his window above the Place des Victoires, Raphael could look down the rue de la Justice and see his parents' first city apartment; and, further on, toward the Porte de Bâle, he could make out the contours of the Nouveau Quartier, where the Koechlins and Dollfuses had broken through medieval boundaries to construct elegant town houses amid a triangular garden park. By the 1860s that "new quarter" was nearly a half century old and fully inhabited, and families like the Dreyfuses searched for other residential districts to develop. Having purchased dozens of parcels of land over the past decade, Raphael could move in many directions. He chose the Quai de la Sinne, along a former moat situated halfway betwen the rue du Sauvage and the Nouveau Quartier.[54]

The new Dreyfus home ranked among the town's more elaborate dwellings. Four stories high, with long, narrow windows, a central balcony with a sculpted stone balustrade, and an entrance framed by garlands in relief, the building had rooms for servants and storage on the top floor. An English visitor to Mulhouse had it right when he described the "fine houses standing in pleasant gardens . . . serious, discreet and dignified," but he had it wrong when he added that nothing was done "for show."[55] The houses on the rue de la Sinne (and Raphael Dreyfus's was one of the first) balanced stately elegance with playful ornamentation, and their architectural styles set them off from the gray flats above shops in the town center and the stark, functional mills to the north.

Escaping the din of newspaper hawkers, wagon traffic, and stonemasons completing work on the Protestant church, the family enjoyed the quiet comforts of the rue de la Sinne, and, for once, they had the added comfort of space. Through the principal foyer of their new home, past Raphael's large office, the parlor, dining room, and kitchen beyond, and near three bedrooms also located on the main floor, a circular stairway led up to more bedrooms, with balconies. Moving from a few rooms to a spacious town house, the family invested a formidable sum in new furniture, and their salon walls, tabletops, and windows would be draped in the luxury fabrics that Raphael had traded as a commission agent a decade before. He could now afford the products of his own success. The tree-lined garden looked out across the Quai de la Sinne toward still-undeveloped pastureland to the south; and in the back, beyond meadows, the spires of Saint Etienne dominated the horizon.

Mathieu Dreyfus, preparing to enter the Collège de Mulhouse, and Alfred, not yet ten, spent long hours working on their lessons in that garden; and they saw little of their father and older brothers. Jacques became partner in the mill when he turned twenty-five in 1869, and every workday, by carriage or on foot, the two directors set off with Léon for the rue Lavoisier.[56]

Henriette Dreyfus commanded the respect needed to manage her "lively" young brother, Alfred. She had her mother's patience, her father's gentle eyes, and a square jaw and sturdy frame. Alfred, slender and fine-featured, had the fair hair, broad forehead, and slightly prominent ears of his father. And from an early age he also had Raphael's blend of curiosity and perseverance. Obeying his elders' every request only after questioning their every motive, he was a dogged and "incorrigible dreamer," a child whose imagination took him on many journeys beyond his tree-lined garden. For good reason his sisters called him "Don Quixote."[57]

CHAPTER III

Germans and French

RAPHAEL DREYFUS'S RIXHEIM DIALECT and German language might have been out of place in the French atmosphere of the Société Industrielle, but they were as important to the workings of his mill as they had been to his father's trade between country and town. The Mulhouse population had doubled in the past twenty years, approaching sixty thousand in the late 1860s, with more than one hundred thousand in the greater *arrondissement;* and while most workers in cotton, wool, chemical, and machine factories had been born in the Haut-Rhin department of Alsace, nearly nine thousand Austrians and Germans, migrating from Baden, Bavaria, and Württemberg, had recently settled in the Mulhouse region. Like an urban archipelago, the neighborhoods of those working-class families spread out toward the town's western and northern hinterlands.[1]

Life on the rue de la Sinne, however, was more uniformly French. On the western side of the family's garden, a new theater, constructed in 1867, aimed to attract a French-speaking clientele. Presenting operas, operettas, and comedies, and mimicking recent Paris trends by adding a small café-concert in the basement, the Nouveau Théâtre emerged as the French counterpart to the German theater near the workers' suburb of Dornach. At the same time, just across the Quai de la Sinne, new rail lines linked the city to Paris, and on those trains came bundles of French newspapers to complement the local *Industriel*

Alsacien. Soon the family's reading would include the *Journal des Débats, Le Siècle, Le Petit Journal, Le Rappel,* or *Le Temps,* a paper founded and financed by Mulhouse entrepreneurs. For young Mathieu and Alfred Dreyfus, deep in their French primers and struggling with introductions to "our ancestors, the Gauls," the lively pages of Parisian broadsheets and newspapers would be a welcome distraction and an entrée into the world beyond Mulhouse.[2]

The recent social and cultural revolution choreographed by Protestant and Jewish industrialists—the insurance plans, workers' savings banks, public baths, housing projects, subsidized shops, and night schools—had aimed to improve the "material and moral" condition of factory hands and ensure the smooth operation of the Mulhouse economy. Those reforms had helped prevent strike activity among local workers, and with the exception of brief periods during the "cotton famine," most wages had risen and most prices had stabilized. In the summer of 1862, when Raphael launched his factory, a few posters appeared comparing the misery of mill hands to the oppression of American slaves; "When a slave is old and can no longer work, his master at least cares for him . . . but for you, free workers, all that is left is misery; and the selfish factory owner [who lives] in opulence [does not] deign to share the scraps he feeds his dogs."[3] But those isolated protests did not give way to widespread disillusionment with the paternalism of Mulhouse industrialists until 1869, when workers—Catholic in religion and, for the most part, German in language—mobilized against the town's Protestant and Jewish *"fabricantocracie."*[4]

Raphael must not have been surprised that Rixheim served as the local base for the most virulent opposition. Established for the defense of "Catholic interests against Protestant propaganda," and obsessed with the conspiratorial trio of Jews, Protestants, and Freemasons, a Rixheim newspaper, *Der Elsässische Volksbote* (*The Alsatian People's Messenger*), played on the German slang of the region and on memories of past conflicts. "In the old days Jews were not considered citizens because the Jewish element did not belong among Christian people," a Rixheim activist observed in May 1870. "But now we call them 'Messieurs les Israélites,' " and now, the paper went on, Jews exploited the law to arrange their finances and manipulated opinion with their "Jewish pen."[5]

The *Alsatian People's Messenger* had stepped up its attacks as a prelude to a spring plebiscite (part of a national referendum on the regime of Napoléon III). Since 1848, when Louis Napoleon had eased toward a Second French Empire by way of the presidency of the Second French Republic, Mulhouse manufacturers had not warmed to his authoritarian regime; while appreciating his respect for order, they remained practical liberals, wary of state intervention. Napoleon III faced many enemies in the twilight years of his empire, but in the eastern provinces, the fiercely independent manufacturers of Mulhouse became his most formidable opponents. They had voted against him at the dawn of his career, and in 1870 they were poised to do it again. For the newspaper *Industriel Alsacien*, the Bonapartist regime was "only a form of absolutism approved by the votes of a deluded population."[6] If the emperor hoped to win the May plebiscite in Alsace, he had to fashion a populist appeal. It would not be difficult for the nephew of a popular legend, a politician who had recently sent representatives to convince Alsatian workers that factory owners were their enemies, and an emperor supported by papers like Rixheim's *People's Messenger*. Napoleon III would score an impressive victory on the May ballot, but he would not be supported by the "industrial and financial aristocracy" of Mulhouse.[7]

For the Dreyfus family, the national plebiscite would be less significant than the forum it provided for a population sharply torn by the divisions of class, religion, and language. Napoleon's campaign had crystallized conflict in the region by exploiting the frustrations of Catholic and German-speaking workers. Most of their grievances were legitimate (the harsh realities that prevailed in mills and foundries confirmed that), but when propagandists attacked the religion and ancestry of the Alsatian "patriciate"—when they introduced the vague but powerful notion of race—they added to their economic protests issues that lay beyond the realm of negotiation. Troubles on the streets of Mulhouse in the weeks and months following the plebiscite would teach Raphael and Jeannette Dreyfus's children more about the complicated legacies of the French Revolution than all the academic exercises they studied in the shelter of their tree-lined garden.

One source of Raphael's capital investment seven years earlier, André Koechlin's huge foundry, became a target for strike activity in the summer of 1870; and when Koechlin joined the Dollfus-Mieg, Steinbach-Koechlin, and Ducommun enterprises to reduce the workday from twelve hours to eleven, strikers moved on to Vaucher, Dollfus-Lang, Schlumberger, and Mieg Frères. Women and children marched with other protesters in long, peaceful processions until early July, when 2,300 workers returned to the Koechlin foundry and set it on fire.

By the second week of July, demonstrations throughout the area involved at least 15,000 Alsatian workers, and town officials had called on mounted troops to stem the violence. Raphael Dreyfus's mill and the neighboring Dreyfus-Lantz enterprise were not hit by the first wave of strikes; either concessions granted by those two companies had preempted troubles, or, more likely, strikes led by machinists and skilled printers had not yet spread to cotton mills. But the Dreyfus family would have heard the "furious shouts and threats," as one report described them, directed against privileged Jews and Protestants in "elegant houses recently built."[8]

Mounted troops restored order and departed quickly, and from his second floor balcony, young Alfred Dreyfus watched the columns of cuirassiers, with heavy armor breastplates and colorful uniforms, gallop out of Mulhouse on July 15, 1870. The festive sight greatly impressed all the Dreyfus children. Mobilized from nearby Belfort, those troops had intervened in time to prevent the strike from spreading to Raphael's factory and had kept demonstrators away from townhouses along the Quai de la Sinne. But if the army had helped limit violence, other factors had brought an end to the strike. The rapid truce fashioned by workers and owners had been prompted by reports of war.[9]

In three weeks' time, many of the cuirassiers who passed under Alfred Dreyfus's window would confront Prussian troops on battlefields at Reichshoffen and Fröschwiller north of Strasbourg, and they would attempt calvary charges across obstacles of stone walls, fences, and vineyards. Cut down by the Germans' modern breech-loading rifles, their bodies, clad in light blue uniforms, would lie "so thickly on the ground" that the landscape would look like "a field of flax." And after Reichshoffen, the Prussians would move south toward Mulhouse.[10]

"Since time out of mind," said one German who spoke for others in 1840, "the French have been known as devious, two-faced, sly, insidious, treacherous people, arrogant and cruel in victory and craven in defeat. They were always dangerous confidence-tricksters, practised swindlers, windbags, babblers, braggarts, hypocrites, liars and thieves. Just about every child knows that."[11] If just about all German children who had grown to military age by 1870 did not share that observer's hatred of the French, they shared a fear of Bonapartist adventurism, and, with the Prussian Chancellor Otto von Bismarck, a desire to secure their western frontier. France had declared war on Germany thirty times over the two centuries prior to 1870, and though a long peace had held since the defeat of the first Napoleon, the image of France remained that of a bellicose neighbor too eager to cross the Rhine. Bismarck wanted "land, fortresses and frontiers which will shelter us for good from enemy attack"; and after the Prussian defeat of the Austrians in 1866 he turned his attention to France. The formation of the North German Confederation in 1867 threatened the balance of power so carefully struck at Vienna a half century before, and tensions increased in early July 1870 when Napoleon III learned of Prussian meddling along France's southwestern border with Spain.[12]

German interest in Spain centered on the throne left vacant after a revolution in 1868. Among the possible successors to Queen Isabella was a German prince with Catholic kin on the Iberian Peninsula and with Bismarck behind his nomination. Leopold of Hohenzollern-Sigmaringen showed little interest in the Spanish crown, however, and his influential relative, Prussian King Wilhelm I, showed even less. But Bismarck convinced the prince of the service he would render to Germany, and with the king's halfhearted support, the "Hohenzollern candidature" was put forward on July 2, 1870. Though more aware than anyone of his late uncle's "Spanish ulcer," Napoleon III could not abide Germans on two frontiers; it was, said the French foreign minister, "nothing less than an insult to France."[13] Convinced of his nation's superiority to Prussia in men, matériel, and military strategy (a misguided opinion that was widely held), and believing that the French army was prepared with food, clothes, horses, breech-loading rifles, and as many as four hundred thousand men with more to come, the emperor and his ministers challenged the Spanish candidacy. But Bismarck knew that Napoleon was deluded by illusions of French grandeur, by a debilitating illness (he suffered agonizingly from kidney stones), and by the pressures of a coterie of imperialist Germanophobes who had the support of the emperor's wife, Eugénie. More important, Bismarck knew that the Prussian army had modernized with striking speed in the past half decade; able to mobilize more than a million men in less than three weeks' time, and with Krupp factories turning out new and powerful cannon, the German states had never been better prepared for war.[14]

Wilhelm defused tensions temporarily when he reconsidered the Spanish plan; and Queen Victoria, along with the king of the Belgians and other European leaders, helped the diplomatic negotiations when they called for a peaceful solution. On July 12, Leopold's name was withdrawn. But French hubris made certain that Bismarck's moment of humiliation did not last long. Napoleon and his ministers announced that the withdrawal of the candidacy was not enough; Prussia must officially "explain" its actions and guarantee that they would never be attempted again. Reassured by General Helmuth von Moltke, commander of the Prussian army, that troops and equipment were ready for mobilization, Bismarck and his agents exchanged a series of telegrams with French officials, the last of which made it clear that the Germans would promise nothing and apologize to no one. That message, Bismarck knew, would serve as a "red rag to the Gallic bull." On July 15, with Parisian crowds shouting "To the Rhine!" and singing the "Marseillaise" (an anthem that Napoleon III's police had suppressed for years), with recruits scrambling to join units throughout France, and with the Belfort cuirassiers called north from Mulhouse, the emperor's government voted war credits. The formal declaration came four days later.[15]

The quick strike by French troops across the Rhine or into the Palatinate never materialized. Instead German soldiers from Baden, Bavaria, Saxony, and Prussia swept into French territory north of Strasbourg. By early August more than half the French reservists had not even reached their regiments, and delayed or poorly routed trains and a lack of adequate maps compounded the crisis (overconfident commanders had sent troops off with maps of Germany, but with few of France). The disasters at Reichshoffen and Fröschwiller were followed by others, and on August 14 nearly forty thousand German troops surrounded Strasbourg. The landscape of that city, like that of Mulhouse, had changed to reflect the peaceful and prosperous years of the nineteenth century; canals had replaced military moats, and the environs had become a patchwork of residential suburbs and factories. Some fortress walls remained, however, to ensure that a direct attack would incur heavy casualties, and given those barriers the Germans opted to besiege Strasbourg. Through early September, the city's library, museums, and Protestant church were destroyed, and entire neighborhoods were demolished before bombs were replaced by slow, persistent shooting from within and without.[16]

Strasbourg held, and Colmar and Mulhouse waited while the key battle of the war brought tens of thousands of French and German troops to the town of Sedan, on the Meuse River near the Belgian border. The battle also drew a gallery of spectators that included, on the German side, Wilhelm, Bismarck, Moltke, and contingents of princes, dukes, and British and American generals. To the French side came Napoleon III on horseback, in a foolish, heroic gesture by a man nearly incapacitated by pain but aware that another major defeat would mean the end of his empire. On the eve of the battle, before Napoleon's arrival, Moltke had realized that the French were doomed ("now we have them in a mousetrap"); and France's General August-Alexandre Ducrot, studying the position of German forces around Sedan, had to agree ("we are in a chamber pot and we will be shit on").[17] In the course of the fighting, which lasted two days, the French commander, Marshal Marie-Patrice-Edmé-Maurice MacMahon, was wounded; soldiers and riderless horses fled from German artillery into nearby forests; and the emperor rode back and forth across the front in a futile attempt to die in battle. The defeat was as rapid as it was humiliating. On September 1, with twenty thousand French taken prisoner (a number that would soon climb to over eighty thousand) and with entire battalions hiding in the woods, Napoleon ordered a white flag raised at Sedan. He asked for an armistice.[18]

For the French the "emperor's war" gave way to a "people's war." On September 4 a mix of moderate republicans and Orleanists proclaimed a Government of National Defense in Paris, and two weeks later German troops surrounded the capital. Far to the east, other troops moved to the walls of Strasbourg, ready to attack, and south of that city they prepared to enter Mulhouse. With military strategies shifting to Paris and its environs, the Vosges Mountains and Rhine Valley had become part of the German rear, and resistance in those regions would be met with draconian measures. If Bismarck's threats never matched those of his wife (all French people should be "shot and stabbed to death," she reportedly said, "down to the little babies"), his warnings were published in the French and German press, and rumors of Prussian designs on Alsace spread as rapidly as the news of French defeats. We "should treat the French as a conquered army and demoralise them to the utmost of our ability," wrote one German general. "We ought to crush them so that they will not be able to breathe for a hundred years." And another general, a foreign spectator at Sedan, offered the wisdom of his own experience during the American Civil War: "The proper strategy consists in . . . causing the inhabitants so much suffering," wrote Philip Henry Sheridan, "that they must long for peace and force the government to demand it. The people must be left nothing but their eyes to weep with over the war."[19]

Alfred Dreyfus called it his "first sorrow."[20] At nine o'clock on the morning of September 16, on the same balcony from which he had watched French cavalry ride off to Reichshoffen, he saw five thousand

German soldiers, part of the Baden corps, enter Mulhouse. They had come to Alsace from a garrison at Müllheim, the native town of Alfred's great-grandmother, only a few kilometers across the Rhine. Mulhouse, situated along a principal rail line running from Germany and Switzerland to Paris, became a hub of troop movements and forced requisitions. The Baden corps stayed only twenty-four hours, but they left a sign of things to come; destroying a railroad bridge over the Ill River, they cut town industries off from markets and sources of fuel and raw materials, and they began the systematic severing of the population from the French interior.[21]

Young Alfred's reaction to the arrival of German troops ("my hatred, the hatred of my family for the foreigners," as he described it later),[22] was less an expression of precocious patriotism than a reaction of fear and anger shared by all the Dreyfuses. Though untouched by invasion or occupation through the early weeks of the war, they had heard of defeats in northern campaigns and of the Germans' push south from Strasbourg. Reports came from Haguenau, Petite Pierre, Bitche, Phalsbourg, and Saverne of "unspeakable panic," and of cruelties, real or fabricated, committed by Prussian soldiers. French dispatches to Alsace confirmed that the fatherland was in danger. As the enemy advanced, observers north and south along the Rhine Valley, and in the French interior, echoed Alfred Dreyfus's reactions. In late September, after Strasbourg fell, one youngster was "consumed with defiance" for the German invaders he watched enter his town with "fife and drums." A textile owner, described in a novel about the war, "had not ceased to rage since the Prussians had invaded the little town." And the response of a character in a Guy de Maupassant story could have been drawn from Alfred's life: "I used to look at [Prussians] out of the window [and] it was more than I could stand. They made my blood boil and I cried with shame all day."[23]

German troops returned to Mulhouse on October 2, marching to the sound of military music and setting up requisition centers at Mathieu Dreyfus's school, the Collège de Mulhouse, as well as at the Ecole Professionnelle and police headquarters. Every visit brought demands for provisions and cash, but when local snipers fired on Germans, Bismarck's generals sent an additional "punitive detachment" of three battalions from a camp near Neuf-Brisach. Two days later, on October 9, Alfred Dreyfus's eleventh birthday, Germans threatened to lay waste Mulhouse—as they had done Strasbourg only a month before—if demands for money and matériel were not met. City leaders rushed to provide 60 wagons, 160 horses, 6,000 flannel shirts, 1,000 loaves of bread, 18,000 cigars, 375 kilos of tobacco, 1,500 bottles of wine, and nearly 50,000 francs in cash. Then, to confirm their true allegiance, they quietly sent supplies of the same value to the French army at Belfort. At the same time, Germans ordered the Mulhouse population to take all weapons to the train station and offered a reward of 135 francs (more than a month's salary for a city mill worker) to anyone willing to denounce his neighbor.[24]

Coming in the wake of labor strikes never fully resolved, German actions rekindled troubles between Alsatian workers and factory owners. It was less a case of divided national loyalties (most workers, though German in language, were French in allegiance)[25] than of class conflict combined with religious prejudice. And the situation deteriorated along with the local economy. In early October workers built barricades near the Place de la Réunion and shattered Town Hall windows until police intervened to put an end to the uprising. Through the fall months, with deliveries of coal and charcoal severely reduced, with rail lines disrupted by troop movements and sabotage, and with Germans ordering factory owners to part with products and cash, industrialists were forced to limit the work week to three days and to let some laborers go. Aware of the "precarious" problems in that area with forty thousand workers, town leaders tried to negotiate an end to the requisitions, but thousands of troops continued to pass through Mulhouse on their way to the French interior. By December, Prussians had destroyed the rail line linking the town to St. Louis and to Basel, and industrialists had been cut off from their primary source of commerce and loans. Raphael Dreyfus, whose ties to Swiss banks remained crucial to the operation of his mill, must have joined other colleagues at the cotton exchange; it had become a veritable "political *salon.*"[26]

Meanwhile, Jacques Dreyfus left the industrial front to his father and sixteen-year-old brother Léon and joined the Légion d'Alsace-Lorraine.[27] The professional French army had failed miserably in the opening weeks of the war, and the new Government of National Defense, under the influence of the republican Léon Gambetta, aimed to push the enemy back with an army drawn from all the provinces—and destined to fail just as miserably. "What we have before us is Prussia; it is the Prussian nation armed," announced Gambetta, and to "confront a nation armed we must also raise an armed nation."[28] Defeats had come so rapidly that nearly one million Frenchmen were still available for service, and in early November a government decree had called for the mobilization of men between the ages of twenty-one and forty. Prussians tried to stem the flight of young men from the eastern provinces to French recruitment centers, but Jacques Dreyfus, just turned twenty-six years old, found a way to volunteer. In keeping with the Byzantine bureaucracy of the French military during those years—the muddled strategies that were so much a part of their defeat—Jacques was sent to Lyon, far to the south, to prepare for war on the Alsatian front. He left Mulhouse only days before Prussians ordered the destruction of all monuments inscribed *Liberté, Egalité, Fraternité.*[29]

In a locality where occupiers threatened residents with fines and imprisonment for simply showing the French flag, Jacques Dreyfus's enlistment would place his family in danger. Since the outset of the war, Prussians had been compiling lists of potential soldiers in occupied territories, and later in the year they issued passports that, if not renewed in person, would lead to punitive measures. Local officials with French sympathies subverted the process and a complete list was never achieved, but the threats of punishment, like the executions of snipers that Bismarck wanted to serve as warnings to others, would be sufficient to put the Dreyfus family on guard.[30]

Much of the combat in the eastern provinces had shifted from cavalry charges and artillery bombardments to guerrilla activities involving groups of *francs-tireurs,* hastily trained militia who cut telegraph wires and sabotaged rail lines. Lyon, where Jacques joined the Légion d'Alsace, became a celebrated center of *francs-tireurs* recruitment; the Italian hero Garibaldi established a unit there to fight for France, and he attracted a bizarre but aggressive mix of provincial patriots and Parisian anarchists. More than fifty thousand *francs-tireurs* operated throughout France, and after November their missions in and around Mulhouse (including the derailment of a troop train between that city and Colmar) brought renewed threats from Prussian authorities. Only days after Jacques left for Lyon, another poster went up in Mulhouse warning those who attempted to join French forces that they, or their families, would suffer "the most severe punishment."[31]

Jacques Dreyfus barely had time to complete his training and return to the front. In late December news reached the Mulhouse cotton exchange that a major battle was unfolding in the region north of Dijon, toward the Vosges. On hearing the reports, town industrialists hoped what the Prussians feared—that French troops would reverse the course of the war and, in a last, heroic assault, push east to the Rhine. But the same freezing temperatures and icy rain that blocked Mulhouse canals also blocked French troops west of the Vosges. Belfort held, but the campaign failed, with one battle costing 4,500 French wounded and 1,500 dead. With the armies of National Defense routed only weeks after Jacques Dreyfus joined their ranks, and with most of the eastern provinces secured by the early days of the new year, the Germans turned to the proclamation of their empire, to the siege of Paris, and to negotiations on the fate of Alsace.[32]

On January 23, 1871, a general alarm in Mulhouse called citizens to the Place de la Paix, close to the Dreyfus house. The crowd learned that King Wilhelm of Prussia had been proclaimed emperor of Germany, and that the confederation of states and principalities that had joined to defeat the French had become a politically united nation. Wilhelm's ceremony had taken place five days before, not in Berlin, but in the chateau at Versailles where Bourbon kings, followed by Bonapartes, had plotted against Prussians for two hundred years. That diplomatic event, designed to match the military humiliation at Sedan, marked the last of many burials of the Second French Empire. With an armistice signed ten days later, a provisional French government gathered to struggle with the harsh terms of a German treaty. But they met in Bordeaux. The capital—along with Lyon, Marseille, Toulouse and other cities—had resisted the demands of both German and French officials, and had held out under siege. Working-class discontent and municipal pride set Parisians against a new French government they perceived as traitorous and concerned only with the protection of property and priv-ilege. On March 1 victorious German troops paraded from the Bois de Boulogne down the Champs-Elysées, but when they returned to camps in the hinterlands, Parisians adopted the methods and language of the first French Revolution and proclaimed a new Commune. It would take more than two months to crush the city's resistance, ending in a civil war the Germans would observe from the periphery of Paris, and not without satisfaction. In late May, French troops broke through the capital's western fortifications and swept into the populous eastern quar-ters. A week later more than twenty thousand Frenchmen and -women were dead, killed by their own countrymen. Thousands more would soon be imprisoned or deported.[33]

There would be no Commune in Mulhouse. All of Alsace, except for the territory of Belfort, remained under German control, and through the weeks surrounding the Commune, while the French As-sembly met at Bordeaux, German troops, joined by German functionaries, kept order along the Rhine. On February 27 occupiers raised the imperial flag in Mulhouse and on the same day ordered town leaders to pay three million francs in reparations. But the key debate centered on annexation. Though overrun by Germans, Alsace and neighboring Lorraine had remained legally part of French territory. Now aware that the enemy had come to stay, representatives from those provinces traveled to Bordeaux to fight against a "dishonorable treaty" that would separate their region from France. Peace could only be maintained by respecting principles of national self-determination, they argued, and the overwhelming majority of Alsatians and Lorrainers were, in allegiance if not always in language, French. But Bismarck saw it the other way. One goal of the war had been to secure "land, frontiers and fortresses" as buffers against French adventurism, and memories of a medieval Germanic empire stretching across the Rhine were as strong as memories of the "old injustices" perpetrated by French kings and a Corsican general. The Germans wanted Alsace-Lorraine, its land, and its industries, and there was little doubt they would have them, with or without the niceties of a legally signed French treaty.[34]

On March 2, in a move that shocked French Alsatians who had sent sons to war, the Bordeaux Assembly ratified the preliminaries of peace and voted 546 to 107 to turn all of Alsace and parts of Lorraine over to the Germans. "You cannot settle a people's fate without their consent," shouted Alsatian representatives to the assembly. And before walking out in protest they proclaimed "forever inviolable the right of Alsatians and Lorrainers to remain members of the French nation. We swear for ourselves, our constituents, our children and our descendants that, in every way and against all usurpers, we will eternally claim that membership."[35]

The Treaty of Frankfurt severed the eastern provinces from France, and on May 21, 1871, Raphael and Jeannette Dreyfus and their seven children became colonial subjects of a German *Reichsland.*

PART 2

Sentimental
Education

CHAPTER IV

Interiors

"My CHILDHOOD passed gently"—Alfred used the word *doucement* to describe the years before the 1870 war—"under the kind influence of mother and sisters, the affectionate protection of older brothers and a father's profound devotion."[1] For more than a decade, from the crowded apartment on the rue de Sauvage to the town house on the rue de la Sinne, the nine family members were separated only during the work hours, which Raphael and the oldest boys spent at the mill and cotton exchange. The youngest sons stayed close to their mother, who never fully recovered from the complications of her last childbirth, while Henriette, Louise, and Rachel, like Chekhov's three provincial sisters, managed the household staff and directed Mathieu and Alfred's early education. With sisters and brothers as playmates and with no need to move beyond the parklike environs of his home, the youngest boy grew up *doucement*, well-supervised, and not a little fussed over.

In less than a year, however, he watched Jacques leave for war and said good-bye to Henriette, the sister who had become "like a mother" to him. Through the network that linked the Dreyfus mill to textile trades of the interior and brought businessmen from Europe and America to Mulhouse, Henriette met Joseph Valabrègue, a fabric merchant from Provence. One of the most prominent Jewish families in the town of Carpentras, site of the oldest synagogue in France, the Valabrègues had long been involved in that region's textile economy. Married in

1870, when she turned twenty-two, Henriette moved to her husband's Carpentras "villa" just before the occupation of Alsace.[2]

But if her departure left a "sad impression" on the boy she helped raise, it also provided the family with an avenue of escape. The same treaty that separated the eastern provinces from France allowed residents to opt for French citizenship if they filed a declaration and moved their domicile no later than October 1, 1872. Raphael could declare residence for the family in Carpentras and join tens of thousands of Alsatians who signed the option papers—some punctuating the ceremony with defiant shouts of "Vive la France!" and most moving to French cities just across the border or on to Paris. As occupation and resistance gave way to the entrenchment of the German administration, it became clear to Raphael that "option" would be preferable to life in a town stripped of French markets and French justice.[3]

Even the children's language had become an idiom of "protest" and a habit that occupiers aimed to break. Early in 1871 authorities ordered that all official communication be conducted in German and, soon after, directed primary schools to teach that language alone. *Reichsland* agents harbored a particular suspicion of the high and official French culture of Mulhouse (they preferred the more Germanic Strasbourg), and from the moment of annexation the linguistic battle set German bureaucrats against local businessmen. Members of the Société Industrielle refused to translate the name of their organization and continued to publish bulletins in French. Some manufacturers organized a Ligue d'Alsace to combat the Germanization of their region and used Swiss newspapers as a forum for their campaign; smuggling French periodicals in from Basel, they helped make Mulhouse "one of the most solid bastions of Alsatian protest against annexation."[4] But resistance to the German language had little hope of success against a colonial administration backed by Bismarck's forces of order. A café-concert song, "The Alsatian Schoolmaster," which described the dilemma, enjoyed enormous popularity: *"La patrouille allemande passe. / Baisser la voix, mes chers petits, / Parler français, n'est plus permis / Aux petits enfants de l'Alsace"* ("The German patrol passes by. / Lower your voices, my dear little ones, / Speaking French is no longer permitted / To the little children of Alsace").[5]

Raphael, whose first language, if not first allegiance, was German, faced different problems on the rue Lavoisier. Train sabotage and troop mobilization had cut his industry off from markets and raw materials during the war, and now his enterprise was about to be drawn into the

Zollverein, the German customs system. Technological innovations, sophisticated management skills, and the growth of French markets had helped Alsatian mills overwhelm most European competitors; and, with Mulhouse alone producing as much cotton as all the states in the Zollverein, the introduction of its goods into the German system on an equal footing would be catastrophic for enterprises across the Rhine. That, Mulhouse industrialists knew, would never be allowed. A compromise agreement fashioned in the wake of the Treaty of Frankfurt postponed economic chaos, but special tariff policies would last only a few months. As the deadline for "option" approached, Raphael searched for a way to save his mill, short of keeping his family under occupation and running the enterprise as a German subject.[6]

He had two choices: He could establish a new factory across the border in Belfort, a territory to the southwest, between the Vosges and the Jura, which was open to French markets and close enough to transfer equipment and draw on the local work force; or he could divide the family, enabling some to become French citizens while others stayed on to manage the business. André Koechlin, the supplier of Raphael's machinery, joined other industrialists and moved branch enterprises to Belfort; but the Dreyfus company was still indebted to Koechlin, and Raphael, though one of the town's more successful factory owners, did not share his colleague's abundant resources. The mill on the rue Lavoisier was only in its seventh year, and the war had taken its toll. Raphael's second choice became his only option when the German state announced its intention to draft Alsatian boys into the military. Residents of the *Reichsland* who had already served with French forces—veterans like Jacques Dreyfus—would be exempted, but Bismarck offered no other concessions. Conscription would begin in the fall of 1872, and in a few years Léon, Mathieu, and Alfred would be pressed into the German army and forced to wear the spiked helmets that had become the most dramatic symbol of the invader and a daily reminder of defeat.[7] In a town where German officers and their families faced hostility in shops and streets, and where the marriage of a Frenchwoman to a Prussian official caused such "general indignation" that Alfred Dreyfus noted it among his most vivid memories of the annexation, the prospect of serving in the enemy camp—a camp that continued systematically to discriminate against Jews in the military—only hastened the family's search for a way out.[8]

As a temporary measure arrived at under the pressure of the citizenship deadline, Raphael asked his oldest son to stay and salvage the family business. In May 1872 Raphael left Jeannette and the children in Jacques' care and traveled south to Henriette's Carpentras. Staying only long enough to declare that town as his official French domicile— and the domicile of the six children who, as minors, were not permitted to opt on their own—he returned to Mulhouse to take advantage of a special provision in the option agreement; with French citizenship confirmed, and with Jacques remaining in the town, Raphael prepared to move the family to Basel. From a temporary residence on the Rhine, at the junction of the French, German, and Swiss borders, he could help direct the mill and hope for changes in the political climate of Alsace.

"He who had sons departed," went a popular Alsatian saying of the time,[9] but Raphael's option, made possible by Jacques' sacrifice, involved much more than saving sons from the German army. In October 1872, with Jeannette too weak to make the journey or unwilling to leave Jacques behind, Raphael took his three daughters and three younger sons along the same southwestern road toward Basel that Jacob Dreÿfuss had traveled as a country peddler—a road that passed by Rixheim.[10] "Perhaps in one sense the war is over," remarked an Alsatian Jew in a novel about the occupation, "but in another sense it has only begun." That family, like the Dreyfuses, faced a new "day of mobilization."[11]

Separated from his home and mother for the first time, thirteen-year-old Alfred spent a depressing autumn and winter in a Basel secondary school (*Realschule*). The institution offered some courses in French, but the primary language remained German, and though the Dreyfus sons knew enough to get by, it was still a hard period of adjustment, especially for the youngest.[12] Nor did Alsatian manufacturers consider Swiss schools the ideal institutions in which to prepare the future leaders of French industry. That training, Mulhouse notables had always insisted, could best be achieved in Paris, at a *collège* or *lycée* designed to ready students for the *baccalauréat* and for entrance into the Ecole Centrale des Arts et Manufactures or the Ecole Polytechnique, the premier schools for young engineers, scientists, industrialists, and military men.[13] Though it was too late for Jacques and eighteen-year-old Léon, Raphael knew the dream was within reach for Mathieu and Alfred. Early in 1873, with their parents, sisters, and elder brothers remaining behind in Mulhouse or in their nearby Swiss refuge, the two boys crossed the Vosges and set off for Paris.

*　　*　　*

"Let's walk together hand in hand, united by the same love for our parents, our Fatherland and our sense of duty," announced the two brothers, André and Julien, featured in *Le Tour de la France par deux enfants,* the most popular school primer of the postwar epoch. Couched in dramatic prose that aimed to teach youngsters that the land of their fathers and their fatherland were synonymous, it recorded a sentimental journey and reminded children that "the memory of our native land, like the memory of our parents, should always live in our hearts." Abstract notions, the preface pointed out, must give way, through "civic instruction," to a clear and concrete knowledge of the nation. Published in 1877, the book would reach 108 printings in the 1880s, and its sales would pass eight million copies by the turn of the century. Readers learned the story of fourteen-year-old André and seven-year-old Julien, two orphans from Lorraine whose father, before his death from wounds sustained in the Franco-Prussian war, had whispered the word "France" to his sons and had heard André's promise that he would protect Julien and teach him the lessons of duty and allegiance. Marching off from their occupied town, the boys followed the "route to France, marking their steps like two young soldiers," and witnessed along the way the glories of industry, agriculture, art, and science in all the nation's provinces. When they first reached the summit of the Vosges and looked west to the interior they cried out, "Beloved France, we are your sons and we want our lives to be worthy of you!"; and many miles later the book ended with the confirmation that André and Julien had remained true to the "great things they had learned to love at such a young age: Duty, Fatherland, Humanity."[14]

Through the half decade before the publication of *Le Tour de la France,* Mathieu and Alfred Dreyfus lived much of its story. More privileged than their fictional counterparts, the boys did not hike around the hexagon with five francs to their name; they traveled amid the comforts of French trains and carried luggage filled with provisions for boarding school. But Mathieu and Alfred, only slightly older than André and Julien, shared the same sense of loss, separation, and adventure. In the space of four years, they would move from Mulhouse to Basel to Paris, and then back to Switzerland and again to Paris, before they parted, with Alfred traveling south to Carpentras and to school in Grenoble and Mathieu settling in Belfort as a French army recruit. As secure and sedentary as the 1860s had been for the Dreyfus children, the 1870s were years of constant movement, with family members drifting apart in what some observers called an ecumenical Alsatian "diaspora."[15]

After a brief time at the Collège Sainte Barbe in Paris, close to the Panthéon and among France's most prestigious secondary schools, Alfred followed Mathieu and transferred to the Collège Chaptal, another school known for rigorous standards and good preparation for the *baccalauréat*. It catered, as one school history put it, "to the elite of the elite."[16] Latin was still part of the curriculum, but physics, chemistry, natural science, history, civics, geography, German, and French grammar and literature made up the core of the program for the school's twelve hundred students. In keeping with the centralized, rationalized sytem of French education, it served as a highly disciplined "forcing house" that turned children into adults as rapidly as possible and demanded quick intellectual achievement. The specter of surprise exams required students to memorize reams of material, and daily dictation demanded the mastery of punctuation, capitalization, penmanship, and spelling. "What distinguishes men of letters from the ignorant and from simple women," men at the Académie Française had announced with characteristic misogyny three centuries before, is "good spelling."[17] Sainte Barbe and Chaptal joined other schools to inflict the same tradition on their students.

When Mathieu moved to an apartment on the rue Soufflot, a few steps from Sainte Barbe, Alfred continued at Chaptal as an *interne*, a word that captured his feeling of confinement. He detested the cavernous brick buildings (the "somber barracks," he later called them) and the "deplorable system," which stifled all "the joy of spontaneity."[18] Barred windows and bare yellow walls added to the cold, institutional image of those "children's prisons." A few years before Mathieu and Alfred arrived in Paris, one author, in a book appropriately titled *L'Education homicide*, had condemned schools that functioned like "monasteries" or "prisons," and he called the entire system a "monument of stupidity and harshness." But a civil servant at the Ministry of Education summarized the majority opinion in a message to teachers: "Coldness is preferable to declamation," he said, and "lack of emotion to the pretense of emotion."[19]

Cold reason reigned in the classroom, but in dormitories young boarders confronted personal dramas. In chronic poor health and suffering bouts of loneliness, Alfred had to deal with notorious *surveillants*, older boys who worked as monitors while learning to be teachers, but whose methods better prepared them for the secret police. A family friend later reported that Alfred, while boarding at Sainte Barbe and Chaptal, could never enter "the society of comrades who hardly understood him." The friend provided no details, but it is likely that Alfred's shy manner and delicate health, combined with the traces of an Alsatian accent (which caused problems for many young easterners in Paris during those years) contributed to his isolation. Moreover, if he was not the only Jewish *interne,* he was among the very few.[20] The experience was so painful that Alfred rejoined his mother in Mulhouse; but in the fall of 1874, just turned fifteen, he was back at a new Chaptal school in the eighth arrondissement on the boulevard des Batignolles.

A massive stone structure indistinguishable from the factories, penitentiaries, and hospitals of the period, it offered all the modern conveniences, though for a youngster reared amid greater comforts it remained an austere place of internment. From dormitory windows Chaptal's students looked out on the confluence of rail lines that swept under new city bridges and led toward the Gare Saint Lazare. Like the Impressionist painters, from Claude Monet to Gustave Caillebotte, who recorded the same scene, Chaptal's boarders watched passenger trains bound for the holiday town of Argenteuil or for the coastal resorts of Deauville and Honfleur. The bustle of street traffic and the clouds of locomotive steam could only have heightened Alfred's sense of solitary confinement.

Upon completing his studies, Mathieu decided not to pursue the onerous *baccalauréat,* or his original intention of applying to the Ecole Polytechnique or the military school of Saint Cyr. There was no need; he planned to follow Jacques and Léon into the textile business, and he had a sufficient background. Returning to Basel, he took a job as a wholesale clerk and joined other family members on trips to Mulhouse. The Germans had not yet sealed the borders of the annexed territories, and family members visited Jeannette and Jacques on a number of occasions. In 1875 they gathered for Jacques' wedding to Louise Wimpheimer, daughter of a Philadelphia industrialist, and then moved apart again—to homes in Carpentras, Basel, or Paris. Taking advantage of a recent law that enabled young men to limit their military service to one year if they paid part of the cost of training, Mathieu, at eighteen, volunteered for the French army. Able to afford the expenses and convinced that Alsatians had a moral obligation to serve France, he joined the 9th Regiment of Hussars in Belfort in November 1875.[21]

With his father and brothers managing the business, Alfred had the time to study and the means to escape the rigors of school life on weekends and holidays. He traveled to Carpentras, where the tree-lined garden of the Valabrègue estate conjured up memories of the rue de la Sinne, and where Henriette's companionship helped him forget the "barracks" at Chaptal. Working part-time with his brother-in-law, he learned the southern French textile trade, and enjoyed his role as the young uncle of Joseph and Henriette's two children. A spacious villa on the southern outskirts of town, the house had become Alfred's home away from home.[22]

Completing course work in Paris in July 1875, he returned to Carpentras to consider the prospect of the *baccalauréat*. It was not a happy one. The arduous written and oral examinations were legendary, the failure rate staggering, and the entire process terrifying for those few students awarded the degree.[23] But with passing marks and an additional year or two of intensive study, Alfred would be eligible to apply to one of the Parisian *grandes écoles* that prepared a select group of young men for leadership in industry and the military. He stayed with Henriette, worked on his lessons, and in the late fall of 1876 took the short train journey east from Carpentras to the Académie de Grenoble. Henriette and Chaptal had prepared him well. At least half the students failed the exams for the *baccalauréat*, but Alfred passed both parts. His high marks on the written work were offset by his mediocre performance on the oral exam—a result perhaps of the boy's shyness and the unattractive, almost monotonous, sound of his voice. Still, he did well enough to move on to the even more torturous phase of preparatory school.[24]

Continuing his academic *tour de France*, he returned to Paris and Sainte Barbe, a *collège* that offered two- and three-year programs for advanced students planning to take the entrance exams required by the Ecole Polytechnique, the Ecole Normale Supérieure, and other *grandes écoles*. Most likely staying with a Valabrègue relative near the Luxembourg Gardens, only a five-minute walk from Sainte Barbe, Alfred studied through the winter of 1876–77 and into the early spring. Henriette, Rachel, and Louise visited him through those months, but, save for a few "promenades" and evenings at the theater, they found it almost impossible to wrench the young man from his books. He worked the same long hours he had maintained while studying for the Grenoble exams, and he paid for it with the shortsightedness that soon required him to wear glasses. Alfred had lived up to the name the sisters had given him a decade before; he was as dogged as Don Quixote and, given the slim chances of entering a *grande école*, as much of a dreamer.[25]

But, perhaps second only to Mathieu, he had a keen intellect, a gift for languages, and a fascination with mathematics, science, and the highly abstract arguments of European philosophy that were so crucial to the "*bac*" and to subsequent examinations. At eighteen he was the beneficiary of his sisters' early tutoring; of a home life in which French was carefully studied and German often heard; of his father's textile society, in which the practical applications of modern science were so important and strong examples of discipline were set; and finally, of an elite Parisian school system geared to preparing boys for the best universities and highest offices of public service and private industry. Very few young men and virtually no women had the opportunity to secure an education like Alfred Dreyfus's (his father had already sent nearly four thousand francs to Sainte Barbe and Chaptal and was prepared to pay the same amount over the next two years), and very few who reached the highest levels of schooling had Alfred's tenacity. To a great extent, French schoolboys were "brought up not to be educated, but to be examined,"[26] and over recent years Alfred had perfected his talent for test taking.

Other applicants to the Ecole Polytechnique shared that talent, however, and of the 236 students accepted, Alfred Dreyfus's exam ranked him only 182nd.[27] But to receive the coveted *baccalauréat* and to move on to the nation's premier *grande école* was a triumph no less significant, and an attempt no less audacious, than his father's decision, nearly twenty years before, to gamble his savings on a cotton mill.

During the months when Alfred struggled with the choice of moving directly into the textile trade or continuing his studies, his brothers urged him to keep the family business as his ultimate goal. He could explore the world of academics or, like Mathieu, enlist for a term in the army, but his focus should remain on Alsace and on plans to establish branch factories in the French interior. Léon and Mathieu, though citizens of France, were working closely with Jacques in Mulhouse (Léon would become a full partner in 1879), and the mill shared in the prosperity that came with the growth of German industry. If the "golden age" of the late Second Empire could not be repeated under the Second Reich, Raphael must at least have been pleased that profits taken from German markets financed his sons' French education.[28]

But Alfred rejected what he called the industrialist's "brilliant situation" and prepared instead for a military career.[29] Henriette, according to a family friend, "impelled by a sentiment natural to an Alsatian in the aftermath of war," encouraged her youngest brother to join the officer corps.[30] Alfred had first felt that sentiment when Prussian troops marched past his Mulhouse window, and recent visits to Alsace had strengthened his resolve; upon hearing German bands celebrating the anniversary of the French defeat at Sedan, he felt "saddened and angry," and vowed to dedicate himself "to the service of the Fatherland." On the short journey from the Mulhouse train station to the rue de la Sinne, he would note the increased presence of Germans in uniform (the garrison had been expanded and the Mulhouse *gare* remained a center of troop movement), and he would hear accounts, accurate or imagined, of the occupiers' arrogance, drunkenness, and violence.[31] The defiance he felt toward the enemy in Alsace had also been nurtured in the classrooms of Sainte Barbe and Chaptal; not a bellicose call for revenge but, like the lessons of *Le Tour de la France*, a constant reminder that families had been divided by force.

Alfred's boarding school curriculum also included lessons of gratitude similar to those repeated by the Mulhouse rabbi, Samuel Dreyfus. "All benefits received lay upon us the duty of gratitude," went one school treatise. "Ingratitude is a sort of treason."[32] In the secular climate of Sainte Barbe and Chaptal, civics lessons stressed patriotism, loyalty, courage, and discipline, as well as a sense of gratitude. But French Jews had other reasons to be grateful, and religious leaders reminded them why; Rabbi Isaac Lévy, for example, an Alsatian contemporary of Samuel Dreyfus, believed that Jews loved France not because it was "powerful and rich" but because it was "good and generous" and because "on its soil grew the noble ideas of tolerance and brotherhood."[33] Alfred Dreyfus's strong desire to manifest his gratitude to France by joining its army could only have been heightened by those lessons, and by his rejection of the conventional wisdom that Jews had a "pronounced antipathy for military service," a "natural timidity" that ill-suited them for "an army career."[34] The young man's exaggerated pride, noted by his sisters long ago, had not diminished, and his quest to prove the totality of his allegiance played an important part in his decision to make the army his life.

But the timing of his application to the Ecole Polytechnique was perhaps the most telling factor of all. Dated May 29, 1877,[35] it came at a moment when war between Russia and Turkey increased tensions throughout Europe, when Germans reinforced the garrison in Alsace, and when a political crisis in Paris threatened to engage the army. Two weeks earlier, President MacMahon, a veteran of Sedan and now leader of the Third Republic, attempted to undermine the power of moderate republicans by restoring, if not a monarchy, then a royalist "moral order." When MacMahon replaced his centrist prime minister with an Orleanist, the Chamber of Deputies was thrown into one of the paralyzing confrontations that would mark the history of the Third Republic. And the key question surrounding the crisis was where the army would stand. In the end it stood where it belonged—it did nothing to intervene—and the failure of MacMahon's challenge to the legislative branch dealt a crippling blow to the power of the French presidency.[36] In the late days of May, when Alfred Dreyfus applied to the Ecole Polytechnique, he could not have been ignorant of those events, or of the sense of adventure that an officer's life promised a young man who, until then, had known only various forms of confinement.

Some family members later pointed to the timid side of Alfred's character as the reason for his enlistment—the shyness he displayed as a child, and the need to retrieve, through flight into the anonymity of the army, the protection he had known in his Mulhouse home. Military life would provide a "sort of cocoon to isolate him from the world."[37] But the same young man had just escaped the stifling isolation of boarding school, and he had just rejected the orderly pattern of promotion through the ranks of industry in favor of a place in a rapidly changing French army. Defeat in 1870 had initiated sweeping reforms, and by the time Alfred prepared for his first autumn at the Ecole Polytechnique, plans were under way to reestablish the army's power and efficiency. "The war . . . marked a profound break in the life of the French army," recalled one cavalry officer; after "the blow of its terrible lesson" came "an uncertainty about the future,"[38] and an effort among military planners to ensure that there would be no more "ruthless" defeats. For a boy just turned eighteen, the army offered more than structure; it promised action, excitement, mobility, and, no less important for the last of seven children, a chance to stand out. "One is somebody" when one dons an officer's uniform, wrote a military observer. "It means something."[39]

No young recruit would be more proud of his uniform than Alfred Dreyfus. At the moment he applied to the Ecole Polytechnique, a government official, responding to the outbreak of the Russo-Turkish war, captured the new climate of military modernization and, indirectly, the sentiments of the youngest Dreyfus son: "The die is cast," announced the French foreign minister. "The great adventure is about to begin."[40]

CHAPTER V

Cavalier

RISING FROM the Left Bank across from Notre Dâme, the Montagne Sainte Geneviève was named for the patron saint of Paris, the fifth-century heroine who helped save the city (then known as Lutèce) from that "scourge of God" out of the east, Attila the Hun. With defense against the barbarian as part of its history and with the majestic Panthéon—Catholic church turned republican temple—at its summit, the "mountain" (really no more than a steep hill) was a fitting location for the Ecole Polytechnique. Founded in 1794, in the wake of the Reign of Terror and amid European war, the school moved from the Palais Bourbon to the Panthéon quarter in 1804. Across the century it attracted the gifted sons of large landowners, high functionaries, industrialists, and professional men, and it produced the nation's leading officers, scientists, and military and civil engineers. When nineteen-year-old Alfred Dreyfus arrived at its gates in November 1878, the most prestigious of France's grandes écoles faced a challenge similar to the one that had prompted its establishment. In the 1790s revolutionary leaders had planned to revitalize an army weakened during the late years of the Old Regime and torn by the divisions of civil war. Eight decades later a new French republic rushed to rebuild an officer corps humiliated by the defeat of 1870. It had been partly responsible, said its critics, for the carnage surrounding the Paris Commune, and it had been largely discredited by the humiliating loss of Alsace-Lorraine.[1]

70

Alfred Dreyfus came to his new school armed with all the paper-work required of entering students. A letter from his father guaranteed payment of the annual tuition and board of sixteen hundred francs, and a medical history provided proof that, aside from a stiff elbow, he suffered no illness or handicap. He was among the youngest members of the entering class—many students had taken up to three years to prepare for the exam—but, more important, he arrived with the habits of home and boarding school: He had been taught to respect authority and discipline, and he was familiar with life in a community of almost monastic austerity. Behind the school's high stone walls, in its vast amphitheaters, laboratories, dining halls, and dormitories, nearly five hundred young men—cut off from *la vie civile* and rigidly monitored from the first study period at 6:00 A.M. to the silence following lights out—continued the lessons of obedience and self-sacrifice they had learned in preparatory school. In their laic cloister behind the Panthéon, geometry was their matins, physics their nones, and national history their evening prayer.[2]

"Recruit, you have been called to wear the uniform of the school," went the official "Code X"—the rules of responsibility read aloud at the opening ceremony in November. "It is an honor which imposes duties upon you. Everywhere and always, respect the uniform." As part of his initiation, Alfred would be passed the sword of a graduating student, and over the next three months he would be disciplined by a second-year recruit appointed by a secretly elected "committee of overseers" and charged with criticizing the young man's every eccentricity. Humiliation was the driving force behind the school's ritualistic "hazing"—its notorious and often violent *brimades*—and the goal was to eradicate all individual particularisms and instill commitment to an elite community of polytechnicians. Day and night Alfred's ways of dressing, walking, working, and eating were tested. His voice, monotone and raspy, would be severely criticized, and his ways of thinking would also interest disciplinarians who demanded allegiance to the extended "families" of school and nation. No less mysterious than the rituals of a Masonic order—and undoubtedly inspired by the Freemasonry of some Jacobins who had helped found the institution—the school's "Code X," along with its own special vocabulary of eight hundred words and expressions incomprehensible to outsiders, were all symbols of militant solidarity and isolation from the secular world below the Montagne Sainte Geneviève.

Since 1830 and 1848, when some Polytechniciens took sides in the Paris revolutions, and especially after the 1871 Commune, the school had discouraged the expression of political opinions. Alfred Dreyfus and his young comrades, the new servants of a moderate republic, were taught to respect the established order. So it went for the expression of religious beliefs as well. The school tolerated diverse faiths and "liberty of conscience," but Catholic, Protestant, Jewish, and "freethinking" students quickly learned that duty, loyalty, and conformity must eclipse all "personal interests." Ordination was at hand, but at the altar of the French army.[3]

Surviving the three months of hazing, Alfred settled in to six-day weeks of course work, drills, and inspections. Professional studies and personal effects were arranged with the same meticulous precision. Assigned numbered seats in dining halls and lecture theaters, students were directed to hang swords on the wall above their beds with hilts facing right, and they placed gloves, collars, underclothes, and toiletries in the same drawers in the same order and the same distance apart. Those quotidian routines were as rigid as the school's two-year curriculum, a complement of courses virtually unchanged over the past half century. Advanced geometry (the most important class) integrated other studies in math, algebra, and calculus; students also learned physics, chemistry, and applied mechanics—the constellation of courses French scientists and civil engineers had studied at the school through the nineteenth century. By the late 1870s new emphasis had been placed on modern languages (German was required and Russian offered) and on French literature and history. Abstract and theoretical, the aim was to achieve encyclopedic knowledge. The lack of intellectual "spontaneity" young Alfred had known at Chaptal, the insistence on deductive reasoning and the suspicion of inductive thought, was raised to a high art at his new institution—a *grande école* of received ideas.[4]

From an early age Alfred had had a talent for science and math; now he added to those interests a sophisticated reading of history, art history, and literature. Montaigne's essays and the recent works of Fustel de Coulanges, historian of antique citadels and medieval fortresses, would emerge as his favorites. During afternoon exercise periods, with gymnastics and fencing, he perfected the one activity that gave him most pleasure of all. He may have been attracted by the prestige of the cavalry or, perhaps, by that vivid memory of cuirassiers riding off from Mulhouse to Reichshoffen. He may also have set out, like an Alsatian Don Quixote on Rosinante, to disprove the myth, widely believed, that Jews had "little aptitude for horseback riding." But whatever his motivation, he cherished the freedom of his daily rides and developed a gift, frequently noted by comrades and superiors, for the art of equitation.[5]

Alfred Dreyfus graduated 128th in his class in 1880. Designated second lieutenant, his good conduct secured him a position as a monitor of second-year students.[6] Two years before, as an entering cadet, he had appeared a half decade younger than his nineteen years; clean shaven and with short-cropped blond hair, light blue eyes, and the narrow shoulders of an awkward teenager, he posed in his Polytechnicien's uniform looking like a schoolboy playing soldier. But with the regime of military life—the marching drills, gymnastics, fencing, and equitation—his shoulders broadened, his appearance changed dramatically, and the timid recruit gave way to a strong self-confident officer. A few years later, posing for a rare photograph out of uniform, he dressed in a fine dark suit and bowler hat, and sported a gold watch fob, an ornately carved pipe, and the traces of his first mustache. Like a character out of Balzac or Flaubert, Alfred Dreyfus looked the part of a young provincial on a private income, proud of his accomplishments and out to conquer Paris.

After the summer of 1880, some of his comrades moved on to the engineering corps and infantry; others, especially the young noblemen, waited out their *passe-temps jeunesse* in the cavalry; and a few graduates left the service for high posts in industry or government administration. But the artillery was the dynamic center of the new French army, and since the early 1870s efforts had been made to bring its officer corps up to full strength. It needed men from the Ecole Polytechnique, and with the majority of students from his class who remained "under the flag" after graduation, Alfred chose the artillery as his career. It would require advanced study at a specialized school of instruction, long hours as a military teacher, and years of nomadic garrison life. Young officers, "camped in France like Turks in Europe," had to be "ready to move their tents at the slightest signal." One contemporary described it vividly: "Am I not the most accommodating man in the world? I am told 'March!' and, like the Wandering Jew, I pick up my walking-stick and hit the road. I am told 'Halt!' and I stop."[7] Grandson of a peddler who had traveled Alsatian roads walking-stick in hand, Second Lieutenant Alfred Dreyfus set off on his own nomadic journey through French garrisons.

Academic and military schedules left little time for visits with family, and the German administration in Alsace had made it increasingly difficult to cross the Vosges from the French interior. While at the Ecole Polytechnique, Alfred listed the provincial town of Bar-le-Duc, two hundred kilometers east of Paris, as his current residence, and he probably made brief trips there to visit his sister Louise and her husband, Arthur Cahn, a local manufacturer.[8] Also within easy reach of Mulhouse and Basel, Bar-le-Duc became a crossroads for family visits, much as the Valabrègues' home in Carpentras had been in the aftermath of the 1870 war. Raphael stayed with the Cahns for a time, leaving Jacques and Léon as codirectors of the mill and Mathieu set to join them as a full partner in 1882. In the early sixties, Raphael often traveled to the cities where members of his family had settled, but he spent most of his time in occupied Mulhouse with his wife and older sons.

The rue Lavoisier factory survived the economic crises of the early 1870s and the flood of English products that inundated German textile markets in 1876. While many Mulhouse enterprises closed down, moved across the border, went public, or merged with other companies, the Dreyfus mill remained an independent family firm, and, thanks largely to Jacques' management skills, it entered a new phase of expansion.[9] Profits from the family's business and property holdings provided substantial dowries for the three daughters (Rachel, the youngest, would soon marry), as well as private incomes ranging from ten to twenty thousand francs per year for each of the four sons. At a time when minor functionaries earned little more than two thousand francs a year and when a second lieutenant's salary was even less, Alfred's income helped cushion the hardships of garrison life and set him off from his poorly paid comrades. Two-thirds of the French officers during that period had no family fortune, and only 20 percent could count on a total *héritage* of twenty thousand francs. With the promise of twenty times that, Alfred Dreyfus was very much an exception—and, by some, very much resented.[10]

Down from the Montagne Sainte Geneviève, he traveled to the Forest of Fontainebleau and the Ecole d'Application de l'Artillérie, from which, in 1882, he graduated thirty-second out of ninety-seven students and showed promise that he would "become a good officer." At Le Mans, a provincial town on the Sarthe River two hundred kilometers west of Fontainebleau, he served in the Thirty-first Artillery Regiment until he moved on to a cavalry division of the same regiment, based in Paris. "Intelligent, conscientious and zealous," according to superiors, he stayed abreast of "maneuvers and theories." His "very bad intonation" hampered his teaching techniques, but he earned praise as an "intrepid horseman." In the spring of 1885, commanding officers approved his promotion to first lieutenant.[11]

In Paris, as in Le Mans, he spent more time with horses, books, and women than he did with fellow officers. Early morning rides in the environs of Le Mans or through the Bois de Boulogne in Paris were followed by drills, instruction, and study. He dined in the officers' mess, and, on occasion, joined other young men of his regiment at haunts like the Café de l'Univers in Le Mans. But unlike comrades whose salaries could barely pay for the "depressing" provincial rooms they were required to rent ("furnished without furniture," as the saying had it), and whose nightly routines were confined to billiards, card playing, and drinking, Alfred had the means to secure the finest lodgings and to break away from the military's *vie communautaire.* He visited family in Bar-le-Duc and Carpentras, and, in 1884, he traveled to an art exposition in Amsterdam. Back at his garrison, he often took long walks alone.[12]

Most of the women he met during those years—at soirées held by provincial notables, on promenades through the fashionable sixteenth arrondissement of Paris, or at the nearby Longchamp racetrack—were his age or older, and most were rich. A few were married, and some had questionable reputations. None of those liaisons, however, developed into serious attachments; not only were the women otherwise engaged, but military codes of conduct contained elaborate regulations that Alfred, a part-time *boulevardier,* tried to follow, with varying degrees of success. Officers often "found their pleasures where they could," but, when indiscreet, they became the targets of "veritable persecution." The crucial point was to avoid scandal and to make public only a courtship that might, with honor, end in marriage. In 1885, when Alfred learned that one of his acquaintances, a Madame Bodson, living on the elegant Avenue Malakoff near the Arc de Triomphe, was becoming known as a courtesan, he quickly broke off the relationship—doing so, it seems, only shortly before Mathieu heard the rumors and reminded his young brother of the rules concerning officers and the offspring of respected Alsatian families.[13]

Twenty-eight years old in 1885, Mathieu had become the intermediary between widely dispersed parents and children. With a private income, an education second only to Alfred's, and two older brothers managing the family mill, Mathieu lived the life of a *rentier*—though not as an idle member of the industrial aristocracy but as an *amateur* of politics, art, music, sports, and literature. His formal education had ended at Sainte Barbe, but he remained an avid student of the classics and of contemporary literature, and he developed a particular interest in the philosophy of the Enlightenment; a bust of Voltaire would soon adorn his library mantel. The tallest and handsomest of the four brothers, he moved with ease through Mulhouse textile society, spending Wednesday mornings at the cotton exchange and joining other city notables on holiday outings to shoot partridge and hare in the eastern countryside. With his parents nearing seventy, Mathieu took charge of family matters, and on January 23, 1886, it was Mathieu who sent word to relatives living away from Mulhouse that his mother had died that morning in the house on the rue de la Sinne.[14]

During the same period, commanding officers filed enthusiastic reports on Lieutenant Dreyfus. He exhibited a "very lively intelligence" and an "excellent memory," and he had worked to improve his voice, though with only moderate success. "Full of spirit" and "extremely qualified" to teach horsemanship to squadrons in Paris, he was an ideal candidate for the Ecole Supérieure de Guerre.[15] That school, not yet a decade old, had been established to prepare staff officers who would work closely with unit commanders, or, in the case of top graduates, with the Army General Staff. Partly inspired by the German example, the aim was to create an elite corps of high administrators who would serve with troop divisions and gain practical experience before entering the military bureaucracy. If the late Second Empire had been top-heavy, inefficient, and far removed from the realities of modern warfare, the early Third Republic would be progressive and prepared. Its new school provided an avenue of promotion for the army's most gifted officers, and for a young man of Alfred Dreyfus's temperament, ambition, and skills it was the logical next step.[16]

Most of the military reforms proposed over recent years were more democratic in nature than the establishment of the Ecole Supérieure de Guerre, and many were the work of a popular minister of war, General Georges-Ernest-Jean-Marie Boulanger, named to the post in January 1886. From his support of striking miners in the town of Decazeville (he ordered soldiers to share bread, not bullets, with workers), and through efforts to relax the draconian regulations of garrison life, Boulanger had secured a reputation as a populist officer of the republic, a colorful minister who stood out from the gray crowd of "Opportunist" politicians. Like the two Napoleons he tried to emulate, he presented himself as a dashing savior on horseback, an embodiment of the true republican tradition, and he found backers to pay for the publicity. Support came first from Radicals who believed the general's republican rhetoric, but by 1888, if not before, the largely subterranean forces of royalism had realized that the autocratic streak in Boulanger's appeal could be used to their own advantage. The man himself—with the fading good looks of a once-dashing actor nearing the end—was a sad case of an ambitious, not terribly intelligent officer whose addiction to drugs (the result of medication for an old wound) and obsession with his mistress distracted him from serious politics. And that left the way open for others to manipulate his image. Defying the army's rule against soldiers running for election, General Boulanger, no longer war minister, mounted a series of campaigns through 1888 that called for revision of the Constitution, dissolution of the Chamber of Deputies, and *revanche* (revenge) against the Germans who had stripped France of Alsace-Lorraine. With promises vague enough to attract a diverse following, Boulanger became a "river into which fed many streams"— most of them polluted.[17]

At his cavalry post in Paris, Lieutenant Dreyfus could not have been untouched by the drama surrounding Boulangism, especially in January 1889, when the general won election to the chamber as a deputy from Paris. On the night of the victory, according to one unconfirmed report, Dreyfus was seen on the fringes of a crowd that had gathered at the Place de la Madeleine outside a restaurant where Boulanger met with political advisers in one room and with his mistress in another. "To the Elysée! To the Elysée," cried supporters, encouraging their hero to stage a coup d'état and march to the presidential palace a few streets away. But the general hesitated, the moment passed, and the republic survived. Within a few months Boulanger, forced out of the army and pursued by the courts, was on a train to Belgium to join his mistress and, after her death, to shoot himself at her gravesite.

If Lieutenant Dreyfus did go to the Place de la Madeleine on that January night, it was not as a demonstrator but, in his habitual way, as a nonparticipant standing aloof from the crowd, uninvolved. Though sympathetic to many of the general's reforms, he would have observed the spectacle with displeasure; through his entire political odyssey, Boulanger violated nearly every code of civil and military conduct which Dreyfus had learned to respect in Mulhouse, at the Ecole Polytechnique, and while serving as an artillery student and officer. With the majority of his comrades, Dreyfus had never wavered from the belief that his duty was to the established order and that the political arena should be far removed from the military parade ground. If he shared the general's obsession with the return of Alsace-Lorraine, he did not share his condemnation of the moderate republic or his vulgar appeals to the crowd. In many ways, Dreyfus was closer to Fustel de Coulanges, the historian he read, than to Boulanger, the war minister he served: "Enough of division, enough of hatred," wrote Fustel. "Accept our government as it is, and as it can be. . . . Our sole objective should be Alsace."[18]

In the late summer of 1889, with the Boulangist adventure nearing its end, Lieutenant Dreyfus began to study for the competitive entrance exams to the Ecole de Guerre, his most exacting challenge to date. He left Paris for the Twenty-first Artillery Regiment and the Ecole de Pyrotechnie based in Bourges, a city in the Berry province of central France and the home of a principal army arsenal. Assigned a teaching post and named assistant to the school's director, he was promoted to captain in September 1889, a few weeks short of his thirtieth birthday.[19]

Through the cold winter days of that year, he rode the six kilometers over icy terrain from his apartment on the Place Parmentier to classes at the Ecole de Pyrotechnie, with his horse "slipping and sliding" along the way. As a Polytechnicien, he was among the select coterie of military teachers trained as special "leaders of men." "The army should not be a school of duty and honor alone," the captain would say about his teaching responsibilities, "but also a school of high morality. . . . Those are the principles I have tried to apply. . . . To be fair toward those who serve well, ready to give them every moral and material assistance, and unsparing toward those who serve poorly."[20] Teaching mathematics and drafting, the captain found himself torn between his students' needs and the pressures of his own preparation for the Ecole de Guerre. Also, life in another provincial garrison ("a tiresome town," as he described it) did not help his state of mind. Bourges "might be a city," he observed, "but its customs have a rustic imprint." On a bleak day early in 1890, with snow turning to mud and with "cursed exams" drawing near, he chastised himself for the "moments of impatience and bad humor I sometimes show when questioning students. . . . It's proof that we often respond with our emotions and that we must make extraordinary efforts to remain absolutely impartial."[21]

Incessant study and teaching chores made for an anxious winter. Every time he began to enjoy a break in the weather—sitting on his balcony above the Place Parmentier, riding in the countryside, or entertaining a woman companion—he would be reminded of the forth-coming exams and "plunge" again into studies of tactics, topography, German composition, and military history. And even more so than in Le Mans or Paris, he had little in common with garrison colleagues. A French officer described the opinion that most soldiers held of bookish types like Dreyfus: "One laughs in his face if, after dismounting from his horse, he gets pleasure from old books; the least one can do is consider him a little touched."[22]

Another artillery officer, however, Captain Paul-David Hadamard, who had known Dreyfus at the Ecole Polytechnique, shared his inter-ests. Those young friends used the familiar *tu* at a time when that informal address was employed sparingly—and when the resolutely formal Dreyfus used it less often than most. Hadamard had also served at Fontainebleau before joining the Fourth Artillery Regiment at Héri-court, a town near the Alsatian border. At some point early in 1889, while still based in Paris, Dreyfus had joined his friend at a family gathering, either at the country house of his colleague's relatives, David and Louise Hadamard, or in their Paris apartment on the rue Château-dun. For Polytechniciens, an event like the one arranged by Dreyfus's friend was a customary way of meeting young women of respected—and respectable—families. Meticulously attired in dress uniforms and white gloves, officers considered those interviews part of their "stra-tegic arsenal"; and parents in search of the right match for an eligible daughter appreciated the ritual no less than the young men they invited to their homes.[23]

Captain Dreyfus met one of David and Louise Hadamard's three daughters, nineteen-year-old Lucie, and over the coming months wrote long letters to her from Bourges. As tall as Alfred, with thick dark hair parted in the middle and pulled back with a bandeau to control her curls, and with brown eyes, broad shoulders, and a slim waistline made slim-mer by the tight lacing of the day, Lucie had been raised at her family's country home at Châtou, near Paris. She may have attended the private Ecole Monceau where one of her sisters had been a student, but tutors and family members directed much of her education. Her first love was the piano, for which she had considerable talent. Lucie's mother, Louise Hadamard, was the daughter of a Polytechnicien, and one of her most celebrated relatives, Adolphe Hatzfeld, coauthored the important *Dic-tionnaire général de la langue française.* Lucie's father, a leading dia-mond merchant in Paris, traced his origins to a prominent family in Metz known for its early involvement in that city's salon culture and its contributions to the local Jewish community. During the Reign of Terror, one ancestor, Rebecca Lambert Hadamard, had appeared before revolutionary officials to protest the "vile plundering" of Jewish cemeteries and to demand that the "cannibals" of the Terror be brought to justice. She met, it seems, with some success. Lucie's early years were more tranquil than Rebecca's, but she shared that woman's spirit, and though she received no formal religious education, she observed the High Holy Days, read the Bible regularly, and shared her family's faith.[24]

The captain enjoyed a substantial private income, but the Hadamard fortune, estimated at nearly 3 million francs, promised Lucie even greater wealth. Dreyfus's comrade had introduced him to a family of considerable note, and to a young woman who would become his wife as soon as the army vetted her fortune and character. Military officials denied many requests from young men who wished to marry the daughters of peasants, petty merchants, or factory workers, and they looked askance at betrothals involving the relatives of actors, musicians, and theater directors. Some of the regulations concerning an officer's engagement had been relaxed over recent years, but Dreyfus still needed to provide a notarized contract detailing his fiancée's dowry; and commanding officers still checked those figures against the minimum dowry required for the rank of captain. Since the minimum would barely cover the cost of Lucie's piano, there was no doubt that the Hadamards were well qualified. Their credentials—economic position, patriotism, and *bonne réputation*—were impeccable. Lucie's dowry would include a trousseau of linen, lace, jewelry, and furniture valued at 20,000 francs; interest at 3 percent on a sum of more than 35,000 francs; and more than 160,000 francs in cash—all of which, thanks to the institutionalized inequities of Napoleon's Civil Code, would be transferred to her husband's name on the day of their wedding. In addition, according to the army's own investigation, Lucie was in line to receive an inheritance of more than 500,000 francs.[25]

With documents scheduled to be notarized in the early spring of 1890, the marriage was planned for April, in Paris. The Hadamards asked their friend, Rabbi Zadoc Kahn, to preside at the wedding at the Temple de la rue de la Victoire; it would be one of his first ceremonies as the new leader of France's Jewish community. Abraham and Brändel's great-grandson would be married by the nation's grand rabbi in the principal synagogue of France.[26]

The youngest and most peripatetic of the Dreyfus children, Alfred would be the last to settle down. Jacques, Léon, and the three sisters had all married by 1889, and all of their spouses had come from families of industrialists or leading merchants; they had secured *bons mariages*. Most recently, in May 1889, thirty-one-year-old Mathieu had married Suzanne Marguerite Schwob, the twenty-year-old daughter of a textile manufacturer in Héricourt. A woman of extraordinary beauty, she was, like Lucie Hadamard, from a family of enormous wealth.[27] The brotherly affection Mathieu and Alfred shared—the closeness they had known since their days working on tutorials and traveling to boarding schools— did not preclude some rivalry; and it may have been more than a coincidence that Alfred proposed to Lucie only weeks after his brother's wedding and that Lucie Hadamard's fortune was superior to that of Suzanne Schwob. But if the two young men were competitors, it was a friendly rivalry and one they never articulated. Their bonds of affection had only strengthened across the years of separation.

Suzanne Schwob's uncle, mayor of Héricourt and a member of its small community of Freemasons, presided at the wedding in the garden of the Schwob estate. A studiously civil ceremony, it was not followed by a second service in the Héricourt synagogue. Freemasonry, with its belief in reason over revelation, had come to France by way of England in the early eighteenth century. Its criticism of the Catholic church had drawn significant numbers of Protestant and Jewish notables to its ranks; its creed of humanity, brotherhood, and progress had attracted the likes of Montesquieu and Voltaire; and, in 1789, its revolutionary dimensions had inspired members of the Third Estate. By the late nineteenth century, the society, which never numbered more than fifty thousand members in France, still appealed to liberal republicans, and especially to provincial notables like Suzanne Schwob's uncle—though the lofty ideals of the early years had given way to more practical considerations. Freemasonry provided a social, political, and economic network for many Protestants and Jews, as well as for lapsed Catholics hostile to clerical influence. Lodges were prevalent in Alsace, and Mathieu Dreyfus was introduced to Freemasonry by industrialist colleagues—perhaps the chemist Paul Jeanmaire and the manufacturer Rudolphe Koechlin—or by the men with whom he went hunting in the Mulhouse hinterlands.[28]

One thing was certain: Since their school years together the youngest Dreyfus sons had traveled in two very different worlds. Mathieu had expanded his contacts with the society of eastern industrialists, and if not yet initiated into a Masonic order, he had joined a brotherhood committed to the liberal republic and to the separation of church and

state. Alfred shared those beliefs, but as a graduate of the most prestigious military school in France, he was poised to enter the ranks of an
army high command dominated by officers who placed little trust in the
parliamentary politics of the Third Republic. Many of those men believed that France needed defending, not only from Germans but from
forces within—from Protestants, Freemasons, and Jews—who, the argument went, undermined the Catholic order and exploited the promises of the Revolution.

Before his wedding Captain Dreyfus would have to survive Bourges, a
difficult task made bearable by immersion in work, by letters exchanged
with Lucie, and by weekend visits to the Hadamards. The young couple
shared news about his garrison life and her entry into Parisian society.
Lucie described promenades through the Bois de Boulogne and the
stifling boredom of weekly "receptions," those special days when visitors came for tea and for what Alfred agreed were sessions of "worn-
out gossip with individuals of little interest." He understood "why some
people have two days of reception," one for "banality," the other for
good times with intimate friends. "For the most part, my isolation
doesn't weigh too heavily," Alfred wrote in the early winter of 1889. "A
few books, a pen and some paper are enough to distract me." But as his
studies for the Ecole de Guerre intensified and his relationship with
Lucie developed, he shared more thoughts about his provincial "prison"
and the "nervousness" that came with overwork. He slept poorly after
returning from weekends of courtship in Paris ("I'll let you guess the
reasons why," he wrote to Lucie), and he tried to tear himself away
from his dreams of evenings with Lucie in front of her fireplace or of
horseback rides in the sun. He described his constant battles with the
rational side of his character. "Reason knocks violently at my door," he
wrote. "It enters . . . and tells me to put an end to all my dreams and
get back to work. As an obedient slave, I do so." Later, he added that
"studies bore me no end, and if I listened only to my heart, I would have
thrown every one of my books overboard long ago. But reason holds me
back." If reason was his monitor, however, *la Veine* (a personification
of good luck) was his bearer of inspiration. She had "extended a helping
hand" at Chaptal, Sainte Barbe, Grenoble, and the Ecole Polytechnique,
and he hoped she would help again in the spring. He asked Lucie not to
tell her family about the Ecole de Guerre exams; "so much chance" was
involved, and he feared that he could "end up failing.[29]

Lucie discovered her fiancé's mercurial moods, the abrupt shifts from lighthearted descriptions of standing watch on a frigid night with a horse whose whole purpose in life was "to return to the stable" to his obsession with work and a relentless perfectionism that made him appear selfish and insensitive. He admitted that it had always been difficult for him to share his private feelings, to "open up," and he agreed that Lucie had a right to know more about the man to whom she was "entrusting" her life. He would try to express himself and to break his "disastrous habit" of taking everything seriously. But he pleaded with her not to interpret his reserved manner as insensitivity: "Surface insensitivity . . . I grant you," he wrote, using the *vous*, the formal address of a proper young suitor. "The real thing, no!" "I hope you'll come to realize," he added, "that however retiring I may be, I love you deeply." Above all, he abhorred clichés—the cheap currency of paramours—and worried that Lucie would think him just another admirer repeating phrases out of an "official handbook for fiancés." He asked, and was given, permission to drop the "hackneyed" address "Dear fiancée" for the simple "Dear Lucie." By the spring of 1890, the relationship had softened some of the hard edges of Alfred's personality, but even his lyrical letters still mixed passion and Polytechnicien logic: "For two instruments to produce a harmonious sound together," he wrote, describing their mutual affection, "they must be in tune, as in music. In physics, it's called 'synchronic vibrations.' "

In the spring Captain Dreyfus took the examination for the Ecole de Guerre—a three-day marathon of military tactics, topography, history, and German—and soon learned that he was the only artillery candidate from Bourges to pass.[30] Final confirmation would not come until late April, but he was confident about the future and convinced that "It was you, dear Lucie, who brought me good luck." After she helped him through those hard winter and early spring weeks, he wrote about how, as a married couple, all their troubles would be lessened by their "community of happiness . . . the ideal of a life together." Preparing to leave Bourges ("in a dozen days I'll be beside you again"), he received telegrams of congratulations from his family, waded through the documents needed to arrange his transfer to Paris ("You have no idea how, in our beautiful land of France, one has to be a rummager of old papers"), and began to plan with Lucie a late spring honeymoon to northern Italy. They agreed not to prepare a rigid itinerary: "Let's just go and see what happens," Alfred wrote in a new spirit of relaxation and adventure. "To plan every day and every hour in advance . . . would be to miss all the unexpected surprises."[31]

CHAPTER VI

Fin de Siècle

LUCIE EUGÉNIE HADAMARD, twenty years old, and Captain Alfred Dreyfus, ten years her senior, filed two marriage documents in April 1890, one with the state, the other with the Consistoire Israélite de Paris. Unlike Mathieu Dreyfus and Suzanne Schwob, married a year before by a Masonic mayor in a provincial garden, Alfred and Lucie would travel between temple and town hall to record their union in the eyes of God and the republic. Shortly before noon on April 18, the Dreyfus and Hadamard families gathered first at the town hall of the ninth arrondissement, near the grand boulevards of central Paris, to fulfill the requirements of the civil wedding. Raphael, seventy-one years old, had come from Mulhouse and, with the Hadamards, witnessed the marriage papers approved by the commanding general of the Eighth Army Corps. On April 21, the day after Captain Dreyfus received confirmation of his acceptance by the Ecole Supérieure de Guerre, the wedding party met again, this time at the Temple de la rue de la Victoire, a few streets north of the Opéra and directly behind the Hadamards' rue Châteaudun apartment.[1] That synagogue, the largest in Paris, had been built sixteen years earlier in response to the rapid growth of the Ashkenazic population, while another temple, on the nearby rue Buffault, served the city's smaller Sephardic community. Part of a large complex of buildings that housed the Consistoire Israélite, the rue de la Victoire synagogue dominated the short, narrow street where young Napoleon Bonaparte and Josephine de Beauharnais had lived and where, a few doors away, one of the city's ten wet-nurse offices was located. On the temple's Roman and Byzantine facade, rosettes crowned five large windows, and the interior, with its high-domed ceiling and chandeliers, housed a massive organ and stained-glass depictions of the twelve tribes of Israel.[2]

To "obtain the religious consecration of their union and the benediction of God," the couple submitted the traditional *ketubbah,* a document that, unlike the state's notarized marriage contract listing Lucie's dowry, confirmed Alfred's financial obligations to his wife in the event of death or divorce. Read aloud by Grand Rabbi Zadoc Kahn and signed by the newlyweds and their fathers, the *ketubbah* set out customary obligations in Hebrew and French and recorded the day of the ceremony in two forms: *21 Avril 1890* and *1er Iyar 5650.* From the synagogue, the wedding party walked the short distance to the Hadamard residence and passed through its grand entranceway, leading to a central courtyard. A lavish celebration followed, and, from the ornately printed place cards to the fine wines and elaborate desserts, the evening had all the elegant touches required of fin-de-siècle society.[3]

Raphael Dreyfus would have recognized the similarities between his son's Paris synagogue and the family's Mulhouse temple, from the rose windows to the interior motifs; and he would have noted how much Zadoc Kahn, son of an Alsatian peddler and educated in Strasbourg and Metz, had in common with Rabbi Samuel Dreyfus. Both men were known for their civic activism, and both had gained a reputation for their French sermons at a time when preaching had become an important part of synagogue services. Responding to members of their congregations who wanted increased use of the national language, shorter worship services, more organ music, and other moderate changes like those that had been part of reform movements among German Jews, both rabbis addressed their community's needs. Grand Rabbi Kahn, however, far surpassed Samuel Dreyfus in effectiveness and oratorical power: "No other preacher of the present time," said a colleague, represents and reflects "the ideas, the sentiments, the sympathies, the joys, the grief, the hope, the aspirations of the community of modern Jews."[4] With his long, dark beard, peppered with gray, and his intense, deep-set eyes peering over small wire-framed glasses, Kahn served as the honorary president of the Alliance Israélite Universelle, and his close relationship with the Rothschilds and other prominent families helped make him the most powerful spokesman for the Jewish community in France. Nonetheless he shared with his Mulhouse counterpart an unflagging commitment to the French nation ("Fatherland and religion," he would tell an interviewer, was the principal slogan of French Jewry), and he emphasized the ideas of duty, gratitude, and allegiance so familiar to generations of Alsatian Jews.[5]

A few months before the Dreyfus-Hadamard wedding, on the centennial of the French Revolution, Zadoc Kahn had talked about the history of the Jews and the traditions of France: "Her principles which constitute the best of her moral patrimony. . . . As for us . . . we will continue to love our country . . . and bear witness, in all circumstances of our gratitude and devotion."[6] A descendant, in spirit, of those Jewish spokesmen who had sent manifestos of allegiance to Rixheim a century before, Zadoc Kahn embodied the marriage of nation and religion, and echoed the beliefs of the Dreyfus family. He reminded his followers that "the Fatherland puts immense claims upon us and we must never believe that we are free of responsibilities. We must at all times contribute to the prosperity [of France], to her grandeur, to the security of her existence."[7] In 1886, for the preface to a book on Jewish life, he described that "valiant France . . . whose name signifies deliverance for all those who suffer oppression; law, equity, protection, tolerance for all who have known the injustices of history . . . Alsatians have always been and will always be doubly French, and Alsatian Jews," he stressed, *encore une fois de plus* (yet again doubly so). It was not the only statement that summarized Captain Dreyfus's feelings about his homeland: "How many of us," Kahn later said, "have left, along with our childhood memories, a part of our heart" in Alsace? And, in a final comment that would apply to the officer married in his synagogue, the grand rabbi added: "Jews above all feel a love for France without limit. . . . They are proud . . . to work for her prosperity and to defend her flag."[8] Patriotism, provincial loyalty, and religious faith were three pillars of a single allegiance.

After approving Captain Dreyfus's marriage, the military bureaucracy permitted a two-month leave at half-pay for the couple's honeymoon to northern Italy. The timing was ideal. Guidebooks designed for affluent European travelers on abbreviated "grand tours" warned against the malaria-ridden months of midsummer and suggested a five- or six-week journey through Lombardy, Piedmont, and Tuscany in April and May. Shortly after their wedding, Lucie and Alfred must have taken the night express from the Gare de Lyon—a train scheduled to cross the Alps by daylight—and they would have followed the route from Geneva through the massive Mont Cenis Tunnel and toward the northern Italian lakes, an excursion they had been planning for months. From Bellagio on Lake Como they traveled south to Florence, the Italian city that most intrigued Alfred. He had read about the cultural history of the northern Italian Renaissance, and he seems to have found in that society's blend of geometric order and high passion a reflection of his own character; his letters to Lucie had talked about his "Reason" vying with his dreams, and no city's art, architecture, and politics captured those tensions better than did Florence. Not surprisingly, his favorite place was the quiet Piazzale Michelangelo, across the Ponte Vecchio, in the hills above the Arno River, set off from the busy attractions of the city center. With one of the many bronze copies of Michelangelo's David at its center and with the eleventh-century church of San Miniato al Monte nearby, the Piazzale looked northeast to the Etruscan hills of Fiesole and below them to the cityscape—to the Palazzo Vecchio, the Duomo, Santa Croce, and a new synagogue that rose up from the eastern quarter near the Piazza d'Azeglio. Completed only eight years earlier, the glistening oriental domes and colorful neo-Romanesque brickwork of the Tempio Israelitico made that synagogue one of Florence's most outstanding monuments. Alfred would be drawn back to the view from the Piazzale Michelangelo many times, and, like other travelers familiar with Florence, he would come shortly before sundown when the mist had cleared from the Arno.[9]

With work at the Ecole de Guerre not scheduled to begin until the fall, the couple took advantage of their return trip from Italy to visit Alfred's family in Mulhouse. German authorities had instituted an obligatory passport for travel into Alsace-Lorraine three years before (a measure that vexed countless families separated by the 1870 war), but the German system, rigid in theory, was not efficient on every front. Like other French citizens visiting family, friends, or Alsatian enterprises, Alfred and Lucie "smuggled" themselves into Mulhouse *en fraude,* as Alfred described it. Traveling north across the Italian and Swiss Alps, they came in the back way, via Basel.[10]

In the nearly twenty years since Raphael had taken the children from Mulhouse to Carpentras by way of Switzerland, the rue de la Sinne and the rue Lavoisier had changed dramatically. The tree-lined garden on one side of the Dreyfus home had given way to new five-story town houses constructed side by side, and the entire street—once a tranquil road overlooking the southern quai—was becoming a crowded thoroughfare with large offices and apartments designed in the elaborate style of neo-baroque châteaus. Jacques, Léon, and Mathieu were moving their families to separate homes in the eastern and southern quarters, while Raphael, alone except for domestic help, remained on the rue de la Sinne. Though his April visit to Paris had been short, it marked the real beginning of his friendship with Lucie. Like Alfred, she had a good knowledge of German, and over the months to come she would correspond with her father-in-law in his first language. Meanwhile, north of the rue de la Sinne, new factory buildings filled of pastureland on which Raphael had built his mill nearly three decades before. Modern boiler rooms, stables, and warehouses had been added to the original buildings—concrete signs of the expansion and prosperity of the family's enterprise.[11]

Returning to Paris, Alfred and Lucie took an apartment in the eighth arrondissement, at 24, rue François Ier. Situated between the Champs-Elysées and the Seine, their street crossed the broad Avenue Montaigne only a few hundred yards northwest of the Pont de l'Alma, one of the bridges Captain Dreyfus could cross to the Left Bank and the Ecole Supérieure de Guerre. Over recent years that arrondissement and other quarters to the west and north had attracted significant numbers of affluent Jews whose families had first settled in central and eastern districts. Since the early 1870s, the city's Jewish population—the vast majority of Alsatian origin—had grown from twenty-four thousand to well over forty thousand; and with the arrival of new immigrants—victims of recent pogroms in Eastern and Central Europe—that population increased in size and diversity. But if Alfred and Lucie Dreyfus had the means to move to more opulent surroundings, most Jewish families remained in the ninth and tenth arrondissements close to the principal synagogues, or in the fourth arrondissement along the rue Vieille du Temple or the crowded rue des Rosiers, where worship services took place not in temples belonging to the Consistoire Israélite but in small, makeshift *oratoires,* or prayer groups.[12] In that dense quarter of central Paris near the Hôtel de Ville, many poor Eastern European Jews, with their traditional dress, dialects, and customs of religious orthodoxy, had more in common with the Dreÿfusses who had moved from Rixheim to Mulhouse a half century before than with the young couple recently settled on the rue François Ier.[13]

Across the Seine the constellation of buildings that made up the Ecole Militaire and the Ecole Supérieure de Guerre looked east toward the semicircular Place Fontenoy and west toward the city's former racecourse and main military parade ground, the Champ de Mars.

During Dreyfus's earlier time in Paris, the Champ de Mars, cleared of the remnants of the 1878 Universal Exposition, had been a vast, dusty rectangle stretching down to the Seine. Cavalry troops had exercised there, treating passersby to the sight of their bright red-and-blue uniforms and shining breastplates, and to the precision of their equestrian drills. By the fall of 1890, however, the parade ground had been reduced by a third to make way for the city's most recent and controversial monument, built for the 1889 Universal Exposition. A useless cast iron monstrosity for some observers, a dramatic masterpiece of modern architecture for others, and a launching platform for a handful of suicidal aviators, the Eiffel Tower and the problems of its technology must have fascinated Captain Dreyfus, that Polytechnicien whose notebooks were filled with the complex equations of civil engineering.[14]

Entering the Ecole de Guerre an unimpressive sixty-seventh out of eighty-one officers, Dreyfus soon attracted the attention of his superiors, much as he had done in the garrisons where he had started slowly, worked doggedly, and advanced quickly. His studies ranged from the hydraulic braking systems of modern weaponry to cavalry and artillery strategy. With most of his instructors advocating offensive warfare (a strategy largely confined to classrooms and not shared by the military hierarchy), his assignments included trips to examine frontier fortresses and transportation networks west of the Vosges and south toward the Alps. The debacle of 1870 had been due in part to a lack of adequate maps, and Dreyfus, whose brother Jacques had witnessed those problems firsthand with the Légion de l'Alsace, could now apply his knowledge of the eastern provinces to topographical studies based on photographs and land surveys. Assessing the capability of rail lines to move troops and matériel across northeastern France toward military centers at Châlons-sur-Marne and Verdun and deep into the Argonne Forest, Dreyfus and his fellow officers mapped out possible scenarios in the event of renewed conflict with the Germans.[15]

After more than a decade of training he was finally involved in projects that fitted his original reason for joining the army—his desire to confront German militarism and ensure the return of his homeland to France. General Jules Lebelin de Dionne, commandant at the Ecole de Guerre, noted Dreyfus's mastery of "military theory and administrative practice," his "good education, work habits and quick intelligence," and his "very good conduct and deportment." Horsemanship and knowledge of German were still cited as outstanding qualities, and though nearsightedness and bad "intonation" remained drawbacks, superiors continued to believe that he would make a fine officer. In a photograph with members of his Ecole de Guerre class, Dreyfus's thin frame, small spectacles, and hint of gray hair made him appear older than his thirty-one years and more bookish than his comrades. But from military study halls to provincial maneuvers, he remained a "spirited" soldier and "very well suited," said Lebelin de Dionne, for "service on the General Staff."[16]

To secure a place on that staff Ecole de Guerre graduates had to rank near the top of their class, and by the summer of 1892 Dreyfus was optimistic that he would emerge with high marks, perhaps in the top ten. During the same summer, probably in conjunction with an army trip to Monaco and to the foot of the French Alps, he stopped in Carpentras, where Henriette found him in "fine health, though a bit thin," and "happier and more content" than ever. "All is well in the countryside," he wrote to one of his nieces, and referring to his many trips for the army he called himself "the Wandering Traveler [who] passes from one land to another." Above all, he felt comfortable in Carpentras with Henriette and her husband Joseph, the first friend he had made outside the immediate family. He had come to their home as a child following the occupation of Alsace, and he had prepared for school exams in the Valabrègue study. As he awaited the results of yet another competition, he believed that the "blue skies, lush vegetation and calm and tranquil atmosphere" of the south helped "ease the nerves."[17]

Before returning to Paris, he visited his father and brothers in Mulhouse. It was his second trip east in two years, and he again followed the example of other French Alsatians who crossed the border without passports. Since 1884 Dreyfus had submitted official requests to visit Mulhouse on at least ten occasions, and most had been refused. Now a veteran traveler impatient with bureaucracy, and aware that frontier authorities habitually just "closed their eyes," he paid another unofficial visit to his family home en fraude.[18]

After two weeks in Mulhouse he rejoined Lucie and, in November, learned the results of the Ecole de Guerre competition. Unlike young Napoleon Bonaparte, whose military genius Dreyfus admired but who graduated from the Ecole Militaire a dismal forty-second out of fifty-eight officers, the captain ranked ninth out of eighty-one. It was a remarkable accomplishment and it made him eligible for a position as a stagiaire (probationer) on the Army General Staff.[19]

* * *

Before taking up his new post he lodged a protest with the commanding officer of the Ecole de Guerre—a dramatic move for a well-disciplined captain who rarely questioned superiors, but not uncharacteristic of a man with a short temper. He had learned during the summer that a member of the examination jury, General Pierre Bonnefond, did not "want a Jew on the General Staff,"[20] a statement that referred to two candidates, Dreyfus and a colleague named Picard, whose promotions were virtually assured. To lower their overall marks, the general had submitted critical reports on their personal character, on the *côte d'amour* of both Jewish officers.

Throughout the summer, Alfred shared with Lucie his concern that Bonnefond's action signaled a larger deception; he feared that no matter how hard he worked he would not succeed on his merits. At one point his anger became so acute that he suffered nightmares. Waiting until November and the announcement of his score (even with Bonnefond's critique he had done brilliantly), he demanded a meeting with General Lebelin de Dionne. "Is a Jewish officer not capable," Dreyfus asked, "of serving his country as well as any other soldier?" Assured that the army never made distinctions based on religious faith, and that "Jewish officers were valued as highly as any others," he emerged from that meeting, and from another with an Ecole de Guerre colonel, "satisfied" that his superiors respected his accomplishments. The most fundamental lessons he had learned at the Ecole Polytechnique—that merit led to promotion, and that duty to the nation eclipsed all personal interests—were honored at the highest levels of the military. Bonnefond, the captain believed, represented an exception to the army's rule of justice.[21]

Events in Paris during the spring and summer of 1892 had helped prompt Bonnefond's attack and Dreyfus's response. In April, Edouard-Adolphe Drumont, recent founder of the Ligue Anti-sémitique de France, launched a newspaper, *La Libre Parole,* which aimed to expose through its "free speech" the perils of Jewish influence; "France for the French!" the paper's subtitle proclaimed. In the spirit of Drumont's dense, two-volume *La France Juive,* published in 1886 and selling one hundred thousand copies in the first year, the newspaper summarized, in vivid prose for popular consumption, the long, corrosive history of the Jews and the crimes of the "sons of Abraham." The time had come, announced Drumont, for "civilized Frenchmen" to challenge the "savage energy of Jewish invaders." Reminiscent of the Alsatian deputy who, during Abraham Dreÿfuss's lifetime, condemned Jews as "Africans" infesting his region, Drumont vilified the "hooknosed tribe" of foreigners who, like microbes, infected the body of the French nation. Pointing to the flood of immigrants from Eastern and Central Europe—many of them orthodox Jews with beards, wigs, clothes, and dietary laws that set them apart—Drumont reminded readers that even the most Frenchified Jews were, under their cultivated veneer, members of the same "foreign tribe."[22] Whether they lived in the poor, crowded *Pletzl* of Paris—the "little square" north of the Hôtel de Ville—or amidst the splendors of the eighth and sixteenth arrondissements, they were unworthy strangers within. Drumont's description of the poet Heinrich Heine captured it all: "The refined Parisian is indeed the brother of the dirty kikes," Drumont wrote. "The Galician kikes with their curly forelocks, who, come together for some ritual murder, laugh with one another while, from the open wound of the victim there runs pure and crimson the Christian blood for the sweet bread of Purim [*sic*]."[23]

No Jew, Drumont insisted, could hide his true allegiance. Always "a nation within a nation," loyal only to the Promised Land of Israel, they could never be true citizens of the French fatherland; their attachments were abstract not organic, legal not real, and their propensity for speculation, avarice, and self-aggrandizement made them responsible for the economic and social upheavals that came with the growth of industrial capitalism. The sooner France took back the mistaken gift of emancipation, the sooner the nation would emerge from the depths of modern decadence, from all the troubles of the urban world that had been the devilish work of conspiratorial Jews. With his anti-Semitic contemporaries in Germany and Austria, and like his predecessors at the time of the Revolution who severed the rights of man from the rights of Jews, Drumont knew how to fashion repeated lies into received ideas. He played on fears that came with rapid ecomomic change and the wave of immigrants from European *shtetls;* and he tapped, for popular political purposes, the reservoir of anti-Jewish legend, religious and secular. "He who has not good memory," Montaigne once wrote, "should never take upon him the trade of lying." Drumont had a prodigious memory for the anti-Jewish legends, which stretched from the Roman era to the day before yesterday, and he invested that memory in his trade of lies.

Killers of Christ and moneylenders of long standing, Jews had moved on to crucify and exploit the French Fatherland. "At the end of this book of history," Drumont wrote in the conclusion of *La France*

Juive, "what do you see? I see one face and it is the only face I want to show you: the face of Christ, insulted, covered with disgrace, lacerated by thorns, crucified. Nothing has changed," wrote Drumont, "in eighteen hundred years. It is the same lie, the same hatred, the same people." The images were familiar (and all the more powerful for it), and the message contained little that was new. During the upheavals of the late 1840s, social critics had twisted old prejudices to new purposes and had condemned the Jews, "people of Satan," as a "horde of leprous" capitalists. Conjuring up the specter of a cabal of Jewish bankers, one writer, Alphonse Toussenel, had called for "Death to parasitism! War on the Jews!" Obsessed with the power of the Rothschilds, Toussenel dubbed that family the "Kings of the epoch,"[24] and in response, the *Archives Israélites* parodied Toussenel's bizarre logic: "If the railroad runs efficiently, it's called the Compagnie du Nord . . . if it runs poorly it's called the Compagnie Rothschild; and when things go wrong it becomes the railroad of the Jew Rothschild."[25] Toussenel was not alone, however, and his contemporary, Pierre Joseph Proudhon, went further. In the guise of enlightened socialism, he insisted that the Jew was "the enemy of the human species. The race must be sent off to Asia or exterminated."[26] Proudhon, Toussenel, and similar critics across Europe—Karl Marx among them—kept an ancient vocabulary of hatred alive. But they attracted few readers during the relatively stable and prosperous years of the Second Empire, and their work had little resonance in France.[27]

Drumont's manifestos, however, were part of the dark underside of popular journalism, which had increased in the wake of a liberal press law passed in 1880 and which had flourished during the Boulangist campaigns and a series of scandals involving high functionaries in the world of banking and government. "Ten years ago," Drumont observed in 1888, *"La France Juive* would have been considered the book of an eccentric . . . two years from now I will be considered too moderate." He was right about the broad popularity of his book (along with Ernest Renan's *Vie de Jesus,* it would become the largest bestseller in late-nineteenth-century France),[28] though he was wrong about his own moderation. By the early 1890s a spate of broadsheets, books, and newspapers echoed his venomous attacks, from *Face aux Juifs!,* which lashed out at the "inferior Jewish race" ("like coolies from the Orient") and called for stripping Jews of citizenship and wealth, through the ephemeral publication *L'Anti-Youtre (The Anti-Yid),* to the long-lasting and widely circulated Catholic newspaper *La Croix,* adorned with a picture of the crucified Christ and filled with hatred for the modern descendants of Judas.[29] The anti-Semites' modern campaign blended vivid images of Christ-killers with the pseudoscience of racialism and pointed to the Jew as the predestined candidate for treason. From moneychangers in the Temple to horsedealers trading with Napoleon's enemies to spies behind the defeat of 1870, Jews had provided abundant evidence, their critics insisted, that they were out to ruin Christianity and France.

Most recently, Drumont and his followers had taken on Jewish businessmen who had conspired, the story went, to exploit thousands of innocent Frenchmen and -women who had invested their life's savings in the Panama Canal Company. Launched by the venerable Ferdinand de Lesseps, builder of the Suez Canal, the Panama Company faced bankruptcy in 1889 and tried to raise state funds through clandestine payoffs to nearly one hundred members of the French parliament. But both the legitimate construction project and the secret campaign of corruption failed, and when Drumont got wind of the scandal he focused on two Jews affiliated with the ill-fated scheme. The Panama debacle, which had been festering for nearly two years by the time *La Libre Parole* appeared, seemed to confirm the anti-Semites' belief that Jewish corruption was at the root of the republic's troubles. And in the summer and fall of 1892, it gave added resonance to warnings that the army, like the Chamber of Deputies, had fallen victim to Jewish machinations. One of Drumont's admirers in the chamber called for legislation to expel Jews from France, and though the bill was soundly defeated, it signaled the emerging political dimension of Drumont's appeal. From investment ventures, banks, industries, and stock exchanges, Jews had spread into the most insidious base of operation—the sacred ranks of the military. At the Ecole Polytechnique and on the General Staff, good Catholics were being pushed out, Drumont warned, by a growing contingent of Protestants, Freemasons, and Jews.[30]

It mattered little that French Jews had fought for the fatherland in Napoleonic campaigns and the Franco-Prussian War, or that hundreds of Jewish officers, generals and colonels among them, were currently serving France with distinction. Anti-Semites agreed only that Jewish presence in the military had increased over recent years—a fact about which they were uncharacteristically correct. In 1892 the number of Jews in uniform was superior, in proportion, to the number of Jews in the general population. But Drumont interpreted that evidence as a sign of infiltration, not patriotism, and just as he inflated population statistics (there were a half million Jews in France, he said, when there were barely seventy thousand), he exaggerated Jewish influence in the army (there were, in fact, only three hundred Jews in an officer corps of forty thousand). With no way to confirm the figures and no desire to do so, the vast majority of Drumont's followers believed what they read, and through the summer of 1892, they read about the inability of the military high command to root out its Jews.[31]

The campaign did not go unchallenged, however, and Dreyfus's experience with Bonnefond at the Ecole de Guerre was only one example among other, more dramatic responses. Within weeks of the publication of the first issue of *La Libre Parole,* French Jewish officers confronted Drumont: "In insulting the three hundred French officers on active service who belong to the Jewish faith," wrote Captain André Crémieu-Foa of the Eighth Dragoon Regiment in May 1892, "you are insulting me personally." The captain's letter and Drumont's response ("If Jewish officers are wounded by our articles, let them choose delegates and we will oppose them with an equal number of French swords") led to a duel in which both men were slightly wounded.[32] A short time later Captain Armand Mayer (like Dreyfus, an Alsatian and Polytechnicien) challenged another anti-Semite, the Marquis de Morès, to a duel. A Spanish-Italian-French nobleman, Morès had been a part-time rancher in the American Midwest until, as he described it, the Jewish-controlled beef trust forced him out of business. Other bizarre exploits took him from railroad dealings in Indochina to membership in Drumont's Parisian circle of Jew-haters. But it was the marquis's duel with Captain Mayer that finally mobilized military leaders, state officials, and Parisian journalists. Armed with a heavy battle sword, which experts from the Ecole Polytechnique later confirmed violated the customary weight for such affairs of honor, Morès needed only a few seconds to perforate Mayer's lung and cut his spinal cord. The captain died that night, and his funeral, presided over by Grand Rabbi Zadoc Kahn and attracting a crowd of more than twenty thousand, became a "spectacular demonstration of public sympathy"[33] marked by military music and students from the Ecole Polytechnique in full-dress uniform. Morès, Drumont, and their allies had gone too far. Following the duel the newspaper *Le Matin* declared that "in one single day, anti-Semites have made Jews more sympathetic than they had made them antipathetic across four or five years of daily attack and slander."[34]

Though Captain Dreyfus seems to have been on assignment in the French Alps at the time of the demonstration in support of Mayer, Lucie and the Hadamards, close friends of Zadoc Kahn and with long family ties to the Ecole Polytechnique, likely attended the funeral and heard the eulogy: Mayer's sacrifice "will not have been useless," announced the grand rabbi, "if it serves to dissipate the fatal misunderstandings, and lets shine forth, through the veil of mourning which covers it today, the flag of France, this glorious and immortal symbol of justice, of concord, of fraternity."[35] Upon returning to the Ecole de Guerre, Captain Dreyfus would have learned the details of the tragedy and heard the strong declaration of support made by the minister of war. "The army makes no distinction among Jews, Protestants and Catholics," the government announced, "and any such division is a crime against the nation."[36]

While anti-Semites played on an ancient language of prejudice, the army's highest officials responded much as they had done decades before during anti-Jewish upheavals in Alsace; they went on record that they would defend the Declaration of the Rights of Man and Citizen. When Dreyfus lodged his protest of General Bonnefond's action in November he did so in the wake of those conflicts and in the spirit of Crémieu-Foa's now-legendary challenge to Drumont ("in the name of Israelite officers").[37] And Dreyfus's satisfaction that the army had responded honorably was reflected in Rabbi Kahn's belief that "all the children of France, following the example of the French army, are part of a single family with one heartfelt passion: to assure the glory and grandeur of the Fatherland, and to guard its good name."[38] Product of a military system that put "the profound cult of honor" above all individual interest, Dreyfus held firm to the belief that religion was a private affair and that race, as he would put it later, had nothing to do with "character." Like those two more celebrated captains, Mayer and Crémieu-Foa, he condemned Drumont's odious campaign as an insult to the army and to the fatherland, and he apologized to no one for his heritage.[39]

Promotion to *stagiaire* on the General Staff prompted two moves. Captain Dreyfus was now assigned to offices at the War Ministry on the rue Saint Dominique, west of the Invalides, and every morning, after brisk gallops through the Bois de Boulogne with David Hadamard, he walked to those offices from his new apartment on the Avenue du Trocadéro, near the Seine. Lucie and Alfred had been planning that move to more spacious quarters ever since the birth of their first child, Pierre Léon, on April 5, 1891.[40]

Born in the apartment on the rue François Ier, the baby was in a "delicate" state for months. It had been a difficult childbirth—Lucie had also fallen ill—and an anxious time for the family. Sharing the prevailing view that the polluted city was no place for an infant in poor health, Lucie and Alfred wanted Pierre to breathe the clean air of Alsace. They also believed, as did others, that hearty wet nurses could only be found in the provinces, and that Alsatians were the heartiest of all. Later in the year, with her husband off on yet another assignment, Lucie regained sufficient strength to travel with Pierre to visit Raphael and to hire an Alsatian wet nurse named Virginie Hasler. Returning to Paris, mother and child slowly improved in health, and a few months later Lucie was pregnant again. On February 22, 1893, only weeks after Alfred began work on the General Staff, a daughter was born in their new apartment. They named her Jeanne, after Alfred's mother.[41]

Army officers based in Paris received a supplement for the high cost of living,[42] but even that income, added to an artillery captain's salary, could not have paid for all the comforts the family enjoyed on the Avenue du Trocadéro. Lucie's trousseau and the couple's combined private income helped them furnish the apartment, pay for servants (among them Jeanne's wet nurse and a family cook), and acquire an extensive wardrobe for city and country, some of it purchased at the Belle Jardinière, the Bon Marché, and other Parisian department stores. Alfred had a wine cellar built for the apartment; he ordered specially tailored uniforms and indulged his taste for chocolates and small cigars; and, though no longer required to exercise horses in military arenas, he continued to secure the finest mounts and best equipment for pleasure rides in city parks. In letters to Mathieu, the family's premier sportsman, Alfred expressed an interest in bird shooting, and turned to his brother for advice on the finest arms. Counseling Alfred on everything from calibers to codes of safety for amateur hunters, Mathieu recommended a sixteen-gauge Hamerless shotgun valued at 550 francs and available at Paris's leading arms merchant, Guinard, on the Avenue de l'Opéra. After more than a decade of nomadic movement through military schools and provincial garrisons, the "Wandering Traveler," as he had called himself, had finally been rewarded, at the age of thirty-four, with the settled, domestic comforts of the Parisian haute bourgeoisie— the life of a rich and gifted officer in a nation at peace.[43]

He regularly left for work at 8:30 A.M. after his morning ride and a brief visit with the children. He walked across the bridge from the Place de l'Alma and east along the quais to General Staff headquarters, a stroll that took no more than twenty minutes. At 11:30 A.M., he returned home for lunch before setting off again, shortly before 2:00 P.M., for the rue Saint Dominique. Rarely staying in his office later than 6:00 P.M., he rejoined Lucie for a quiet dinner followed by an evening at the symphony or a rubber of bridge with the Hadamards and family members visiting from the provinces. Most of the time, however, the couple spent alone, taking short promenades through their *quartier* and returning to read by the fire. They were building a considerable library in the new apartment, with titles that reflected their varied interests—from six-volume sets on Napoleonic campaigns, cavalry tactics, and military fortifications to histories by Fustel and Ernest Lavisse, Balzac novels, Shakespeare plays (translated into French), and a broad range of literary magazines and Parisian periodicals.[44]

They also took advantage of evenings and Sundays alone to talk about the children's discipline. Raised in similar environments, Lucie and Alfred had been sheltered by parents and older siblings. But the Hadamards had been stricter than the Dreyfuses and less willing to pamper their children. While Alfred had enjoyed the comforts of his Mulhouse garden and the gifts of toys and books for good behavior, Lucie had rarely been rewarded with more than a slice of fruit, and, it seems, she had been occasionally, though not abusively, punished. Worried that Pierre's delicate health and highly sensitive nature were signs of general weakness, Lucie's instinct was to balance her affection for the boy with a firm hand. Alfred's feelings, however, the result of his own upbringing and his methodical interest in philosophies of child rearing, led him to reject corporal punishment. Fear encouraged weakness, he believed, and following the tenets of the eighteenth-century philosophes he so admired, he insisted that education, reason, and "moral influence" would mold the strongest character.[45]

Through their early years Alfred and Lucie had been surrounded almost exclusively by parents, sisters, brothers, and family servants, and after their marriage they made little effort to change those habits or to cultivate new friendships outside their tightknit family circle. But there were other reasons for their restricted number of friends. Alfred never felt comfortable in the presence of strangers. His sisters had noted his reserve as a child when visitors called at their home, and they had seen how playful he became when alone with the immediate family. Later that shyness bordering on timidity became a reserved, highly controlled public manner seeming, at times, like arrogance. The private struggles he described in his early letters to Lucie from Bourges—the difficulty he had "opening up," the tensions he grappled with between disciplined work and the desire for spontaneity—had their public manifestations. From his school years in Paris through his work on the General Staff, he impressed colleagues as a proud but distant man who kept himself under tight rein. The many stages of isolation in boarding schools and garrisons had not encouraged expansiveness, and the contrast with his closest brother's self-assured manner must have intensified his sense of awkwardness. Even their voices confirmed the difference: Mathieu's was pleasant and sonorous, Alfred's harsh and metallic. In appearance and personality Mathieu had an elegant, aristocratic manner his brother could admire but never duplicate. As one observer put it, the textile manufacturer had the strong bearing of a distinguished military officer, while the career soldier with the pince-nez had the pallid, distracted look of a reserved and serious scholar.[46]

But Alfred had ventured into a world of obstacles Mathieu had never confronted. Self-assurance in the familiar circle of Mulhouse industrialists was more easily achieved than in the often-hostile society of Parisian *grandes écoles* and military politics—a society that forced the issue of religion and "race" in a way Mathieu rarely encountered in Mulhouse. And for a boy raised by three sisters and sheltered through his most formative years, it was a hard world in which military life required the assertion, as one witness described it, of strong "male sentiments" and "virile habits" of audacity and courage.[47] Alfred fought to prove himself through hard work and merit, and not through affluence or privilege; he still possessed the traits his sisters had attributed to their "Don Quixote," and for more than a dozen years he passed every test that Paris and the army had set before him. As a young, ambitious provincial alone in the capital he had "thrown down the gauntlet" before Paris and all it represented; but unlike the Balzacian characters who made the same gesture with tragic results, Dreyfus had, so far, succeeded brilliantly. Sacrificing the comfortable life of an industrialist, he had survived years of discipline in dormitories and garrisons and earned the right to be proud. Even Mathieu commented on his brother's "exaggerated pride" and "passion for the military métier."[48] Nonetheless, Alfred was not a *fanatique militaire*—a *"fana-mili"* in the vocabulary of the fin de siècle—but a patriot whose code of honor was built on a sense of duty to the fatherland and a spirit of self-abnegation. "Fatigue, danger, death, all that is nothing!" wrote one student of military discipline. "For a young, well-bred and spirited man to blindly submit himself to the will of countless superiors, to bow down to discipline . . . is to deny all personal feeling and to become a passive instrument."[49] Though far from passive (he admitted that his "nervous temperament" often made him "hotheaded"),[50] Dreyfus had become the willing instrument of the army to which he had devoted his life. Shaped by the austerity of the Ecole Polytechnique, he was an ascetic in uniform whose two transgressions were ambition and pride and who had only two demands— that his attainments be respected and his contributions justly rewarded. Those demands were the principal reason why he had challenged Bonnefond's threat to his advancement, and why he made few friends on the General Staff. Montaigne's comments on ambition fit the officer who read the essayist so often: "Let us reply to ambition that it is she herself that gives us a taste for solitude," Montaigne wrote. "For what does she shun so much as society? What does she seek so much as elbowroom?"[51]

Dreyfus's professional zeal and personal pride elicited both admiration and hostility on the General Staff. As he passed through its four sections and learned, along with twelve other *stagiaires,* the details of fortifications, artillery strategy, troop movements, and intelligence, he continued to win the praise he had known throughout his career. A "very intelligent officer . . . with extensive knowledge," wrote one colonel in the fall of 1893. "He wants to—and should—succeed." But alongside high marks for his "gifted" and "quick" mind and his language skills, there appeared, for only the second time in his career, criticisms of his "pretentiousness," and, as Colonel Pierre Fabre of General Staff put it, problems with his "character." He was ambitious and "perhaps too sure of himself." The language was reminiscent of Bonnefond's earlier critique, and it revealed, among other prejudices, a desire on the part of some officers to rid the Etat-Major (the General Staff) of its Jewish *stagiaire.* For the aristocrats who still made up an influential force in the high command—and who, threatened with extinction in republican France, insisted more than ever on the "qualities" of breeding and race—Captain Dreyfus was a parvenu, an *arriviste* with abundant talent and little grace. As the son of devout Jewish parents and the husband of a woman whose faith was genuine and intense, he would not curry favor at the expense of his family's honor. He would not do at the Etat-Major what he had refused to do at the Ecole de Guerre.[52]

For other colleagues, many of them avid readers of *La Libre Parole,* Dreyfus was a target of envy. Struggling to emulate their betters, most staff officers scraped by on an annual salary which barely matched a month of the captain's private income. Not even the old military proverb—"Second lieutenants amass debts, lieutenants pay them off, and captains put money in the bank"[53]—could apply to the Etat-Major's new *stagiaire*. He had entered the military already armed with enormous wealth, and, no less irritating to those officers who struggled through the ranks, he had come as the product of the elite Chaptal, Sainte Barbe, and Ecole Polytechnique. He had traveled through a different world than many of his colleagues, and, rumor had it, those travels had included excursions into the demimonde of Paris racetracks and courtesans' salons.

Though mostly the wishful thinking of envious men deprived of access to that rarefied society, the rumors had some substance. As a young officer in Paris, Fontainebleau, Le Mans, and Bourges, Dreyfus had rejected the company of garrison colleagues for study alone or for rendezvous *"dans le monde."* He dined at the fashionable Cercle de la Presse on the Boulevard des Italiens; he frequented Longchamp and Auteil (though more as a horse lover than as a gambler); and he enjoyed a few liaisons with women of considerable means and cultivated, though sometimes idiosyncratic, tastes.[54] Furthermore, his reputation at the Etat-Major in 1893 was not helped by stories of his involvement in a sensational murder trial three years before, a Parisian *crime passionnel* that the popular press had covered in all its sordid details.

As a young lieutenant in Paris in 1884, Dreyfus had made the acquaintance of a woman married to an industrialist in the town of Juvisy, south of the capital. Strikingly beautiful and from a good family, Madame Dida—who was, like her husband, in the first stages of an addiction to morphine and cocaine—had a penchant for collecting young male admirers. In 1884–85 she exchanged a number of letters with Dreyfus. The lieutenant's friendship with the woman ended after only a few meetings when her father told him about Dida's husband, her two young children, and her unbalanced state. Appealing to Dreyfus's honor, the father asked him to break off the relationship. The woman continued to leave desperate messages at his Paris quarters, but the lieutenant kept his word and never saw her again. Six years later, however, the father reappeared to ask for help. Madame Dida's husband had died in the interim, and a Russian fortune hunter named Pierre de Wladimirof had proposed marriage. With a stylish blond mustache and long side-whiskers, and turned out in a black frock coat and high starched collar, Wladimirof was handsome, tall, and twelve years Madame Dida's junior. He was also a high society con artist. With the woman in the worst throes of her drug addiction, the courtship, which included late nights at the Moulin Rouge and Chat Noir, was a stormy one. Accepting Wladimirof's proposal, then refusing and accepting again, Dida went with the Russian to a country inn south of Paris. Wladimirof brought a loaded revolver (a purchase he had made by pawning one of his fiancée's jewels) and threatened to kill himself if she rejected him. In the hotel Dida finally decided against marriage, and during the ensuing argument she called Wladimirof a "crazy man." He shot her five times. He would later insist, unconvincingly, that he thought there were six bullets in the chamber and that he was saving the last for himself. Attempting to explain his actions by slandering Dida, Wladimirof named a string of the woman's previous lovers. Called to testify at the trial held in Versailles in January 1891 were a Parisian industrialist, a wine merchant, and a young attaché at the Ecole de Guerre, Captain Alfred Dreyfus.

On assignment and unable to attend, Dreyfus agreed to the father's plea for support and submitted a deposition that echoed the testimony of Madame Dida's other friends: Dreyfus was "indignant" that Wladimirof would attempt to save himself by sullying the character of a "charming woman" Dreyfus had known "in fashionable society" but with whom he had "never been intimate." With the help of his counsel, the celebrated Parisian criminal lawyer Maître Edgar Demange, the Russian tried to convince the jury that he, as much as Dida, had been a victim of passion. The prosecutor, however, accused the "sharper, thief and murderer" of being made desperate not "by passion" but by desperately "bad finances." The well-publicized double suicide in 1889 of Austria's Crown Prince Rudolph and his mistress, Marie Vetsera, at Mayerling, outside Vienna, was a recent and vivid memory, and the prosecutor, who knew it would move the jurors, contrasted the prince's heroism with the criminal cowardice of the bogus count Wladimirof. In the end the Russian's histrionic call for mercy had some impact on the jury; convicted with extenuating circumstances, he received a sentence of twenty years at hard labor.[55]

Dreyfus had kept his promise to Madame Dida's father, but it was an embarrassing episode, one of the kind young Polytechniciens were taught to avoid, and one surely known to the captain's associates on the General Staff. After his marriage in 1890, he severed ties to the Parisian society in which he had met Madame Dida, though in the months following Pierre's birth, when Lucie was ill or away in Mulhouse, he was tempted to revisit the life he had known as a young *boulevardier*. In his *quartier* near the Place de l'Alma he met Marie Virginie Déry, a socialite well acquainted with a number of French officers, and he visited her on two or three occasions at her apartment on the rue Bizet. But that relationship—and another with a woman he met at the racetrack and again near the Place de Clichy—was brief and never serious. Dreyfus had always preferred the company of cultivated women to the male society of army colleagues, many of whom he found petty and boorish, and he had many opportunities to contrive a double life of domesticity and the *petites aventures* so common for men of his station. He might have taken a mistress, had it not been for his devotion to Lucie ("my love for my wife overcame the desire of my senses")[56] and for her readiness to stand her ground. With Mathieu and the Hadamards, she monitored Alfred's movements and reminded him of his responsibilities as husband, father, officer, and gentleman.

Thus nothing came of the captain's brief return to "fashionable society." He settled into his work routine at the Etat-Major and into a comfortable life with Lucie, the children, and family visitors. But those changes did not alter the attitudes of officers who either disapproved of or envied his past, and who, above all, resented his promising future. As he moved through the stages of the General Staff he made no attempt to downplay his achievements, hide his wealth, hold back his opinions, or change his solitary work habits. And as relations with associates became strained and the influence of Drumont continued to grow within army circles, the captain renewed his conviction that it was "absurd to bore oneself with a society of tiresome . . . disagreeable, often spiteful and envious men."[57] He saw copies of *La Libre Parole* on the desks of some colleagues, but attached little importance to those "displays of human foolishness."[58]

He was not entirely isolated, however, and not all officers were part of the despotic "satrapie," as one of Dreyfus's friends later called the inner circle of the Etat-Major.[59] Occasionally the captain walked home in the evening with an officer or two who lived in the sixteenth arrondissement, and they shared common interests in hunting, horsemanship, and more. But toward most of his colleagues he remained correct and distant. He worked diligently at every task assigned to him as a *stagiaire* (even the most severe critics could not deny his talents), while showing little of his closest brother's diplomacy. In his own estimation he was neither "compliant . . . nor a flatterer." If there was to be a politician in the Dreyfus family, it would not be Alfred but Mathieu, who had patience with critics and an instinct for compromise.[60]

* * *

On returning from maneuvers in Beauvais in early December 1893 and another assignment in Le Mans, the captain received word that his father had fallen critically ill. Coming at a time when he was making the choice to "stay aloof" from military society and "be contented with the happiness" of close family ties,[61] it was particularly shocking news. Granted emergency leave from the War Ministry and a travel permit from the German Embassy (a request often refused French officers even in times of family crisis), Alfred rushed to Mulhouse and to Raphael's bedside.[62]

He had barely two days with his father in the house on the rue de la Sinne. At 5:00 A.M. on Wednesday, December 13, surrounded for the first time in years by all his children, Raphael died. He was seventy-five years old. On the next afternoon, the industrialist's longtime friends and associates gathered in the late autumn cold outside the Dreyfus home and followed the funeral cortege north along the same route Raphael had taken in 1860 to survey the pastureland where his factory would be built. Turning west, the procession entered the Jewish section of the Mulhouse cemetery, a flat, open space with dense rows of small stone markers chiseled with Hebrew inscriptions and dates recorded according to the Jewish calendar. Jacob Dreÿfuss had been the first member of the family to be buried in that plot, and Raphael, alongside Jeannette and the two infant daughters they had lost many years before, was the last.[63]

If Raphael's legacy to his seven children was far superior in worldly goods to the inheritance he had received from his own father, many of the lessons were the same. Tutored by Jacob in the village markets of Alsace, Raphael, in turn, had taught his sons the intricacies of the textile trade and, no less important to him, the duties that came with membership in the Mulhouse "patriciate" and with citizenship in France. He had been the patriarch of a family of *protestataires,* Alsatians who had opted for France, and it was the nature of that patriotism, extended from province to nation, which set him off from his own father. While Jacob Dreÿfuss brought the family out of a hostile countryside into *"la ville la plus française de l'Alsace,"* Raphael Dreyfus, in name and allegiance, led them deeper into the French interior. That he stayed behind in his native province under German occupation was not a sign of divided loyalties, just as it was not for Jacques, Léon, and Mathieu, who had also stayed on, or returned, to live and work in Mulhouse. It was a practical strategy to save the family's resources and the personal statement of a patriot—of Alsace and of France—who never accepted the inevitability of permanent occupation.[64] As a devout Jew, a man of Scripture and of the belief, strengthened through his own lifetime, that France was a land of promise, he may well have found in his later years as father and grandfather new layers of meaning in Isaac's words to Jacob: "God almighty bless you and make you fruitful . . . that you may become a company of people . . . that you may take possession of the land of your sojournings which God gave to Abraham."

Raphael's legacy included a fortune generated by a thriving industry. By 1894 the mill was paying annual property taxes commensurate to those levied on the Koechlin-Schwartz, Schlumberger, Dreyfus-Lantz, and other leading Mulhouse enterprises.[65] In addition to regular payments over recent years, each of the children received an additional 250,000 to 300,000 francs on Raphael's death. Added to other savings, that sum would have brought Alfred and Lucie an annual income of nearly 35,000 francs in 1894 had a fire not destroyed some of the factory's buildings and machines in late August. In response the sons followed in their father's bold footsteps and channeled the large insurance payment they received into the rebuilding and modernization of the existing factory and into the construction of a new cotton-spinning mill in Belfort, across the border in French territory. In order to raise additional capital, they took Raphael Dreyfus et Compagnie public, selling stock and transforming it into a *société par actions,* though the name remained along with the family's controlling interest.[66] Jacques planned to oversee the new Belfort operation from his base in Mulhouse, while Mathieu, assisted by Léon, would take charge on the rue Lavoisier. Cotton industries throughout the region were entering a new era of "spectacular progress" following economic depression in the 1880s and early 1890s, and in September 1894 Mathieu shared his optimism in a letter to Alfred: "If we are able to move ahead next January and February with the completely new factory . . . and with heavy machinery, we can hope, given the current price of raw cotton and thread, for a fine inventory in 1895."[67]

As general manager of the family's holdings, Mathieu divided Raphael's house into apartments, kept his brothers and sisters informed of the search for rental income, and distributed the cotton mill's profits. He had recently moved with Suzanne and their two infant children, Emile and Magui, to a large house near the southern canal of Mulhouse, on the tree-lined Altkircherstrasse. Notwithstanding German street names (in place for two decades), most of the merchants and manufacturers who lived in Mathieu's *quartier* and who gathered at the cotton exchange continued to use French—often with a vengeance. The Dreyfus brothers negotiated in German with workers, bureaucrats, and associates across the Rhine, but French remained their first language. "The most solid bastion of protest against annexation," Mulhouse was the only Alsatian city in which French progressed after 1870, and, to a great extent, its survival had been the work of the stubbornly patriotic *haut patronat*, which included the Dreyfus family. The Société Industrielle still refused to translate its name or to publish its newsletter in German, and it was not uncommon for Alsatians to confront occupiers over issues other than language. Mathieu knew that well; at some point in the early 1890s, hearing a German slander France, Mathieu challenged him to a duel. Neither man was injured, it seems, but the incident added to the family's local reputation as "ardent and irreproachable patriots." So too did the recent actions of Jacques' family; taking advantage of a German law permitting emigration to France when children reached the age of seventeen, Jacques' two oldest sons opted for French citizenship and left for Paris to prepare for entrance exams at the Ecole Polytechnique and Saint Cyr. Having made that choice, they were prohibited by German authorities from returning to live in Mulhouse.[68]

In the months following Raphael's death, optimistic letters from Mathieu, and reports of the expansion of the family enterprise, must have helped raise Alfred's spirits. By the early summer of 1894, he had reimmersed himself in work at the Etat-Major, and in late June he was encouraged by a meeting with General Raoul de Boisdeffre, the army's new chief of staff. Dreyfus accompanied the general on a trip to the town of Charmes, near Epinal and the Vosges Mountains. At dinner, conversation turned to recent artillery tests conducted in Calais and Bourges, a subject Dreyfus knew well. Given his prodigious memory and interest in artillery modernization, the captain impressed his companions with his sophisticated analysis and mastery of detail. After dinner Boisdeffre invited Dreyfus to join him for a walk, and for more than an hour along the banks of the Moselle River the army chief of staff and the second-year *stagiaire* discussed military matters while other officers trailed behind. Dreyfus returned from that trip with a profound appreciation of General Boisdeffre's goodwill, and with renewed faith that the high command valued his efforts.[69]

It must have made the family's annual holiday all the more enjoyable. Packing baby carriages, summer wardrobes, servants, and Hadamard in-laws into train compartments at the Gare Saint Lazare, Alfred and Lucie took the family along the route from Paris to the Normandy coast that had become so popular with Parisian vacationers. Two decades before, as a boarder at Chaptal, young Alfred had heard those trains pass under his dormitory window, and, with other *internes,* he must have dreamed about their destinations. Now a seasoned traveler, he knew the pleasures of Normandy at firsthand. Dotted with private villas and elegant "watering places" (*stations balnéaires*), and catering to tourists from both sides of the Channel, the strip of coastline between the Orne River and the Seine was gaining the reputation as "le 'Far West' de la France"—but a Far West of fin-de-siècle "luxury and high life." At Trouville and Deauville, yachtsmen, horsemen, and other fashionable types strolled along boulevards facing the beach or went "five o'clocking" at tea shops, while at the smaller resorts of Villers-sur-Mer and Houlgate, preferred by the Dreyfuses and Hadamards, modern hotels, villas, and swimming clubs shared the coastline with old fishing harbors and roughhewn timber houses. On the beach at Houlgate, beneath the dark cliffs known as the Vaches Noires (Black Cows), Lucie would keep young Jeanne shaded from the summer sun while Alfred helped Pierre, not yet four years old, run through the seaweed and sand. On the rocks below the Vaches Noires, according to tourist guidebooks, fishermen invariably met with good luck.[70]

PART 3

The Affair

CHAPTER VII

Reunion

ON WEDNESDAY, October 31, 1894, Lucie Dreyfus sent an urgent telegram to Mathieu at the Mulhouse cotton exchange. He must come to Paris immediately. The message contained no details and no mention of Alfred, but Mathieu assumed that his brother had fallen ill or suffered an accident. Taking the night train, he arrived at the Gare de l'Est before dawn the next morning, and when he saw his sister Rachel alone with Lucie on the dimly lighted platform, he feared the worst.[1]

From the early days in Mulhouse, Mathieu had been his brother's keeper and closest companion, even from afar. While Jacques and Léon worked in their father's mill, the younger boys stayed behind, the focus of their sisters' attention. They moved to Switzerland together and crossed the Vosges, and when they separated—one in Alsace, the other in Paris—they believed that they were working toward a common goal on the front lines of industry and the military, toward the reunification of the family that could only come with the reunification of the homeland and the fatherland. And just as Alfred admired his closest brother's social graces, Mathieu, who had dreamed of a military career, respected his younger brother's success. Jacques and Léon were of another generation, with other interests, and, to a certain extent, another language. Alfred was Mathieu's *ami d'élection,* his "friend of choice."[2] During the all-night train journey from Mulhouse, and as he walked down the platform toward Lucie and Rachel the next morning,

111

Mathieu was increasingly certain that "something grave" had happened to his brother. His mind raced through "every possibility," but the reality surpassed anything that his "imagination could conceive."[3]

Accused of high treason, Alfred had been arrested two weeks before and held under strict secrecy by military authorities. Lucie had not been allowed to see her husband or write to him, and only in the last few hours had army officials given her permission to contact the family. Lucie's words were like a *coup de massue*, a "physical blow," which left Mathieu stunned. His brother was a patriot ("honor itself"), and whatever his faults his strongest trait was "perfect loyalty." The one crime impossible for the son of a family of Alsatian *protestataires* to commit was treason.

"What do you know?" Mathieu asked Lucie. "Nothing at all," she responded, "I've been unable to get any details from the officer in charge of the investigation." Realizing that their "excited and troubled" exchange was attracting the attention of passersby, Mathieu sent Lucie and Rachel off to the Avenue du Trocadéro apartment and remained, for a moment, alone on the train platform. He rehearsed the words "prison, crime, treason" and felt as if it were all a dream. Never doubting his brother's innocence, he searched for an explanation: "Was he the victim of some hateful plot, of vengeance, of an error?" Leaving the Gare de l'Est, Mathieu passed news vendors hawking papers with accounts of an espionage trial in the making. Headlines still focused on the death, a few days before, of the Russian Czar Alexander III, but when the Havas Press Agency released the first report on the "high treason" of a French officer, journalists rushed to investigate. On October 31 *Le Soir* published the essential detail, Dreyfus's name. Wasting no time, Drumont's *La Libre Parole* added the critical adjective to its November 1 edition: "Arrest of a Jewish Officer, A. Dreyfus."[4]

Mathieu rejoined Lucie and learned that she had not seen Alfred since Monday morning, October 15. The previous Saturday the captain had received orders by special messenger to appear at the Etat-Major for an inspection of staff officers. He found it peculiar that a general inspection, usually conducted in the afternoon, had been rescheduled for Monday morning, and, more perplexing, he wondered why the note stipulated that he dress in "civilian clothes." It was also strange that the messenger had returned later on Saturday to demand a written receipt confirming acknowledgment of the order. By the next evening, however, when the couple played bridge at the Hadamards, as they did every Sunday, and as they shared memories of Alfred's festive thirty-fifth-birthday party the week before, the captain put his queries aside and assumed that the staff meeting promised nothing out of the ordinary.[5]

Punctual to a fault, he always returned home for lunch at noon. On that Monday, however, it was not Alfred who came to the Avenue du Trocadéro apartment, but two men from the Etat-Major, Commandant Mercier du Paty de Clam and Armand Cochefort, a police functionary assigned to the army's Criminal Investigations department. With du Paty's first words, "I am, Madame, on a sad mission," Lucie cried out, "My husband is dead!" Confused by the commandant's evasive response ("No, worse than that"), Lucie asked if Alfred had suffered a riding accident. "No, madame, he is in prison." The men told her neither the charges brought against her husband nor the prison in which he was held. Du Paty, with his monocle, massive handlebar mustache, and exaggerated military bearing, had a foppish side to his character and took pride in being a lady's man. But his moods were mercurial (as his part-time transvestism confirmed) and his temper vicious. He was a "disturbing character," according to one diplomat who knew him, "with a morbid mentality, a shadowy and unhinged imagination, a strange mixture of fanaticism, extravagance, and folly"; he was out of a "tale of Hoffmann." During the first meeting with Lucie and the interrogations that followed, du Paty made halfhearted attempts to calm the young woman while condemning her husband as a "wretch, scoundrel, and coward." With Cochefort, he searched the apartment, noted the amount of cash in drawers and in Lucie's purse, and then left with a threat. Aware of Lucie's frequent contact with the Hadamards and family members in Mulhouse, he insisted that she tell no one of her husband's arrest. "One word, a single word uttered by you," du Paty warned, "and he will be ruined. The only way to save him is through silence." Confiscating letters, account files, army notebooks, maps, and volumes of military history, the two men moved on to interrogate the Hadamards and to search their apartment on the rue Châteaudun.[6]

Lucie, twenty-four years old, was now alone with Pierre and Jeanne. Sharing her husband's respect for the military, and convinced that the Etat-Major would quickly realize its error, she followed du Paty's order and spoke only to her mother. The next day, with Madame Hadamard, she gathered letters Alfred had written from Bourges during their courtship (correspondence overlooked by du Paty) and delivered them to General Staff headquarters in the hope that her willingness to cooperate would be rewarded with news of Alfred. It was not, and for more than two weeks she clung to the single thread of evidence that her husband was still alive—a note du Paty had dictated to the prisoner: "I assure you of my honor," Alfred had written, "and my affection."[7]

Every second or third day the commandant returned to search the apartment more thoroughly. His questioning of the family's former Alsatian wet nurse, Virginie Hasler, who occasionally received German-speaking friends, so traumatized the woman that she suffered seizures of vomiting, a display that heightened du Paty's suspicion that the servant was involved in a cover-up. Meanwhile Lucie's frustration increased when, with perverse pleasure, du Paty asked about the captain's history of "intimate relations" with Parisian women and when he reported that her husband had "taken ill" in prison.[8] Still offering no details of the charges brought against the captain, he told Lucie, "It is my absolute conviction that your husband is guilty. Imagine a circle," he said, "in which I put a certain number of officers likely to have committed the crime . . . it retracts more and more, until finally only one name remains, that of your husband, at the center of the circle."[9] Taunting Lucie, du Paty hoped to break her resolve and extract a confession. But with every interview she became more determined: "I tried to show him his error," she later said. "I told him about my husband's character, about his frankness, integrity and loyalty, and about his sense of duty and love for the fatherland." She described how they were together constantly, and how he never went out alone except to staff headquarters. He was innocent, she insisted, and the General Staff had made a grave error. But it did no good. The strength of Lucie's character, her "incredible *sang-froid*" noted by du Paty, only heightened her inquisitor's suspicions. A young woman with a traitorous husband should be much less composed.[10]

Finally, in late October, aware that Parisian newspapers planned to break the story, du Paty allowed Lucie Dreyfus to contact her family. By the morning of November 1, as she waited with Rachel on the platform at the Gare de l'Est, Lucie knew only that Alfred had been accused of transmitting military secrets to a foreign power and that the Council of Ministers was about to consider an indictment. Du Paty sent a calling card informing her of that meeting, and, with characteristic sadism, hinted that there was "still hope . . . I shall pass by during the day." When Lucie handed du Paty's card to Mathieu two weeks of isolation came to an end, and the family—the brothers, sisters, and in-laws congregating in Paris—began to fight for Alfred's release.[11]

At midday on November 1, Mathieu sent Jacques' eighteen-year-old son Paul, a student in Paris, to du Paty with a message. He wished to meet the commandant either at General Staff headquarters or at the Avenue du Trocadéro apartment. Paul returned with news that du Paty agreed to the interview, and with a strange story of the commandant's "spontaneous" condemnation of Captain Dreyfus. "Your uncle is a wretch," du Paty had shouted at the young man, "a two-faced monster leading a double life—normal and correct with his wife, secretive and mysterious with loose women." Launching into a nearly incoherent account of the death of his own wife, and of the "indignity" of "treason" against women, the officer frightened Paul Dreyfus and reduced him to tears. "I have searched for the truth," said the commandant. "Your uncle is guilty."[12]

Accompanied by the archivist from the army's intelligence bureau, Félix Gribelin, du Paty returned to the apartment he had searched so many times over recent days. To shield Lucie from the strange commandant's outbursts, Mathieu took the two men into a separate room and asked the charges brought against his brother. "I can tell you nothing," said du Paty, "except that he is guilty." "We are among people of honor," responded Mathieu. "Surely without betraying some confidence you could tell me the charges and whether it is possible that an error had been made." But Mathieu did not know the nature of the man he faced; du Paty refused to comply and repeated that there was not the "slightest chance" that the prisoner was innocent. "Besides," said the commandant, "he has already made a partial confession, and I expect to obtain a full one." Du Paty's earlier warnings had kept Lucie from demanding more information, but Mathieu refused to remain silent. "I know [my brother's] entire life," he said, "I was raised with him, I lived with him. . . . He has hidden nothing from me, and nothing in his character suggests the possibility of such a crime." As he had done with young Paul Dreyfus, du Paty responded by condemning the captain's "obscure, mysterious life," his "monstrous" duplicity and womanizing; and he rejected Mathieu's comment that even if Alfred had had relationships with women, the fact did not make him a traitor. "You are convinced of his guilt," said Mathieu, "I am not." And he proposed the ultimate test. "Let me see my brother alone, under any conditions you wish. Place witnesses in an adjoining room or behind doors. . . . I swear on my honor that I will ask him if he committed the crime, if he is guilty or not. And if he confesses, I shall hand him the gun with which he will commit suicide." With the brother showing the same determination as the wife, du Paty shouted, "Never, never! One word, a single word, and there will be a European war." Without elaborating, he ended the interview and added that he, du Paty, would "soon be delivered from this nightmare. Tomorrow your brother's case will be referred to the Conseil de Guerre, and next week he will be judged." Pointing to his forehead, he intimated that the prisoner was insane, but Mathieu now realized that du Paty was the true lunatic, and he feared what could happen to his brother "in the hands of that man."[13]

Telegrams and letters went out from Paris through the first week of November calling family members from Mulhouse, Héricourt, Bar-le-Duc, and Carpentras. Staying with Lucie or the Hadamards, or taking rooms at the Grand Hotel on the Boulevard des Capucines, Alfred's sisters, brothers, and in-laws gathered each day at the apartment on the rue Châteaudun. Mathieu described the "continuous comings and goings, from morning till night," the intense discussions about how the family should proceed, always in a "low voice, as in the house of a dying man." And he described the abrupt change of subject every time young Pierre and Jeanne entered the room.[14] Told that their father had left on an army assignment, they were the only youngsters amid the growing contingent of adults (Mathieu and Suzanne had left their two children with grandparents in Héricourt). Meanwhile, hoping to win the support of influential colleagues in Mulhouse, Jacques and Léon traveled back and forth as Alsatian liaisons, while Henriette, who had been ill, remained in Carpentras. She received daily letters from her husband, Joseph Valabrègue. "Our dear Alfred cannot possibly be guilty," he wrote on November 6. "There is certainly some inexplicable plot against him. . . . Have faith. . . . Soon I hope to have more reassuring news." But with no details of the case and no word from the prisoner, letters to the provinces could speak only of the family's commitment: "Lucie is astonishing," Valabrègue wrote. "Her confidence, her faith in her husband's honor, which we all share, is so firm, so noble, that it does us all good."[15]

But letters filled with hope also described the dark side of the family's days in Paris, especially the "squalid contents of news reports," the sensational stores of treason and Jewish conspiracy Henriette and others would soon read in local editions. Papers of every political stripe capitalized on the scandal, publishing rumors culled from unidentified sources at the Etat-Major or overheard in cafés, gambling dens, hotel lobbies, and the quarters of gossiping concièrges. Editorials asked if

Dreyfus betrayed his country for Germany or Italy or both, if his motive was greed or revenge, and if women were involved—an angle that editors, with an eye to selling papers, hoped to exploit. On November 9, *La Libre Parole* published a statement by General Bonnefond, the officer who had tried to block Dreyfus's promotion to the Etat-Major. "You know [that] we buy our information on foreign armies [from] Italian Jews, German Jews, Rumanian Jews; [they] sell us all . . . we need. And you want to place Jews on our General Staff? Why would a French Jew behave any differently than the others?"[16] The governments of Germany, Italy, and Austria denied any knowledge of Dreyfus and made certain that Parisian newspapers published those denials, but the nationalist press ignored the disclaimers or defined them as part of a foreign cover-up.[17]

Journalists questioned everything but the captain's guilt and "Jewish" treachery. From *La Libre Parole* to the widely circulated Catholic paper *La Croix* to the enormously popular Parisian daily *Le Petit Journal,* reports of treason on the General Staff seemed to confirm Drumont's warnings of the past decade ("Concerning the Judas Dreyfus . . . I have been warning you!"), and Drumont had not laid the groundwork alone. Throughout the summer before Dreyfus's arrest, the front page of *Le Petit Journal* had carried a serial, a *roman-feuilleton,* which told the story of a bizarre case of forgery and espionage among officers attached to the War Ministry. Complete with a cast of artillery captains, former Polytechniciens, bellicose journalists, and suspicious Jewish gamblers, that popular fiction, combined with Drumont's "facts," helped prepare the reading public for revelations of scandal within the military—and for the involvement of a Jewish officer.[18] Dreyfus "entered the army with the premeditated plan of committing treason against it," reported *La Libre Parole* on November 14. "As a Jew and as a German he detests the French. . . . German by taste and education, Jew by race, he does their work and nothing else." He was the agent of an "occult power," other papers insisted, "of a high international Jewry which is out to ruin the French people and to monopolize the land of France." "The affair of Captain Dreyfus . . . is only an episode in Jewish history," *La Libre Parole* instructed readers. "Judas sold the compassion and love of God . . . Dreyfus has sold to Germany our mobilization plans." The "homeland" of the Jews, another report insisted, "is to be found where the money is good."[19]

With newspapers as their only source of information, the family read scores of fabricated accounts of their own recent and distant his-

tories. "It was a torrent against which we could do nothing," wrote
Mathieu. "All the newspapers were hostile or frightened. It was impossible to publish a line of protest against the infamous lies they were
spreading." Denied access to the publishers of *Le Temps, Les Débats,
Le Figaro,* and other papers, Mathieu found only one sympathetic journalist, Emile Bergerat, who agreed that the captain had "the right to be
innocent."[20] But Bergerat's articles remained exceptions to the rule of
presumed guilt. *Le Jour* told of economic troubles at the Dreyfus mill in
Mulhouse and of the family's desperate need for cash: "What methods
would they employ?" the journalist asked, and he answered by suggesting that the brother, "the French army officer," would sell secrets to
the enemy. On November 7, newspapers ran the story of a mysterious,
black-candle ceremony at Zadoc Kahn's synagogue, a ritual to mark the
"excommunication" of Dreyfus; and though Grand Rabbi Kahn protested the absurdity of the reports,[21] readers unfamiliar with Jewish
customs were ready to believe in the sinister nature of Israelite congregations. Above all, journalists ignored three generations of the family's history in "the most French city of Alsace" and concentrated instead
on the Dreyfuses' supposed allegiance to the enemy across the Rhine.
"The frightful Jews, vomited up into France by the ghettos of Germany,
can barely jabber our language," went one report, and others described
the "hereditary stains," the "curses," which marked all Jews however
French they might be in appearance. For Drumont the Dreyfuses and
Hadamards were dangerously "refined Parisians," families who spoke
good French only to facilitate their infiltration of French society. Were
you to slap Dreyfus's face "with his own epaulets," Drumont wrote,
"you still would not succeed in implanting in his brain ideas he does not
possess about honor, duty, and the homeland." Those are "legacies,"
Drumont concluded, which are "transmitted through innumerable generations. They cannot be improvised."[22]

Reading that litany of contempt, Joseph Valabrègue asked how it
was possible, "if there is justice in the world," that an innocent man
could be so vilified, how "entire families could be dishonored for the
single reason that they observe a different religion than the majority of
the nation?"[23] That Valabrègue even posed the question was a sign of
how quickly the climate had changed. His family in Carpentras, like the
Dreyfuses in Mulhouse, had known many forms of prejudice, but they
had not witnessed in their lifetime the "torrent" of bigotry that accompanied Alfred Dreyfus's arrest. Violent language, a staple of fin-de-
siècle politics, had not given way to violent acts, as it had done so often

in Alsace, but with the mobilization of the popular press and with anti-Semites applying their familiar vocabulary to contemporary issues, words could soon be followed by deeds.

A stream of anonymous letters arrived at the Hadamard apartment, and though most of it was hate mail, some of it promised assistance, including prison escape plans and clues to the "real traitor"—all for a fee. Desperate for any news, the family fell victim to an array of tricksters. A former supporter of Drumont, a naturalized Frenchman of Italian origin named de Cesti, admitted his past involvement in anti-Semitic circles but insisted that he possessed information confirming the captain's innocence. De Cesti, with a contact at Cherche-Midi prison, brought reassuring news of Alfred's health and protestations of innocence. It was the only concrete information the family had received since the arrest and it seemed genuine. On a subsequent visit to the rue Châteaudun, de Cesti suggested that another officer, Donin de Rosière, had suspicious contacts with the German Embassy in Paris, as well as a private life marked by bizarre love affairs and bad finances. Perhaps he was the traitor. For two thousand francs to cover expenses, de Cesti offered to investigate the officer, and the Hadamards agreed. But Mathieu, cautious from the outset, launched his own investigation and confirmed that de Rosière, though a strange character, was not a traitor. De Cesti, on the other hand, proved to be "a swindler involved in every kind of sordid affair, a very dangerous man."[24] That experience, coupled with the virulence of press reports and the presence of police agents following the family day and night, drew the brothers, sisters, and in-laws even closer together. The rue Châteaudun apartment became the headquarters of a family reunited but under siege.

Resolved to devote their considerable fortune to securing Alfred's release, the family began the search for a lawyer. Through a relative of the Hadamards, Lucien Lévy-Bruhl, a professor of philosophy at the Lycée Louis-le-Grand in Paris, Mathieu was introduced to René Waldeck-Rousseau, one of France's most politically astute lawyers. But, unfamiliar with military tribunals and concerned about the political implications of defending a man universally assumed to be guilty, Waldeck-Rousseau refused to take the case and advised Mathieu to contact Maître Edgar Demange.[25]

On first impression, it was odd advice. In 1892 Maître Demange had defended the Marquis de Morès after that notorious anti-Semite killed Captain Armand Mayer in a duel; and two years earlier, in another trial exploited by the popular press, he had won a reduced sentence for

Madame Dida's murderer. When Mathieu came to Demange's office to ask for help, it was not the first time the lawyer had heard the brother's name: Captain Dreyfus had submitted a deposition for the prosecution in the Wladimirof case.[26] But Demange, a "fervent Catholic and profound admirer of the Army," was also a consummate professional; he listened to Mathieu's request and agreed to take the case if certain conditions were met. "I will be your brother's first judge," he told Mathieu Dreyfus. "If I find in his dossier any charge whatsoever which leads me to doubt his innocence, I will refuse to defend him. This proposition is extremely serious." He added: "The day the public learns that I have turned down your brother's case, it will conclude that he is guilty, and he will be irredeemably lost." Mathieu agreed to the conditions without hesitation, and on December 3 Maître Demange received permission to review the prisoner's file.[27]

That night he called Lucie and Mathieu to his office and "with profound emotion" said, "If Captain Dreyfus were not Jewish, he would not be in Cherche-Midi prison." He had been accused of treason based on a single, unsigned, undated document that had been transmitted to "a foreign power," and that, Demange was told, contained classified military information. The handwriting had a certain resemblance to the captain's, but two of three experts had insisted that Dreyfus was not the author. That was all. There were no other charges and no other evidence. "It is an abomination," said Demange. "Never have I seen such a dossier. If there is justice, your brother will be acquitted."[28] On the following day, six weeks after Alfred Dreyfus had lost all contact with his family, Demange met the prisoner at Cherche-Midi and learned the details of his arrest and interrogation.

Shortly after 8 A.M. on Monday, October 15, in civilian dress as ordered, Dreyfus had walked along the banks of the Seine to General Staff headquarters on the rue Saint Dominique. Lieutenant Georges Picquart, who had been one of his instructors at the Ecole de Guerre, directed him to the office of General Boisdeffre, the chief of staff he had so impressed only a few months before. Dreyfus was surprised that other officers, normally called to general inspection, were not present. Nor was Boisdeffre. Instead, he found Commandant du Paty de Clam and three strangers in civilian clothes. Displaying a black silk glove on his right hand, du Paty announced that he had injured his finger and asked the captain to take dictation while they waited for the general to arrive. Dreyfus found du Paty's sharp behavior and "constricted voice" somewhat odd—a feeling intensified by the presence of the three men who lurked near the back of the room—but taking dictation was as natural to that former *interne* as his instinct to follow orders. Seated at a small desk with du Paty at his side, Dreyfus began writing a note that dealt with sensitive military matters. Again, he was surprised that an officer would so readily share information concerning weaponry and army maneuvers, especially in the presence of civilians.

"What's the matter?" interrupted du Paty. "You're trembling." "Not at all," Dreyfus responded, taken aback by the hostile tone. It was a chilly autumn day, and his hands were cold from his walk along the riverside. He resumed writing, but du Paty stopped him again: "Pay attention!" he shouted. "This is serious!" Believing that his penmanship somehow displeased the officer, Dreyfus made an effort to concentrate. Suddenly du Paty placed his hand on the captain's shoulder and raised his voice as if to reach an audience beyond the office walls. "I arrest you in the name of the law," he announced. "You are accused of the crime of high treason."[29]

Everything about Alfred Dreyfus's personality ill prepared him for that moment: his stiff military bearing and awkward manner; his monotone voice and inability to express himself without sounding detached, calculated, or self-possessed; and, perhaps most important, his discomfort in the presence of strangers, a timidity always hidden behind a rigid exterior. "Coldness is preferable to emotion," schoolmasters had taught their charges when Dreyfus boarded at Chaptal, "and lack of emotion to the pretense of emotion." And long ago he had admitted to Lucie that his greatest fault was an inability "to open up," to make people look beyond his *insensibilité extérieure*. He had so internalized his feelings over the years, so carefully built a carapace around his public self, that when he tried to protest his innocence and convince du Paty that a "horrendous error" had been made, the commandant found it all too much like the entreaties of a criminal who had planned his response in advance; it was all "too theatrical." And on this morning the captain lacked even the security of his uniform—the military garb that, as Mathieu had noted so many times, had become his mantle of honor and pride. There was a mirror in Boisdeffre's office, and witnesses thought that Dreyfus tried to sneak a glimpse of his "performance" in the midst of his protestations. If so, it would not have been unusual for a self-conscious man in a state of panic, desperate to appear convincing.[30]

Feeling as if he had been "struck by a bolt of lightning," Dreyfus thought it was all a dream or that du Paty had been overcome by some sudden madness. But as the commandant read aloud the article on treason from the French penal code, Dreyfus knew that the nightmare was real. Reaching to the table, du Paty pushed aside a dossier and revealed a pistol. "I am innocent!" the captain called out. "Kill me if you wish!" "It is not for us to do that work of justice," the officer responded, "it's for you." Now almost completely out of control, and still ignorant of the specific charges brought against him, Dreyfus lashed back with a torrent of protest. As the three men rushed to search him ("Take my keys. Open everything in my home. I am innocent!"), he insisted that he had never contacted foreign agents; that he was a good husband and father; that he was an officer beyond reproach, an Alsatian devoted to the army and to the nation. Turning to face du Paty, he must have conjured up memories of his confrontation with General Bonnefond. Someone, he shouted, would pay.[31]

The dictation had taken ten minutes, but the interrogation that followed lasted two hours. The strangers in civilian clothes—Cochefort, from Criminal Investigations, his secretary, and Gribelin, from the intelligence bureau—joined du Paty to grill Dreyfus about trips to the provinces for the General Staff and about his work with the technical section of the artillery. The captain learned that a certain document implicated him as a spy and that the army was conducting a thorough investigation of his background. But that was all. Demanding more details ("Show me proof of the infamy you say I've committed!"), he was ignored. "If the actions you accuse me of were confirmed," he admitted, "I would be a miserable wretch, a coward. . . . It is my honor as an officer that is at stake," he added, "and no matter how painful my situation becomes, I will defend myself to the end. . . . I want to live to prove my innocence."[32] Aware that it would be impossible to exact a confession or a suicide, at least for now, du Paty closed the interrogation. At noon, under strict secrecy, the captain was transferred to Cherche-Midi prison.

Amid bouts of panic and anger, Dreyfus had struggled in Boisdeffre's office to maintain his composure and appeal to the reason of his accusers. On arrival at Cherche-Midi, however, locked in a dark cell on a row with condemned criminals, his pocket watch taken from him and all sense of time lost, he suffered what the prison commander described as a complete nervous breakdown. "I had before me a true madman," reported Commandant Ferdinand Forzinetti.[33] Through the afternoon of October 15 and across the three days and nights that followed, Dreyfus, "walled in alive," paced his cell "like a wild beast." Shouting out his innocence and calling for his wife and children, he beat his head against the cell wall and drew blood. Remembering Bonnefond's insult, he cried out, "My only crime is to have been born a Jew!"[34]

Ordered not to speak to the prisoner, guards in the corridor listened to his shouts. His voice growing hoarse, he collapsed on his prison cot only to be jolted awake by nightmares. He ate nothing and drank only broth and a taste of sugared wine. Forzinetti tried to calm him, but the commandant could not satisfy the prisoner's demands. Above all he wanted his family; and he wanted a pen and paper to write to the minister of war. Officials from the General Staff, worried about the efforts of "upper Jewdom" to secure the prisoner's release and wanting Dreyfus held in the strictest secrecy, had ordered Forzinetti to deny those requests. By the afternoon of the captain's first day at Cherche-Midi, however, Forzinetti, convinced of his innocence, had become his first ally.[35]

Meanwhile, du Paty—who thought it unwise to put those "who are not Frenchmen of France" in sensitive military positions[36]—became his most implacable enemy. On the night of October 18, believing that the prisoner was ready to confess, du Paty prepared the next phase of interrogation. To take Dreyfus "off guard," the commandant wanted to enter the cell quietly and shine a powerful projection lamp in the prisoner's face. But Forzinetti refused to comply. Instead du Paty and the archivist Gribelin took Dreyfus to a room nearby. Ignoring a law dating from the thirteenth century, which required authorities to inform prisoners of the charges brought against them, du Paty refused Dreyfus's demands for information and again ordered him to take dictation. Forcing the prisoner to write seated, standing, lying down, quickly and slowly, with and without gloves, right-handed and left-handed, in French and in German, du Paty repeated, with variations, the words, "I am off to maneuvers," a phrase, Dreyfus soon realized, which appeared in the incriminating document. Every second or third night the interrogators returned armed with new questions and new methods; once they brought examples of Dreyfus's handwriting (short phrases taken from his personal papers) and placed them in a cap along with fragments clipped from photographed copies of other documents. Ordered to identify which examples were in his own hand, Dreyfus made the distinction without fail and continued to thwart du Paty's schemes.[37]

Frustrated by the prisoner's resolve, the commandant turned from dictation to rapid-fire questions about Dreyfus's military career and access to classified information. The treasonous document, which the prisoner had still not seen after ten days of interrogation, contained information on artillery and troop maneuvers—information, du Paty suggested, which could only have been compiled by a *stagiaire* moving through the offices of the Etat-Major. Dreyfus's notebooks and accounts of trips to provincial garrisons emerged as evidence, not of his professional interest in military strategy but of espionage; and his "remarkable memory" for maps and plans, his desire to work alone, and his fluent German added to the profile of a spy. All the qualities for which he had been rewarded as a young officer rising through the ranks were, when read by du Paty, hints of his treachery. So was his background. While most officers of Alsatian origin were considered zealous patriots and "doubly French," Dreyfus's trips to the "lost province" under the guise of family visits must have included rendezvous with German agents. The more the prisoner stressed his "devotion" to Alsace and to France, the more du Paty thought he protested too much.[38]

Throughout those nights of inquisition, Dreyfus tried to marshal the strength needed to answer the barrage of questions with clarity and thoroughness. Struggling for control, he explained his limited access to classified information at the Ecole de Guerre and Etat-Major and tried to convince du Paty of his family's patriotism. Trips across the Vosges, he told his interrogator, were not unusual; countless French Alsatians had been making the journey, with and without approval, for the past two decades. "I swear on my children that I am innocent," Dreyfus repeated. "I have absolutely no idea what you want of me. Perhaps if you showed me the incriminating document I would understand. After eleven days," he concluded, "I still do not know what you accuse me of doing." But du Paty only repeated that documentation was surfacing to confirm the captain's treason, and he pressed on.[39]

With sleepless days following nights of interrogation, and with no news from his family, the prisoner edged toward suicide. Reveling in the tricks of mental torture, du Paty would suddenly break the regular schedule of questioning and disappear for three or four days at a time—adding to Dreyfus's confusion—and then return with queries about the officer's reputation as a womanizer, queries which suggested that Dreyfus's contact with Parisian women, some of them foreign, had included espionage. When the prisoner protested, du Paty quickly turned to another line of questioning, or noted the physiological "evidence" of Dreyfus's guilt. Like Drumont, who informed readers that the "grasping and light-fingered" hands of the Jews "betrayed their race," du Paty believed that any movement in the prisoner's legs signaled guilt, "be-

cause the movement of the feet is linked to the movement of the heart."
Mathieu Dreyfus was right; his brother's interrogator was "mad." He
was also relentless.[40]

The prisoner's "mental state is indescribable," Forzinetti reported
to superiors. "Since his last interrogation . . . he has had frequent
fainting-spells and hallucinations; alternately sobbing and laughing, he
says that he is losing his mind. Still protesting his innocence, he cries
out that he will go mad before that innocence is recognized. He constantly demands to see his wife and children; and he fears that he will
succumb to an act of desperation, despite all the precautions which have
been taken, or that he will be overcome by madness."[41] The only
response to Forzinetti's appeal, however, was an increase in the number of guards assigned to the prisoner and a visit by an army doctor who
prescribed sedatives.[42]

Finally, on October 29, du Paty showed Dreyfus a photograph of
the key document. "Do you recognize this letter as being in your handwriting?" the commandant asked. Though exhausted and sedated, the
prisoner immediately felt a "sense of deliverance." The handwriting,
though similar, was clearly not his. A *bordereau,* or "memorandum,"
rather than a letter, the one-page document listed five topics to be
covered in a subsequent communication. Carefully analyzing its form
and content, Dreyfus explained why he could not possibly be its author:
the document referred to hydraulic braking systems for 120-millimeter
cannon, a topic Dreyfus had not studied since the Ecole de Guerre, and
then only cursorily; it mentioned a "project for a firing manual" about
which he knew nothing; and as for a "note pertaining to Madagascar,"
the captain had never been involved with an assignment concerning that
location. Supposedly written only a few months before, the memorandum ended with the words "I am off to maneuvers." But official records
would confirm that Dreyfus had not been on maneuvers since the previous year. There was reason for hope.[43]

Du Paty told the prisoner, however, that "experts" had officially declared that the letter was written in his hand and ordered him to copy it
yet again. "Do you not acknowledge a peculiar resemblance?" "Yes, in a
few details," said the captain. "But I repeat that I did not write it . . . and
I want to be heard by the Minister [of War]." Du Paty ignored the request
and closed the session. The next morning he announced that the minister would see Dreyfus if—and only if—he wished to confess. "I repeat
that I am innocent, that I have nothing to confess. It is impossible for
me, confined within the four walls of a prison, to explain this appalling

enigma. Give me access to the head of the department of criminal investigations and I will devote my entire fortune, my entire life, to solving this affair."[44] But the "maddening mystery" was far from over.[45] Du Paty informed the Conseil de Guerre that sufficient proof existed to open an official inquiry, and on November 5, two new interrogators, Commandant Bexon d'Ormescheville, judge advocate, and his clerk, Vallecalle, began another round of questioning within the confines of Cherche-Midi.

The Paris prefect of police had rushed to compile a dossier on Dreyfus's private and professional life based on interviews with colleagues and acquaintances. It uncovered nothing that pointed to espionage. Officers from the Ecole de Guerre and General Staff recalled Dreyfus's "exaggerated diligence" and "lack of modesty" ("too sure of himself for his age . . . a bit of a boaster," said one witness), and still others described his habit of working alone or choosing the company of women—and horses—over that of most colleagues.[46] Though Dreyfus may have seemed peculiar to some, his actions were far from criminal, and had the police dossier been the only source of evidence, the army might have terminated the investigation. But du Paty provided other information. While the prefecture compiled its evidence, the Statistical Section of the General Staff, the command post for military counter-espionage, amassed its own documentation under the direction of a former police agent named François Guénée. Slapdash, sensational, and fabricated from a network of unreliable informants, it was a dossier of rumor and innuendo. A notorious "peddler of gossip" who frequented bistros, brothels, hotel lobbies, news office corridors (*La Libre Parole* provided Guénée's most creative sources), and the strategically placed rooms of Parisian concièrges, the agent turned up half-truths about the captain's past involvement in "fashionable society."[47] Dreyfus listened to d'Ormescheville redefine his recent history, from women friends he had known as a young lieutenant to outings at Longchamp and Auteuil. His liaisons could be part of a clandestine network of espionage, the judge advocate insinuated, and his racetrack visits suggested a compulsive addiction to gambling that required infusions of cash from enemy agents. Had Dreyfus not known a number of "foreign" women, like the Austrian Madame Déry who lived in his *quartier* and whom he had met on two or three occasions? Could those women not have taken classified documents from his pockets in the dead of night? Jilted by Dreyfus, could they not have sought revenge? And his involvement in the Dida case, an affair complete with a bogus foreign aristocrat and rumors of drug addiction, only seemed to confirm the officer's sordid past. In fact, Dreyfus had circulated in the fasionable society of Paris and the provinces, but Guénée's reports painted the picture of a Jew infiltrating the demimonde.[48]

Candid about his visits to racetracks and Parisian clubs, Dreyfus was also adamant that he had no interest in gambling, and that his relationships with women involved nothing out of the ordinary. He had made mistakes, but what young man alone in Paris or the provinces had not? Over the recent past he had settled into a normal life with his wife and children, and, from the Ecole de Guerre to the Etat-Major, he had worked with diligence and devotion. He was rich, with no need to trade in secrets; and as a patriot, he had only contempt for the enemy that had divided his family by force. Once more he challenged his interrogators to provide proof of his "treason." But D'Ormescheville was as deaf to the prisoner's attempts to respond logically to each accusation as du Paty had been. The judge advocate operated with the confidence of an inquisitor who held the ultimate proof of wrongdoing, while the prisoner operated as the victim of a "plot," a "machination." Through it all, Dreyfus never questioned the motives of the military high command or doubted the honor of his superiors.

As the second phase of interrogation came to an end, D'Ormescheville asked the prisoner if he had anything more to say. "I have been held in secret for six weeks," he responded, "six weeks during which I have suffered the most appalling martyrdom an innocent man could tolerate. . . . From a family of *protestataires,* I left my position in Alsace to serve my country with devotion. Today as yesterday, I am worthy of leading my soldiers into battle."[49] Dreyfus had tried every method of defense, from measured reason to passionate outbursts, but after more than forty days in solitary confinement—sedated, forced awake, and sedated again—he had to struggle to distinguish nightmares from reality. To his accusers, that final statement, like the protests on the day of his arrest, sounded hollow, melodramatic, and unconvincing. With D'Ormescheville's report in hand, military authorities chose December 19 for Alfred Dreyfus's court-martial.

CHAPTER VIII

Justice

DURING HIS LONG-DISTANCE COURTSHIP with Lucie Hadamard, Dreyfus had sent letters from his "provincial prison" at Bourges describing the couple's future "community of happiness." Lucie had helped her anxious fiancé through the hard weeks of preparation for the Ecole de Guerre exams, and her confidence, the captain believed, had brought him "good luck." Four years later, on December 5, 1894, in the first letter he was permitted to send his wife, the prisoner recalled the life that "smiled on them" until the moment he was accused of "the most monstrous crime . . . a soldier can commit." As he had done from Bourges, he described his isolation and recounted his inner dialogue. But now, instead of a young officer's debate between reverie and reason, it was a prisoner's struggle between panic that edged toward madness and a resolute, logical "conscience" that told him, "Hold your head high and look at the world face on. . . . It is a terrible test, but one must suffer it." Army censors prevented him from detailing his interrogation, but, in his own desire to spare his wife the details—and in his fear that he would "go insane" if he relived the "nightmare"—Dreyfus censored himself. "Don't worry about the unevenness of my letters," he cautioned Lucie shortly before his court-martial. "You know that I cannot write to you in my usual way."[1]

Having lost control over the present, he sought solace in the past and future. "Do you recall the story I told you about my trip to Mul-

128

house a dozen years ago," he wrote to his wife, "when I heard a German band celebrating the anniversary of [the French defeat at] Sedan? . . . I cried with anger and swore to devote all my energy, all my intelligence, to serving my country against those who insulted the grief of Alsatians." And in a refrain that ran throughout his letters, he asked how "dear France, whom I love with all my soul, all my heart, could accuse me of such an appalling crime."[2] From the moment of his arrest, Dreyfus had joined his fate to the promise of French justice, a promise that, for him, had not been broken. "I place my hope in God and in justice," he told Lucie in his first prison letter, and as his trial approached he declared himself ready to appear before his judges as he would "one day appear before God, head high and conscience clear." He was not an observant Jew, nor did he share his wife's strong faith. A consummate Polytechnicien, he had become skeptical of established religion and certain only of the "cult of humanity" represented by *la grande famille française.* But in the spirit of those Jewish notables whose manifestos of deliverance had been read aloud to his ancestors a hundred years before, he believed that the divine call for justice had been answered by the Revolution's Edict of Emancipation. His was a strict— even religious—faith in France.[3]

The nation, with the military as a reflection of its will and grandeur, had taken on a spiritual authority Dreyfus venerated. "If I did not have my honor to defend," he told Lucie on December 7, "I assure you that I would prefer death; at least all this would be forgotten." But personal honor alone would not be enough to sustain him. He considered the attack on his integrity an assault on the entire officer corps, "of which I am a part, and of which I am proud," and, with the same flourish of self-importance that prompted colleagues to criticize his "pretentious-ness," he extended his individual struggle to a defense of the French military. Clad in soiled civilian garb in his prison cell for more than seven weeks, however, he felt increasingly isolated from that military corps and its discipline, stripped of the self-image he had so carefully culti-vated since his days at the Ecole Polytechnique. That school's "Code X" had instructed young recruits, "Everywhere and always, respect the uniform . . . it is an honor which imposes duties," and no soldier had adhered to the code more meticulously than had Alfred Dreyfus. On December 8, in anticipation of his courtroom appearance, he asked Lucie to send his best dress uniform, finest kepi, and white gloves to Cherche-Midi. He would manifest his allegiance in every way: "They will see on my face, they will read in my soul . . . my innocence." He remained confident that "loyal and honest soldiers . . . will one day recognize, I am sure of it, the error which has been committed."[4]

Despite having only letters and reports from the lawyer Demange by which to gauge her husband's condition, Lucie sensed the fine line between his desperation and desire to fight. Proud of his courage, she was also well aware of his nervous temperament, and she feared that his exaggerated commitment to military honor might push him to the noble solution of suicide. Attempting to enlarge the boundaries of his obligations by reminding him of his duty as a father, she described how eagerly the children awaited his return. She shared the quotidian details of their family life (the cod-liver oil she gave the delicate Pierre for energy, the robust health of their daughter Jeanne), and she inserted a message from their three-year-old son, a note her mother helped the boy write: "My Papa . . . you must return on the train quickly before it gets cold so that I can give you a good kiss [un bon bec]." Dreyfus read the note from "Pierrot" and cried; but he also gained confidence, looked forward to the moment of reunion with his family, and, as his court-martial approached, promised Lucie that, for her and for the children, he would not take his life.[5]

Still prohibited from receiving visitors, he asked his wife to serve as "interpreter," to convey the message to their families that they were "linked in a firm alliance which nothing can break; our honest and respectable life, all of the past of all of our families, [and] our devotion to France provide the best proof of who we are." While urging Lucie to guard her health "for the children's sake," he also implored her to devote all her efforts and intelligence—and, if necessary, their "entire fortune"—to finding the real traitor, the "wretch" responsible for their plight: "Money is nothing, honor is all," he told Lucie, and he knew that the other guardian of that family honor would be Mathieu. "We have always been more than brothers," he wrote Mathieu on December 12, "we shared thoughts and hopes in common. . . . What sustains me, what allows me to keep my head high is my clear conscience, my life entirely devoted to honor . . . I defy anyone to take it from me." Through his early days as a boarding student, homesick and unable to fit in with schoolmates, Alfred had turned to Mathieu for companionship and protection. Now, confined "like a lion in a cage," he asked his older brother to "move heaven and earth" to secure his release.[6]

Mathieu began by engaging Maître Demange and continued by enlisting, with the help of Jacques and Léon, the aid of influential Alsatians.

Through November and early December, the population of Mulhouse greeted reports of the captain's arrest no differently than did the population of Paris; the overwhelming majority believed what they read or read what they wanted to believe and assumed that the government had proof of Dreyfus's intrigues with a "foreign power."[7] Only close friends and fellow industrialists rallied in support. Some reserved judgment on the captain, but most confirmed their readiness to help the brothers. "Let me say that the immense bad fortune which has just struck your family," Michael Diemer-Heilman wrote Mathieu in early November, "does not diminish in any way the genuine feelings of esteem and sympathy I have always had for you and your brothers, Jacques and Léon." The family's doctor, a "devoted old friend" of Raphael's, would soon contact Léon and offer to contribute fifty thousand francs toward "finding the criminal";[8] and other members of the Alsatian elite, former friends of Raphael's and current associates of his sons, pursued leads in European diplomatic circles and in the French high command. Theodor Schlumberger and M. Mieg-Koechlin approached the German chancellor and learned that his government denied any relations with Dreyfus (though the Germans would not intervene on the captain's behalf for reasons of "foreign affairs"); and Rudolphe Koechlin, along with a French officer from Alsace, gave Mathieu and Léon letters of introduction to yet another officer born in Mulhouse. The chief of the Statistical Section of the General Staff, Colonel Jean-Conrad Sandherr, directed the office responsible for uncovering the *bordereau* and calling for Dreyfus's arrest.[9]

As the command post for French counterespionage, the Statistical Section masterminded "the picking of locks, the bribing of servants and prostitutes, the stealing of letters and forging of documents."[10] An intelligence bunker in back rooms on the rue Saint Dominique, its workings were a mystery to all but the initiated. The unit served as a clearinghouse for clandestine lists of potential spies, and, over recent years, under Sandherr's direction, it had become so obsessed with fears of infiltration that the five officers assigned to the unit suspected the patriotism of colleagues in adjoining offices. In its eagerness to protect national security, the office—investigating thousands of foreigners residing in France—expanded the repertoire of its "enemies list" to include French citizens, especially Alsatians whose allegiance might extend to the wrong bank of the Rhine. The irony was evident (scores of high-ranking French officers were of Alsatian origin), but so too was the explanation: Many of those officers had learned their bigotry at home. In 1870 Sandherr's father, a Protestant converted to Catholicism, had marched through Mulhouse shouting "Down with the Prussians of the interior!" which in local parlance meant, "Down with Protestants and Jews!" He had been among those demonstrators whose "furious shouts and threats" kept the Dreyfus family off the streets and behind locked doors on the rue de la Sinne.[11] Later, at a military ceremony in the Vosges, Colonel Sandherr confirmed that he was his father's son. Seeing an Alsatian Jew moved to tears by the commemoration, he told a colleague that he distrusted those tears: "Why? Because I distrust the Jews." When another officer from Mulhouse suggested to Sandherr that it was impossible for an Alsatian like Dreyfus, "product of our great military schools and son of a rich and respected family, to have turned against his country," the colonel agreed only in part: "You're right, it would be incomprehensible for others, but he's a Jew."[12]

If Sandherr had prejudged Alfred Dreyfus in every way, he revealed none of that when Mathieu and Léon came to his home on the rue Léonce-Reynaud with letters of introduction from Rudolphe Koechlin and an Alsatian commandant. Cordial and correct, he told his visitors that he was aware of their reputation in Mulhouse, of their "very French sentiments," and he sympathized with the brothers. When Mathieu followed Demange's lead and said that Captain Dreyfus had been the victim of a plot "because he's a Jew, because there are those who want to run him out of the military," Sandherr protested that the army did not condone "such ideas." Describing the "passionate" hatred du Paty had shown toward his brother, Mathieu questioned the expertise of handwriting analysts and expressed his concern that the court-martial would be held in closed session, with his brother's case hidden from public scrutiny. And he added that he would devote his "entire life and family fortune to discovering the truth." Sandherr would later accuse Mathieu Dreyfus of attempting to bribe him; but for now he ignored the comments and simply confirmed that a "long and serious inquiry" had led to the captain's arrest. "It would not be very practical," he concluded, for the family to conduct their own investigation. The brothers left Sandherr's home with the realization that their powerful connections in Mulhouse would have little influence in Paris.[13]

"We must not linger on discouragement," Mathieu told the family, "because discouragement leads to inaction, and that would be our disarmament." If the likes of Sandherr and du Paty were to be witnesses for the prosecution, Mathieu had to find character witnesses for his brother. He met with only limited success. Lévy-Bruhl, Lucie's relative and a distinguished academic; Arthur Amson, an industrialist; Dr. René Vaucaire, a physician; and Rabbi Jacques-Henri Dreyfuss of Paris (no relation but a family friend) all agreed to appear at the court-martial. But Mathieu needed military men to confirm his brother's loyalty. From instructors and administrators at the Ecole de Guerre to the captain's former colleagues and superiors in Paris and provincial garrisons, Mathieu received either polite rejections or hostile tirades against the "traitor." As a young officer, his brother had remained aloof from barracks life, and Mathieu learned the price of that bad diplomacy; he found only one officer, Commandant Clément, who promised to testify. Eventually, after much prodding by the family, four other officers agreed to submit depositions describing the captain as a "good and loyal soldier." It was a courageous group of witnesses, but a weak alliance with which to confront the minister of war and the entire high command of the General Staff.[14]

A few days before the court-martial, and prior to the interview with Sandherr, Demange had asked Mathieu to go to the clerk's office at the Conseil de Guerre to pay for the copying of legal briefs (regulations prohibited lawyers from settling accounts directly). Accompanied by Demange's secretary, Mathieu learned that the clerk, Vallecalle, had access to the *bordereau*. When the secretary asked to see it, Vallecalle agreed, most likely for a fee paid by Mathieu. Locking all the doors, he fetched the Dreyfus dossier and showed the men the small, single sheet of lightweight paper. "Stupefied" by the document, Mathieu noted only a "vague resemblance" to Alfred's handwriting, and, more important, "striking differences which lept to the eye."[15] He reacted precisely as his brother had done when du Paty first brought the *bordereau* to Cherche-Midi: The army's case could not possibly stand on such thin evidence. Demange had recently informed Mathieu that military officials considered the document a masterful example of "self-forgery," a highly technical achievement on the part of Dreyfus, designed to disguise his own hand. That convoluted thesis had been developed by Alphonse Bertillon, head of the "anthropometric service" at the Prefecture of Police. Jean Casimir-Perier, president of the French Republic, would call Bertillon "completely insane . . . given to an extraordinary and cabalistic madness"; his "unintelligible jargon," "grotesque gibberish," and "strange looks" put Casimir-Perier in mind of "a lunatic escaped from the Salpêtrière or Villejuif!"[16] But Bertillon enjoyed the confidence of the General Staff, and when Mathieu glimpsed the *bordereau* (before the clerk heard a noise and quickly closed the dossier), he realized why the army had been forced to resort to Bertillon's absurd theories. He also wondered why the General Staff was pursuing a major case of treason with such limited evidence. Disquieted by rumors that the army would demand a trial in closed session, Mathieu was increasingly certain that his brother had been the victim of a conspiracy.

Before dawn on December 19, Captain Dreyfus crossed the rainswept rue du Cherche-Midi and, surrounded by guards, entered the former Convent of the Good Shepherd, a somber stone building constructed in the seventeenth century on land confiscated from Protestants and now serving as a prison annex. The court-martial was scheduled for noon, but by late morning the combination of winter weather and reports that the trial would be closed to the public had limited the crowd to barely thirty curious onlookers. Meanwhile, inside the cramped, high-ceilinged courtroom, journalists, clerks, and witnesses awaited the arrival of the seven military judges. Heavy, threadbare draperies covered four bay windows and kept the room close and dim. At first denied permission to enter, Mathieu and Jacques, the only two members of the family to attend the proceedings, appealed to the commandant in charge and, after much difficulty, were allowed to stand in the back of the room. They had not seen their brother in over four months, and when Colonel Maurel of the Conseil de Guerre ordered, "Bring in the accused," Mathieu, sweating in the midwinter cold, felt his throat tighten and his legs nearly give way.[17]

Clad in the crisp, brass-buttoned uniform with gold braid and epaulets that Lucie had sent to Cherche-Midi, the captain entered the hall with his head high. Flanked by a lieutenant of the Republican Guard, he moved with a firm military step to his place facing a crucifix, which hung above the judges on the courtroom's far wall. The prisoner's thin frame, dull complexion, and prominent cheekbones, like the streaks of gray in his close-cropped hair, were evidence of more than eight weeks in his Cherche-Midi cell. But Mathieu was not the only observer to find the captain "very much in control."[18] Saluting the tribunal, he responded to the colonel's opening questions in a clear, calm voice: "Your age?" "Thirty-five." "Your place of birth?" "Mulhouse, Alsace." In a letter to Lucie the night before he had said that he was "ready to appear before soldiers, as a soldier who is blameless. . . . I have nothing to fear."[19] For all but his most rabid critics, the captain's entrance into the hushed courtroom confirmed that confidence.

Maître Demange knew, however, that his client had everything to fear from a closed session and a court-martial whose members included not a single artillery officer. Over previous days, the lawyer had attempted to convince government officials that a public trial would be in the best interests of both the army and the accused; through his friends, Waldeck-Rousseau and Joseph Reinach, an influential member of the Chamber of Deputies, Demange sent his appeal to the minister of war, General Auguste Mercier, and to President Casimir-Perier, along with assurances that "diplomatic questions" would be treated with "the greatest reserve." But none of Demange's emissaries met with success. For months the nationalist and anti-Semitic press had been attacking Mercier for the breakdown of military order and for his inability to rid the General Staff of treasonous Jews, Protestants, and Freemasons. Dreyfus's arrest only confirmed their belief in Mercier's "human idiocy" and, in turn, intensified the minister's desire to limit the damage. As the trial began, courtroom observers anticipated the call for a closed session, and when Demange referred to a "single piece" of incriminating evidence against Dreyfus, the judges immediately stopped the proceedings, ignored the lawyer's protests, and adjourned to consider the judge advocate's request that the court-martial be closed to the public for reasons of national security. After only fifteen minutes of deliberation, the Conseil de Guerre returned with its unanimous verdict and ordered the room cleared. "Their bias," Mathieu noted, was already "evident." Leaving to rejoin the family at the Hadamard apartment, the two brothers asked a small group of friends—including Sam Wimpheimer, Jacques' young American brother-in-law—to wait in the corridors of Cherche-Midi, and to telephone with any news. They began a three-day vigil.[20]

Black-robed lawyers and colorfully uniformed prosecutors and witnesses surrounded the seated figure of Captain Dreyfus. The rest of the hall was now empty except for Louis Lépine, the Paris prefect of police, and Commandant Georges Picquart, charged by Mercier, the minister of war, and by Boisdeffre of the General Staff to keep them informed of events. For Dreyfus the parade of witnesses rehearsed, yet again, all the rumors recounted over weeks of interrogation in Cherche-Midi: the suspicious trips to Mulhouse; the overzealousness of a junior officer curious about troop deployment; the insistence that Dreyfus's handwriting matched the *bordereau;* the lurid stories of gambling, womanizing, and more. Prepared for that litany of lies and half truths, the prisoner remained quiet, exhibiting a confidence which worried the prosecution. If his voice was "atonal and without effect," as Lépine reported, his attitude, according to Colonel Maurel, was soldierly, "strong and absolutely correct."[21] Only once during the first day of testimony did Dreyfus break his rigid shell of discipline. Hearing the words "crime of high treason" he "reacted vehemently," as his ally Joseph Reinach would later describe it, "evoking his Alsatian birth, the rich industry he abandoned for army barracks . . . his patriotic ardor, happy life and promising career." Why would he jeopardize all that? "For a little gold which he did not need? for the pleasure of shame?" Commandant Picquart found the prisoner's outburst "a bit theatrical," however, and not well received by the judges. Given his voice and awkward manner, Dreyfus made a stronger impression when silent and stoic.[22]

Through the afternoons and evenings of testimony, he listened and learned. Officers recounted the history of the *bordereau,* its discovery by an agent in a foreign embassy in Paris, and their realization that the memorandum must have been written by a member of the General Staff who had access to its many offices—in other words by a *stagiaire* moving through the various sections of the Etat-Major. Two officers involved in the first stages of the investigation, Lieutenant-Colonel Henri d'Abboville and Colonel Pierre Fabre, told how they settled on Dreyfus as a prime suspect, and, after comparing his handwriting, how they reported their findings to superiors. In sixteen years of military life, since he first arrived at the gates of the Ecole Polytechnique, Dreyfus had received only two negative assessments of his performance and personality: one from the anti-Semite Bonnefond at the Ecole de Guerre, and the other from Colonel Fabre at the Etat-Major: "An incomplete officer," went Fabre's description in 1893. "Very intelligent and devoted, but pretentious and not able—from the point of view of character, conscience and manner of service—to fulfill the conditions necessary for employment on the General Staff of the Army."[23] In contrast to his superior, Boisdeffre, Fabre had no appreciation of the captain's talents; but Boisdeffre, whose support on that summer night in the Vosges five months earlier Dreyfus recalled and never doubted, remained conspicuously absent from the Cherche-Midi trial.[24]

Despite its impressive array of witnesses, the prosecution's case was not going well. Picquart mentioned the obvious lack of evidence and the "emptiness" of the judge advocate's arguments, and he feared that acquittal was a distinct possibility. Lépine agreed, as did another courtroom observer, Commandant Hubert-Joseph Henry, a member of the Statistical Section and director of its vast subterranean network of undercover agents. The first staff officer to see the *bordereau*, Henry had worked for months with his friend du Paty to prepare the dossier against Dreyfus. Son of a peasant from the Marne, and veteran of the 1870 war, the broad-shouldered and brutish Henry had none of the social graces of his General Staff comrades and only a rudimentary education; but he compensated with energy, ambition, and a willingness to follow any order. An avid admirer of Edouard Drumont and a firm believer in the perils of Jewish infiltration, he aimed to save the prosecution's case.[25] Having testified in the early stages of the trial, he secretly sent word to one of the judges, an old friend, that he wished to be recalled and asked a specific question regarding "the presence of a traitor" in the Deux-ième Bureau, the intelligence section, of the Etat-Major. Taking the stand, he announced in a loud voice and with sweeping gestures that "an absolutely honorable person" had alerted him the previous spring to a traitor within the ranks. That same informant had later provided more details and identified the officer. "There he is," Henry shouted as he pointed to Dreyfus. "That man is the traitor!"

The prisoner and his lawyer immediately stood up to protest the introduction of hearsay evidence; objecting to the illegality of Henry's remarks, they demanded the name of the informant. But Henry, con-fident that the judges would respect the army's need for secrecy, pointed to his own military cap and announced that "there are secrets in an officer's head that even his kepi should not know." Dreyfus and Demange pushed their protest, but the judges never intervened: "We will not ask you the name," they assured Henry, "but do you affirm on your honor that this traitor was attached to the Deuxième Bureau, and that it is Captain Dreyfus?" Turning to the crucifix, Henry said, "I swear it."[26]

However crude, the commandant's testimony clarified the essen-tial debate: The seven military judges of the court-martial would be forced to weigh the prisoner's word against that of a General Staff officer, a war veteran and personal friend of the court, who had, under oath and with access to the most sensitive documentation, named the traitor. In his character and in the content of his testimony, Henry defined the conflict; it would be the inner circle of the Etat-Major, many of its members disciples of Drumont, against a Jewish *stagiaire*.

Subsequent witnesses, for and against the accused, did little to undermine the commandant's testimony. With labyrinthine charts and photographic enlargements, Alphonse Bertillon contradicted grapholo-gists who insisted that Dreyfus could not have written the *bordereau*.

Arguing that the captain had borrowed, as part of a cunning decoy, the penmanship of his wife Lucie and brother Mathieu, Bertillon also maintained that clues to the traitor's finances were embedded in the document's lettering. Without explaining his method, he announced that Dreyfus had received the sum of five hundred thousand francs. Looking on, the prisoner attached no importance to Bertillon's testimony; he considered it, as did most observers, "the work of a madman."[27]

Defense witnesses offered more straightforward accounts. J. H. Dreyfuss, the grand rabbi of Paris, believed in the "moral affinities between the two races," the Jews and the French. Like his superior, Zadoc Kahn, he defined the French as "this elect people of modern times, spreading abroad the blessed notions of liberty, equality and fraternity."[28] For the rabbi, Captain Dreyfus represented all those qualities as an upstanding family man and dedicated officer. But from Grand Rabbi Dreyfuss to Professor Lévy-Bruhl and the captain's former military colleagues and Mulhouse acquaintances, witnesses repeated what the court already know: The Dreyfus family enjoyed a solid reputation as French patriots, and the accused was a man of formidable intelligence and profound loyalty. Du Paty, always bothered by the family's prestige and Dreyfus's apparent lack of motive, intervened with his own theory about the traitor's Alsatian contacts. A "considerable indemnity" the family had received following a recent fire at their cotton mill had not been a legitimate transaction at all, du Paty suggested, but a clandestine payment for Dreyfus's treason. On the next day, however, the last of the trial, Maître Demange produced telegrams from Mulhouse insurance executives that confirmed the family's story and left the prosecution with the key dilemma it had faced from the outset: the question of motive.[29] For Henry, du Paty, and the coterie of officers steeped in Drumont's theories of eternal Jewish treason, the motive was evident; for the seven judges of the court-martial, however, Demange increasingly feared that it was irrelevant. Accustomed to criminal proceedings in which motive was crucial and doubt led to acquittal, the lawyer had been frustrated in every phase of his argument.

Mathieu and Lucie met the lawyer every evening and, with other family members and friends, began to share concern about the trial's outcome. Only the prisoner remained confident. If he had not won the sympathy of his judges, he had won their respect. Responding to their questions with logic and objectivity—"as if forgetting that he himself was on trial"—he drew on his memory for details, and his ability, shaped at the Ecole Polytechnique, to present tighly reasoned arguments with

the precision "of a mathematician at a blackboard." He continued to
believe that "good soldiers would make good judges." On the night
before the verdict he told Demange how often over the past weeks he
had contemplated suicide, "how many times I thought that it would be
better to die than to support this horrible martyrdom." But he had
resisted that temptation ("for my wife, my children . . . my name") and
was now certain, after nine weeks of isolation, that the family would be
reunited the next day.[30]

On Saturday, December 22, Mathieu and Demange shared a carriage to the rue du Cherche-Midi. Before entering the courtroom the
lawyer summarized the captain's chances: "If an order has not been
given to condemn him, he will be acquitted this evening."[31] Mathieu
returned to Suzanne and then joined Lucie and the rest of the family at
the rue de Châteaudun. He knew that Demange's closing remarks would
last until midafternoon and expected a verdict no later than 5 P.M. "The
hours seemed interminable" for Mathieu, and at 7, with Lucie "wandering from room to room," there was still no word. Thirty minutes
later the phone rang, and a friend of the family, Dr. Weill, heard the
verdict. In a unanimous decision, the captain had been convicted of
treason and sentenced to "perpetual deportation."[32]

"Like an automaton," Mathieu stood up, took his hat and prepared
to leave for Demange's office. Suzanne asked Dr. Weill to "not leave
him alone." Told by the lawyer's secretary that he, Mathieu, had done
everything possible for his brother, that he had done his "duty,"
Mathieu, still in shock, responded simply: "It is beginning." Maître
Demange arrived, having just seen the prisoner: "I implored him to . . .
live until tomorrow," the lawyer told Mathieu, "and I refused to leave
until he gave me his word that he would not take his life." Forzinetti, the
prison commandant, assured Demange that he would keep a constant
watch. Mathieu searched for an explanation, but Demange had none to
give; he did not know what transpired in the deliberation room. "My
brother must sign his petition for appeal," Mathieu said before leaving.
"Make him sign it tomorrow."[33]

Two months before, on the platform of the Gare de l'Est, Mathieu
had heard newspaper hawkers announcing the arrest of a Jewish officer
for the crime of high treason. Now, as his carriage crossed onto the
Right Bank, and as evening editions arrived on city streets, he heard
their calls again, "shouts which followed me all along my route." He
would not return to Mulhouse. Rejoining Lucie, he promised to stay in
Paris and "search for the truth."[34]

* * *

During the judges' deliberation, Captain Dreyfus had waited in the prison infirmary adjoining the courtroom. In accordance with military law, he would not be present when his verdict was read in public session. Aware that decisions to acquit were pronounced quickly and without debate, Dreyfus became increasingly anxious as the time stretched on. He paced the room. Finally, after an hour, the door opened, Demange entered and, without a word, took the prisoner in his arms. They moved to a dark vestibule off the courtroom where Judge Advocate Brisset, surrounded by military guards, read the verdict by candlelight. At attention, his arms straight against his body and showing no emotion, Dreyfus listened: "To-day, 22 December 1894, the First Court Martial . . . has unanimously declared Captain Alfred Dreyfus of the 14th artillery regiment, probationer of the General Staff, guilty of having delivered to a foreign power, or to its agents, a certain number of secret or confidential documents concerning national defense . . . in order to obtain for that power the means to commit hostilities, or to undertake war, against France." And then the sentence: "Accordingly, the Court unanimously condemns the above mentioned Dreyfus to the punishment of deportation in a fortified place and to military degradation."[35]

The official act of judgment went on to confirm that the prisoner had been born in Mulhouse, the son of Raphael Dreyfus and Jeannette Libmann, and that, conforming to the code of military justice, he would pay the expenses of his court-martial.[36]

CHAPTER IX

"France for the French!"

SURROUNDED BY SOLDIERS in the Cherche-Midi vestibule, Dreyfus maintained his self-control. But when prison guards led him back to the infirmary, the stoic discipline he had displayed like a badge of honor for four days gave way to panic. He hurled himself against the wall, as he had done on the night of his arrest, and beat his head and limbs "like a madman." One guard seized him by the waist and tried to calm him, but without success. Having come to his trial meticulously clad in his finest dress uniform, he was taken back across the deserted street at midnight with his officer's cloak wrapped around his arms like a straitjacket, the hood pulled over his head. "My only crime is to have been born a Jew!" he cried out to Forzinetti as he had done two months before. "Why did I ever enter the Ecole de Guerre?" And he demanded a revolver from the prison director who had become his friend. But Forzinetti understood Dreyfus's character and the language needed to control him and stayed through the night to talk "soldier to soldier" about honor, justice, and the shame of accepting defeat. Taking his own life would be a confession of guilt, Forzinetti told him, and by the time the commandant left the cell Dreyfus had promised "if not to live, at least to wait."[1]

Through letters and messages relayed by Maître Demange, the family immediately redoubled its efforts to give the prisoner hope. Still prohibited from visiting Cherche-Midi, his wife, sisters, brothers, and

141

in-laws tried to exact a promise from afar: that he would draw on his courage "still once again" and live to sign his appeal. "Write your uncle Alfred the most affectionate letter possible," Joseph Valabrègue told his son; he "needs all of our love, and he deserves more than all of it." "You must live for the children," Lucie wrote the morning after the conviction, and "for me." Later the same day she promised, "Everywhere you go, or where they send you, I will follow. . . . We will raise our children together and give them a spirit tempered against the vicissitudes of life." Even Jeanne's wet nurse, she said, was committed to stay with the children and follow the family into exile. "Think of the good years we have had together," Lucie wrote, "and the ones we will have again." And she pledged to take care of him as he had taken care of her when she was ill. "Gather your forces and fight," she exhorted her husband. "We will fight together. . . . What would become of me without you? I would die of sorrow if I no longer had the hope of being beside you again."[2]

Informed by Demange of the family's "terrible ordeal," the prisoner wrote his closest brother about the grief they shared seeing their name "reviled and dragged through the mud." He asked Mathieu to "attempt everything, even the impossible," but confessed that he was "wavering between two resolutions," between engagement and suicide. He wanted to be "finished with this sad life. . . . It's cowardly, I know, but at least I would find oblivion in all the silence of the grave."[3] Thoughts of death brought thoughts of providence, and, on the day after his trial and for the first time since his arrest, he asked to see Zadoc Kahn, a fellow Alsatian and the man who had officiated at his wedding four years before. The prisoner wanted to be "comforted" by the rabbi's "warm and eloquent words."[4]

Through his friend Louis Lépine, Kahn had been trying to help Dreyfus's cause for weeks, and when he received the prisoner's appeal he quickly wrote to General Félix-Gaston Saussier, the military governor of Paris, asking authorization to bring Dreyfus "religious support." But Saussier referred the grand rabbi's letter to the judge advocate, and the request was denied: "Given the nature of the crime for which Captain Dreyfus has been condemned," the military prosecutor replied, "it is my opinion that he see no one."[5]

In complete isolation across the days and nights following his court-martial, Dreyfus was kept alive by Forzinetti's surveillance, Demange's support, and a flood of family letters. But it was to Lucie, above all, that he turned for hope: "You are the single thread that attaches me to life," he wrote on December 24, and, admitting that her "heroism" had won him over, he reconfirmed a belief he had held since his years in Mulhouse and later in Carpentras, with Henriette: "Decidedly," he told Lucie, "women are superior to us . . . I am proud of you and I will try to be worthy of you." In a letter to his brother Léon he said that "Lucie's love and the profound affection of all of you has sustained me"; calling on the imagery of the officer corps, he promised to defeat the enemy "or at least die in the breach."[6] He signed the appeal for review, but with little hope of success. It would take months, he knew—perhaps years—for Demange and the family to uncover the truth and secure his release.

A few days after her brother's conviction, Rachel Dreyfus Schil wrote to the minister of war in the family's name. Appealing to his honesty, influence, and patriotism, she asked General Auguste Mercier to overturn the decision made "in the shadows of a closed session" where no one heard the captain's defense. "Think of the martyrdom of this man," she wrote, "for whom the only crime is to have been born a Jew; think of the horrible agony of his wife and family, all of whom are good French men and women." Ambitious and easily frightened by attacks from the nationalist press, Mercier ignored Rachel's letter ("no response" was scribbled across its first page), contributing to the family's growing sense of powerlessness and isolation.[7] "No hand was held out to us" after the condemnation, said Mathieu, "and every door was obstinately closed. On the street, people who knew us . . . fled from us. We were the plague-stricken."[8]

As the government ignored them and many friends turned away, new enemies, inspired by the nationalist and anti-Semitic press, forced family members into their homes for protection. In a wave of euphoric self-congratulation, La Libre Parole, La Croix, L'Intransigeant, and scores of other newspapers—left, right, and center—applauded the army's victory and offered General Mercier absolution for his earlier sins. The "sacred military" had been purged of a traitorous Jew, and if a French law dating from 1848 prohibited capital punishment for "political crimes" (a law not a few politicians and army officials worked feverishly to overturn), there was at least the satisfaction of knowing that Dreyfus would be publicly humiliated and sent to suffer in perpetual exile. Confirming the widespread belief in the captain's guilt, hostile reactions came from everywhere, including from significant numbers of French Jews rushing to distance themselves from the traitor. Concerned that the individual's crime would be imputed to his community of coreligionists, to his "race," they aimed to make their opinions known. Journalists Isadore Singer and Joseph Aron, fervent patriots who had been battling anti-Semitism, felt that Dreyfus should be shot or "subjected to the 'pitiless penal code of Moses'—death by stoning, with the grand rabbi of France casting the first stone."[9] But if some French Jews joined the assault while others remained silent, the most vitriolic attacks still came from Drumont and his allies, and, as expected, they moved beyond concerns about a single officer. "Jews out of France!" Drumont wrote on the day of Dreyfus's conviction, "France for the French!" A recent raving by the Marquis de Morès was put forward as advice: "Yes, mothers of France, in order to revenge themselves on our patriotism, the occult chiefs of Judaism have decided that next year Israel would eat unleavened bread saturated with the blood . . . of Christian babies. . . . We must destroy the Jews," the marquis insisted, "chase every last one of them from our midst, or perish at their hands."[10]

On Christmas Day the Orleanist newspaper *Soleil* reminded readers that "Dreyfus is a man without a country, a man of a special race; this is not a Frenchman," and another journalist from the same paper added a perverse twist: "As a Jew, Dreyfus did not betray his Fatherland, which is the temple of Jerusalem. A passive and disciplined soldier in the Judeo-Masonic International, he recognizes the grand master of that society as his leader. He obeyed, just like those who follow him will obey."[11] In the December 27 edition of *La Libre Parole*, Drumont invited Germany "to erect a statue of Dreyfus"; as a child he had come to France from Alsace only to betray the nation, and he had entered the Ecole Polytechnique, the Ecole de Guerre, and the Etat-Major in order to intercept defense secrets and sell them to the Prussians.[12]

In Paris, Mulhouse, Belfort, and Carpentras, family members read "all these infamies and lies," as Henriette described them in a letter to her son. "In what mudhole," she asked with disgust, had the minds of these hostile critics been "petrified?" More than ever, the family felt the impact of the captain's conviction, and, through late December, the potential for violence. Police reports from Belfort described members of Jacques Dreyfus's family moving in with Mathieu's in-laws, the Schwobs, in nearby Héricourt, "not daring to show themselves." In Paris, Jacques' two oldest sons were forced to abandon their preparation for the Ecole Polytechnique and Saint Cyr and return home; and the two youngest boys would soon be chased from their Belfort *lycée* when the school principal could no longer protect them. Léon and his wife

Alice "hid themselves from the eyes of Mulhousiens," according to one police agent, and met only with a few "intimates." For safety Henriette instructed other family members to send her news in double envelopes addressed to a local friend in Carpentras. And Mathieu and Suzanne, concerned about their children, Emile and Magui, left them with grand-parents in Héricourt while they moved from the public Grand Hotel in Paris to a private apartment on the Boulevard Haussmann. Within days they would move yet again, to the rue de la Victoire close to the synagogue and in a building adjoining the Hadamards' on the rue Château-dun. Taking precautions against threats, the family drew closer to-gether in an alliance led by Mathieu, an alliance critics would soon define as the nucleus of a "Jewish syndicate."[13]

Through the last week of December, Lucie enlisted the help of her mother and sisters to gather provisions her husband would need for his long imprisonment. Concerned about his uniform, torn on the night of his conviction, and about his soiled laundry and lack of winter clothes, Lucie offered to pack a valise and deliver it to the Cherche-Midi guard. Dreyfus, his scrupulous sense of order now intensified by his need to control some aspect of his daily life, compiled a detailed list for his wife. Knowing that he would soon be prohibited from wearing his uniform, he asked her to pack his best civilian clothes, including "a black winter suit, eight starched collars, four new ties, three night shirts and a pair of warm slippers (size 41) that can be put on easily." He would need a nail file, an extra pair of pince-nez and, as the hard days of winter ap-proached, a heavy, dark gray macfarlane cape he suggested Lucie buy at the Belle Jardinière department store. "A macfarlane will be more useful during my travels," he admitted, "than my winter overcoats which are too elegant for the torture I am about to undergo." And for "distraction during the long days of isolation," he asked his wife to purchase a sturdy portable inkwell ("so that it doesn't spill in trans-port"), and an English grammar book with exercises suited for a class-room of one ("since I will be my own professor"). Encouraged by her husband's plans for the future, Lucie wrote back that she and Mathieu would also study English: "The best method, you know, is to read a lot and to familiarize yourself with the vocabulary. But it's the pronuncia-tion," she confessed, "which is really difficult." Her comments must have reminded Alfred of his early lessons in French pronunciation, but Lucie's advice was sadly ironic as well; in his "perpetual exile in a fortified place," he would be forced by prison authorities to remain silent.[14]

The couple also made plans for Pierre and Jeanne and for the Avenue du Trocadéro apartment. "Buy the children toys for New Year's Day," the prisoner wrote on December 26, "and tell them they're from their father; the poor things are just beginning life and they must not suffer our troubles." Though always less lavish than her husband, Lucie agreed to "spoil" the children with games and chocolate cigarettes. Pierre and Jeanne had been in the care of the Hadamards while Lucie worked with Demange and Mathieu, but they would now move permanently with their mother to the rue Châteaudun, where they would await their father's return from his "long voyage." Meanwhile, in a series of letters, Lucie and Alfred unraveled the intricacies of their apartment contract and the clause that allowed them to break their lease under extraordinary circumstances ("Sadly," the prisoner noted, "that's the case"). They shared all the details of what to pack, and they talked about the sadness of leaving a home "filled with excellent memories." Among the personal effects that conjured up those memories were cases of fine wine that Raphael had collected in Mulhouse. The first anniversary of Raphael's death had just passed, and Lucie described to her husband how Mathieu had taken the family to synagogue services. "For a long time last night," the prisoner wrote on the morning of December 31, "I also thought about my poor father, and about the entire family. I won't hide from you the fact that I cried. . . . But the tears comforted me." So too did the realization that his father, an Alsatian *protestataire* proud of his son's military service, never witnessed his humiliation.[15]

Delivering books and clothes to Cherche-Midi, Lucie confessed that, "for a moment, I had the feeling of being close to you. I wanted to shatter those cold high walls which separate us, and I wanted to hold you."[16] It had been ten weeks since Dreyfus had left the Avenue du Trocadéro for General Staff headquarters, and his wife still waited for permission to pass inside the prison gates.

On New Year's Eve, du Paty returned to Cherche-Midi to inform the prisoner that his appeal had been denied. Anticipating a violent reaction, he posted a guard outside the cell, but Dreyfus remained calm. Supported by family, Forzinetti, and Demange, he had controlled his panic over recent days and prepared for the degradation and deportation to come. If anything, he now welcomed the voyage as an escape from the scene of his disgrace. On this visit, however, du Paty came with an offer from the Ministry of War. If Dreyfus exposed his network of treason, or if he admitted that he had written the *bordereau* as a ploy to obtain more sensitive documents from the German and Italian attachés in Paris, the government could recognize extenuating circumstances, and, perhaps, lighten the prisoner's sentence; it could, du Paty intimated, cancel the public degradation or arrange for Dreyfus's wife and children to accompany him into a relatively comfortable exile. The commandant and the prisoner spoke for an hour, but the more Dreyfus insisted on his innocence—he would never betray his country, nor would he engage in counterespionage without orders from superiors—the more his interrogator pushed for a full confession. Finally, when du Paty reverted to his old ways and suggested that Lucie was part of the "conspiracy," Dreyfus's patience broke: "Enough!" he told his most dogged enemy. "I am innocent and your duty is to pursue your investigation." "If you are innocent," du Paty responded, "you are the greatest martyr of all time."[17]

As soon as the commandant left, Dreyfus wrote his wife. "The appeal is denied, as expected. I've just been told. Immediately request permission to see me." Now certain that the degradation ceremony would take place, he asked Lucie to send his sword, which would be taken from him and broken in front of fellow soldiers. It would be a "cruel and horrible punishment," Dreyfus admitted, but he was now "ready to face it with the dignity of a clear and tranquil conscience." Late that night he also recounted the du Paty interview in a letter to Demange, and he wrote to the minister of war: "I have received, by your order, a visit from M. le Commandant du Paty de Clam to whom I have declared that I am innocent and that I have never committed the slightest indiscretion of any sort. I am condemned; I have no favor to demand; but in the name of my honor, which I hope will be returned to me one day, it is my duty to ask you to pursue your investigation. After I am gone, continue the search. It is the only favor I ask."[18]

On the morning of January 2, 1895, Forzinetti told Dreyfus that his wife would visit him that afternoon. "I hope to see you in just a few minutes," the prisoner wrote, "and to draw strength from your presence. We will support each other against everything. I need your love to carry on." Waiting in his cell, he became more anxious and he spoke to Lucie by letter: "Since four o'clock this afternoon my heart has been beating so fast it is about to break. You're still not here; the seconds seem like hours. I listen to hear if someone is coming to fetch me. I hear nothing, I wait." The long weeks of late-night interrogations, the breakdowns after his arrest and conviction, and the sedatives had taken their toll, and when a guard arrived to lead the prisoner downstairs, he nearly collapsed. Forcing himself upright, he entered the dark Cherche-Midi basement, "a veritable ice-house," where he could barely see his wife through the thick wire latticework of the two partitions that separated them. Military officials had ordered Forzinetti to keep the couple at a distance, not to allow them to touch. Surrounded by guards and struggling to see more than their silhouettes through iron grates, they spoke only for a short time before the prisoner reached the end of his strength. "My hand is still not steady," he wrote minutes later from his cell, and "I needed to hide myself in order to cry. But don't think that my spirit has diminished," he assured his wife. "It is only my body which is a bit weak after three months of confinement." Their talk, "even through prison bars," had done him good. Above all, he told Lucie, "I felt how courageous and spirited you are, so full of affection. . . . As for me, you must have sensed that I am ready for everything; I want my honor and I shall have it; no obstacle will stop me."[19]

Lucie had to be supported by Forzinetti during the brief meeting, and in the shadows of the prison basement she could only discern that her husband had lost weight, that he was "pale and troubled." "I wanted to tell you so many things," she wrote that night, "I wanted to give you courage, to comfort you . . . but I couldn't find the words."[20] The next day she lodged a protest with the military governor of Paris: "Please accord me authorization to speak with my husband other than through a double partition, so that I may embrace him. You are too good-hearted a man," she told General Saussier, "to refuse a wife's legitimate request after such a cruel separation."[21] Forzinetti, also angered by the army's inhumane treatment of Dreyfus, appealed to Saussier that the couple be allowed to meet in the prison commandant's office, in his presence. "Relatives of many convicted men had obtained the privilege of using the 'special visitor's room,' " Forzinetti wrote, and "it could be granted to Madame Dreyfus."[22] Saussier relented—immediate family could visit the prisoner—and on the evening of January 3, Dreyfus and his wife held each other for the first time in nearly twelve weeks.

That night Lucie had gone to Cherche-Midi with her mother, and the next morning she brought her husband's closest friend. "When my brother saw me," Mathieu later wrote, "he threw himself in my arms and shouted, 'Why am I cursed, Mathieu? What is this fate that haunts me?' " As a young lieutenant he had been reprimanded by his older brother when romantic liaisons or difficulties with fellow officers threatened his career and the family's reputation. Mathieu had always set the standard, and now, controlling his own emotions, he promised to do everything within his power to discover the truth. He reminded his brother that "suicide would be considered a confession of guilt," and, for the last time before the degradation, he asked him to live "for his wife, for his children."[23]

Originally scheduled for the morning of Friday, January 4, the degradation was postponed a day. Military authorities offered no explanation, but some observers thought it fitting that the traitor be publicly condemned on the Jewish Sabbath.[24] The family would not attend. "Do everything possible," Joseph Valabrègue wrote his son, "to stay away from this appalling ceremony."[25] More than the danger if they attended, which was real, the family knew that Alfred could not bear them to witness his disgrace. "I will resist," he wrote his wife. "I shall draw strength from your love, from the affection of all of you, from my dear children, from the supreme hope that one day the truth will be known." He told the Valabrègues that he felt as if he were in the middle of a "bad dream. But, alas, it's reality! You believe, my dear Henriette, that there is a God. How can he allow such injustice, such wretchedness! . . . I had hoped until this last moment for a divine intervention which would expose the real traitor. But now I know that we must count only on ourselves." Still, he promised to face his sacrifice "head high," a pledge he made in a wave of letters that went out from his prison cell. "You can be calm," he told Léon and his sister-in-law Alice. "From the moment I understood that I must live, that I had no right to abandon the struggle, I regained all my energy. I will endure everything, as I have so far . . . without weakness." On the eve of his degradation he wrote Demange: "To tell you that my heart will not be tortured when they strip the badges of honor for which I have worked so hard would be to lie; I would, a thousand times, prefer death. But you have informed me of my duty," he told Demange, "and you have given me faith." He promised the lawyer that he would march to his punishment "head high."[26]

And he did. Across the days following the "execution procession," some newspaper sketches and magazine caricatures would show the traitor with head bowed and body stooped in defeat.[27] But those illustrations were as inaccurate as the editorials that accompanied them. Head up and with exaggerated military discipline, Dreyfus faced his degradation as he had faced his morning drills at the Ecole Polytechnique or, more recently, his court-martial; and he held that rigid control from the moment guards entered his cell at 7:30 A.M. on Saturday, January 5. After loosening his epaulets, brass buttons, and gold officer's braid so they would tear away more easily, and after scoring his sword so that it would break swiftly and cleanly, the guards brought him to the Cherche-Midi gates where he was searched and handcuffed. Forzinetti, more than ever convinced of Dreyfus's innocence, protested the treatment, but to no avail. Shaking the prisoner's hand, he turned him over to the Republican Guard. Mounted troops surrounded a black prison wagon drawn by four horses, and the cortege galloped southwest down the rue du Cherche Midi toward the Ecole Militaire.[28]

Crowds had started to gather in the "piercing cold" outside the ornate iron gates that separated the Cour Morland, the main courtyard of the Ecole Militaire, from the public Place de Fontenoy to the east. The golden dome of the Invalides dominated the northern horizon, and some spectators climbed to the roof of the immense, iron-framed Galerie des Machines, built for the 1889 Universal Exposition. Military authorities directed journalists, diplomats, and dignitaries to reserved sections inside the courtyard; Léon Daudet, Maurice Barrès, and other political commentators and literati joined a contingent of international journalists that included Theodor Herzl, a Hungarian Jew on assignment for the Austrian newspaper *Neue Freie Presse*. Nearby, undoubtedly attracting the most attention, Sarah Bernhardt waited with another group of notables under the elaborate stone reliefs of mythological figures that ran across the building's eighteenth-century walls. It was a cloudy morning; it had rained the night before, and the footing of the Cour Morland had turned to icy mud. Shortly before 8 A.M. Dreyfus's wagon sped past the crowd and toward a garrison office where, under the watch of Captain Charles Lebrun-Renault of the Republican Guard, the prisoner would wait until the bells of the Ecole Militaire struck nine.[29]

Newly returned from the colonies and aware only of Dreyfus's "crime and race," Lebrun-Renault watched his charge "more with disgust than with pity"; and his almost palpable contempt intensified the prisoner's anxiety. In a nervous, staccato monologue that was, more than anything, an attempt to steel himself for events to come, Dreyfus, despite prohibitions of silence, rehearsed all the arguments he had marshaled against du Paty, d'Ormescheville, and the judges of his court-martial. He was the "innocent victim of a terrible error," and his lawyer would expose the truth, even if it took two or three years. "I entered the Ecole Polytechnique at eighteen years of age," he told his guard. "I had a magnificent military career in front of me, a fortune of five hundred thousand francs. . . . I have never been a womanizer. . . . I have no need of money. Why would I betray my country?" Lebrun-Renault remained indifferent, moments of silence passed, and Dreyfus began again; he described his last meeting with du Paty and his refusal to bargain away his honor. "Now, it's finished," he said; he would go into exile, probably to the fortress for political prisoners in New Caledonia, and, within three or four months, he hoped that his wife and children would join him. As the hour of his degradation approached, he asked his guard to tell the sergeant major who would strip his insignias "to please go about his busines quickly." Instead, Lebrun-Renault alerted superiors that his prisoner was prepared to create a scene, to protest his innocence in front of the assembled troops.[30]

Bells sounded, military drums rolled, and four artillery soldiers, sabers in hand, led Dreyfus into the Cour Morland. Every regiment of the Paris garrison had been ordered to send two detachments to the ceremony—one of soldiers in arms, the other of young recruits. Like the ritualistic hazing process Dreyfus had known as a first-year cadet at the Ecole Polytechnique, the "degradation" of an officer was a didactic ritual designed to instill the fear of humiliation. Moving diagonally across the courtyard's vast expanse and toward a general on horseback at its center, Dreyfus marched under the chiseled inscription "Ecole Supérieure de Guerre." It was the place where he had spent the most important part of his military career and where "every wall, every stone, recalled images of his past."[31] Now, on a terrace "which dominated the sad and imposing spectacle," military students watched the traitor walk below. In lock-step with his guards, he stumbled briefly, then regained his balance. "Look how he holds himself upright, the scum," remarked someone in the distant crowd, but the nearly four thousand troops had been ordered to remain still and silent. The guards retreated, leaving their prisoner alone in front of General Darras and Vallecalle, the clerk of the Court-Martial. In a loud, clear voice Vallecalle read the act of judgment, saluted Darras, and stepped back. Dreyfus, heels together and at attention, remained silent. Standing in his stirrups, the general raised his sword, looked down at the prisoner, and announced, "Alfred Dreyfus, you are not worthy of bearing arms. In the name of the French people, we degrade you!"[32]

In fulfillment of the promise he had made to himself and his family, the prisoner broke his silence, raised both hands, forced his head even higher, and shouted: "Soldiers, they are degrading an innocent man! Soldiers, they are dishonoring an innocent man! Long live France! Long live the Army!" Another silence followed, broken seconds later by the crowd beyond the courtyard gates chanting "Death! Death!" Quickly a sergeant major approached Dreyfus and slashed the gold braids from his cap and uniform; he stripped the regiment numbers from his collar, ripped off his brass buttons and, kneeling down while the prisoner remained at strict attention, tore from Dreyfus's pants leg the red stripes he had worn since his entrance into the Ecole Polytechnique. Finally, he took the sword, broke it over his knee, pulled off the captain's scabbard and leather belt, and threw the pieces to the ground. With his kepi now misshapen and threads hanging from his uniform (his "black rag"), Dreyfus repeated his protest: "I am innocent!"

Stepping over the pile at his feet, he moved off the narrow cobblestone pathway that ran down the center of the Cour Morland and began the "degradation parade" around the courtyard's muddy periphery. He knew the regulations and seemed to lead his guards "like an officer commanding his squadron." Soldiers gazed past him without a word, while dignitaries and journalists recorded their impressions. Maurice Paléologue, a diplomat from the Ministry of Foreign Affairs, had come to the degradation with Colonel Sandherr. Taken aback by Dreyfus's stiff, monotonous appeals, he told Sandherr: "If I were innocent I would rebel, I would struggle." "It is clear that you do not know the Jews," responded the officer. "The race has neither patriotism, nor honor, nor pride. For centuries they have done nothing but betray."[33] A journalist covering the event for La Croix would call Dreyfus's shout of "Long live France!" the "last kiss of Judas," and the reporter from La Libre Parole said that "it was not a man being degraded for an individual error, but an entire race whose shame was laid bare."[34] Léon Daudet followed the proceedings with opera glasses and described the traitor as a "rigid puppet, pale and weasel-faced . . . with a body . . . stripped piece by piece of all the things that had given him social value and rank." When he shouted out his innocence "his voice was toneless," said Daudet. "He no longer had an age, a name, a complexion. He was the color of treason . . . a wreck from the ghetto." The traitor could never share "the single faith . . . which safeguards our race, our language, our blood, and which keep us all in solidarity. . . . This wretch is not French."[35] Maurice Barrès examined every movement and noted that Dreyfus's "foreign physiognomy, his impassive stiffness, the very atmosphere he exuded revolted even the most self-controlled of the spectators." Another observer, Raphael Viau, listened to the prisoner's "hoarse" cries of innocence; he felt the agony "in the pit of [his] stomach," said Viau, and, from a distance, he heard the "relentless shouts,

'Death! Death!' " Sarah Bernhardt, the only witness with credentials to judge the "parade" as performance, remained silent, but she believed the prisoner's protests, and, like the journalist Herzl who stood "huddled in a heavy coat" nearby, became convinced of the captain's innocence.[36]

When Dreyfus passed a special section reserved for officers' wives, the women began their own chants, and one, near the parade line, spit in the prisoner's face. Moving on, he called out, "I swear on my wife and children that I am innocent! Long live France!" At the high gate facing the Place de Fontenoy, Dreyfus stopped and turned to the crowd. Police agents tried to push spectators back from the iron bars, but they surged forward and greeted the prisoner's protests with a torrent of hisses and shouts of "Traitor! Traitor! Death to the Jew!" Nearing the end of his march, Dreyfus stopped again in front of the press: "Tomorrow you will tell all of France that I am innocent," he said. But the journalists, like the coterie of army wives, broke the silence that reigned within the courtyard and lashed back: "Shut up, you wretch! Coward! Judas! Filthy Jew!" For the first time, Dreyfus interrupted his litany and cried out, "You have no right to insult me!" But he was moved on by the Republican Guard, handcuffed, and pushed into the waiting prison wagon. The driver, who later called it "the most beautiful day of my life," whipped his horses into a gallop and headed north toward the Avenue Bosquet and the Pont de l'Alma. The entire spectacle had taken ten minutes.[37]

Crossing onto the Right Bank, the prison wagon sped through the Place de l'Alma and past the eastern end of the Avenue du Trocadéro. Dreyfus had not seen his home in three months, and the fleeting sight of the place "where I left all my happiness," he later wrote, "was a cruel agony."[38] Along the route, crowds recognized the prisoner's cortege and shouted, "Traitor! Death to the Jew!" as they hurled stones at the wagon's wire-mesh window. Minutes later, at the Central Prison Depot, Dreyfus was dragged from room to room, photographed, searched, measured, and stripped of his uniform. Now in the hands of civilian officials, he came under the authority of the Minister of the Interior. The process took three hours, and when the director of the depot told his prisoner how sad he was to inscribe the words "crime of treason" next to the name of a French officer, Dreyfus responded, "I understand your indignation. . . . But I am innocent."[39]

CHAPTER X

The Voyage Out

TRANSPORTED BACK across the Seine at noon, inmate number 164 arrived at the civilian Santé prison south of the Collège Sainte Barbe and the Ecole Polytechnique. Before leaving the Central Depot he had told its director that he would face his ordeal with "confidence in God," and when he entered his Santé cell, close to the panic which had overcome him at Cherche-Midi, he prayed for strength. In the evening, he rallied long enough to write his wife and family. "I promised not to desert my post," he told his brothers and sisters, "and I have kept my pledge. . . . But today has laid me low. . . . All I ask at this moment, since I am of no use to you here, is that they send me away as soon as possible." He might still have "the courage of a soldier who confronts death without fear," but, he asked, "do I have the courage of a martyr?"[1]

Sparing Lucie the details of his degradation, he said only that it was like "a hallucination" until "my torn and soiled clothes shocked me back to reality, and the look of contempt on those around me made it all too clear why I was there." Again, he had paid the price for his inability to articulate his deepest feelings. "If only we could open a man's heart with a scalpel," he said, and expose the soul, "then all the worthy people who saw me pass by would have read . . . 'This is a man of honor.' " Dreyfus understood the contempt felt by the soldiers lining the Cour Morland. "In their place I too would have been unable to contain my scorn upon seeing an officer who had betrayed his country," he told Lucie. "But that is the tragedy, the traitor is not me!"[2] Denied access to the prisoner immediately after his degradation ("I so much wanted to be close to you," wrote his wife, "to comfort you"), the entire family was finally granted permission to visit twice a week in the presence of the Santé warden. During those brief meetings, and in scores of letters, they struggled to understand the events of January 5. "Decidedly," Henriette told her children, "everything that this poor, unfortunate man does turns against him. His cries of innocence should have moved the crowd," she said, "but, on the contrary, they defined those shouts as cynicism. . . . I ask myself how he will be able to resist all this torture." "What a hideous morning! What fearful moments!" Lucie wrote shortly after receiving news of the degradation parade. "No, I cannot think of it; it makes me suffer too much. . . . You promised me to be brave, and you kept your word." "That day, that Saturday, remains engraved in my spirit," the prisoner said later, and to his brother Léon he described how "day and night I dream of this atmosphere of infamy which surrounds my name."[3]

As he awaited news of when and where he would be deported, Dreyfus fought to separate the iniquity of his conviction from the ideal of French justice he had never doubted. The degradation had shaken one faith—more than ever he questioned his physical ability to sustain the "tortures" still to come—but it strengthened his belief in "providence," "justice," and "France." In time his innocence would be "recognized and proclaimed by this beloved France, my Fatherland, to whom I have always devoted my intelligence and my strength"; and to whom, as a soldier, he had always wanted to "consecrate" his blood.[4] When he spoke of duty to the land of one's fathers, of heroic sacrifice, and of readiness to shed blood for France, he employed the same vocabulary as his most virulent critics; the spirit of "national energy"—which Barrès, Daudet, Drumont, and others defined as foreign to Protestants, Freemasons, and Jews—was the source of Dreyfus's strength. And his family echoed that faith: "Yes, we must hope," Lucie wrote, "that France, our dear Fatherland, for whom we are ready to pay with our blood, will one day recognize its error and see in you one of its most courageous and noble citizens."[5] Writing to his brothers and sisters, the prisoner said that he "must do as Lucie does, and tell myself that there is justice in this world." He promised his wife that "together in exile, proud and worthy of one another, we will show that our . . . thoughts have always been . . . of France." Finally, to Mathieu, he said that "our two souls are as one; I feel everything that you suffer. . . . But the hour will sound when all of France will recognize that I am one of its worthy sons." As Dreyfus's letters blended with his private prayers, he invoked those professions of faith with increasing intensity. "When they return the golden officer's braids that I am as worthy to wear today as I was yesterday, and when I am finally leading our brave soldiers again," he told his wife, "I will forget everything, the sufferings, the tortures, the outrageous insults. . . . May God and human justice make that day come soon!"[6]

"Material" conditions, physical survival, now concerned him more than "moral" strength. "What a part these miserable nerves play in human life," he complained to Lucie. "Why can't we entirely separate our material character from our moral character so that one has no influence on the other. My morale is still strong," he insisted, "and ready for everything. But for nearly three months my nerves have been stretched to the limit . . . and I have not even had the resource of hard physical exercise to overcome them."[7] His Santé prison routine—which he described in meticulous detail, from his 6:30 A.M. shave to his last meal of bread, jam, and chocolate at 8:00 P.M.—included only thirty minutes of walking in an open air space barely six meters square. But Dreyfus had been plagued by "miserable nerves" long before his arrest and the breakdowns he suffered at Cherche-Midi. As a student he had struggled with bouts of nervous tension brought on by overwork, and he had always looked forward to weekend trips to Carpentras, which, he said, "helped ease my nerves." Before that, in Mulhouse, his sisters had described his "delicate" constitution and tendency to be both "proud and timid." But if, before his arrest, Dreyfus had exhibited symptoms of neurasthenia, he now moved beyond that vague affliction and suffered the very real hardships of solitary confinement. As they had done at Cherche-Midi, prison doctors prescribed sedatives.[8]

The afternoon of January 17, Henriette's daughter visited her uncle and found him "no longer himself." Though still "courageous and resolved to live," his suffering was obvious and "intense." Dreyfus told his young niece that he was suffocating within the four walls of his cell and that he was desperate to leave Paris, the sooner the better. He would rather "mount an assault on ten fortresses singlehandedly, than be here, powerless, inactive and waiting passively for the truth to discover itself."[9] Deported, he would at least be cut off from the daily reminders of his past; he would be far from the Ecole Militaire and the Ecole Polytechnique. And in exile he would be reunited with his wife and children. Officials from the Ministry of the Interior had not yet announced the prisoner's final destination, but he knew that his first stop would be at the citadel of Saint-Martin de Ré on an island off the west coast of France. He would have a room and courtyard there, he told his niece, and conditions would be better.

He was wrong. Within hours after Henriette's daughter left Santé prison, his treatment deteriorated. Returning to his cell, he received news that Lucie, who had been ill and ordered to rest, would visit him in two days' time. But late that night he was suddenly awakened by a deputy from the Interior Ministry. Handcuffed, half-dressed, and without his pince-nez, he was dragged from bed and hoisted into a horse-drawn van. The trip from the Santé prison past the Salpêtrière hospital to the Gare d'Orléans lasted only minutes. Guards hurried him through the station's freight entrance onto the platform and into a special train car with a row of miniscule cells, each one large enough to accommodate only a seated man. In leg irons and handcuffs, Dreyfus's limbs went numb. Without food or drink, and "shaking with fever," he waited all night for the train to depart. The next morning, after many appeals, guards gave him coffee, bread, and cheese, and minutes later the journey began.[10]

Traveling southwest from Paris through Orléans, Blois, and Niort, the prison train arrived at the port town of La Rochelle at noon. Much like the republic of Mülhausen, La Rochelle had been a stronghold of Calvinism in the sixteenth and seventeenth centuries, though its history had been more violent than its Alsatian counterpart; exposed to the threat of naval attacks by the English, the coastal town had been the setting of constant warfare until Cardinal Richelieu conquered the Huguenot resistance and the port became a passageway for Protestants escaping to Britain and North America. In the winter of 1895, however, only the round fortress towers guarding the port remained as monuments to the wars of religion, while at the train depot nearby, small crowds habitually gathered to watch the arrival of La Rochelle's new generation of transients—convicted murderers, thieves, and political prisoners en route to exile.

Transporting Dreyfus in secret, officials anticipated no incident at La Rochelle; but curious passersby noted police agents milling near one train car and suspected that it carried special cargo. Rumors spread, the number of onlookers increased, and, at one point, the prisoner's name was overheard. Cramped in his dark cell through the afternoon, Dreyfus listened to the crowd become "more and more agitated." At nightfall, deputies unlocked his leg irons, threw his macfarlane over his shoulders, and tried to hurry him past the station's arrival gate. But the mob, now armed with lanterns, pushed forward to separate Dreyfus from his guards. "Into the water!" they shouted, "Death to the traitor! Death to the Jew!" Beaten with canes and fists, spat upon and struck by a French officer using the butt of his saber handle, Dreyfus did not try to escape. The demonstrators thought they were "'confronting a traitor," he said later, "the vilest of wretches," and he understood their anger. Finally pulled from the melee by two policemen, he was locked into a waiting van, "a sad collection of rags," *La Libre Parole* reported the next day, "almost worthy of pity." At a "triple gallop" the wagon headed toward the dock of La Palice with the crowd running behind, gathering up stones and breaking the van's window "into a thousand pieces." Hurried onto the small launch *Nénuphar,* Dreyfus embarked for the Ile de Ré.[11]

Though indifferent to the prisoner's plight, many news reports expressed shock at the savagery of the mob and condemned the slipshod way authorities had transported the prisoner. Drumont's paper, however, offered another explanation for the events at La Rochelle: "The Jews had too little time to organize a serious kidnapping in Paris," the story went, but on the train platform at La Rochelle "the supposedly hostile demonstrations were provoked by friends of the Jews who rushed toward Dreyfus not to lynch him, as it seemed, but to tear him from the hands of the police." Still, Drumont warned, "The Jews do not feel defeated: they are preparing to begin again."[12]

The night crossing from La Rochelle to the fortress at Saint-Martin de Ré took one hour. With his hands frostbitten, with his wrists and ankles bruised from the iron restraints, and with no eyeglasses, the prisoner walked through the snow from the landing dock to a stone entranceway adorned with royal images of the Sun King. At the Ecole Polytechnique and Ecole de Guerre, young Lieutenant Dreyfus had studied the citadel of Saint-Martin de Ré. Built by the royal architect Vauban for the defense of the realm in 1681, the fortress—a perfect square surrounded by a deep moat and four bastions—was as impregnable as it was Cartesian; and its barracks, said local historians, possessed "that family air which always marked the military buildings of Louis le Grand." During the Revolution, Count Mirabeau had been imprisoned in those barracks for the crime of treason, and with the Reign of Terror, Jacobins had used the citadel as a holding camp for thousands of priests who refused to take the revolutionary oath. Many of those "non-juring" clerics perished at Saint-Martin de Ré. Through the nineteenth century its constellation of central buildings had become a penitentiary and processing depot for criminals and political insurgents caught on the wrong side of Parisian barricades; it was the last stop on the way to New Caledonia and other islands of exile.[13]

Stripped and searched in the prison registry, Dreyfus entered his cell at 9 P.M. In a remote corner of the compound, separated by a high wall from the courtyards and buildings used by other inmates, his quarters were designed for constant surveillance. Two guards on two-hour shifts watched every movement through a large grated transom directly above his cot, and during the brief daily exercise period guards lined the walls around his yard. Special regulations required that Dreyfus be stripped naked and searched every day, and the letter-writing privileges he had known at Cherche-Midi and Santé were revised; prohibited from contacting any member of his family except his wife, he was given a pen, ink, and a single sheet of paper twice a week, all of which he had to return after each use. The small cigars that helped ease his nerves—and to which he had become addicted—were also prohibited.[14]

During the nearly four months since his arrest, Dreyfus had written his wife at least two or three times a day. From the outset prison rules had forced him to "speak only of family affairs and private concerns." Censors studied every word and held back every note that seemed to violate those orders, and, by late January, Dreyfus knew that his protests of innocence, his demands for justice, his pledges of allegiance, his dedication to the children's honor, and more had become a string of monotonous pleas. "You must succeed in proving to all of France," he wrote Lucie yet again, "that I am a worthy and loyal soldier who loves his country above everything, having always served it with devotion. It is the principal and primordial goal, more important even than my own person."[15] Driven to repeat those appeals, he apologized to his wife for having lost the tone and "style" that had distinguished his early notes to her from Bourges. Those letters of courtship had been full of plans for the future, and, amid complaints about military exams and provincial boredom, there had been humor and a lightness of touch. Now "my style is baroque and desultory," he wrote on January 31, "my brain is wasted, my focus gone . . . I stammer day and night, awake and in my dreams."[16] His letters had become like the incantations of an anchorite, a series of formulaic prayers through which he hoped to hold on to his sanity, conjure up the truth, and will his release.

He could not recount his prison routine in detail, but it soon became clear to Lucie that conditions on the Ile de Ré were deplorable. Joseph Valabrègue called them "absolutely barbarous . . . monstrous and revolting," and told Henriette about the family's protests to government officials, all of which were rejected or ignored. Again Dreyfus wrote directly to the minister of the interior: "In a century like ours, in a country like France," went his letter of January 26, "it is impossible that, with the powerful means of investigation at your disposal, you cannot shed light on this tragic story. . . . In the name of everything that is dear to you, pursue your investigation." And he asked the minister for permission to write his wife more than twice a week, and to be able to work in his cell—"that is all that this most unfortunate of Frenchmen demands." That letter, like all the others, was never answered.[17]

With no word from her husband, Lucie telegraphed the warden of Saint-Martin de Ré and prepaid the cost of a return wire. He did not respond. For ten days officials held back all of Lucie's letters, and the prisoner began to fear that something have happened to her or to the children. Rereading old correspondence "four or five times, until, little by little, the written words transformed themselves into spoken words," he imagined his wife close to him and he waited for new letters to filter through.[18] He may never have received Lucie's note of January 27 suggesting that he ask Zadoc Kahn to designate a rabbi in the vicinity of the Ile de Ré to come and "comfort him." Four weeks earlier, when Dreyfus's first request to see the grand rabbi was denied, Santé officials had sent a prison chaplain to his cell instead. Now Lucie encouraged her husband to try again, and to meet with "a minister of our own faith." Religious help, she said "would be a great consolation."[19] But either the warden of Saint-Martin de Ré intercepted Lucie's letter, or Dreyfus, rejected once, refused to submit himself to yet another humiliation.

In the second week of February, when Lucie finally received permission to visit Saint-Martin de Ré, preparations for her trip triggered the first family quarrel since Dreyfus's arrest—a sign that the tensions of the past sixteen weeks were taking their toll. With Mathieu busy working alongside Demange, Léon had promised to accompany his sister-in-law on the difficult journey west. She had been in frail health, and Mathieu, keeping all newspapers out of sight, had tried to spare her the "scenes of savagery" that accompanied Alfred's arrival at La Rochelle. Mathieu knew that Lucie could not travel alone, and he counted on his older brother's assistance. At the last moment, however, Léon remained in Mulhouse complaining of "too much work and a nervous stomach," excuses that hurt Lucie's feelings and brought the wrath of

Mathieu, who accused his brother of a hopeless "lack of energy." Joseph Valabrègue, constantly traveling between Carpentras and Paris, immediately volunteered his services, and late on the night of February 13 he accompanied Lucie and Léon's wife, Alice, to the Gare d'Orléans. They arrived in La Rochelle at sunrise, just in time to catch the morning launch, and, after settling in at an *auberge* (carefully registering under Valabrègue's name), they walked through the village of Saint-Martin de Ré toward the citadel.[20]

The weather was "glacial" but sunny, and the winding roads leading up from the white sand seashore must have put Lucie in mind of her trips with her husband and children to the Normandy coast. Like Honfleur and Villers-sur-Mer, the Ile de Ré was dotted with small fishing ports, and, along its high banks, old houses with ornate wooden carvings were the domestic monuments of shipbuilders and merchants. In contrast to the fashionable "Far West de la France," however, Saint-Martin de Ré and its environs had not been overrun by holidaygoers from Paris and London; its local industries—fishing, winegrowing, and salt—remained much as they had been since Cistercian monks helped develop them in the twelfth century. The odor of seaweed, codfish, and salt permeated the island and, to the distress of local *vignerons,* infiltrated the wine. "I think this is absolutely one of the ends of the world," an observer had written a few years before Lucie Dreyfus's visit, "with a little imagination you could transport it into any hemisphere."[21]

Shortly after 10 A.M. Lucie and her in-laws arrived at the citadel's immense central courtyard. Convicts at work and troops in the midst of morning exercises watched the three civilians, and, noting Lucie's black mourning dress, recognized the wife of the prison's most celebrated inmate. After a thirty-minute wait, a guard ordered Madame Dreyfus's two companions outside the citadel walls. In the cold wind, Joseph Valabrègue and Alice Dreyfus walked along the stone embankment until Lucie rejoined them an hour later and described her first meeting with her husband in nearly a month.[22]

Taken to a narrow room with whitewashed walls, Lucie had waited at the end of a long table as guards bolted the door behind her. A short time later, the prison director entered, moved to the middle of the table and listed the conditions of the visit: Madame Dreyfus could have thirty minutes, during which time she could not approach her husband or discuss anything concerning his case; she could not utter the name of any individual without first identifying that person; and under no circumstances could she speak in a foreign language. Through a window looking out onto an adjoining courtyard Lucie saw Alfred approach surrounded by two guards. It was, she later said, a "harrowing vision." Stooped over and appearing much older than his thirty-five years, his complexion had turned to a jaundiced yellow, his cheeks were sunken, his hair and beard had grown out (officials had not trusted him with a razor), and the small round eyeglasses he now wore instead of pince-nez had also transformed his appearance. When he entered through a door at the far end of the room, he too was taken aback; he had not been informed of his wife's visit. Keeping the couple at a distance of four meters and remaining as a barrier between them, the warden placed his watch on the table and monitored their conversation. Unable to discuss the issues that most consumed him, Dreyfus stared at Lucie while she spoke about his courage and, in sweeping generalizations, about the family. The prison director cut the meeting short after twenty minutes.[23]

The next day, under the same conditions, Dreyfus tried to rally while his wife discussed plans for her return the following week. She would bring new clothes, clean linens, and English grammar books, and perhaps she would have news from the minister of the interior about their place of exile. She already knew (but was prohibited from telling her husband) that the *Journal Officiel* had announced a "law of exception" inspired by General Mercier and passed by the Chamber of Deputies on February 9; it declared that the Iles du Salut off French Guiana had been reinstated as an official "place of deportation in a fortified locale." The "islands of salvation," once called the "Devil's Islands" (*Iles du Diable*), had been renamed by eighteenth-century travelers seeking to escape the tropical diseases of the mainland. For colonists and criminals, however, the islands lived up to their former name. Precisely a century prior to the "law of exception" voted for Dreyfus, two French revolutionaries had been the first deportees sent to French Guiana; and both Napoleons had continued to ship political enemies and common criminals to Cayenne and to the nearby islands—the Ile Royale, the Ile Saint-Joseph, and the smallest and most barren island, which kept the name Ile du Diable. In one year alone, under Napoleon III, 2,500 men had died of malaria, dysentery, and other diseases, and though the functionaries of the Third Republic preferred the less-murderous climate of New Caledonia, Dreyfus's conviction rekindled interest in the South American islands. Convinced that an international "Jewish syndicate" would arrange his escape from New Caledonia, journalists and politicians lobbied for the Iles de Salut as the next best thing to capital punishment. Whatever the final destination, however, the prisoner's wife had studied the regulations and knew that deportees had the legal right to be joined by their spouses and children; if she could not tell her husband about the "law of exception," she could at least give him hope by repeating her commitment to accompany him on the voyage out.[24]

In fact Dreyfus would have welcomed news that the government had chosen an isolated locale for his deportation. Over recent weeks he had constantly asked to be thrown "incognito onto a deserted island . . . where I will never see another human being until the day . . . the truth is discovered." He repeated his appeal in a letter to the colonial minister: "I beg you to send me to my place of exile without requiring me stop at yet another prison depot. . . . Send me to any deserted island you wish . . . any dungeon . . . but save me from the sight of those who have a justified contempt for a traitor, for the most miserable of wretches. . . because a traitor I am not." Dreyfus would have his wish, but his wife would not. Through a distant relative, a former naval officer, Lucie tried to contact the colonial minister for authorization to sail with her husband on the same ship, and to learn the day of his departure. But she heard nothing.[25]

A week later she returned to Saint-Martin de Ré carrying books, a small medicine chest, lightweight cotton clothes, and a mosquito net. On the afternoon of February 21, the prison director, Picqué, allowed the couple forty-five minutes together, again in his presence, but when Lucie asked to hold her husband's hand, the request was refused; Picqué feared that the Jewess might transfer information through some kind of "cabalistic sign." But Lucie persevered. Earlier in the day, she had seen a large ship anchored near the citadel and sensed that the prisoner's voyage was imminent. She wanted to touch her husband, to kiss him, and she asked the warden to tie her hands and lead her across the room. Picqué refused, and, losing patience, sent Dreyfus back to his cell. With the next visit scheduled for the following week, Lucie left for La Rochelle and the evening train to Paris.[26]

Knowing that Dreyfus would be moved that night, the warden nevertheless said nothing to the prisoner or his wife. Shortly after Lucie's departure, a guard ordered Dreyfus to pack his belongings into a single valise and small duffel bag. Stripped and searched, he was led by six guards to a launch at the citadel's dock. With the government anxious to avoid yet another demonstration, police had cordoned off the public route to Saint-Martin de Ré. The citadel's stone embankment was deserted. Dreyfus's launch traveled south to the Ile de Aix, near the port town of Rochefort, and, in the middle of the night, he boarded the steamship *Ville de Saint Nazaire*. Ordered by the colonial minister never to speak to the prisoner, guards arranged the transfer in complete silence. Locked into a wire-mesh cell just below the bridge, exposed to the wind, Dreyfus waited for the ship to sail. He was given no food, and the temperature plummeted to seven degrees. Later a guard threw him a hammock, but, unable to sleep and overcome with "sorrow and despair," he crawled into a corner of the cell and wept. Twenty-four hours later, the *Ville de Saint Nazaire* weighed anchor. It was February 22, 1895, the second birthday of Dreyfus's daughter Jeanne.[27]

Manacled in his iron cage, with armed guards watching him day and night, the prisoner still had no idea of his destination. On the fifth day, he was allowed on deck for one hour, but kept at a distance from other prisoners—the usual cargo of murderers and thieves. His rations came in old tin cans which, as the days passed, littered his cell floor. Bitter cold gave way to warmer temperatures, and then to torrid heat, and by the eighth day Dreyfus knew the ship approached the equator. The route to New Caledonia, a forty-day journey, would have taken them south from La Rochelle through the Strait of Gibraltar and toward the Suez Canal. But the *Ville de Saint Nazaire* had steamed west, and at 1:30 P.M. on March 12, after a voyage of fifteen days, it dropped anchor in the harbor of the Ile Royale. Strategic studies of French territories, along with conversations overheard on ship, helped Dreyfus identify the three islands off French Guiana. Eleven kilometers from the mainland, forty-four kilometers northeast of the coastal town of Cayenne, and situated only five degrees north of the equator, the Ile Royale and its smaller neighbors were known for their desolation, disease, and unbearable heat. Victor Hugo, who knew something about life in exile, had called French Guiana "the dry guillotine." With the temperature reaching 104 degrees on the day of Dreyfus's arrival and "without a breath of wind," the prisoner remained in his ship's cell exposed to sun while authorities prepared his transfer.[28]

Ordered to heft his own belongings onto a launch, he set off with a special contingent of functionaries and guards. His misshapen felt hat and threadbare clothes were a striking contrast to the colorful dress uniforms of colonial officials who surrounded him; and behind his wire-rimmed glasses and gray beard, witnessess noted the waxen, sweaty look of a newly arrived deportee. They had seen it many times before. Unsteady from the long voyage, he had to be helped by a prison worker up the rough stone steps leading to the island's administration buildings. That pathway, like the gardens, lawns, and cobblestone roads lined with mango trees, had been built by generations of convicts sentenced to hard labor in double chains and under the regime of the cudgel (bastinado); they had turned the central quarter of the Ile Royale into a garden oasis amid the dreary landscape of the Iles du Salut. The prison complex in which Dreyfus would be temporarily held included a hospital, chapel, offices, and cell blocks, and all of it, said local observers, had the look of a former convent. On reaching the plateau, Dreyfus heard three long blasts and turned to see the black smoke of the *Ville de Saint Nazaire*. The ship, his last link to France, was steaming south toward Cayenne to discharge its load of criminals at the mainland prison.[29]

For thirty days Dreyfus waited in a small guard's room converted into a prison cell. On the second floor of the central building, it looked out on a yard where convicts sentenced to solitary confinement—barefoot, hands tied behind their backs, and watched by guards armed with revolvers and rifles—took their daily exercise. But Dreyfus never joined them. Directives from Paris insisted on "absolute secrecy," and authorities ordered that his shutters be kept closed and that he never be permitted outside. Every day, straw-hatted convicts, many of them Arabs who spoke no French, brought food and water and fetched the prisoner's wooden waste tub. With his scissors and razor taken from his valise on arrival, his hair and beard grew longer, and with rations often inedible and the tropical heat oppressive, he continued to lose weight. Like every other European who came to French Guiana, Dreyfus fell victim to intestinal parasites ("homicidal vapors" in the local parlance), and to the fever that accompanied dysentery. In early April he began to drink enormous quantities of water, took to his bed, and finally called for the prison doctor. Along with the chief guard, Pouly, the doctor, Major Debrieu, sympathized with Dreyfus's plight and tried to improve his condition; but both officers were under the orders of Commandant Bouchet, director of the prison, and Bouchet, like his Parisian counterpart, du Paty, was obsessed with maximizing Dreyfus's punishment. Told that the prisoner could be neither hospitalized nor assigned a nurse to monitor his fever, Debrieu prescribed quinine, sedatives, herb tea with a tincture of opium, and, temporarily, a healthier diet of broth, meat, eggs, and milk. Bouchet approved: "I would much prefer to keep him healthy than sick," noted the commandant. "He'll be less of an encumbrance for us all."[30]

By mid-April Dreyfus regained his physical strength, though guards still noted his "nervous" and "overexcited" state. Unable to sleep, he wrote scores of letters to his wife and family by the red-tinted light of his single wall lantern, then tore them up and drafted them again. "I will not recount my voyage," he wrote on the day he arrived. "I was transported in a way befitting the vile scoundrel that I am taken to be; it is only just." In separate letters to his brothers, sisters and wife (but in nearly identical phrases) he spoke of Pierre and Jeanne and revealed the depth of his despair: "A thousand times I would rather know that my children were dead than to think for a single moment that they would live with their name dishonored."[31] He implored the entire family to press the investigation and he urged Lucie to write. "Send a telegram," he said, when the truth has been uncovered. "I await it every day like the messiah." But it never came, nor did any letters from his family through late March and April. Total isolation fueled his *nervosité* and kept prison officials on guard against a suicide attempt.[32]

Finally, at 2 P.M on April 14, he was taken from his room for the first time in a month. Blinded by the light and weak from fever, he was helped down the flagstone path toward the shore. From a dock below the island's Grand Mamelon, its highest hill, Dreyfus watched a whaleboat cross the rough waters between the Ile Royale and the Ile du Diable. Though only a few hundred meters away, the Ile du Diable had little in common with the archipelago's principal island; barely one thousand meters long and two hundred meters at its narrowest point, it was a "thin tongue of land" covered with dry brown bushes and chalky volcanic rocks the color of lead. With virtually no beachfront, its steepest cliff emerged directly from the sea to a height of sixty feet. The island owed its name to the violent agitation of the surrounding channel waters, whipped up by a powerful current from the north, and infested with sharks.[33]

While the Ile Royale received the most dangerous criminals and the Ile Saint Joseph housed anarchists and the insane, only lepers had lived on Devil's Island, the least habitable of the Iles du Salut. Tending goats and picking wild tomatoes and coconuts, their community of eighteen had been housed in a small complex of ramshackle huts. Dreyfus, "whose hideousness," according to Commandant Bouchet, "was a thousand times more frightening than that of the wretches who had preceded him" on Devil's Island, had to wait for colonial officials to transfer the lepers and burn the remnants of their colony—to "purge it of its vermin."[34] When the prisoner and his escort disembarked on the Ile du

Diable all that remained was a small stone cabin with a corrugated iron roof and, nearby, a hut for five guards and their superior. Dreyfus would be the island's only inmate, and his every movement would be followed by sentries on the spot and by others manning a telescope on the Ile Royale. Behind the prisoner's cabin, Bouchet pointed out wooden posts that marked the boundaries of an exercise area, a barren space exposed to the full force of the sun. Dreyfus could never walk there unaccompanied, and when work crews of convicts or provision boats from the Ile Royale approached, he would be taken to a far corner of the field or hurried back to his cell until the island was deserted again. If unidentified ships came closer than three miles, guards would open fire, and if the prisoner attempted to escape, the order from the colonial minister was clear: "Blow his brains out."[35]

Locked in his stone hut—his *case*—at 4:00 P.M. on April 14, Dreyfus changed into the uniform of a deportee for the first time: cotton shirt, canvas jacket, flannel belt, and cloth pants. He kept only his felt hat—a hot and impractical souvenir from Paris. The cabin, four meters square and with two small barred windows, had an iron cot, an whitewood table, two rush-bottomed chairs, a washstand with a "regulation prison basin," and, later, a large bucket from the main cistern. Warm and stagnant, the water that Dreyfus used for washing, cooking, and drinking became a "repulsive sink of mosquito larvae," a "cemetery" for insects swarming through his hut, and a reservoir of disease. The cell's grated, padlocked door looked directly onto an anteroom where a guard was always on duty. Under the watch of his jailers, the prisoner had no corner of privacy and, in the space behind his cabin, not even an outhouse. A wooden waste tub was placed near his cot. At night the guard's lantern flooded light into his cell, and every two hours, as Dreyfus described it, "an infernal noise of keys striking iron" jolted him awake and announced the change of shift. "Impossible to sleep," he made a record of that first night: "The guard walks in front of this cage like a ghost appearing in my dreams, and every sort of creature crawls over my skin."[36]

On Devil's Island, Dr. Debrieu's special diet gave way to standard provisions delivered from the Ile Royale: coffee, moist sugar, rice, a half loaf of bread a day, meat three times a week, and, on occasion, canned pork or canned beef. Wild goats, brought onto the island for its leper colony, provided milk, but officials debated whether the herd should remain. Like Ulysses escaping the cavern of Polyphemus, Dreyfus might grab hold of a goat, authorities feared, and swim out to sea.

Sharks would certainly destroy them, but Bouchet and his subalterns took no chances and the goats were removed.[37] With only fetid water to drink—from old cartons of condensed milk—Dreyfus's dysentery became chronic. Though required to cook his own food, he had, for a long period, no plates, utensils, or iron grate for a fire. Much of the time the meat was rotten and the coffee berries unroasted, and Dreyfus chucked it all in the sea, choosing instead to subsist on bread and water. He requested a drinking glass or cup, but officials worried that he would use the shards to cut his throat or attack a guard; after much delay, they sent along two iron mugs instead. At first the prisoner washed clothes and bedlinens in a small pool of brackish water near the shoreline below his cabin; but that routine required a guard to stand watch in the sweltering heat. Soon they sent his laundry to the hospital washroom on the Ile Royale, where workers ripped open the hems of every item and searched for clandestine messages. Under strict orders never to address his guards, Dreyfus could not protest this or any other treatment, nor could he request provisions except in writing. After five months of submitting appeals that were denied or ignored, he opted for the regime of silence.[38]

It was a pervasive silence, broken only by the clatter of padlocks and the sound of the sea. On the evening of his first day, he started a journal destined for his wife: "Today I begin the diary of my sad and tragic life." He described the view through his barred window, "the billowing clouds and filtered moonlight which give the ocean a silver hue. . . . The sea evokes memories," he wrote, thinking back, perhaps, to the Normandy coast, "of happy moments close to my wife and children." But the rough channel waters pounding against the rocks that formed the contour of the island "roared and bellowed" at his feet and reminded him that those happy moments were lost: "What has happened to the precious dreams of my childhood," he asked that same night. "To the hopes of my mature years? Nothing remains alive in me." And in another journal entry: "I have followed step by step the horrible road which has brought me to this point . . . leaving a piece of my soul at each detour along the way." He felt betrayed not only by some unknown criminal and tragic judicial error, but by the very "cult of reason" that had sustained him in the past: "I believed in the logic of things and of events, I believed in human justice! Everything bizarre or outlandish hardly entered my mind. But alas! What destruction of all my beliefs, of all my sane reason." His thoughts returned to suicide, and then to the promise he had made his wife not to desert his "post," and, finally, to the sound of the sea: "What an echo to my soul! The foam of the waves . . . is so soft and white that I would like to fall upon it, and be lost."[39]

In Paris a month before, while her husband was in middle passage on the *Ville de Saint Nazaire*, Lucie had purchased books describing the history, climate, and vegatation of French Guiana and the plight of prisoners in Cayenne and on the Iles du Salut. She shared her research in a letter that she hoped would greet Alfred upon arrival—it did not, but Lucie had no way of knowing: "Take quinine as soon as you feel feverish," she said. "And moderation, I don't have to advise you on that. I know that you neither eat nor drink too much, but don't work too hard; it seems that for Europeans who are not accustomed to hard labor it's the most dangerous thing they can do. Keep yourself occupied intellectually: read, work, interest yourself in the books that I send you, write, edit. . . . Above all, write to me, that's all that I desire."[40]

He did—for nearly four and a half years.

CHAPTER XI

Mathieu

WHEN DREYFUS changed prisons in January 1895, from Santé to Saint-Martin de Ré, France changed presidents of the republic. The captain's trial and degradation did not prompt Casimir-Perier's resignation, but the espionage case was one more drama the fifth leader of the Third Republic could do without. He was exhausted. The Elysée had become his "galley," a "bogus setting in which one does nothing but receive blows without being able to return them," and he talked constantly about "escape." Casimir-Perier's predecessor had been assassinated by an Italian anarchist wielding a six-inch knife and shouting "'Long live the Revolution!" and while the new president had dealt quickly with "propagandists by the deed" and other "associations of evil-doers," he could not control the anarchy of French party politics. An orderly man of conservative tastes, he was frustrated by challenges to his authority and put off by the vulgarity of parliamentary factionalism.[1]

The balance struck by those fraternal twins of the early Third Republic, Léon Gambetta and Adolphe Thiers—the blend of Gambetta's Jacobin democracy and Thiers's conservative Orléanism—had disintegrated under the impact of universal male suffrage, the growth of the industrial working class, and the proliferation of political movements on the Left and Right. General Boulanger's campaign of the late 1880s, calling for "revision" of the Constitution and "dissolution" of the Chamber of Deputies, and attracting discontents from both extremes, was only the most publicized threat to the centrist, or "Opportunist," Republic. More important, because more focused on specific issues, were movements launched by anticlerical Radicals and, increasingly, by socialists. Forty independent socialist deputies sat in Parliament in the early 1890s, and, in alliances with Radicals of various stripes, they made life difficult for Casimir-Perier's thinning coterie of conservative supporters. As a major investor in the Anzin mining and metallurgy company in northeastern France, the president had come under attack from the populist right wing as well as from the left: "The mansion that Casimir-Perier inhabits," Drumont wrote in 1894, "the princely luxury which surrounds him, the carriage in which he travels, all these he owes to those unfortunate miners who have passed their bleak hard lives in the black depths of mines under the perpetual threat of pit-gas." Sick of the slander and needing neither the prestige of the presidency nor its perquisites, Casimir-Perier resigned in January 1895.[2]

If the republic's fifth leader had been indifferent to the trappings of the office, its sixth, a former leather merchant from Le Havre (a "self-made man" as the French liked to put it in English), would have a passionate interest. Much about Félix Faure was passionate and expansive—his prodigious appetite, his penchant for immaculately tailored clothes, his weakness for women. Only his politics were moderate, and that augured well in the climate of divisiveness that marked the epoch. An early supporter of Léon Gambetta, one of the founders of the Third Republic, Faure, like others present at the creation, had drifted toward the center of the political spectrum. As minister of the navy, he had become something of an expert on economic and colonial questions, and those assets, along with an elegance which "inspired confidence," helped make him the preferred candidate for the presidency over Eugène Henri Brisson, the choice of socialists and some Radicals, and René Waldeck-Rousseau, the lawyer Mathieu Dreyfus had approached to defend his brother. But Waldeck-Rousseau, a decent if dreary man, had been only recently elected senator, while Félix Faure had cultivated the public support of colleagues with the same smooth charm he used to nurture his private liaisons.[3]

A new president meant a new prime minister, and that change of government raised hopes. When Henriette's daughter visited the Santé prison in mid-January, she thought that the "parliamentary mess" might postpone her uncle's deportation.[4] But the republic's bureaucracy, accustomed to revolving-door cabinets, pushed forward. "You can imagine with what impatience I await the formation of the new government,"

Lucie had written her husband shortly after Faure's election. "Never have politics interested me so much, since I must appeal to the Ministry in order to . . . rejoin you, to embrace you."[5] Appeal she did, only to hear one official say that life for a woman on the Iles du Salut "would be impossible. . . . You have no idea what you would be exposing yourself to down there." Lucie agreed that the climate would be too harsh for the children—she would leave them with grandparents—but she insisted that she could "survive anything . . . I fear no deprivation." Wanting to be finished with the traitor, however, and with his family's endless appeals, the new government under Prime Minister Alexandre Ribot broke the law concerning deportees and denied Lucie Dreyfus's request to join her husband.[6]

In the wake of his brother's degradation, Mathieu began the battle against indifference, against the public's rush to forget. "I understood my task," he later wrote, "to undertake, without tiring and without being discouraged by anything, a personal campaign of propaganda in every milieu I could penetrate; to make recruits and to ask them and all our friends to help . . . find the criminal."[7] With the exception of Maître Demange, Commandant Forzinetti, Grand Rabbi Kahn, and a few others, however, friends and colleagues had either abandoned the family or had given up hope; and in the public arena of the Palais Bourbon—in corridors, cloakrooms, or on the Chamber floor—Mathieu had no parliamentary allies to keep his brother's case alive. Auguste Lalance, former deputy from Mulhouse, and Joseph Reinach, Opportunist deputy from the Basses-Alpes department, were among the few who questioned the intrigues of the General Staff and expressed doubts about Dreyfus's guilt. But when it came to the traitor, the majority of Radicals, socialists, and centrists shared the views of Bonapartists, royalists, and professional anti-Semites. They disagreed only on the severity of Dreyfus's punishment and on the political ramifications of his case. Jean Jaurès, deputy from the southeastern mining town of Carmaux, and the Chamber's most articulate independent socialist, reiterated the standard attacks on Jewish capitalism and asked why the government saved a bourgeois officer and sent him into exile while they executed "simple soldiers, without pardon and without pity."[8] But those were only details of the debate. A consensus emerged on its broadest outlines, and by the opening weeks of 1895 deputies and senators turned to other issues on the political agenda. For all but a few journalists from *La Libre Parole*—obsessed with the fear that Dreyfus would be liberated by German-Jewish comrades and hoping to maintain the extraordinary newspaper sales of previous months—the case had become old news.

Trying to rekindle interest and rally support, Joseph Valabrègue accompanied Mathieu on visits to politicians, business leaders, and newspaper editors; and though often disappointed, they sensed that a subtle change had occurred since the degradation. "More than a few people now believe in Alfred's innocence," Valabrègue told Henriette, "but not one has the courage to write it directly, and newspapers do not want to publish anything favorable." Léon Dreyfus would also report that reliable sources in eastern France knew of officers who "dared" to question the captain's guilt, though they would not take a public stand. Even the prisoner anticipated the dilemma in a letter to Lucie: "No matter who is convinced of my innocence," he wrote shortly after his arrival on Devil's Island, "they will do nothing to change our situation. We are often paid off with words and illusions; but nothing can save us if it is not my rehabilitation. . . . Knock on every door," he urged the family. "Use every means to uncover the truth. All methods of investigation should be attempted; the goal is my life, all of our lives."[9]

With "a silence of death hovering around the family," Mathieu attempted everything from sessions with a psychic to a meeting, via an intermediary, with Félix Faure. A relative of Mathieu's wife who lived in Le Havre knew that the president's friend and former physician, Dr. Gibert, believed in the captain's innocence. The relative also knew that Gibert experimented with hypnosis, much like his Parisian counterpart, Jean-Martin Charcot, who had treated hysteria through hypnosis and whose discoveries had influenced a student from Vienna, Sigmund Freud. Among Gibert's patients was a woman named Léonie, noted for her powers of clairvoyance. She had attracted the attention of "mental pathologists" on both sides of the Channel (including founders of the Society for Psychical Research, an English group that numbered Gladstone, Ruskin, and Tennyson among its members), and Gibert believed she could penetrate the mysteries surrounding Dreyfus's arrest. The doctor invited Mathieu to come to Le Havre.[10]

But Mathieu had to proceed with caution. Gibert, considered bizarre and rebellious by conservative members of the medical community, could be yet another charlatan out to exploit the family. Confidence tricksters and fortune hunters still pursued the Dreyfuses and Hadamards, as did undercover agents sent by du Paty to entrap them. From the outset of the scandal, the Statistical Section of the General Staff had identified Mathieu as "the keenest member of the family,"[11] and du Paty's fervor did not decline with the captain's conviction. His henchmen opened Mathieu's mail, bribed his cook, housekeepers, and concièrge, and followed him through the streets of Paris. Demange advised Mathieu to keep no important papers in his home, to watch his servants, and to avoid the crowded department stores of Paris, where an agent might slip an item in his pocket, arrest him for shoplifting, and ruin his reputation. In early January, learning from Demange that he was about to be arrested as his brother's accomplice, Mathieu had sent a vigorous protest of du Paty's "odious accusations" to Sandherr: "It is time, Sir, that these insinuations stop." And reminding the colonel of the family's reputation in Mulhouse, he added that "You, better than anyone, know who we are."[12]

Given that onslaught of undercover agents, crooks, and crackpots, Mathieu understandably greeted Gibert's offer of a clairvoyant with skepticism. But the doctor's credentials were impeccable, his friendship with President Faure too promising to resist, and the family had no other leads to pursue. In February, with Lucie preparing to leave for the Ile de Ré, Mathieu set off on his own "very interesting voyage" to Le Havre.[13]

Léonie, a peasant woman in her fifties, as stout as her doctor was slight, sat on a sofa in Gibert's office waiting for Mathieu. Eyes closed and already in a deep trance, she wore the bonnet and provincial garb of her Normandy region. The doctor directed Mathieu to a chair facing her. Taking his thumbs, stroking them, scratching them, Léonie spoke hesitantly, with long periods of silence: "You are his brother," she said. "Your wife is with you, you have two children, a little girl and boy who are not with you; they are with their grandmother; your brother is away, he suffers much." Suddenly the woman dropped Mathieu's hands and spoke as if facing the prisoner: "Why are you wearing glasses? Who gave you those glasses?" Mathieu corrected her and said that his brother always wore pince-nez. But, in a fit of anger, she shouted back, "I know what I am saying, I say glasses, they are glasses." Mathieu's relative could have supplied the doctor and Léonie with the details about the family, all of which were correct; but the woman was clearly wrong about Alfred's pince-nez. A few days later, however, Mathieu learned that Alfred had worn wire-framed eyeglasses during his meeting with Lucie at Saint-Martin de Ré; it was a "stunning" confirmation of Léonie's statements. But Mathieu, still the supreme rationalist, searched for scientific explanations. He studied histories of mesmerism and clairvoyance, and, returning to Le Havre on numerous occasions, he learned from Gibert how to put the woman into a hypnotic trance. He tested her by writing down a word or a sign and by placing the paper in Léonie's hands. "Without that one cannot live," she said before opening an envelope that contained the word "hope," and it was not the only time she passed Mathieu's examinations. Anxious to know something about his brother's conditions in exile, Mathieu would later put the woman to sleep and urge her to "go to Devil's Island" for news of the prisoner.[14]

At Gibert's suggestion Mathieu brought Léonie to Paris. Since the previous November, family members had created their own enclave of provincial migrants in the capital—in hotels, townhouses, and apartments in or near the Hadamards' *quartier*—and now a Norman psychic became part of that Dreyfus reunion. Staying first with Rachel Schil on the rue de l'Arcade, a few streets west of the rue Châteaudun, she then moved in with Mathieu and Suzanne on the rue de la Victoire. Nearly every morning, in the apartment or on walks through the Bois de Boulogne, Mathieu interrogated the woman. His children, Magui and Emile, visiting from Héricourt, would sometimes play in the park with their cousins Pierre and Jeanne, and, from a distance, without understanding the curious sight, they would watch Mathieu, tall, top-hatted, and elegant, hypnotize a squat, corpulent peasant in a strange provincial bonnet.[15]

Léonie's most revealing "vision" had come early in the sessions at Dr. Gibert's. "What are those documents shown to the judges in secret?" she asked deep in a trance. "Don't do that; it's not good," she went on. "If Monsieur Alfred and Maître Demange saw them it would ruin their effect." Mathieu tried to understand. "They are documents you know nothing about," Léonie told him. "You will see later." A short time after that session, at an early morning meeting in the Elysée Palace, Gibert and Félix Faure discussed the Dreyfus case. Describing the prisoner's "honorable family," the doctor insisted that there was no motive for treason. "Richest of the young captains at the Etat-Major, what could he possibly expect from the Germans? Nothing but contempt."[16] President Faure, however, in office for barely a month, confessed that Dreyfus had been convicted not on the basis of the *bordereau* but "on documents given to the judges in the deliberation room, documents which neither the accused nor his lawyer could be shown for reasons of State." Gibert expressed shock at that obvious violation of the law; he warned his friend not to be implicated in "this crime" and, at Mathieu's prompting, showed the president a letter the prisoner had written to his wife after the riots at La Rochelle ("I ask for no mercy, but I demand the justice which is the common right of every human being"). Though moved by the letter, Faure had no doubts about the captain's guilt or the integrity of the army's investigation and refused to pursue the matter further. Before leaving, Gibert asked if he could repeat the president's comments to Mathieu Dreyfus in confidence, and, surprisingly, Faure agreed. A humane gesture, but politically foolish, it gave Mathieu the hope that his brother's conviction could be reversed on a technicality; if he could not discover the real traitor he could at least expose the judicial error.[17]

Barely a month after Gibert's meeting, Maître Demange also learned about the secret documents through associates at the Palais de Justice. In particular he described an item containing the phrase "that scoundrel, D. . . ," which army intelligence had intercepted from a "foreign power" and inserted, without Demange's knowledge, into the trial dossier. By the summer of 1895, as a result of a peasant woman's vision confirmed by one of France's leading lawyers and by the president of the Republic, Mathieu knew that his brother's court-martial in closed session had been "a farce."[18]

Through the fall and winter, however, and into the following year, Mathieu had nothing more than hope. If queried, Faure would deny his statements to Gibert, and the General Staff would refuse any comment for reasons of national security. The case was closed, and Mathieu felt powerless. He called it "the most painful and sad period of my life." Still followed by half a dozen agents, he and his wife adopted an alias, "Mr. and Mrs. Mathieu," and asked the Valabrègues to sign rental leases and other documents. They were not alone. After the degradation ceremony, many Dreyfuses, of no relation to the family, abandoned the name, which had become synonymous with treason. For Mathieu, however, the irony intensified his frustration: In order to launch his "campaign of propaganda in every milieu" he had to surrender temporarily the very name for which he was fighting. Meanwhile, his brother's letters, which began to arrive in Paris via the colonial minister in midsummer, repeated the leitmotiv of "rehabilitating" the family name: "Our goal," he wrote, "is the honor of the name which our parents gave us, pure and undefiled."[19]

Mathieu could cope with police agents and the logistics of protecting his family, but the prisoner's letters began to "haunt" him. "The obsession with my brother on Devil's Island," he said, "never left us."[20]

Those letters, with countless variations on the single theme of survival, always included declarations of confidence in the family and the army. They repeated the prisoner's certainty that "the truth," "the light," would one day be uncovered, and, almost without exception, they closed with a call for courage: "Fear nothing," he wrote Mathieu in July 1895. "I will go to the end of my strength without weakening, for Lucie, for my children, and finally for my name."[21]

But Mathieu and Lucie soon detected desperation in the tone and content of Alfred's letters. He began to speak of "situations which a human being cannot bear indefinitely." "I have suffered enough," he wrote on another occasion. "Human strength has its limits, and my anguish overwhelms me." He continued to insist that he could survive the "accessory conditions" of his physical existence—"the climate, the complete isolation, the perpetual silence as profound as that of the tomb"—but he worried about "fits of delirium," about nerves "stretched like the cords of a violin." He counted the days ("I dare say, even the hours") and wondered how long he could maintain "the almost super-human force" he needed in order to resist. "There are blows," he wrote Mathieu, "which, repeated often enough, take their toll on everything that is noble and elevated in one's being. . . . In the long run, the heart rebels . . . the soul is drained, and a single desire emerges: to be finished with such hell." "I would like to close my eyes and no longer see, no longer think, no longer suffer."[22]

Nearly every letter reaffirmed his belief that Mathieu would be the agent of his liberation. He reminded his brother that, unlike their parents and sisters, and unlike Lucie, they shared a skepticism concerning "divine intervention" and a common faith in the role of "human will in earthly matters." "Religious doctrine," the prisoner wrote in the fall of 1895, "beyond its moral value, is the domain of dreams; of thoughts which leave sad realities behind and escape into the ideal, into a world where truth, beauty and perfect justice reign . . . these are the confused aspirations of our existence, to move toward a more perfect humanity which we do not see on earth and which we would like to believe—in order to console ourselves about distressing realities—is elsewhere." For Alfred, whose religious skepticism was not new, but whose opinions had been reshaped by the events of the past year, it was "precisely the sight of suffering, of human injustice," which argued against the notion of divine intervention. "Being numbed by the passivity of religious resignation . . . is the fate of the weak," he said. "Those of strong spirit are sustained by their conscience, their duty, which makes them act and press toward their goal with a will and vigor that nothing can stop, nothing can bend. I am sure," he told his brother, "that you possess that . . . strong spirit, and that it will never desert you, come what may." In a refrain that heightened Mathieu's "obsession" with the prisoner in exile, Alfred confessed that "I think of you night and day."[23]

"Every passing hour," Mathieu knew, was a "century of suffering" for his brother and "another step toward death."[24] Each time Lucie received an envelope from the colonial minister she hesitated, knowing that it contained either a letter from her husband or news of his death. When "two lines in a wretched newspaper" (probably *La Libre Parole*) announced that the prisoner had fallen ill, Lucie passed "the most horrible day" of her life; "I know the importance of the freedom of the press," she wrote, "but those two lines were a terrific blow."[25] Congregating through the summer of 1895 in a home rented by the Valabrègues in Saint Cloud, south of Paris, family members wrote to Alfred, and always on the same theme: He must "endure his present misery" and have faith. But the prisoner's depression was acute, and Mathieu was forced to respond with a challenge: "I beg that you continue to be what you always were, strong and calm, and God, who is just, will not allow an innocent man to pay for a guilty one. I count on your moral energy, my dear Alfred, and I hope."[26]

Mathieu searched for new avenues of appeal. Months of working through intermediaries, however, and countless investigations by the family's private detectives achieved nothing. They were unable to move politicians or penetrate the General Staff, and Mathieu found no way to reach the "objective of highest interest"—the German Embassy, in which the *bordereau* had been found. Convinced that the real traitor must be known to that embassy's personnel, he sought ways to approach its military attaché, Colonel Maximilien von Schwarzkoppen.

Like many of his European contemporaries, Mathieu believed in the superior reputation of British detectives, in the qualities of phlegmatic detachment and impartiality that set them off from their continental counterparts. Having witnessed the links between politics and police work in France, Mathieu decided to seek professional help across the Channel. On April 15, 1896, with Jacques Dreyfus's brother-in-law Sam Wimpheimer along as translator, Mathieu dodged undercover police in the Gare Saint Lazare and boarded a train bound for Dieppe and London. Through the Cook Detective Agency in England, he engaged the services of a "young and skillful investigator, a perfect gentleman," who had been educated at Oxford and who spoke fluent German and French. The agent would attempt to infiltrate the society of German diplomats in Paris, as would another Cook employee, "an intelligent and clever" woman with a "respectable air" whose aim it was to befriend the English wife of a German Embassy guard suspected of contacts with the French government. Under the pretext of traveling to France to educate her daughter, the woman moved into a furnished apartment in the guard's building, a flat found and paid for by Mathieu. But investigations by foreign detectives required not only exorbitant sums of money (which the Dreyfuses and Hadamards provided) but time to cultivate leads. Mathieu called it "difficult and delicate terrain," and Cook expressed his concern that a dramatic move was needed to break the silence surrounding Dreyfus's case—a case "generally forgotten."[27]

In the late summer of 1896, Clifford Millage, Paris correspondent for the English newspaper the *Daily Chronicle,* agreed to help Cook mobilize support. Millage's pecuniary interests were in line with his personal convictions; he received substantial payments from Mathieu but also believed in the captain's innocence and knew of similar "favorable" sentiments among other English journalists.[28] If most foreign observers had never questioned Dreyfus's guilt, many had criticized the sordid details of his degradation and deportation. With economic and imperial rivalries exacerbating their deep-seated contempt for the French, the English condemned the excesses of the French military high command and the vitriol of the nationalist press. For many English observers the Dreyfus scandal underscored the hypocrisy—and bad form—of their oldest enemy.[29]

Millage and Cook believed that by placing stories describing the prisoner's "lamentable existence" on Devil's Island in British and French newspapers, they could break the public's indifference and the government's intransigence. They proposed spreading a rumor that Dreyfus had escaped. "Some kind of sensational story was needed," Mathieu agreed, but he worried that the government, under pressure from the likes of Drumont, would respond by imposing even more "painful punishment" on his brother. He insisted that the rumor be so "improbable" that after creating the desired impact, it would immediately be denied by the colonial minister. His English comrades concurred, and on September 3, the *Daily Chronicle* announced that "Captain Dreyfus had escaped from the Iles du Salut aboard an American vessel." Neither the "source" of the story (a newspaper called the *South Wales Argus*) nor the American ship ever existed, but the Havas Press Agency immediately reprinted the article in French papers. "Stirring up emotions in Paris," as *L'Eclair* reported, it described a sensational scenario that included Lucie Dreyfus ("obviously well furnished with money") arranging the escape from her base in Cayenne. As expected, government officials denied the rumor (after cabling the Iles du Salut) and called it "absolute fantasy." Following Mathieu's wish that the story be discredited, Georges Hadamard told reporters who had rushed to the rue Châteaudun that his sister had never received permission to travel to French Guiana and that she was presently living in seclusion in a house outside Paris. The family, Hadamard said, though committed to securing the captain's release, would never support an escape attempt.[30]

The ploy had worked; the lie was exposed and journalists and politicians began to reconsider the case. *La Libre Parole* and *L'Intransigeant* surprised no one with revelations of a Jewish-led "Escape Syndicate," or suggestions that Dreyfus's "gold" could easily corrupt poorly paid guards on Devil's Island, while other observers, including the influential Paul de Cassagnac—Bonapartist and anti-Semite but also a friend of Demange—expressed new doubts about the captain's court-martial and conviction.[31]

Mathieu's fears, however, were also realized. On September 4, the colonial minister, André Lebon, cabled French Guiana and ordered Dreyfus confined to his cabin and locked into "double shackles at night." A young cabinet member with unbridled ambition and a blind commitment to Drumont's brand of anti-Semitism, Lebon knew that the *Daily Chronicle* story was false and that the prisoner could not possibly escape from an island secured by guards and surrounded by sharks. But the minister feared the criticism of *La Libre Parole* as much as he admired its founder, and worried that if "yesterday's lie" became "tomorrow's truth," if Dreyfus did escape, his political future would be doomed. And beyond politics, Lebon seems to have been particularly sadistic and unmoved by the Dreyfus family's tragedy; reading their correspondence, he found the letters stereotypical, banal, and without a trace of genuine emotion. The family, he believed, showed no faith in the captain's innocence. For the prisoner Lebon would become the most evil player in a drama that had its share of diabolical actors: "His heart," Dreyfus would later say of Lebon, "was in his ministerial portfolio."[32]

It took two days for workers on the Ile Royale to reconstruct a hospital bed equipped with an iron "bar of justice," similar to an old wooden pillory, which guards would clamp over Dreyfus's ankles at night. On September 6, adhering to the rule of silence and not responding to the prisoner's demands for an explanation ("you are driving me to the grave!"), they forced him into the "'double buckle.'"[33] He was just recovering from his most severe bout of malaria, and now, for more than forty nights, in torrid heat, with spider crabs, mosquitoes, and ants crawling over his body, he was immobilized, his ankles raw and bleeding. Released from the shackles during the day, he suffered temporary paralysis of his back and neck, and, though desperate for air, he could not leave his cabin. At his small table, surrounded by old food cans filled with foul-smelling oil to repel insects, he described his "tortures" in his journal and in letters to Lucie and the family. "These nights in irons!" went the entry of September 8, "without knowing why. . . . In what atrocious nightmare have I been living." And later the same day: "I cannot take it any longer, everything is giving way in me." He wrote his last testament: "I leave my children to France, to my dear Fatherland. . . . If these lines reach you," he told Lucie, Pierre, and Jeanne, "believe that I have done everything humanly possible to resist." Two days later, "broken in body and soul," he abandoned the diary that had become his private dialogue with Lucie. It would be three months before guards unbolted his door, and by that time another order from Minister Lebon had been followed. A thick double fence, seven feet high, with planks hewn from the walaba wood of French Guiana, surrounded his cabin. Blocking the light and air from his window, it cut off his view of the sea, his one "supreme comfort."[34]

Before Mathieu learned the full consequences of the *Daily Chronicle* story (and he learned them, he said, through Léonie's psychic "travels" to Devil's Island),[35] he was encouraged by news reports that reopened the debate over the court-martial. *Figaro* and Cassagnac's *Autorité* hinted at irregularities that should be investigated, but the most important article, entitled "The Traitor," appeared in *L'Eclair*. Though hostile to Dreyfus and full of lies and half truths, it presented a detailed account of events from the day of the captain's arrest, and it exposed for the first time the existence of "decisive" secret documents communicated to judges in the deliberation room, "out of the presence even of the accused." According to *L'Eclair*, a letter from the German Embassy in Paris to the Italian Embassy, photographed by French agents in September 1894, contained the sentence: "Decidedly, that animal Dreyfus is becoming too demanding." Well documented, serious in tone, and seemingly objective, the *L'Eclair* article purported to provide "irrefutable proof" of the captain's treason. Reprinted in other newspapers, it pleased Dreyfus's enemies and, according to some observers, relieved many Jews who noted that the anonymous journalist had been careful to avoid the religious dimensions of the case: Dreyfus did not represent his people, went this interpretation; he was "a monstrous exception."[36]

From Demange's contacts at the Palais de Justice the previous year, Mathieu had learned that the German Embassy document mentioned only the initial "D" ("that scoundrel, D . . .") and not Dreyfus's name. Mathieu and his lawyer assumed that the General Staff had planted the newspaper story to put an end to the growing controversy, and they reckoned that the minister of war would publicly deny its most damning revelation—that Dreyfus's rights as a defendant had been violated. When the government remained silent, however, Demange drafted a petition to the Chamber of Deputies. Signed by Lucie Dreyfus as the legal guardian (*tutrice*) of her husband's interests, it stated that "after debates cloaked in the most complete mystery, because of a closed session, a French officer has been condemned . . . on the basis of an accusation . . . which neither the accused nor his counsel could discuss. This is a negation of all justice." The petition reaffirmed Lucie's belief in her husband's innocence and announced a new campaign: "Despite all the odious and absurd calumnies spread in public and in the press, I have remained silent. Today it is my duty to break that silence and, without commentary, without recrimination, I address you . . . the sole power to whom I have recourse, and I demand justice."[37]

The Chamber rejected the petition "for lack of proof," and even though *Figaro* and other newspapers published its contents, neither the government nor *L'Eclair* responded to its allegations. "The public conscience should have been aroused" by revelations of a miscarriage of justice, Mathieu had thought, the appeal should have "provoked universal condemnation."[38] But "there was nothing," only the tired incantations of the nationalist press: "After Catholics who believe in the divinity of Jesus," *L'Intransigeant* observed in an article on Dreyfus, "the most influential people are the Hebrews who crucified him."[39] And another petition submitted by Lucie in September, to a spiritual rather than a temporal authority, also met with silence. Helped by the "imaginative" English journalist Millage, Lucie drafted a letter, in Latin, to Pope Leo XIII. Its florid language confirmed Millage's hand, but its message echoed other appeals made by Lucie to French officials. "The wife of a Captain of Jewish extraction" humbly asked for the "pity and compassion of the Father of the Catholic Church." Summarizing her husband's plight, Lucie noted that "Christians were beginning to greatly fear that antisemitic prejudices have had much to do with this affair." She knelt at the feet of "the Vicar of Christ . . . just as the daughters of Jerusalem had turned to Christ himself." But the pope ignored Lucie's appeal; he had only recently "rallied" to the Third Republic in the hope of pushing back the tide of anticlericalism in France, and he had no intention of rallying to a Jew condemned for betraying the powerful neighbor he was trying so hard to tame.[40]

On the second anniversary of his brother's arrest, Mathieu began to break the pattern of private initiatives cautiously followed and move toward a more public campaign. It was a difficult decision, and one with which he never felt comfortable; his "natural inclination" had been to employ quiet methods and to work through established channels. Like the prisoner on Devil's Island, he never questioned the integrity of the nation's institutions and never doubted their "disinterestedness." Those institutions, born of the Revolution, deserved respect. In the spirit of young Alfred Dreyfus's "sacrifice" of his position in Alsace for a career in the military, it was a matter of gratitude strengthened by the belief that the family lived in an epoch of social progress. "We live in the hope," Rachel Schil wrote to her brother in exile, "that the truth will be discovered . . . it is inevitable in a century like ours." And Alfred told his wife that "light" would soon be shed on the "mystery" of his case because "anything else is impossible in our epoch."[41] The family had faith in the institutions of their "fatherland" not because of some reactionary predilection for law and order, but because across the decades, French law, if not always French legislators, had respected the covenant of emancipation. For the Dreyfuses, Hadamards, Valabrègues, Schwobs, and other family members, the captain's arrest was a "tragic error" committed by individuals who were either criminal or misguided; it had nothing to do with the failures of French "Justice," a word the prisoner capitalized so often. "Above all, and no matter what the cost," Alfred would announce from Devil's Island, "the interests of the country must be respected." "Search for the truth with energy and decisiveness," he urged Mathieu, "but always for France and with France."[42]

In concert with Demange and Zadoc Kahn, who also believed in "religious respect for the law,"[43] Mathieu had vetoed political protests from the outset. Shortly after the degradation, Arthur Lévy, a Bonapartist writer convinced of Dreyfus's innocence, had drafted a petition to be submitted to deputies, senators, judges, and members of the French Institute. Sent under Lucie's name and distributed to the press, it would politicize the case and force the government to respond. Author of a book entitled *Napoléon Intime,* Lévy must have been inspired by similarities between the old hero on Saint Helena and the new martyr on Devil's Island; but Mathieu held firm against entering the political arena. He rejected Lévy's petition as well as similar efforts by other allies. The climate was already too charged, Mathieu believed, and he preferred to appeal to the reason and compassion of government officials. Grand Rabbi Kahn, who approved of that strategy, would have defined it as a secularized version of *shtadlanut,* the maintenance of discreet but effective contacts between Jewish leaders and government officials. Like the *shtadlan* of a traditional community, chosen for his refined manners, appeal to reason and justice, and ability to "turn enemies into good, if temporary, friends," Mathieu took on the combined roles of "diplomat, advocate, and intercessor."[44]

But along with his instinct for compromise, he had a sense of the right moment for engagement, and while pacifying anxious allies, he laid plans for a future campaign. After the captain's transfer from Cherche-Midi, Forzinetti had given Mathieu copies of the judge advocate's indictment, which the prisoner had secretly annotated in his cell. "They will be useful one day," Forzinetti told Mathieu, "if you decide to launch a campaign in the press."[45] All materials relating to a trial were classified, and public disclosure would surely lead to Forzinetti's discharge and to a jail sentence for Mathieu. Knowing that his humiliation would delay his brother's release, Mathieu again proceeded with caution. He kept a copy of the transcript in Paris, and sent Georges Hadamard to Basel, the town that had served so many generations of the Dreyfus family, to deposit the originals with Henriette Valabrègue's daughter, who lived there. Searching for a way to put the report to use, to expose the court-martial's "judicial error," he was helped by Rachel and Louise. On a visit to Santé, the sisters had been advised by the warden (like Forzinetti, another convert to Dreyfus's cause) that only two writers had the talent to articulate the family's campaign: Edouard Drumont and Bernard Lazare, a young poet and journalist with anarchist sympathies. Strange choices both, but Lazare, a Jew from southern France and author of a recent history of anti-Semitism, would at least share Mathieu's belief that suspicion had fallen on Captain Dreyfus "because he's a Jew" and because "there are those who want to run him out of the military."[46]

Offspring of an assimilated but observant Jewish family in the Provençal town of Nîmes, Lazare Bernard, as he was first called, had come to Paris in 1886 at the age of twenty-one. After attending the Ecole Pra-

tique des Hautes Etudes, he transposed his name, abandoned academe
and the remnants of his religious faith, and entered the world of the literary avant-garde. Often described as "pugnacious," the young poet,
with his monocle, mustache, and pointed goatee, gained a reputation as
an independent critic and a man of passionate political beliefs. While many
of his contemporaries drifted into the heady atmosphere of "art for art's
sake," Lazare remained on the literary barricades of Paris, hurling salvos
at comrades who refused to recognize the link between art and politics.
Angered by the injustices of a corrupt capitalist society, he fought with
intensity and not a little ruthlessness: "Hatred is in literature, as in politics, as in art, a primordial and indispensable passion," he would write in
1895. And in a statement that captured his somewhat convoluted theory
of literature and life, he said, "He who does not know how to hate does
not know how to love what is for him beautiful."[47] So it was for the anarchists of the age, and, as journalist, lecturer, and witness for the defense in a series of trials, Bernard Lazare joined their ranks. Though
more engaged than other intellectuals and artists of the time—whose
anarchy remained largely confined to the quest for a pastoral utopia—
Lazare never took to the streets with "propagandists of the deed," who
assassinated politicians, bombed the Chamber of Deputies, and dyna-
mited bourgeois restaurants. But if Lazare's anarchism rarely moved beyond the boundaries of art, it was never frivolous. Committed to social
justice, the writer was a revolutionary with talent, and, as his recent book
had shown, he had a keen sense of the scourge of anti-Semitism. He
deserved Mathieu's attention.

He might never have tolerated it, however, were it not for Joseph
Valabrègue and family connections in the Jewish communities of Provence. Shortly after Dreyfus's arrest, Lazare expressed no interest in
the prisoner, who, as an army officer and son of an industrialist, represented everything wretched in contemporary society. Late in 1894
Lazare had written two articles attacking the anti-Semitic aspects of the
case, but when approached by the editor P.-V. Stock about becoming
involved in the captain's cause, he refused. "Why should I?" he responded. "I don't know him or his family. Of course, if he were some
poor devil, I would be worried about him soon enough, but Dreyfus and
his people are very rich, they say."[48] Lazare had no desire to rally to a
bourgeois in trouble.

In order to enlighten the writer about the facts of the case, Joseph
Valabrègue contacted members of his family who had settled in Carpentras. Jewish communities in Lazare's Nîmes and Valabrègue's Car-

pentras had enjoyed close ties for centuries. As the capital of the Comtat, the Provençal territory held by the papacy until the French Revolution, Carpentras had been a principal economic center in the region. With its large Jewish population, its influence reached to settlements of coreligionists in outlying villages and towns, and west to Nîmes. Using his connections, Joseph Valabrègue secured a letter of introduction from Lazare's relatives—and from another Carpentras notable, Alfred Naquet—and went to see the writer in Paris.[49]

With good diplomatic sense, Valabrègue focused not on Dreyfus's patriotism or privileged background, but on the anti-Semitic dimensions of the case and on the violation of Dreyfus's civil liberties. Lazare listened "cordially and with sympathy" and agreed to see the prisoner's brother. During a series of meetings through late February and March, Mathieu told Lazare about the *bordereau*, the disagreement among graphologists, and the "inquisitorial methods" of the prosecution; and he asked the writer to use the prisoner's annotated transcript to compose a "memoir" exposing the "judicial error." Eager to push the case into the political arena, Lazare agreed: "From that moment," he later recalled, "three people took an active interest in that poor man's fate: Demange, Mathieu and me."[50] He was only partly correct: He underestimated Valabrègue's contributions, and he had not yet met Forzinetti, Dr. Gibert, or Lucie Dreyfus.

Written in a clear, vigorous style, and with a journalist's dispatch, Lazare's manuscript summarized the facts and exposed, with a surgeon's precision, the lesser known fantasies, conspiracies, and lies perpetrated by "dangerous maniacs" like the so-called handwriting expert Bertillon. A tour de force of political journalism, at once passionate and measured, it promised to mobilize allies and shock the government into action. With a draft completed in the early summer of 1895, Lazare read it aloud to Mathieu and to Lucie, whom he met for the first time. Never doubting the writer's brilliance or the power of his account, the family hesitated nevertheless and, in so doing, marked the beginning of a long and at times acrimonious struggle over the methods and timing of the propaganda campaign. Mathieu, seconded by Demange, decided to wait for a more "favorable occasion" to publish Lazare's manuscript, while the impatient writer rejected "foot-stamping in place." He had only contempt for the discreet avenues of influence pursued by the lawyer and Mathieu Dreyfus, and he considered the family's prudence as misguided as their strange obsession with the hypnotic visions of Léonie.[51]

In this case, however, Mathieu was the patron and Lazare the artist, and publication of the pamphlet would have to wait. Now engaged in the battle, the writer returned to journalism and to assaults on those anti-Semites who had prepared the ground for Dreyfus's arrest and who continued to wield power in military and political circles. Through 1896 the Jewish anarchist Lazare taunted the Jew-hater Drumont ("You are not invulnerable, neither you nor your friends"), and he faced the editor of *La Libre Parole* in a duel in which neither man was injured. Waiting for Mathieu and Demange to break free from their passivity, he also composed a series of articles on the "atavistic pusillanimity" of French Jews. Those essays, informed by Lazare's experience with the Dreyfuses, signaled a shift from the writer's earlier belief that assimilation into "the mass of the nation" would bring an end to anti-Semitism. As a hostage to Mathieu's caution, Lazare recast his views on the political behavior of French Jews and, eventually, on issues of Jewish nationalism. He condemned the "deplorable habit learned from old persecutions . . . of not protesting . . . of waiting for the storm to pass, and of playing dead so as not to attract the lightning."[52]

United in their goal of saving a victim of anti-Semitism, Bernard Lazare and Mathieu Dreyfus remained divided in their definitions of state power. For the anarchist it represented oppression, while for the patriot it stood for protection. Lazare's comments on Jewish "pusillanimity," though sweeping enough to carry a grain of truth, could not apply to Mathieu's actions—or calculated inaction. Far from "waiting for the storm to pass," he waited for it to build, and in the autumn of 1896, when the *Daily Chronicle* and *L'Eclair* articles returned his brother's case to the public arena, he contacted Lazare and asked him to update his manuscript for publication. Mathieu arranged for Lazare to travel to Brussels (where the pamphlet would be printed to avoid legal action in France), and in early November three thousand French notables— judges, journalists, deputies, and senators—received copies of *A Judicial Error: The Truth About the Dreyfus Affair.*[53]

The press, police, and government officials reacted to the pamphlet, but "glacially," as one observer put it, and in a wave of protest.[54] *La Libre Parole* circulated the rumor that Lazare, a Jewish anarchist in need of funds, had been paid five thousand francs by the Dreyfuses and Hadamards; a tradesman by race, he acted as a wholesale merchant of propaganda designed to discredit the army and embarrass the nation. In the Chamber of Deputies, politicians who read the pamplet (and more who did not) repeated their belief in Dreyfus's guilt and extended their accusations to other family members. One story had Lucie's father traveling to Italy to sell documents relating to the defense of the Alps. The newspapers *Radical* and *Paix* published David Hadamard's angry protest, but guilt was presumed and innocence never considered. Still, Lazare's pamphlet kept the story alive and moved a minority of "individual spirits" who doubted Dreyfus's guilt.[55]

Joseph Reinach—member of the Chamber of Deputies, friend of Maître Demange, and an early advocate for the captain he did not know— met Bernard Lazare shortly before the pamphlet's publication. Though he detested the writer's anarchism, Reinach had been impressed by his battle against anti-Semitism. "We are each of us being attacked as Jews," Lazare would tell the politician. "This is why we can forget our economic and philosophical differences and agree on the fight to be waged against anti-Semitism."[56] With characteristic bravado Lazare would also concede that, "after me, you were the first and most ardent Dreyfusard."[57] Reinach believed that only a united front could secure the captain's release, a well-orchestrated campaign which would pillory French officials without tarring French institutions. A masterful arbiter, Joseph Reinach would win Lazare's respect and Mathieu Dreyfus's lifelong friendship.

Ally and biographer of Léon Gambetta, veteran of the bitter struggles of the early Third Republic, Reinach would also be, by the end of his career, the veteran of no fewer than thirteen duels, including two with a former Gambetta colleague, Paul Déroulède, who began his political life as a poet of nationalism and closed it as a strident anti-Semite. Brandishing swords or pistols in the Bois de Boulogne or political rhetoric on the Chamber floor, Reinach's opponents must have been intimidated by his physical presence. Stocky rather than portly in middle age, he had the thick neck, massive chest, and muscular arms of a brawler—if Lazare acted pugnacious, Reinach, with his wide-set eyes and dense brown beard, looked it. But the look deceived; salon habitué, patron of the arts, lover of ballet and opera, he was a man of refined tastes, and a gifted, though at times grandiloquent, essayist, biographer, and historian. With boundless energy and a capacious intellect, he would bring political wisdom to the Dreyfus campaign and the needed ingredient of influence. Sharing Mathieu's aristocratic manner, flirtation with Freemasonry, and unwavering patriotism (he had served as secretary-general of the Ligue des patriotes in the 1880s), he also knew the sources of Bernard Lazare's anger. Neither the industrialist from Mulhouse nor the *littérateur* from Nîmes had ever experienced the cascade of bigotry anti-Semites had heaped on Reinach across nearly two decades of political life. And the worst was yet to come.[58]

Edouard Drumont had cut his teeth on the Reinach family. Much of the language and imagery the editor of *La Libre Parole* marshaled against Dreyfus had been used a half decade before on Baron Jacques de Reinach, Joseph's cousin and father-in-law. Implicated in the Panama scandal, the baron had been accused of influence peddling in the Chamber of Deputies. After panicking and attempting to placate Drumont and his allies, the financier died on the eve of his court appearance; the popular press called it suicide, while others insisted that the relentless assaults by anti-Semites had brought on a massive heart attack. Whatever the case, Jacques de Reinach's sordid biography cast a shadow over his entire family, and most especially over his cousin. Joseph Reinach became his relative's "beneficiary," both for socialists, who believed that Judaism was synonymous with capitalism, and for political anti-Semites, who needed no justification other than "race." Though born in Paris, Reinach fell into that vast category of "German Jews" Drumont dubbed as "enemies within." So too did his no-less-talented brothers, Théodore and Salomon, classical scholars, prolific writers, and, with Joseph, famous for their extraordinary triumph at the general examinations of all *lycées*. In Parisian fin-de-siècle circles, the Reinach brothers were known as a trio of intellectual brilliance, and, for those threatened by such things, their success seemed, as one contemporary put it, like "an act of violence."[59] Mortified by competition, anti-Semites met violence with violence: Léon Daudet, who had attended Dreyfus's degradation and described the captain's "weasel-faced" and "foreign" physiognomy, had much the same to say about Joseph Reinach and his brother Théodore: "When they entered the drawing room," Daudet wrote, "one after the other, the effect was prodigious. It was Orang leading Outang."[60] The Reinachs, like the Dreyfuses, responded to those slurs with what Théodore had called in 1886 "the silence of disdain."[61] A decade later Joseph kept the disdain, but, with his more militant friend Bernard Lazare, he joined the growing contingent of Dreyfus supporters—"Dreyfusards"—to break the silence.

In the closing weeks of 1896 press reports confirmed that the legal case threatened to become a political *affaire*. On November 10, on the heels of Lazare's brochure, the Parisian daily *Le Matin* published a facsimile of the *bordereau*, the "incriminating document" that had never been seen in public. One of the handwriting experts had kept a photograph of the memorandum, and when the trial became front-page news two years later, he secretly sold the item to *Le Matin*. Mathieu called the newspaper's revelation "an event of the highest importance," which gave him "the greatest joy." Acting to capitalize on the "considerable publicity" unleashed by the *bordereau's* appearance, Mathieu paid for posters that displayed examples of the captain's handwriting alongside the facsimile of the memorandum. That striking image of Dreyfus's innocence would move the public, the family believed, and force the government to respond.[62]

By the early spring of 1897, graphologists hired by Mathieu had confirmed the differences between the prisoner's handwriting and that on the *bordereau*. The family found a new ally when Gabriel Monod—medieval scholar, former teacher of Bernard Lazare, and a Protestant who would suffer his share of Drumont's vitriol—submitted a comparative study concluding that Dreyfus was innocent. Other French experts concurred. But Mathieu, so certain that this would be the key to his brother's release, engaged an additional half dozen graphologists from Switzerland, Belgium, England, and the United States at a cost of more than seven thousand francs—though some, like Monod, refused a fee. Every expert reaffirmed that the *bordereau* could not have been the work of Alfred Dreyfus. Mathieu wrote to his brother, but could only communicate a vague expression of hope: "The long hours that you pass down there in complete isolation, we pass with you in our thoughts," Mathieu said, "but our future goal must make us forget our present sadness."[63]

In midsummer the family received the first sign that their efforts had made an impact beyond the circle of the already converted. It came in a confidential letter from Joseph Reinach, which Lazare delivered to Lucie Dreyfus. For months Reinach and another former Gambetta ally, Arthur Ranc, senator from the Seine department, had been trying to enlist the support of Auguste Scheurer-Kestner, the highly respected vice president of the Senate. Also a veteran of Gambetta's republican fraternity, the Alsatian Protestant from Mulhouse, owner of a major chemical enterprise in nearby Thann, had been approached by Mathieu shortly after the captain's arrest and, later, by Lazare and Demange. With his long white beard, aquiline features, and tall, angular frame, Scheurer-Kestner had the "austere look of a sixteenth-century Huguenot." A statesman with considerable influence, he would have made a powerful ally; but, like most other Alsatians, he expressed "profound pity" for the sons and daughters of Raphael Dreyfus without questioning the army's findings. As "the protector of all Alsatians in France," the senator had a "vague and sad reaction" to the first reports of Dreyfus's arrest and harbored early doubts that an officer from Mulhouse, of considerable wealth and good reputation, could betray his fatherland. Also, targeted by the nationalist press as part of the Protestant-Masonic-Jewish cabal, he agreed that Drumont and his followers "dishonored our country and our century." And finally he could empathize with the prisoner's plight; arrested as a rebellious republican by Louis Napoléon's "praetorian guard," he had known the hardships of political imprisonment. But life after Gambetta had tamed the old rebel, and the army he reviled under Napoleon III he revered under the Third Republic. According to Reinach, he firmly believed in the new officer corps and, much like Alfred Dreyfus, "worshipped" the military uniform with "superstitious veneration."[64]

Now, however, Reinach's letter to Lucie Dreyfus announced that the vice president of the Senate believed in her husband's innocence. He had been given proof that, for the moment, must remain confidential. Moving through established channels (he called himself just a simple "bourgeois impassioned against injustice"),[65] Scheurer-Kestner aimed to rehabilitate the image of his homeland by liberating his fellow Alsatian. Reinach's letter filled Mathieu "with joy and confidence," and for Lucie it represented the "first glimmer of hope"; it gave her "strength to live."[66] With only the most unregenerate Protestant-haters doubting Scheurer-Kestner's integrity, the family's campaign would finally be recognized; the government would listen to the nation's most prominent senator.

No drama could penetrate the stillness of August in Paris, however, and when the Parliament went on holiday, Scheurer-Kestner went with it. Journalists and Dreyfus supporters pressed on through that unusually hot and humid summer, and with politicians absent and hard news scarce, the rumors spread. By September the senator's commitment to the prisoner was widely known, and, through letters to colleagues from his home in Alsace, Scheurer-Kestner did his part to convince the intransigent and motivate the indifferent. He insisted that the captain's fate was linked to the fate of the republic: "I tell you that Dreyfus is innocent," he wrote. "I tell you that we know it. . . . I tell you that such things are unacceptable in the nineteenth century [and] that they dishonor the Republic."[67]

Through a mutual friend in Mulhouse, Scheurer-Kestner invited Mathieu to come to Basel, near the senator's home in Thann. Their secret meeting took place in a private dining room at the Hotel Zuber, an establishment named for the Protestant who had transformed the Dreÿfuss village of Rixheim into an industrial town a century before.

During the meeting the Alsatians discussed the strategy of the case, and, without divulging the information he had promised to keep confidential, Scheurer-Kestner tried to encourage the family's investigation. "Look in the military directory for an infantry commandant with two names and from an aristocratic background," he instructed Mathieu. "He is intimately linked with an Israelite who had been attached to the War Ministry, but who is now in the reserve; I cannot tell you more; I am bound by my word; but search thoroughly and you will find the name." Mathieu noted that the secret was "suffocating" Scheurer-Kestner—that his compatriot, "visibly upset" and "anxious," wanted to reveal more. Immediately on returning to Paris, Mathieu tried to follow the senator's leads, but aristocrats with hyphenated names, genuine and bogus, dominated the military directory, and Scheurer-Kestner's clues, though tantalizing, "were too imprecise."[68]

Through the early fall the senator's conversion began to draw the wrath of the nationalist press. *Patrie* called him a naive old man who had been "duped by scum"; Gaston Méry, a friend of Drumont, named the senator as a key figure in a "Jew-loving, Huguenot cabal"; and provincial editions of *La Croix* announced that "after a long, occult fermentation, the Jewish conspiracy has suddenly exploded, and the noise from that hellish machine has reverberated everywhere, with the rapidity of thunder."[69] Drumont also turned on the Protestant politician and seized the opportunity to make another suggestion concerning the Jewish prisoner: "I do not believe that outside the synagogue," he wrote in early November, "there would be many tears in France if an 'intelligent bullet' suppressed a cursed being who . . . has been the disgrace and scourge of his country."[70] Along with Parisian editorials, Scheurer-Kestner's involvement in the case prompted private letters and petitions, especially from fellow Alsatians who either condemned the senator as an accomplice to treason or applauded his courage. "Wretch, sold off to Germany," went one diatribe. "You should be named the first stool pigeon of the Prussian police. . . . You're a filthy German in the pay of the Jews and you're well known for your links to our worst enemies." Most letters took it for granted that "an Alsatian is incapable of betraying his country," though not all agreed that Scheurer-Kestner and Dreyfus were bona fide Alsatians. The Protestant's "disgusting and ignoble conduct" convinced many "True Frenchmen" that some "Alsatians are nothing more than Prussians." "You are an old blackguard, rogue and traitor," said one observer who spoke for others, "a dirty Prussian like all the rest of your Protestant and Jewish coreligionists."

Slowly, however, the anonymous ravings of self-professed defenders of the French faith were counterbalanced by letters of support and gratitude. Many Alsatians who had remained silent for three years, out of conviction or cowardice, now moved to the side of their celebrated compatriot: "You are . . . as immortal as Voltaire who also had to fight, almost alone, against popular prejudice," went one note from Strasbourg. "I can assure you that nearly all Alsatians and Lorrainers, regardless of religious or political opinions, are with you in the fight for justice, law and truth." Though a bad student of public opinion, the writer captured the spirit of Scheurer-Kestner's struggle, and he was not alone: "You are the last true representative of Alsace in the Parliament," another letter proclaimed. "Dreyfus, a Mulhousien and a French soldier, is two times our compatriot. Save him."[71]

But Dreyfus could only be saved by evidence that a judicial error had been committed or by the identification of the real traitor, and Scheurer-Kestner would comment on neither issue. Nor would he do anything to embarrass the republic. Summarizing his goals in a letter to Reinach, he said that "it is necessary to rescue the individual, restore honor to his family—and save the republican government. Such interests are sacred."[72] He did not need to read his mail to know the perils of a propaganda campaign that played on religion, race, and politics, and though respectful of Lazare the Dreyfusard, he vigorously opposed Lazare the anarchist Jew. Learning that Mathieu planned to rerelease Lazare's pamphlet with the facsimile of the *bordereau,* Scheurer-Kestner warned, in the frank way for which he was known, that "the affair should not become Jewish." Prudence, not prejudice, lay behind that warning (or so Joseph Reinach said of the senator who had called anti-Semitism "the shame of the nineteenth century"), but Scheurer-Kestner would not join an effort that, to his mind, threatened to divide the nation.[73]

Mathieu was now constrained by his even-more-cautious fellow Alsatian. Faced with yet another delay, he carried stacks of the *bordereau* facsimile and copies of letters the prisoner had written to his wife and attempted, with Lazare, Reinach, and others, to win over politicians and literati. Henri Rochefort and Maurice Barrès, self-professed guardians of social justice, but prisoners to their own anti-Semitism, refused to help, while other notables joined the effort—from Lucien Herr, Alsatian, socialist, and librarian of the prestigious Ecole Normale Supérieure; to the popular but controversial novelist Emile Zola.[74] For Mathieu, however, that celebrated gallery of new campaigners would contribute less to the cause in the late fall of 1897 than an unknown

Parisian stockbroker waiting for a horsedrawn omnibus on the Place de la Madeleine.

His name was de Castro, and, glancing at a poster he had purchased from a vendor on the *grands boulevards,* he recognized the handwriting on the *bordereau.* Returning to his office he searched through papers of former clients and found letters written in a hand identical to that on the memorandum. By this time Parisians who had been following the case knew that the Hadamard apartment on the rue Châteaudun served as the Dreyfus family's base of operation, and de Castro sent word that he wished to meet the prisoner's brother. November 1897 marked the third anniversary of Mathieu's arrival in Paris, three years of rushing to follow every lead and of running into dead ends. He must have greeted the unknown stockbroker's invitation with skepticism, but, true to his early promise to enter "every milieu," he met de Castro at a private businessman's club on the Boulevard Montmartre.[75]

And he learned the traitor's name. With the letters of de Castro's former client spread on a table next to the poster, Mathieu was "immediately struck by the extraordinary resemblance of the handwriting." Having spent many hours with "magnifying glass in hand," he had become an amateur graphologist, and he noted the unique dotting of the *i* and the *g* that appeared more like a *y.* Cross-checking the letters and the memorandum "slowly and with care," he identified every peculiarity and knew that he had found the criminal. Finally, on the reverse side of one letter he read the signature of the man responsible for his brother's dishonor, a name he had never heard before. The stockbroker told Mathieu that Commandant Marie Charles Ferdinand Walsin-Esterhazy, a French officer of Hungarian descent, had been a singularly "detestable" client, always short of money and with a notorious reputation as a gambler, womanizer, crook, and swindler. De Castro believed that the major was still attached to the Seventy-fourth Infantry Regiment, based in Rouen.[76]

"Suddenly I was seized by a profound distress," Mathieu later wrote. "What if Walsin-Esterhazy was not the same man whom Scheurer-Kestner knew to be the traitor?" Mathieu rushed directly from de Castro's club to the senator's Paris quarters and tried to convince him to break his silence. But his fellow Alsatian, honor bound, would not divulge what he knew. "Then I will tell you the traitor's name," Mathieu declared. "It's Esterhazy." And Scheurer-Kestner, feeling a "weight lifted from his shoulders," said, "Yes. It's him."[77]

CHAPTER XII

Banquo's Ghost

ACROSS THE YEARS on Devil's Island, Mathieu's brother held back his anger at "the real traitor"—for him, the unknown traitor—and rarely expressed desire for revenge. Only on a few occasions, amid hundreds of letters and countless diary entries, did he try to imagine the criminal's mind and motives. And when he drifted into those "dreams," in the throes of malarial fever or depression brought on by the "perpetual silence" that surrounded him, his rage surfaced with uncharacteristic venom: "The wretch who committed this infamous crime will be unmasked," he wrote more than two years before his brother discovered Esterhazy, "and if I could take hold of him for only five minutes I would make him suffer all the tortures that I have had to endure. . . . Without pity, I would rip out his heart and entrails."[1] On New Year's Eve, 1895, after a long period of driving rain, insufferable heat (the temperature approached 120 degrees in mid-December), and a bout of malaria, Dreyfus composed a letter to his wife full of affection and hope. Then, turning to his journal, he unleashed his anger: he saw himself putting "a knife to the throats of the traitor's miserable accomplices," punishing them for the "vile and base schemes they had plotted against our country"; and later he dreamed of "skinning" them alive, "piece by piece," until they confessed.[2]

But, like cannon blasts fired toward vessels sailing too close to Devil's Island, Dreyfus's fits of anger served as warning signals that he

195

was losing control. Revenge could only be corrosive, another infectious disease to combat, and the traitor, when discovered, deserved only the silence of disdain and the swift punishment of French justice. "We must face the reality," Dreyfus admitted to his wife, and not descend into "bitter and acrimonious personal attacks. We must look higher." "I will repeat again today what I have said from the first day: above all human passions, above all human error, there is the Fatherland . . . and it will be my supreme judge."[3]

Montaigne, one of the prisoner's closest companions in exile, had envied those who could "rest on the soft pillow of faith." But for Dreyfus keeping the faith was the hardest challenge of all. Rest through death ("eternal repose," he called it) remained a constant seduction.[4] After six months on Devil's Island he suffered a fainting spell and felt his heart stop; instead of panicking, however, he languished in that moment of release, of "parting without suffering." "If only I were alone in the world," he had written earlier. "I would have been in the grave a long time ago." And it was not the only time he described "the peace of the tomb," the one place where he would no longer be plagued by "human deception." If he had no wife and children, he confessed, and no responsibility to his family name, he would willingly die to escape his "madness."[5] Montaigne, building on Cicero, had believed that "to philosophize is to learn to die," to deal with the fear and torment of our mortality; but the prisoner on Devil's Island, who imagined the comfort of death and feared life in exile, noted next to the quotation from the essayist that "death takes us all, the humble and great." Using his journal as a forum for a vast gallery of literati, Dreyfus did as Montaigne had done and called on Horace to make his point: "We are all forced down the same road," wrote the poet, "Our fate, / Tossed in the urn, will spring out soon or late, / And force us helpless into Charon's bark, / Passengers destined for eternal dark." It is better, the prisoner concluded, "to philosophize in order to learn how to live."[6]

If Chaptal, Sainte Barbe, and the Ecole Polytechnique had introduced Dreyfus to the philosophers, poets, playwrights, scientists, and historians who, along with spider crabs, mosquitoes, and the occasional boa constrictor, would populate his Devil's Island cell, those schools, with their relentless drills and inspections, had also shaped his meticulous sense of order and almost pathological obsession with routine. From the "somber barracks" of boarding school, where *surveillants* monitored every *interne* and punished every transgression, to the garrison at Bourges ("my provincial prison"), Dreyfus had spent the greatest part of his life learning lessons of obedience, self-sacrifice, and discipline; he was the product of institutions cordoned off, as the Ecole Polytechnique would put it with pride, from *la vie civile*. Much about that austere, regimented existence ("monastic" was the adjective most often used to describe it) appealed to the youngest and least demonstrative son of Raphael and Jeannette Dreyfus, though it always battled with the restless side of his "Don Quixote" character. "Reason knocks violently at my door," he had written Lucie from Bourges, "and tells me to put an end to all my dreams and get back to work. As an obedient slave . . . I do so." If there could be such a thing as a dress rehearsal for Devil's Island, Dreyfus had lived it in dormitories and garrisons, and he tried to put its lessons to use in exile. For more than four years, when not paralyzed by fever or depression, his highly structured agenda of "work, study and meditation" joined "love for the Fatherland and for humanity" to form his strategy for survival.[7]

By the late spring of 1895 the routine was set. To save himself from the debilitating heat of the midday sun, he awoke at 5:15 A.M., and when provisions were available (and edible) he prepared a small plate of vegetables and a tin mug of coffee or tea. He made up his cot, washed, and received daily rations at 8:00 A.M. Prohibited from possessing a razor, knife, or scissors, he never shaved, and his hair and beard, rapidly turning gray, would be cut only infrequently by an inmate sent from the Ile Royale. After lunch (at 10:00 A.M.) Dreyfus remained under the cover of his sweltering but shaded stone hut, sweeping the floor, mending torn clothes, reading, and writing letters. Constantly sweating through his prison garb, he washed again, and in the late afternoon, with an armed guard always at his side, he worked outside fetching water, cutting wood for his cooking stove, and, on occasion, gathering cucumbers or tomatoes from plants first cultivated by the island's leper colony. Sometimes he would venture out toward midday to consult his primitive sundial. (His gold watch, confiscated by guards at Cherche-Midi and later returned, never worked properly.) To determine the meridian, he attached a vertical plumb line made with a string and pebble to a broom handle, and "stupefied" his guards: "They probably wondered," he said in a rare moment of levity, "if I was signaling some balloon in the sky to come and rescue me."[8]

More often than not, his meager harvest of fruits and vegetables, like food sent from the Ile Royale, gave him agonizing stomach cramps. With the formidable sum of five hundred francs per month (his *masse*, or "spending money," deposited by Lucie in Paris) he could order provisions from Cayenne, and by the summer of 1895, he began receiving, on an irregular basis, boxes his wife filled with items from Félix Potin and other Paris shops and delivered to the Colonial Office on the rue Oudinot. Containing condensed milk, Vichy water, coffee, cigarettes, pipe tobacco, chocolate, biscuits, and quinine, the packages were searched and, it seems, pilfered by local officials. At one point, having watched guards rip into Lucie's carefully prepared parcels, Dreyfus asked his wife to stop sending the provisions: "It's probably a childish request," he wrote, "but your packages are the object of thorough searches, and I feel each time that it is like a slap in your face." Lucie knew their importance, however, and as they continued to arrive, guards carefully rationed their contents. Worried that Dreyfus would scrape the tips of matches to prepare a suicide potion or set fire to his cabin, they handed out the small matchboxes one by one, and they limited his tobacco ration (inmates on the Iles du Salut were known to consume huge quantities in attempts to choke themselves to death). Dreyfus smoked constantly to calm his nerves, to "intoxicate" himself as other prisoners did, and when tobacco ran out he filled his pipe with dry tea leaves.[9]

He called the period after 6:00 P.M., when sentries locked him in his *case*, "the longest moment" of the day. Kept awake by light pouring in from the adjoining annex, and often too exhausted to read or write, he listened to the "continual comings and goings" of guards whose wooden clogs pounded against the hard ground. The periodic nightmares he had suffered long before his imprisonment now became constant and violent, and in those early morning hours when at last he fell asleep, he would jolt himself awake with a scream. At first sentries rushed into his cell, but the nightmares soon became as routine as the rancid food and dysentery, and the prisoner was left alone to shout himself into exhaustion or, more often, as official reports noted, to cry himself to sleep. Night after night, guards ignored his outbursts and used the bureaucrat's abbreviation to describe his condition: *RDN*, they marked on the prisoner register—*rien de nouveau*—"nothing new."[10]

Even when confined to his hut by malaria, colic, or dysentery, Dreyfus recorded with Cartesian precision his temperature, pulse rate, doses of quinine and drugs, and campaigns against insects ("I scratch myself bloody"). He gauged the "violent palpitations" of his heart, described the "boiling hot liquids" used to combat fever, and watched his cabin thermometer rise degree by degree, hour by hour. And when strong enough to put pen to paper, he charted it all like a Polytechnicien listing the ingredients of chemical compound.

His worst attack of malarial fever came with the heavy rains of June and July 1896. Late one night, in a fit of delirium, he stumbled over his washtub, bloodied his nose and forehead, and fell unconscious. Orders from the colonial minister kept the main hospital off limits ("I must die on my own miserable litter," Dreyfus later remarked), and the prisoner could receive no more than cursory medical care on the spot. Able to digest only crackers dipped in wine, he tried to nurse himself with drugs parceled out by prison guards, but his condition deteriorated. Wanting Dreyfus debilitated but not dead, the commandant, urged on by Dr. Debrieu, finally sent an inmate to prepare food and mix the mustard flour footbaths that were a common prescription on the Iles du Salut. By late July, the patient began to regain his strength thanks to the combined efforts of a strange alliance: the inmate helper, Amadou Thiam, undoubtedly chosen because he spoke no French; the prison doctor; and, secretly, the wives of a few guards who, from their mainland homes, often "came to the rescue" of ailing deportees by collecting fresh food for them.[11]

If Dreyfus's fundamentally strong constitution helped him survive the many diseases of Devil's Island, his guards, including one "courageous and loyal man" who had been more compassionate than most of his comrades, were often overcome by illness and forced to leave the island. Malarial fever also took its toll among prisoners across the narrow channel, on the Ile Royale and Ile Saint-Joseph, and Dreyfus, overhearing descriptions of burials at sea, would imagine his own body wrapped in the regulation gray linen shroud, weighted with a piece of iron, and slipped into the archipelago's shark-infested waters. He did not know that colonial officials had drafted special plans for their most notorious deportee; unlike a common criminal whose death would give rise to no controversy and whose cadaver would be of no interest to German agents or the international "Jewish syndicate," Dreyfus's body would be photographed, embalmed, and shipped back to France the way it came—"under heavy guard."[12]

Only medical crises and the rare, special visits of government functionaries broke the "profound, eternal and torturous silence" that reigned on Dreyfus's island. "Still alone, never speaking to a single person, never hearing a human voice," he noted in his journal in June 1895, and many times thereafter. He hoped for "one sympathetic word,

one friendly look" but heard nothing except the incessant waves pounding "on this rock thrown into the middle of the ocean." "It is worse than
the tortures of the Middle Ages," he wrote, "which broke only the
body, and which never lasted as long."[13] At times he defied orders and
spoke to his guards, and at times they refrained from reporting him to
the commandant. But those were brief moments of human sympathy
amid long months of hostility and "perpetual silence," and more often
than not he would be shouted down, threatened with draconian punishment, and told to put his protests in writing. By his second year in exile,
his voice had become so hoarse from lack of use that on those occasions
when officials demanded a response he found it difficult to translate his
thoughts into coherent sounds; like a stroke victim struggling to articulate the simplest statement, he agonized over every word and, according to medical reports, spoke only "with great effort."[14]

Every day and night on Devil's Island his primary struggle remained the
same as it had been at Cherche-Midi, Santé, and on the Ile de Ré.
Prepared to deal with physical suffering, he feared the loss of his "lucidity," the waves of "incoherence," the prospect of going completely
and irrevocably insane. Trying to battle insomnia and calm his chronic
nervosité and *tension cérébrale,* he forced himself to stay awake during
the hot, languorous midday hours—the customary time of *sieste* in
French Guiana—in the hope that he could sleep at night. He occupied
that time with chores, English lessons (using the exam books Lucie had
sent from Paris), letter writing (often tearing up ten drafts for every
one he sent), and drawing designs and copying literary aphorisms and
mathematical theorems on sheets of foolscap.[15]

Far from random sketches or haphazard private thoughts, however, those "scribbles," as he called them, were the methodical hiero-
glyphics of a Polytechnicien walking the razor's edge of a nervous
breakdown. Remembering his university courses in solid geometry and
integral and differential calculus, he reconstructed complex problems
and moved with sophisticated skill to their logical end. He determined
the position of points and planes, the Cartesian coordinates of his equations, and he lingered over the shapes of cones and triangles as if they
were pieces in a jigsaw puzzle he had solved many times before. Exercises against boredom, they were, more important, problems he could
master with satisfaction. Interspersed with those formulas were rows
of bizarre, at times freakish, arabesque designs, also drafted with geometric precision. They covered hundreds of notebook pages, from mar-

gin to margin, and, with Cartesian axes as their foundation, they were
Dreyfus's attempt to impose a rational structure on the blank space of
his foolscap. He never commented on the origins of those labyrinthine
motifs, or on their symbolism, if any; at times they appeared like dissected specimens of the human brain, while at others they had orna-
mental qualities that suggested sculptural reliefs. Lucie had sent her
husband a number of art history books, and it is possible that his designs
were inspired by pictures of classical Corinthian capitals with their elaborate interlacing patterns (one of his sketches captured that motif) or by
reproductions of the swirling forms of late antique and early medieval
manuscript illuminations. Like those minutely detailed pages ("as complex as any mathematical group theorem"),[16] Dreyfus's designs seemed
to have been drawn with compass and ruler, and with a militant preference for abstraction over objectification. Though his manuscript pages
contained an occasional landscape and architectural sketch, they never
depicted a human figure or face. Relentlessly abstract, the patterns
were, perhaps, visual expressions of the prisoner's disgust with "human
deception," a pictorial record of his quest "to look higher," as he often
told Lucie, "above human passions."[17]

    If so, they had more than pure ornamentation in common with the
manuscript illuminations of eighth- and ninth-century Celtic monks in
windswept island monasteries. For scribes who labored for days on a
single page of microscopic spirals, the act of illustration was, above all,
a spiritual exercise, "another way to attain communion with God." Their
work paralleled the "austere self-discipline" that characterized their
"ascetic practices,"[18] and the geometricity they imposed upon anarchic
forms reflected their belief in divine order over the chaos of temporal
life. Though the prisoner on Devil's Island often used a Christian vocabulary to describe his plight (he spoke of his "trappist" existence on
that "lost rock," of his "calvary" and "martyrdom" and that of his
family),[19] his spiritual strength, his "moral force" as he put it, did not
issue from Christian sources. "Duty," "country," "family," and a belief
in "justice," which combined the Judaic traditions of his family with the
ideals of the French Enlightenment, were the divinities he worshipped.

    Whatever the talismanic qualities of those arabesque designs, their
specific forms may have been prompted not by classical motifs or medieval illustrations but by memories of images closer to home. Growing
up in Mulhouse in the 1860s, Alfred and Mathieu had witnessed the
most dramatic event in their *quartier*—the massive renovation of the
Protestant church of Saint-Etienne, a building located only meters from

the family apartment. For a half decade, the youngsters watched stone-masons reconstruct the neo-Gothic church, and, like other spectators, they must have noted its most peculiar and, for some, outlandish feature—thousands of small, bulb-shaped sculptures that crowned its columns and ran up its spires like decorations on an elaborate wedding cake. Thirty years later the prisoner's notebook designs had many of the same features. But those church arabesques also resembled other patterns familiar to the Dreyfus family in Mulhouse—fabric designs produced by the leading members of the local *patronat* (many of them elders of Saint-Etienne) and the city's Jewish textile manufacturers. *Toiles peintes* remained the dominant industry in late-nineteenth-century Mulhouse, and those luxury materials repeated the rococo patterns that adorned walls, drapes, cushions, and furniture in public buildings, private salons, and in the Dreyfus family homes. Strikingly similar arabesques adorned Dreyfus's Devil's Island notebooks and provided the only ornamentation (along with painted wooden frames containing photographs of Lucie and the children) in his stark cell with its whitewashed walls.[20]

The prisoner's letters and journal entries confirmed that "immersion" in geometric patterns and mathematical theorems helped calm his nerves. But cabin fever could be as torturous as malarial fever, and the sedatives to which he was now addicted were rarely an effective antidote. As a young officer he had relieved the strain of study and the loneliness of garrison life with late night "promenades"; now, as a middle-aged prisoner, he tried to reconstruct some of that routine. When his health permitted, he walked the periphery of the field behind his hut and, later, the small yard marked off by the high wooden fence. Those double-time marches, however, drew protests from guards who refused to tolerate the heat. When the commandant ordered Dreyfus to slow down or face the consequences, the prisoner again turned to his journal, the single outlet for his anger: "I am pursued everywhere, and everything I do is wrong. When I walk too quickly, they say I exhaust the guards who must follow me; when I announce that I will no longer leave my hut, they say they will punish me."[21]

"They'll have me whipped for speaking true," laments the Fool in *King Lear*, "Thou'lt have me whipped for lying; and sometimes I am whipped for holding my peace."[22] Dreyfus's private language of protest and desire began to echo that of the literary characters who shared his exile. The Fool, the old king, Othello, Banquo, Polonius, and the Prince of

Denmark became, with their creator, "immortal friends" whom Dreyfus described "sleeping on the bookshelf" of his cell, always ready to be invited down for a conversation. And across the years, on irregular schedules determined by the moods of functionaries in charge of Dreyfus's reading materials, those "immortals" were joined by many others. In addition to the dozen Shakespeare plays he "read and reread" on Devil's Island (first in French and later, haltingly, in English) he spent long hours with Montaigne and Montesquieu, Voltaire and Rousseau, Balzac and Hugo, Tolstoy and Dostoyevsky, Nietzsche and Ibsen. He read the memoirs of Chateaubriand, Napoleon, and Madame de Staël, and the most recent novels and short stories of Maupassant, Bourget, Loti, and Barrès. As he had done at the Ecole Polytechnique and in the library of his Paris apartment, he studied scientific and literary periodicals (*L'Année scientifique, La Nature, Revue des deux mondes, Revue rose, Revue bleue, Revue de Paris*), and he reread the historians Michelet, Taine, and, above all, Fustel de Coulanges. From Descartes and Kant to Pasteur and Claude Bernard, it was, for the most part, a repertoire of the modern age of science and reason, a handpicked gallery of rationalists whose beliefs fitted well with Dreyfus's own predilections. But those writers also shared space on the prisoner's shelf with romantic novels and treatises on medieval art, and with four Bibles and three boxes of religious sermons.[23]

"My isolation doesn't weigh too heavily," the young captain had written his fiancée from Bourges in 1889. "A few books, a pen and some paper are enough to distract me."[24] Six years later Lucie became the distant organizer of her husband's distractions, his research librarian. Along with securing food and tobacco at Parisian shops, she traveled through the city in search of books and periodicals colonial authorities would deliver on an average of every three months (newspapers, she learned, were prohibited). "I know your tastes," she wrote Alfred in August 1895, and her own wide intellectual interests, coupled with her husband's keen knowledge of recent literary trends, helped her fill each box with a dozen books and a dozen contemporary journals. That routine lasted barely a year, however; after the summer of 1896, government officials refused to forward the packages Lucie brought to the rue Oudinot. In response she increased her husband's monthly stipend so that, when permitted, he could have books sent from a small shop in Cayenne or from the even-smaller prison library on the Ile Royale.[25]

A passage from Horace, used by Montaigue to describe the importance of private journals, could apply to the prisoner who turned his diary into a meeting place for celebrated authors: "He would confide," wrote Horace, "as unto trusted friends / His secrets to his notebooks; turn there still: / Not elsewhere, whether faring well or ill. / So that the old man's whole life lay revealed / As on a votive tablet."[26] Dreyfus did not simply "reread" the authors he had known as a student, he confided in them and read them anew, with an eye for language that captured his own plight and with a desire to both break the boundaries of Devil's Island and articulate the measure of his despair. And so it went for the contemporary novelists he read for the first time in exile. He traveled with that enormously entertaining chronicler of escape, Pierre Loti, to the deserts of Galilee and the exotic ports of the Far East, and he could not help but reflect on the amorous adventures of his own youth as he charted the erotic escapades, real and fabricated, of the licentious naval officer Lieutenant Loti. Paul Bourget's *Voyage en Amérique*, a less titillating account, served as another temporary passport out of prison, as did Saint-Simon's voyeuristic memoirs of the Sun King's court and Nikolay Gogol's dramatic story of the Cossack past, *Taras Bulba*.[27]

For the most part, however, Dreyfus preferred interior journeys. *Post tenebras spero lucem* ("After the shadows I hope for the light"), he scribbled on a notebook page, and as silence "weighed more heavily" on him and his own "interior life intensified," he searched for that light in the books he read. He called on other, more eloquent voices to help define the sources of his strength.[28] The principal leitmotiv of his "study and meditation" was best summarized in the simple question posed by the author he read most often and most carefully: "What do I know?" queried Montaigne, and Dreyfus, asking the same question of himself, responded with hundreds of axioms, borrowed and original, clichéd and creative, and with long disquisitions on books and articles he examined "like a military professor demonstrating the mechanics of a rifle."[29]

Reading Descartes, he noted that "the native quality of a true Frenchman" is reflected in the "principal, dominant role played by reason. . . . France has carried rationalism, intellectualism, to its highest power," the prisoner observed in his journal, "by disengaging it from political or religious interests, and by giving it a philosophical dimension." He praised the French notion of "noblesse oblige," the idea of generosity, which had nothing to do with aristocratic birth and everything to do with transcendant values. And he maintained that "there is no other nobility than moral nobility; whether rich or poor, whether dressed up with a particule or not, the noble man is an honest man."[30] Above all, he looked for (and found) in Descartes, Montesquieu, and others those "heroic" qualities of "courage and disdain for death" (he borrowed the words from Montaigne),[31] of "liberty, enlightenment and progress," which characterized the "soul of the French nation." Over and over again, he repeated that France must never renounce the key ingredients of its "true moral power"—its "ideal of generosity" and "spirit of impartiality." Along with *justice, duty, honor* and *truth*, the words *disengagement* and *disinterestedness* appeared most often in Dreyfus's notebooks and letters. And for good reason: They represented the foundation of his faith. Through four generations, his family had been the beneficiaries of the distinterested ideals of the French Revolution, and now, though the background of his arrest remained a mystery to him, Dreyfus knew that he had been the victim of some "plot," some "ambush," engineered by traitors who had violated those sacred tenets. He both feared and reviled human selfishness, which he saw as antithetical to the French spirit, and he turned to another of his "immortal" companions, the sixteenth-century writer La Rochefoucauld, to illustrate the point: "Eternal virtues are lost under the pressures of self-interest," Dreyfus wrote, "much like rivers disappearing into the sea."[32]

Not every author, French or foreign, met his rigorous standards. He dismissed Cesare Lombroso's radical theories on "genius and madness" (undoubtedly finding them void of any moral dimension), and he called the Italian criminologist's work "naive" and "puerile." In contrast, he admired Hippolyte Taine's scholarship, though he considered the historian's famous formula—*race, milieu, moment*—too sterile and restrictive. In his view it should be a quartet, not a trio, and it should, Dreyfus noted, embrace "the individual." Jules Michelet and Fustel de Coulanges had always been more to his liking; the first because he probed not only "facts, but the soul of the people who lived those facts"; and the second because he "disengaged himself from all bias and captured in his work "the highest quality of all: impartiality." That theme, along with the quest of the individual to rise above his troubles and master his fate, ran throughout Dreyfus's notebooks, and he searched for those messages in every literary genre. "I have just reread Ibsen's most recent play, *John Gabriel Borkman,*" he wrote in 1898, "and I have hardly understood the moral value of the work." He considered Ibsen a "great intellect" whose power had been weakened by an abandonment of moral and social issues; the playright's early depictions of individuals striving for "good" through "noble efforts" had given way to limited concerns with the arid problems of psychology and the loss of will. And for Dreyfus, Ibsen's characters had, as a result, lost their soul.

Likewise reading excerpts from Maurice Barrès' novel *Les Deracinés,* Dreyfus called it a "very original" story by a "very bizarre" man. He did not know that his allies in Paris had asked the influential Barrès to join their cause, to no avail, but he captured the writer's few strengths and many weaknesses when he described his "novel of national energy" as an odd mix of "lofty ideas," "petty vilifications" (*dénigrements*), and "narrow social views."[33]

Tolstoy and Dostoyevsky, on the other hand, were among the few undisputed heroes in Dreyfus's literary circle. Locked in cosmic struggles against "interior passions" and despair, their characters fought "to disengage themselves from the exterior oppression society weighed upon them." With none of Ibsen's middle-class neurasthenia or Barrès's strident chauvinism, the Russian novelists presented "magnificently human" dramas that, Dreyfus intimated, best reflected the nature of his own condition. If Montaigne's essays provided the model for his catalog of human limitations and human potential—for his journal entries on vanity, faith, education, and more—the players who inhabited the pages of Tolstoy and Dostoyevsky, whether triumphant or doomed, brought those eternal truths to life.[34]

But above them all was Shakespeare. Not the playwright dissected by Taine in his study of English literature (and stripped, according to Dreyfus, of all grandeur), but the humorous, passionate, sympathetic Shakespeare the prisoner "never understood better than during this tragic epoch," and who, like Dreyfus, may also have turned to Montaigne as a source of inspiration. Distracted and enlightened by what he called "those most delicious comedies," *The Merry Wives of Windsor* and *As You Like It,* Dreyfus found in *King Lear, Othello, Hamlet, Macbeth,* and *Richard III* poetic variations on the themes he had been attempting to describe in letters to his wife and family. "Money is nothing, honor is all," he had insisted, but Iago put it better, and in one letter Dreyfus reminded Lucie of those lines from the third act of *Othello* they had read together in French translation: "Who steals my purse steals trash; 'tis something, nothing; / 'Twas mine, 'tis his, and has been slave to thousands; / But he that filches from me my good name / Robs me of that which not enriches him / And makes me poor indeed." Commenting on the quote, Dreyfus told his wife: "Yes, the wretch who stole my honor has made me poor indeed."[35]

Shakespeare provided a fresh vocabulary to relieve the monotony of the prisoner's prose, but more important, he introduced into the "silence and solitude" of Devil's Island other intrigues, other stories of foul play, false hearts, and human courage, which helped Dreyfus feel less alone. The prisoner copied "that admirable line Shakespeare put on the lips of old Polonius" ("This above all: to thine own self be true, / And it must follow, as the night the day, / Thou canst not then be false to any man"), and he learned from *Lear*—that most "heart-rending play" that exposes all the "steps of human misery"—the "bitter irony of Shakespeare's moral philosophy." For Dreyfus *Lear* was the definitive treatise on the "weakness of the human condition," a confirmation of how "the wicked rarely profit from their crimes, while the good are rarely rewarded for their Virtue."[36] All of Shakespeare's works became a compendium of allegories of all of Dreyfus's dilemmas; ignorant of the details concerning his own tragedy, his own arrest and conviction, and desperate to make sense of his ordeal, Dreyfus cast the unknown characters of his case in Shakepearean roles—the good, evil, and indifferent players who populated the back rooms of the General Staff and plotted against France in foreign embassies. And in one sense at least, he saw himself as that ill-starred army officer who had refused to partake in Macbeth's "dishonorable enterprise." Devil's Island might destroy Dreyfus in the end, but he promised his wife that the truth would out, "because like Banquo's ghost I will emerge from the tomb in order to shout 'courage, courage' to you, to everyone, with all my soul . . . and in order to remind the Fatherland that it too has a sacred duty to fulfill."[37]

Since the days in Santé prison, his first classroom of one, Dreyfus had been studying English to break the "terrible monotony of waiting," and in the hope that he could better grasp the essence of Shakespeare's plays. Functionaries who examined the prisoner's every word considered those English exercises "insignificant," but when rumors spread in Paris that his dictionaries and primers might be code books linking him to foreign co-conspirators, officials ordered a full-scale *fouillé*, a surprise ransacking of all his possessions. Late at night, with guns and truncheons drawn, guards stormed into his cabin, cut through his mattress, searched his laundry, tore off the heels of his shoes, and ordered him to strip. Reports filed later described Dreyfus laughing at the absurdity of it all, and when guards found no code book on his person or on his shelf, they allowed him to keep his "insignificant" English books.[38]

Returning to his studies, he copied English exercises for three and four hours a day. He had a gift for languages (fluent in German, he also had a good knowledge of Italian and Latin), and by his third year in exile, thanks to the popular "Ollendorf method," he was reading *Othello* in

English and transcribing his favorite Iago speech ("He that filches from me my good name . . ."), though not without errors. In a whisper, he recited long lists of idiomatic expressions, and even the phrases he chose to memorize suggested that government officials were wrong again: For the prisoner, English provided more than an "insignificant" distraction. "What does that prove?" "Can you disprove it?" began one list of fifty English phrases in his journal in 1898. "I can prove that it is not true." Even his grammar exercises interlaced allusions to his case, and he learned other phrases that signaled his resolve: "At least I have my duty," he wrote in English; and he translated the sentence "Nothing will last forever." One day, he hoped, after his acquittal or after his death, his wife would receive his journal, and next to the French dedication, "Pour ma chère Lucie," he copied, in English, the lines Hamlet, "his hot love on the wing," had sent Ophelia: "Doubt thou, the stars are fire; / Doubt that the sun doth move; / Doubt truth to be a liar; / But never doubt I love!"[39]

A disciplined officer who, in society, had always seemed rigid and sober, without lightness and without passion, Dreyfus appeared more complicated in his prison journals and in his reveries more like the French essayist he admired: "I am by nature not melancholy," Montaigne confessed, "but dreamy."[40] Despite all the apologias for reason and rationalism that ran throughout his diaries, Dreyfus still used Shakespeare's characters to express his longings, and Shakespeare's poetry to confirm his faith in dreams.

For Lucie, every letter from her husband represented a document of survival, tangible proof that he had not succumbed to the ravages of disease or to his own depression. "I am strong, my dear Alfred," she wrote in March 1896, "so have no fear; when you feel most discouraged, most sad, tell me all your thoughts and describe all the bitterness in your heart."[41] He did, and as his wife examined those letters like a physician feeling a patient's pulse, she sensed, in the slightest shift of style or language, her husband's changing moods. And she fashioned her responses accordingly, with a call for patience ("think only of the goal, the end," she wrote, "and wait with patience and courage") or, in desperate times, with an appeal to his sense of duty as a husband and father.[42] Lucie had always been a strong, articulate partner in a marriage of equals; she had always spoken her mind, from the early days of courtship when her fiancé's ambition made him appear distracted and "insensitive," to the months after Pierre's birth when Alfred's eye had wandered to other women. Now Lucie brought those qualities of self-assurance and, when necessary, sternness to the letters she sent to Devil's Island, and she urged her husband to redirect his focus from the present. She conjured up memories of "splendid walks and beautiful evenings when we would discuss the future so enthusiastically. . . . We made projects and we built on dreams, and soon the day will come when we shall do it all again."[43] The hundreds of letters they exchanged, and the hundreds more they drafted and never sent, were transcripts of an ongoing conversation, a desultory dialogue between a husband and wife who were surrounded—by guards or by family and friends—but who both felt the isolation of imprisonment. "My thoughts never leave you for an instant," Alfred wrote, "neither during the day nor at night, and if I listened only to my heart, I would write you every moment of every hour."[44]

For more than four years, the couple clung to their photographic images. In Santé prison, while awaiting his deportation, Alfred had asked Lucie to send a picture he would place between those of Pierre and Jeanne. "Your three images before my eyes will be the companions of my sad solitude." Lucie admitted that she was embarrassed to pose for a photographer, but she agreed to do anything that would give her husband "a few minutes of contentment." It gave him much more than that, and as he sat at his small table before the wood-framed "portraits" of his wife and children, he recorded in his journal that "I must live for them." In those "numerous moments when profound disgust with human iniquities and lies" swept over him, when he "faltered," he would look at the photographs of Lucie, Pierre, and Jeanne and "whisper, very low, the three names . . . which are my talisman, my strength." And in her bedroom in her parents' apartment, Lucie did the same: "Sometimes I have such a need to confide in you," she wrote late one evening, "to tell you my hopes, to lean on you . . . that I embrace your photograph. I hold it with all my strength, I speak to it and I want to bring it to life. I search in that image for your look, so kind, so gentle, and then I am seized by sadness and I return to painful reality."[45]

Protecting her children from that same reality and keeping up the charade of the captain's "army voyage" (the children were shielded from news by "a miracle of tact and discretion," said one family friend), Lucie showed Pierre old photographs of his father on horseback, and the boy, in turn, shared memories with his sister Jeanne, who "listened with respect."[46] Two years old the day her father sailed for Devil's Island, Jeanne grew quickly, and her features, according to Lucie, changed more radically than Pierre's. Both children had curly brown hair, but Jeanne's blue eyes, fair skin, rosy cheeks, and hearty appearance contrasted with her brother's dark eyes, olive complexion, and thin, delicate frame. Jeanne looked like "one of those big, blond Alsatian babies raised in the open air of the countryside," Lucie told her husband. "No one would guess that she's Parisian." She resembled members of the Dreyfus family (Lucie saw a "striking likeness" in Alfred's baby picture), while Pierre had the more angular features of the Hadamards. In personality, however, the boy shared many of his father's traits ("frank, honest, and a bit demanding"), while his sister was robust, playful, headstrong with her wet nurse, and something of a "show-off." Jeanne learned to charm "those people who would spoil her."[47]

One of her most attentive relatives, Aunt Henriette, had offered to take the children to Carpentras. She wanted them to escape the polluted air of Paris—as young Alfred had done on trips to Provence to visit his "second mother"—and she wanted to give her sister-in-law more freedom to work with Mathieu and Maître Demange. But Lucie could not bear to be separated from both her husband and her children ("It's selfish, isn't it?" she commented to Alfred), and she did not want to interrupt the tutorials she conducted every morning, with long-distance collaboration from Devil's Island.[48]

"Given their extreme youth," she wrote Alfred, "I cannot yet reason with them; I can only make them obey and inculcate in them a sense of absolute openness and candor." She noted that a "soft, tender touch" worked best with Jeanne, while the highly sensitive Pierre needed a "firm and tenacious hand." The couple had discussed that "hand" before, and it was an issue on which they had disagreed. But Alfred now added a new dimension to his philosophy of child rearing; in concert with Montaigne, whose comments on education the prisoner read with care, and with Rousseau, whose *La Nouvelle Héloïse* stressed the "admirable idea of the complete renewal of the moral being," Dreyfus offered his advice. "There is a sort of servility about rigor and constraint," Montaigne had argued, "and I hold that what cannot be done by reason, and by wisdom and tact, is never done by force. I was brought up that way." Also brought up that way, Dreyfus reminded his wife that he was not a "partisan of corporal punishment. . . . A soul guided by fear," he said, "will always be weak." "You've told me about Pierre's sensitivity (*sensibilité*) and about your ways of combating it," he went on. "If it is in fact sentimentality (*sensiblerie*), then yes, a thousand times yes. But if it is sensitivity, compassion, then no; you must leave it be and add to it a dimension of energy, of will." Pierre should never be allowed to become "self-involved" (s'absorber dans son soi); "through regular physical exercise, reading and commenting on works which teach . . . qualities of bravery, energy, and endurance, he should be taught, above all, the noble cult of honor." A child must be sent out into the world "not only with the intellectual baggage taught in school, that alone does not suffice," Dreyfus agreed, "but with a moral sentiment so strong, so unbreakable, that death alone can master it."[49]

If Dreyfus agreed with Montaigne on philosophies of child rearing, he parted company with the essayist on attitudes toward women. A mother's role should be confined to early "nurturing," Montaigne believed, and he described the "ordinary weakness of the sex," that "disordered appetite and sick taste that they have at the time of their pregnancies" and that "they have in their soul at all times." Mothers must give way to fathers in the realm of education, Montaigne believed, because women lack the "force of reason" so crucial to the formation of strong and virtuous youngsters.[50] Everything in Dreyfus's life exposed the absurdity of that view; raised by his sisters, and especially by the sensitive but strong-willed Henriette, he was now sustained by a wife who educated his children and fought for his release. If anything, Dreyfus tended to idealize women as "invincible" symbols of energy and honor. In one letter, he had told his wife that "women are decidedly superior [to men]. . . . I love you deeply, you know that," but he added that Lucie's courage and devotion had increased his admiration: "Today I . . . venerate you. You are a saint, a noble woman. I am proud of you and I will try to be worthy of you." In his journal he observed that "if women created neither the Illiad nor the Odyssey, if they invented no railroads, they do something much greater than all of that: on their knees are formed the most excellent things in the world—an honest man and an honest woman."[51]

In 1895, when Pierre turned four, his mother supplemented his studies with colorful images d'Epinal, popular mass-produced lithographs that, as one contemporary put it, used pictures to "engrave ideas in the soul." Strips of vignettes, sixteen or twenty to a page, depicted scenes of kings and queens, soldiers and emperors, flora and fauna, and they told stories of chivalry and romance, astrology and apocalypse. Those simple pictorial narratives would introduce Pierre to the principal figures of French history, to the grandeur and heroism of Joan of Arc, the Sun King, and Napoleon, and the captions beneath each image would help him learn to read and write.[52]

And so, too, would religious studies. Lucie informed her husband that it was "time to speak to Pierre about God," and, without divulging the details of his father's troubles, to "teach him a little prayer in which he will ardently ask justice for his poor Papa."[53] Lucie did not list the sources she used to instruct her son, but it is likely that she turned to her rabbi, Zadoc Kahn, for guidance, and that she referred to two popular children's books of the epoch—Salomon Ulmann's *Catéchisme, ou éléments d'instruction réligieuse et morale à l'usage des jeunes israélites,* and Michel Mayer's *Tsidkath Elohim: instructions morales et religieuses.* Both books focused on the respect French Jews owed their fatherland, and the messages of both would have pleased Lucie's husband.[54] "Alongside intellectual instruction," he observed in his journal, "should be placed moral education, without which the first is meaningless. Moreover, Philosophy and Religion have a common ground, which is to say the essential and eternal truths of all morality. . . . And it is this . . . which one must teach independent of any Creed." Had Dreyfus been able to join his wife for Pierre's morning tutorials, he would have stressed the universal dimension of an "ethical education," and concentrated not on the rites of Judaism, but on its elements of justice. If he was not "a believer," he proclaimed himself "hostile to no faith [and] a sympathetic witness to those who believe; [I am] aware of the moral beauty of faith, but always on the condition that it does not become an abstract formula, a narrow idea." Dreyfus remained confident that, with the help of his wife and brother, his children would learn the "elevated ideas" of truth and justice.[55]

In the spring of 1895, Pierre composed his first letter, guided by his mother's hand: "Mon petit Papa," it began, "Pierrot kisses you lots and misses you, just as Mama does. You must return. I always say my prayer in bed. I ask God that Papa and Mama stay healthy and that Pierrot be well-behaved." Lucie added a postscript from Jeanne, who sent kisses and asked for candy, and a few months later another letter dictated by her daughter requested a "pretty pink doll . . . Jeanne remembers her father very well, you know, but I want you to come home soon." By November 1897, the third anniversary of Dreyfus's imprisonment, his son was writing on his own. "Are you pleased with your . . . Pierrot?" the boy asked, and he promised to put "beautiful flowers" in his father's room when he returned. At six Pierre was "reading constantly," and at seven he showed a particular aptitude for arithmetic and geography, two subjects at which his father had also excelled.[56]

Across the years on Devil's Island, Dreyfus responded to his children's every letter ("When Papa returns from his voyage," he wrote Pierre, "you will fetch him at the train station, with Mama, with little Jeanne, with everyone."). He could deal with memories of his son and daughter, and he could write about their future. ("We will take refuge in our mutual affection. . . . We will live again in our children to whom we shall devote the rest of our days.") But when he lingered on the sadness of not watching his children grow up and on the fear that he might never see them again, he felt his "strength falter," his "throat tighten," his "heart break." Often finding it too difficult to write them directly, he asked Lucie to act as the intermediary for his private messages of affection, just as she had become the spokesperson for his public protests of innocence.[57]

In the early spring of 1897, Dreyfus sensed a change in the tone and content of his wife's letters. "The first two years were particularly atrocious," Lucie admitted, "we were in the blackest night; but now if you only knew how our burden is less heavy, if you only knew the mountains we have moved, and how the route still to travel has become so much shorter." In fact the prisoner could never know the details—censors made certain of that—but he could, as Lucie hoped, read between the lines and find that his family had reached a new phase in the struggle for his release. In midsummer, immediately upon learning of Scheurer-Kestner's interest in the case, Lucie tried to send a letter which, without mentioning the senator's name, announced that a high political dignitary had joined their cause. But André Lebon, the minister responsible for the draconian "double-buckle" of the previous year, refused to forward the letter to Devil's Island, and Lucie was forced back on sweeping statements of hope. "Decidedly," she wrote in August, "we are entering a better period. . . . This time we have definitely found our way . . . I am distressed that I cannot explain more," she continued, "but there are things so momentous, so important, that one dare not express them on a piece of paper." A short time later, still trying to raise her husband's spirits, she sent another letter of encouragement: "If I could only speak to you openly, to tell you all the vicissitudes of this horrible drama and the different steps we have taken to arrive at the truth. You would be soothed and your hope would be immense." Not all of Lucie's letters made it past government censors (weeks went by with no news at all), but Dreyfus received her optimistic note of September 1: "We see the clear path opening out before us. I can only press upon you to have confidence, not to grieve any more, and to be very certain that we shall attain our end."[58]

All those entreaties remained an enigma to the prisoner, however, and at the same time that his family promised an end to his "calvary," colonial authorities promised to harden the physical conditions of his exile. Minister Lebon increased the number of guards (from five to ten and finally to thirteen) and in the summer of 1897 ordered the construction of a more secure prison complex on the highest slope between the quai and the former leper camp. For weeks guards kept Dreyfus locked in his stone hut while sixty convicts sent from Cayenne and the Ile Royale built a slightly larger wooden cabin with an adjoining guards' barracks. Another fence, enclosing an exercise area, would prevent Dreyfus from seeing anything but the open sky above, and, most important, he would be in clear view of the island's new thirty-foot observation tower. Equipped with a Hotchkiss cannon powerful enough to destroy vessels penetrating the three-mile limit, the tower was manned day and night. After three years, Devil's Island had finally been transformed into the "fortified place" required by the Parliament's original "law of exception," and when the prisoner moved to his new quarters, with its bleak yard and iron-mesh windows, which allowed little ventilation, he was convinced that "They will bury me here."[59]

The new permanence of his imprisonment contrasted with his family's insistence that liberation was near. "Our hopes are stronger than ever," Mathieu wrote in the spring of 1898, and Lucie spoke of the "final phase" of the case ("We are in full possession of the truth . . . my hand trembles, I am so happy"). But when those dramatic statements were not followed by concrete news, Dreyfus succumbed to the consequences of rising expectations and fell into the deepest depressions he had known since his arrival on Devil's Island. In a letter to the president of the republic, he described his "physical and moral strength diminishing every day. . . . I ask only one thing of life: to be able to go quietly to my grave knowing that my children's name has been cleansed of this horrible stain." For months, Lucie received only brief notes, and their depressing tone and staccato style testified to her husband's mental state. At one point, when he intimated that he no longer had the will to write, she begged him not to deprive her of "the only thing which I cherish in life." During the same period, more allusions to suicide appeared in his notebooks, and when a prison official visited his cabin in the fall of 1898, Dreyfus, "desperate and overexcited," announced that he had decided "to be finished with life . . . I have had enough." He wept when the official told him to think of his wife and children, and that night sentries expected a suicide attempt.[60]

But Dreyfus held to the promises contained in his family's letters, and three weeks later, at 12:30 P.M. on November 16, 1898, he received a telegram from the governor of French Guiana. On behalf of the colonial minister, the governor announced that "the Criminal Branch of the Supreme Court of Appeal has declared acceptable in form the application for a revision of your judgment and has ordered that you be notified of this decision and be invited to set forth your defense."[61]

After forty-eight months in prison and forty-three months in exile, it would now be "a matter of weeks," Dreyfus recorded in his journal, "before I set out to be with my wife, my dear children, my family." Immediately, he began to dream of the "long days of rest which would follow so many long days of trial." As a fitting complement to the news of his pending liberation, guards opened the gates of his wooden fence and allowed him to walk along a path marked off by a low stone wall. For the first time in two years he could see the ocean. Gathering up rough, brown volcanic stones, he built a sturdy bench—a chair of rock that later prisoners on Devil's Island would call "Dreyfus's bench"—and he sat in silence, looking out to the horizon or making notes in his journal. Facing east, he recalled how, in the early days of his exile, he had watched for steamships carrying letters from home, and how he had turned "toward France," as he put it, "in the hope that one day my Fatherland would call me back."[62]

In December 1898 Dreyfus received further confirmation that his case had been reopened, and he read the public prosecutor's summary of events "with profound astonishment." For the first time, he learned of his brother's accusations against a certain Commandant Esterhazy— the "miserable wretch" who, until now, never had a name—and he tried to make sense of the prosecutor's allusions to forgeries, confessions, an officer's suicide, and other "incidents, the meaning of which escaped me." He hoped that additional reports would clarify his questions, but they never came. And through yet another season of intense heat and tropical disease, he waited for word of his departure. Like the strange quiet that followed the torrential storms of French Guiana, however, the news of his pending release gave way to another long period of silence. Officials held back Lucie's letters entirely or delayed them for weeks, and Commandant Deniel, the chief administrator of the Iles du Salut, exploited his final time of control over Dreyfus by inflicting the small tortures that satisfied that bureaucrat's sadism; "misplacing" written requests for provisions, he also refused to answer Dreyfus's questions about the postponement of his departure.[63]

Deniel and all he represented put the prisoner in mind of a flock of hens that populated the field behind his cabin. He had been observing their Hobbesian universe and recording their curious ways. "They are numerous," he wrote, "and, moving along next to each other, they march back and forth through the rare herbs and lichen with a dignified air and an indifferent look. Some of them, however, are the object of strange treatment. . . . Each time they approach their feed, they receive from their companions a quick, hard peck. Ordinarily so sweet and placid, those irresponsible hens seem to obey some kind of perverse instinct. But is there not a similar law which triggers the evil passions of men and reduces them to tormenting each other in a manner that is sometimes cunning and sometimes bold [?]. . . They open the wound which another suffers."[64] After nearly five years of solitary confinement on "a rock tossed in the sea," Dreyfus understood the parable. He had learned much about his companions' capacity for evil; he had learned it from du Paty and André Lebon in Paris, and from Commandant Deniel and many of his guards on Devil's Island. Victim of their "iniquities," he had also become, in his notebooks and letters, a chronicler of their "perverse instincts." To a great extent, the experience had intensified the misanthropy he had always felt as a proud man awkward among men.

But if he had failed in company, as Montaigne had put it in another context, he had triumphed in solitude. He had survived, and he owed that survival to the family who had never wavered in its affection or its confidence; to the "immortal companions" whose stories of human weaknesses and human courage gave him strength; and to France. He had been telling Lucie "from the first day" that "above all human passions, above all human error, there is the Fatherland . . . and it will be my supreme judge." And his last letter from Devil's Island confirmed that his faith had not diminished. He still expressed profound respect for the army to which he had devoted his life, and he still capitalized the key word: "My confidence in the Justice of my country is the same," he wrote on June 1, 1899. "It will be the honor of this noble France, the honor of our dear army, to finally arrive at a solution to this horrific judicial error, and to its reparation."[65]

Four days later, the chief guard entered his cabin and handed him a document: "The court rescinds and annuls the judgement proclaimed on 22 December 1894 against Alfred Dreyfus," it read, "and remands the accused to a court-martial. . . . As a result of this decision, Captain Dreyfus ceases to be subjected to the regime of deportation and becomes a simple prisoner; he is restored to his rank and allowed to again wear his uniform." The report ended with news that "the cruiser *Sfax* leaves today [from Martinique] with orders to take the prisoner from Devil's Island and bring him back to France."[66]

Dreyfus's reaction was one of "immense, unutterable joy. . . . I was finally escaping the torture rack (*chevalet de torture*) to which I had been nailed for five years. . . . Happiness replaced the terror of inexpressible anguish, and the day of justice had finally dawned for me." He sent a telegram to Lucie: "Courage, my spirit is with you, with the children, and with everyone. . . . Waiting with immense joy the moment of happiness, of holding you in my arms."[67] He spent his final hours with two men who, along with the prison doctor Debrieu, had shown him some compassion: the mayor of Cayenne and the guard who had brought him news of his release. When asked for souvenirs of his time on Devil's Island, Dreyfus, embarrassed that he had nothing of value, gave the men the thermometers he had used to gauge his fevers and told them to choose among his books and clothes—his "rags."[68]

He kept Shakespeare's plays and Montaigne's essays, however, the most sacred texts of his exile. They had spoken to him when no one else would, and when death seemed certain. And just as he could use their language to articulate the measure of his despair, he could use it to celebrate his emancipation. He could call on Montaigne, who, in his turn, had called on Horace: "Brave men who had endured with me / Worse things, now banish cares with revelry; / Tomorrow we shall sail the mighty sea."[69]

CHAPTER XIII

The Tutorial

AT 7:00 A.M. on the morning of June 9, 1899, Dreyfus began the first leg of the Atlantic crossing that would take him from the midwinter of equatorial Guiana to the midsummer of metropolitan France in three weeks' time. Boarding the "cockleshell" launch he had watched navigate the channels of the Iles du Salut, he left the "cursed island" where he had "suffered for so long" and headed toward the war ship *Sfax* anchored in the deep waters of the Ile Royale bay. Armed with leather briefcases and official documents of transfer, police functionaries—not military guards—accompanied the captain on that first voyage out. Having come to Devil's Island as a *condamné*, a convict, he would depart as a *prévenu*, a prisoner still officially accused of a crime but confident that exoneration awaited him on the French mainland. And he would not wear military garb until he arrived home; even if his old uniform had not been lost or destroyed by prison officials, it would no longer have fitted his emaciated frame, and, stripped of gold braid, epaulets, and brass buttons, it would only have conjured up memories of his public degradation. Instead, he wore a misshapen white hat and a simple dark suit procured by the mayor of Cayenne, one of his few allies in exile. Forced to wait beside the *Sfax* for two hours, their launch buffeted "by the great waves of the Atlantic," Dreyfus and his entourage became seasick; but by late morning the prisoner had been installed in a special cabin with a barred porthole and an armed guard. A few hours later "the spectre of

Devil's Island disappeared behind the bluish mist of the Guiana sea coast."[1]

With his keen interest in military history, Dreyfus must have known that he sailed toward his personal victory on a ship of conquest. Named for the Tunisian port taken by the French in 1881, the *Sfax* was a monument to the colonial adventure that, after Islamic revolts had been suppressed in the holy city of Kairouan, consolidated French control. Imperial troops gave way to imperial entrepeneurs out to exploit the rich olive groves of Sfax, but on his voyage home Dreyfus would have thought only of the great Tunisian campaigns he had studied as a young officer eager to lead his own "soldiers into battle." Exile had put an end to those dreams, but now, by the grace of General de Boisdeffre, the army chief of staff whom Dreyfus believed to be "the author of the revision of his case," the captain, certain that he would soon be promoted, could return to a military command in France. On June 18, when the *Sfax* took on coal at Cape Verde off the West African coast, Dreyfus asked for authorization to send de Boisdeffre a telegram of "remerciements."[2]

Twelve days later, "after five years of martyrdom," Dreyfus saw the coastline of France. "I returned in search of justice," he wrote; "the horrible nightmare had come to an end."[3] But the silence that reigned on Devil's Island continued aboard the *Sfax,* and officials never told the prisoner the details of his landing. On the night of June 30, in the midst of a torrential rainstorm, he was ordered to jump from the cruiser's side ladder into a small dinghy; he injured both legs, and, as the boat headed toward the coast, he was seized by fever and chills. Finally, at 2:15 on the morning of July 1, he set foot on French soil. But instead of the festive homecoming he had imagined, he arrived on a dark, deserted beach and found only the "anxious faces" of policemen and mounted troops. Hurried into an open carriage and taken to a special train, he traveled in the company of thirteen policemen and four detectives—all silent. Nearly three hours later the train stopped between stations, and the prisoner was transferred to yet another carriage. Only at dawn, as the procession galloped through the streets of a large provincial city and toward a military prison, did Dreyfus learn that he had disembarked near Quiberon, on the southern coast of Brittany, and that he had been taken to Rennes, the place, he thought, where his innocence would be proclaimed and his "nightmare" would end.[4]

If his return had been "sinister," a letter awaiting him in prison promised hope. "I want you to receive a word from me when you arrive," Lucie had written, "and I want you to know that I am close by, in the same city, with my heart beating with joy and emotion." Through a local Protestant pastor, the Dreyfuses had rented the house of a widow, Madame Godard, for the duration of the captain's retrial; shaded by trees and surrounded by a high wall with an iron gate, the house was situated on the same narrow street as the military prison. Lucie's note, written while her husband was en route to France, described him traveling closer to Rennes, "each hour, each minute," until the couple "found themselves in each other's arms." Lucie had acknowledged in letters to Devil's Island that they would be "much older," in many ways, when they finally met again, and that their "characters would be markedly different." But she had also admitted that they now shared "something more than the immense fondness" they had always known; they shared "an indefinable feeling created by the community of our sufferings."[5]

Less than three hours after arriving in Rennes, Dreyfus learned that his wife would meet him in a few minutes in an adjoining room. Suddenly, uncontrollably, he cried ("tears I had not known for such a long time"). In pain from the injuries sustained a few hours before, and physically and mentally exhausted, he was unprepared for the one reunion he had dreamed about through every day and night in exile. "Taking hold" of himself as he had done prior to meetings with Lucie at Cherche-Midi, Santé, and Saint-Martin de Ré, he fought back his tears and joined his wife for the first time since the early spring of 1895.

"There are no words with enough intensity," he later wrote, "to describe the emotions we felt upon seeing each other again. There was everything, joy and grief." But mostly there was silence as the couple, in the presence of a guard, tried to "read on each other's face the traces of pain." For Lucie, who wanted to speak "of a thousand things, of the children, of the family, of those who love us both," there was the fear that her husband could not support the weight of it all so soon; and for the prisoner, whose monologues on Devil's Island had been "whispered" to Lucie's photograph, to his "talisman," there was the awkwardness of dialogue and the paralysis of embarrassment over his physical condition. On the morning of his arrest nearly five years before, he must have been at the peak of physical health; more wiry than muscular, he had profited from holidays on the Normandy coast and morning gallops through the Bois de Boulogne. He had strength and stamina. But now the ill-fitting suit from Cayenne seemed to hang on his body, as if from a mannequin, and though he was only thirty-nine, his thinning hair had gone almost completely white. Since his early bouts with malaria, he suffered sudden flushes of fever that turned his sallow face bright red and exaggerated his prominent cheekbones. His voice was strangled and almost inaudible; not only had years of silence damaged his larynx and vocal chords, but malnutrition and disease had inflamed his gums and rotted his teeth. He could utter only raspy, hissing sounds. To maintain a facade of dignity during his reunion with Lucie—to appear the "Stoic" she had always admired—he forced himself to remain as quiet and motionless as possible.[6]

"The meeting between the prisoner and his wife was . . . less sensational than one would have supposed," went a police report from Rennes, "and the couple seems to have been particularly reserved."[7] But Lucie knew the meaning of that "reserve," and though she rushed to telegraph allies in Paris with the good news of the captain's arrival ("Saw my husband this morning," she informed Maître Demange, "found him well morally and physically"), she confessed her concerns in private to family and close friends. After arranging for daily one-hour visits to the military prison, she began another letter-writing campaign designed to raise her husband's spirits and prepare him for the trial scheduled to begin on August 7. "My poor friend," she wrote on the day of their first meeting, "you have not spoken for nearly five years, and you have suffered every martyrdom." But "you are still valiant and courageous," she added, and "worthy of all the admiration, all the numerous testimonials I have received for you from France and the entire world."[8]

That letter provided the first indication to Dreyfus that his case had moved beyond the realm of military tribunals and judicial bureaucracy. It had attracted national and international *témoignages;* great "men of character" had taken part in the "terrible drama," as well as men so "base and vile that they deserve only pity." Dreyfus dared not "interrogate" his wife on the details of his case—he feared that it would be too "painful"; and, for her part, Lucie preferred to let Mathieu and the lawyers recount the events that had transpired since her husband's deportation. She did alert Alfred, however, that preparation for his retrial would be more complicated than he had imagined: "These will be days of work for you," she wrote, "as you inform yourself of all that has happened."[9]

Like the Devil's Island cabin that served as Dreyfus's classroom of one, the visitors' area next to his Rennes cell became a study hall in which he learned, as he put it, "my own history."[10] Maître Demange arrived on July 3, and, with another lawyer retained by the family—the young, energetic, and eloquent Fernand Labori—began a month-long private tutorial with Dreyfus as their pupil. Outlining the chronology of his case, they introduced the players and the legal and political intrigues that had turned the court-martial into an "affair." "I listened breathlessly," Dreyfus wrote, and heard "the long series of misdeeds, villanies and crimes against my innocence." The lawyers brought stacks of documents and trial records that the prisoner annotated late into the night; then, rising between 4 and 5 A.M., he read more dossiers and "passed from one surprise to another" as he attempted to assimilate the "mass of formidable facts." Studying the history of the past four and a half years, he learned that among all the allies noted for "heroic acts" and "supreme efforts" on his behalf, Mathieu had been the most "admirable." With "courage, wisdom and will," he had been the agent of his brother's liberation—"the most noble example," Alfred wrote, "of fraternal devotion."[11]

Mathieu found his brother "visibly" exhausted, but "calm . . . and extraordinarily confident," and he joined Demange and Labori to tell the prisoner of the other allies recruited to his cause. Dreyfus finally heard the names of the early supporters who had helped the family "amidst all the adversity"[12]—from Dr. Gibert, Bernard Lazare, and Joseph Reinach to Gabriel Monod and the other experts who had examined the *bordereau*. He also heard how that coterie attracted the wrath of Drumont, Rochefort, and others who defined every action by Mathieu and his supporters as the work of a clandestine Jewish syndicate: "The Jew has not changed," Drumont had announced. "He is still the same cursed creature that we have had to slaughter and hang . . . because he has always organized Dreyfus's affairs."[13] The more Mathieu drew confederates to the cause, the more he seemed to fulfill the anti-Semites' prophecies. Newspaper editorials, political speeches, and popular caricatures depicted the Dreyfuses and their comrades as "hook-nosed" co-conspirators; and though the family expended enormous sums to counter that propaganda with images and publications proclaiming the captain's innocence, the anti-Semitic press was too sophisticated in its organization and simple in its message, and belief in the captain's guilt was too widespread.[14]

Dreyfus learned that a key moment had come in the summer of 1897 when Mathieu and Scheurer-Kestner, working independently, identified the author of the *bordereau*. Obsessed on Devil's Island by the nameless "wretch" responsible for his "torture," Dreyfus now had a focus for his anger. The traitor, described by Mathieu as "a great bird of prey," proved even more wretched than the prisoner had imagined.[15]

Marie Charles Ferdinand Walsin-Esterhazy, though born in Paris, was the descendant, albeit illegitimate, of a Hungarian family of diplomats, soldiers, and princes with huge landholdings in the Holy Roman Empire. Some accounts traced the family's origins to the Crusades, while others, more legendary, reached back to Attila the Hun. By the late 1860s, however, when Esterhazy joined the French army, he had only the family name and none of its wealth. Through influential relatives, he received a series of promotions and served with the Foreign Legion, the Army of the Loire in the 1870 war, and the Army Information Service in Paris. During the Tunisian campaign of 1881–82, he was stationed in the port town of Sfax (one of many ironies Dreyfus would encounter while studying his case). A pathological gambler, Esterhazy became a pathological swindler as he attempted to settle his mounting debts. He married a countess from Lorraine for her money, but his profligate life with courtesans and gamblers kept him on the brink of bankruptcy. And he sold favors of every kind to any buyer. In the early 1890s, while contributing scurrilous articles to *La Libre Parole*, he simultaneously presented himself as a defender of the Jews—for a price. Having served as a second to the Jewish Captain Crémieu-Foa in that officer's duels with anti-Semitic journalists, Esterhazy believed that he had the credentials to solicit funds from Jewish notables; he coaxed money out of Baron Edmond de Rothschild and received the support of Grand Rabbi Zadoc Kahn. But his duplicity soon became obvious. Compared by those who knew him to a character out of Balzac, the commandant had much in common with the blackmailer Vautrin in *Le Père Goriot*, whose first name was "Cheat" and who believed only in "events" and never in "principles." But Esterhazy also went the way of Balzac's villains and paid for his sins. By 1894, "the fallen, exhausted adventurer," suffering tuberculosis, insomnia, and the claustrophobia of a provincial infantry post in Rouen, "was gasping for breath amid the thousand intrigues he had woven around himself."[16]

Espionage was not a surprising choice for a man with only one allegiance—himself—and for an officer who had always hated the high command. "The French have not understood me," he would write. "So much the worse for them."[17] But Dreyfus had been in prison for nearly two years before Esterhazy's contacts with the German military attaché in Paris were discovered by the officer who had replaced Colonel Sandherr as chief of army intelligence.

For the Dreyfus family, Lieutenant Colonel Georges Picquart was an unlikely hero. An Alsatian Catholic, he made no secret of his anti-Semitism. He had been indifferent to the student Alfred Dreyfus whom he had taught at the Ecole de Guerre; but from the October morning in 1894 when he met the captain at the War Ministry and brought him to du Paty—and from the day of the degradation, when he described the "traitor" calculating the weight of his gold buttons and braid like a Jewish moneylender—Picquart had been convinced of the prisoner's guilt. He read Dreyfus's Devil's Island mail and ordered all letters examined for invisible ink—for the secret "occult" messages Jews were believed to exchange so naturally. But if Picquart shared his comrades' bigotry, he did not share their refusal to believe, in the face of new evidence, that anyone but the Jew Dreyfus could have written the bordereau. Picquart was an anti-Semite, but he was not a fool or a coward.[18]

Early in 1896 he discovered a letter-telegram on thin blue paper (a petit bleu) addressed by the German attaché, Schwarzkoppen, to Esterhazy—proof that the French commandant was in league with the enemy. During a secret investigation Picquart noted that Esterhazy's handwriting was identical to that on the "Dreyfus" bordereau; and he learned the details of the commandant's sordid biography. "He's an adventurer, a blackguard, a cheat, a swindler," reported one police agent, "a pimp, a pillar of the brothel and the bawdy house, and he sweats vice, wickedness, and treason."[19] Though familiar with the hyperbole of the French secret police, Picquart realized that, in this case, the profile fitted the man. But when he informed superiors of his belief that the wrong officer had been exiled, he was ordered to divorce the Esterhazy question from the Dreyfus case. "What does it matter," said the deputy chief of staff, "if that Jew stays on Devil's Island?" Picquart paid the price for his revelations; he was transferred out of the Intelligence Service and sent to a post in North Africa.[20]

Convinced that officers had conspired to protect Esterhazy, Picquart prepared a statement to be opened in the event of his death. He also shared his findings with his friend and lawyer, Louis Leblois, another Alsatian. But months passed before Mathieu learned that Leblois had passed the news to his Alsatian compatriot Scheurer-Kestner. Only in the summer of 1897 did the senator identify Esterhazy as the traitor; and only in the late fall of that year, when rumors spread in the Parisian press, did Mathieu decide to condemn Esterhazy, formally and publicly. Late on the night of November 15, with legal advice from Demange and Leblois, Mathieu composed a "letter of denunciation" addressed to the minister of war, General Jean-Baptiste Billot: "The sole basis of the accusation brought in 1894 against my unfortunate brother," he announced, "is an unsigned, undated letter establishing that confidential military documents were delivered to an agent of a foreign military power. I have the honor of informing you that the author of that document is M. le Comte Walsin-Esterhazy. . . . I cannot doubt, Mister Minister," Mathieu concluded, "that knowing the author of the treason for which my brother was convicted you will act swiftly that justice be done." Leblois, who mailed the letter, knew the significance of that challenge to the high command; for the rest of his life he would hear the sound of the letter falling into the mailbox on the Place de la Bourse.[21]

A few days later the minister of war met Mathieu Dreyfus's challenge and opened an inquiry in the Chamber of Deputies. Now publicly accused but privately confident that no panel of politicians or military judges would dare convict him, Esterhazy fought back with characteristic insolence. He invited an official investigation, and, as the few newspapers in France that supported Dreyfus's cause published more profiles of the decadent commandant, Esterhazy demanded that his name be cleared and his honor restored. "As an innocent man," he wrote the army's general investigator (with that investigator's prior knowledge and editorial assistance), "the torture I have been enduring for fifteen days is superhuman. . . . As an officer accused of high treason, I have a right to . . . the highest form of military justice. . . . I await to be called before the Court-Martial of Paris." Like a beleaguered prime minister sensing the opportune moment to call an election, Esterhazy knew that his constituency of protectors might defect if he waited any longer. The army cooperated and scheduled the commandant's trial for January 10, 1898.[22]

Interviewed by officers in charge of the pretrial inquiries, Mathieu realized that Esterhazy's day in court would be a travesty of justice. "Not for a single instant" did investigating officers "search for the truth," Mathieu observed; their goal was to portray Esterhazy as "an innocent victim of a plot concocted by Picquart . . . with the complicity of the Dreyfus family." The army's handwriting experts determined that Esterhazy had not written the *bordereau;* instead, the "real traitor" had attempted to implicate the commandant by mimicking his handwriting. But the majority of "experts" testifying for the prosecution in 1894—all but the "madman" Bertillon who had his own convoluted thesis—had declared that the memorandum was in Dreyfus's hand, and that no "mimicking" was involved. Noting this "absolute contradiction," this "new fact," Mathieu and Lucie Dreyfus filed civil suits against Esterhazy in order to intervene in his court-martial and focus on the *bordereau*. Demange would act for Mathieu, and Fernand Labori would represent Lucie. Interrogating Esterhazy, they would expose his treason.[23]

But minutes after the court-martial convened, in the same Cherche-Midi annex where Dreyfus had been convicted three years before, the judges rejected the civil suits—a decision that confirmed the court's belief that ex-Captain Dreyfus had been "lawfully convicted."[24] With no opportunity to link Esterhazy to the *bordereau*, Mathieu knew that an acquittal was certain.

In the prison at Rennes Alfred Dreyfus read the court-martial transcript and learned from his lawyers the unrecorded incidents—the litany of Esterhazy's lies, the bogus findings of the army's graphologists, the confrontations between Picquart and officers who attempted to smear his character, and, most painful for Alfred, the account of his brother on the witness stand. On cue from the general in charge, officers and others in attendance had cut across Mathieu's testimony with howls and laughter, and when Mathieu proclaimed, "I defend my brother in every respect," he was shouted down. Nor did the epithets end with the verdict of not guilty—a unanimous decision, reached after only two days of testimony and three minutes of deliberation; Mathieu had to push his way through a "menacing crowd" of more than one thousand gathered on the rue du Cherche-Midi. Subjected to his own "parade of degradation," he was besieged by the same shouts his brother had heard in the courtyard of the Ecole Militaire—"Long live the Army!" "Long live France!" "Death to the Jews!" On Devil's Island the prisoner could only imagine his family's plight; but now, reading the history of his case, he knew the meaning of Lucie's reference to their "community of . . . suffering."[25]

However, Esterhazy's trial signaled a new era of combat. The family's affair became "the Dreyfus affair" when the case moved "outside the legal process" to be judged in the arena of public opinion.[26] New and powerful supporters rallied to the ideas of social justice that the prisoner of Devil's Island came to symbolize. The Alsatian Jew from a privileged background who had devoted his life to the French army had attracted

little sympathy and even less support; but the victim of corrupt institutions infested by clericalism and royalism was someone who made the
battle worthwhile. Elevated into a Manichean conflict between justice
and fanaticism, between the individual and the state, the case began to
attract an extended cast of players. While on Devil's Island, Dreyfus had
drawn the historic parallels between his plight and that of others con-
signed to some kind of outer darkness—from Banquo's ghost to Napoleon shipped off to another island exile—but how he learned that he had
not been alone in drawing those comparisons. During his absence, and
particularly after 1898, he had emerged in the public imagination as a
"modern Judas" for some and as a "modern Calas" for others.

Joseph Reinach, an early ally, had been accused of looking for "a
new Calas" to support. One politician, alluding to the involvement of
Reinach's cousin in the Panama scandal, suggested that he forget
Dreyfus and try to rehabilitate his own family instead. That remark in
the Chamber, which led to a duel in the Bois de Boulogne, was not
the only reference to Dreyfus and the eighteenth-century Protestant
Calas. "I will give you only one piece of advice," Reinach had told
Scheurer-Kestner, "reread the Calas Affair . . . the same arguments
[are there], only the names have changed." The Protestant Scheurer-
Kestner received similar advice from coreligionists who stressed the
similiarities between the two victims of religious intolerance.[27] As a
result of "judicial errors" perpetrated in secret, both men had been
tortured for crimes they did not commit; both had fought to save the
honor of their family name; and both had been defended by "great
men of character."

Jean Calas had worked as a textile merchant in the southwestern
city of Toulouse. His region, like the Dreyfuses' native Alsace, had
been a center of religious violence for seven centuries—from the public
executions of Albigensian heretics to the persecutions that followed the
revocation of the Edict of Nantes—persecutions that led to the mass
exodus of Huguenots. Calas's family had remained in Toulouse, however, and for Protestants who stayed in French territory, any overt
profession of faith brought renewed threats of torture and execution.
On the night of October 13, 1761, when Calas's son was found hanged
in the family's shop, a rumor spread that the young man had wanted to
convert to Catholicism and that his father, in league with a "secret
synod" of Protestant elders, had conspired to kill him. Marc-Antoine
Calas was, in fact, a suicide, but anti-Protestantism kept the rumor of
murder alive. Marc-Antoine's father refused to announce the suicide—

as a "self-slayer," the boy's naked body would be dragged through the streets and "cast forth unburied." Jean Calas protested his innocence but said nothing more, and his silence was defined as an admission of guilt. On March 9, 1762, only one of Calas's thirteen judges voted for acquittal. Taken to the church of Saint-Etienne, with a rope around his neck, he was forced to kneel in repentance. At the Place St. Georges the executioner shattered Calas's arms and legs and pounded his kidneys with a square iron bar. Strapped to a wooden wheel, he lived for two hours while the prosecutor and a priest worked to extract a confession: "You poor wretch, look at the burning stake that will turn your body to ashes; tell the truth." Calas's only response was to look away; finally he was strangled "to end his suffering." His remains were burned and scattered to the wind. On the way to his death, Calas had cried out to the crowd lining the streets, "I am innocent!"

The Protestant's case did not become an "affair" until the philosophe Voltaire intervened and fought for the family's "rehabilitation." In the year of Calas's arrest, Voltaire had little interest in the plight of that obscure cloth merchant and little patience for his religious faith; but when he learned the details of the case, he realized that Calas and his family had been victimized by the forces of fanaticism. Befriending the "admirable" Madame Calas, Voltaire published essays that mobilized support in France and throughout Europe. "Shout everywhere, I beg you, for the Calas," he wrote, "and against fanaticism, for it's l'infâme that has caused their misery." In 1763 an appeals court allowed the family's request for a hearing, and two years later, after "monstrous judicial errors" had been exposed, Louis XV officially rehabilitated the Calas family. They received compensation from the state, and Voltaire received the pleasure of having again "cut the serpent's head of fanaticism."[28]

More than a century later, Emile Zola, whose novels had examined social injustice in France for more than two decades, interrupted his "tranquil existence" and redirected his talents to the world of nonfiction. He became the Voltaire to Dreyfus's Calas. Like the philosophe, Zola was at the crest of his career, admired by radical critics of the status quo (again like Voltaire) and vilified by reactionary defenders of French morality. Depending on the point of view, he was an eloquent champion of social change or a dangerous "pornographer." Voltaire had entered the Calas case at a moment when religious intolerance had reemerged to intensify the conflict between enlightenment and obscurantism; and Zola joined the Dreyfus cause at similar moment, when resurgent anti-

Semitism, rampant in the military but not limited to its ranks, challenged the legacies of the Revolution. Rallying to Dreyfus, Zola could not help but mobilize—and divide—public opinion.[29]

He had learned the details of the case from Scheurer-Kestner in the late fall of 1897. Amid all the striking parallels with the Calas affair, however, Zola, unlike Voltaire, could still save the victim. His first articles, published in *Le Figaro* prior to Esterhazy's court-martial, examined Scheurer-Kestner's role as a defender of Dreyfus and analyzed the judicial errors committed since the captain's arrest. *"C'est scientifique,"* Zola said of the case, and he dissected its history with the blend of strict logic and high passion that distinguished his naturalistic novels. In a pamphlet entitled *Letter to Youth,* he encouraged students of the Latin Quarter, the future intellectual leaders of France, to rally to the Dreyfus cause; and in a *Letter to France,* he appealed to the "commonsensical people" of the nation who might succumb to the "ferocity of fear, the shadows of intolerance."[30] The first phase of Zola's involvement attracted only limited commentary. One letter, from an admirer, captured the broad significance of the prisoner's torment; the writer, Abraham Dreyfus, though unrelated to the captain, announced that he suffered, as a French Jew, "the same anguish so admirably expressed" by Zola. "Now I count on you alone," that Dreyfus admitted in December 1897. "But what will you do? What can you do?"[31]

He could do a great deal. On the morning of January 13, 1898, in response to the Esterhazy verdict, Zola published an open letter to the president of the republic, Félix Faure. He had worked on the document for two days, and had brought a draft to the offices of *L'Aurore* newspaper on the night of January 12. Supported by the paper's director, Ernest Vaughan, and encouraged by one of its leading columnists, the Radical and recent convert to the Dreyfus cause, Georges Clemenceau, Zola searched for the most powerful headline for his manifesto. Clemenceau suggested the key words of its final paragraphs, and on the following morning three hundred thousand copies of *L'Aurore* were hawked on the streets of Paris and provincial cities with the bold headline J'ACCUSE.[32]

Zola knew the art of diplomacy and opened his letter with an almost obsequious acknowledgment of President Faure's patriotism and honor. But he quickly turned to the "stain" that had defiled the republic, and to a description of the nights he had spent "haunted by the specter of the innocent man dying [on Devil's Island] amidst the most frightening tortures, and all for a crime he did not commit." Without divulging the source of his information, Zola informed the public of the discoveries made by Picquart and by Mathieu Dreyfus's private agents; the captain had been framed and Esterhazy had been aided and abetted by members of the General Staff—and most especially by the "criminal" Commandant du Paty de Clam, a "diabolical" man with an "extraordinary and demented imagination." Du Paty, Zola announced, "is the entire Dreyfus Affair." But the commandant did not work alone, and Zola, aware that he was exposing himself to prosecution for libel, listed the rogues gallery of co-conspirators. He accused General Mercier, minister of war at the time of the captain's arrest, "of having become an accomplice out of weakness of intellect at least"; he accused General Billot, one of Mercier's successors, "of having had in his hands certain proof of Dreyfus's innocence and of having suppressed it"; he accused Chief of Staff de Boisdeffre and Deputy Chief Charles-Arthur Gonse "of being complicitous in the same crime, one undoubtedly out of clerical passion, the other perhaps out of that esprit de corps which makes the offices of war a holy, unassailable ark"; and he accused all the handwriting experts, army investigators, and military judges who had condemned Dreyfus and aquitted Esterhazy of lies, fraud, and juridical crimes. Zola did not know those men, he confessed, and he held against them neither "malice nor hatred." For him, they were "nothing more than entities . . . of social wickedness"; and Zola's letter to the president of the republic was nothing less than "a revolutionary means of hastening the explosion of truth and justice."[33]

But *J'Accuse* hastened a counterattack from the army and an explosion of popular violence. The minister of war brought suit against Zola and *L'Aurore* for libel. Maître Labori, Zola's lawyer, marshaled all his gifts of theatricality and attempted to turn the process into a second Dreyfus trial, but the judges suppressed evidence and convicted Zola without addressing the substance of his manifesto. Sentenced to one year in prison and three thousand francs' fine, he lodged a series of unsuccessful appeals through the spring and early summer of 1898 and then fled to London to avoid imprisonment—much as Voltaire had fled to Switzerland when the French state lost patience with his radicalism. Zola's name was stricken from the rolls of the Legion of Honor, and his chances of election to the Académie Française—always an unlikely proposition for such a controversial social critic—were doomed.

The military high command dealt with Picquart as well. Dismissed from the army in February, he was subsequently imprisoned for exposing military secrets. Key Dreyfus supporters in the two houses of

Parliament were also dispatched. Scheurer-Kestner was stripped of his
Senate vice presidency, and his constituents mailed in their opinions of
the Alsatian Dreyfusard and his comrades: "You are all a band of German Jews," went one note, "traitors to your so-called Fatherland. Riff-
raff, sluts, pigs . . . and you [Scheurer-Kestner] are a filthy ass." Joseph
Reinach, recipient of similar diatribes, lost a parliamentary election and,
with it, his authority to interrogate government officials in the Chamber
of Deputies.[34] For more than three years Mathieu Dreyfus had worked
to organize a group of powerful and articulate allies, and in the final days
of 1897, he had sensed that victory was at hand. But by the early
summer of the following year many of the family's most effective supporters had been imprisoned, forced into exile, or chased from their
positions of influence.

Since the captain's degradation, the anger provoked by his "treason" had been largely confined to epithets hurled by journalists and
courtroom demonstrators. Allusions to Dreyfus in a parliamentary debate, a café-concert, or a theater performance would, on occasion,
incite troublemakers—as they did in December 1897 when references
to injustice and intrigue in a play featuring Sarah Bernhardt prompted
jeers, hisses, and anti-Dreyfus slogans. With the Esterhazy trial and
Zola's response, however, words gave way to actions. The captain's
allies and enemies took up pistols and swords in a series of duels, and
through January and February riots erupted in Paris, provincial cities,
and, bloodiest of all, Algeria. Citizens out to defend the army—or to
exploit the climate of anarchy for personal ends—turned on Jews, and
on their homes and businesses. In league with Protestants and Masons,
they had humiliated France and its military.

During Zola's trial crowds surrounded the defendant and two of his
friends, Joseph Reinach and Yves Guyot, director of Le Siècle, shouting,
"Into the water with the traitors!" Students and unspecified "demonstrators" in Versailles, Reims, Lille, Nantes, Caen, and other cities and
towns attacked Jewish shops and synagogues while shouting "Kikes to
the water!" "Death to the Jews!" "Down with Dreyfus!" "Down with
Zola!" "Long live the army!" Four thousand people demonstrated in
Bordeaux following the publication of J'Accuse, and police turned back at
least a thousand who marched on the synagogue. A poster in Saint-
Etienne implored patriots to "Imitate your brothers of Paris, Lyons,
Marseille, Nantes, Toulouse," and to "join with them in demonstrating
against the underhand attacks being made on the Nation." In one brief
period, nine towns reported significant injuries, and arrests were made

in twenty localities, with more than two hundred demonstrators apprehended in Paris alone. In Algeria—with its huge population of fifty thousand Jews, distrusted by French settlers and detested by Arabs—crowds were fired up by Max Régis, a comrade of Drumont's and a future mayor of Algiers. Vigilantes assaulted Jews, sacked their bazaars, and pillaged their homes.[35]

Since the captain's court-martial, the Dreyfuses, Hadamards, Valabrègues, and other members of the family had been receiving hate mail and death threats—including one unsigned note, Mathieu later learned, from Esterhazy. They had assumed names and changed lodgings on numerous occasions, either to avoid detection or because they were chased out by nervous landlords; but undercover police had still followed them and du Paty's agents had harassed them. Across the border from Mulhouse in the territory of Belfort, where Jacques Dreyfus had lived as a French citizen since 1897, periodic threats had forced Jacques' family to find shelter in the home of a neighbor. After January 1898 those troubles intensified, and family members throughout France kept shutters bolted and doors locked "in order to avoid," as one friend put it, "surprises in the night." In Bar-le-Duc, where Dreyfus's sister Louise Cahn lived, demonstrators ransacked Jewish shops and chased the local rabbi from town; far to the south, in the Valabrègues' Carpentras, posters sent from the offices of *La Libre Parole* announced a gathering at the Place du Théatre: "All patriots disgusted with the intrigues of Jewish vermin will gather today," the poster proclaimed, "in order to form a procession to the town hall with shouts of 'Down with the traitors! Down with Dreyfus! Down with the Jews! Long live the Army! Long live the Republic!' " Another poster was affixed to the Valabrègue house ("Down with the Syndicate of Treason!"), and in the garden behind, where young Alfred Dreyfus had relaxed from the rigors of boarding school, hooligans mounted a train bridge that crossed nearby and hurled rocks at Dreyfus's children. Anticipating troubles in Paris, Lucie had thought that Pierre and Jeanne would be safe in Carpentras.[36]

Mathieu and Suzanne had kept Emile and Magui in Héricourt with Suzanne's family, but during one visit to Paris the youngsters had to be protected from drunken soldiers. As a gang chanted "Down with Dreyfus!" outside the apartment window, the family's Alsatian cook threw open the shutters and brandished a knife. Those hostile pilgrimages to the Dreyfus and Hadamard homes continued through the early months of 1898, and Lucie's letters to her husband in exile, though never mentioning the details, suggested their constant presence: "So quickly

I am pulled from my dreams [of you]," she wrote in March, "by a commotion outside, and I return abruptly to reality." She considered sending Pierre and Jeanne to friends in Switzerland, but she could not tolerate the separation of her entire family.[37]

Concerned that his presence would incite demonstrators, Mathieu had not attended Zola's trial. On other occasions, however, when meeting allies or following the leads of his agents, he confronted "sinister crowds," and he might have heard the popular song which described him as the "traitor's" brother, that "crafty Yid."[38] Exhausted and overworked, Mathieu found a "sympathetic atmosphere" in the offices of *L'Aurore,* a place where he could be among friends. But on more than one night crowds gathered outside on the rue Montmartre. Having to return to his family, Mathieu "took his life in his hands," as Georges Clemenceau warned him; surrounded by comrades, he escaped the "howling mob" by running toward the labyrinthine corridors of Les Halles market. The quiet diplomacy and detective work of the early years had given way to meetings held in barricaded offices, to street fights, and to families under siege.[39]

One isolated act of violence in 1898, however, a suicide, signaled the most important turning point of the affair. Its announcement filled Dreyfusards with hope. Missing from Zola's list of du Paty's accomplices was an officer who had testified for the prosecution during the 1894 court-martial. Commandant Henry, later head of the Intelligence Bureau, had announced that the Etat-Major had proof of Dreyfus's treachery, but that matters of national security prevented disclosure. Henry, it turned out, had guarded more than his share of secrets under his kepi, not only during the court-martial but through the following three and a half years. Along with du Paty and the army's archivist Gribelin, he had protected Esterhazy (at one point, Henry sent his comrades in false beards and dark glasses to calm the anxious Esterhazy in a Paris park); and to ensure that the Dreyfus dossier contained sufficient "proof" of guilt, Henry set up his own cottage industry of forged "evidence." A letter manufactured in 1896—from the Italian military attaché in Paris to his German counterpart—mentioned "relations with this Jew . . . Dreyfus." But on reviewing the file a few months later, an officer noticed that the letter was an obvious forgery; Dreyfus's name had been added to an insignificant diplomatic note. On August 31 Minister of War Godefroy Cavaignac confronted Henry and he confessed, suggesting that an overzealous commitment to preserving the honor of the military had prompted his patriotic mistakes. Sent to the prison fortress of Mont-Valérin, Henry was found twenty-four hours later with his jugular cut, a shaving razor in his hand, and the stench of rum permeating his cell.[40]

Army Chief of Staff de Boisdeffre resigned that day, Cavaignac a few days later, and within two weeks du Paty had been retired on half pay. In late September, Esterhazy, who had fled to London, confessed that he had written the *bordereau*, not as a spy, but under orders from Colonel Sandherr, head of the Statistical Section. It was a convenient scenario (Sandherr had died of natural causes in 1897), but given Esterhazy's diversionary tactics and demented mind, it was never clear whether he had done the deed as part of a plot of counterespionage or as a ploy to entrap a Jewish *stagiaire*. The evidence suggested, however, that Esterhazy peddled secrets in an attempt to extricate himself from debts incurred in a life of debauchery.

"We leapt with joy," said one of the Mathieu's confederates upon hearing of Henry's suicide and the events that followed; it was as if a "bolt of lightning had stricken [our] adversaries."[41] On September 3 Lucie Dreyfus petitioned for appeal of her husband's court-martial, citing the "new evidence" needed for an official review; and allies regrouped to prepare for the captain's retrial. The League of the Rights of Man, founded by a former minister of justice, Ludovic Trarieux, and a coterie of prominent socialists and Radicals, stepped up the fight against militarism and clericalism. The Dreyfusard cause gained one of its most eloquent converts when the socialist Jean Jaurès, long indifferent to the Jewish captain and his "bourgeois civil war," realized that Dreyfus had been victimized by the forces of reaction. Through this same period, Marguérite Durand and the journalist known as Séverine launched a feminist newspaper, *La Fronde*, to support not only women's issues but the Dreyfusard cause. The paper applauded Lucie's energy and devotion and compared contemporary society, as one *La Fronde* columnist put it, to "a patient struck by cancer." Other "Women's Leagues" commended the prisoner's wife as a tireless social revolutionary. Lucie Dreyfus had never accepted that role, but she had won the admiration of women in France and throughout Europe and America for her "dignified" and "courageous" conduct during the years of her husband's exile.[42]

Hopes ran high in the early days of 1899, but barriers still blocked the prisoner's return. The Chamber of Deputies insisted that the case be reviewed by a special combined meeting of appeals courts; and the army did not relent on the question of Picquart, now the most celebrated figure of the affair. He remained in Cherche-Midi prison, still accused of violating espionage laws. And if Dreyfusard leagues intensified their campaigns, anti-Dreyfusard groups responded in kind—from Déroulède's old Ligue des Patriotes to the new Ligue de la Patrie Française and the revivified Ligue Antisémitique de France, founded by Drumont and taken over by the no-less-virulent Jules Guérin. Those organizations worked with *La Libre Parole* to solicit contributions for Colonel Henry's widow. Joseph Reinach had publicly announced that Henry had been Esterhazy's accomplice in treason, and Madame Henry had promptly sued Reinach. In an appeal entitled "Le Monument Henry," Drumont encouraged patriots to rehabilitate the colonel ("the victim of duty," the "martyr for patriotism") and help pay for the widow's legal expenses. From every corner of France came a total of 131,000 francs raised by 25,000 contributors, many of whom sent editorial remarks: a waiter in Paris, "insulted in a gross and cowardly manner by a filthy Yid by the name of Dreyfus," offered his few francs; and a small officer's mess, "unfortunate to have to eat with a Jew," pooled their contribution. The wife of one soldier wanted "to defend the honor of the army against Reinach, Ltd."; a sewage worker confessed that he "would not dare to touch Reinach for fear of being polluted"; and a group of officers stationed "on the frontier" waited with impatience "for the order to try their new cannon and new explosives on the 100,000 Jews who poison the country" (they inflated France's Jewish population by 20,000, but Drumont had inflated it by more than 400,000). Candidates for the Ecole Polytechnique protested "the Jewish invasion," as did "patriotic feminists" (*La Fronde* did not speak for all Frenchwomen), and others signed on with references to "Jewish vermin," "the Jewish plague," and the "Synagogue lice." One enthusiast supported the subscription "For God, the Nation and the extermination of the Jews."[43]

The riots had subsided and a minority of Frenchmen and -women had accepted the possibility of a new Dreyfus trial. But the opponents of "revision" remained strong, and the deeply held prejudices that gave force to their campaign had not been shaken by Henry's suicide, Esterhazy's flight, or du Paty's humiliation. Yesterday's heroes had defected, but their many admirers fought back, now frightened of losing the advantage they had held so long.

If popular reactions placed the Dreyfus family and their allies in danger, official intransigence provided the most solid obstruction to the captain's retrial, and with every delay Mathieu thought of his brother on Devil's Island: "Do we have the right to wait?" he asked himself. "Will he be able to support his martyrdom for so long? This was my great preoccupation, my eternal obsession." Not every government official held firm against the prisoner. In the summer of 1898, before Henry's suicide, Prime Minister Henri Brisson, known for his Radical anticlericalism and Freemasonry, thwarted an army plan to arrest Mathieu Dreyfus and fourteen of his confederates; and in the early fall, reeling from the resignations of three ministers of war, Brisson—improbably—sent an aide to query Mathieu on an appropriate candidate for the post. "I was just a bit surprised," went Mathieu's understatement. "Given my situation over the years, I had not expected to be asked to find a Minister of War." With the advice of Joseph Reinach and Dr. Gibert, however, he suggested one candidate, who declined the post, but another proponent of revision, General Charles Chanoine, accepted.[44]

The most immovable object, however, was at the top. In the four years since Dr. Gibert had appealed to the president of the republic, Félix Faure's political ambitions and acute sense of caution in all but his intimate life had made him unwilling to challenge the military and risk the consequences of greater social unrest. Given the fickle nature of Third Republic politics (not one president had served an entire term), Faure had enjoyed a long tenure in office; and his accomplishments in foreign affairs, especially in relations with France's powerful ally and economic partner, Russia, had been considerable. It seemed that he would remain in the Elysée Palace frustrating Mathieu Dreyfus's efforts for years. But that final barrier fell on the evening of February 16, 1899, when the president died of a cerebral hemorrhage. That the sturdy Félix Faure would no longer lead the republic was a shock; that he had died in a back bedroom of the presidential suite in the arms of his mistress surprised no one. Only the "adversaries of revision" regretted the demise of the "mediocre" Félix Faure. "They had lost in him," Mathieu observed with understandable bitterness and some exaggeration, "their most devoted servant."[45]

Meanwhile the proponents of revision gained a new president with none of Faure's panache but with a reputation for managing scandals, and with a sense of moderation that had been lacking in nearly every government leader over the past four years. Emile Loubet had barely returned to Paris from Versailles, the site of his presidential election by the Chamber and Senate on February 18, before crowds began shouting "Resign!" "Down with Dreyfus!" and, as a reminder, "Panama!" Having served briefly as prime minister in 1892, Loubet had tried to limit the damage of the Panama scandal, and, like most politicians, had been accused of graft by the nationalist press. Loubet may have been "clumsy" in his policies but he was not corrupt in his person, and now, as a veteran inured to hostile crowds, he had the right credentials to extricate the republic from a battle that had gone on too long.[46]

He would need that expertise. On the day of Félix Faure's funeral—a public extravaganza not unlike the one arranged for a different sort of romantic, Victor Hugo, fifteen years before—Loubet's enemies, who were Dreyfus's enemies, attempted to stage a coup d'état. "To the Elysée!" shouted the crowd gathered at the Place de la Nation, and while Maurice Barrès and other anti-Dreyfusards looked on, Paul Déroulède, the aging but still enthusiastic founder of the Ligue des Patriotes, led his paramilitary troops. The coup failed when the army, refusing to storm the presidential palace, arrested Déroulède; but the incident, however much a comic opera in retrospect, confirmed that tensions surrounding the Dreyfus affair had not diminished with the death of Félix Faure. The case had become a national and international scandal, with its "train of prejudices, hatreds and passions," as Mathieu described it, and the spirit of politics, not the letter of the law, would determine its outcome. A few years earlier, Prime Minister Loubet, wanting to "steal a march" on the German emperor, who had been planning a world's fair for Berlin, called for a Universal Exhibition to be held in Paris in 1900. Arrangements for that manifestation of French grandeur were under way, and it promised to be even more spectacular than the 1889 exhibition. Loubet would not have an embarrassing scandal, marked by Parisian coups and parliamentary chaos, ruin his best-laid plans. The Dreyfus affair needed a political solution, and quickly. Later, the poet and journalist Charles Péguy—Catholic, socialist, and Dreyfusard—would look back on that critical moment and summarize it best: "Everything begins in faith," Péguy observed of the affair, and "ends in politics."[47]

But for the prisoner in exile and for his family waiting in Paris an honorable end was all that mattered, and in the spring of 1899 it drew near. The United Courts of Appeal, after another interminable period of political maneuvers and legal inquiries, set aside the 1894 condemnation and referred the case to a new court-martial in the provincial city of Rennes. Dreyfus would have his wish. He would be judged by his peers.

His family gathered with supporters in the Hadamards' apartment on the rue Châteaudun, much as they had done on the night of the first verdict four and a half years before. But now the circle of friends had expanded to include men and women who had either been convinced of Dreyfus's guilt in 1894 or indifferent to his plight. They felt the camaraderie of veterans who had survived a war. Telegrams, letters, cards, and flowers were "heaped in a colossal pile" on David Hadamard's billiard table, and, "with transports of joy," as one friend described it, the crowd celebrated the news of "revision" and the "triumph which seemed definitive."[48]

Only Lucie Dreyfus was absent. She had taken Pierre and Jeanne to relatives in Châtou, the place of her birth on the outskirts of Paris. Stricken by pleurisy earlier in the year, she had not completely recovered; but no less important, too many promises had been broken since that day when du Paty had come to her home and had asked her to have faith in the army. She would attend no celebration until her husband's innocence had been proclaimed; and, as she had done throughout the affair, she would continue to wear black.[49]

At some point during his prison tutorial in Rennes, Alfred Dreyfus received a letter from Emile Zola. "If I have not been one of the first to send you all my sympathy, all my affection, upon your return to France," Zola wrote, "it is because I feared that my letter would be incomprehensible. I wanted to wait until your admirable brother had seen you and told you of our long combat." Applauding the prisoner's "courage" and "faith," Zola turned to the battle still ahead; having learned the character of his Calas, he said all the things that Dreyfus needed to hear. "At this hour, your great task is to bring us . . . justice," he wrote the captain, "to finally calm our poor and noble country." It is "the honor of the army that you will save, this army that you have loved so much and in which you have placed all your idealism. Don't listen to those who blaspheme, who would like to exalt [the military] through lies and injustice. It is we who are its true defenders." The day was approaching, Zola promised the prisoner, when the army would be not only a manifestation of "power" but of "justice."[50]

With the help of that letter and hundreds of others, Mathieu instructed his brother on the essential features of his "affair." Though still concerned about Alfred's physical ability to withstand another trial, Mathieu had been impressed by his lucidity, by the quickness with which he had comprehended his situation. In preparation for his defense, Dreyfus filled more than a hundred pages with columns of anticipated questions and accusations, and in his quest for objectivity, he listed his responses in the third person singular.[51] The Polytechnicien had survived Devil's Island only to become, it seemed, even more methodical in his deliberations, in his cultivation of what he called that "principal, dominant role played by reason." Now, having listened "breathlessly" to the litany of "villainies" which had occurred during his absence, he would try to meet Zola's challenge and live up to the promise he had repeated as a private incantation in exile. While others engaged in "bitter and acrimonious attacks," he would "look higher . . . above all human passions, above all human error."[52]

CHAPTER XIV

Extenuating Circumstances

CAPITAL OF THE DUCHY of Brittany under the Old Regime and *chef-lieu* of the Ille-et-Vilaine department under the new, Rennes had gained a reputation as a major university and administrative center of western France. Nantes, due south, and Brest, on the Atlantic Coast, enjoyed more thriving economies; and historic Quimper and St.-Malo, with their Breton customs, dialects, and monuments, attracted more travel writers and, increasingly in that age of train excursions to folkloric sites, more tourists. At the confluence of the Ille and Vilaine rivers, the ancient city center of Rennes drew its share of sightseers, but it was a "lusterless" provincial town compared to its Breton neighbors, dominated by institutional architecture and surrounded by a ring of new *quartiers* with standardized stone houses and hotels, cafés, and shops designed "in the latest style . . . on the Parisian model." Proud of its modern comforts, Rennes could easily accommodate the mass of journalists, officers, and functionaries expected for Dreyfus's retrial. More important, the forces of order, mobilized to prevent riots on the Parisian model, appreciated the distant location 360 kilometers west of the capital, and the fact that only eleven Jewish families resided in the city. Anti-Dreyfus demonstrations had been reported the previous year, but Rennes had quickly returned to its "habitual" calm, and now, with a good number of town dwellers on holiday by the sea or in the countryside, many avenues were deserted and businesses closed. A sweltering

The Mulhouse apartment in which Léon, Rachel, Mathieu, and Alfred Dreyfus were born. With the prosperity of their cotton mill, the family would move to more luxurious quarters in the early 1860s. *Inset:* Raphael Dreyfus and his wife Jeannette Libmann Dreyfus, about 1875, after their thirtieth wedding anniversary and the family's option for French citizenship. (*Private collection*)

Right: Mathieu Dreyfus, painted by Madame du Pury in the 1870s, after completing his studies in Paris. (*Private collection*)

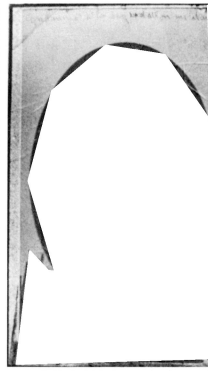

Right: Alfred Dreyfus at the Ecole Polytechnique, 1878–79. Later, the school album photograph was mutilated and the word "traitor" scribbled in the right margin. (*Archives de l'Ecole Polytechnique*)

Below: Lucie Eugénie Hadamard, about the year of her marriage to Alfred Dreyf (*Private collection*)

Left: Dreyfus, the young officer, about out of uniform and sporting the ornate watch fob, and silk tie of a provincial o private income. (*Private collection*)

Le Petit Journal

Le Petit Journal
Le Supplément illustré
CHAQUE JOUR 5 CENTIMES
CHAQUE SEMAINE 5 CENTIMES

SUPPLÉMENT ILLUSTRÉ
Huit pages : CINQ centimes

ABONNEMENTS

PARIS
DÉPARTEMENTS
ÉTRANGER

Sixième année   DIMANCHE 13 JANVIER 1895   Numero 217

LE TRAITRE
Dégradation d'Alfred Dreyfus

Dreyfus's degradation at the Ecole Militaire
included the stripping off of his braid and buttons
and the breaking of his sword—the ultimate symbol of dishonor.
(*Courtesy of Christian and Nicolas Bailly and the Jewish Museum, New York*)

A police identification photograph taken
immediately after Dreyfus's degradation.
He is thirty-five years old.
(*Courtesy of Mr. and Mrs. Herbert D. Schimmel
and the Jewish Museum, New York*)

Joseph Reinach,
republican politician,
Dreyfusard, and prem
historian of the affair.
(*Private collection*)

Dreyfus's Devil's Island notebook. Under a quote from Shakespeare ("he that filches from me my good name...") are the bizarre designs the prisoner repeated on hundreds of notebook pages. (*Bibliothèque Nationale, Paris*)

Edouard Drumont and the anti-Semitic newspaper he founded.
"The Traitor Convicted," reads the headline after the verdict at Rennes.
"Down with the Jews!" (*Roger-Viollet, Paris*)

Family reunion, Carpentras, 1899. *Standing, left to right:* Henriette Valabrègue, Lucie and Alfred Dreyfus, Alice and Léon Dreyfus. Young Pierre is in front of his father, and Jeanne is on Joseph Valabrègue's knee. (*Private collection*)

The former Devil's Island prisoner (*right*) has put on weight— and a smile. He stands in the garden at Carpentras with Mathieu, the brother who saved him. (*Private collection*)

Pierre and Jeanne Dreyfus capture the festive mood at the Valabrègue estate following their father's return from his "long army voyage." (*Private collection*)

Dreyfus leaving his "rehabilitation" ceremony at the É[cole] Militaire on July 21, 1906, with the Legion of Honor pin[ned] to his uniform. (*Private collect*[ion])

The Dreyfuses' Swiss retreat, about 1908. *Left to right:* Hélène Naville, Pierre and Lucie Dreyfus, Philippe Naville, Mme. Naville's brother, Eugène Naville, and Alfred and Jeanne Dreyfus. (*Private collection*)

Jacques Dreyfus and his American wife
Louise Wimpheimer, about 1910. Their
youngest son, René, would fly the real
thing over the Western Front during the
1914–18 war. (*Private collection*)

ounded by applauding admirers, Dreyfus,
urer on the "History of Syndicalism in
ice," walks through a popular quarter of
s, about 1908. (*Roger-Viollet, Paris*)

Marguerite ("Magui"),
daughter of Mathieu and Suzanne Dreyfus,
shortly before her marriage to Adolphe Reinach.
(*Private collection*)

A union of Dreyfusards, Belfort, 1912. The father of the bride is seated with Madame Joseph Reinach to his right, and Jeanne Dreyfus (*far right*) sits in front of her smiling father, Alfred. In the background, to the left of the bearded and hatted Théodore Reinach, is Lucie Dreyfus. (*Private collection*)

His affair over, his innocence proclaimed, Dreyfus relaxes on Lake Geneva. (*Private collect.*

"I tell you that to stand for peace today is to wage the most heroic of battles." Jean Jaurès, former Dreyfusard, under the Socialist flag, May 1913. Jaurès split with the Reinachs and Dreyfuses over the question of war. (*Roger-Viollet, Paris*)

tenant Adolphe Simon Reinach before leaving he front in August 1914. (*Private collection*)

Mathieu and Suzanne Dreyfus's only son, Emile, during the "Great War." (*Private collection*)

Alfred and Lucie Dreyfus's only son, Pierre, veteran of Verdun and the Somme, wears one of his many military medals. (*Private collection*)

"The Tiger," Prime Minister Georges Clemenceau, about 1918. (*Musée Clemenceau, Paris*)

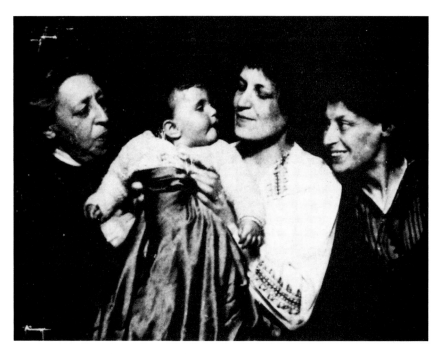

Four generations of women on the World War I home front. Louise Hadamard (*left*) and Lucie Dreyfus (*right*) look on as Jeanne Dreyfus Lévy holds her daughter, Simone. (*Private collection*)

Armistice and the return of the "lost provinces." Mathieu Dreyfus's grandchildren Suzie, France, and Jean-Pierre Reinach in Alsatian costumes, November 1918. (*Private collection*)

Lucie Dreyfus in the Parc Monceau
Paris, with her granddaughters
Madeleine (*left*) and Simone (*right*).
(*Private collection*)

"The admirable brother."
Mathieu Dreyfus in retirement,
about 1928. (*Private collection*)

Alfred Dreyfus thirty-five years after Devil's Island, the rosette of the Legion of Honor in his buttonhole. (*Private collection*)

Jean-Pierre Reinach, a
lieutenant in training with
Gaullist resistance in Engl
enjoys a leave before his
mission to France in 1942.
(*Private collection*)

Madeleine Lévy, Alfred Dreyfus's
favorite grandchild and a member
of the "Combat" Resistance movement in Toulouse during World
War II. (*Private collection*)

summer in Rennes was an ideal time to limit the drama of Dreyfus's second court-martial.[1]

"Parisians," the customary term for outsiders in the provinces, began arriving in late June and early July, and not all came from the capital. Hundreds of other visitors—newspaper correspondents, photographers, political caricaturists, legal experts, and assorted curiosity seekers—traveled from America, Great Britain, and every major European city. Police cordoned off an area in one of the newer neighborhoods south of the Vilaine River, and through August and early September attention would be focused on that restricted zone, which contained the military prison, the house rented by the captain's family, and, a few hundred meters away, the high school chosen as the site for the court-martial. Located on a main thoroughfare leading to the train station, the sprawling three-story *lycée,* with its rose-brick facade, ornate stone reliefs, and spacious inner courtyards, had been built in 1863 and surrounded by a high iron gate—a feature security officials found especially attractive.[2]

Lucie Dreyfus arrived in Rennes on June 28. Dressed in black and accompanied by her father and brothers, she had hoped to avoid the crowds expected for the trial. But a throng of reporters, photographers, and "curious onlookers"—moustached men in summer suits and straw hats—immediately surrounded Lucie at the train station and followed her to the Godard house and, later, to the military prison. Lucie often expressed her "hatred of publicity" and her embarrassment at being photographed, but with Dreyfus behind prison walls, Dreyfus's wife attracted the attention of journalists in search of a story. They gathered every day to record the visits of family and supporters—from Mathieu and Suzanne Dreyfus to Bernard Lazare and Maître Demange—and they shadowed Lucie on her walk to the prison. Friends opened broad black umbrellas in an attempt to shield Lucie from "insolent" reporters and photographers, but, taller than most of her entourage and virtually the only woman in the crowd, she provided an easy target. Soon abandoning her daily walks, she traveled the short distance to the prison in a closed carriage surrounded by police guards ordered to "remove Madame Dreyfus from public curiosity."[3]

Attacks on the prisoner's wife, in words or deeds, seem to have come from only a handful of anti-Semites. News reports confirmed that no "shouts or incidents" greeted Lucie in Rennes and noted that crowds often responded "with sympathy." Dreyfusard newspapers, out to glorify the noble wife, may have overstated the case, but Lucie's quiet dignity helped "turn public opinion" in her favor. She made it clear, as one police agent said with relief, that her family had no interest in inciting trouble, that they planned to remain "in the strictest intimacy . . . far from all commotion, and strangers and adversaries to all demonstrations." Having done precisely that for nearly five years, Lucie would not change her habits at the moment of her husband's homecoming.[4]

Mathieu Dreyfus, on the other hand, had been marked as an *agent provocateur.* The same journalists who convicted the prisoner before the fact, condemned the prisoner's brother, the "crafty Jew" responsible for the "Syndicat's" campaign. They pursued him in Rennes with no less diligence than they had in Paris, and police responded by assigning detectives to protect Mathieu, as they had done for Lucie. Aware of the antagonistic attitude of many police agents, however, the family mobilized its own private contingent of bodyguards, led by twenty-six-year-old Paul Valabrègue, Henriette's son, who came to the job with experience: He had helped Mathieu through the most perilous months of the affair in Paris, and six years earlier, while in the cavalry, he had served as a military bodyguard to Queen Victoria during a winter holiday in Nice.[5]

But the greatest challenge for the forces of order would be getting Alfred Dreyfus through the trial alive. One nationalist commentator announced that if the prisoner was acquitted "it will be the duty of every patriot to kill him."[6] Police reported rumors of assassination plots ("Captain Dreyfus's life is in great danger in Rennes," went one telegram of early July), and stressed the need for nearly two hundred mounted police, along with other troops to secure the city's restricted zone; additional agents would be assigned to other *quartiers.* The mayor ordered posters calling for calm, and not a few officials commented that the normally "sleepy" provincial town might awaken on the first days of the trial to the worst violence it had known since the Catholic and royalist revolts of the French Revolution. Given the influx of potential troublemakers—from highly cultivated literati to highly motivated street brawlers—the fears were well founded.[7]

Train junkets subsidized by anti-Dreyfusard leagues brought newspaper hawkers and professional demonstrators from Paris (plied with free wine, a few francs, and the promise of a good time). Max Régis, the anti-Semitic activist largely responsible for recent pogroms in Algeria, planned to join confederates in Rennes; and in the neighborhood where former minister of war General Mercier, Dreyfus's chief accuser, had rented a house, army officers and nationalist politicians joined "the squireens of provincial Brittany and many ecclesiastics" to form an enclave of anti-Dreyfusards. Police took note of all those groups, as they did of "the opposite camp"—the reporters, intellectuals, anarchists, and radical politicians who gathered at the Hôtel de France and, in the nearby countryside, at the Auberge des Trois Marches, the "veritable general headquarters" for all the "chiefs, champions, missionaries and proselytes of Dreyfusism."[8]

As the trial approached, a wave of inflammatory articles and caricatures appeared in the provincial and Parisian press. Henri Rochefort suggested that Dreyfus had dared not return to France as a free citizen, but as a guarded prisoner, because he knew about "*la loi Lynch*"; and song sheets, adorned with grotesque pictures of the Jewish captain, played on the French words for "guilty" (*coupable*) and "circumcision" (*couper*): "*Il n'est pas coupable!!!*" ("He is not guilty!!!") went one caption, "*Il est déjà coupé!!*" ("He is already cut!!"). [9] Another broadsheet, sent to Brittany from Paris on the eve of the prisoner's arrival, carried the bold announcement: "He is returning, the kike!"[10] Pseudoscientific racialists echoed their more popular counterparts and helped raise tensions: "Rennes is a sacred battlefield," wrote one theoretician, "what is involved is not the fate of a poor little Jewish Captain, but the eternal struggle between Semitism and the Aryan. . . . I really believe that the Jew is born of a special category of anthropoid," this observer concluded, "like the black man, the yellow man, or the redskin." And all of them, he added, were "deficient."[11] A poster, printed in Paris, carried the title "New Predictions from the Prophet," and described "How the Dreyfus Affair Will End,"; all of Israel "will be chased from France, disappearing in a cloud of dust and smoke . . . engulfed forever. It is the ruin, the death, the horrible slaughter of a race butchered by the hatred it had created across the centuries. . . . Long live France," the poster went on. "Long live the Army!" Closer to Rennes, *Le Patriote Breton* provided one of the few venomous references to Lucie Dreyfus; in the typical fashion of a promiscuous Jewess, the paper suggested, Dreyfus's wife had given birth to an illigitimate baby eight months earlier, a child now secreted away in Paris.[12]

While angry words kept police on the *qui vive,* reports from Paris and provincial cities heightened concerns in Rennes. In early June, Parisian demonstrators wearing the bluet of anti-Semitic leagues and the white carnation of the newly formed royalist Action Française had gathered at Auteuil racetrack in the Bois de Boulogne to protest the presence of Emile Loubet. As the president prepared to watch a stee-plechase, hundreds of "society people and stable boys"—from the Marquis de Dion, recent founder of the Auto and Aéro clubs of France, to a squadron of younger, less distinguished agitators—surrounded his podium and chanted the familiar chorus of nationalist refrains. One royalist, looking not at all out of place in the entourage of genteel racing enthusiasts, slipped through a ring of guards and charged forward to beat the president with his cane. Police intervened, and only Loubet's top hat was damaged, but the incident sparked counterdemonstrations through June and July. Temporary coalitions of socialists, anarchists, radical republicans, and unaligned Dreyfusards responded to the assault on Loubet—with one meeting held, appropriately, at Longchamp racetrack, west of Auteil. Thousands of police and soldiers were deployed to prevent violence, a force, Joseph Reinach reckoned with intentional exaggeration, equal to Bonaparte's army in Egypt.[13]

At the same time, the Jewish Consistory in Paris received urgent reports from provincial rabbis. Relative calm had been established over the months since the anti-Semitic riots of 1898, but the announcement of Dreyfus's retrial sparked new incidents and raised new fears. In late June in Versailles, seven followers of the Ligue des Patriotes broke into the synagogue, confronted the watchman, and raised truncheons shouting "Death to the Jews!" "Long live Déroulède!" "Down with the Yids!" They pummeled the guard "unmercifully," and when the rabbi tried to intervene, they told him, "Go back to Berlin, filthy Jew!" and then beat him across the face with the jagged end of a broken cane. While the rabbi's wife fled for cover and an assistant ran for help, the gang defaced the synagogue and promised to return "to put a match to it." Police apprehended one of the assailants, and government officials promised the rabbi that the synagogue and Jewish-owned shops in the area would be placed under "the strictest protection." But the rest of the gang escaped, and, like the racetrack demonstrators in Paris, they fitted the profile of thugs catching trains to Rennes. President Loubet, more fortunate than the Versailles rabbi and watchman, put it best: "I am not hurt," he said after the Auteuil incident. "But this is a lesson."[14]

By dawn on August 7, the lesson had been learned in Rennes, and the city had all the appearances of a "fortress . . . under siege." To avoid the midsummer heat, the trial would begin at 6:00 A.M., with the prisoner escorted to a side entrance of the *lycée* thirty minutes before. Armed guards flanked the captain, and inside the school's iron gate, a double line of soldiers turned their backs on him as a sign of dishonor. Nearby, mounted patrols galloped along the avenue with "sabers rattling," as Mathieu described it, while police with rifles and revolvers kept watch throughout the area. Special agents combed the school's basement in search of bombs, and clerks stationed at the public entrance on the north side collected all canes and umbrellas, the now-notorious weapons of anti-Dreyfusard agitators. By the time the court convened, no incidents had been reported, and anxieties over street riots had been eclipsed by the high anticipation of Dreyfus's entrance into the school's auditorium, its *salle des fêtes.*[15]

Though more spacious than the Cherche-Midi annex in which the first court-martial had been held, the hall shared one prominent feature with that earlier locale: A white plaster crucifix hung on the wall directly behind the elevated stage. A long table provided for the seven military judges (all graduates of the Ecole Polytechnique) filled the stage, and, immediately below, former cabinet ministers, generals, and other high-ranking officers sat in red velvet armchairs. Scores of less notable witnesses filled benches farther back. A spectators' section was located at the extreme rear, and armed guards lined the room's periphery. Reporters worked at banks of whitewood tables running along the southern bay of high windows (four hundred journalists held press passes in Rennes), and directly across from them on another raised platform, Demange and Labori, in full black robes with long white collars, prepared for the opening session. A simple straight chair placed in front of the defense table for Captain Dreyfus provided a striking contrast to the plush furniture set out for his chief accusers.[16]

Observing the room, with its proscenium stage and ornate escutcheons carrying the names of Renan, Chateaubriand, and other Breton luminaries, one spectator was put in mind of a grand but slightly decrepit casino at a provincial spa. Another witness, the diplomat Maurice Paléologue, asked himself if "such a theatrical hall did not involve the risk of transforming the proceedings into a play and exaggerating still further the dramatic elements in the case, which ought to be decided in cool and calm surroundings." The metaphor occurred to many others: spectators had come "as if to the theater," reported a journalist from *L'Aurore,* and Joseph Reinach, who remained in Paris and received descriptions of the trial from Mathieu, agreed: "Still one act to play in the fever of the battle," he wrote, "and then the curtain will fall, the lights will dim, and the actors will give up their costumes and become themselves again, the good, the mediocre and the others."[17]

Only family, lawyers, and prison officials had seen the captain since his return from Devil's Island. The rest of the audience waited and wondered if the images they held of the prisoner would match the reality. For more than four years, painters, lithographers, caricaturists, and song-sheet illustrators had made Dreyfus the most familiar public figure since the two Napoleons and the ill-starred General Boulanger— perhaps even more familiar, given the revolution in newspaper circulation and the technology of popular imagery. For the sympathetic, there had been saccharine scenes of a handsome patriot gazing out from his Devil's Island cabin to the Atlantic and the fatherland beyond; and for the hostile, there had been the countless grotesqueries, the pen-and-ink caricatures of a Germanic Jew, stoop-shouldered, double-chinned, and slothful. All the propaganda, whether financed by the Dreyfus family or by Edouard Drumont, had attempted to represent a simple, striking icon, not a detailed human likeness. In the popular imagination Alfred Dreyfus had become everything but real; and now, in Rennes, he would be expected to fit an image already drawn and play a role already written.[18]

While Lucie remained in isolation in the Godard house (she would receive constant reports from family messengers), Mathieu took his place at the back of the hall. Unable to watch his brother's "first contact with humanity in five years," he closed his eyes when the prisoner was summoned. Others, however, stood up to observe—and later record—every move. In a new artillery officer's uniform, with gold braid, buttons, and epaulets, with new boots, spurs, cap, white gloves, and sword, Dreyfus entered through a north door behind the defense table. Accompanied by a guard, he marched at the brisk soldierly pace he had shown at Cherche-Midi and in the courtyard of the Ecole Militaire. But as he climbed the steps of the platform and approached his judges his movements became more deliberate, more labored. Séverine, of *La Fronde*, described him as "precise" and "self-controlled," with "an incredibly strong spirit and a disdain for posturing." Eugène Naville, a Swiss philanthropist who had become a close family ally, noted Dreyfus's "cool reserve," the bearing of a "mathematician." But he was "like a phantom," Naville added, "who had the best of years of his life taken away from him . . . and who had returned from hell."[19] Others commented on Dreyfus's ghostly appearance, his white hair and jaundiced skin, and, most of all, his "used-up" body. His legs, injured while disembarking from the *Sfax,* were weak, and the arm that had bothered him since his days as a cadet at the Ecole Polytechnique was held close to his side and appeared slightly deformed. "His arms were withered," said Paléologue, "his knees so thin that they seemed to pierce the cloth of his trousers. . . . Only the staring eyes behind his pince-nez gave some slight animation to his cadaverous face."[20] Able to digest only milk and biscuits since his return, the prisoner had lost more weight, and though military officials had added thick padding to his uniform, few in the audience were fooled. He's "a little old man," wrote a correspondent from the London *Times,* "a little old man of thirty-nine." Jean Jaurès, reporting on the case for *La Petite République,* described "how deep my feeling of pity was when I first saw him. . . . His whole presence reveals depths of unspeakable suffering." And Maurice Barrès, who had not come to praise Dreyfus, could still pity him; he looked like "a miserable human rag," and when his face suddenly flushed with fever, Barrès was put in mind of "a little pig turning pink." Not all the "perfumes of Arabia or waters of Jordan or gold itself," the writer concluded, "could conceal the stench of treason."[21]

By the time Mathieu had the courage to look up, his brother had saluted the judges with a "crisp, automatic gesture" and had started to respond to questions. Deportees who survived their exile often returned from the imposed silence of the Iles du Salut or New Caledonia with speech impairments; radicals shipped out in the wake of 1848 were not the only prisoners to come back with "croaking" voices.[22] But Dreyfus had not returned to France to rest and recuperate; he had to defend himself in a cavernous school auditorium, in a public performance. As a young officer he had received poor marks for his weak voice, and now that handicap would plague him again. With his semi-paralyzed throat and missing teeth, he emitted hoarse, mostly inaudible sounds, and his sentences were cut short by his lack of breath and stamina. Listeners compared the sound to recent inventions: Dreyfus spoke "like a phonograph," said one witness; his voice seemed to be coming from "a distant place," noted another, "heard through static, like a voice transmitted by telephone."[23] Mathieu knew that if his brother tried to overcome that disability and shout out his responses he would sound "artificial." Only by "hiding his troubles" would the prisoner impress his judges. To save his case, Mathieu thought, he must rely on the same "heroic stoicism" that had saved his life on Devil's Island.[24]

Not unaware of his own dilemma, the captain aimed to preserve his strength and resist all pressure to "play a role." He believed in arguing his innocence through "moderation" and "without violence," and, consistent with his character, he maintained that a powerful defense need not resort to "shouts and sentiments . . . pompously expressed." He was "entirely incapable" of that behavior, not only because of his immediate lack of physical strength, but because of his long-held belief that posturing was an odious and counterproductive form of self-indulgence. Critics would contrast his comportment with that of the theatrical Esterhazy, the officer who had seduced his own court-martial audience with histrionic gestures. But Esterhazy was guilty, and that was the point. Dreyfus would risk the criticism of those who defined his reserve as arrogance, his rigidity as disdain, and he would continue to believe that "reason" alone would guide his judges.[25]

So many of the witnesses in Rennes had appeared at the 1894 court-martial and at the trials of Esterhazy, Zola, and Picquart that they had become known as "the personnel of the Affair"; and to those spectators and correspondents who had followed the history of the case, the testimony sounded like a stale performance by a tired traveling repertory company. "How many ruins and wrecks there were among them!" Paléologue said of the politicians and officers who took the stand. "All those whom the Dreyfus case has morally killed were there; it was like a necropolis." Mathieu had the same impression: "Is there nothing under these uniforms all embroidered in gold?" he asked. "[Is there] neither heart, nor conscience?" Three key figures—Esterhazy, Henry, and du Paty—were missing, but all the others had come to repeat (with General Mercier) their absolute certainty of Dreyfus's treason or to insist (with Picquart) on the captain's innocence. Across the five weeks of the trial, the prosecution would call seventy witnesses; the defense only twenty.[26]

The army's most celebrated handwriting "expert," Bertillon, led the judges yet again through his "thaumaturgic spells," and the prosecutor suggested that the same "cryptographological tricks" that Dreyfus employed on letter drafts to his wife from Devil's Island had been used on the *bordereau*. It became clear that military officials aimed to revise Esterhazy's revelation (that he had written the memorandum under Sandherr's orders) and convince the court that the scandalous commandant had worked as Dreyfus's intermediary in espionage. General Staff officers rehearsed their suspicions of the captain's interest in eastern fortifications and railroad networks; they reminded the court of his unreported trips to Alsace; and, repeating old allegations, they referred to Dreyfus's gambling and womanizing. The prisoner listened with no sign of emotion ("wrapped in a cloak of iron," noted one reporter), though he seemed ready to object to the personal insults when the prosecution mentioned his affair with Madame Dida, a woman notorious for "paying her lovers." Through it all, judges allowed the prosecutor and his witnesses to digress, intervene, and comment at will, while statements by the defense were frequently cut short. At one point Dreyfus protested the "impossibility of being able to defend himself," but that intervention was also ignored, and the captain did not press his superiors.[27]

With signs of emotion from the prisoner so rare, any incident, however fleeting, attracted comment. Hearing his early ally, Commandant Forzinetti, describe his fits of panic in Cherche-Midi prison, Dreyfus confirmed the testimony and admitted that he had come close to suicide. Without the support of his wife, he said, who had implored him to live for her and for their children, he would not have survived the torture of his degradation and exile. Conjuring up memories of Lucie's appeals, he began to "sob," as witnesses described it, when he told the judges, "If I am here, it is to her that I owe it."[28] On another occasion, after examining the *bordereau,* the "infamous yellowed paper," and repeating that he was not its author, he reaffirmed his innocence: "For five years, my colonel," he said to the chief judge, "I have suffered everything, but, once again, for the honor of my name and that of my children, I am innocent." Only isolated words could be heard throughout the hall, but spectators could see the prisoner's legs tremble and his face go white. "For me, who knows him so profoundly," Mathieu wrote that night, "who knows that he does not express himself outwardly, that he cannot, I wanted to weep for him when . . . his voice choked and when his eyes filled with tears but he could not cry." But again the prisoner recovered quickly, "as if seized by regret that he had lost his military bearing."[29]

Most often the focus of the crowd fell on two figures: Dreyfus and General Mercier, the former minister of war, in his velvet armchair "two steps" from the prisoner. For Mathieu, "the vile Mercier dominated the drama of Rennes. He commanded, directed, and inspired the army of forgers, of false witnesses . . . [who] moved to his orders."[30] Joseph Reinach and other Dreyfusards had been publishing attacks on Mercier, but not all of Mathieu's confederates agreed that the minister had had knowledge of Esterhazy's treason from the first hour. In *J'Ac-*

cuse, Zola had attributed the the general's complicity to "a weak mind" and nothing more, while others found Mercier's certainty of Dreyfus's guilt—his inability to comprehend that the army could commit an error—to be infinitely more frightening than any premeditated involvement in a conspiracy. Whatever the timing and extent of his complicity, however, it seemed that nothing could shake Mercier's faith, and, for that reason above all others, he emerged as Dreyfus's most formidable opponent. Mathieu was right; the former minister of war dominated the drama at Rennes, and, most worrisome, he outranked every one of the prisoner's seven judges.

Taking the stand early in the trial, Mercier repeated his belief that if no "certain proof" existed of the captain's espionage, circumstantial evidence coupled with the general's own "moral conviction" should "suffice in the eyes of the law." During his long testimony, he recounted events in a low, calm voice (Dreyfusards described it as the sound of "nasty old women"); but if he showed outward signs of confidence, he also signaled his fear that "the ground," as one observer noted, "was slipping out from under him." His hands trembled, his throat went dry, and he frequently interrupted his statements for a drink of water ("much like a speaker at a conference"). The peroration of his testimony, memorized in advance, led to the one confrontation between Dreyfus and his chief accuser. Maintaining his "deferential" attitude throughout the trial, the captain would counter accusations with the logical responses he had prepared on paper for more than six weeks in his prison cell. But with Mercier he faced a man unmoved by reason. "If the slightest doubt had crossed my mind," the general announced to the court, "I would be the first to tell you so, for I am an honest man and the son of an honest man." Then, turning to the defendant for the first time, Mercier added, "And I would be the first to say to you, 'Captain Dreyfus, I have made an honest mistake.' " But the prisoner cut him off and rushed toward the witness stand: "Then say it, say it," Dreyfus shouted in a strangled voice, "because you are lying!" Mercier recoiled and tried to respond ("I have just said . . ."), but Dreyfus interrupted him again ("It is your duty!").[31]

Pulled back to his chair by a guard, the prisoner heard the audience erupt into applause, cheers, and hisses. Enemies and allies alike seemed relieved that Dreyfus had broken through his carapace of prudence. For one reporter, it was a "superb" display, a moment of "extraordinary emotion . . . that brought tears to one's eyes." For most others, however, the captain's one grand theatrical gesture had failed. "Oh, the idiot," an actor who had come to Rennes from Paris remarked. "How I would have screamed that out!"[32]

Maurice Paléologue's fears that the court-martial would degenerate into a theatrical performance proved correct. Dreyfus, fighting for his life, thought that the truth was all that mattered; he had thought that at Cherche-Midi and through all his years on Devil's Island. Mathieu, Demange, and Labori may have outlined the major events of his "affair," but they had not prepared him for a case with the "allure of drama," as Joseph Reinach defined it, "in a country where the aesthetics of the theatre prevail." One journalist, sympathetic to Dreyfus, captured the disappointment: "We would like to see the attitude of a hero," he wrote, "but this hero, of the most frightful adventure, has the look of an impeccable functionary." Condemned by critics who exalted form over substance, who wanted a victim worthy of the tragedy, Dreyfus, who had read Shakespeare to learn about the human condition and not about artifice, suffered for being himself and not Hamlet.[33]

With each session suspended at midday in anticipation of the sweltering afternoon heat, the captain returned to his prison through the same double phalanx of armed guards that assembled inside the school's iron gate every morning. By showing their backs to Dreyfus those soldiers achieved two goals: they focused their attention on crowds of journalists and paid demonstrators and enacted their ritual of dishonor. But just as there was a limit to Dreyfus's patience with Mercier, there was a standard of military behavior he insisted on maintaining with pride. Confronting an infantry lieutenant outside the *lycée,* Dreyfus reminded the junior officer that he should salute an artillery captain in uniform. The lieutenant followed the order, the prisoner returned the salute, and the incident was "widely commented upon" in Rennes.[34]

But the strength that Dreyfus marshaled in public took its toll in private. Malarial fever persisted and he continued to lose weight. Guards noted that he "hardly touched his food," even though he received the same meals as the prison staff. Sensitive to the abrupt change of climate, he suffered chills and wore layers of heavy clothing in the middle of the scorching Breton summer. Plagued by memories of the "double buckle" on his Devil's Island cot, he slept fitfully in the Rennes prison, jolted awake by nightmares. With little rest and no appetite, he needed energy for the long court sessions; he added a caffeine-rich kola extract to his cups of milk ("in order to keep myself upright"), and, continuing a practice that seems to have led to an addiction on Devil's Island, he took stimulants (*médicamentation énergique*) every morning. On the brink of physical and emotional collapse, he could only hope that a decision was near. By the end of the first week, Lucie was more anxious than ever about her husband's condition; police agents described her leaving the Rennes prison "in tears."[35]

Meanwhile, other trial participants—witnesses, journalists, and spectators—settled into less dramatic routines through August and early September. On Saturday evenings some visitors returned to Paris or set off on short holidays in the countryside or at the shore north of Rennes. During the week, they awaited the afternoon arrival of Paris newspapers at the train station and heard the odd sound of hawkers selling morning editions as the sun began to set: "Read *Le Matin,*" they shouted outside Rennes cafés, "the evening paper!" Merchants appreciated the unusual profits of August, and, with strangers overwhelming the city and legends of the "Jewish syndicate" widely publicized, some small shopkeepers and tradesmen called the foreign coins they exchanged "dreyfusardes." Late afternoon "siestas" were followed by dinners in restaurants and rented houses that divided Dreyfusards and anti-Dreyfusards as clearly as did the seating arrangements in the Rennes *lycée*; and after those same groups walked along the quais of the Vilaine River and returned to their lodgings to sleep until 4:30 A.M., the city fell quiet.[36]

On the morning of August 14, however, the monotony ended when Fernand Labori failed to appear in the courtroom. At 6:35 A.M. word came that Dreyfus's lawyer had been shot in the back near one of the bridges across the Vilaine. His assailant, pursued by Picquart, had disappeared into a forest on the city's outskirts. Semi-paralyzed, Labori was forced to roll over on his briefcase in order to prevent passersby from stealing his trial documents; other witnesses ignored the stricken man until Dreyfusards arrived to call police. "Political passions, religious fanaticism," Mathieu wrote of the incident, "had suffocated every human sentiment in the hearts of those men. The legends of the Jewish traitor, of the Syndicat of treason, of foreign gold—all those lies, widely circulated and interminably repeated by the press, had turned people into beasts with disturbed minds." That, Mathieu concluded, "explained the crime." But there was more. The night before the attack, Mathieu had met Labori in his lodgings, and, with windows wide open, the lawyer had railed against the "misèrable" army officers and politicians who frustrated his defense efforts and turned the tide against acquittal. Since the Esterhazy and Zola trials, Labori had not hidden his contempt for the high command and for the cabinet ministers who had framed Dreyfus and blocked his return from Devil's Island. The evidence seemed clear: The lawyer's assailant must have been in the pay of the captain's enemies.[37]

"It takes more than a bullet from a revolver to kill me," Labori told Mathieu shortly after the assault, "it takes a cannonball."[38] Eight days later the lawyer returned to the defense table more committed than ever to taunting the prosecution. He insisted that if the government wanted an end to the affair it should contact German officials and verify the links between Esterhazy and attaché Schwarzkoppen (some initiatives had been attempted, but without results). And he fought the testimony of a surprise witness for the prosecution. A former Austrian lieutenant with a perverse personal history that rivaled Esterhazy's, Eugène Lazare de Cernuski announced that while based in Vienna in 1894 he had heard colleagues identify Dreyfus as a German spy. But Cernuski offered no proof, and when it became obvious that the officer, who claimed descent from a tenth-century Serbian dynasty, should have been vetted more thoroughly, the prosecution called for a closed session. Aware of the history of closed sessions in the Dreyfus case, Labori exposed the Austrian as an army deserter, an inveterate liar, and swindler, and announced that if foreign witnesses were fair game he would call Schwarzkoppen and Schwartzkoppen's friend, the Italian attaché Alessandro Pannizardi, to Rennes, a strategy approved by Mathieu. But Labori went further. Consulting neither his client nor his defense colleague, he telegraphed the German emperor and the Italian king; he wanted them to order their attachés to confirm that Dreyfus had never engaged in espionage.[39]

If that grandiloquent appeal, like most of Labori's dramatic petitions, led nowhere, it fitted the lawyer's style. He "fulminated" against the prosecution with "swollen phrases and melodramatic gestures" (one observer called it the "the kind of eloquence least suited to a military audience"),[40] and his radical irreverence clashed with Demange's cautious methods and respect for authority. Both lawyers enjoyed solid reputations and considerable wealth, and, not surprisingly, both accused each other of errors in strategy and style. By early September in Rennes, their conflict seemed irreparable, and the audience took note: "It appeared to me," Maurice Barrès wrote, "that there was a priest's hatred between those two robes."[41] They fought over who should be "leading counsel," over who should prepare closing arguments, and, most important, over how vigorously they should condemn the army and the government. "We are not here to try the General Staff," Demange reminded his bellicose associate. "We are here to concentrate on Captain Dreyfus." During afternoon meetings even the prisoner had to act as referee and remind his lawyers that guards and inmates could overhear their arguments. The black comedy of it all was not lost on Dreyfus; exhausted, feverish, and unable to eat or sleep, he was forced to soothe the nerves of the two professionals who had come to Rennes to save him.[42]

Mathieu began to wonder if his brother's fate might be decided by the bad temper of his lawyers rather than by the deliberation of his judges. Nearly every day he had to fill "the sad and miserable role" of arbiter, of "buffer," as he called it, between Labori and Demange. At one point, lamenting that "everything is lost," that "we will all be sent to Cayenne," Labori threatened to quit the case if not given free rein. To appease him, Mathieu wrote a letter on the spot, formally requesting the lawyer to remain in Rennes. It was as if Labori needed a written record to preserve his reputation if the captain was reconvicted. Accustomed to fighting on two fronts—to dealing with his brother's enemies and settling quarrels among his allies—Mathieu drafted the letter without hesitation; he would do everything necessary to keep the focus on the defendant. Furthermore, he respected Labori, and if he did not agree with his tactics he understood his desire to expose the corruption of the military high command and to defend the republic while defending Dreyfus. Labori had literally risked his life for those ideals.[43]

But Mathieu also knew that unbridled anger had never worked in his family's favor, and he refused to adopt the methods of his adversaries. Nor would he turn his back on Demange, the lawyer who shared the family's belief that respect for French justice must be maintained. For nearly five years Maître Demange, a devout Catholic and patriot, had devoted his energies and risked his reputation to defend a Jewish officer. Smeared by the nationalist press and criticized by many Dreyfusards as ineffective at best and cowardly at worst, he had never wavered in his commitment, nor had he allowed personal considerations to jeopardize the captain's case. "Demange thought only of Dreyfus," wrote Joseph Reinach, "he saw only Dreyfus"; and he considered Dreyfus's closest brother one of his most "faithful" confidants. Between sessions in Rennes, Mathieu and Demange would take long walks together, always shadowed by police agents, and, on occasion, they would enter a church. While Mathieu stood to the side, his friend knelt and prayed "for the triumph of justice." When Labori attempted to wrest control of the trial from Demange, and when he demanded that the prisoner distance himself from Mathieu as well, he made his worst tactical error. Courtroom strategies could never take precedence over Dreyfus's sense of obligation to his brother and his first counsel.[44]

With the presentation of evidence coming to an end, Mathieu had to find a way to reunite the lawyers. The rivalry had engaged principal Dreyfusards in Rennes and in Paris, and divisions among allies had become as perilous as the confrontation between the defendant and the General Staff. With Picquart and Clemenceau supporting Labori's strategies, but with Lazare opposed and Reinach leaning toward moderation, Mathieu realized that any decision would be met with protest. The only solution was to present Labori with the opinions of their supporters, and to let the lawyer decide for himself. Convinced that the Dreyfus family would veto his attacks on the army and the government, Labori announced that he would not present a closing argument. He made it clear that a strategy of deference would not work against an enemy that deserved only contempt. But in the end he stood aside for Demange.[45]

Like heated debates in the meeting rooms of Dreyfus's supporters, final statements in the Rennes *lycée* centered on a question of trust. Long before the retrial, when the General Staff and government officials learned that the wrong man had been sent to Devil's Island, the honor of the army took priority over the rights of an individual. Members of the high command knew that they had to be like Caesar's wife, and when shadows of suspicion fell on them, they chose to hide their crimes and protect their criminals. Henry's suicide, which the Dreyfus family had hoped would break the cycle of secrecy, only sharpened the divisions: Henry became a "martyr" of the fatherland, a patriot who took his life when his attempts to protect the army failed. Though never admitting their mistakes, members of the Etat-Major readily confessed that the case of a single captain could not be allowed to endanger the reputation of the entire army and, by extension, the security of the nation.

"I am convinced of Dreyfus's innocence," admitted one officer who captured the essence of the dilemma, "but if it were for me to judge, I would condemn him again for the honor of the army." The Lord Chief Justice of England, sent by Queen Victoria to report on the Rennes court-martial, learned the same lesson from his coachman; riding to the *lycée* one morning, the justice shared his opinion that Dreyfus was innocent. "And the generals?" the driver asked. "Are they guilty?" From that moment the English peer realized that the case "was no longer a question of justice." Others had known it all along: "An army which does not know how to defend its honor against a band of Jews," Drumont wrote in *La Libre Parole,* "will not know how to defend the Fatherland against a foreign invasion." Still another journalist, referring to the prisoner and Mercier, put it simply: "Between the Jew and the General, choose." Barrès said much the same thing: "The choice is clear," he wrote a month before Rennes. "Dreyfus or our principal leaders. . . . On the one hand, there is Dreyfus's honor; on the other, there is the honor of all the ministers and generals who have sworn to Dreyfus's guilt."[46]

Exploiting that choice in his closing remarks, the prosecutor repeated the old accusations and at first infuriated Dreyfusards in the audience. But the weakness of his case, coupled with his ineptitude, quickly turned their anger to amusement, and renewed their hopes for a favorable verdict. For his part, Demange had to convince the judges that "Dreyfus's acquittal would not mean the conviction of his superiors."[47] He had to depict Mercier as an individual who had made a tragic error and not as a general whose opinions in Rennes, directed at a tribunal made up of junior officers, were synonymous with marching orders. Returning to a meticulous presentation of the physical evidence, and, above all, to the question of the *bordereau,* Demange spoke for seven hours over a two-day period. "The lawyer's voice was pleasant," said one spectator, "paternal . . . almost good natured; one would say that he was trying to tame the stubborn and pacify the irritated."[48] Unlike Labori, who would have focused on the certainty of Dreyfus's innocence, Demange emphasized the doubt surrounding the captain's guilt. "That doubt is enough for me," he announced. "That doubt is an acquittal." And he honored the army, if not all its officers, in a way that repulsed Labori and satisfied their client. Addressing the "honorable witnesses" and "loyal judges," Demange added a final compliment: "I have confidence in you," he told the court, "because you are soldiers."[49]

Dreyfus, moved by his lawyer's eloquence, had used those same words on the eve of his first trial; his judges would treat him fairly, if they treated him as a fellow officer. That certainty persisted in Rennes, though it had been undermined by the one betrayal that shocked the prisoner more than any other; from the day of his arrest, he had believed that the Army chief of staff, General de Boisdeffre, had been fighting for his release. As an officer who had never enjoyed the patronage of a military mentor, a custom so common in the French army, Dreyfus had held to the memory of his summer meeting with Boisdeffre in 1894. Walking along the banks of the Moselle near Epinal, the young captain had impressed the chief of staff and had come away convinced of the general's goodwill. Four years later, from Devil's Island, Dreyfus urged his wife to enlist the general's help ("he has never refused us justice"), and on his voyage home he tried to send the chief of staff a telegram of gratitude. Even through the weeks of his prison tutorial, when his lawyers and brother exposed Boisdeffre's complicity, Dreyfus clung to the hope that his superior had not joined the ranks of his accusers. But when the general testified in Rennes the final hope was lost. With a "melancholy" attitude, as Joseph Reinach later described it, and never daring to look toward Dreyfus, Boisdeffre reaffirmed his "absolute belief" in the prisoner's guilt. The defendant, who was allowed to address the witness, had nothing to say to the man whom he had "placed so high." With Boisdeffre's defection, the captain had to rely more than ever on his first article of faith: To secure justice he would "look higher," to the rule of law that, though threatened by bitter men, existed outside the realm of human passions.[50]

For the final session, police barricades outside the courtroom were quadrupled, spectators were searched, and even opera glasses were confiscated. To maintain calm, the court barred two groups of potential troublemakers: military observers and women. Before the closing arguments, Dreyfus had followed his regular routine: He entered the hall, saluted his judges, and turned to his lawyers with a slight bow. This time, however, Demange and Labori took his hand, a gesture that, according to witnesses, seemed to surprise and move the prisoner. At the close of the session, the court asked for his final statement: "Before my country and the army, I affirm that I am innocent," he said. "For five years I have undergone the most frightening torture for the unique goal of saving my name and the name of my children. Today, I am convinced that I have attained that goal," he concluded, facing his judges, "because of your loyalty, and your sense of justice." Now "horribly pale," Dreyfus had come to the end of his strength, and his last words faded into "a sort of hoarse muttering."[51]

The court adjourned, guards led the prisoner to a nearby room to await the verdict, and Mathieu pushed through crowds to join Lucie and other family members and friends. They had shared similar vigils over recent years, and their gatherings had grown through each phase of the affair. In the past the Dreyfuses and Hadamards had always limited their society to kin and very few friends, but with the captain's case their city apartments and country houses had become Dreyfusard salons, meeting places for politicians, journalists, academics, and literati. With few exceptions, all those allies had come to Rennes full of confidence that the retrial would be "the last step," as Mathieu thought, "of our calvary." The highest judicial body in France had voted unanimously for revision of the first court-martial and, by implication, for Dreyfus's acquittal. There had been reason for hope.[52]

But the captain wanted to be judged by fellow officers, not by civilians, and across the weeks of his second trial most of those officers had shown that they honored a different set of rules than those of the republic for which they stood. If Dreyfus's allies still thought it "impossible that the army would knowingly condemn an innocent man," Dreyfus's enemies, who had the first court-martial to give them hope, thought it equally "impossible that the army would . . . condemn itself."[53]

It would not. At 4:45 on the afternoon of September 9, after one hour of deliberation, the military judges found Dreyfus guilty of the crime of high treason. Lucie's brother, Georges Hadamard, brought the news to the family, and in an antechamber of the *salle des fêtes,* Labori brought it to Dreyfus. Maître Demange had broken down on hearing the verdict; unable to face the captain, to relive the experience of the first court-martial, he asked his colleague to be present when the prisoner heard the decision. In 1894, in a dark vestibule off the Cherche-Midi courtroom, Dreyfus had reacted to his conviction with stiff military bearing; but immediately following the reading of the first verdict he had lashed out "like a madman," beating his head against the wall and forcing his guards to restrain him. There would be none of that in Rennes. He was now a product of Devil's Island, and if the army had not broken his spirit, it had broken his body. He listened to the verdict without emotion: "In the name of the French people, the president has posed the question: Is Dreyfus guilty? . . . By a majority of five votes against two, the Court-Martial has responded: Yes, the accused is guilty." Embracing Labori, the prisoner said simply, "Console my wife."[54]

FRANCE IS SAVED, ran the headline of Henri Rochefort's *L'Intransigeant* the next day. "What ecstasy there is in all French hearts, and what rotten luck for the hook-nosed Yids." Savoring their victory, Rochefort and counterparts at other nationalist papers took parting shots at the "treasonous" politicians and notables who had rallied to Dreyfus and defiled the fatherland. "The debauched Reinach," always a favorite target, received the most cutting blows: "In his imbecile conceit he had counted on the millions distributed by Godfather Zadoc [Grand Rabbi Zadoc Kahn] to achieve the liberating rehabilitation of his Dreyfus," declared L'Intransigeant; but now he would "find himself down on his immense derrière among all the Yids who will be yelling their heads off, clamoring for their money back, like crowds at a box office after a tenor, overtaken by hoarseness, has told the manager that he cannot go on."[55]

Dreyfusard journalists, if less scatological, were no less passionate in their response to the verdict. Under the title "The Innocent Condemned," L'Aurore attacked "the abominable judgment" and looked to the future: "We know that this judicial lie is not the last word of the affair, and that the forgers, victorious today, have only put off the hour of their own imprisonment. We count on tomorrow," the paper went on. "France cannot let itself be dishonored in the eyes of the world by five officers, Jesuits and idiots, who aimed to cover up the crimes of their chiefs." For Yves Guyot's Le Siècle, those officers had passed a verdict "which will remain a model of cowardice and jesuitism." Away from the glare of journalism, Dreyfusards exchanged letters with commentary on the case. In a note to "My Dear Little Mama," Marcel Proust, an avid follower of the affair, if only through newspapers studied in his shuttered bedroom, called the verdict "sad for the army, for France, and for the judges who have had the cruelty to ask an exhausted Dreyfus to make another effort to be brave." The novelist was most sensitive to the "physical strain" on the prisoner, to the burden of "having to display moral fortitude when he is already broken." For Emile Zola, who also lashed out against the "jesuitical" court, "the transcript of the Rennes process, when published in full, will stand as the most execrable monument of human infamy. . . . The ignorance, the folly, the madness, the cruelty, the lies, the crime, will have been exposed with a shamelessness that will make future generations tremble from shame."[56]

For hundreds of anti-Dreyfusard demonstrators gathered outside the Paris offices of La Libre Parole, however, the night of the verdict marked a moment of jubilation. Drumont's paper announced the good news from Rennes by filling office windows with colorful Venetian lamps and by hanging huge banners reading "France for the French" from the balcony above the Boulevard Montmartre. For nearly six hours crowds

paraded through the *quartier* shouting "Long live Drumont!" "Long live
the Army!" "Death to the Jews!" and after taking over a local brasserie,
they ended the night singing the "Marseillaise." At the same time, far
to the east, near Alsace, demonstrators in Belfort celebrated with identical slogans while they smashed the windows of Jacques Dreyfus's
home. The police, after dispersing the crowd, stood guard all night.[57]

If the army followed the letter of the law it would sentence Dreyfus
to "perpetual deportation" and "imprisonment in a fortified locale," and,
after another public degradation, return him to Devil's Island. But the
verdict had not been unanimous, and, more important, it had come with
a qualification that angered the captain's friends and enemies and fooled
no one. The judges announced that "extenuating circumstances" prevailed in the case, and though they never explained the statement, few
observers needed a translation. "Do they imagine," asked *L'Aurore*,
"that we will accept their vile poison just because they serve it up with
a bit of honey?" The army preferred "an injustice to a disorder," as
Goethe had put it in another context; politics had informed their verdict,
and politics would determine the "traitor's" punishment. Navigating
their way past the Scylla of military honor and the Charybdis of social
revolution, the judges aimed to appease both camps by first upholding
the status quo and then by qualifying the verdict. The specifics of
Dreyfus's fate would come later; for now, he was sentenced to ten
years "detention" and given credit for the five years he had already
served.[58]

Accompanying Lucie to the military prison, Mathieu and Suzanne
found the captain outwardly calm. But when Mathieu asked him to
renew his strength in order to continue the battle and possibly confront
another degradation, his brother reacted with sudden anger: "I will not
undergo a new degradation," he shouted. "I will not wear my uniform
again so that it can be defiled a second time; I will be dragged, carried
by force . . . never, never." The family was most distressed, however,
by another comment: Dreyfus wanted his children brought to Rennes.
To see Pierre and Jeanne "in these conditions," Mathieu thought, "to
give those children, who still knew nothing about the drama, a frightening and indelible vision of their father in prison, locked in a narrow
cell . . . surrounded by soldiers and guards, could only be the last
request of a man who felt the end was near."[59]

As he had done so many times when his brother seemed to have
lost all hope, Mathieu acted quickly to push the case forward. Joining
the "rapid exodus" from Rennes, with hundreds of spectators, wit-

nesses, journalists, and government officials, he took an express train to Paris on the afternoon of September 10. Over the next two days he would hold meetings with old and new allies, and he would search for a way to preserve his brother's honor without sacrificing his life. A formal appeal was already under way (Dreyfus signed the petition three hours after the verdict). But that would take time, and, after two convictions, a favorable decision would take a miracle. Besides, as Mathieu told supporters, the captain "will not live six months if he stays in prison."[60]

The only other option, a presidential pardon, required political maneuvering in the corridors of Parliament and the Elysée, and, even more problematic, in the meeting rooms of Dreyfusard supporters. Mathieu had been exploring the possibility of a pardon with Joseph Reinach and Henri Mornard, a lawyer with political connections who had represented the family before the appeals courts. But Mathieu had not yet discussed the idea with his brother. He knew that Alfred aimed for the complete recognition of his innocence, for the rehabilitation of his family name, and he knew that a pardon would secure only his brother's release, not his liberation. Mathieu also sensed that most of their confederates would agree; they had not fought for a Pyrrhic victory.

Reinach believed, however, that a pardon, offered within forty-eight hours, would serve as a clear rejection of the army's judgment; and it would save Dreyfus's life. He could then recuperate and renew the legal battle in freedom. That the question could even be contemplated was a testimony to the transformation of French parliamentary politics across recent months, changes that had occurred, in large part, as a result of the Dreyfus affair. Félix Faure had engineered his own demise, but he had been replaced by a president who wanted an end to political chaos. Only a few weeks before the Rennes court-martial, that president had chosen a prime minister, René Waldeck-Rousseau, who numbered Demange among his closest friends and Reinach among his political allies. With the establishment of a clearly republican government on June 22, 1899 (dominated by cabinet ministers who believed in Dreyfus's innocence), Mathieu's odyssey had come, in a sense, full circle. In the fall of 1894, he had approached the lawyer Waldeck-Rousseau to represent his brother and he had been referred to Demange; now Mathieu would ask the prime minister to secure a presidential pardon.[61]

And he would receive it, but not without endangering the Dreyfusard alliance. Across the forty-eight hours following his brother's reconviction, Mathieu had to draw on every diplomatic skill he had learned since 1894. In many ways, he had become the prime minister of his own shadow government, the leader of a cabinet that included many of France's most influential politicians, journalists, and academics. More than any other single figure, Mathieu had been responsible for the establishment of that Dreyfusard organization, and, like other leaders of coalitions, he had been forced to deal with strong-minded personalities with wildly divergent opinions. All of his supporters—the anticlericals, the socialists, the anarchists, the old Gambettist republicans—had shared the common goal of bringing Captain Dreyfus home from Devil's Island and proclaiming his innocence. But if, on the journey to Rennes, factionalism had been kept to a minimum, the arrival of the prisoner marked a new phase of divisiveness that jeopardized Mathieu's work. He had tried to finesse the feud between Demange and Labori, and he would never know the extent to which that rivalry had contributed to his brother's verdict. But now the conflicts over methods in Rennes would be played out in Dreyfusard debates over a presidential pardon. Mathieu faced a coalition disintegrating into pockets of special interest, most of them worthy, all of them influenced by the affair, and many of them no longer focused on the fate of the prisoner who had inspired their alliance. Dreyfus's cause had done better with Dreyfus on Devil's Island.

Returning to Paris, Mathieu went directly to Joseph Reinach's home near the Parc Monceau and met with Bernard Lazare. Lazare had also attended the Rennes trial, but serious disagreements had strained his alliance with the family. Above all Mathieu had criticized Lazare's tendency to stress the anti-Semitic dimensions of the case, and to do so publicly. That assessment, Mathieu believed, was both dangerous, because divisive, and reductionist, because it ignored the vast number of anti-Dreyfusards who cared a great deal about the army's reputation and not at all about the "Jewish question." For Lazare, however, anti-Semitism was no longer a passing sickness in France, as he had once believed, but an incurable disease. Over the past two years, he had begun to look on the captain's struggle as a metaphor for the experience of all oppressed Jews: Dreyfus "incarnates, in himself," Lazare wrote shortly before Rennes, "not only the centuries-old suffering of this people of martyrs, but their present agonies. Through him, I see Jews languishing in Russian prisons . . . Rumanian Jews who are refused the rights of man, those of Galicia . . . the Algerian Jews, beaten and pillaged." Dreyfus inspired Lazare to think of "all of those whom desperation drives to seek some haven . . . where they will at last find that justice which the best of them have claimed for all humanity."[62] Dreyfus had inspired similar responses beyond France. As Paris correspondent for a Viennese newspaper, Theodor Herzl had witnessed the 1895 degradation and the crowds chanting, "Death to the Jews!" Herzl's vision of a separate Jewish state, explored in his 1896 pamphlet *Der Judenstaat*, was shaped by more than the captain's degradation, but Dreyfus's tragedy gave his dreams added urgency. If religious tolerance and racial harmony were impossible in France, the home of the Rights of Man, they were, Herzl was now convinced, impossible everywhere.[63]

Lazare's conversion to Jewish nationalism was passionate and not without irony. Disillusioned by the broken promises that reached back from the affair to the Revolution, Lazare had turned against the ideals Dreyfus continued to revere. When it came to national allegiance, Lazare had been radically transformed by Devil's Island and all it represented, while Dreyfus, insulated from debates over the place and fate of French Jewry, returned from his exile with, if anything, a heightened sense of patriotism. He believed that faith in his fatherland had saved him. But if Lazare championed a cause that angered many of his old confederates, he did not, in the end, abandon the prisoner who had been his inspiration. Unlike Labori, Picquart, and others who would continue to fight the Dreyfus family over different issues, Lazare agreed to work with Mathieu and remain, for now, within the disciplined ranks of Dreyfusards.

Joseph Reinach respected Lazare but shared none of his notions of what it meant to be a Jew in France. He rejected the idea of Jewish nationalism, and insisted that Zionism, by its very nature, preached division, not unity, and placed some "sort of ethnic solidarity" above the interests of the French nation. The movement was misguided, unpatriotic, and undoubtedly "a trap set by the anti-Semites for the naive or thoughtless"; it was "destined for a pitiful failure."[64] Later, in a note to Reinach's brother, Salomon, Mathieu would also warn against what he perceived to be special interests threatening the common cause: "Neither the government nor Israel nor any familial or personal sentiments influence our decisions. They are exclusively subordinated," he stressed, "to the goal we pursue . . . inflexibly: the honor of our name."[65] Joseph Reinach agreed, and in response to the First Zionist Congress, held in Switzerland, he announced that the "French fatherland was given to the Jews by the Revolution—the anti-Semites will not take it away from them, and the Zionists at Basel will not determine any Jew to renounce it."[66] Through all the years of the affair, Reinach refused to write the obituary for the promises of emancipation. He had been a beneficiary of those promises, and, like the Dreyfuses, he had believed that gratitude, in the form of patriotism, had been part of the original convenant. For good reason, he had emerged as the family's close friend and ideal ally.

And Mathieu would need as many allies as he could find to press the case for a presidential pardon. His quick diplomatic tour of Paris took him from Reinach's home to a confrontation with Georges Clemenceau. A fierce defender of Labori's methods during the Zola trial and the Rennes court-martial, Clemenceau, now approaching his sixtieth year, had made his mark as a brilliant and contentious politician and journalist, a radical enemy of clericalism, militarism, and all forms of centrist "Opportunism" that stifled social change. Though a native of the Vendée region, he had little in common with his counterrevolutionary countrymen. From the days of the Paris Commune through the Boulangist years and beyond, he had supported democratic movements that promised reforms, and then turned on those movements with vehemence when they shifted course to the center or right. As an elected member of the Chamber of Deputies or as a journalist looking on, he reveled in toppling governments that had neither the courage nor the talent to effect the revolutionary changes he envisioned—from the separation of church and state to the recognition of trade unions and more. Tested by nearly three decades of political wars, Clemenceau was wiser than his friend Labori, more calculating in his strategies and focused in his goals (Mathieu noted his "ruthless logic" and his sharp intelligence, "like the point of a sword"); and, on a personal level, he was more respectful of Mathieu's political acumen. But Clemenceau, later dubbed "the Tiger," shared Labori's instinct to attack. He, too, wanted to look beyond the legal case of an individual officer—a man he found unsympathetic and uncomfortably conservative—to the political drama of an entire nation.[67]

Describing his brother's condition and stressing the urgent need for a pardon, Mathieu asked Clemenceau to exert his influence with Waldeck-Rousseau, as Reinach and Henri Mornard had done in recent meetings with the prime minister. "My heart says yes," Clemenceau responded. "My reason says no." He explained that it would be impossible to mobilize support if Dreyfus were at liberty. Followers would be galvanized by an innocent man still in prison, but a family man returning to the bourgeois comforts of home would be met with indifference. In the arena of public opinion (and no politician could take the pulse of that opinion better than Clemenceau) a pardon would be looked on as a "solution," as an end to the affair.[68]

From his meeting with Clemenceau, Mathieu went on to poll other supporters in the newspaper rooms at *L'Aurore* and *Radical* he had frequented so often. Later, accompanied by Reinach, he met with Alexandre Millerand, the new minister of commerce and the first socialist named to a cabinet post under the Third Republic. Millerand's news was encouraging but mixed; a pardon could be secured, but, given a legal technicality, the prisoner would have to first withdraw his appeal. Millerand and Reinach urged Mathieu to return to Rennes and present the option to his brother. If he accepted, he could be free the following day.

But Mathieu would not go without the support of the two Dreyfusards most opposed to accommodation: Clemenceau and Jean Jaurès, the socialist who had joined the cause in its eleventh hour. Mathieu had little sympathy for Jaurès's assaults on industrial capitalism, but since their first meeting in 1898 the manufacturer from Mulhouse and the socialist from the working-class town of Carmaux had developed a firm friendship. Their political persuasions were as different as their appearance; tall, slim, mustachioed and impeccably dressed, Mathieu towered over the broad-shouldered and full-bearded Jaurès, whose tie and high starched collar were always a bit off center. With all their differences, however, they had been united in the campaign for the captain, and now Mathieu hoped that Jaurès would be more amenable than Clemenceau— that he would understand the need to postpone politics.[69]

Millerand invited that coterie of Dreyfusards to his offices at the ministry, and into the night they discussed the pardon and the prisoner's fate. "You know my feelings," Mathieu told the group. "I will do nothing without your consent. If you say yes, I will accept [and pursue the pardon]; if you say no, I will refuse. After the admirable support you have given me," he concluded, "my duty is to not separate myself from you. Your decision will be mine." Reinach argued the practical and humane reasons to secure a pardon, while Clemenceau said that "sentiments" should not influence such a grave decision. The debate became heated. When Clemenceau insisted that he was not without feelings, that he had, in fact, cried during his earlier meeting with Mathieu, Reinach responded caustically, "that proves that you cannot cry two times in the same day." Jaurès, hostile to the pardon at first, was won over by Reinach and Millerand. Clemenceau, however, held out until Mathieu announced that he would not act if the group remained divided. Pacing the minister's office, upset by the consensus of his colleagues,

Clemenceau turned to Mathieu and admitted, "If I were the brother, I would accept."[70]

Armed with Millerand's promise that he would approach the prime minister and the president the next day, Mathieu boarded the night train for Rennes at the Gare Saint Lazare. He carried a letter from Minister of War Gaston de Galliffet to the director of the military prison, which would enable him to meet his brother in private. At 6:00 A.M. on September 12, Mathieu and Alfred were alone for the first time in over five years.

Describing the events of the past two days, Mathieu lobbied his brother with the same arguments he had used to convince his supporters. "I was resolutely hostile to the idea at the beginning," Alfred later wrote, "because I had a thirst only for justice." But Mathieu explained that a pardon would have a "considerable impact" (as the government's thinly veiled condemnation of the army's verdict); and he reminded Alfred of his duty to his wife, children, and family. Mathieu had played that role with his brother many times before; having taught him how to behave as an officer and a gentleman, he would now suggest the choices he should make as a prisoner promised his freedom. It took two hours, but Alfred finally agreed to accept the pardon and bring the five years of his "physical and moral torture" to an end.[71]

Secret telephone conversations between Mathieu in Rennes and Millerand in Paris were followed by a new round of train trips to the capital. President Loubet, living up to his image of dogged caution, feared that the army would not tolerate intervention in its affairs so soon after the verdict. Loubet wanted to pardon Dreyfus, but not at the expense of a military backlash, and events in Paris only increased his desire to wait for a moment of calm. Through the final days of the court-martial, as one police agent had reported, the forces of order thought "less of Dreyfus in Rennes than of Paris in full revolt." Anti-Semites and militant nationalists confronted socialists and anarchists, with each group invading the other's political rallies, and with injuries reported among demonstrators and police. In the wake of the racetrack incidents of the early summer, nationalist agitators, including the indefatigable Paul Déroulède, had been arrested, while their paramilitary followers, led by Jules Guérin, had taken refuge in the offices of *L'Antijuif* newspaper on the rue de Chabrol, close to the Gare de l'Est. During the month of the Rennes trial and through most of September, Guérin's armed troops, under siege by Paris police, held out behind the iron fence and steel-lined shutters of "Fort Chabrol." It became a piece of street theater, widely reported by the press, and Loubet had good reason to reconsider the timing of Dreyfus's pardon.[72]

Under pressure from his newly formed government, however, and after a personal intervention by Demange, the president agreed to sign the pardon as a humanitarian gesture on the condition that medical reasons could be documented. Mathieu returned to Paris yet again, and then traveled back to Rennes with a physician, Dr. Delbet, the only official visitor, the prisoner later noted, to show any sign of human sympathy. Delbet's report left no doubt; Dreyfus was completely exhausted (*épuisé*) and, along with mulnutrition and malarial fever, showed symptoms of tuberculosis of the spinal marrow (*tuberculose de la moelle épinière*). If he were not freed immediately, the medical report concluded, his health would deteriorate "without hope of recovery," and he would be dead within months.[73]

At the next meeting of the Council of Ministers, Galliffet submitted the letter of pardon to President Loubet. "The highest function of government," wrote the minister of war, "is to respect, without distinction and without reservation, the decisions of the courts of justice. Resolved to fulfill that duty, it should also concern itself with issues of clemency and public interest. . . . The government would respond poorly to the wishes of the country, eager for peace, [if] it did not endeavor to erase all the traces of a painful conflict. It is up to you, Monsieur le Président," Galliffet concluded, "through a noble humanitarian act, to perform the first work of bringing the peace that public opinion demands and that the well-being of the Republic dictates." On September 19, 1899, three weeks short of the fifth anniversary of the captain's arrest, the president of the republic signed the pardon that annulled Alfred Dreyfus's ten-year sentence and canceled his second military degradation.[74]

Mathieu arranged for a statement from the captain—drafted by Jaurès on the night of the meeting in Millerand's office—to be published immediately. "The government of the Republic grants me my freedom," went the announcement. "It is nothing to me without my honor. Beginning today, I shall persist in working toward a reparation of the frightful judicial error whose victim I continue to be. I want all of France to know through a definitive judgment that I am innocent. My heart will be at rest only when there is not a single Frenchman who imputes to me the crime committed by another."[75]

Dreyfus left Rennes the way he arrived—in the middle of the night and surrounded by guards. They took him to a train station in the hinterlands and then to Nantes, where they were joined by Mathieu. Hoping to keep Dreyfus from becoming a target of renewed demonstrations, Prime Minister Waldeck-Rousseau had asked Mathieu to send his brother to the Channel Islands or some distant locale. But Mathieu refused; such a choice would appear cowardly, he said, and given the sympathy for the Dreyfusard cause outside France, it might lead to events that would embarrass the republic. Instead he would take Alfred to the first place of refuge the family had known in France after the German occupation of Alsace: He would take him to Carpentras, and to Henriette, who had always been his "second mother." Five security agents and Paul Valabrègue, acting as bodyguard, accompanied them, and Mathieu carried a revolver.[76]

CHAPTER XV

Homecoming

"EVERYTHING AMUSED ME, everything interested me," Alfred Dreyfus wrote of his train journey. "It felt as if I had returned to life after a long and horrible nightmare." With security agents in a neighboring compartment, he sat with his brother and nephew and, with a "sense of joy," looked out at the villages of the Vendée and, further south, at the roads leading to the port town of La Rochelle. He could only be "amused" by the irony of it all; his last voyage through that region, his last view of the French countryside in daylight, had come in January 1895 when his prison wagon, pelted by rocks, had sped away from the La Rochelle train station at a "triple gallop." Now, amid the first-class comforts of the Nantes-Bordeaux express, Dreyfus savored his freedom, and, his brother noted, he began to relax.[1]

The rest of the entourage, however, prepared for trouble. Though rumors of the captain's destination had been off the mark (a reporter for *Le Petit Journal* cabled that Dreyfus would leave for England on a French torpedo boat), it would be difficult to avoid notice all along the nine-hundred-kilometer route to Carpentras. Waldeck-Rousseau had insisted that the group avoid Paris and take a secret and circuitous route; they would change trains in Bordeaux, Sète, Tarascon, and Avignon, and then travel the final twenty kilometers to the Valabrègue house in two closed carriages. But when the express arrived at Bordeaux at 4:38 P.M. on September 20, and the party had to leave the train

269

to wait for their connection east, it became clear that local journalists had been alerted by their counterparts in Rennes. "The telegraph," Mathieu observed, "had obviously worked." With crowds gathering on the quai and the chief security agent paralyzed by the fear of a demonstration, Mathieu took charge. He separated the group and had Alfred and a friend (a reporter from Le Figaro) enter the station's Hôtel Terminus from a back corridor. The ploy worked, and through the early evening, while crowds assembled outside the hotel's private dining room, Alfred received "the most singular service" he had ever known. Eager for a glimpse of their notorious guest, all the waiters of the establishment filed through with appetizers, main courses, desserts, bread, water, and wine. As the security chief continued to "lose his head" and imagine the "massacre" about to take place, Alfred remained the most "tranquil of all."[2]

He drifted into a private reverie, distracted not by the crowds below but by the strange look and feel of the objects that surrounded him: the whiteness of the starched linen napkins, the touch of the silverware, the reflections of the shimmering crystal goblets and decanters. For thirty-five years those had been the unexceptional utensils of his daily life, the necessities never questioned; but after five years of tin mugs and cartons of condensed milk, they had become new luxuries to be appreciated and examined. Most of all, he was fascinated by the intensity of the hotel's electric light. Lucie's family had been one of the first in Paris to install an incandescent light bulb in their apartment, but that gadget had been a curiosity, an exception to the rule of candles and gas lamps. In 1889 the Universal Exposition—the largest and most successful yet—had been illuminated by gas (only the elevators of the Eiffel Tower were powered by electricity), but the Universal Exposition now in preparation for 1900 would be distinguished by its thousands of bright bulbs and its "Palace of Electricity." With a Polytechnicien's interest, Dreyfus had read about the technological improvements of the period in the science journals he had received on Devil's Island. Now the theories became realities as he watched the flood of "radiant electricity," as one novelist had put in 1898, bringing the "immortal transformation" of night into day.[3]

The telegraph and telephone, though established prior to the captain's arrest, had only recently become weapons in the journalists' arsenal; reporters used those inventions to "scoop" competitors, and, perhaps more than ever before in France, they relied on them for daily articles on the Rennes court-martial. At the same time Dreyfus must have learned from his family of the controversy surrounding yet another new technology, the cinema, and specifically an eleven-reel movie entitled *The Dreyfus Affair* (or *On Devil's Island*) by the pioneer filmmaker Georges Méliès. After studying photographs and sketches, Méliès, who had built the world's first film studio, restaged the principal events of the prisoner's case and of his life in exile. An ironmonger with a striking resemblance to the celebrated prisoner played the leading role. When audiences protested the sympathetic portrait of the "traitor," however, the government, worried about the real drama unfolding in Rennes, banned Méliès's film, as well as a six-part "docudrama" on the affair by the Pathé brothers.[4]

It would take time for Dreyfus to learn about those and other innovations that had taken place during his years in prison. For now, as he waited in the Hôtel Terminus, other images would capture his attention, images that Mathieu and Paul Valabrègue took for granted. Given his interest in horses and horsemanship, from his daily rides to his racetrack visits, he could not have helped but notice the many modes of transportation competing with horsedrawn carriages and omnibuses. Bicycles, like light bulbs, were not new in the late 1890s, but now their numbers were unprecedented (contemporaries confirmed the "bicycle boom" of the decade), and their designs had changed radically during Dreyfus's exile. With wheels of equal size and pneumatic tires now common, bicycles attracted novelists and illustrators intrigued by the "cult of speed" and, no less important, by the changes in fashion that cycling helped influence. On the roads leading into Bordeaux and along the quais of other provincial train stations, Dreyfus would see fewer women clad in tight-waisted dresses with enormous bustles, and fewer with the massive, heavy hats so common in the 1880s. Fashions looked sleeker, dresses clung rather than flared, and there were more French variations on bloomers in evidence, at least among women who were more audaciously *sportive*. In fact, Dreyfus's route had taken him to a city in the avant-garde of sport and sporting fashion in France; the Cyclistes Girondins had been founded in Bordeaux only two years before, as had the region's Auto Club. The novelist Paul Adam (when not vilifying Dreyfus) had written in 1898 about the "new automobilism" of the age, and in the same year Henry Adams had worried about the impact the automobile would have on travelers to France's historic monuments, tourists who would motor to medieval cathedrals and pass "from one century to another without a break."[5] As he peered through his train window or onto the streets in front of the Hôtel Terminus,

Dreyfus felt himself passing from one century to another after the hiatus of Devil's Island.

Tensions in Bordeaux might have put Mathieu in mind of close encounters with Parisian crowds, but no troubles developed (only isolated shouts of "Down with Dreyfus!" and "Long Live Dreyfus!"), and the remainder of the trip to Carpentras passed without incident. Police had worried about the Mediterranean city of Narbonne, where Dreyfus's train would stop in the middle of the night (Freemasons had hoisted their flag there to celebrate the captain's pardon, and local royalists had protested); but aside from a small crowd that tried to approach Dreyfus's compartment only to be blocked by security agents, that brief stop proved as uneventful as those in Sète, Tarascon, and Avignon. When the party arrived at Villemarie outside Carpentras at ten o'clock on the morning of September 21, most journalists were heading south to Marseilles. Reckoning wrong about Dreyfus's destination, they had lost their quarry.[6]

Nearly twenty-five years had passed since Henriette's closest brother had spent his vacations in Carpentras, studying for the *baccalauréat* and playing with his nieces and nephews, including Paul, the family bodyguard who would now remain in Provence, along with three inspectors, to protect his uncle. Situated in the forested Quintine *quartier,* five hundred meters from the town's periphery, the estate at Villemarie, bordered by the Auzon River, a high train trestle, and full, arching trees, provided the security the family would need. News of Dreyfus's arrival spread quickly, and, like nearly every other good-size town in France, Carpentras had local commentators who expressed their opinions on the Rennes verdict. For the most part, the news had been greeted with relief, though a socialist demonstration a few days prior to Dreyfus's arrival had prompted the *Journal du Comtat* to attack the town's "numerous Yids" and their "poor fin de siècle martyr."[7]

Henriette and Joseph Valabrègue had lived with that language since the fall of 1894. As prominent members of Carpentras's Jewish community (Joseph's brother, Adrien, was president of its consistory), and as kin of the prisoner, they had served as ideal targets for demonstrations. "If we are not mistaken," the Catholic paper *La Croix d'Avignon et du Comtat* reported a few days after Dreyfus's arrest, "one of the Captain's sisters lives in Carpentras. Besides, Jews are almost all relatives." To clarify its stand, the paper added, "France committed an immense mistake the day that . . . it gave the Jew his citizenship." Two years later, when the publication of Bernard Lazare's Dreyfusard pamphlet raised tensions in the Jewish communities of southern France, a police agent summarized the situation in Carpentras: "The prisoner on Devil's Island has a sister [here] who is married to M. Joseph Valabrègue, an Israelite . . . with an important wholesale textile business which has branches in Avignon and Orange. Since the condemnation of her brother," the report continued, "Madame Joseph Valabrègue has withdrawn into her country house . . . and has broken off all social relations." While Joseph shuttled to and from Paris, Henriette remained "withdrawn," especially through the early months of 1898, when anti-Semites and Dreyfusards began shooting at each other in Carpentras, and when candidates in the May 1898 election capitalized on the close presence of the prisoner's family. "Our town is impassioned," announced one journalist. "Political parties have momentarily disappeared; there is now only the Dreyfusard party and the anti-Dreyfusard party." Posters calling for the "Expulsion of the Semites" appeared during the campaign, and in response Joseph Valabrègue sued the leading anti-Semitic candidate for defamation. According to *La Croix,* Mathieu Dreyfus traveled from Paris to testify for his brother-in-law, and then left when he confronted the "animosity that [Carpentras] harbors against Jewish traitors." Valabrègue lost the suit and paid court expenses, but, in the end, the anti-Semite fared no better. He lost the election.[8]

One spectator who published his "impressions" of the Rennes trial and of Dreyfus's return to Carpentras acknowledged the long history of anti-Jewish violence in Provence, but got it wrong when he described Carpentras' "progress toward tolerance," and when he reported that Dreyfus would be greeted in that "Meridional city . . . without a shout, without a demonstration." A gang chanting "Down with Dreyfus!" surrounded Villemarie barely twenty-four hours after his arrival, and as they confronted another group shouting "Long live Dreyfus!" they staged a classic *charivari,* complete with late-night processions and "violent racket." The prefect of the Vaucluse alerted guards that Dreyfus might be poisoned or shot, and letters sent to Villemarie confirmed the need for increased security. The author of one note addressed to the family of the "new Judas" hoped that a "Saint Bartholomew's Day . . . will come soon, and that [your race] will not live to see the year 5660 of the Hebraic era." Another writer warned that Dreyfus would soon be impaled by "the dagger of a true Frenchman" who would spill his blood "for the fatherland"; and still another announced that he had purchased "a revolver and six bullets" to use in the name of Frenchmen "who had voted for [Dreyfus's] death." Through it all, local reporters who praised Edouard Drumont as "a profound philosopher and talented journalist" reminded their readers of the "leprous . . . Hebraic morals" that had "infected" their town across the centuries, and of the celebrated synagogue, "the Palace of Usury," which had been built "from the fruits of [the Jews'] insolent plunder."[9]

Dreyfus had chosen Carpentras, with its mild autumn and winter climate, its clean air and good memories, as the ideal retreat after five years in prison. With the security provided by Villemarie, the Valabrègue house and garden would serve the purpose well. And if troublemakers lived close by, that would have been the case in almost any French town. Besides, Dreyfus had learned in prison cells and on Devil's Island how to block out the world and create an enclave of calm. "The emotion was indescribable," he wrote of his first days in Carpentras, and he was not referring to local politics. "It was finally a time of peace and relaxation," he said, "in this long series of sufferings that had been the lot of us all."[10]

Playing her part in the scheme to confound journalists, Lucie Dreyfus first went to Paris from Rennes and then traveled south to be with Alfred on the night of his arrival in Carpentras. Having put away her black mourning clothes, she came dressed to celebrate "this first day of our real reunion," as Alfred described it, the first time in five years that they would be together without a double iron grille or a long prison table to separate them. The couple remained silent on the subject of their first night alone (there would be no letters now to record their intimate feelings), and said only that they were able to "see each other again, finally, in freedom."[11]

The next day David and Louise Hadamard brought eight-year-old Pierre and six-year-old Jeanne to the reunion that Alfred had anticipated with both joy and anxiety. Most of all, he worried that the children would be "shocked" by a father who had become a stranger to them. But Lucie had raised them on memories and had kept their father's photographs, on horseback and in uniform, close by. As the years passed, the children had written more often, guided by their mother's hand, and every letter had repeated the happiness they would feel upon greeting their father after his "long voyage." Coincidentally, a letter from Emile Zola arrived in Carpentras the day after the reunion with the children and captured the scene. Imagining Dreyfus in the "intimacy of his family," where "all the abominations of the street die on the threshold of the home," Zola described Pierre and Jeanne sitting on their father's knee while he told them, finally, "the entire tragic history" of the years just passed. "And they will be very proud of him," the letter went on, "they will carry his name with glory . . . the name of a worthy man and a stoic who has purified himself [through suffering] to the point of the sublime."[12] Always as much a romantic as a naturalist, Zola may have overstated the case; but Dreyfus did sit with his son and daughter in the Villemarie garden and did tell them, eventually, the story of his "long voyage."

Pierre would later recall his arrival in Carpentras as his second clear childhood memory (the first had come when he learned that news of Emile Loubet's election would please his mother and he ran home to announce that victory, which he did not understand, "with great satisfaction"). He remembered approaching Villemarie and seeing his mother next to a man with white hair and "clothes which floated on his thin frame." The man seemed "weary," said Pierre, "but he looked at us with such emotion that we returned his kisses and immediately welcomed him as our papa." The instant the children "threw themselves into my arms," as Alfred described it, "they made me forget so much sadness, so much sorrow."[13]

Curious about the "mystery" that seemed to "exist . . . in the life of my parents," Pierre questioned them over the months that followed, and they recounted the "broad outlines" of the captain's case using a colorful *image d'Epinal*—a popular illustration manufactured in the eastern French town of Epinal—which "retraced the principal stages" of the affair. Lucie had used the same type of teaching tool to introduce the children to the history of France, to its kings, generals, and heroes. Stencil-colored lithographs with four rows of four captioned pictures, those images of the affair had been produced in profusion over the past two years, and the one shown to Pierre, entitled *Histoire d'un Innocent*, summarized the case from the time of Dreyfus's arrest through Henry's suicide and Esterhazy's flight. Undoubtedly part of the propaganda financed by Mathieu, its message was as tendentious as that of its "Epinal" counterpart, *Histoire d'un Traitre*, published by anti-Dreyfusards a year later, and the captions of both were in simple prose, easy for youngsters to read. Pierre learned the story of "the young Alsatian officer on the General Staff, very intelligent, patriotic and well-behaved, named Dreyfus." Vignettes introduced all the "jealous, scheming, deceitful" officers who plotted against the captain, as well as the protagonists, the "magnificent" Picquart and the courageous "defenders of justice," Zola, Lazare, Jaurès, and others. In one domestic scene, Pierre saw himself, next to his sister and mother with his head buried in his arms, crying "Mama! Where is my father?" Printed late in 1898, prior to the call for revision of the case, the lithograph ended with a scene of hope: An angelic image of Marianne floated over Dreyfus's head and returned his kepi while an officer in full-dress uniform presented a medal to the captain. "One day soon," the caption read, "they will return Dreyfus's officer's stripes, and glorious France will have nobly atoned for the injustice done to one of its most devoted soldiers."[14]

Despite all the embellishments, the *image d'Epinal* that Alfred and Lucie showed Pierre was accurate—until the final scene. Dreyfus could not be reinstated into the officer corps until "new facts" emerged to reopen his case and secure his acquittal. He had been pardoned at Rennes, not "rehabilitated," and as soon as his health permitted he would direct the next phase of the legal battle. But if his first outings with Lucie and the children in Carpentras were any indication, it would be a long while before he had the strength to manage his own affair. He could not walk more than a few hundred meters, and on nights when his malarial fever returned, he hallucinated that he was still trapped on Devil's Island.[15]

Like latter-day pilgrims en route to a celebrated shrine, Parisian Dreyfusards made their way south to meet the man they had defended. The first visitor, appropriately, was Dreyfus's first ally outside the immediate family. Convinced of the captain's innocence on the night of his arrival at Cherche-Midi, Commandant Forzinetti, the prison director, had risked his career and, later, his life to support the family's cause. Dreyfus embraced his "brave" friend at Villemarie, and the men shared memories of their last moment together, when the commandant, in protest, turned his prisoner over to the guards who would take him to the "degradation parade." Dreyfus paid Forzinetti his highest compliment when he called him a "courageous and loyal soldier."[16]

Like most of the visitors to Carpentras, Gabriel Monod had never met Dreyfus. Founder of the *Revue historique* and distinguished professor at the Ecole Normale Supérieure and the Ecole Pratique des Hautes Etudes, Monod had been asked by Mathieu to examine the *bordereau* in 1897. With his former student, Bernard Lazare, he became a principal organizer of the Dreyfusard cause in intellectual and academic circles, and, as a Protestant with a scholarly interest in German history, he felt the wrath of nationalist groups out to identify "traitors" within the enemy camp. In Carpentras, Dreyfus must have shared with the professor his interest in historiography—in the works of Michelet, Taine, Fustel, and the other scholars he had read on Devil's Island. "It is not your honor alone [which is at issue]," Monod had written the prisoner in Rennes, "it is that of the fatherland and the army." Impressed with all the allies who came to pay their respects, Dreyfus felt a special camaraderie with Monod, the man he called "a secular saint."[17]

Lucie received friends and admirers as well, including Hélène and Eugène Naville, who traveled from their Geneva home. Like so many other Swiss and French Protestants, the Navilles had been converted to the Dreyfusard campaign by their coreligionist Scheurer-Kestner. Through his articles in the *Journal de Genève,* Eugène Naville became one of the captain's most eloquent defenders outside France, and on his trips to Paris he worked with Mathieu, Jaurès, Reinach, Anatole France, and others engaged in the battle for "revision." Hélène often accompanied Lucie at times when it was perilous to be in public; and with expertise gained as a volunteer for the Red Cross (an organization her husband helped direct in Switzerland), she cared for Lucie during her long bout with pleurisy. In 1898, under the pseudonym Villemar (from the name of the Valabrègue estate), she wrote *Dreyfus Intime,* a short history of Alfred's life. Based on interviews with his sisters and brothers, it drew a human portrait of a man who existed only as an abstract symbol. The Navilles' stay in Carpentras served as a reunion with Lucie and as an introduction to her husband, and the couple came away feeling like Dreyfus's "old friends." Most of all, they were impressed by his "serenity" and absence of anger. "I understood that this man was perfectly composed," Eugène Naville observed in his journal, "and that his ability to survive the most horrible torment he owed to his extraordinary moral strength."[18]

Dreyfus finally met Joseph Reinach, that staunchest of defenders who, most recently, had been counseling Mathieu on how to manage his brother's recuperation ("Above all, keep him out of the cold, and always make him come in *before* the sun sets. It's essential.").[19] Reinach had remained in Paris during the Rennes court-martial in order to stay close to the politicians who would determine the prisoner's fate, and to avoid the demonstrators who, on seeing one of their favorite targets, would undoubtedly cause trouble; if the name Rothschild had become synonymous with Jewish "usury," the name Reinach had served a similar purpose for anti-Semites obsessed with Jewish "infiltration" of parliamentary politics. Joseph Reinach stayed away from the courtroom dramas because he was most effective in the corridors of political power and in his book-lined study where he wrote countless letters, pamphlets, and newspaper articles in defense of a man he had never met. He had met Dreyfus's brother, however, and their alliance developed into an enduring friendship. As Mathieu's confidant, Reinach gained a special insight into Alfred Dreyfus's character long before the return from Devil's Island. "For many partisans," he would later write, the prisoner "played his role poorly, because he played none at all; he remained simply himself." And if those partisans mistook Dreyfus's "modesty" for "curtness," if they found his expressions of gratitude inadequate and wanted his heart "to overflow," Reinach realized that the captain's "simplicity" was his strength, and that he would never "exploit his suffering." In October 1899, as he approached the garden at Villemarie, and as Lucie introduced her husband ("as if she needed to identify him"), Reinach knew what to expect. The two men shook hands, and, "without apparent emotion," Dreyfus said, "Thank you." That simple greeting, Reinach observed, was "equally worthy of him and of myself."[20]

The visits of family, friends, and allies continued through the fall and winter. But leisurely reminiscences of the past gave way to strategic planning for the future when Waldeck-Rousseau proposed amnesty "for all criminal acts or misdemeanors connected with the Dreyfus affair or comprised in any lawsuit relative to any of those acts."[21] Mathieu called the planned legislation "shameful, wretched." Even though it would let the Rennes verdict stand and leave open the possibility that Dreyfus could overturn that decision, it also meant that Mercier and his co-conspirators would escape the punishment they deserved and that the family would find it virtually impossible to uncover the "new facts" needed to pursue the case. Every Dreyfusard condemned the government's plan, and none more passionately than Dreyfus himself: "The project . . . deprives me of my most cherished hope," he wrote the president of the Senate's amnesty commission, "that of seeing my innocence legally proclaimed. . . . I have solicited no indulgence; the right of an innocent man is not clemency, it is justice." And, he went on, the government's plan would "leave me disarmed against injustice."[22] Dreyfus filed his protest immediately upon hearing of the proposed law. But preparations in the Senate continued, driven as much by pressures from outside France's borders as from within.

From Esterhazy's trial and the riots that followed J'Accuse, to the charade of Dreyfus's reconviction "with extenuating circumstances," foreign reactions to the French political, judicial, and military systems had gone from bad to worse. Confidential reports submitted to the minister of foreign affairs from French embassies and consulates throughout Europe and America in 1898 had confirmed "the sad impression" the affair was making abroad. The "entire press" of the United States, "even the most moderate newspapers," said one diplomat, "attack the government and France with extreme violence and in conspicuous bad faith." Later, on the eve of the Rennes verdict, a letter from a private citizen in New Jersey to the Paris "Chief of Police" warned that "if Dreyfus is convicted . . . it will be unsafe for Frenchmen to travel in this United States of America." From Rome, Vienna, and Madrid came other reports chronicling "unfavorable impressions" and outright "hostility." Not surprisingly, German newspapers, in Berlin and Cologne, lashed out at the government's handling of the affair in editorials that were "hateful," "intemperate" and "violent"; but so, too, did the Dutch, who called it "the greatest scandal of the century." Other communications from Holland said that Protestants equated the situation in contemporary France with that of the "Saint Bartholomew's Day Massacres and the dragonnades"; and members of another Protestant community—the "French-descended Huguenots established in the United States"—wrote from their newspaper's headquarters in Springfield, Massachusetts, to protest the "fanaticism" and "intolerance" rampant in France. Crowds in Brussels formed a "public cortege" in the late spring of 1898, with a carriage decked out to represent "the Apotheosis of the Prisoner Dreyfus," and, according to the French embassy in London, every British newspaper expressed its hostility toward France and its support of the prisoner. One member of the Reform Club aimed to start a "public subscription" to raise money for Dreyfus and to put an end to the "revolting" scandal. On a business trip to Romania in 1898, Eugène Naville learned from colleagues of their disgust with the affair ("as in all the countries of the world," he added), and those comments were similar to the one received by a French general from a "highly placed Russian" whose "educated countrymen were incensed with France. . . . Make no mistake about it," he warned, "in our century of steam power, no country can turn inward and isolate itself from world opinion. France is judged, and judged very severely, by every foreign land." A Viennese newspaper announced that the French army had suffered a "domestic Sedan, the repercussions of which will be more profound and more lasting than that of September 1870." Closer to home, Mathieu received an assessment from a Mulhouse industrialist: "Here [in Alsace], as in Switzerland and beyond, people are asking if France has gone mad."[23]

With few exceptions, diplomats in the field and specialists in Paris attempted to explain away those reactions as the inspiration of foreign Jews out to humiliate France. "Many of the large newspapers are in the hands of the Jews," went one report from the French embassy in London, "and those that are not . . . are in the hands of the Protestants." When demonstrators in Brussels criticized French handling of the affair, their comments were considered understandable in a city "which has been one of the most active theatres of operations for the Israelite Syndicate," a syndicate whose moneylender (according to this particularly paranoid official) was "the Jew . . . Consul General of Italy." The report from Brussels ended with a rousing confirmation that "the Great Nation [of France]" is superior to Belgium, with its "noisy little people, conceited and thankless." But if every form of xenophobia appeared in French assessments of foreign reactions to the affair, the principal worry remained the Jews, and nowhere were they more powerful (French perceptions had it) than in Central Europe. Austrian newspapers were bound to attack the army and support the "ill-starred" Dreyfus, observers insisted, since those papers were "almost entirely in the hands of the Jews"; and though some anti-Jewish journalists, officers, and diplomats in Germany had the "wisdom" to believe in Dreyfus's guilt, they had no hope of countering the pervasive influence of "the Semites."[24] In the final years of the century, Edouard Drumont's message had reached beyond his traditional readership of petty shopkeepers, rural priests, and disaffected aristocrats to a significant part of the French diplomatic corps; they reckoned, as the majority of the French General Staff had done, that only Jews could find something lacking in France.

But in the late summer and fall of 1899 the problem of foreign reactions would not go away, and even the most rabid anti-Semites could not accuse groups like the "Swedish Association of the Blind" (which sent a letter of support to the prisoner who had also lived in the dark, "in chains") of conspiring with the "Jewish Syndicate."[25] When Queen Victoria expressed her displeasure with the affair, the international repercussions were clear. After Rennes, where the British Lord Chief Justice had witnessed the court-martial, the queen announced her "profound sorrow" on hearing news of the verdict and, in a phlegmatic turn of phrase that nonetheless captured her abhorrence of French politics, she declared Dreyfus's condemnation to be "in defiance of good sense."[26] The British ambassador in Paris believed that "no impartial foreigner" could contemplate the case "without a sensation of pity, very much allied to contempt," and he admitted to his own feeling of "mental nausea."[27]

Coming in letters, telegrams, and newspapers, British responses to the Rennes decision were the most numerous, and most did not trouble with the diplomatic niceties of the queen and her ambassador. Even the staid London *Times* showed its anger: It had "no hesitation in affirming that the sentence . . . constitutes in itself the grossest and . . . most appalling prostitution of justice which the world has witnessed in modern times." The paper concluded with an attack on France's most cherished image: "Never before—in a country which claims to march at the head of civilization—[has a nation] so flagrantly, so deliberately, so mercilessly trampled justice, honor and truth under foot!"[28] One Englishman told Mathieu not to "despair with the sentence those cowardly traitors have passed on your brother . . . the poor fellow is the daily talk of every true British subject all over the world." He exaggerated, but in Hyde Park and in the East End "considerable crowds" and "hundreds of speakers" gathered to condemn the Rennes verdict. And while one group of Frenchmen and -women resident in England sent a petition of "sympathy" to the captain, others confronted pro-Dreyfus demonstrators in London and shouted "Down with the Jews!" "Long live the Army!"[29] On September 11, 1899, a one-line telegram sent to the president of the French Republic "on behalf of sixty-five Englishmen and eight Germans" summarized the tone of foreign reactions, and, to avoid any misunderstanding, they sent it in French: *"Monsieur, vous êtes chef d'un sale peuple"* ("Sir, you are the leader of a filthy people").[30]

That animosity had not been spontaneously induced by the Dreyfus case. A long history of Anglo-French hostility shaped responses to the affair, as did recent conflicts over issues that had nothing to do with the captain's plight. The armies of Britain and France had been shadowing each other across northern Africa for decades, and in 1898, those two rivals, the world's most formidable imperial powers, had come to the brink of war in the eastern Sudan, where, their eyes on Egypt, they had faced each other at the fortress of Fashoda on the Nile. Vastly outnumbered, the French had been forced to pull back, and that humiliation in the desert, widely reported by an international press eager for stories of imperial conquest, had strained relations in the governmental offices of the metropole. A year later, with the outbreak of the Boer War, relations deteriorated further. Roundly condemned by most of Europe for its imperial aggression against the Dutch settlers of southern Africa—for a war waged in pursuit of diamonds and gold—Britain received its most virulent criticism, not surprisingly, from France. "In the throes of a veritable Anglophobic madness," as Mathieu Dreyfus described it, Paris soon became so "violently pro-Boer [that] to speak English on the streets . . . was dangerous."[31]

Another long-standing rivalry, however, brought the focus back to the Dreyfus affair. The Universal Exposition scheduled to open in Paris in April 1900 was only the most recent in a string of world's fairs that dated from the late eighteenth century but that had been crowned by the hugely successful Crystal Palace exhibition in London in 1851. Arenas for the celebration of industrial progress, those expositions, which attracted millions of visitors to thousands of exhibits from scores of countries, served the double purpose of fostering international trade and, for the host country, national grandeur. If Britain frequently got the best of France in colonial competitions, the French Republic outdid its chief rival in international pageants. The organizers of the 1900 Paris Universal Exposition aimed to draw even more visitors than the thirty-two million who, in 1889, had marveled at the Galerie des Machines, the Eiffel Tower, and, on that centenary of the Revolution, the pantomime of a prisoner escaping the Bastille. In 1889 visitors had left behind a surplus of eight million francs, and 1900 promised even greater profits.[32]

President Loubet and Prime Minister Waldeck-Rousseau may have recognized the inequities of an amnesty bill that would protect the most sordid criminals in the Dreyfus case. But Loubet had promoted the 1900 exposition, and Waldeck-Rousseau—who approached issues, it was said, with "the cold eye of a fish in aspic"—had no intention of presiding over its failure; because fail it would if France did not do something to improve its image abroad. As early as March 1898, one diplomat learned that Holland and Switzerland would "refuse any participation in the exposition" and the same question was discussed "in German industrial circles." Too many perils existed in France, according to one group of Germans, "a country where all rights are violated, where only the antisemitic and chauvinist population makes the law, and where anyone who doesn't share their passions runs the risk of being hurled into the Seine." The hypocrisy of that statement mattered less to the French government than the threat of a boycott. But the height of the crisis came with the Rennes verdict eighteen months later. "Foreign commission agents have been ordered by their enterprises to purchase no fashion articles in France," reported the director of the Galeries Lamartine department store in Paris, and witnesses in Vienna, Budapest, Brussels, Rome, Milan, and Naples confirmed more threats of a boycott, while French agents in Britain predicted the "failure of the Exposition."[33]

Those pressures influenced Loubet's decision to pardon Dreyfus ("The Exposition," Minister of Commerce Millerand had asked. "Is the Exposition not in danger?"); and a friend of the Dreyfus family, their fellow Alsatian Lalance, confirmed the need for a period of calm. "It is in your interest," he wrote the captain late in September 1899, "and above all in the superior interest of France that the agitation surrounding your name stop, [and] that there be a truce of one year. . . . The Exposition must run its course before you will be able to open the campaign for rehabilitation effectively. Have patience until then," Lalance urged, and "the rest will come in time."[34] Dreyfus respected the "sane reason" and "generous heart" of that fellow *protestataire*. But plans for the exposition conflicted with plans for his own legal struggle when the government decided that contempt from abroad could not be swept away by a pardon alone, and that only an amnesty could put an end to hostilities. For Dreyfus and many of his allies, however, French grandeur would be best served if the government acted on the ideals of the Revolution—ideals they were about to package for commercial consumption at a world's fair.

Though his fevers and nightmares persisted, Dreyfus regained sufficient strength in Carpentras to protest the amnesty legislation as it made its way through committee debates. He also worked on his case and turned to the mass of letters he had received since Rennes. Pierre and Jeanne watched their father at his desk "examining documents and covering great sheets of foolscap" with his fine—and now infamous—handwriting. Letters of support came from old acquaintances and new, from friends of friends, and from allies he had never met—with many addressed in care of Mathieu, internationally known as the manager of his brother's "affair." A young assistant professor of history on a research trip to Paris from the University of Chicago asked Mathieu "to communicate to your brother the encouragement and sympathy of the Faculty of an American university," and an old associate of Dr. Gibert's (that Dreyfusard from Le Havre who had died early in 1899) wanted to treat Alfred's illnesses; like his late colleague, the doctor specialized in "therapeutic hypnotism," which worked wonders, he said, on "stomach disorders." A physician from the Loire-et-Cher department suggested a glass of "beef blood" (taken while still warm) as the perfect cure for anemia; and still another suggestion came from a celebrated American author with a fanatical distrust of the French ("The unspeakables!" Samuel Clemens called them. "I don't think they have improved a jot since they were turned out of hell!"). Clemens, it seems, considered Dreyfus a victim of Gallic evils, and wanted to help. He asked an acquaintance in England to suggest to Madame Dreyfus the services of a Mr. Kellgreu; he "can cure any disease that any physician can cure," the writer insisted "and . . . in many desperate cases he can restore health where no physician can do it." Dreyfus used the Valabrègues' doctor in Carpentras, but the friendly letters he received were far better antidotes to his troubles than the spells and potions that were suggested.[35]

Dreyfus also developed at Villemarie a research habit he would never break as he studied his affair. Clipping and annotating every newspaper article that referred to his case, he flagged errors and confirmed accurate insights; and while he filed most reports away for future reference, he shared the more comical or bizarre passages with family and friends. If public passions had ebbed, outlandish rumors had not, and one, in December 1899, had Dreyfus preparing to stand for a senatorial election in the Seine-et-Oise. A short time later, Le Siècle, reporting on an article from the New York Herald, said that a junta in the Philippines had hired the captain "to reorganize the Tagales [Tagalog] troops"—a story that so amused Dreyfus that he sent it to Joseph Reinach with a note asking "how far the imagination can go." In the spring of 1900 he responded to a request from the New York Journal that he comment on the South African war and on the delegation of Boers just arrived in the United States. "Profoundly touched" that his opinion had been solicited, he said that his legal situation made it impossible for him "to take part in the discussion," and he ended with a statement carefully worded to avoid criticism of the English (his greatest supporters) and of the Boers (with whom he may have sympathized): "I hope from the bottom of my heart, and for the cause of humanity, that the United States will find a way to bring an end to this war in which the two adversaries have shown such admirable qualities of sacrifice and courage." Learning, long after others had learned, that he had become an international celebrity, Dreyfus tried to develop the diplomatic skills he would need as a public figure; those skills, however, came more naturally to his brother Mathieu. [36]

Entrepreneurs soon realized that Dreyfus's *affaire politique* could be turned into a profitable *affaire commerciale*. Offers had started to arrive while the prisoner still awaited his verdict in Rennes, and most had come from abroad—an indication, perhaps, that French business-men anticipated that more problems than profits would be associated with Dreyfus. Literary agents from England and America proposed lucrative book contracts, and a lecture agent from Liverpool promised more than one hundred thousand francs if Dreyfus traveled to England and the United States to speak on the "genesis" of his affair. Those offers and others like them could have helped defray the costs of his case, but Dreyfus had neither the stamina nor the desire to exploit his own recent history; and while his family had spent large sums over the past six years, they had no need to commercialize the case in order pay its expenses. [37]

Dreyfus would publish his memoirs in France, not abroad, and he began to outline that project in Carpentras with the long-distance help of Joseph Reinach, who was at work in Paris on his own history of the affair. The two men shared information and, later, chapter drafts, and if Reinach knew the case far better than its central figure did, Dreyfus could comment on the personal passages of his friend's volumes. He explained the topography of Devil's Island, and suggested that David Hadamard be referred to as his father-in-law, not as a "diamond trader" (a term, Dreyfus said, which sounded "a bit too vulgar"). Though "grateful" for Reinach's "passionate" and "admirable" account, Dreyfus later admitted one regret: The author was not hard enough on their adversaries and too hard on their allies. Supporters may differ on tac-tics, Dreyfus observed, but they all had "courage." Examining Rein-ach's massive work like a meticulous amateur editor, Dreyfus approached the history of his case just as he had approached its court-room debates—with his "tendency toward objectivity." [38]

Despite Reinach's admonitions to keep warm in Carpentras, Drey-fus reported that he dealt with the "Siberian cold" that swept through Provence in the winter of 1899 better than the general population (all "burrowed in at home"). [39] He could not, however, bear the heat that was sure to hit by early summer, and doctors advised him to continue his recuperation in a more moderate climate. It is also likely that life within the garden walls of Villemarie, ideal for an invalid, had become claustrophobic for a man with renewed energy. Given the dangers involved, he rarely ventured beyond the boundaries of the Valabrègue estate, and he may have started to wonder if his true freedom would ever come—the freedom to walk along a city street with Lucie and the children, to visit parks, shops, theaters, and galleries, as he had done with his wife so many years before. The climate of Provence—natural and political—suggested that it was time to move. But the family's options in France were limited.

Numerous supporters, known and unknown, had invited the Dreyfuses to share their villas, country cottages, and seaside retreats. A friend of the Hadamards, a physician, offered his home in Cannes; a group of citizens in the Michigan village of Otsego wanted to purchase a house for Dreyfus in the hope that he would settle there; yet another American offered the gift of a "well-built, three story and basement family residence on Walnut Street" in Louisville, Kentucky. Dreyfus may have appreciated the idea of a quiet life near thoroughbred horse farms, but he wanted, if he could, to remain in France. That choice would also lead him to reject an invitation made by Lady Dorothy Stanley to stay in her country home in England, with its "cows and chickens," its "pure milk and fresh eggs." Lady Stanley's husband, the celebrated explorer Henry Morton Stanley, had spent nearly as much time in the jungles of Central Africa as Dreyfus had in South America, and "Bula Matari" (the "Stonebreaker") knew what it was like to survive malaria, dysentery, and equatorial heat. But for Dreyfus a move to England would trigger accusations of "flight"; Esterhazy had escaped to London and still lived there, and Zola had fled to England in the wake of J'Accuse.[40]

If the situation in France remained too perilous for the family, one foreign country could provide a safe haven without political repercussions. Switzerland had served as Raphael Dreyfus's base until his children moved to the French interior after the Franco-Prussian War, and both Mathieu and Alfred had returned south of the Rhine on many occasions—Mathieu had apprenticed with a textile firm in Basel, and Alfred, like other French Alsatians blocked from the Reichsland, had used Switzerland as his back door into Mulhouse. If leaving Carpentras for England might prompt criticism that the family preferred a country hostile to France, the same could not be said of the Francophone town of Geneva, where Eugène and Hélène Naville opened their home to the Dreyfuses in April 1900. Like most other Swiss Protestants who took notice of the affair, the Navilles had denounced the General Staff with-

out condemning the French nation. "Too often foreigners are reproached for having rallied to Dreyfus because of their hatred for
France," Naville noted in his journal. "On the contrary, it was our great
attachment to France, our affection, which inspired all our efforts to
oppose the abominable judicial crime which defiled its history." Educated at the Ecole de Commerce in Mulhouse and recipient of the
Legion of Honor for his services to wounded French soldiers in the 1870
war, Eugène Naville was the perfect ally. Dreyfus's return to Switzerland would be almost like coming home.[41]

Awakened by news of the pending move, police agents and journalists, like wasps mobilized after a long winter, sent a flurry of telegrams to their superiors. With the family able to keep their destination
secret until the last moment, rumors spread that Dreyfus had been
spotted in Montpellier, or that he was en route to Biarritz or Lyon or
Bellegarde near Orléans. One report said that he had finally chosen
England as his place of refuge. By April 20, however, when the family
departed from the Carpentras train station (accompanied again by their
bodyguard, Paul Valabrègue), most reporters identified Geneva as the
final stop. The move came at a curious moment. The Universal Exposition had just opened in Paris, and the most successful "entertainment," with its 21,000 square meters of "artificial mountains, fir forests,
Alpine torrents, chalets, pastures with herds of cows and sheep" and
three hundred actors playing peasants, was a recreation, near the banks
of the Seine, of Switzerland.[42]

On a promontory fifty meters above Lake Geneva, near the village of
Cologny and a twenty-minute walk from the center of Geneva, the Villa
Hauterive had much in common with Villemarie. Surrounded by high
trees and set off from the main road, the Navilles' home—though more
spacious than the Valabrègue estate and more sumptuous in its architectural details—provided good security. Alfred and Lucie soon learned,
however, that the Genevois had little in common with the citizens of
Carpentras; they left the family in peace. From the terrace at Hauterive, Dreyfus looked out across the lake—with its sailboats, tour
boats, and "silver reflections" in the afternoon light—to the crests of
the Jura Mountains on the French border, still covered with snow in late
April. Geneva, nestled in a pass between the Alps and the Jura range,
could be seen through the trees that lined the villa's garden. Dreyfus's
view was, in a sense, the mirror image of the one he had known as a
child in Alsace; with his hometown situated near the northern reaches

of the Jura foothills, his view south from Mulhouse had stretched down the mountain range toward Switzerland.[43]

"What an exquisite rest this was for all of us," Dreyfus wrote, "after so many painful years." Respecting their guests' need for quiet, the Navilles arranged only a few activities: Eugène Naville's eighty-year-old mother asked for a dinner with the famous captain as her special "birthday present"; Dreyfus spent an afternoon at the lakeside summer house of the Baroness de Rothschild, a friend of the Navilles; and, on one brief outing, he joined friends for lunch at the cure center of Thonon-les-Bains in the nearby Haute Savoie—a visit that passed without incident, despite *La Libre Parole's* insistence that "hostile shouts" had greeted Dreyfus along the way. Lucie and Alfred took an occasional boat trip with their hosts on the lake, but they preferred the quiet promontory of Hauterive to the busy world below. If "the scenery is wonderful," Dreyfus confessed in a letter to Joseph Reinach, the "general impression" of the populated areas near the lake "is less favorable." There were, he said, too many tourists.[44]

Devoting most of his time to trial transcripts and other documents that might reveal the "new facts" needed to reopen his case, Dreyfus also responded to critics who defined his pardon as an admission of guilt or who accused him of abandoning his battle for the soft life of retirement on a private income. In letters to editors and notes to supporters, he stressed that he could do nothing until he had concrete evidence; for Dreyfus, as Reinach noted, "the law . . . was the law."[45] If criticisms had come only from the usual sources—Drumont and his followers—Dreyfus could have saved his energy and ended his long-distance self-defense campaign. But many of his most influential allies were turning against him—or turning away.

In the late fall of 1900, Mathieu wrote to Cologny and confirmed that supporters "misinterpreted" Dreyfus's absence and demanded that he return to Paris. "Esterhazy in London, Dreyfus in Switzerland," said one confederate. "That does not sound good." Too many rumors were circulating that the captain had given up the fight or feared for his life. Mathieu understood his brother's need to recuperate, and he believed that Alfred should avoid the "personal risks" he would confront in Paris. But the infighting that contaminated Dreyfusard circles in Rennes continued in Paris, and Mathieu faced the collapse of his alliance. If Reinach, Demange, Zola, and a few others still cared about Dreyfus's personal well-being, Picquart, Labori, and Clemenceau put the politics of the case above the interests of a man for whom they had no affection.

They wanted to press the ideological fight, and they could not do it with its symbol relaxing on the shores of a Swiss lake.[46]

The split between Mathieu and Labori had become serious. The lawyer stepped up his diatribes against Demange and insisted that his former partner had fallen victim to Waldeck-Rousseau's political caution. Labori ordered Mathieu to break with his first counsel ("It's either him," he warned, "or Picquart and me"), and he again accused the Dreyfus family of a cowardly strategy of deference to the government. After one sharp exchange in Paris, Mathieu tried to calm Labori and make him understand that no conspiracy of surrender existed, and he repeated that the family had no intention of turning against Demange. But Labori, on the verge of physical violence, rushed at Mathieu and shouted, "Demange knows things I don't know. Maybe your brother confessed to him." Mathieu, his patience gone, wanted to go at Labori's "throat," but contained his anger out of respect for the lawyer's past efforts. Before walking out Mathieu simply said, "You are mad, Labori, ruthlessly mad."[47]

Clemenceau was different. With that Dreyfusard, Mathieu enjoyed a better relationship, a feeling of mutual respect that dated from their strategy sessions in the offices of *L'Aurore*. But Clemenceau echoed Labori's demands. As a politician who had built his career on the ruins of governments he had destroyed, he had no time for Waldeck-Rousseau's bland republicanism; and as a Radical, he had no stomach for Demange's Catholicism. Like Labori, "the Tiger" wanted to wrest control of the affair from tame politicians and atavistic believers. Furthermore, his hostile attitude toward Mathieu's brother seemed a curious contradiction: Self-professed champion of the downtrodden, Clemenceau rarely, if ever, thought of Alfred Dreyfus as one of the oppressed. And when the veil—always a thin one—was lifted to expose Picquart's true contempt for the Dreyfus family, a contempt shaped partly by that Alsatian's anti-Semitism, Mathieu knew that the solidarity of 1898 had been shattered by special interests and private prejudices made public.[48]

Dreyfusard critics had good reason to question the government's commitment to the case. A few months earlier, during parliamentary debates over the amnesty question, Waldeck-Rousseau tried to bury his greatest problem with a single proclamation; confirming what Dreyfus called his "lack of moral courage," the prime minister announced to the Chamber that "the Dreyfus Affair is over."[49] He was right, at least when it came to the center ring of French politics. With the key figure out of exile, with the officers who had engineered his convictions about to be protected by an amnesty law, and with world opinion assuaged, for the most part, by the proposed legislation, the case no longer inspired the passion it had when Zola published *J'Accuse*. Reinach, who always painted a grand canvas, compared it to a "flood" that had inundated the political life of France until it drew back, after the second court-martial, like "the ebbing waters of the Nile."[50] Mathieu admitted that he could "arouse new and violent polemics" and bring about, perhaps, "the fall of the government" that Labori and others so desired; but Mathieu and his brother saw "no material or moral advantage" in that strategy. Letting their gratitude get the best of their anger, they refused to attack the men who had lobbied so "courageously" for the prisoner's pardon.[51]

The family deferred to the prime minister but never accepted his obituary of the affair. Dreyfus left Switzerland and returned to Paris to keep his case alive and to help the brother who had helped him. Waldeck-Rousseau "was mistaken when he said that he had seen the last act played out," Dreyfus announced. "He had seen only the next to the last act."[52]

CHAPTER XVI

Legions of Honor

ONE YEAR after royalist gangs smashed his top hat at Auteuil racetrack, President Loubet, so often under siege, scored his greatest triumph. Through the spring and summer of 1900 he staged a Universal Exposition that shattered all records and outgrossed—in receipts and matters of taste—the extravaganza of 1889. As promised, the "World's Fair truce" pushed the Dreyfus affair into the background, and the threatened boycotts never materialized. More than fifty million visitors (eighteen million more than the previous exposition) passed through the thousands of national and international exhibits which covered scores of acres on and near the banks of the Seine in western Paris. And gigantism provided the fair's only unifying theme—from the 106-meter-high Ferris wheel and the cavernous movie house, to the electrified "palace" and the ornate Alexandre III bridge, dedicated to the late czar of France's giant Russian ally. Even the feasts were gargantuan; Loubet hosted one banquet for more than twenty thousand mayors and deputy mayors from villages and towns throughout France, and many of those local functionaries, on their first trip to the capital, must have associated the City of Light not with the old Sun King but with new incandescent bulbs.[1]

Adhering to a schedule that the government must have appreciated, if not ordered, Dreyfus and his family returned to Paris in the aftermath of the exposition. The electric-powered "moving sidewalks"

291

had stopped, and the Swiss "peasants" had turned in their wooden clogs, but many of the monuments remained, and most were situated in the family's former neighborhoods. The Grand Palais and the Petit Palais dominated the cityscape just east of the apartment in which Pierre had been born, and directly across the Pont de l'Alma from Alfred's last home on the Avenue du Trocadéro, workers dismantled the remnants of "Old Paris," a shaky stucco and plaster recreation of medieval stone turrets and steeples. From the Ecole Militaire to the *quartier* of the Ministry of War and north across the river toward the Champs-Elysées, the exposition had encompassed the entire area of Paris that Dreyfus knew best and that he had not seen in more than a half decade.

"What tragic events had occurred since I left my home . . . never to see it again," he recalled on that late November morning when he returned to Paris. For Lucie and Alfred 1900 marked their tenth wedding anniversary, but with most of their married years spent apart, they came to the capital like newlyweds, resolved to look forward and not back—to obliterate, as Alfred put it, the "sad and depressing images of the past" that the city conjured up. Again, like a young couple starting a new life, they moved in with Lucie's parents on the rue Châteaudun. For Pierre and Jeanne, who held only vague memories of the apartment they had shared with their father, the Hadamards' was home. [2]

Shortly after his brother's arrival in Paris, Mathieu made his own voyage home—to Mulhouse. His daughter, Magui, had been only three years old and Emile still an infant when his odyssey began in 1894, and though Suzanne brought the children to their father's temporary apartments on the rue Téhéran and the Boulevard Haussmann, they had spent most of the years of the affair with their grandparents in Héricourt. Now, in the fashionable Faubourg du Miroir quarter of Mulhouse, Mathieu reunited his family in a new three-story home with verandas and balconies. Designed in an architectural style as oxymoronic as its name ("bourgeois classique"), the house was situated close to those of old colleagues—the Jeanmaires, Koechlins, Schlumbergers, and others—who had become Dreyfusard allies. In the Faubourg du Miroir, at the cotton exchange, and in the countryside surrounding Mulhouse, Mathieu tried to reestablish his former routine of family life, work, and sport; and he did it with an expanded circle of friends. After years on one kind of chase with Joseph Reinach in Paris, he invited his comrade on another, to hunt partridge and hare in the forests of southern Alsace. [3]

Assuming more control over his own affair, Alfred found the

quarrels among allies in Paris more "painful" and "nerve-racking" than
the "base attacks" of his adversaries, which, he said, left him "indifferent." Hoping to focus exclusively on his case, he spent much of his
time acting as an arbiter of Dreyfusard conflicts. He tried to soothe
damaged egos and move his supporters toward "the final triumph."
But his diplomacy could not succeed where his brother's had failed.
Labori and Picquart rejected the captain's overtures, and though the
Hadamards and Navilles tried to arrange meetings of reconciliation,
the invitations were ignored. Fissures had run throughout the Dreyfusard alliance for well over a year, and the final split with Labori and
his comrades came when the lawyer ordered Dreyfus to keep his
brother in Mulhouse and off the case. "Placed between fraternal devotion and gratitude toward defenders [who had become] demanding
and intransigent," Eugène Naville observed, "Alfred had no choice but
to side with his kin." In making that decision, he was "excommuni-
cated" by Labori and Picquart, "two of his most ardent champions."[4]

But Naville had it only half right: Dreyfus did the excommunicating.
He reconfirmed his "indissoluble ties" to his brother and wrote Labori
a final letter. "I profoundly regret not being able to resolve a situation
that I find deplorable and that I did not create. For my part, I have done
everything humanly possible." Mindful of the lawyer's past efforts,
Dreyfus ended his letter with a gesture of friendship that neither Labori
nor Picquart would ever return: "Please believe," Dreyfus wrote the
lawyer, "that I will be eternally grateful for your admirable devotion
during these ill-fated years, and that I will be happy, whenever the
occasion presents itself, to shake your hand." In his private journal,
however, Dreyfus recorded his decision on those who had insulted his
brother and jeopardized his case: "The incident," he noted, "is closed."[5]

Reflecting on the steady dissolution of the Dreyfusard camp, Joseph Reinach pondered its inevitability. Many of those who supported
the cause had begun to realize that "there are no demigods, no perfect
heroes," and that when martyrs are "unnailed" from the cross, "they
are no different from other men." Whatever harmony existed at the
height of the affair, it was eclipsed when politics and personalities became more important than the common struggle for an ideal. Reinach
only hoped that "history" would reunite men like Dreyfus and Picquart,
because "history," he said, "is more tolerant, and therefore more just."[6]

In the spring of 1901 Dreyfus and Reinach celebrated the publication of
their very different histories of the affair. Recounting every intrigue that

had led to the captain's arrest, Reinach's massive volume introduced all the players and described the months leading to Devil's Island. In a letter to his friend, Dreyfus admitted that his own book would serve a different purpose, and that it would contain none of the "anecdotes" that Reinach captured so brilliantly. Unlike Robinson Crusoe, Dreyfus observed in good humor, "whose single goal was to live on his island and who had good reason to describe his life there. . . . I have another duty to fulfill, and everything unrelated to that obligation cannot appear in my account." His "duty," as he put it in the preface, was to "tell the story of . . . the five years when I was cut off from the world of the living," from the events in France which "remained unknown to me until the trial in Rennes." Presenting a selection of letters he had written to Lucie and to government officials from Paris prisons and from Devil's Island, he hoped to mobilize support for the final revision of his case.[7]

Published in May 1901, *Cinq années de ma vie* enjoyed immediate success in France and, in many translations, abroad. Wanting to avoid any appearance that he was out for profit rather than for "an essentially moral goal," Dreyfus had asked his publisher, Eugène Fasquelle (who numbered Zola and Reinach among his authors), to publicize the book only briefly and "with dignity." Fasquelle agreed and launched a campaign in France that Dreyfus deemed "perfectly correct"—though foreign distributors irritated the novice author with their "unseemly publicity." Having known only the career of an army officer, Dreyfus took pleasure in his brief moment as a "professional" writer; he worked on the editing and marketing of his book and enjoyed signing copies for allies and family members. Emile Zola's *La Vérité en marche*, a compilation of essays and letters on the affair, also appeared early in 1901, and the two men exchanged copies of their books with inscriptions that confirmed their mutual "admiration and affection." Dreyfus sent twenty copies to Henriette in Carpentras and asked that she distribute them, above all, in "popular quarters" where "one cannot buy the book," he said, "and where it most needs to be read." Amid all the celebrity, he did not lose sight of his goal. The anti-Semitic press greeted the release with predictable slurs (Maurice Barrès was not alone in accusing Dreyfus of cashing in on his own "treason"). But Joseph Reinach's assessment of his friend's "little book" spoke for more reasonable critics. Noting its simplicity and the way it "profoundly moved" the reader, Reinach also agreed with another Dreyfusard, Julien Benda, who had been struck by the captain's "almost pathological" desire to speak of himself "as if he were someone else." Directed toward its goal with surgical precision, *Cinq années de ma vie* was an accurate reflection of the man, but so too were the passionate letters it contained.[8]

The work that went into that book, along with the work that went into battling contentious colleagues, exhausted Dreyfus and brought on a recurrence of malarial fever. He was ordered to bed. "The doctor finds him much weaker, much less robust than last year," Mathieu wrote a friend late in 1901. "He is haunted by his case, obsessed by it night and day."[9] He returned to Switzerland in an attempt to regain his health and avoid the foul weather of Paris, but his own impatience, coupled with renewed accusations that he had abandoned the struggle, drew him back to France. Finally, after seven years of travel, forced and voluntary, he decided in the early months of 1902 to search for a permanent home for his family in Paris.

With Reinach serving as their informal realtor, Alfred and Lucie found an apartment in the eighth arrondissement on the Boulevard Haussmann, just south of Reinach's Parc Monceau villa. After they paid the deposit, however, the manager of the building broke the contract. Not surprisingly, the incident made good copy, and many journalists, eager to show dissension within the ranks of French Jews, traced the problem to a familiar source. The international banker Edmond de Rothschild owned the building (according to *Le Matin* and *La Libre Parole*), and when he received a telegram confirming Dreyfus's offer, he ordered his agents to get rid of the new tenant "at any price." Another story had Alphonse de Rothschild scolding his younger brother and volunteering personally to find a home for the Dreyfus family. But the most likely scenario appeared in *Liberté:* If Rothschild did own the building—and the rumor was never confirmed—he must have been deluged by complaints from residents who protested Dreyfus's presence and threatened to move out. Whatever the case, Alfred and Lucie did not press the issue and settled for the return of their deposit. *Le Matin* noted that Dreyfus had at least been saved an "unsightly" view; on the small square below the apartment, at the juncture of the Boulevard Haussmann and the rue d'Argenson, stood a "pitiful statue on a thick pedestal." Or so *Le Matin* described it. But Dreyfus, who had promised to return from exile "like Banquo's ghost," would have been pleased to look out on a likeness of William Shakespeare.[10]

It took months for the family to find a home in a building with an owner who would tolerate them. Finally, a lawyer and art collector, Gustave Dreyfus, with no relation to the family but with the courage to confront the dangers involved, rented them a fifth-floor apartment at

101 Boulevard Malesherbes. It was even closer to Reinach and the Parc Monceau, and it soon became clear that tenants had good reason to be concerned. Only a few "curious onlookers" had gathered in front of the Hadamards' when Dreyfus first returned to Paris late in 1900, but the author of *Cinq années de ma vie* had reemerged as a public figure, and, more important, his old allies, and especially the "Dreyfusard" government of Waldeck-Rousseau, had come under attack from clericals, royalists, and militant nationalists. Elections in the spring of 1902 had brought a majority of republicans, Radicals, and moderate Socialists to the Chamber of Deputies, but Paris, voting the other way, had become a nationalist enclave. Disgusted with the prime minister's long run (Waldeck-Rousseau had set a record for the Third Republic), and incensed by his Law of Associations, which aimed to control religious orders, anti-Dreyfusards condemned the new policies of their old enemies. Waldeck-Rousseau did not help matters in the summer of 1902 when he retired (voluntarily) and proposed as his successor an even more committed anticlerical, the sixty-seven-year-old senator from the Charente, Emile Combes. As prime minister, Combes would have no fewer than ten Freemasons in his cabinet, and, within days after taking office, he would sign decrees closing down more than one hundred religious schools throughout France.[11]

If Captain Dreyfus had worn thin as an issue in his own right, he could still serve as a symbol of a political system overrun by godless republicans and treasonous Jews. And Dreyfus's apartment could provide a target for the government's critics, as well as for those who enjoyed manifesting their bigotry whatever the political climate. In the period from Panama to the affair, Edouard Drumont and his followers had turned anti-Semitism not only into an ideological tool but into a new kind of urban sport, and the rules of the game had not been forgotten with Dreyfus's release from prison. On June 6 *La Libre Parole* published the address of that "Great Piece of Filth," Dreyfus, and advised tenants to make certain that the apartment is "vigorously disinfected."[12] In the weeks and months following those revelations, police agents and journalists reported the responses. Shops lined the building at its street level, and on the window of one vacant store, formerly a wine merchant, a poster read "Attention! The Great Bartender of Devil's Island opens soon. German wines and liquors. . . . And please note, maps and secret documents from the General Staff will be delivered to all customers!"[13] The apartment's concierge intercepted letters addressed to "the Jewish traitor" and delivered them to the prefecture of police.

"Twelve bullets in the body, that's what traitors deserve," began one note signed by "a patriot of Paris," and it went on to describe the iron grillework of the apartment's balcony; it must "remind you of the bars of your cage on Devil's Island," the "patriot" concluded, a cage "you should never have left." Another note, to the building's owner, condemned the "bourgeois justice" that had set the "millionaire traitor" free, and the authors of that letter, "a group of workers from Clichy," underscored their final sentence: "Since Dreyfus is living in your building," they announced, "we shall blow [it] up."[14]

Had that particular threat been carried out, Dreyfus's enemies would have destroyed an empty apartment. Either anticipating trouble or, more likely, ignoring it, Alfred, Lucie, and the children had left Paris in early June to pursue the seasonal routine of "bourgeois millionaires" at the seaside north of Dunkirk. But they received more threats after returning to their new apartment. *L'Intransigeant* linked anticlerical politicians to the nation's most notorious turncoat and warned that the affair was not over. The captain's supporters agreed, of course, for other reasons, and through the following year, when they stepped up the campaign for revision, their opponents responded with new suggestions of how to deal with Dreyfus. Drumont wanted him deported across the Channel ("where there are no traitors on his scale . . . and where he would be, without doubt, a great success"), while a group of "independent anti-Jews" made Drumont look benevolent when they called for the "execution" of the man they "still considered guilty."[15]

That announcement, police confirmed, went beyond "violent polemics." Undercover agents had exposed a plan to kidnap Dreyfus and "put an end to his Affair." Jules Girard, founder of *L'Action Nationale*, a publication that had fallen on hard times and needed the customers that a sensational kidnapping would insure, had assembled a gang of café waiters, failed artists, part-time actors, and full-time anarchists, many of them past and present members of the Antisemitic League of France. They had stationed men on the Boulevard Malesherbes to determine Dreyfus's routine, and they had planned to seize "the traitor," smother him with a cloth drenched in chloroform, and hurry him into an automobile waiting nearby. Taken to a secret location (many of Girard's followers volunteered their apartments), he would be held until all attempts to reopen his case were abandoned. If they were not, police evidence suggested, Dreyfus would be executed, like those "traitors and speculators" decapitated during the Revolution, their heads "shown to the people." Finally, if Dreyfus's kidnapping failed, Girard had ordered his men to march to the Parc Monceau to try the same methods on Joseph Reinach as he took his "daily promenade."[16]

The prefect of police sent his director of investigations to alert Dreyfus—and, presumably, Reinach—to the plot. But by now Dreyfus had been exposed to every conceivable form of abuse, from newspaper articles smearing his ancestry to hate mail containing bomb threats and promises of assassination scrawled by semiliterate madmen. He "smiled" on hearing the details of the latest "wild plan" and suggested that his kidnapping would serve no purpose. The fight for his innocence would continue in his absence. But police took the threat seriously and sent guards to the Boulevard Malesherbes to protect the family and their visitors.[17]

Accustomed to living behind shuttered windows and bolted doors, Dreyfus and his wife invited to their apartment those allies who had not defected. Lucie managed her household with the same orderliness with which Alfred managed his case, and she kept careful lists of guests and dinner menus. Family members from Paris and the provinces were the most frequent visitors, but on some evenings Reinach, Demange, the Navilles, and the Mathieu Dreyfuses would join Gabriel Monod, Jean Jaurès, and the lawyer Henri Mornard. Francis de Pressensé, "the most prominent representative of the Protestant conscience in the ranks of the Socialists," came regularly, as did another leading Protestant politician, the Radical Socialist Ferdinand Buisson, a former professor of pedagogy, and, like so many of his Dreyfusard comrades, a Freemason. Buisson's personal history had something in common with that of his host; in defiance of Napoleon III's autocratic regime, he had chosen voluntary exile in Switzerland.[18] "Within the limits of life," Dreyfus wrote, "one of the most beautiful things is to be surrounded by warm and sure friendships, and one must seize them precisely because they are so rare." After the troubles with Labori, Picquart, and Clemenceau, Dreyfus appreciated friends on whom he could "count absolutely," without worrying about "hidden motives." They made it possible, he said, "to smile at the inherent sadness of life."[19]

If friends gave him pleasure, however, there was much sadness during those years. Between 1899 and 1903 no fewer than six of Dreyfus's most important supporters died. Dr. Gibert had been the first, a few months prior to the Rennes trial, and Scheurer-Kestner had died on the day of Dreyfus's release—the day his pardon took effect. Bernard Lazare, only thirty-eight years old, lost a long battle with cancer on

September 1, 1903. And the two relatives who, along with Mathieu and Lucie, had worked the hardest for Alfred's release—David Hadamard and Joseph Valabrègue—also died in that short span of time.[20]

No individual Dreyfusard had done more to turn the case into an affair than Emile Zola, and on the night of September 28, 1902, Zola fell victim to carbon monoxide poisoning in the bedroom of his Paris apartment on the rue de Bruxelles. Servants had closed the fireplace draft, unaware that coals still smoldered, and the room had filled with fumes overnight (though another report had it that debris blocked the chimney). Zola collapsed as he tried to open a window, and his wife fell unconscious but survived. Rumors soon spread that the notorious Dreyfusard had either been murdered or committed suicide; but an autopsy, along with blood samples taken from Zola's wife and the couple's pet dog, seemed to confirm that it was an accident. Dreyfus learned of the tragedy within hours, and, at dawn, rushed the short distance from his apartment to the rue de Bruxelles. He arrived just as Madame Zola, still unconscious, was being taken to a hospital. Returning for Zola's vigil, and every night for four nights to console his widow, Dreyfus mourned the *grand romancier* who had saved his life. He sat for hours in front of Zola's body, watching his friend's favorite cat perched on its master's chest, and he thought not only of the writer's "creative power" but of his "generosity." Only a few months before, Zola had rallied again to Dreyfus's defense when the nationalist press spread new rumors that the captain had "confessed" his crime: "Today, as in the past, I affirm his innocence," Zola had written in *L'Aurore*, "and I have for him the greatest admiration and the greatest fondness."[21]

Madame Zola shared her husband's affection for the captain, but faced a delicate problem. She worried that Dreyfus's presence at the funeral—to be held at the Cimitière du Nord in Montmartre—would trigger demonstrations and place him and other mourners in danger. Joseph Reinach agreed, as did the Paris prefect of police. They urged Dreyfus to remain in seclusion, but he protested. "You are asking me to commit an act of cowardice," he told Reinach, and though his friend preferred to call it "an act of sacrifice," Dreyfus insisted that insults hurled by "miserable" troublemakers would not prevent him from fulfilling his "duty" to Zola's memory.[22] The fears proved well founded on the eve of the funeral, when journalists, as eager to beat dead horses as live ones, slandered the "pornographic and dung-drenched" novelist and threatened violence if Dreyfus joined the cortege. *L'Intransigeant* ordered all "republican patriots" to go en masse to the cemetery and to remain silent unless "the spy in the service of the enemy has the audacity to slip himself in. . . . Do not tolerate that provocation," Rochefort's newspaper concluded, "that supreme insult to the Fatherland."[23]

Dreyfus did not join the group that set off from the Zola home at 1:00 P.M. A crowd estimated at more than twenty thousand followed the cortege on its short journey north, accompanied by mounted troops prepared for trouble. At some point along the route, however, between the Place Blanche and the cemetery entrance, Dreyfus appeared among the mourners, flanked by Mathieu, Jaurès, Lazare, and other friends acting as human shields. The service began; Dreyfus heard Anatole France's eulogy to the author of *J'Accuse,* and, with others, he filed by the coffin. By the time the two hundred demonstrators outside the gates began shouting "Dreyfus to Noumea!" (a penal colony in the South Pacific) and "Zola to Charenton" (a prison and insane asylum near Paris), and by the time troops galloped into that mob, Dreyfus had left the cemetery by a side exit. One police agent submitted a report by telegram at 2:45 P.M.: "It is all over; Dreyfus has returned to his home without incident." Outsmarting the crowd, he survived that rare public appearance and fulfilled his duty to Zola.[24]

Less than two weeks later, on the night of October 15, Alfred, Lucie, and other family members were visiting the Hadamards on the rue Châteaudun when Lucie's father suffered a massive stroke. He died at three o'clock the next morning. Family members attributed his death to the pressures of the past decade. David Hadamard had protected his daughter throughout the affair, and he had stayed by her side in Rennes, visiting the military prison and fending off crowds with his open umbrella. With Mathieu and Reinach, he had been portrayed as a key leader of the "Jewish syndicate," and those accusations were helped along by stereotypes pinned on prosperous Jews involved in the gold and diamond trade. On October 20, Zadoc Kahn officiated at his friend's service, and nearly three thousand mourners attended—a confirmation of Hadamard's important association with the synagogue on the rue de la Victoire. Had the event not followed so closely on Zola's funeral, demonstrators might have tried to attend as well; but Hadamard's death, unlike Zola's, did not provoke Parisian crowds, and the service passed without incident.[25]

Still, police agents had prepared for trouble, and while Dreyfus tried to console his wife, he also had to deal with the distractions of armed guards who surrounded them. That experience, along with the troubles associated with Zola's funeral, convinced Dreyfus that Reinach and the others were right: He should no longer attend public events, not for his own protection (if anything, he preferred to defy the crowd) but for family and friends who might be threatened. After receiving news of Joseph Valabrègue's death in Carpentras, Dreyfus explained his decision in a letter to Henriette. But first he recalled how his brother-in-law had welcomed him to Villemarie thirty years before, how he had made a new home for a boy who had been forced to "abandon" his native Mulhouse. He recounted the years of the affair when Joseph had worked so selflessly. "I cannot offer you consolation," Dreyfus wrote his sister. "We have just lost one of our dearest friends, and my grief echoes yours. But we can recognize, simply, that we have obligations in life, and that, however great our afflictions and pains, we will face them courageously until our turn comes."[26] If Dreyfus felt a duty to attend any funeral, it was Joseph Valabrègue's, but he knew the climate of Carpentras, and he cared too much for his sister to risk the violence that his presence might incite. He asked Lucie to attend the funeral in his place, and the family understood.

Nine months later, however, many of Bernard Lazare's supporters did not understand when Dreyfus stayed away from the funeral of one of his most courageous and gifted allies. Only a small group of mourners followed Lazare's hearse—a traditional "hearse of the poor" as he wished it—to the Montparnasse cemetery. It was early September and the relentless flight from Paris for late summer holidays had much to do with the small size of the service and with its particular social complexion. *Le Siècle* reported the presence of Mathieu and Léon Dreyfus, but few other prominent veterans of the affair joined the procession of family, old anarchist comrades, and, in the greatest numbers, Jewish immigrants. Alfred Dreyfus's conspicuous absence fueled suspicions that he had rejected Lazare. Critics called it proof of his ingratitude.[27]

It was true that the captain and the Jewish nationalist had held conflicting views on the lessons of the affair and, later, on the intersection of politics and religion. Lazare tried to convince Dreyfus that he had been the victim of more than a "judicial error"; he had suffered, Lazare believed, as so many generations of Jews had suffered, from the blight of anti-Semitism that ran through Western culture. After reading *Cinq années de ma vie*, Lazare offered his own assessment of Dreyfus's inner strength: "You are, perhaps, more Jewish than you think," he wrote, "through your incoercible hope . . . your almost fatalistic resignation. It is this indestructible foundation which has come to you through your people [*peuple*]; it is what has sustained you."[28] "People," in another sense, meant "nation," and while Dreyfus may have acknowledged the importance of his wife's faith and the legacy of his parents' Judaism, he would insist that France, not Israel, had sustained him. For Dreyfus, emancipation was a fact rooted in history, not a dream to be realized in some future utopia; it had been achieved under the Revolution, and all Frenchmen should protect its promise. Dreyfus looked back to revolutionary edicts of liberation with gratitude, while Lazare, who once shared those sentiments, felt an equally passionate sense of betrayal. And, finally, Dreyfus believed that one of the key elements of the Revolution, which he saw as the final act of the Enlightenment, had been the struggle for a secular state. It had not yet been achieved, but in the third decade of the Third Republic it was close to realization. Only a few days after Lazare's death, Dreyfus told a friend that while all "professions of belief are worthy of respect," they should remain "in the private realm and have nothing to do with the duties of a citizen. The separation of Church and State," he said "is the solution we must attain." Zionism aimed for a very different solution, and Dreyfus, like Joseph Reinach, considered that movement an "anachronism" in modern society.[29]

But if Dreyfus rejected the idea of Jewish nationalism, neither he nor his family had been blind to the role that anti-Semitism had played in his arrest and deportation. At Cherche-Midi, Commandant Forzinetti had heard his prisoner shout "My only crime is to have been born a Jew!" and during the first trial Dreyfus's sister, Rachel, had used the same words in her appeal to the minister of war ("Think of the martyrdom of this man, for whom the only crime is to have been born a Jew").[30] Later Mathieu suggested that a climate of anti-Semitism had enabled Labori to treat the captain so reprehensibly: "If Alfred were not a Jew," Mathieu told a friend, "if this atrocious antisemitism, this disgraceful mark on so many minds . . . was not at the root of all this hatred, Labori would be strongly and universally criticized. But what is there to say?" Mathieu concluded, "If Alfred were not a Jew he would not have been sent to Devil's Island."[31] There was, however, a profound difference between recognizing the existence of anti-Semitism in French society and defining it as eternal.

Alfred Dreyfus seems to have harbored no personal animosity toward Bernard Lazare. The two men had stood side by side at Zola's funeral (one report suggested that Lazare had helped shield Dreyfus from the crowd), and immediately on hearing of his ally's death Dreyfus told Reinach of his "profound sorrow at the loss of his friend, so loyal and so good."[32] Even Dreyfus's absence from the Montparnasse service—which police considered an arena of potential violence—might have been a sign of respect for the family's tranquility (as it had been a few months before when Joseph Valabrègue had died) rather than an advertisement of disapproval. No evidence survives to confirm that Dreyfus contributed to a collection that Zadoc Kahn took up for Lazare's widow, but given Reinach's involvement in the project and the close ties of the Dreyfuses and Hadamards to Grand Rabbi Kahn, it is likely that the captain was among the "handful of wealthy Jews" who offered support; three years later he would be one of the first to volunteer his contribution to a monument in Lazare's honor. The Jewish nationalist, with his "gaze lit by a flame fifty centuries old," as Charles Péguy described him, had pledged his loyalty to a movement Dreyfus did not recognize; and the captain, rigid in his allegiance, often lost patience with patriots who strayed from the fold. But as a selfless advocate of justice, Lazare deserved respect. And he got it—at least from the man whose affair had inspired his conversion.[33]

Among the friends who had joined Dreyfus at Zola's funeral, Bernard Lazare represented the allies of the first hour, while Jean Jaurès stood for those who had waited until the eleventh. And Jaurès, like Lazare, championed an ideology that often ran counter to Dreyfus's vision of France. A leading socialist in the Chamber, Jaurès had spent most of his political life attacking industrial capitalism and the profits reaped by families like the Dreyfuses. From the moment of the captain's arrest and well into 1898, he had dismissed the bourgeois Jewish officer whose problems diverted the government from more significant issues. But Jaurès had always been less dogmatic than other socialist colleagues, his ideology made room for people amid the theories, and when he realized that Dreyfus was a target of reaction, he rallied to the captain with the same vigor he brought to the defense of coal miners and glass blowers in his native region. He shared Reinach's energy, Lazare's sensitivity, and Mathieu's personal concern for the well-being of the affair's principal victim.

Jaurès met Dreyfus for the first time in 1901, long after his alliance with Mathieu, and over the next two years he joined the brothers in the search for "new elements" to reopen the case. They focused on the mystery that still surrounded the Rennes verdict, "with extenuating circumstances." Convinced that members of the high command had transmitted a "secret document" to the seven judges (as the army had done in 1894), they launched an inquiry to determine how the court-martial had reached the decision that both Dreyfusards and anti-Dreyfusards had called "absurd." One elusive piece of "evidence" that might have appeared in the deliberation room at Rennes—and that had long hovered in the "shadows" of the case, as Mathieu described it—was the original sheet of paper from which the *bordereau* had been traced. Or so the story went. Never seen but always rumored to be the single most dramatic document of the affair, it allegedly contained annotations by Dreyfus's main contact across the Rhine—the German Emperor Wilhelm II. In a case full of fantasies, the *bordereau annoté* ranked with Bertillon's "thaumaturgic spells" and Henry's secret agents in dark glasses and false beards. But few doubted the document's existence. Dreyfus's enemies believed that the General Staff kept it secret for reasons of national security, while Dreyfus's friends called it "the fake of fakes," one of the many pieces of counterfeit evidence fabricated in the back rooms of the Etat-Major. "The 'imperial forgery' existed," Mathieu wrote. "It was there [in Rennes]," and the "hardened criminal Mercier had it handy."[34]

So powerful was the mystery surrounding the annotated *bordereau*, and so great the fears that its appearance might spark new domestic and foreign troubles, that politicians ignored it, like an unwelcome guest, in the hope that it would go away. But after the elections of 1902 the complexion of the assembly changed; moderate republicans, Radicals, and Socialists now dominated the political arena, and many of those deputies did not need to be convinced of the captain's innocence. Like the defendant himself, however, they needed "new facts" from which to launch the final revision. Dreyfus sensed that, and for months he combed trial transcripts and other sources in search of references to the *bordereau annoté,* and he clipped hundreds of articles on the subject from scores of newspapers. Serving as a research assistant on his own case, he consulted Jaurès and encouraged him to bring the issue before the Chamber.[35]

On April 6, 1903, the Socialist deputy exposed the "secret role" that the "imperial forgery" had played in the affair. He hoped to convince colleagues that the annotated *bordereau,* when uncovered, would provide a crucial new fact, and that all the bogus evidence and false testimonies presented at the two trials would reveal even more. Across two days, Jaurès captivated his audience, as he had done so often in the Chamber, fighting back insults from the nationalist right and convincing skeptical comrades on the left that the Dreyfus case was not a bourgeois battle, but a struggle against reaction. Jaurès crafted his appeal to avoid explicit condemnation of the military and its judicial officers, but his message was clear: Clericals, neoroyalists, nationalists, and anti-Semites were losing their hold on the republic, and it was time that they lost their hold on the affair as well. Dreyfus had read a draft of the speech and, in form and content, had proclaimed it "perfect."[36]

General Louis André, minister of war since the spring of 1900, addressed the assembly and agreed with Jaurès that "the conscience of the country has been singularly alarmed by the appearance of extenuating circumstances in an affair of this nature." André's allegiance to the military was not blind, and, like Picquart before him, he aimed to get at "the truth of the Affair"; he accepted "entirely the task of launching an administrative inquiry." The political climate had merely shifted, however, it had not reversed, and the Dreyfusards achieved only a partial victory. The assembly voted down Jaurès's motion for an inquest, leaving the minister of war to pursue a "personal" investigation of the documents related to the affair. And he would do it during that long period of customary political calm in Paris when deputies adjourned for their summer vacation.[37]

"Overjoyed" by André's commitment but "profoundly disappointed" by the assembly's vote, Dreyfus defied calls for caution and submitted his own request for an investigation based on new facts. Like the lists of questions and answers he had compiled in Rennes, his eight-page letter to the minister of war examined the results of his own research into the "imperial forgery" and the false testimonies of witnesses for the prosecution. Dreyfus promised not to "retrace" the history of his "existence since 1894," but he could rarely resist an opportunity to remind superiors of the tortures he and his family had suffered. As he summarized his case, he employed the same stylistic device he had used so many times before: He told his story in the third person singular. "Absolutely innocent of any crime," Dreyfus wrote of himself, "he tries in vain to unravel the mystery, he shouts his innocence . . . and he awaits the supreme joy of attending his rehabilitation." When he asked for the minister's help, however, he returned to the first person: "Victim of criminal maneuvers and of a violation of the law committed twice in my case, I appeal to the highest officer of military justice."[38]

Eugène Naville noted that Jaurès's speech and André's inquiry marked a turning point when the affair entered "a period of new gestation." He was right, but the gestation would prove interminably long and fraught with false alarms. Nearly ten years had passed since Dreyfus's arrest, and, as Reinach would put it later, Voltaire had needed only three to rehabilitate Calas. General André and his associate, Captain Antoine-Louis Targe, sifted the evidence for over seven months before presenting their findings to the minister of justice, and though they never located the *bordereau annoté* (no investigation ever would), they uncovered the two letters from the Italian military attaché to his German counterpart that Colonel Henry had altered. Learning the results of the inquiry, if not the details, Jaurès called Dreyfus to his apartment late in November 1903 to announce "the happy news." With "new facts" now established, Dreyfus submitted another petition for the revision of his trial ("because I must have all my honor, for my children and for myself, because I have never failed in my duties as a soldier and a Frenchman"). The judges of the Criminal Chamber announced a public hearing, and through the spring and summer of 1904, all the players in the affair who had not died or fled for cover returned to the witness stand for what they hoped would be the final rehearsal for the last act.[39]

Dreyfus had faced his first court-martial in a state of shock; after a nervous breakdown on the day of his arrest, he was sedated through the weeks that du Paty pressed him with questions and threats. Five years later, he returned to France a victim of Devil's Island, and though he found the energy, through hope, to prepare his arguments, the aftereffects of malaria and dysentery took their toll. At both trials he could not adequately contribute to his defense. But by the summer of 1904 he had mastered all the details, and, thanks to visits to Cologny, he had regained much of his strength. As he had done as a young officer keeping physically fit in provincial garrisons, he pursued a regime of exercise in Switzerland to prepare for the legal battle; he hiked the roads and trails leading from Hauterive to the shoreline of Lake Geneva, and after nearly a decade away from his favorite sport, he took long rides on one of Naville's Irish mares. His host noted his "spirited" horsemanship and confirmed that Dreyfus was well rested and "full of hope about the resumption of the Affair."[40]

In June 1904, with the Criminal Chamber's preliminary investigation nearing its end, Dreyfus asked permission to be heard. "For the first time in my life," he wrote, "I walked across the threshold of the Palais de Justice where my name . . . had echoed so often." He wanted to expose, "documents in hand," the "audacious lies" of his accusers; but, no less important, he wanted to explain his character in a public forum. Every trial transcript and newspaper report he had studied had made some reference to his lack of passion, to his inability to play the lead role in a high drama. "Dreyfus's heart," said one military observer in Rennes, "has not spoken." Referring to that quote and to others that "dumbfounded" him, Dreyfus offered the Criminal Chamber his opinion on the difference between theatricality and justice: "I believe in reason; I believed that reason in such matters in which the emotions of the heart can offer no explanation, no mitigation, should be a judge's sole guide. It is natural to look for pity when one is at fault," he continued, "because in certain cases the heart excuses many mistakes. But, here, we have had an affair that concerns an innocent man. . . . I had only one duty: To appeal to the reason and conscience of my judges." Wanting to set the public record straight, he restated his "patriotic sentiments" ("my life is there to prove them") and, in a rare expression of revenge, launched a long overdue attack on du Paty—for having "terrorized my young wife." He closed with his own final verdict: "It is I who have pity for those who have dishonored themselves by condemning an innocent man through criminal means."[41]

On the basis of new evidence and the powerful arguments of Dreyfus's counsel, Henri Mornard, the Criminal Chamber voted to move the case to the High Court of Appeal. Dreyfus's public apologia, however, met with less sympathy. "Word has it," *La Presse* reported, "that he made a rather unfortunate impression." Even Joseph Reinach noted that Dreyfus's forty-minute address to the Court had been received with "disappointment." He displayed the "same punctilious stoicism, the same pride (that one admires, but that leaves one cold)," and, again, he refused to give his audience the "shout of anger," the cry of a "wounded and bleeding animal," that it wanted to hear. "Incapable of not controlling himself," as Reinach knew so well, Dreyfus "did not cry out."[42] *La Libre Parole* insisted that the entire inquiry "smelled of the Jew," that Dreyfus's "shadow hovered over the room," and Drumont's newspaper combined the two issues that, in its opinion, most threatened the moral fiber of France—anticlericalism and the affair: "Instinctively, we raise our eyes to see if an image of the traitor has replaced the Christ banished from our halls of justice. But, amazingly," *La Libre Parole* announced with confidence, "Christ is still there."[43]

The bureaucratic machinery of the United Chambers of the High Court of Appeal would lumber through two years of delays before reaching its final verdict. Long "judicial vacations" slowed the process, but the most formidable barriers were political, and they included a new "affair" involving the minister of war. While investigating Dreyfus's dossier, General André also channeled his republican enthusiasm into purging the army of all anti-Dreyfusards who, in the vocabulary of the time, fit the broad definition of "Jesuits." Mounting a private system of internal espionage, the minister compiled information on the religious and political beliefs of fellow officers (who attended mass and who, in André's opinion, had the good sense not to), and he secretly noted those findings—which would determine promotions and demotions—on thousands of small pieces of paper (*fiches*). In league with zealous associates, the minister recorded rumors garnered from concierges, shoemakers, tailors, and grocers; but his best informants came from the ranks of Masonic lodges, and especially from the anti-Catholic section of the Grand Orient of the rue Cadet. The old threat of "Protestants, Jews, and Freemasons" out to ruin France took on new meaning in 1904 when nationalists in the Chamber exposed André's *affaire des fiches* and when the minister, attacked by the right and abandoned by most of the left, was forced to resign. General André came to symbolize the "fanaticism" of unchecked Dreyfusards, the excesses of republican virtue, and his scandal delayed the revision he had hoped to expedite.[44]

The Combes government, a runner-up to Waldeck-Rousseau's in the game of ministerial longevity, could not survive the *affaire des fiches* and fell in January 1905. The septuagenarian Combes gave way to the only slightly younger Maurice Rouvier, a former prime minister whose background as an international banker had embroiled him in the Panama scandal and who now hoped to moderate the anticlerical wars waged by his predecessor. But Rouvier lasted only four weeks, and Prime Minister Ferdinand Sarrien, another moderate republican, would hold on for barely eight months. The presidency of the republic, however, continued to function on schedule; after a full term of seven years, Loubet was replaced in February 1906 by Armand Fallières, a solid Dreyfusard, an old comrade of Scheurer-Kestner's, and a politician with a particular interest in foreign affairs. None of those new republican leaders aimed to deny Dreyfus's final appeal, but none wanted the affair to slip from the judiciary and return to the streets. The streets were busy enough. Industrial strikes heightened domestic tensions already strained by conflicts over the separation of church and state, and on the international front, German challenges to French designs on Morocco led to heated debates over military preparedness and France's need to strengthen its recent Entente Cordiale with Britain. Dreyfus's case would have to be delayed; the republic could tolerate only so many civil wars.

The High Court of Appeal waited for the legislative elections of

April 1906 before moving on to Dreyfus's revision. While the Sarrien ministry, formed in the wake of those elections, included many Dreyfusards (Clemenceau became minister of the interior), the election campaign confirmed that the case no longer excited public passions. After a dozen years and two trials that had reshaped the political landscape of France, triggered riots, and placed the existence of the republic in danger, a wave of indifference greeted the hearings of the High Court in June and July 1906. Only a small coterie of Dreyfusard and anti-Dreyfusard veterans gathered for the last battle in their long war, and the prefect of police provided the clearest proof that times had changed when he ordered no extra security precautions at the Palais de Justice.[45]

The revision process took place in an atmosphere of "calm," Eugène Naville noted in his diary, primarily because the evidence was obvious to all but the most unregenerate anti-Dreyfusards. There were no more surprises. Esterhazy, still in London, had not retracted his "confession" (though he continued to insist that he had written the *bordereau* under orders), and most of the witnesses for the prosecution who had met with success in 1894 and 1899 had been exposed as dupes, liars, madmen, or misguided defenders of military honor. A committee of university mathematicians disposed of Bertillon's graphological theories with the contempt they deserved, and Maître Mornard went over the old ground of Henry's forgeries and the more recent "revelations" of witnesses like Cernuski, the Austrian deserter who had embarrassed everyone in Rennes, his French military paymasters most of all. Across the three weeks leading up to the closing arguments, the main drama within the Palais de Justice involved the small audience, and especially those Dreyfusards whose rivalries had not abated. Two years earlier, during the Criminal Chamber's investigation, Labori had walked out in protest when Henri Mornard spoke favorably of Captain Dreyfus's personality, and Picquart had approved his friend's gesture by proclaiming, loud enough for the court to hear, "Well done, well done." In 1906, with the deliberations of the High Court drawing to a close, Mathieu Dreyfus, full of confidence and hoping to repair the divisions of the past, walked over to Picquart and put out his hand. But in a gesture of public insult that "stunned" Emile Zola's widow standing nearby, the Alsatian officer turned his back on the Alsatian Jew. Angered but not surprised, Mathieu said of Picquart: "He has all the rights, and I have all the duties."[46]

On the evening of July 11, 1906, as the law required and as he had done twice before, Alfred Dreyfus awaited his verdict outside the courtroom. On this occasion, however, he did not pace a dimly lit antechamber under the watch of armed guards but waited with Lucie and the children in the company of friends in the apartment on the Boulevard Malesherbes. "We don't know how long the deliberation will take," Suzanne Dreyfus wrote her mother in Héricourt. "We will wait—how impatiently!—at Alfred's home for them to come in an automobile and tell us the verdict."[47] Since Rennes, there had been a question as to whether that verdict would—or should—be final. Mathieu had tried to convince his brother that if the High Court voted in his favor the case should not be sent forward to a new military court-martial (in legal terms, an annulment of the Rennes verdict "sans renvoi," without referral to another court, would be possible since no criminal charges against "the convict" would remain and since Dreyfus had no interest in monetary compensation).[48] But the captain, who had always wanted to be judged by his fellow officers, resisted until Mathieu, who had made an art of instructing his headstrong brother on the need for compromise, outlined the options and the obvious risks. A decision by the highest court in the land would restore the family's honor, while the deliberations of seven new military judges could well end in a third disaster. Alfred agreed to abide by the verdict.

It arrived at 6:30 P.M.—by automobile, as promised. The judges of the High Court of Appeal had voted thirty-one to eighteen to annul the verdict of the Rennes court-martial sans renvoi and rehabilitate Alfred Dreyfus. "It was the end of my torment which had lasted twelve years," Dreyfus wrote, "the end of my anguish over the future of my children."[49]

At noon the next day, the chief presiding judge read the formal verdict in the Palais de Justice. For more than an hour he revisited the principal events, people, and documents of the case, focusing on Henry's forgeries and on the bordereau and confirming that "no referral to further adjudication is in order." To avoid sending the case back to a military court-martial, the civilian judges had applied a liberal reading of Article 445 of the Criminal Code, and anti-Dreyfusards would soon "brandish" that article as a "talisman" in their attacks on the corrupt republic.[50] But now the judgment was final, and it would be posted in Paris and Rennes and published in the Journal Officiel, "as well as in five newspapers to be chosen by Dreyfus." In addition it would also appear, "at the expense of the Treasury," in fifty other Parisian and provincial newspapers" of Dreyfus's choice. Finally the presiding justice ordered that the "judgment be entered into the registers of the Court Martial of

Rennes, and that mention of it be made in the margins of the annulled decision."[51]

Over the days that followed—after telegrams of congratulations arrived "from all countries" and after a "numerous crowd" of family and friends came with "arms full of flowers"—Dreyfus settled into his study on the Boulevard Malesherbes. He wrote to the widows of Bernard Lazare and Emile Zola and to other supporters, and he noted in his journal that he had "never doubted the triumph of justice and truth." His faith in France had been "unshakable." With the same care he had brought to the theorems and arabesques in his Devil's Island notebooks, he clipped the announcements of his innocence from Parisian and provincial newspapers and pasted them into a diary destined for his children.[52]

When the High Court's annulment of the Rennes verdict reinstated Dreyfus's civil liberties, Minister of War Eugène Etienne (André's successor) set out to reestablish the captain's military rights and privileges. Given his accomplishments over the years prior to his arrest, Dreyfus would have been promoted to major (*chef d'escadron*) by 1901; and if his exemplary record had continued, he would have become a lieutenant-colonel soon after. A number of officers of his generation had reached that level as early as 1903. But the minister recommended Dreyfus's promotion only to major, a rank that made him subordinate to nearly one hundred artillery officers with less seniority. Picquart, on the other hand, was promoted two full ranks to brigadier general—and retroactively from 1903. The minister's decision ("fair for Picquart, but not for Dreyfus," said more than one observer) may have been influenced by his cabinet colleague Georges Clemenceau, who had "lost interest" in Dreyfus after the pardon and who had always preferred Picquart. But, no less important, the government worried that the military high command and its parliamentary supporters would tolerate only so much indulgence toward Dreyfus; he may not have been a spy (as the likes of Mercier, now a senator, continued to insist), but he had inflicted a dozen years of humiliation on the army of the fatherland. The captain's reinstatement was a political necessity, not a cause for celebration.[53]

Approving Minister Etienne's proposal, the Senate added a statement that cloaked the final injustice under dignified prose: "The Government is powerless to repair the immense material and moral prejudice suffered by the victim of such a deplorable judicial error. At the very least, it wishes to return Captain Dreyfus to the situation in which he would have found himself had he pursued the normal course of his career."[54] But that was the point: The same reactionary forces that interrupted the "normal course of his career" prevented its honorable resumption. Dreyfus confessed to Joseph Reinach—and later to the president of the republic—that the "joy of victory" had been "tainted": "I felt that I had done my duty," he wrote Reinach, but "the government has not done its [duty]. . . . I will never recriminate, but I will not give up my dignity, no more today than when I was on Devil's Island, and I will leave the service at the hour and at the moment that I judge most opportune." Realizing that at his age (forty-six) and in his condition he would never attain the high rank that had always been his goal, he decided to remain in the army for one year. He would prove to his critics that he could serve effectively, and, perhaps, he would retrieve, however briefly, a semblance of his military life before his affair.[55]

If he had been "stunned" by the injustice of his promotion, he was heartened by the announcement that he would be named a chevalier of the Legion of Honor. The distinction came almost automatically to officers of long tenure above the rank of captain, but the general in charge of the Council of the Order in 1906 made a point of separating himself from anti-Dreyfusard officers when he publicly recognized his comrade's sacrifice: "I could, by considering only . . . Dreyfus's years of service," the general announced, "limit myself to saying that the recommendation is made in conformity with the regulations. . . . But it is incumbent upon us to fulfill another duty. . . . We must consider our decision to be a rightful compensation for a soldier who has endured a unique martyrdom." The Council of the Order of the Legion of Honor approved the award unanimously; President Fallières, a veteran Dreyfusard, signed it; and arrangements were made to knight Dreyfus on July 21 at the Ecole Militaire, only steps from the site of his degradation.[56]

Joseph Reinach had wanted the ceremony to take place in the grand Cour Morland, on the precise spot of the captain's humiliation. It would be a powerful statement of rehabilitation, a closing of the circle, and the minister of war, more generous with symbols than with promotions, agreed. But Dreyfus, afraid that the memories would overwhelm him, refused. Even the neighboring Cour Desjardins, its gray walls topped by a panoply of flags and with cavalry stables at each end, would bring back memories not only of the degradation, but of the time when he was stationed at the Ecole Militaire as a young lieutenant full of ambition. Dreyfus prepared for his ceremony with a mix of joy and trepidation. He must have been pleased that the army had restricted the witnesses to immediate family members and a few journalists (Reinach, one of the many Dreyfusards who could not attend, defined the event as "discreet" to the point of "secrecy"); and he must have also taken comfort in knowing that Commandant Targe, General André's assistant in the inquiry that led to Dreyfus's revision, would stand beside him and receive a rosette of the Legion of Honor. But he worried about his physical ability to see the ceremony through.[57]

Called from an orderly room off the courtyard at 1:30 P.M., Dreyfus came forward, his head high and his pace rapid and "automatic." It was the march of self-control he had used on the day of his degradation. From second-story windows looking out on the Cour Desjardins, family members, reporters, and photographers watched Dreyfus pass two batteries of artillerymen and two squadrons of cuirassiers. His "very pale" face turned a sudden, feverish red. In the "heavy silence" that followed, as he stood at attention before the commanding officer, his thoughts "took flight" and the memories returned—"the shouts of the crowd, the atrocious ceremony, my stripes torn away . . . my sword broken and lying at my feet in crossed pieces." As his heart "raced" and he began to sweat, he had to call on "an immense effort of will" to hold himself upright. When a colonel called out "At ease!" Dreyfus, alone among the soldiers in the courtyard, did not move.[58]

The sound of trumpets finally "wrenched" him from his "painful dreams." Brigadier General Gillain, a senior officer in ceremonial dress, decorated Commandant Targe and then turned to Dreyfus: "In the name of the President of the Republic," he announced, "and by virtue of the powers invested in me, I name you . . . Chevalier of the Legion of Honor." He lowered his sword to Dreyfus's shoulder three times, pinned the cross on his black tunic, and, "near tears," embraced Dreyfus, saying, "I am happy to have been charged with the mission I have just accomplished." The order "Forward, march!" echoed through the courtyard. Preceded by a flourish of trumpets, artillerymen and cuirassiers filed out saluting Dreyfus with their sabers as they passed. Having decided to retire from the army, Dreyfus must have looked on that ceremony as a symbolic finale; he had always believed that the image of cuirassiers in Mulhouse in 1870 had inspired his decision to make the army his life.[59]

Shouting, "Long live Dreyfus!" the small group of witnesses entered the Cour Desjardins, and the new chevalier of the Legion of Honor responded with words similar to those he had used to answer other shouts nearly a dozen years before: "Long live the Republic!" he said. "Long live truth!" Anatole France, one of the few allies outside the family in attendance, greeted Dreyfus and called the ceremony "the coronation" of their "work of justice"; and even General Picquart was sufficiently moved to shake the hand Dreyfus offered. Photographers, lugging cumbersome machines the size of small suitcases, captured the final moments, including one picture of Dreyfus embracing his wife. Never comfortable in front of cameras, Lucie stood at attention while her husband leaned forward to kiss her. Her thick black hair, smooth skin, and straight posture provided a striking contrast to Alfred's grayness to his weathered face and stooped shoulders. A moment later, fifteen-year-old Pierre ran across the courtyard and into his father's arms. But as other well-wishers drew near, "the emotions became too intense," and Dreyfus, with sharp pains in his chest, asked to be taken home.[60]

In Mulhouse the French-language newspaper *L'Express* received a letter to the editor that commented on Dreyfus and on the finale of his affair: "What a relief for . . . other citizens of Mulhouse," an Alsatian remarked. "It had seemed that a little of the mud that had covered him had spread to us as well." But now the city was "cleansed of the stain of having given birth to a traitor against his fatherland."[61] At the same time, in Paris, the main publication of the Jewish Consistory announced that "the Dreyfus Affair has concluded for the Israelites and its conclusion would make us love even more, were that possible, our dear country." Another periodical summarized what it believed was the most significant legacy that the triumph of justice had left for France and for French Jews: "The Affair . . . had particularly fortunate results for our coreligionists," wrote the *Univers israélite,* "for in giving birth to the Dreyfus Affair, anti-Semitism had died."[62]

CHAPTER XVII

Great Expectations

ON THE LEFT BANK, in a corner of the seventh arrondissement dominated by government offices and public monuments, the rue Barbet-de-Jouy ran near the Church of St. Louis and the Hôtel des Invalides. The Ecole Militaire lay just to the west, and a few blocks north were the sprawling headquarters of the Ministère de la Guerre. Nearly every Thursday, shortly before noon, Dreyfus returned to that *quartier* he knew so well to meet with a group of professors and politicians, many of them deputies and former or future prime ministers, and all of them Dreyfusards. Old age and ideological quarrels would alter the list of luncheon guests invited to the elegant town house on the rue Barbet-de-Jouy, but across the dozen years following 1902, Dreyfus joined the historians Daniel Halévy and Gabriel Monod, the Socialist deputies Aristide Briand and Jean Jaurès, and those republicans of different Radical and Masonic stripes, Henri Brisson, Joseph Reinach, and Emile Combes. Their conversations ranged from the Parisian performances of Eleonora Duse and Sarah Bernhardt through the curriculum at the Sorbonne to working-class upheavals in France, revolution in Russia, and threats posed by the rapid buildup of the German military.[1]

Presiding over those luncheon debates was the Marquise Arconati-Visconti, the owner of the town house and the founder of the Thursday meetings. Sixty years old when she first met Dreyfus (though admitting only to fifty), the marquise had, despite her aris-

315

tocratic title, impeccable republican credentials. Born Marie-Louise-Jeanne Peyrat, she was the daughter of a journalist who challenged the Second Empire and raised his family in the Jacobin "cult of the French Revolution." After studying at the Ecole des Chartres, Marie Peyrat, with a trousseau of only "a dress and a pair of shoes," married Gianmartino Arconati-Visconti, an Italian nobleman of enormous landed wealth and the son of a patriot of the Risorgimento. The marquis shared his father's progressive politics and developed ties with a number of prominent European republicans, including Victor Hugo, who would serve as a witness at the Peyrat–Arconati-Visconti wedding—a studiously civil ceremony—in 1873. Thirty-three years old at the time of her marriage, the marquise was widowed only three years later and became the sole beneficiary of extensive landholdings in Italy, Belgium, and France. Continuing her father's tradition of public service, though on a scale he had never achieved, she channeled much of her wealth into educational and philanthropic organizations, endowing chairs at the Sorbonne and the Collège de France (including one for Gabriel Monod), establishing scholarships to encourage the study of history and medicine, and creating a foundation to aid families of policemen injured or killed in the line of duty. She would also donate one million francs to the University of Paris for the construction of an Institute of Geography. Scolding the modern generation for "calculating" profits and not "redressing human injustice," she aimed to continue the fight for social and political reform begun by her father and carried on by her husband.[2]

The republican marquise did not, however, reject the aristocratic comforts to which she became quickly accustomed. She kept the palaces and villas in Milan, Florence, and above Lake Como, and, when not in Paris, spent most of her time at the Château Gaasbeek near Brussels, a fanciful estate owned by the Arconati-Visconti family since the eighteenth century, adorned with medieval castle turrets and beech-tree-lined paths named after the new proprietor's favorite republican luminaries, Léon Gambetta, Alphonse Peyrat, and, eventually, Alfred Dreyfus. It had been Gambetta who, in the late 1870s, had encouraged the marquise to establish a salon devoted to politics on Thursdays and art on Tuesdays. Special weekly *"jours"* of dining and conversation were a common practice in Parisian society, and the Tuesday group on the rue Barbet-de-Jouy would compete with other gatherings, including one convened by the poet Mallarmé on the same day, and another held by Madame Geneviève Straus, one of the mod-

els for Proust's Duchesse de Guermantes and the marquise's rival for
the attention of Joseph Reinach, Daniel Halévy, and other politicians,
artists, and literati. Given the marquise's striking beauty and exotic
tastes (she often dressed in antique robes, prompting Reinach to call
her that "pretty Macedonian"), the rumor spread that her relationship
with the "bohemian" Gambetta involved more than a shared interest
in republican ideology. Admitting that Gambetta had dubbed her his
Clio, the marquise denied having been his mistress; but at a time
when conventional wisdom had it that attractive women of independent wealth were better suited for lovemaking than policy-making, her
protestations were ignored. As a public and private confidante of a
founder of the Third Republic, she gained a reputation as a keeper of
the Gambettist legacy.[3]

Like so many of Gambetta's disciples, she joined the Dreyfusard
cause with the zeal of a republican proselytizer. She saw the affair as a
battle between the forces of enlightenment and clerical reaction and as
an occasion to reform the nation's sclerotic institutions. "History will
never understand," she would later write Dreyfus, "how in the nineteenth century, in republican France, the great leaders of the army
were able to . . . fabricate forgeries and build lies upon lies without
finding judges who would dare to condemn them. . . . When a country
opens its innards for others to see how it digests, the sight is ugly and
dangerous."[4] At the height of the affair, the marquise contributed financial support to *L'Aurore;* she insisted that her servants read only
Dreyfusard newspapers (her concierge was called "Zola" by comrades
in his *quartier*); and she pasted political posters to her door on the rue
Barbet-de-Jouy. Upon learning of her physician's anti-Dreyfusard sympathies, she changed doctors, and when Paul Déroulède tried to launch
a coup d'état in 1899, she hurried to the Place de la Concorde so that
she could shout—and order her coachman to shout—"Vive la République!" in protest at the reactionary event.[5] By 1900 Dreyfusards
dominated her Thursday salon, and by 1902 she had been introduced—
probably through Joseph Reinach—to Alfred Dreyfus, a man she considered a certified republican hero.

The marquise and her most celebrated Thursday guest (*"jeudiste"*)
found many things in common, from their bouts with rheumatism and
fever (the veteran of Devil's Island offered the marquise his expertise
on quinine and other medicines) to their interest in medieval art and
Wagner's music. Often arriving at the rue Barbet-de-Jouy two hours
before other guests, Dreyfus would learn the topics of the marquise's

Tuesday salon—the debates among artists, collectors, and curators—and he would hear about the university courses she had audited on Dante, Machiavelli, and modern European philosophy. She called herself "an old student," and, like her new friend, she constantly applied the lessons of the past—of republican Rome or revolutionary France—to the contemporary political and cultural scene.[6]

Early in their friendship, Dreyfus and the marquise exchanged letters on a topic that had intersected with the politics of the affair: the alleged "bankruptcy of science." According to essayist Ferdinand Brunetière, a member of the anti-Dreyfusard Ligue de la Patrie Française, modern science had created an arid, positivist atmosphere stripped of mystery and transcendent values. The Catholic church, said Brunetière, protected those values, and it was no coincidence that the essayist's most influential work on the subject had carried the title "After a Visit to the Vatican." For the marquise, daughter of a fierce republican who had proclaimed "Clericalism, there is the enemy!" Brunetière's reactionary call threatened the victories of the Dreyfusard coalition and especially the separation of church and state. "When civil society allows congregations to teach," an angry marquise confessed to Dreyfus, "it is the suicide of liberty." And though her friend left room for compromise, he agreed that the law of separation promised "the emancipation of the mind." But most of all Dreyfus reproached Brunetière "for having ignored the conquests of science. . . . [Its] progress has been enormous," and to say that it "will give us every happiness is to misunderstand it, because it can only assure us more truth every day, beginning with more justice."[7]

However self-effacing Dreyfus may have been in public—insisting that his cause mattered more than his person—he reveled in the marquise's attention and appreciated the opportunity to "escape the banalities that one hears at most dinner parties." Until the final revision of his case, he spent "nine-tenths" of his time, as he told his friend, "running left and right in search of information" for his appeals, and he regretted that so few hours were left for "intellectual work." He cherished the quiet reunions with his family and needed the periods of rest in Switzerland and along the Normandy coast. But he missed grappling with the subjects that had intrigued him as a student and that he had continued to explore as a prisoner in his classroom of one. The marquise's Thursday salon provided a forum for Dreyfus's continuing education and a change of scenery for a man who had always been restless.

Lucie knew that side of her husband's character well. In the early years of their marriage she had been forced to deal with the lingering habits of his bachelorhood. More recently, after their long separation, her concerns had focused on Alfred's physical and emotional health. But she understood his impatience with family gatherings ("I am already so old," he would tell Joseph Reinach only half in jest, "because I play bridge!"), and she seems to have approved of his Thursday diversion. After being forced into the public arena, Lucie must have savored the end of that nightmare and enjoyed the steady return of the privacy she had always preferred. She was still, as Alfred put it, the most important "confidante of all my thoughts," but she no longer placed political intrigues high on her agenda. Her husband could discuss those issues elsewhere.[8]

Through the early years of the new century, the marquise's salon reflected the ideological realignments which followed the affair. From Waldeck-Rousseau's "Government of Republican Defense" through Emile Combes's government of anticlerical offense, the Dreyfusard coalition (the so-called *bloc des gauches,* or leftist bloc) had remained united, if not harmonious. With the dual victory of Dreyfus's rehabilitation and the separation of church and state, however, the terrain of commonality gave way to a battleground of factionalism. The old differences between Mathieu Dreyfus and Picquart, Reinach and Clemenceau, and Demange and Labori had centered on the strategies of the case and on the prejudices of its major players. But the new divisions encompassed the entire network of Dreyfusards, and their disagreements concerned the very nature of parliamentary politics in a rapidly changing world. In the context of the Arconati-Visconti salon—a group that represented a microcosm of republican politics—the deepest schism divided Radicals satisfied with anticlerical victories and socialists fed up with bourgeois coalitions and ready for a turn toward social revolution.

Above all, Jean Jaurès, the marquise's most influential socialist guest, wanted his friends to move beyond their obsession with what another socialist had called "monk-hunting."[9] Jaurès saw his allies drifting into semiretirement from the truly radical questions that faced the republic. As long as working people remained victims of the capitalist system, Jaurès argued, the affair's struggle for justice must be renewed and redirected. From barely one hundred strikes per year in the 1880s, the numbers had more than quadrupled through the 1890s, and by the early years of the new century the frequency of strike activity—and the fears it engendered—increased along with the sophistication of working-class organization. More than one thousand strikes were recorded in 1904 alone, nearly double the number of the previous year; and in the months and years that followed, labor unrest intensified, with the participants ranging from miners, metal workers, and agricultural laborers to school teachers, lithographers, and *coiffeurs*. In Paris and provincial cities, labor exchanges provided job placement services, libraries, and meeting halls, but, as "local points of crystalization for the workers' movement," those *bourses du travail* also served as centers for propaganda and strike coordination. No less important, the legalization of trade unions in 1884 had led, eleven years later, to the formation of the Confédération Générale du Travail (CGT), a national organization that would subsume the *bourses du travail* after 1902 and press the campaign for an eight-hour workday. Most worrisome for the forces of order, the CGT would also condemn the army as "the main bulwark of the exploiting capitalist state" and champion the revolutionary ideology of "anarchosyndicalism."[10]

In the early 1890s the assassination of a president, the dynamiting of bourgeois restaurants, the nail bombing of the Chamber of Deputies, and other forms of "propaganda by the deed" had been, in keeping with the spirit of anarchism, largely unorganized and individual affairs. Politically engaged artists and writers like Bernard Lazare may have been uncomfortable with extreme forms of terror, but they appreciated the theoretical aspects of a movement that promised to destroy state institutions and create a new world of decentralized communities open to individual expression. Long on utopian reveries and short on hard facts, anarchist theories could appeal to a wide spectrum of the disenchanted. By the turn of the century, however, the remnants of fin-de-siècle anarchism had been neutralized by the combination of state repression, economic upturn, and a long run of governmental stability.[11] Realizing that any new attempt to achieve social revolution would require (paradoxically for anarchists) strong local and national organization, the CGT devised the doctrine of "direct action syndicalism," or "anarchosyndicalism." Trade unions (*syndicats*) would be the vehicles for the destruction of industrial capitalism, and all participation in bourgeois governments—all attempts to reform the system from within cabinet coalitions—would be condemned.

For a brief moment at the height of the affair, leftist factions in and out of parliament had fought in concert against Dreyfus's enemies. "We entered into the Dreyfus Affair," the anarchist Sebastien Faure reminded his associates in 1903, "not to defend the Captain . . . a product of that bourgeoisie that we combat, but to defend a man who suffered, a man whom we knew to be the victim of racial hatred [and] militarism. . . . We acted for the deliverance of all of society's victims." But when the prisoner returned from exile and became "only a man who peaceably enjoys the revenue of his great fortune," most of the left rejected "the old soldier." He had "turned his back on us," they said, when he reassumed his commission in the army. "The Dreyfus Affair," Faure announced, "is finished."[12]

Politics as usual was finished as well. In 1905, after years of infighting over the tactics of social change, after conflicts between orthodox Marxists and pragmatic socialists, those diverse members agreed to form the Unified Socialist Party, a group that became the French Section of the Workers' International (SFIO). Jean Jaurès argued for some measure of cooperation with bourgeois reformers, but to no avail; the SFIO, with Jaurès finally in agreement, proclaimed its support of the CGT and the doctrine of revolutionary syndicalism. It also moved in that year of international crisis—with Russia in the midst of revolution and Germans challenging French designs on Morocco—toward a policy of antipatriotism as well as antimilitarism. Led by one of the most inflammatory figures on the left, the journalist, history professor, and "traveling salesman of socialism" Gustave Hervé, the pacifism of many members of the SFIO, and their call for a "general strike" in the event of war, deepened the divisions between old Radicals and new socialists. "[For] the poor," Hervé would proclaim, "nations are not loving mothers; they are harsh stepmothers. . . . Our nation can only be our class." That sort of rhetoric produced the final tear in the already threadbare alliance of Radicals and socialists known as "Combism."[13]

As long as Jaurès fought for Dreyfus and for the separation of church and state, he enjoyed the marquise's admiration (she saw him as a "second Gambetta") and largesse. She raised funds for *L'Humanité*, the newspaper launched by Jaurès in 1904, and though she never liked the title ("I find it pretentious and puerile"), she very much liked the idea of an official organ of "Combism" that turned the screws on clericals and anti-Dreyfusards. But when Jaurès's paper began to preach class conflict, and when the socialist fraternized with "antipatriots," he fell from grace on the rue Barbet-de-Jouy. After 1906, a year marked by an unprecedented number of violent strikes and threats of a "general strike" to paralyze the republic, the marquise asked how she could

322 * THE AFFAIR

"continue to receive" Jaurès in her home. The man who "shook Hervé's hand" had become a stranger, "an obsequious valet of anarchy. . . . I despise him," the marquise told Reinach in 1907. "I vomit him up." And with every anarchosyndicalist proclamation and every proletarian revolt, her rancor increased; "Take care," she warned Jaurès. "You are bringing on yourself, on your memory, the hatred of all those who love France."[14]

If the Parisian Belle Époque had a goddess of vengeance to rival the Furies of Greek mythology, it was the Marquise Arconati-Visconti on witnessing Jaurès's "betrayal" of Gambetta's dream. And as the dream unraveled, the marquise did not limit her anger to revolutionary socialists. During the same period, though for very different reasons, she attacked the policies of Georges Clemenceau, one of the leading figures in the radical pantheon but, because of long-ago quarrels with Gambetta, never welcome in the marquise's inner circle. Many years before, Edouard Manet's portrait of young Clemenceau showed the deputy from Montmartre standing alone, his arms firmly crossed and his expression full of confidence; thick, arched eyebrows, high cheekbones, and a drooping black mustache accentuated his "Asian cast of features," and his posture suggested more than a hint of imperiousness. Nearly three decades later, the mustache had turned white and the wiry frame had filled out, but Clemenceau, at sixty-five, still had the energy and audacity of his early years. And on October 25, 1906, he found the one prime minister he could support without qualification: himself. Few politicians of the early Third Republic came to the post with more experience, and none disappointed so many comrades so quickly.[15]

First as minister of the interior and then as prime minister, the Tiger changed his ideological stripes, or so it appeared to commentators on the left who condemned his repression of working-class demonstrations. For three years he presided over a government that arrested union leaders, fired protesting teachers, and used soldiers to break strikes from Paris to the winegrowing regions of the Midi. In the end twenty workers were killed and nearly seven hundred wounded, and thousands more were apprehended by troops in the service of a former radical who took to the intrigues of police work with the same enthusiasm that he had shown for toppling "reactionary" governments. Progressive hero of the Dreyfus affair, Clemenceau now served as the nation's "first cop" (le premier flic de France); and through it all, while many of his former allies criticized his heavy hand, he maintained that his commitment to social justice had not diminished. Meaningful reforms could only be realized in a society that respected law, order, and the protection of civil liberties, he said, and when socialists turned against the government of the republic they placed themselves "on the other side of the barricades."[16]

Clemenceau and Jaurès accused each other of hammering the last nail into the coffin of the Dreyfusard coalition. For the socialist the Tiger was an authoritarian at heart and, though keen on democratic rhetoric, fundamentally hostile to the poor. "It is absolutely useless to argue with Clemenceau," Jaurès told Dreyfus, who knew from firsthand experience. "He always wants to have the last word, and he always finishes an argument with violence and brutality." For the prime minister, however, Jaurès declared himself an enemy when he incited workers to attack the reformist republic born of the affair. "Do you know how you can always recognize a speech by Jaurès?" Clemenceau once remarked. "All the verbs are in the future tense." Prime ministers dealt in the hard facts of civil society, the Tiger would maintain, while Jaurès dealt in dreams.[17]

Meanwhile, for the Marquise Arconati-Visconti, both men qualified as dismantlers of the *bloc des gauches* and as potential traitors to the republic; Jaurès had traveled too far to the left, and Clemenceau had not adequately defended the center. Convinced that anarchists presented a double-edged threat to France—as domestic warriors and international pacifists—the marquise chastised Clemenceau for "lacking the courage to reestablish order."[18] The nation's first cop had been too indulgent with the nation's internal enemies. Though raised in the "Jacobin cult of the French Revolution," the marquise acknowledged no similarities between the *sansculottes* of the past and the proletarians of the present; the former had marched to defend France from counterrevolutionary Prussians, while the latter were retreating into antipatriotic organizations at a moment when France was again threatened by German militarism. Though still opposed to nationalists and Catholic neoroyalists, the marquise believed that the affair and the law of separation had effectively defeated those enemies and that the most urgent need was for "national concord" and preparation for war abroad. She had not forgotten the lessons learned from her father and Gambetta—that France must be defended by vigilant patriots—and as "a good republican" with a clear conscience she condemned the revolutionaries who sabotaged that legacy. She damned Jaurès's "humbug" about the rights of the proletariat and announced that she would trade it all for "one good cannon."[19]

No one, not even the Marquise Arconati-Visconti, could rival Alfred Dreyfus's patriotism. But if those friends shared a commitment to the republic, they held different opinions on socialism and on the matter of Jaurès and Clemenceau. Unlike the marquise, Dreyfus thought that the Tiger had gone too far; his response to working-class upheavals had been a manifestation of that "politics of force and violence" that Dreyfus called "absolutely contrary" to the modern "temperament." By overreacting to strikes, the government had created the "grave situation" of intensifying working-class hostility to the republic; for Dreyfus, Clemenceau's repression was a form of "authoritarian conduct which no longer responds to modern social conditions."[20] In his Devil's Island notebooks and in the diaries he kept through the years that followed, Dreyfus often spoke of a "politics of character" devoid of "personal interest," of leadership that, though "wise and firm," was distinguished by the ability to "seize the true aspirations of a people, and to understand the great needs of a nation." Clemenceau had brought to his new post the "intelligence" that Dreyfus considered essential to the political "elite," but the old radical had not brought the equally important ingredient of "decency." Honoring the fact that "the most admirable page in [Clemenceau's] career had been his attitude during my affair," Dreyfus never publicly condemned his former ally, but he numbered himself among those republicans who had greeted Clemenceau's coming to power "with joy and hope," only to be "deceived."[21]

In his private correspondence and conversations, Dreyfus concentrated on the prime minister's flawed domestic policies (Zola's widow agreed that her husband would have condemned Clemenceau's treatment of the working class);[22] but Dreyfus confronted other problems with the new government when Clemenceau named Georges Picquart minister of war. Angering anti-Dreyfusards for obvious reasons, the appointment also shocked colleagues who had worked with Picquart during the affair and who knew that he had neither the expertise nor the temperament for such a post. He had helped lead the Dreyfusard battle with heroism, but when it came to leading the army of the republic, scores of other officers were better qualified.[23] Clemenceau trusted Picquart, however, and manipulated him with ease, and the prime minister enjoyed his friend's appointment as a symbolic gesture of revenge; to elevate to minister of war an officer who had been victimized by the General Staff would confirm the Dreyfusards' victory and Clemenceau's personal triumph.

Meanwhile, for Alfred Dreyfus, Picquart's advancement created a personal and professional dilemma. In the fall of 1906, after taking up his duties as artillery commandant—first at Vincennes, east of Paris, and then at Saint-Denis, to the north—Dreyfus decided to appeal for his promotion to lieutenant-colonel. If the problem were not rectified, he would retire, because, as he put it, he could no longer tolerate "the feeling of being bypassed for having spent five years on Devil's Island." It was a difficult decision for a man who had always wanted to be judged on his merits and it was made more difficult by the fact that his petition had to be submitted to Clemenceau's minister of war. In late November 1906, Dreyfus met Picquart in the minister's office on the rue Saint Dominique. Both men must have recalled the October morning twelve years before when Picquart had led the captain into a neighboring room with Commandant du Paty de Clam. Their 1906 interview proved no less frigid. Besieged with requests for Dreyfus's promotion (from Joseph Reinach, the Zola family, and others), Picquart believed that the campaign had been orchestrated by Dreyfus himself. While the general dealt with his junior officer as if he had come to Canossa to plead for special dispensation, Dreyfus, who had always given Picquart higher marks for courage than for character, refused to beg indulgence. He tried to convince the minister that the promotion was warranted given his years of service, but Picquart ignored the petition and, finally, rejected the appeal.[24]

Dreyfus's misfortune had been largely responsible for the rise to power of Clemenceau and Picquart. Those allies had fought valiantly for the captain's cause, only to treat the affair's central figure with a contempt that rivaled that of their reactionary predecessors. For Clemenceau the insult to Dreyfus may have been yet another gesture of revenge, punishment for the man who, by accepting a presidential pardon, had terminated the heroic phase of the affair. For Picquart, heard to say that "we have done enough for Dreyfus," it may have been an expression of jealousy fused with anti-Jewish prejudice.[25]

Finally, for Dreyfus, retirement would mean the end of a long period of unease over his place in the military. "What good does it do to drag this thing out," he asked Reinach. "When one faces a surgical operation, how much better to do it quickly than to make the patient wait." He had hoped that the "solemn proclamation" of his innocence in 1906 would terminate his "ordeal." But it did "nothing of the sort. . . .

I must remain the victim until the end." He would try to take comfort in the thought that "the injustice which I have suffered . . . will have served the cause of humanity and developed the sentiments of social solidarity." And he would try to fulfill a promise he had made to himself long before. While reading Montaigne on Devil's Island ("Now, the aim of all solitude," the essayist had written, "is to live more at leisure and at one's ease"), Dreyfus had confessed his own "desire for the solitude of retirement." He wanted "to forget in calm all the sadnesses of the past and be born again to life."[26]

He submitted his request for retirement based on seniority and did not, he made it clear, tender his "resignation." Having served as *chef d'escadron* for less than two years, he was retired at the lower rank of captain, with a pension of 2,350 francs for nearly thirty years of service, and with no compensation for his time in prison or in exile. His immediate superiors, unlike the minister of war, closed his dossier with a glowing report. Citing his "excellent conduct," "wide learning," and "very lively intelligence," they called his years in the military "worthy of praise" and added that, despite his age, he was "perfectly suited to render the finest service to the Artillery or to the General Staff as a Major or Lieutenant-Colonel in the reserve." In the event of war, the report concluded, Alfred Dreyfus would be assigned to the military command of Paris.[27]

If Dreyfus had little in common with Clemenceau and Picquart beyond the affair, he shared with Jean Jaurès a mutual admiration and, for a time, a close working partnership. He praised the "penetrating eloquence" and "tight logic" of his socialist ally, and he admitted that Jaurès "possesses the most excellent spirit I know." Mathieu held the same esteem for "our friend Jaurès," for his "modesty, generosity and great courage." During the fight for revision the entire Dreyfus family disagreed with supporters who believed that their socialist colleague had become too "visible," too ready to "monopolize" the case for his own ideological ends. "Jaurès involved himself in the Affair because of his conviction and his role as a public man," Dreyfus had said in his defense in 1903, "and I defy [anyone] to find a deputy in Parliament who dares to take such initiative." While other supporters lost interest in the case, Jaurès maintained his commitment. He spent hours with the Dreyfus family in their Boulevard Malesherbes apartment, and when his young daughter, Madeleine, fell ill, Alfred Dreyfus was one of the first visitors to her bedside.[28]

As the ideological quarrels between Jaurès and the Marquise Arconati-Visconti intensified, Dreyfus served as intermediary between his two strong-willed colleagues. Given the contests he had refereed since Rennes, he had the experience. In his opinion the marquise had chastised Clemenceau for the wrong reasons; she had called him indulgent in the face of social disorder when she should have called him dictatorial. And though Dreyfus joined the marquise in criticizing Jaurès's alliance with antipatriots, he had a more sympathetic view of the industrial proletariat. "The great development of industry has increased human misery," Dreyfus had written while in exile, and "everything possible must be done to ease the plight of the unfortunate. But above all," he added, "it is the suffering of poor children which must be alleviated; first and foremost those little ones must attract all our attention."[29]

"Recently I walked by a pastry shop," Dreyfus wrote the marquise, "where I saw two poor children peering in the window with hungry eyes at all the good things they could not have. I bought them a treat, and I assure you that their joy cheered me up all day long. You see, as painful as my life has been, and I believe that it has been one of the most painful, one can still find happiness." On another occasion, while still serving as artillery commandant, Dreyfus sent Joseph Reinach a report on the low wages and "tenuous financial situation" of his *gardiens de batterie;* he asked Reinach to intervene in government circles on behalf of those "modest employees" who are not fairly compensated and who are "excellent servants of the State." A short time later, when criticized for supporting an impartial investigation of two strike organizers arrested by Clemenceau's troops, Dreyfus defended his action: "How is it that I have no right to give my opinion on a question of justice!" he demanded. "Victim myself of a denial of justice . . . it is my duty to come to the aid of other victims . . . whatever opinions they may profess."[30]

Raised and educated to respect order, authority, and hierarchy, Dreyfus's instincts were conservative and his attitudes toward the working class, shaped by his father and brothers in Mulhouse, were paternalistic. But the obedient soldier had returned from six years in solitary confinement with an empathy for the oppressed and a commitment to radical, though not revolutionary, social change. "We are in a remarkable period of transition in History," he wrote. "We are cheerfully throwing off our old used clothes in order to move toward new horizons where Humanity will find, if not happiness (because suffering and pain will always exist), at least more joy in life with every passing day. I am not a socialist," he went on, "in the sense that I am not a collectivist, but I believe that people who struggle and work have a right to their share of happiness, and that we must strive to give it to them." He condemned the "subversive theories" of anarchosyndicalists for endangering the nation, but he insisted that trade unions operating within the law must be treated fairly. "To want to take away the workers' right to unionize, which brings with it the right to strike," he commented during the labor crisis in the Midi, "is to want to reduce them to a kind of slavery."[31]

From his years growing up in the industrial society of southern Alsace, through his Polytechnique drills on the responsibilities of serving "the French people," to the lessons of Devil's Island and his alliance with Radical and socialist leaders, Dreyfus had formulated his own brand of "solidarism." Officially elaborated in the 1890s, that doctrine of social justice had been taken up by many veterans of the affair—some of them, like Ferdinand Buisson, Dreyfus's close associates. Solidarists envisioned society as a "chain of individuals associated in a common task to which everyone has obligations"—or, as one of the founders of the Radical party, Léon Bourgeois, maintained in a modern variation on Rousseau, society should be built on a "quasi-contract of association." Believing that social peace could only be achieved through class cooperation, solidarists treated advocates of class conflict and capitalists who placed profits over people as common enemies of the progressive state. Opponents of collectivism and of unbridled economic liberalism, they wanted to protect workers from exploitation while preserving private property and free enterprise. They searched for a "middle way," a third way, and Alfred Dreyfus stood firmly in their centrist camp.[32]

Also in that camp, though more interested in its philosophical underpinnings than its political framework, was Emile Durkheim, son of a rabbi in the province of Lorraine. To the west of Mulhouse, just across the Vosges, Durkheim's town of Epinal had also been occupied during the Franco-Prussian War, and, like Dreyfus (who was the same age), the young Lorrainer had migrated to Paris in the 1870s to pursue his studies. Though he majored in philosophy at the Ecole Normale Supérieure, Durkheim followed wide-ranging interests, and one professor who profoundly influenced his intellectual development, Fustel de Coulanges, was the same scholar who would later shape—from afar—Alfred Dreyfus's views of history and the origins of French institutions. Fustel's example encouraged Durkheim to apply scientific methods to the examination of human society and, specifically, to the role of religion in social life. In a series of works Durkheim explored how "the individual is dominated by a moral reality greater than himself; namely collective reality." Concentrating on "the importance of communal sentiment, collective ideals and religious symbols in social life," Durkheim's sociology, though never an official creed of the solidarist movement, reflected its belief in "civic morality," "social justice," and "organic solidarity."[33]

The Dreyfus affair represented for Durkheim a moral crusade waged in defense of those "collective values." By violating the "natural rights" of an innocent individual, anti-Dreyfusards had threatened "the moral unity of the nation"; and by rallying to the captain's cause, through "the book, the public lecture and popular education," Dreyfusards had, in turn, forced the community to rise above its "moral mediocrity." It was a heroic moment of "idealistic spontaneity," and Durkheim engaged the campaign in essays that responded to Catholic propagandists, and in university lecture halls, where anti-Semitic students tried to shout down their "traitorous" teacher.[34] Much like the man he defended, Durkheim considered anti-Semitism to be not an ineradicable disease in French society but "the consequence and the superficial symptom of a state of social malaise."[35] He believed, again like Dreyfus, that at moments of "public madness" the government had a responsibility to act on the promises of protection guaranteed by the edicts of emancipation: "The government should take it upon itself," Durkheim wrote at the height of the affair, "to show the masses how they are being misled and not allow itself to be suspected of seeking allies within the party of intolerance."[36] To secure order and unity the French government should honor the moral principles on which the revolutionary state had been founded.

Descendants of devout Jewish families who had known the consequences of social disorder on two sides of the Vosges, Durkheim and Dreyfus rejected the traditionalism of their ancestors for a new faith in a secular and all-inclusive community. But they could not sever themselves entirely from the traditions of their parents; and their belief in what Dreyfus, echoing Durkheim, called "social solidarity"[37] could be traced, at least in part, to the practices of social justice that distinguished the Jewish communities of Epinal, Mulhouse, and Rixheim. Durkheim's concept of "organic solidarity," though influenced by Enlightenment philosophes and mid-nineteenth-century positivists, had also been informed by the "unusual solidarity" of Jewish communities, those "small, compact and coherent [societies]," as Durkheim defined them, "with a strong feeling of self-consciousness and unity."[38] The Revolution had swept away the legal autonomy of the Jewish *kehillah,* the body that dealt with the social needs of the Jewish community, but customs of charity and justice, captured in the single Hebrew word *tzedakah,* remained vigorous in the postrevolutionary world in which Rabbi Moïse Durkheim and Raphael Dreÿfuss had worked and worshipped. Following the biblical entreaty to "open wide your hand to your brother, to the needy and to the poor, in the land," Jews in the eastern French provinces had insisted that the poor must always be cared for "because nature and religion demand it."[39]

While many customs of mutual aid disappeared with the secularization that marked nineteenth-century society, the lessons of social responsibility and the idea of an organic, interdependent community survived the exodus from country to town. In the Mulhouse of Alfred Dreyfus's childhood, Jewish and Protestant industrialists had anticipated the solidarist recipe. "Manufacturers owe their workers something more than a wage," announced one Alsatian entrepreneur,[40] and they acted to fulfill those obligations with insurance plans, housing projects, and subsidized shops that aimed to improve the plight of the proletariat while counteracting the seduction of trade unions. To raise capital for renovation and expansion, many industries, the Dreyfus mill included, became joint stock companies, a strategy that, according to solidarists, created the ideal social organization—"a class of owners who work and of workers who own." Strong defenders of their local turf, Mulhouse manufacturers would have rejected the solidarist belief that the state should intervene as the principal guardian of social justice, but the more enlightened among them would have agreed that "for a director of industry . . . to be 'liberal' [requires] proof of a broader vision, of commitment to the general interest, indeed, to generosity."[41]

As advocates of industrial progress who condemned capitalism devoid of social conscience, and as moral conservatives who championed radical reform,[42] Dreyfus and Durkheim traveled strikingly similar routes to their concept of "social solidarity." And both men also supported the early humanitarian socialism of their mutual friend Jean Jaurès. There is some evidence that Durkheim, a classmate of Jaurès's at the Ecole Normale Supérieure, had helped recruit the socialist to the Dreyfusard cause, and that he had done so with another *normalien,*

Lucien-Lévy Bruhl, a relative of Lucie Dreyfus. Like Jaurès in the years after Rennes, Durkheim tried to redirect the "energies" of the affair; "the moral agitation which these events have provoked," he wrote, "has not yet been extinguished." The fight must continue, and "it is indispensable for us to keep our social energies, in a manner of speaking, perpetually mobilized."[43] Jaurès had expressed identical sentiments to his comrades on the rue Barbet-de-Jouy. But for Durkheim, as for Dreyfus, the key moment of division came when Jaurès failed to condemn the policies of the SFIO and the pronouncements of antipatriots like Gustave Hervé. "I am quite aware," Durkheim wrote at the time, "[that] when people speak of destroying existing societies, they intend to reconstruct them. But these are the fantasies of children. One cannot in this way rebuild collective life."[44]

Dreyfus understood Jaurès's dilemma, his personal desire to work with the reformist bourgeoisie and his ideological commitment to French socialism. Hoping to at least slow Jaurès's drift away from the moderate *bloc des gauches,* Dreyfus had arranged a private meeting with his ally in the spring of 1905. He recorded its outcome in his diary, and the tone was sad. Reaffirming his "profound attachment to the person of Jaurès" and his "esteem for his character," he expressed regret that his friend would remain in the socialist camp "under such conditions." His appeal to Jaurès failed. "Once upon a time," Dreyfus wrote, "there was an avant-garde party that called itself the *jaurèsiste* party." But it had been "decapitated." Like a family member in mourning, and with more sympathy than the Marquise Arconati-Visconti ever marshaled for her former friend, Dreyfus wondered why "this poor Jaurès . . . did not remain himself."[45]

With the *bloc des gauches* quickly becoming a petrified artifact of the affair, Dreyfus spent his early retirement trying to understand its demise and to comprehend the "loss" of Jaurès. During a visit to Villers-sur-Mer on the Normandy coast, he talked with workers in that small port town—"men whose lives are so precarious"— and resolved "to consecrate a part of my time . . . to the great duty we owe toward the proletariat." Examining the question like a Polytechnicien studying a chemical compound, he read the newspapers and manifestos of French syndicalism. "At this moment, it is the most vital question for France," he told Joseph Reinach, "and it can become dangerous [not only because] of the impatience and extremism of syndicalists, but because of the fright and comprehension of the propertied classes. . . . I believe that we have a pressing obligation," he repeated in the language of a dogged solidarist, "to find a path of bold wisdom between these two perils." In another letter, he admitted, "There are movements that cannot be stopped, and so it goes for the trade union movement. I have been thinking about it for a long time," he wrote, and "the most prudent way of keeping that movement from anarchism and from compromising the very existence of the Republic, is to search for a way to organize it. It is the most urgent problem to resolve."[46]

In February 1908 Dreyfus addressed the Combat à la Villette, a revolutionary syndicalist organization based on the northeastern margins of Paris, near the city's slaughterhouse. The group had invited Dreyfus (an indication, perhaps, that his sympathies toward trade unions had become well known), and he shared the platform with three other speakers, including Albert Lévy, treasurer of the CGT and a notorious "ultra" who believed that the street, not the parliament, was the place to stage a worker's revolution. Recognizing his role as the token "bourgeois intellectual," Dreyfus seized the opportunity "to make contact with this milieu and to take its pulse." As a reserve army officer condemned by many anarchists as a deluded patriot and as a target for deranged extremists of all stripes, Dreyfus's safety could not be guaranteed (the assassination plot thwarted in 1904 had been followed by other threats). But having spent nearly five years surrounded by sharks on Devil's Island, he did not hesitate to test the troubled waters of a revolutionary *quartier* that, chances are, he had never visited before.[47]

Not surprisingly, his call for "legislative reforms to aid the legal organization of the working class" fell, for the most part, on deaf or hostile ears. The CGT treasurer—one of three Jews on the platform, as Dreyfus noted with "curiosity" but without comment—controlled his "extraordinary violence" in the presence of the meeting's celebrated guest. And at the end of the conference at least one union member complimented Dreyfus's "energy and will" and suggested that the working-class community take inspiration from his speech "to organize itself within the law and . . . without violence." Dreyfus later told Reinach that he had been "very well received" by the workers of La Villette; he had studied "the spirit, the inclinations and the culture of anarchists *sur le vif* [from life]," and he had reconfirmed his stand against "violent solutions." He had seen little difference between the antiparliamentary platforms of the extreme left and the policies embraced by the radical right, above all by the Action Française, a neoroyalist organization founded by Charles Maurras at the height of the affair. "In my opinion," Dreyfus wrote, "[anarchosyndicalists] are infinitely closer to Charles Maurras in the modes of action they extol than they are to socialists of the color of Jaurès."[48]

A few weeks after Dreyfus addressed the workers of La Villette, the Action Française, on the tenth anniversary of its founding, launched a newspaper of the same name, "a daily organ of integral nationalism." The commentators who would rally to Maurras's movement constituted a rogues' gallery of anti-Dreyfusards, many of whom, like Léon Daudet and Maurice Barrès, had attended the captain's degradation and followed the case to its bitter end. While much of their vocabulary was indistinguishable from the stylish paranoia of Drumont's *La Libre Parole* (they, too, condemned the conspiracy of Protestants, Freemasons, and Jews), the organization led by Maurras had added a new ingredient— the call for a royalist restoration. Portraying the French Revolution as the first act of a long tragedy that had destroyed order, religious faith, and national grandeur, the Action Française pressed the attack against secularism and parliamentary democracy. Three French republics were three too many, and the third must be swept out for a modern monarchy. Defining France by what it was not—and it was not a haven for "foreigners, half-breeds, and Jews"—the group aimed to unify the nation through the exclusion of its internal enemies.[49]

Maurras's troops had a hard time of it in the years immediately following Rennes, when Dreyfusard governments imposed their will on the army, the church, and other bastions of reaction. But with the disintegration of the *bloc des gauches;* the climate of violence encouraged by the "ultra" wing of the newly unified left (and inflamed by Clemenceau's repression); and, finally, the buildup of the German military, the Action Française portrayed itself as a champion of social order against anarchists, collectivists, and godless republicans and as a defender of the French fatherland against the enemy across the Rhine. Maurras's well-armed battalions of royalist Catholic students, the "Camelots du Roi," stepped up their demonstrations and "libelous campaigns"; and as proof of their effectiveness, they attracted the attention of the government's Criminal Investigation Department. The founding of the *Action Française* newspaper in 1908 only confirmed in print what was obvious in the streets; a "nationalist revival" had emerged to challenge the hegemony of Dreyfusard radicals and to reverse the course charted by the victors of the affair. "One could have thought nationalism dead and buried," observed a contemporary newspaper. "But here it is again . . . and on the Boulevard Saint-Michel cudgels are selling like hotcakes once more."[50]

In the summer of 1908 Dreyfus learned at first hand that his suspicions were correct, that Maurras's "modes of action" had much in common with the extreme left. Two years earlier, on the day following Dreyfus's revision, the Chamber of Deputies had voted to move Emile Zola's remains from the Montmartre cemetery to the Panthéon, the grand repository of French heroes. Delayed by nationalist protests and bureaucratic inertia, the transfer was finally approved in the spring of 1908 by the government of Georges Clemenceau, Zola's old comrade. The novelist and defender of Dreyfus would be interred near Voltaire, the defender of Calas, and the event would be marked by a celebration at the Place du Panthéon, only a few steps from the Ecole Polytechnique. Alfred Dreyfus would attend, and he would be surrounded by old friends in a familiar locale. Meanwhile, in the weeks prior to the ceremony, the Action Française condemned Zola's proposed "pantheonization," and encouraged its followers to protest the government's "profane" act. Zola's widow received anonymous notes from "young patriots" who warned that if her husband's ashes went to the Panthéon a "bloody drama" would ensue and his remains would end up not in the nation's sanctuary but in the Seine. A poster that appeared in Paris in April insisted that Zola's "rightful place was in the excrement that he loved so much"; and late on the night of June 3, the eve of the ceremony, hundreds of nationalists shouting "Spit on Zola!" marched through the Latin Quarter to confront counterdemonstrators shouting "Long live Zola!"[51]

Under the headline TO OUR FRIENDS OF THE LATIN QUARTER, the June 3 issue of *Action Française* prepared its legions for the following day: "Patriotic students, who do not want France devoured alive by the Jew and the alien, we call on your energy, your solidarity, your spirit of organization." Léon Daudet went on to attack "the foreigners of the interior" and the republic itself ("that constitutional wound through which all poisons penetrate the social body"), and he railed against the "supreme shame" of honoring Zola, "the great alien . . . the protector of the Jewish Traitor. . . . [We] are here," he argued, "to give form and clarity to legitimate national anger. A committee for the surveillance of aliens, based in the Latin Quarter, is an urgent necessity," he wrote, "and, of course, we put at the disposition of that committee the offices of the Action Française."[52]

Daudet's public announcement had been preceded by a private

meeting of the star chamber of the Action Française. The main topic, according to one undercover police agent, had concerned the proposed "assassination of Dreyfus" during the Zola ceremony and the measures that would be taken "to facilitate the assassin's escape [and] protect him against the possible reprisals of the crowd." A well-heeled royalist put up twenty thousand francs for the execution of the Jewish traitor, but Maurras vetoed the plan. "By liquidating Dreyfus," he maintained, "the Action Française would lose its best weapon against the Republic." Not all members agreed—some wanted to keep their "options open"—but any fatal attack would not have Maurras's official approval.[53]

Late on the morning of June 4, a clear but sweltering day, Armand Fallières, the president who had signed Dreyfus's revision, approached the Panthèon along the rue Soufflot. Two lines of soldiers stood between the president's carriage and a large crowd of students shouting "Down with Zola! Down with Dreyfus!" Prepared for trouble, police arrested demonstrators who refused to move on, as well as a handful of young men brandishing knives. Within a cordoned-off section of the Place du Panthéon most of the surviving notables of the affair, including the rivals of recent years, gathered for the solemn ceremony. Clemenceau and Picquart were there, along with Jaurès and Briand, and Alfred Dreyfus sat between Lucie and Mathieu, with Pierre, Jeanne, and Mathieu's wife, Suzanne, nearby. When the minister of public education finished a speech honoring Zola's devotion to France, an army band struck up the familiar *Chant du Départ*.

Rising to join the official cortege, Dreyfus suddenly heard a gunshot behind him and to his right. As he turned he glimpsed a revolver pointed at his chest and instinctively raised his right arm as a "shield" of protection. A second shot pierced that arm before Mathieu, Suzanne, and members of the Zola family surrounded Alfred and wrestled the assailant to the ground. Others on the platform tried to attack the gunman, but Mathieu held them off. A physician hurried the victim into a police station nearby and treated the wound; the muscles of Dreyfus's forearm had been severed, but his movement in self-defense had deflected the bullet, which might otherwise have proved fatal.[54]

Allies and enemies alike responded to news of the attack with "general astonishment." Dreyfusard newspapers called it "the most odious and cowardly assault"—"doubly so," noted *Aurore*, "since Dreyfus was surrounded by his children." For *Gil Blas*, "the truly guilty parties were those fanatical [journalists] who spread their incivilities every morning . . . with vulgarity and brutality." Notes and telegrams of sympathy arrived at the Boulevard Malesherbes, including one letter from a Dreyfusard who had followed the affair's principal actor since the day of his degradation: "You have suffered again," Sarah Bernhardt wrote, "but you should suffer no more. The flag of truth . . . snaps louder than the barking of the dog pack. . . . Look around you, near and far . . . and you will see a multitude of people who love you and defend you against cowardice, lies and forgetfulness."[55]

But the dogs still barked. "We will probably have the good fortune," Henri Rochefort observed with sarcasm, "of preserving [Dreyfus]. . . . But if, instead of a glancing wound, he had been killed, the rest he is now enjoying would be absolute." Like other members of the radical right, Rochefort laid the blame at the doorstep of the republican government for its "premeditated provocation of the people" and for its insistence that the army humiliate itself by participating in an homage to the "Venetian eroticist," Zola. Dreyfusards should consider themselves lucky that their hero, "that dear child of Israel," received only "an insignificant wound." The *Action Française,* not entirely surprised by the incident, called the gunshot an echo of the people's anger. "Do you want Zola out of the Panthéon?" Léon Daudet asked his readers. "Do you want to bring Dreyfus to the execution stake? Do you want to break the Jewish yoke? Then call forth, demand, invoke your King!"[56]

Sixty-six-year-old Louis-Anthelme Grégori, a diminutive, gray-bearded former playwright who had turned to journalism and to an expertise in military affairs, had probably acted on his own, though he must have been aware of the bounty on Dreyfus's head. A *normalien* more in the mode of the anti-Dreyfusard Brunetière than of his fellow alumnus Jaurès, he had worked with Edouard Drumont on the illustrated edition of *La France Juive.* "The Dreyfus Affair and the demolition of our army by the Jews had profoundly disturbed [Grégori]," went Drumont's understatement, and during the Panthéon ceremony, when he heard the praises of Zola's patriotism, he decided to fire, "not on Monsieur Dreyfus," as he insisted at his trial, "but on Dreyfusism." It was, he said, "a purely symbolic act"; and that argument would serve as the crux of his defense. Grégori's sister told police that her brother was "incapable of performing such an act with premeditation"; his devotion to France had been confirmed by his fifteen duels with antipatriots, and "his idolatrous love for the Fatherland," the sister went on, "must have prompted that . . . moment of patriotic exaltation."[57]

During the trial, held in September, Grégori's lawyers attempted to reopen the Dreyfus case by repeating old rumors about the captain's alleged "confession" of his crime. But after fourteen years, two court-martials, and a final revision, the Dreyfus family would have none of it. Having learned from previous mistakes, the victim of Grégori's attack addressed the court "in a strong and harsh voice" and stood up "in anger" to remind the lawyers that the High Court of Appeal had proclaimed his innocence. Jeers and hisses came from one section of the room, while shouts of "Bravo! Bravo!" came from another. Mathieu, who no longer possessed the patience he had shown throughout the affair, found his voice growing louder as he testified; he lashed out at Grégori and his supporters, shouting, "You are liars and cowards!" In the midst of the melee, André Gaucher, an Action Française member who had himself volunteered to assassinate Dreyfus, disrupted the trial with references to Article 445, the section of the Civil Code that had enabled officials to hand down a "trumped-up verdict" in 1906 and avoid a new court-martial.[58] The judge jailed Gaucher for contempt, but Grégori would not join his comrade behind bars. The jury promptly acquitted Dreyfus's assailant, suggesting that his "passionate" deed was not premeditated and that the patriot had not been responsible for his actions. Like the wave of *crimes passionels* that marked the period, Grégori's act had been prompted, the jury suggested, by blind devotion. Eugène Naville, attending the trial as one of Dreyfus's bodyguards, knew better: The jury, he reported succinctly, was "antisemitic and anti-Dreyfusard."[59]

The Action Française and like-minded nationalists had scored a double victory: Thanks to Grégori's poor marksmanship, their principal symbol of republican decadence had survived to be attacked in other ways on other occasions, and the fledgling crusade for integral nationalism had been blessed by a bonanza of free publicity. "Grégori's courageous attack struck Dreyfus in the arm," the newspaper *Gaulois* announced the day after the trial, while "the verdict struck Dreyfusism in the heart." *La Libre Parole* published a letter from Grégori thanking his comrades for their moral support, and Drumont responded by launching a subscription for Grégori in the spirit of Colonel Henry's "Monument."[60]

For Dreyfus the battle did not end with Grégori's release. Through the fall of 1908 and for at least three years thereafter, he attempted to sue the nationalist press for "injury and defamation." Only one decision seems to have gone in his favor—when a judge ordered *Action Française* to pay a small fine and to publish all the "letters to the editor" that Dreyfus had written in protest of slanderous reports. For Maurras, however, the judgment and the "traitor's" correspondence—Dreyfus's doomed efforts to correct in rational letters all the irrational propaganda of the nationalist right—only served to keep the movement alive. During that period, police received "strong" rumors of plots by "young royalists" to kidnap Dreyfus, and in February 1909 a gang of sixty "well-dressed, top-hatted young men brandishing canes," the customary weapons of the Camelots du Roi, invaded the family's apartment building on the Boulevard Malesherbes. Shouting "We must have the Jew!" they reached the elevator, which they vandalized, before being chased out. The demonstration confirmed that Dreyfus had not lost his appeal as a nationalist target, and though Maurras's legions continued to insist that he was nothing but a "pure symbol," they never explained why guns, cudgels, and canes were needed to fight an abstraction.[61]

Nor did the *Action Française* press the issue alone. When Dreyfus wrote in protest to yet another newspaper, *Autorité,* its editor shot back in print with a virulence that rivaled the old attacks by Drumont and the contemporary variations by Daudet: "You are a nobody as a Frenchman and a nobody as a soldier," announced Guy de Cassagnac, son of the old Bonapartist, Paul de Cassagnac. "Instead of a sword, straight and bright, you have preferred the nib of a pen stained with ink, and the scribe in you has killed off whatever remained of the officer after the last braid had been torn from your uniform. I would like to pity you," Cassagnac went on, "because compassion is Christian, but I cannot. Your cold insolence, your crafty hypocrisy, all of which I saw lurking in the sinewy . . . signature at the bottom of your typewritten letter (because today you're careful to compose your *bordereaux* on a machine!), leaves in us nothing but an insurmountable disgust. You resemble, sir, a game of cards, however strange that comparison may seem. . . . It would be wise, as they say in bridge, for you to play the dummy, the dead man."[62]

Dreyfus did not abandon his crusade of writing letters to editors, and he continued to address the urgent issues of the day. He presented his lecture, "The History of Syndicalism in France,"[63] and on the occasional Thursday at noon he shared his opinions at the Arconati-Visconti salon. But after Grégori's attack and the resurgence of threats, he sought places of security for his family; the "nationalist revival" had revived Dreyfus's own need for sanctuary. Furthermore, his nightmares, fevers, and chronic fatigue had not abated, and doctors put him on a strict diet and ordered a regimen of exercise in the fresh air. He returned with Lucie to the northern Italian towns where they had spent their honeymoon more than twenty years before, he visited the Navilles' home above Lake Geneva, and he joined his sisters—also on holiday—for boat trips and walks in Switzerland's Bernese Oberland. Dreyfus escaped Paris as much for its pollution as for its politics, and, with Lucie, he resolved to devote the rest of his days to their children.[64]

PART 4

The Thirty Years' War

CHAPTER XVIII

Heirs Apparent

PIERRE AND JEANNE DREYFUS, like their closest cousins, Emile and Magui, grew up amid an illustrious troop of "uncles" and "aunts." Joseph Reinach, Jean Jaurès, Gabriel Monod, the Navilles, the Marquise Arconati-Visconti, and, until their deaths, Scheurer-Kestner, Zola, and Lazare were not "Dreyfusards" to the children but kindly members of a new extended family. They helped Lucie maintain the secret of the captain's "long army voyage," and when Pierre and Jeanne learned the truth about their father's exile, family friends helped shield the youngsters from dangers that had not abated. On the steps of the Panthéon, Grégori's bullet had narrowly missed the children, and on the Boulevard Malesherbes the assault by the Camelots du Roi had reconfirmed the need for tight security.[1]

Confined to homes in Paris, Carpentras, and Geneva through the affair and its aftermath, Pierre and Jeanne enjoyed only the occasional companionship of Mathieu and Suzanne's son and daughter and of Joseph Reinach's children, Ado and Lili. The other Dreyfus cousins—the children of Jacques, Henriette, and Rachel—were either much older or kept close to home in Belfort or Carpentras. Mathieu had insisted that his son and daughter remain in seclusion with Suzanne's family in Héricourt, but those youngsters, eager to rejoin their parents, made plans to run away. They packed a change of clothes in small sacks made of old material from their grandfather's Mulhouse mill. That particular journey

343

never came about, but Suzanne brought Emile and Magui to Paris to visit their father and to play with Pierre and Jeanne and Ado and Lili Reinach. As soon as the adults disappeared into libraries or drawing rooms for their mysterious conversations, the children dashed through apartment corridors dancing the *tanzette à la schnellette,* a rapid Alsatian step which Emile and Magui taught their Parisian cousins and friends.[2]

Unlike Lucie, who revealed nothing to Pierre and Jeanne about their father's exile, Mathieu Dreyfus and Joseph Reinach told their children about the affair at an early date—though unbeknownst to the parents, the youngsters had already coaxed the information from the family's servants. Reinach dedicated his first volumes on the case to "My son, Ado," and in 1898 the boy wrote a poem about the captain's affair that he presented to "Magui Mathieu Dreyfus," his childhood sweetheart. Covering seventeen pages in an awkward scribble, those verses applauded the heroism of Magui's uncle: "Who is the cause of the struggles and the fears / Of the battles, the shouts . . . and the tears / It is an innocent man unjustly condemned / Of the greatest and most infamous of crimes / . . . It is, in one word, the greatest martyr since Jesus / The Captain of the General Staff, Dreyfus." Ado described how "nothing, nothing was too tough for this Jew," and he warned that enemies who wished to make the captain "an outcast of a great nation / Will one day witness his rehabilitation!"[3] A sophisticated achievement for an eleven-year-old, the poem may have been helped along by Joseph Reinach, just as Ado's precocious courtship of Magui Dreyfus may have been inspired by his father's example: When asked, at the age of seven, what he wanted to be when he grew up, Ado had said that he would, like his father, pursue "politics and ladies."[4]

When left alone to play with Ado and their cousins, or when querying the domestic staff, Pierre and Jeanne may have learned something about their father's notoriety, though they never broached the subject with their mother. Forbidden topics marked those early years, but the period following the captain's return proved even more difficult. After Rennes the children heard their father having nightmares and witnessed his attacks of fever and fatigue. They noted his "constant tension," his "preoccupation with the official recognition of his innocence," and for much of the time "laughter and gaity" were in short supply in the Dreyfus home. Pierre would later recall his father's kindness during those years, but he would also describe the "oppressive ambiance which weighed upon us all." Obsessed by the struggle for revision, Dreyfus seems to have been equally obsessed by the need to divorce his public agenda from his private life; he taught the children only the outlines of his case, and once told, the story was rarely repeated. Popular illustrations of Dreyfus holding his son and daughter and telling them the history of his affair ("*Père, une histoire!*" went the caption of a celebrated sketch by Félix Vallotton) were more charming than accurate. Dreyfus had resolved to focus on the future, and though Pierre and Jeanne wanted to know more about their father's exile, their questions were discouraged and to them the details of the affair remained a mystery.[5]

Dreyfus tutored his children in other subjects, however: Latin, German, French grammar, mathematics, science, geography, and history. "My husband and I are working together," Lucie wrote a friend, "to manage the children's training and education. For Pierre, it is interesting," she said, "while for Jeanne, who is just starting out, it is a matter of patience."[6] When his health permitted, Alfred took his son on mountain hikes in Switzerland, forced marches of sorts to strengthen the frail boy, who had always been a prime candidate for cod-liver-oil potions; if Pierre wanted to emulate his father—as he did with his meticulous stamp collection—he would have to balance his sedentary habits with vigorous exercise in the open air. Pierre was a diligent student, but he never enjoyed the wide-ranging instruction Alfred had received from sisters and tutors in Mulhouse; the upheavals of the affair had seen to that. Nonetheless he showed an aptitude for science and mathematics, and by his eleventh year he was ready to enter a Paris *lycée*.

Jeanne's education would follow a different course. She would not pursue the *baccalauréat* but instead study language, literature, and household management, first under her parents' guidance and then at a private school on the rue Alphonse de Neuville, just a few hundred yards west of the family apartment. Directed by two teachers known for their Dreyfusard sympathies, the Villiers school offered both personal instruction and personal safety. In addition, as her mother had done, Jeanne learned embroidery and studied music (*solfège*) every Thursday afternoon.[7]

Pierre began the first phase of his formal education as an *externe*, a day student, at the Lycée Condorcet on the rue Caumartin. Also near the Boulevard Malesherbes, it met the family's requirements for security and academic excellence. Honoring the enlightenment philosopher and revolutionary advocate of public education for all citizens, the school reflected only part of Condorcet's dream: Its clientele learned to believe in unlimited progress, but, as a private institution with a stiff tuition, the *lycée* did not concern itself, as Condorcet might have hoped, with the abolition of inequality through public education. When Pierre studied there, most of his fellow students were the affluent sons of doctors, lawyers, magistrates, and industrialists, and its distinguished alumni, from the historian Hippolyte Taine to the portrait photographer Nadar, secured its reputation as a fashionable secondary school for the elite.[8]

Other graduates, arguably the most talented of all, were the three Reinach brothers—Joseph, Salomon, and Théodore—and for a brief time Pierre attended Condorcet with Joseph's son, Ado. Four years older than his friend, Ado had also been tutored at home, by instructors specializing in Latin and Greek, and by family members celebrated (and reviled) in Paris for their intellectual brilliance. Recalling the difficulties of his own school years and aware that his son would face the same prejudices, Joseph Reinach employed a coach to teach the boy *la boxe,* an English sport à la mode in turn-of-the-century Paris. Ado was a slight youngster, and when he entered the lycée ahead of his class and younger than his colleagues, his father's fears were realized. Using the cover of "anti-Dreyfusard" politics to justify their hooliganism, students hurled ink at Ado and pierced his neck with needles. The boy's boxing skills could not deter that onslaught, and without informing his son, Joseph Reinach hired a security agent to follow him. With Pierre confronting similar attacks at school, it is likely that his family also called on the detectives they had employed for protection throughout the affair.[9]

If Pierre had the gift of dogged concentration, Ado had a mind that wandered and a curiosity that could not be satisfied within the stifling confines of Parisian classrooms. After passing his *baccalauréat,* he made one unsuccessful attempt to enter the Ecole Normale Supérieure and then decided to follow the example of his uncle Salomon, a renowned archaeologist. At the Sorbonne, the Collège de France, and the Ecole des Hautes Etudes, Ado took courses in ancient history, epigraphy, and Hellenic religions; and by 1911 he had traveled to Greece, Italy, Turkey, and Egypt. He participated in archaeological digs in Galatia, south of the Black Sea; in Koptos, on the eastern bank of the Nile; and at sites on the islands of Thasos and Crete. He published his first monograph (*L'Egypte préhistorique*) at the age of twenty-one and went on to compile a critical bibliography on Homer and to publish the findings of his explorations in Koptos. Ado Reinach may not have enjoyed his father's success as a student, but he shared, as a fellow classicist put it, his "insatiable curiosity."[10]

Pursuing a more traditional course of study, Pierre Dreyfus, his *baccalauréat* in hand, entered his father's former school, the Collège Chaptal, where he concentrated on mathematics and modern languages (recent alternatives to the classical curriculum) and prepared for the entrance examinations required by the *grandes écoles*. During the affair, his older cousins, Jacques Dreyfus's sons, had suffered guilt by association with the "traitor" and had been forced out of the Ecole Polytechnique. More than a decade later, with the nationalist revival rekindling anti-Semitic sentiments, Alfred Dreyfus's son would surely be subjected to the same harassment if he tried to follow his father as a Polytechnicien. Hoping for a career in industry, Pierre applied instead to the Ecole Centrale des Arts et Manufactures, an institution as prestigious as the Polytechnique but with greater concentration on the practical matters of business and engineering. In September 1910, at the age of nineteen, Pierre passed the entrance examination and took pride, as his father had done more than three decades before, in being accepted by a *grande école* on his first application.[11]

While Pierre, Jeanne, and the Reinach children enjoyed the privilege of Paris's finest schools, Emile and Magui Dreyfus, growing up in Mulhouse, attended small private classes arranged by French families who refused to patronize German-controlled institutions. Their principal tutor was a Swiss Protestant with French sympathies, and for examinations they traveled to a school in Besançon, in French territory, where Emile passed his *baccalauréat* in 1906. Visiting the Dreyfuses in Mulhouse during those years, Eugène Naville noted the city's "heavy, melancholy atmosphere," the consequence of an oppressive "administrative and military bureaucracy," and he remarked how "French society" was forced to "live within itself." On the streets of their native city, Emile and Magui joined other children to taunt German officials. Because the shout "Vive la France!" was outlawed in Alsace, the youngsters sneaked up behind Germans in uniform and chanted "Vive la . . . Vive la . . . Belgique!" Young Parisians like Pierre, Jeanne, Ado, and Lili had to learn the largely abstract subject of "Alsace-Lorraine" as part of their curriculum of patriotism, while for Emile and Magui it was a concrete reality, a homeland waiting to be liberated by the "mother country."[12]

After 1908, to avoid the requirement that they declare citizenship in the German *Reichsland*, Emile and Magui, now teenagers, moved back to the house in which they had spent most of the affair—their maternal grandparents' estate across the Vosges in Héricourt. Raised in part by the Schwobs, a family known for its Freemasonry, Emile and Magui received no religious schooling, nor did the Reinach youngsters. Among the children of the affair, only Pierre and Jeanne seem to have had formal religious instruction. Lucie read the Bible at home, and on High Holy Days and on the anniversary of a family member's death she took the children to synagogue. Grand Rabbi Kahn, Lucie's relative by marriage, believed that the affair and its attendant anti-Semitism should prompt Jews to break their "religious stagnation" and encourage in their children a strong "Jewish consciousness."[13] The rabbi's appeal met with little success in the assimilated Jewish community of Paris, but Lucie, who had drawn strength during the affair from the two faiths of patriotism and religion, did her part to provide spiritual instruction for her son and daughter during their most formative years. Later, when Alfred joined his wife as the children's tutor, the philosophy of the enlightenment assumed a greater role in their curriculum. But if Alfred was not "a believer," he was "a sympathetic witness to those who believe—I am aware of the moral beauty of faith," he had written on Devil's Island, "on the condition that it does not become . . . a narrow idea."[14]

Despite their differences all the Dreyfus and Reinach children learned to share one faith without qualification: the belief in *revanche*, the return of Alsace-Lorraine to France. An articulate spokesman for the lost provinces in the Chamber of Deputies, Joseph Reinach displayed on his desk a silver medal celebrating the "marriage" of Mulhouse to France. And Alfred Dreyfus had joined the officer corps expressly to achieve the goal of reunification. With every accusation of his "treason" he had reminded his judges that he was the son of Alsatian *protestataires*. His entire family had, in fact, violated the first half of Léon Gambetta's old axiom: French citizens should "never speak" about the lost provinces, Gambetta had suggested, but "always think" about them. But the Dreyfuses did both. Like the statue representing Strasbourg, which remained under a black shroud of mourning on the Place de la Concorde, and like school maps with the region of Alsace-Lorraine marked in red, symbols of the lost provinces played a central role in the children's education. "The image of the Rhine," Alfred Dreyfus had written, "should never be erased from our memory."[15]

That dream of reunification applied to the family's two industries as well—to Raphael Dreyfus's original factory and to the branch managed by Jacques in Belfort. The division of those enterprises reflected the forced separation of the family itself, and part of their definition of *revanche* included the hope of one day consolidating the Mulhouse and Belfort mills under common French ownership, to the benefit of French markets. With the rate of economic growth increasing throughout industrialized Europe after the hard years of the early 1890s, Raphael Dreyfus et Compagnie entered a new phase of expansion; the Mulhouse factory added offices, an archive, and new machinery in 1905, and a half decade later the complex of buildings on the rue Lavoisier, now a half-century old, were joined to a modern three-story addition.[16]

In 1911 Mathieu lost the partner who had helped maintain the family's first enterprise throughout the affair. Léon Dreyfus's death, at the age of fifty-seven and probably as the result of a stroke, was unexpected, though he had been in poor health for most of his life. The complaints of a "nervous stomach," the periods of weakness bordering on paralysis, had been related to Léon's long bout with diabetes. Unlike the brothers and sisters who made frequent trips to Paris during the affair, and unlike Henriette, whose Carpentras home had become the family's provincial base of operations, Léon remained confined in Mulhouse by the responsibilities of business and by his illness. He had promised to accompany Lucie to the Saint-Martin de Ré prison in 1895, but, at the last minute, could not. And four years later, during the retrial in Rennes, the family received another report of his troubles: "Léon is in a pitiful state," wrote an Alsatian friend, "because he lacks the strength to react," and because, without children and without family, he and his wife "are very much alone and very unhappy."[17] Growing up in the shadow of his older brother Jacques, and never receiving the education enjoyed by Mathieu and Alfred, Léon spent his adult years as the most isolated of the seven Dreyfus siblings. He followed the affair from afar, and though he organized support in Mulhouse, the case that reunited his family had, in many ways, passed him by.

Jacques Dreyfus sent his older sons, Charles and Maurice, to take over Léon's responsibilities on the rue Lavoisier. But if Jacques was a full partner in the enterprise, just as Léon had been, Mathieu had emerged as the first among equals. He had served as his father's principal assistant until Raphael's death, and he had continued to make key business decisions during the affair. Now, with Jacques approaching sixty-seven and Mathieu nearing fifty-four, the time had come to prepare a new generation and to name an heir apparent. While the family would continue to share the profits of Raphael Dreyfus et Compagnie,

Mathieu's son, Emile, and Jacques' son, Charles, would preside over the factory's reinstatement as a French Alsatian enterprise at the hour of *revanche*.

Or so Mathieu hoped. But life under German occupation had instilled in Emile the same sentiments felt by his uncle Alfred four decades earlier. He believed that a member of the Dreyfus family should serve as a career officer in the campaign for *revanche*. While fulfilling his compulsory military service in 1912, Emile announced that he planned to make the army his life, a decision shaped by his family's commitment to the lost provinces and prompted by recent events that had raised the prospect of European war. In that same year, asked if he ever thought about war, Joseph Joffre, the new French chief of staff, replied, "Yes, I do think about it. I think about it all the time. We shall have war. I will make it. I will win it." Emile echoed Joffre's thoughts, and he was not the only young Frenchman to change his career plans in order serve his fatherland.[18]

Tensions between France and Germany had been rekindled a few months before when a German gunboat, the *Panther*, dropped anchor in the Moroccan port of Agadir. Kaiser Wilhelm II aimed to protect German nationals from French-inspired revolts in the region, but, no less important, the naval display served as a symbol of Berlin's "muscular diplomacy." The crisis passed when France ceded part of its holdings in the Congo to Germany in return for a free hand in Morocco, but if the *Panther* sailed home in peace, diplomatic waters remained troubled. A series of alliances and "friendly agreements" forged over recent decades—especially those involving France, Russia, and Britain on the one hand and Germany, Austria-Hungary, and Italy on the other—were being tested by nationalist upheavals in distant Balkan states whose names the vast majority of Europeans could neither pronounce nor locate on a map. Bosnia-Herzegovina and other provinces on the southern margins of the Hapsburg Empire had significance for France because of the role they played for France's premier ally, Russia, and for that power's interest in maintaining a presence in the region between the Black Sea and the Mediterranean. Russia's ties to Serbia, across the southern border from the Austro-Hungarian Empire, provided a constant threat to political and military leaders in Vienna and Berlin; and every push for independence by Serbian nationalists within lands recently annexed by Austria-Hungary placed further strains on an already precarious balance of European power. "The war between Serbia and Austria . . . is inevitable," the head of Serbian military intelligence announced in 1912. "This war must bring about the eternal freedom . . . of the Balkan peoples."[19]

Given the agreements signed by European states, however, a conflict between Austria and Serbia could just as easily bring about the mobilization of their closest allies, Germany and Russia. And in the event of war, the Third French Republic would rally to its militantly antirepublican partner, czarist Russia. Reflecting their common goal of containing Germany—now the strongest military and industrial nation on the European continent—the Franco-Russian alliance also reflected close economic interests. With Russia receiving 25 percent of France's entire foreign investment, the Third Republic had good reason to protect its autocratic ally. Largely responsible for building the railroad system that stretched east to the Siberian frontier and to Pacific ports, France had long encouraged its citizens to participate in Russia's economic development. Since the 1880s huge loans had been arranged by the Rothschilds and other French bankers, and thousands of investors, the Reinach family among them, would later purchase shares in capitalist ventures like those launched by the Compagnie du Chemin de Fer d'Olonetz (Olonetz Railway Company)—investments that promised a 4.5 percent return, "guaranteed by the Imperial Government of Russia."[20] Czar Nicholas may have been "a throwback to the Middle Ages," as Alfred Dreyfus called him, a tyrant "who has forgotten that time marches on,"[21] but the czar's state had been propped up by an infusion of French francs, and that economic reality, along with the belief that pressure on Germany's eastern front would help France retrieve Alsace-Lorraine in the event of war, made the Franco-Russian alliance both shrewd and popular. A French diplomat called it the "perfect . . . 'mariage de raison,' " and "to be convinced of this," he added, "one needs only to examine a map."[22]

In fact French officials had spent a great deal of time examining maps since the Franco-Prussian War, a habit they had not pursued with sufficient diligence before it. In 1912 Emile Dreyfus prepared to join an officer corps armed with sophisticated maps that his uncle Alfred, fresh from the Ecole de Guerre, had helped draft two decades earlier. Those plans of fortresses, garrisons, and rail lines reaching from Paris to Châlons-sur-Marne, Verdun, and the Argonne Forest had been updated over recent years, and so, too, had the personnel of the General Staff. The radical republican attempt to purge reactionary officers in the wake of the Dreyfus Affair had led at first to the "profound demoralization" of the military; but with every display of German belligerence support for the high command returned, and by 1912 French officers enjoyed a new and positive image as soldiers on the front line of the "nationalist revival." The Action Française may have hoped for legions led by Catholic royalists, but as Emile Dreyfus's decision indicated, the renaissance of nationalism proved more democratic than that. One of its principal leaders, Raymond Poincaré, elected prime minister in 1912, emerged not from the troops of Charles Maurras but from the ranks of Dreyfusards and anticlericals. His allegiance to the captain had been marked by caution, conservatism, and a desire to protect his own political future, but the moderate republican's intense nationalism reconfirmed that France's "revival" had gained a broad base of support. Committed to military preparedness, to the Russian alliance, and, as a proud Lorrainer, to the goal of *revanche*, Poincaré would succeed Armand Fallières as president of the republic in 1913. He would name Alexandre Millerand, the socialist who had choreographed Dreyfus's pardon, minister of war; and he would choose Aristide Briand, Dreyfus's luncheon partner on the rue Barbet-de-Jouy, as prime minister. The reactionary right had never enjoyed a monopoly on patriotism, and by 1912 it had lost its corner on militant nationalism.[23]

"A new generation of officers, more independent-minded and open to the modern spirit," Mathieu Dreyfus had said in the aftermath of the affair, "must show that the army and the nation are one." If not, he warned, "all the gains of recent years . . . will be lost." A decade later, his own son wanted to be part of that "new generation," and Mathieu, though disappointed that Emile would not succeed him in the family business, supported the choice and spoke of the special obligations. "Because of the name you carry," Mathieu wrote, "your duty is even more exacting than that of your comrades."[24]

But if Mathieu gave his blessing, Ado Reinach, completing his own military service, felt a "duty" to change Emile's mind. Close friends for more than a dozen years, those young men were about to become brothers-in-law. In a civil ceremony reminiscent of her own parents' wedding, Magui Dreyfus would marry her childhood sweetheart, Ado Reinach, in the garden of her uncle Jacques Dreyfus's Belfort estate, and two of the most prominent families of the affair would be united. Ado, wanting to protect his old friend and future brother-in-law from both the dangers and the boredom of a military career, offered his advice to Emile.[25] "You are attracted by the charm of good camaraderie," he wrote, "of the grand task of forming soldiers in a time of peace and of leading them under fire in a time of war; as an energetic and zealous youngster you thought you would find that in the army, and you hope to find it there even more today." Ado realized that Mathieu and Alfred had served as role models for Emile ("are they not both military men, with their self-discipline and with the ardor for action that they manifested during the Affair?"), but Ado warned against such an "ideal" vision of army life and implored his friend to be more "realistic." He must see not only the "glory" and "grandeur" but "the perils, the boredom and the servitude." Furthermore, he must recognize the consequences of his family background. "When one carries your name, when one is the son and the nephew of those men whom you would have the perilous honor of representing in the army, mediocrity, however honest it may be, is not permitted."

By remaining in the army Emile would do a disservice to the very fatherland he wished to protect, Ado implied, and to the father who had helped build one of the great industries of Alsace. After the long struggle of the affair, Mathieu needed a rest and he needed his son's support. "If you pursue a military career, your father may have to sell the industry," Ado told Emile, "and what a heartbreak it would be to see that beautiful tradition shattered, to have your grandfather's creation, maintained and developed through so many difficulties, abandoned by his grandchildren." With the loss of the Mulhouse and Belfort mills would come the loss of the "five percent return" they provided as well. "You know the cost of modern life very well," Ado said, "and you know that the name you carry requires a certain style of living. . . . Soon you will marry and raise a family. Do you have the right to condemn them to a narrow life when it could be a generous one?" Sensing that Emile worried about the "monotonous routine of business" in provincial Belfort, Ado suggested that the boredom of "garrison life in a little town" would be even worse. "How much better to be the leader of hundreds of workers," he said. "In the army you are a slave to regulations, but in industry you enjoy a relative freedom which permits you to . . . work for progress [and] for the welfare of others. . . . I don't envy a colonel," Ado observed, "I envy the director of a grand industry."

He then turned to the one argument he hoped would sway his friend, to the future of the lost provinces. He imagined Emile raising "one more Alsatian family on the breach," at the foothills of the Vosges, "a family which will continue . . . the traditions of honor . . . work and energy. . . . Is that not a fine prospect," he asked, "to be one of the great cotton manufacturers of France on the frontier of Alsace?" He described Belfort, with its many émigrés from southern Alsace, as "the most beautiful creation of Mulhouse, the gift of Mulhouse to France. . . . A soldier's duty tempts you, my friend, but . . . as a good Frenchman, doubly French for being Alsatian, where does your duty lie? Is it not in Belfort maintaining the legacy of your grandfather, the enterprise which, thanks to the following generation, became one more link between the mother country and the annexed lands? I know very well that the brutality of the Germans may break that link. But will you help them by not staying and honoring your duty to preserve Mulhouse industry?" Continuing to emphasize the military aspects of industrial leadership, Ado again called on the vocabulary of war: "The post of combat for you is in Belfort . . . where you will be able to preserve a French enterprise in the face of the Germans. Among all the factors pushing you toward the army, what is the most heroic motive? It is that an Alsatian, a Dreyfus of Mulhouse, a Dreyfus of the Affair, plays his role . . . in the defense of the nation. . . . The family has maintained that role against all odds for decades," Ado concluded, "and now you, as the 'heir-apparent,' can maintain it as well, for the grandeur of France on the frontier of Alsace."[26]

At the same time that Ado Reinach appealed to his young friend's national and provincial patriotism, a French author, Roger Martin du Gard, completed a novel on the generations shaped by the affair. *Jean Barois* traced the odyssey of a man raised in a Catholic home and his intellectual journey toward a new faith in science. Launching a monthly literary review ("a hymn to progress"), Barois joins the Dreyfusard cause with high ideals: "It was a wonderful century," says one of his colleagues, "which began with the Revolution and ended with the Affair." But if the Dreyfus campaign transcended party politics and national chauvinism (the "rattling of the patriotic saber"), the years that followed brought disillusionment and factionalism, and by the novel's final chapters a new breed of "patriot" has emerged to lead a more "action-oriented" France into the twentieth century—and to prepare the nation for war. Two students, one from the Ecole Normale Supérieure and both in their early twenties, come to see the middle-aged Barois. "Your generation, Monsieur," they announce, "unlike ours, was satisfied with abstract theories. . . . Well, that sterile, navel-gazing contemplation may be good enough for Orientals, but . . . the France that has been through the Agadir crisis and lives under the German threat has no use for it!" Born again to the Catholic faith, those young critics believe in "Discipline," "Heroism," "Reconstruction," and "our national prestige," and though Barois condemns their credo as "the vulgar instinct of self-preservation," they present themselves as proud representatives of France's future.[27]

Much of the language used by the new nationalists in *Jean Barois*— or by old nationalists like Maurice Barrès—echoed the patriotic sentiments expressed by other Frenchmen who shared neither the political ideology nor the religious fervor of the reactionary right. "Discipline," "heroism," "energy," "action," and "national prestige" played an important part in Ado Reinach's entreaty to Emile Dreyfus, and when Ado asked his friend to remain "on the breach" in Alsace, "in the face of the Germans," he depicted the lost provinces much as the Lorrainer Barrès had depicted them only a few years before—as "the forward bastions" of France.[28] Along with Pierre Dreyfus, who began his two-year military service at a garrison near Héricourt in 1912, Emile and Ado exhibited none of the hard-edged pride displayed by Martin du Gard's young men, and shared none of their religious fervor. But if their differences were many, they nevertheless had more than age, education, and social class in common. The pervasive fear of German imperialism had blurred the distinctions between the chauvinistic nationalism captured in *Jean Barois* and the inclusive patriotism honored by the Dreyfuses and Reinachs. Old antagonists had not become new friends, but they had come to share a common enemy in Germany, and, in the broadest terms, they all defined the "nationalist revival" as a struggle for "French civilization." The reserve officer Alfred Dreyfus called for "the intense military preparation" of the fatherland and for a vigorous high command that would not repeat the errors of 1870; and his brother Mathieu, watching German dirigibles fly over Mulhouse and hearing German occupiers shouting *"Deutchsland über alles!"* condemned the "brutality" of those violators of his homeland who considered themselves members of "a superior race."[29]

Convinced of his responsibilities to the family enterprise, Emile Dreyfus agreed to at least postpone his decision on a military career. He would complete his required army service and then return to the "front line" of industry in Belfort, just as Ado, having fulfilled his military obligations, would rejoin his bride Magui in Paris and resume his scholarship and his archaeological explorations in the Mediterranean. Pierre Dreyfus's term with the Seventh Artillery in eastern France was scheduled to end late in 1914, at which time he hoped to complete his studies at the Ecole Centrale and look for a position in a Paris-based industry.

With every passing month, however, the likelihood of a peaceful return to civilian life seemed more remote. Across Europe, nations responded to Germany's military buildup with their own calls for large standing armies and modern matériel, and in France only Jean Jaurès and a handful of his comrades openly resisted the march toward war. Even the socialists' ranks had been depleted by the exodus of supporters convinced that national defense was now a greater priority than international brotherhood. Gustave Hervé, France's most notorious antimilitarist, suspended his definition of parliamentary republicans as "traitors to the working class" and called for a coalition of patriots; and with few exceptions, Radicals and Radical Socialists rallied to President Poincaré's campaign for military preparedness. Witnessing that "irrational" flight to the brink of war, Jaurés tried to expose the specious arguments of bellicose patriots: "Today you are told: act, always act!" Jaurés would announce to a meeting of students and workers. "But what is action without thought? You are told: brush aside the party of peace; it saps your coverage! But I tell you that to stand for peace today is to wage the most heroic of battles."[30]

Through the summer of 1913, Jaurès focused his energies on the fight against legislation calling for three years of military service, a law proposed by Jaurès's former socialist colleague Aristide Briand. With Germany increasing its forces at an unprecedented rate, the French government advocated the "three-year law" (instead of two years of service) as a crucial ingredient in the nation's defense recipe. It quickly became a litmus test of allegiance, dividing "patriots" and "antipatriots." But Jaurès criticized the law not only as an act of aggression; he saw it as a wrongheaded solution to the strategy of defense. Too much of a pragmatist to deny the need for a national militia, Jaurès believed that a powerful reserve force—a contingent of citizens ready to defend French territory as the soldiers of the Revolution had done—would save the enormous expenditures required by a large standing army. And on that point he won the support of Alfred Dreyfus. Though retired, Dreyfus had been working as a reserve *chef d'escadron* on studies of troop mobilization in the region north of Paris. Recognizing that in wartime the majority of combatants would be drawn from the reserves, he advocated a short term of active service coupled with frequent reserve exercises and the development of an "extremely well-prepared career officer corps"—a General Staff, in other words, with more knowledge than that of 1870 and more integrity than that of the 1890s.[31]

Logical answers to the question of national defense carried little weight, however, against a government and popular press inflamed by anti-Germanism and more taken with symbols than solutions. The Chamber of Deputies and the Senate approved the three-year law, and though Jaurès never stopped condemning the legislation, he turned to other tactics. Encouraged by socialist political victories throughout industrialized Europe—and above all by the French elections of April– May 1914, when the Socialist party garnered an unprecedented 1,400,000 votes—Jaurès believed that the combined strength of the European proletariat could prevent the catastrophe of war. If the laboring classes presented a common front against the political and military handmaidens of capitalism—if they united to proclaim a general strike in the event of war—governments would be forced to step back from the politics of confrontation. Not suprisingly, the Action Française condemned Jaurès as a traitor, and the socialist acknowledged that he and his followers had become candidates for "assassination."[32]

They were not alone. Late in the morning of June 28, 1914, Jaurès's campaign for a peaceful solution to the crisis in Europe was all but destroyed by an assassination in the Bosnian city of Sarajevo, far from the centers of diplomatic power. Archduke Franz Ferdinand, the crown prince of the Austro-Hungarian Empire, had come to Bosnia with his wife, Sophie, symbolically to reassert Hapsburg control over that troubled Balkan region. A few days before, young members of a secret nationalist organization, the Black Hand Society, had slipped across the border from Serbia to join other "Young Bosnians" in a plot to assassinate the archduke with pistols and primitive hand grenades. Most of the seven coconspirators were teenagers, including a student, Gavrilo Princip, known to Austro-Hungarian police as a Bosnian rebel with allegiance to Serbia. Positioned along Sarajevo's Appelquai, on the bank of the Miljaka River, the young men failed in their first attempt to stop the royal motorcade, but when it returned forty-five minutes later, and the archduke's driver made a wrong turn and stopped his car, Gavrilo Princip dashed forward, pointed his pistol, closed his eyes, and fired. Franz Ferdinand and the archduchess died within minutes, and police immediately apprehended their eighteen-year-old assassin.

Had the threats and counterthreats that followed the killings been limited to political leaders in Vienna and in the Serbian capital of Belgrade, the war—if there was to be one—might have been contained within southeastern Europe. But the archduke's uncle, the octogenarian emperor of Austria and king of Hungary, Franz Joseph, could not resist the pressures that came from his dominant and more energetic neighbors to the north—his allies in Berlin. Through late July, while Austria-Hungary, prompted by Germany, sent impossible ultimatums to Serbia, the alliance systems forged to protect the balance of power in Europe set about destroying it. When Russia announced its intention to defend Serbia and its interests in the region, Germany stepped up its own plans, already under way, to protect Austria-Hungary. The Third French Republic, committed to join Russia in the event of war and fearful of a German invasion through Alsace-Lorraine, prepared to mobilize its military and naval personnel. Meanwhile, England waited.

"Each nation has taken to the streets of Europe brandishing a lighted torch," Jean Jaurès proclaimed, "and now the fire is raging." On July 20, in the pages of his newspaper *L'Humanité*, the socialist, under constant attack as a German sympathizer, tried to warn his countrymen about the consequences of war in the modern age. He described the Apocalypse. War in the twentieth century would mean "millions and millions of men . . . destroying each other," Jaurès wrote. "The financial resources of the nations devoured day by day—in the service of death; economic life suspended, credit broken down, unemployment aggravated; the machine gun and typhus decimating both the vast armies and the civilian populations." As the fever pitch of European militarism intensified, so, too, did Jaurès's plea for reason and negotiation. Imagining war and its aftermath, he declared, "What sorrow, what barbarism, what seeds of revolt! What a prodigious tension of nerves as a result of contradictory reports, as a result of the vicissitudes of victory and of disaster! Only death will be assured of a constant, monotonous triumph—over victors and vanquished alike!"[33]

Jaurès's close friend and old *normalien* classmate, Lévy-Bruhl, worried that the socialist did not fully comprehend the German threat or the dangers of antiwar manifestos at home. Knowing that Mathieu Dreyfus had heard reports of German military maneuvers and the repression of French patriots in Alsace, Lévy-Bruhl arranged a meeting between the two friends. For more than two hours, Mathieu recounted to Jaurès the facts he had learned in Mulhouse about the nature and extent of Germany's military buildup, and he concluded with a word of concern for the safety of his old ally. With journalists damning Jaurès's "treason against the homeland" and with the Action Française encouraging attacks on the "Prussian Jaurès"[34] (just as it had encouraged the elimination of the "Jew Dreyfus" six years before), Mathieu counseled caution: "My friend, if I had your notoriety, I would never place my name on a document [of protest] which might weaken the defensive forces of France." Silent for a moment, Jaurès then confided to Mathieu, "If you are right, I will be the first one killed."[35]

On July 28, a few days after Mathieu's visit to Jaurès, Austria-Hungary declared war on Serbia, and for the seventy-two hours that followed, the hope of localizing the conflict in the Balkans faded as European powers took further steps toward mobilization. SANG-FROID, declared the title of Jaurès's editorial on July 29. "We must have time for wisdom and reason," he wrote, "for the forces of law, democracy and peace [to have] their hour." The following day, Jaurès joined members of the International Socialist Bureau in Brussels, and, despite Mathieu's advice, signed a manifesto against war. Returning to Paris, he continued his campaign for peace in the back rooms of the National Assembly and in his offices at L'Humanité, where he promised to "expose everyone responsible for this crisis. . . . I will write," he announced, "a new J'Accuse!"[36]

A short time later, at 9:40 P.M. on July 31, as he sat with colleagues at the Café du Croissant near the headquarters of L'Humanité, Jean Jaurès met his own Grégori. Unlike Dreyfus's assailant, however, Raoul Villain, a twenty-nine-year-old worshipper of the Action Française, accomplished his deed. With a high-caliber nickel-plated revolver in one hand and two typed pages of Maurice Maeterlinck's symbolist poem The Blue Bird in the other, Villain—tall, thin, and elegantly dressed in a suit and straw hat—pushed aside a screen that separated Jaurès's table from the sidewalk terrace. He fired two shots into the back of the "traitor" he had been stalking for days. Jean Jaurès became the third casualty of a world war not yet fully declared, and, like the Austrian archduke and archduchess in Sarajevo, he died within minutes, murdered by a nationalist fanatic. "The grief we suffer," L'Humanité announced the next morning, "is felt not only by workers and socialists, [but] by all men of conscience who wish, at this moment of anguish and gloom, to direct all peoples toward a future of conciliation and concord." The assassin, however, had the last word. "I punished him," Villain wrote from prison, "and my act was the symbol of a new day."[37]

A few hours before the assassination, Germany had sent ultimatums to France and Russia demanding that those powers suspend mobilization plans. On August 1, the government of the Third Republic informed Berlin that France would act "in accordance with her interests," and on the same day Germany declared war on Russia. Posters appeared throughout France calling for general mobilization, and President Poincaré's cabinet, led by Prime Minister René Viviani, a socialist who had helped Jaurès launch *L'Humanité* a decade before, made the final preparations for war.[38]

The Dreyfuses and Reinachs prepared as well. As for so many families caught in the midst of their summer holidays in 1914, mobilization meant a rapid return to Paris from seaside villages and mountain retreats. Anticipating the call to arms, Ado Reinach had left Magui and their two infants, Suzie and France, in the small Breton port town of Perros-Guirec on July 30. With his father-in-law, Mathieu, Ado took rooms at the Grand Hotel in Paris and immediately wrote to Magui with a description of the city's intense activity. He noted the "good will and good humor" that reigned "everywhere" as Parisian families made last-minute arrangements. "Hearts may be anxious," he said, but "faces are smiling; it is a glorious spectacle, and *worthy*," he underlined in his letter, "*of France.*" A thread of hope still remained that war could be averted: "Everything depends on . . . Emperor Wilhelm II," Ado believed. "Let's hope that this . . . leader of men will feel his responsibility before God and before history." But if Ado was optimistic, he also inserted in his letter detailed plans for his family's quick return from Brittany. He asked Magui to reserve train compartments for herself, the children, the wet nurse, the three governesses, and the maids. If necessary, after a brief reunion in Paris, he would send the entire party, with Mathieu in charge, to Switzerland or Carpentras, the places of sanctuary members of the Dreyfus family had used so often in the past.[39]

Twenty-three-year-old Emile Dreyfus, a civilian for less than a year, rushed to rejoin the 32nd Artillery at Fontainebleau, while his cousins, Jacques' sons, enlisted in Belfort.[40] Also in that eastern French territory, and still in uniform, Pierre awaited orders at a garrison near Héricourt. His parents and sister were vacationing with the Navilles in Geneva (and celebrating Jeanne's engagement to a young physician, Pierre Paul Lévy), but with news from France becoming more "worrisome" every hour, the family cut their visit short. "Delicious stay from 20 to 30 July 1914," they wrote in their old friends' guest book. "Hurried and anxious departure on night of 30 July." Lucie headed north to Héricourt to say goodbye to Pierre but could not cross the border before the 7th Artillery transferred her son to another post near the

German frontier. "The poor woman," Eugène Naville wrote after Lucie's return. "Her entire life is riddled with catastrophes that she bears heroically." Worried that he would miss the mobilization of reserve officers, Alfred took a night train to Paris with his daughter. At the Geneva station a flourish of drum rolls called soldiers to arms to protect Switzerland's "neutrality and integrity," and though that spectacle greatly impressed Alfred Dreyfus ("the emotions were indescribable"), it could not compare with the delirious chaos he would witness on arriving in Paris.[41]

The first link in the "sacred union" of all French parties had been forged in 1913, when the moderate republican Poincaré had called on the socialist Viviani to form a government. One year later, in the early hours of August, that coalition extended to other politicians who crossed the center aisle of the Chamber of Deputies to shake hands and share their commitment to the defense of the fatherland. Meanwhile other, less public gestures also confirmed the solidarity of the "sacred union" and the triumph of the "nationalist revival": Ado Reinach's father, Joseph, joined the Ligue des Patriotes, an organization founded by Déroulède, an old enemy with whom Reinach had fought a series of duels in the 1890s; and at a social gathering in Fontainebleau an aged Catholic aristocrat, a *"militariste enragé"* from Lorraine, struck up a friendship with Emile Dreyfus. Congratulating the young man for having the courage to join the army, especially given the notoriety of his name, the Baron d'Harcourt, an anti-Dreyfusard comrade of Déroulède's, proclaimed that political divisions were a thing of the past: "With the dangers now facing France," he told Emile, it was "a joy to shake the hand of a Dreyfus." Late into the night, the Catholic baron and the offspring of France's most vilified Jewish family sang military songs and drank toasts to their fatherland.[42]

Approaching his fifty-fifth birthday in the summer of 1914, Commandant Alfred Dreyfus received his mobilization orders on August 2. Posted as an artillery officer in the fortified zone north of the capital near Saint-Denis, he would serve under General Joseph Gallieni, the military governor of Paris. "Now have courage!" Dreyfus wrote the Marquise Arconati-Visconti on the day his orders arrived. "Germany is the basest of nations and it deserves a vigorous dust-up (*coup de torchon*)." Only in uniform and in the service of *revanche*, Dreyfus confessed, would he feel that his rehabilitation was complete. Nearly twenty years had passed since the prisoner on Devil's Island had written his family about the goal he wanted most to achieve: "When I am finally leading my brave soldiers again," he announced, "I will forget everything, the sufferings, the tortures, the outrageous insults. . . . May God and human justice make that day come soon!"[43] It came on August 3, 1914, when Germany declared war on France.

CHAPTER XIX

Pro Patria Mori

On the evening of August 7, 1914, Pierre Dreyfus joined fourteen thousand other soldiers mobilized from Belfort to prepare for the invasion of Mulhouse. Two nights before, bayonets fixed, those troops had chased a German brigade from the nearby town of Altkirch, and Pierre, having fought "with courage" in that battle, had been promoted from corporal to sergeant (*maréchal des logis*). While French Alsatians greeted the liberators of Altkirch with "enthusiastic shouts of joy," enemy troops fell back to Mulhouse and its northern and eastern hinterlands. At 6 P.M. on August 8, French cavalry galloped through the streets of *la ville la plus française de l'Alsace* and, after drawing sniper fire from doorways, windows, and roofs, forced the retreat of German units and cleared the way for the Seventh Corps. Accompanied by an "immense procession" of jubilant citizens, Pierre Dreyfus entered Mulhouse along the same road that his grandfather had taken from Rixheim eighty years before. Marching down the rue du Sauvage near the rue de la Justice, he passed the apartment in which his father had been born, and he helped secure the city's northern periphery in the shadow of Raphael Dreyfus et Compagnie on the rue Lavoisier.[1]

"Children of Alsace," began a proclamation by General Joffre posted in Mulhouse and distributed throughout France on the morning of August 9, "after 44 years of painful waiting, French soldiers are marching again on your native soil. They are the first workers in the grand task of *revanche*. What emotion for them, what pride. . . . The French Nation unanimously urges them on, and in the folds of their flag the magical words of law and liberty are inscribed: Long Live Alsace! Long live France!" In a telegram of congratulations to his chief of staff, the minister of war noted how the "moral situation" in France had been bolstered by the "energetic and brilliant offensive in Alsace,"[2] and on a troop train near Verdun, Emile Dreyfus, preparing for his own "grand battle on the banks of the River Meuse," closed a letter to his mother with the exclamation, "Long live Mulhouse! Long live Alsace!" On another train, near Troyes, Ado Reinach applauded the "glorious brigade" from Belfort, which included Dreyfuses in its ranks (along with Pierre, Ado was probably referring to Jacques' sons, Charles, Maurice, and René), and he hoped that their "brilliant exploits" were only an "hors d'oeuvre." Always the scholar, Ado promised to deposit a copy of Joffre's historic proclamation in the Mulhouse Museum, and he told Magui that he would see her again "in two months' time in French Mulhouse."[3]

To the west, in Paris, Commandant Alfred Dreyfus felt "profound emotion" when he learned that Mulhouse had been taken. "Our confidence is boundless," he said, and though he knew that a "grand conflict" against the "barbaric, arrogant and hegemonic" enemy would follow, he had the "firm hope . . . that this marked the beginning of an era of victory."[4]

Like the entire high command, however, he was wrong. French troops held Mulhouse for barely forty-eight hours before German units launched another invasion. After securing reinforcements, the French retook the city and raised the tricolor, but Germans tore it down a few days later and reestablished control in the wake of fierce house-to-house fighting. With light summer rain and heavy ground fog covering the Rhine Valley, and with machine-gun fire echoing throughout the region, battles continued in the Hardt Forest and in outlying *bourgs*, including Rixheim. "Reports have it that villages attacked by the Germans have been the scene of unknown savagery," *L'Humanité* announced in mid-August. "Our troops have found houses burned and bullet-riddled cadavers of local residents obstructing roads." Hoping to fan patriotic flames, newspapers exaggerated the scope and one-sidedness of the "savagery," but casualties on both sides were real and significant. Over a two-week period, the French lost three hundred thousand soldiers and nearly five thousand officers in the "Battle of the Frontiers," and by late August the General Staff learned that it had played directly into German hands. The "shock line" of this war would not be the Rhine Valley, as it had been so often in the past, but the forests and plains of southern Belgium and northeastern France.[5]

Adhering to its Plan XVII, the French high command had hoped to stage a lightning push through Alsace-Lorraine and across the Rhine. Sending eight hundred thousand men straight toward the eastern frontier, they had aimed to turn the tables of 1870. But the enemy had followed its own prewar plan, devised by the military strategist Count Alfred von Schlieffen, and after invading neutral Belgium in early August, German armies swept into France and turned south toward a lightly defended Paris. With Plan XVII a "complete and bloody failure," French armies rushed to protect the capital along the Marne River, and among the troops called back across the Vosges was Sergeant Pierre Dreyfus. Joining his cousin, Emile, also sent to the Marne, Pierre engaged the enemy only a few kilometers from his father's military post near Paris, and for two months his parents received no news of his fate.[6]

On the eve of his own departure for the front, shortly after the declaration of war, Ado Reinach pledged to fulfill his military duty in a way that would be "worthy of the Fatherland." Whatever happens, he wrote his parents, "let us say together, 'Long live France, Immortal France.' " And he looked forward to the day when the "triumphant [nation] will applaud those brave soldiers who secure the frontier of the Rhine and reestablish peace and the balance of power for France and for the world." Despite the rain that fell during his final hours in Paris, Ado described the "magnificent" and "unforgettable" scene of flowers and songs and a "river of tricolor flags." While loading cavalry horses onto special train cars, Ado learned that he would be sent to the front earlier than expected, and that he would have no time to say good-bye to his family. "Perhaps it is wise," he wrote his parents, "to avoid a meeting over which the word *dernière* would hover. . . . Your son leaves," he said, "with the beautiful and comforting image . . . of his family remaining at their civilian posts . . . doing their best for the nation under threat." Later that day, pulling out of the Gare du Nord and settled in a "comfortable First Class train compartment" with fellow officers, he wrote another letter to Magui. "All that is left," he announced, "is to roll on—toward victory." And as his train passed wheatfields in the environs of Nogent-sur-Seine, he hoped that his destination would be Alsace, "by way of Sarrebourg and Mulhouse. . . . May God have it!"[7]

Like thousands of other leavetakings in August, Ado Reinach's efficient departure from Paris confirmed the success of mobilization plans drafted and revised so many times since 1870—plans Alfred Dreyfus had helped formulate as a *stagiaire* on the General Staff. Nearly two million men were called to arms in the opening days of the war, and of the more than four thousand trains that brought them to their posts, only nineteen ran late.[8] But Ado's train did not take him to Alsace. After stopping in Troyes, the lieutenant was ordered northeast to Saint-Mihiel on the rolling plains of the Meuse region between Bar-le-Duc and Verdun.

Early in his travels, he described the mix of "hatred" and "intense respect" that German military strength inspired in French officers, and he contrasted those passionate opinions with the dispassion of the local population he encountered in the countryside. "These placid Lorrainers," he wrote in early August, "appear no less indifferent than the livestock they tend. . . . Perhaps familiarity with the frontier and its dangers . . . has contributed to their blasé attitude." They had to "realize," Ado warned, "that perils have finally passed from theory to imminent action." Eager for his own "action" in battle, Lieutenant Reinach, with the Forty-sixth Infantry Regiment of the Third Army, wrote his family at least twice a day, and complained only of the interminable waiting. Exercises in the "terrible heat," which took a toll on "poor foot soldiers," left Ado "indifferent"; he was "a well-equipped horseman" and, as a veteran archaeologist, "habituated to the sun of the Orient." "Still another day of country life," he wrote from a village near St. Mihiel, "beautiful weather [and] nature smiling. We have not moved at all, nor have we seen or heard anything move around us." Though encouraged by early reports of victory in Alsace, Ado felt disappointed that he could not join his Dreyfus in-laws on the banks of the Rhine, and as a symbol of both his frustration and his "dream," he changed the name of the "excellent mare" he rode as a cuirassier. "I have rebaptized her," he wrote his wife, "and called her 'Mulhouse.' "[9]

Finally, on August 13, marches and maneuvers gave way to battle, and Lieutenant Reinach experienced his "first true day of war." Covering seventy kilometers in seven hours, his unit engaged German cavalry across the Meuse countryside. And Ado fired his revolver for the first time in combat. As a "historian and critic," he wrote Magui, he wished he had time to "narrate the scenes of cavalry troops at a grand trot stirring up as much enthusiasm as dust, the dust of a glorious history, I would call it." But the detached "observer," as he labeled himself, had become a central actor in the making of history, and Ado, "surrounded by torment," had lost the luxury of academic reflection. The routine of military exercises had been replaced "by a life-and-death struggle," he told his father, and "that truth is slowly entering into the spirit of officers and their men." In the wake of battle, Ado confronted "the most painful" responsibility of war: the duty shared by all officers to "inform the families of those comrades who had been killed under one's eyes." He described the "nobility of their final moments" and told his wife that the stories he would recount upon his return would be both "beautiful" and "atrocious."

But the lieutenant also spoke of the heroism of survivors, including four "young and distinguished Semites" who served in his battalion. "Eberstein, Bénac, Bernheim and Rosenfeld . . . honor the race," Ado said, "by facing all the troubles of military life—troubles exacerbated under such circumstances—with courage." Admitting that it had taken time for him to develop the aggressive instincts of a "warrior," Lieutenant Reinach now promised to serve those men who had won his respect. He would also avenge his fallen soldiers and help "deliver the world," as he put it in a letter home, from "German Imperialism."[10]

Not until late August did French officials realize that uncensored letters from the front might compromise the war effort by exposing the location of military units and by revealing disenchantment with the strategies of the General Staff. Ado's early letters chronicled his movements through specific towns and villages along the banks of the Meuse River, and after the losses in Alsace and the failure of Plan XVII, he shared his anger in notes to his father. Aware that some censorship had already begun, he sometimes wrote his criticisms in Latin, and while he praised common soldiers, he questioned, as the good son of a good Dreyfusard, the actions of military and political leaders. "They do not seem to have profited from the lessons of 1870," he reported on August 27, and on the following day he contrasted the sophisticated "industrial organization" of the German military with the "poorly managed operations" of the French high command, whose strategies "break down with deplorable ease." Victory was "not in doubt," he insisted, but he had more confidence in his men than in his "grands chefs."[11]

German troops scored a series of victories as they pushed through Picardy, Champagne, and Lorraine, and between August 22 and 26, Ado's regiment tried to slow the march of the German Fifth Army on the edge of the Ardennes Forest. "The most essential thing for you to know," Ado wrote his wife, "is that I am in excellent health, and that

these first engagements have left me unhurt, physically and morally."
On August 28, he described how Magui (whose name, Marguerite,
means *daisy*) had protected him in the midst of combat; while others
called to mind " 'the grace of God,' " he said, "I pick a daisy from the
flower-scented fields that have been plowed up by artillery shells."
Concerned about the families of less-fortunate comrades, he asked
Magui to do volunteer work for an organization based at the Invalides in
Paris; he wanted her to help "the widows of soldiers and officers from
this regiment which has lost 700 men." And on August 29, after billeting
six thousand troops in a village of three hundred residents, he profited
from a few hours of morning rest to send his wife "another letter of
endearment." He thanked her for the packages of food and clothes she
had sent to the front, and he told her how happy he was to know that
Pierre, Emile, and all the other "soldiers of our family are still intact and
at their posts."[12]

Magui Dreyfus Reinach would never hear from her husband again.
On the night of August 30, the lieutenant returned from a mission as a
liaison officer to find his company decimated and leaderless. Germans
had attacked a short time before and had pulled back to a *petit bois*, a
small wooded area, nearby. Taking command, Ado ordered his men to
secure an abandoned farmstead between the properties of "Tyranes"
and "Bellevue," bordering the village of Fossé; and then, on his mare
Mulhouse, his armor breastplate and high plumed helmet making him an
easy target, he galloped with more than a dozen troops into the neighboring forest. By a clearing, at the edge of a large pond, the lieutenant
and his comrades engaged the enemy. The stillness of that August night
would be broken by gunfire and the rallying cry—*Boutez en avant!*
("Drive forward!")—but given the darkness and the confusion of battle,
the few cuirassiers who returned to the farmstead a short time later
could not confirm if their lieutenant had been shot, drowned, or taken
prisoner.[13]

"Think of the mothers who have remained without news of their
sons," a French politician wrote during the war, "of the nightmare
visions that haunt their sleep, of the . . . false hopes attended by the
sickening grief of disappointment, the agonized waiting of those who
cannot bring themselves to believe the worst. They are wracked by
suspense," the writer concluded, "their life is one torment: they are
determined to find the truth."[14] Wives like Magui Reinach were determined as well, and through the fall of 1914 she did everything possible,
short of entering the battlefields of the Ardennes, to learn her husband's

fate. Her father-in-law rejoined his old colleague, Mathieu, and appealed to politicians, officers, and private citizens for help, much as they had done during the affair. The Princess Marthe Bibesco, one of Joseph Reinach's oldest friends, wrote to her diplomatic contacts in Romania, Austria, and Spain, and the former Dreyfusard Eugène Naville used his influence as a director of the Swiss Red Cross. But they learned nothing. In mid-September, *Le Temps* raised the family's hopes when it listed Adolphe Reinach among the "wounded," but the newspaper soon acknowledged the inaccuracy of that report. Meanwhile, the minister of war in Berlin informed the Red Cross that Lieutenant Reinach was not in German custody.[15]

The International Agency of Prisoners of War—with Eugène Naville among its directors—had received 150,000 requests for information on French soldiers, and in October 1914 the Geneva office alone processed up to 10,000 letters a day. Like the Red Cross, however, that organization found no trace of Ado Reinach. At same time, in response to a telegram from Mathieu, Naville located a woman living in Switzerland who had gained a reputation for work with families of missing soldiers. Mademoiselle Martin, a former teacher, accepted no fees for her services, and in late October she carried a letter from the Red Cross (to avoid suspicions of espionage) and traveled into French territory to begin her search. Her efforts, like those of other individuals contacted by Ado's family and friends, were heroic—and futile.[16]

In January 1915, having exhausted every option, Eugène Naville came to Paris to help the Dreyfuses and Reinachs face the reality of Ado's loss. But Mathieu "trembled with a formidable hatred of the Germans" and insisted on continuing the search. Joseph Reinach, having just learned that his son-in-law, Lili's husband, had been killed in battle, also clung to the hope that Ado was still alive, and he, too, implored his Swiss friend to press the investigation. While Naville noted in his private diary that the two families were "deluding" themselves, he honored their requests and launched a new round of inquiries.[17]

Mathieu Dreyfus's insistence had less to do with delusion, however, than with a practical need to protect his daughter's physical and emotional health. In January 1915 Magui was seven months pregnant with a child conceived in the final days of a Breton summer holiday on the eve of her husband's departure for the front. Magui may have been "strong," "stoic," and "patriotic" ("May France have many Magui Reinachs!" Naville declared),[18] but she could not survive, her family believed, without hope. Writing from an encampment not far from where his friend had disappeared, Emile Dreyfus tried to keep Ado's memory alive, while preparing Magui for the worst. "How many times I think of him," Emile told his sister, "of his ardor and intensity . . . which glorifies our soldiers, and of his admirable devotion." Fellow officers, inspired by Lieutenant Reinach's example, often spoke of his "sublime act of courage." And in the midst of war that legacy of heroism, Emile tried to convince his sister, had become more important than life itself. "You see, my dear, death is nothing for us. For so long now, we have lived by its side every day."[19]

For the Dreyfus family, the early spring of 1915 marked the celebration of a birth and the beginning of a period of mourning. On March 27, in the apartment she had shared with Ado on the rue de Liège in Paris, and in the midst of a bombardment by German zeppelins, Magui Dreyfus Reinach—"almost a widow," as Naville described her—gave birth to her third child. It was her first son, and she named him Jean-Pierre.[20]

A few days before the baby's birth, Magui's eldest uncle, Jacques Dreyfus, devastated by the recent death of two of his sons at the front, had suffered a stroke at his home in Belfort. Though seventy years old, Jacques had been in good health prior to the war, and his brothers and sisters were certain that grief had caused his death. "He died," they said, "of a broken heart." Using the black-bordered stationery that had become so common across Europe since the late summer of 1914, the family exchanged letters of sympathy. From Paris, Lucie wrote Henriette in Carpentras and recalled how Jacques had stayed behind in Mulhouse after the 1870 war to manage the family mill, to care for his mother, and to allow his brothers and sisters to settle in French territory as French citizens: "What a tragic destiny for that ardent patriot," Lucie said. "After so many sacrifices for his country, he died without knowing the joy of . . . *revanche*, without witnessing the return of Alsace to France." At his post north of the capital, Alfred was "cruelly stricken" by news of his oldest brother's death; but the commandant, in his role as the family's expert on war, added that even more "courage" would be needed "for the ordeals that the future still holds for us."[21]

"What sadness to see members of our family disappear one after the other," Jacques' nephew, Emile, wrote from the front, "and especially in *our* family which has always been more unified than others since the great crisis which did so much to draw us together. . . . But whatever happens," he concluded, "the soldier must laugh at defeat, he must pass it by with disdain, always and everywhere whispering one single word: Hope."[22]

As a second lieutenant with the Thirty-second Artillery, Emile Dreyfus had fought close to his cousin Pierre at the Battle of the Marne. Many weeks passed before Alfred and Lucie learned that Pierre had survived that first major campaign of the war, but Emile's notes to his parents, "full of confidence and hope," arrived regularly and captured the battle's intensity. Through four days in early September, Emile slept a total of six hours (in one brief period, five hundred German shells fell on the small area where he was posted), and by September 9, two of the three captains in his outfit had been killed. "Spoiling for a finish" to the war after so many early retreats, General Joffre had envisioned the Marne as a decisive battle: "Let us stop looking back," he told his troops, "let us be killed on the spot rather than go back again." Emile echoed his commander in chief when he reported that his men had been ordered "to stop falling back." If necessary, he said, "we would die on the spot."[23]

After six days of conflict (the men "fire, they fire, they fire," went Emile's description), and after troops from the new Sixth Army had been rushed to the front from Paris in a fleet of twelve hundred taxis, French units pushed forward across "a terrain covered with the cadavers of our soldiers." Further on, entering an area "piled high with mountains of dead German troops," and realizing that "victory" had been achieved, Emile was "overtaken by a mad explosion of joy." Officers, enlisted men, and gunners threw themselves on captured German horses, wagons, and trucks, and "ran toward cannon which they embraced like children." French armies and the British Expeditionary Force had halted the German march on Paris and had destroyed the Schlieffen plan. And Emile, amid mounds of enemy dead, had felt the "unparalleled joy" of having fought "for our beautiful France and our sweet Alsace."[24]

In private journals and in letters from the front ("from my pothole," as Emile called it), soldiers often contrasted the "civilized" and "savage" sides of war, the conflict between French "enlightenment" and German "barbarism." The experience of Second Lieutenant Dreyfus, however, like that of his cousins and friends, confirmed that the struggle was not limited to the collectivities of nations or "races"; it went on within the hearts and minds of individual soldiers. No member of the

Dreyfus family had a gentler, more "civilized" nature than did Mathieu's twenty-three-year-old son Emile; known for his "good humor" and "noble character," he filled his letters with descriptions of the colors of the French countryside and with lighthearted comments on the follies of war. In October 1914, instead of sending his mother a standard postcard or note, he mailed an official pink tax form with a revised "balance sheet"; promising a "sum total" of "1,000 kisses," he marked "10 paid at the time of departure" and "990 still due." Later, he asked his parents to send books to the front, which, "after so many horrible sights," would "nourish my spirit with more artistic visions." And in his military kit, alongside pistols and bayonets, he carried a violin. On Christmas Eve, 1914, accompanied by a flutist and a small choir, Emile staged an ecumenical concert for his men, and then, with the tobacco, chocolates, handkerchiefs, and other "precious objects" that his family had sent to the front, he held a lottery. "Every soldier," he made certain, "drew a winning number."[25]

But the same young officer who spoke of the "cult of the Beautiful and the True" had climbed over "mountains" of dead Germans at the Marne with a sense of "joy." After "vagabonding from east to west" and engaging the enemy in house-to-house battles through villages along the Oise and Somme rivers, he described "the monstrous, unqualifiable joy that one feels when killing the *Boches*. . . . Every time I move to our forward trenches," Emile wrote his sister, "I grip my good Lebel [rifle] and fire over and over again on the German trench across from us, in the hope that some bullets will reach their target and have a destructive effect. The distance is not great," he went on, "no more than one hundred meters, but those monsters [with their distinctive helmets] are careful not to show their pointed heads." Emile, Ado, and Pierre had all confessed that "hatred" and "agression" had not come naturally to them in the opening days of the war; "Never, at the outset," Emile wrote, "were we able to loathe" the Germans. They condemned the kaiser's imperialism and rallied to the defense of the French fatherland with a patriotic sense of mission which was indistinguishable from a youthful sense of adventure; but when they set out from Paris and Belfort in August 1914, they entered the war with respect for the German "military machine" (as Ado had put it), and with no personal rancor toward the soldiers they were about to confront. Their hatred was abstract. "Now, however," Emile wrote home early in 1915, "as a result of their atrocities, we feel even more than a sense of hatred; we feel a passion." Within weeks following the outbreak of war, every officer in Emile's original battery had perished, and, later, with his best friend lost in battle, with two cousins dead at the front, and with countless comrades killed or maimed at his side, he was no longer motivated solely by the "sacred goal" of *revanche*. Every personal loss increased his drive for revenge, and though he maintained his "good humor," it was a strategy of survival, an echo of the absurd world in which he found himself. The "joy" of mobilization in Paris, marked by a naive and blissful ignorance and by a nationalism blind to its consequences, had given way to the education of war and to the very different "joy" of battle.[26]

For Emile, Pierre, and thousands like them, the campaign at the Marne had signaled the end of a brief war of "movement" and the beginning of a long war of "stagnation."[27] German strategists and their French and British counterparts had envisioned huge armies sweeping across vast battlegrounds, but by the winter of 1914–1915, Allied and enemy troops, armed with machine guns and spades, the essential tools of trench warfare, had dug into a narrow strip of landscape running from the North Sea to the Swiss border. And to try to move those winding, subterranean communities, supported by sandbags and wooden planks and separated by barbed wire, was like "trying to bite through a steel door with badly fitting false teeth."[28] Lamenting the action-filled "wars of old," Emile contrasted "the cut and thrust" of Napoleonic sabers "under the sun of Austerlitz" with twentieth-century trench battles fought "in the dark of night." For us, he wrote Mathieu, "the enemy is invisible." But not, he might have added, inaudible. In those hours when both sides honored unofficial cease-fires, Emile arranged "tea-bridge" parties in his bunker, and as he played cards with fellow officers he could hear German troops singing hymns eighty yards across no-man's-land.[29]

If censorship prevented Emile from revealing the position of his unit, his letters described in detail the social world within his trench. "Among our ranks," he told his mother, "is an eleven-year-old gunner, the son of a refugee. . . . A model soldier, he knows all the rules and proudly wears the gold stripes of a corporal." The boy fought alongside the oldest enlisted man in the outfit, "a fifty-four-year-old soldier whose son is also in the army." Another comrade of Emile's, an Alsatian who had crossed the border to fight for France at the outset of the war, knew "only a few vague French words," but his presence and his distinctive accent always conjured up "fond memories of home."[30] And if that Alsatian, following the habit of other provincials, shared family recipes with the company cook, the aroma of home also permeated Emile's trench; reporting from another arena of battle, Rudyard Kipling described the smells of Alsatian "cookery" emanating from makeshift kitchens in trenches "among the wooded hills."[31]

As the temperature plummeted below 15 degrees, Second Lieutenant Dreyfus confessed that the battle against the elements was often worse than the fight against the Germans. "What a horrible winter!" he wrote his mother. Sporadic snowfall, followed by two months of frigid, "torrential rains," filled his trench with thick, icy mud, making it impossible to light fires with "green, damp wood." Imagining their return to Mulhouse, he promised his family that they would "light fires in the hearth on the Faubourg du Miroir and burn bad memories." In charge of antiaircraft guns, Emile also had difficulty determining the flight path of German planes in the gray winter sky above (though he admitted that enemy pilots, less audacious than the French, made fewer costly mistakes). When alone in his bunker, his underground "rabbit cage," Emile fought the cold by dancing the "Tango Argentin" and the *tanzette à la schnellette*—variations, he wrote Magui, "on the steps we shared in the old days in apartment corridors . . . in Paris." He danced to fill his "spirit with happy memories" and to circulate the blood in his "frozen toes." And when carried away by the exercise, the six-foot-tall officer struck his head on the low ceiling of his private "ballroom. . . . It is a mistake," he told his sister, "which the best professor of dance formally prohibits."[32]

White snowdrops, the first flowers to signal the coming of spring, appeared in Emile's "corner of France" in March. "Delightful blossoms with slender petals . . . decorate our table," he told Magui, "a beautiful display for men habituated to the sad and atrocious spectacle of war. . . . The heart of that little flower is black, it is true," Emile went on, "but our [hearts] are still black as well, are they not? A tint of mourning covers our beautiful France." White flowers also pushed through the muddy ground near the wooden crosses of fallen soldiers, "as if those pretty guardians of the dead intentionally honored the defenders of the land." Emile called them a "symbol of hope for the living," but he realized near the end of a letter to Magui that rhapsodic descriptions of the French countryside must give way to the job at hand: "I am leaving for the forward trenches where I will order my men to fire on the enemy," he told his sister. "I will become a solder again, and no longer have the right to dream." A few weeks later he returned to the subject, however, when more colorful blossoms appeared in the fields near his trench. On the back of one postcard to his mother, below the word *soleil*, he sketched a single sunflower.[33]

Across the ten months since he had rejoined the Thirty-second Artillery, Emile had moved from the Marne region, north to the Oise, the Somme, and the Pas de Calais. Periodically relieved of duty on the firing line, he would spend a short time with other members of his unit in support trenches and in reserve in nearby villages or towns. Through the late spring and summer of 1915, the stalemate on the Western Front continued, and in the month of May alone, in the Artois region, close to the Belgian border, the French lost more than one hundred thousand men for an advance of barely two miles. More often the total territory of "conquest" was measured in yards. The only significant movement of troops seemed to be occurring far to the south, in the Dardanelles, where the Allied forces of Britain, France, Australia, and New Zealand engaged Ottoman Turkish armies and their German allies on the Gallipoli Peninsula. By midsummer, however, that campaign, marked by early and disastrous defeats for the Allies, had entered its own phase of stagnation.[34]

For Second Lieutenant Emile Dreyfus, as for Sergeant Pierre Dreyfus, in a trench not far from his cousin on the Aisne River, the most notable victory during those months was survival itself—and the triumph of good weather over bad. Lounging on a folding beach chair a friend had sent from Paris, Emile enjoyed the warm "breeze from the north"; and as he luxuriated in that momentary role of "a perfect sybarite," he wrote long letters home. In early July, with his father about to celebrate his fifty-eighth birthday, Emile imagined Mathieu surrounded by serenading grandchildren, by Ado's and Magui's three infants, and he explained how birthdays had no significance on the battlefront. "Everyone is the same age in the face of the enemy," he told his father, "in the face of artillery shells, and we will only keep track of such things again when victory comes."[35]

The same letter also commented on the recent shortage of matériel and on the faulty production of artillery shells—information that military censors, fallible and overworked, had not deleted from Emile's correspondence. Only a few weeks before, he had reported that French troops "had never been better equipped or better prepared," but now his outfit struggled along "with many cannon out of use. . . . Only when we are better armed," he wrote, "will we pierce the enemy lines as we wish." And good strategy was lacking as well. After taking an enemy trench, Emile's troops were at the mercy of German artillery, which "bombarded their former positions with extreme violence. It is at that moment," he said, "that we lose so many men." Emile looked forward to the time when "orders from on high would no longer stop us at conquered positions but authorize us to push forward; then we will easily break through the first barriers of the current front." To do this, however, French forces needed "masses of heavy artillery and tons of munitions."[36]

In August 1915 Emile marked the first anniversary of the war with his first leave. Mixing tradition and practicality, his parents planned a summer excursion to Villers-sur-Mer in Normandy, a coastal village near Deauville and Honfleur that the family had visited many times before. Trying to maintain some semblance of normal life in the midst of war, the Dreyfuses and Reinachs, along with other city dwellers who could afford it, kept to the custom of August holidays and traveled west, away from the dangers of Paris and the battlefields beyond. During his few days at the family's rented villa on a promontory above the Baie de la Seine, Emile consoled his sister (who still clung to the hope that Ado would be found) and played with his two nieces and his six-month-old nephew, Jean-Pierre. Half in jest, Emile reported that since rejoining the army he had grown even taller, and photographs taken in the Villers-sur-Mer garden show Magui's children perched on the lap of a slender, long-legged French officer with a pencil-thin black mustache that made him look only slightly older than his twenty-four years.

While on leave, Emile would share the news of family members at home- and battlefronts. His cousin Pierre, still awaiting his first leave, had taken part in nearly every major campaign since the outbreak of the war, from Altkirch and Mulhouse to the Marne, Soissons, the Oise, and the Aisne. Pierre's father still served as a commandant in the "immense fortified camp" that protected Paris. Lucie and Jeanne were doing volunteer work in Paris hospitals for the Red Cross, and Jeanne's fiancé, Dr. Pierre-Paul Lévy, a major in a military hospital, had requested ambulance duty at the front; he wanted, the family reported, "a dangerous posting." Mathieu and Alfred's sisters, Rachel Schil and Louise Cahn, had resettled with their husbands in Henriette's Carpentras, where they were joined by the widows of Léon and Jacques. Meanwhile, Magui's father-in-law, Joseph Reinach, now fifty-nine years old, remained in Paris, giving speeches and publishing essays that applauded the heroism of French soldiers and portrayed the war as a defense of Gallic civilization against Teutonic imperialism. At the same time, Joseph Reinach persevered in the search for his son.[37]

Emile and Pierre, like Ado before them, pointed to their families' labors at home as an inspiration for their own sacrifices at the front and as evidence of the totality of war. Ado Reinach had imagined his parents working at their "civilian posts," doing their duty "for the threatened country," and Emile Dreyfus, in words reminiscent of the English soldier-poet, Rupert Brooke, had stressed the importance of knowing that in "some beautiful corner of our dear France," as he put it, loved ones were committed to their men on the firing line. Even the feelings of "contentment" that families represented for soldiers in battle—like the image of Magui, which meant so much to Emile—were part of the work of war. Knowing that her brother would return to the trenches and perhaps to the same fate as her husband, Magui had to conceal her fears and provide Emile with the happiness he needed at Villers-sur-Mer. It could not have been easy, but in early September, Emile traveled back to the firing line with fond memories of the "delicious calm . . . of the seaside" (where "I was spoiled like an old man of pleasure"), and with compliments for his family's "moral courage." They exemplified, he wrote, "the admirable . . . soul of France."[38]

Back at the front, Emile described the fraternity of the trenches in his letters home. "In the face of danger everyone is a brother," he had written early in 1915, "and acts of devotion are the consequences of that union. I believe that men at the front, under enemy fire day and night, become better for it. Their bad prejudices and bad instincts disappear . . . and with death a constant threat they are compelled to search within themselves for the sources of the admirable strength and courage which always urges them on." For Emile, as for so many of his cousins and comrades, "memories" were the sources of their strength—"the memory of a wife, a child, a family that one has left in order to defend the Family of us all." To fulfill one's "military duty, as well as a Duty much more far-reaching," Emile said, "and to fulfill it fifty meters from the enemy, in a meter of water, under machine-gun fire night and day . . . all of that brings out the best in us!"[39]

Within three weeks of his return to the front, Second Lieutenant Dreyfus realized his consummate duty at an observation post in a forward trench in the Champagne region southeast of Reims. He had "the good fortune to arrive on the firing line," he wrote his mother, "at a moment when there was lots of work to do," and that activity helped distract him from the languorous memories of his seaside holiday.[40] After a summer lull on the Western Front, Commander in Chief Joffre tried to break the stalemate with another major offensive by French and British troops in Artois and, simultaneously, by the French alone in Champagne. Thirty-five divisions—nearly five hundred thousand men—

amassed along the region's chalk flats, and Emile and Pierre Dreyfus joined their ranks. With little protection in that open, sparsely wooded area, French forces dug new trenches, many of them three to five miles long.[41]

The Battle of Champagne began on September 22, 1915, when nine hundred heavy and sixteen hundred light guns fired on German positions, and when Joffre sent off yet another declaration to his troops: "Your enthusiasm," he promised, "will be irresistible!" (*"Votre élan sera irrésistible!"*). But the Champagne landscape was only relatively flat, and Germans controlled the heights of its gently rolling hills. Breaking through the first enemy line, French armies did not have the artillery to reach the second, and a brief battle of movement gave way to another episode of bloody trench warfare. In the final week of September, with French armies under intense bombardment, the high command sent down an order much like the one that had led to success at the Marne: Try again, the generals commanded, "whatever the cost."[42]

On September 27, after three days and three nights of directing artillery fire from a forward trench, Emile Dreyfus was struck by the shrapnel of a German shell. It tore into his skull in four places and exposed his brain, but when gunners carried him back to the main trench he was still alive. With other gravely wounded soldiers unable to survive transport to distant medical units, Emile was taken to a field hospital in the nearby village of Mourmelon-le-Grand, and two days later, through the family of another officer of the Thirty-second Artillery, Mathieu received the first report—a report without details—that his son had suffered "a severe injury."[43]

Denied an official *laisser-passer* to travel to the front, Mathieu immediately phoned the one former Dreyfusard who could cut through military regulations better than any other. Elected to the parliamentary Army Committee a few months before, seventy-four-year-old Georges Clemenceau gave his friend a handwritten "pass," an entirely unauthorized document that carried only the power of Clemenceau's name. But that was enough. Hours later, Mathieu, his wife, Suzanne, and their daughter, Magui, left Paris for Châlons-sur-Marne, the city closest to Mourmelon-le-Grand. The only civilians permitted to enter that war zone, they drove across fields pockmarked by artillery shells and finally found Emile in a large hut (*baraquement*) on the outskirts of a French encampment. "Nearly motionless on his stretcher," as Mathieu described the scene, and with "most of his face obscured by bandages," Emile had fallen into a "partial coma." But he regained consciousness and recognized his family. "Amidst the groans of twenty other wounded soldiers and the whistling of German shells above," Suzanne Dreyfus nursed her son. She would remain at Emile's side for fifteen days, returning to Châlons-sur-Marne with Mathieu and Magui for only a few hours sleep each night.[44]

Shortly after the family's arrival, the commandant of the field hospital announced that Second Lieutenant Dreyfus had been named a chevalier of the Legion of Honor. In a "solemn" bedside ceremony, with the medical officer pinning a medal on his patient's hospital gown, Emile Dreyfus became the second member of his family, after his uncle Alfred, to be awarded the Legion of Honor.

A few days later Emile's condition deteriorated, and, as Mathieu described it, "the agony began." The family received permission to stay in the field hospital through the night, but "a downpour" of German shells scored a direct hit and "violently hurled Suzanne and Magui to the ground." Covered with debris but unhurt, they were evacuated to bunkers a few hundred yards away. A procession of medics carried stretchers across "a terrain plowed under by shells, through a night illuminated by the explosion of German bombs," and in a "cold, wet and suffocating bunker a few meters underground," Suzanne placed her winter coat over her son. When enemy shells "moved on to ravage other sites," as Mathieu reported, an order came to move the wounded to yet another field hospital.

The next morning, with a second German strike expected in twenty-four hours, the commandant ordered the Dreyfus family to leave the war zone immediately. He showed them the ruins of the first field hospital (where "only a miracle" had saved them) and insisted that they could do nothing more for Emile. "He is in a coma," the doctor said. "There is no more hope." Magui left for Paris that morning, but Mathieu and Suzanne stayed through the afternoon, watching their son on his stretcher, "his eyes closed, his body jolted by sudden chills, and his life leaving him, little by little."

Two days later, on October 22, 1915, Mathieu Dreyfus received a telegram in Paris: "Your son has just died peacefully," it read, "never having regained consciousness after your departure." The following day, another note informed the family that Emile had been buried near the Mourmelon-le-Grand field hospital, in grave number 109, section 37; if desired, relatives could transfer his remains to another location at the end of the war. From the mayor of the eighth arrondissement of Paris came an official letter urging Mathieu to be proud that his son had "fallen gloriously on the field of honor for civilization and for the existence of France itself." And still another official communication carried the signature of the French commander in chief; citing Emile Dreyfus's "bravery and initiative since the outbreak of the war" and describing his "noble attitude and sang-froid under fire," General Joffre announced that the second lieutenant, a chevalier of the Legion of Honor, had been awarded the Croix de Guerre with palm.[45]

In a handwritten memoir destined for his grandchildren, Mathieu recalled those October days and the cavalry charge fourteen months earlier when Lieutenant Reinach disappeared. "My dear children," he wrote, "think often of your Papa Ado and your Uncle Emile. They were two beautiful spirits. Let the example of their lives always sustain you and always encourage you to do good works. And you, Jean-Pierre," Mathieu wrote the boy who had never known his father and could not remember his uncle, "I am certain that you will be, like them, an honorable man, a brave Frenchman. And if the Fatherland ever calls on its children again . . . you will do your duty as they did theirs."[46]

CHAPTER XX

Revanche

POSTED NOT FAR from Mourmelon-le-Grand, Pierre Dreyfus, recently promoted to second lieutenant, received permission to "visit and embrace" Emile before he died. He arrived in time and stayed long enough to arrange a temporary marker in the military graveyard nearby. Those two Dreyfus cousins, both twenty-four years old in 1915, had shadowed each other across the fields, forests, and riverbanks of northeastern France for thirteen months. They had always been very different in personality and appearance; the tall, thin, and fine-featured Emile had the look of an aristocratic officer and, like his father, a confident, quick-witted charm; while Pierre, smaller, round-shouldered, and with his own father's quiet, serious demeanor, appeared, in photographs sent from the front, more like a hard-fighting enlisted man. But looks deceived, and "in the face of danger," as Emile had said, "everyone is a brother." Pierre had fought courageously at the Marne, as his cousin had done, and a year later he too served in the ranks of Joffre's "irresistible" strike force. The slaughter in Champagne took Emile Dreyfus and 145,000 other Frenchmen, while Pierre, through a combination of dogged discipline and blind luck, survived to fight again.[1]

In the spring of 1915, Lucie had asked her son to request a forty-eight-hour leave; she had not seen him in nearly a year. "In our outfit," he responded, "such permission is never granted! And besides, that's only right. Why give an officer a leave and not his men?" Furthermore, to break the routine and enjoy a family reunion might lead, Pierre believed, "to demoralization. . . . No, the best leave that one could grant us is that of pushing on." Pierre received his wish at the Aisne in late spring, where he fought while "swimming in a sea of mud," and at Champagne in the early fall. "Those ten days of combat were harder than the ten months which had preceded them," he told his parents, but "I am happy to at least be moving forward." Enthusiasm gave way to frustration, however, when Joffre's campaign failed to break the German line and when French forces dug in yet again along the Western Front. Finally, in November 1915, after nearly sixteen months of combat, and after sleeping, when he could sleep, on the dirt floor of his Champagne trench ("awakened by the penetration of cold and rain"), Pierre surprised his parents and returned home on a six-day leave.[2]

He spent one day at his father's post ten kilometers north of Paris at Montmorency. Serving as special assistant to Colonel Goëtzmann, artillery commander of the capital's northern fortified zone, Alfred Dreyfus had taken charge of what he called his own "factory"; he directed the mounting of cannon and the preparation of other armaments sent to the front, and helped inspect the ring of trenches that protected Paris. His thinning hair and thick mustache now almost completely white, the fifty-six-year-old officer, never fully recovered from the maladies of Devil's Island, bundled himself up against the winter wind with heavy coats and special woolen muffs and took long drives through his sector in an open car. He slogged through trenches "in detestable weather," as he described it, "with mud up to my knees," and he remained in surprisingly good health and "full of spirit" through it all. He continued to feel "much more rehabilitated by his active army service," said his friend, Eugène Naville, "than by the official judgment of the High Court of Appeal."[3]

The commandant's most intense activity had come in the opening weeks of the war with the capital in the midst of mobilization and enemy troops approaching the Marne. Riots had swept through Paris, forcing French families with Germanic names to bolt shutters and doors and pressuring businesses like the Brasserie Viennoise on the Boulevard Montmartre to pull down their German-related signs. Gangs shouting "To Berlin!" pillaged the stores of potential "traitors," including establishments owned by Alsatians, and as they waved tricolor flags they continued their march west of Paris toward Neuilly. By late August, most of those demonstrators had left for the front, but the chaos of war preparation continued in the capital and its environs. A mammoth German zeppelin dropped the first bombs on the city on August 30, killing one old woman and spreading the fear of future aerial invasions. And in the Bois de Boulogne, the two racetracks that Alfred Dreyfus had visited so often—Longchamp and Auteuil—became pastures for beef cattle and other livestock, as they had been during the siege of the Franco-Prussian War. Across town, the Bois de Vincennes served as a depot for military matériel. In early September, with Germans massing only a few kilometers to the east, and with enemy airplanes dropping leaflets on the capital ("There is nothing you can do but surrender"), the French government followed another lesson learned in 1870 and decamped to the port city of Bordeaux. "The . . . Government of the Republic [has] left Paris to give new impulse to the national defense," announced Alfred Dreyfus's superior, the military governor of Paris. "I have received a mandate to defend Paris against the invader. This mandate," General Joseph Gallieni declared, "I shall carry out to the end."[4]

Demonstrations within the capital and the threat of invasion from without had prompted Dreyfus to send his wife and daughter to the home of Hadamard relatives in Lyons. Only after the victory at the Marne did Lucie and Jeanne return to Paris and to volunteer duty at the Saint-Louis Hospital in the working-class quarter of Belleville. In barely a month's time, Paris, that hub of mobilization, had become a "demi-desert," and by the winter of 1914–15, when Eugène Naville visited his friends, an eerie calm had descended on the capital. Restaurants and cafés closed early ("when street lights were dimmed by half in order to baffle German aviators"), and if metros and trams followed their regular schedules, buses no longer "rolled through the streets like thunder"; most had been commandeered to deliver supplies to the front. In August hundreds of thousands of recruits had made their way through the Gare du Nord and the Gare de l'Est, but in subsequent months most troops in the city were late foreign arrivals (especially English and African soldiers) or wounded men returning from the front. Despite some sights and sounds of normal big-city life (the taxis that had shuttled troops to the Marne were back "circulating as rapidly . . . as in ordinary times"), Paris seemed on most days "as quiet as a provincial town."[5]

As a young officer Alfred Dreyfus had detested the provincial quiet of garrison towns, and thirty-five years later he wanted to move beyond the secured outskirts of Paris and "take part in combat." Maintenance of the fifty-kilometer ring of trenches and artillery posts around the capital required constant work, but it was "a monotonous life" compared to the battlefront, and Dreyfus "waited with great impatience for the order to move forward." He "wanted the satisfaction," as Lucie told a friend, "of crushing the enemy." Earlier than most observers, Dreyfus had announced that "the war will be long, very long," and he had advised family and friends to marshal their "courage and will in order to destroy Prussian militarism once and for all." He no longer spoke of the achievements of German civilization, of the works of Kant, Goethe, and Wagner he had so admired; instead, he described a "ferocious and barbaric people . . . incapable of any noble or elevated feeling," a people obsessed "by the cult of force." And now the commandant wanted to match his words with deeds by joining the younger men of his family on the firing line. His superiors, however, concerned about his health or worried about rekindling anti-Dreyfusard protests within the army, denied his request to serve at the front and delayed his promotion from cavalry major to lieutenant colonel. For now at least, he would have to fight vicariously, through his son and nephews.[6]

After visiting Montmorency, Pierre spent the rest of his six-day leave with his mother and sister in the family apartment on the Boulevard Malesherbes. Lucie, now forty-six, had recently recovered from a major operation. She had received "radiotherapy treatments" for fibroid tumors during the spring of 1915 and had then undergone surgery at a clinic near the Boulevard Saint-Germain. Given her weak state, and the rudimentary methods of anesthesia and blood transfusion of that time, the procedure was far from routine, and doctors warned Alfred Dreyfus that his wife's "chances were only six in ten." But the surgery was a success, and in July, after the commandant returned to his post, Jeanne took her mother to Deauville for a summer of recuperation. By the time of Pierre's visit, Lucie had resumed her volunteer work in Paris and admitted that seeing her son in good health and in good spirits was, for her, the most effective therapy of all.[7]

Second Lieutenant Dreyfus left the comforts of his Paris apartment in late November and returned to the rat-infested trenches of Champagne. By January 1916, he had been relocated again, to the town of Bar-le-Duc, where he would prepare for yet another move, forty miles due north to the Verdun salient. French, British, and Russian military leaders, along with representatives of their new ally, Italy, had recently met at Joffre's Chantilly headquarters north of Paris to plan strategies for the new year. After seventeen months of war, they searched for ways to engage the enemy simultaneously on the Western, Eastern, and Italian fronts. They decided that the key sector of action would be along the Somme River, where British and French lines joined, but after plotting that offensive, the French high command received reports that German armies had mobilized near the town of Verdun on the Meuse River. In accordance with Joffre's belief that citadel battles were a thing of the past, the guns of Douaumont, Vaux, and other forts in the Verdun region had been dismantled and all but two French divisions had been called back. In late January and early February, however, Joffre recognized the need for reinforcements.[8]

Preparations to join the first wave of troops on the northern road from Bar-le-Duc to Verdun would prevent Pierre from attending a special family gathering in Paris. On January 26, 1916, at a town hall near the Champs-Elysées, twenty-two-year-old Jeanne Dreyfus married Dr. Pierre-Paul Lévy, a former resident physician in a Paris hospital and now an army medical officer at the front. The groom had secured an eight-day leave, and after the wedding the couple would journey south for a brief honeymoon in the Midi. Officiating at the civil service (the private "religious blessing," according to the wedding announcement, would follow later at the synagogue), the mayor of the eighth arrondissement cited the achievements of his distinguished guests and revisited the triumphs of the family's affair. "How can my thoughts not return to an epoch which the war itself will not efface from our memory," he asked, "to an affair which History will always hold in its archives . . . and which will always be debated." Turning to Mathieu Dreyfus ("the model of fraternal devotion") and to Lucie and to Emile Zola's family, also in attendance, the mayor applauded their "courage and sacrifice." And addressing Jeanne's father, on leave from Montmorency and in full-dress uniform, the mayor added that "the present war is in many ways similar to your cause. The world struggles for the rights of nations, as it struggled for the rights of a man; it fights against the despotism of Force, as it fought against the despotism of blind faith. . . . Today," the politician told Commandant Dreyfus, "you have reentered with joy the ranks of that army which was the passion of your youth. . . . You are ready to shed all your blood for your fatherland, [and] you are ready to sacrifice your son . . . who has fought valiantly for eighteen months at nearly every point along the immense Western front." Finally, the mayor directed his closing remarks to Jeanne: "If your childhood years have been sad," he said, "the years to come will be so much more joyful; for having paid a heavy debt to misfortune . . . you have earned your happiness."[9]

A marriage ceremony in the midst of war might provide an oasis of optimism, but the promise of happiness could not be fulfilled while Jeanne's brother fought at Verdun. The northern road that Pierre and his comrades—including his aunt Rachel's son, Louis—took from Bar-le-Duc would become known as the *voie sacrée*, the "sacred path" over which thousands of trucks would carry provisions to hundreds of thousands of French troops trapped along a jagged eight-mile front. If the ancient town of Verdun had had strategic significance for Attila the Hun in the fifth century, or for the armies of Napoleon III in 1870, it had virtually no importance in 1916. Far to the east of Paris, and far from the Somme where Joffre planned the major confrontation with enemy armies, the Verdun region, with its fortresses perched on rolling hills and overlooking fields and forest copses, no longer served as an "indispensable anchor of the Allied front."[10] It was a strategic irrelevance. But to lose Verdun would be to sacrifice a historic symbol of French defense, and, in a war that had degenerated into murderous struggles over a few meters of useless territory, the symbol of Verdun became a political priority for French and Germans alike.[11]

The chief of the German general staff, Erich von Falkenhayn, chose the citadel town and its hinterland forts not for a battle of cavalry charges and decisive forward movement but for a calculated war of attrition. The code name for the operation left no doubt about its goal: *Gericht,* they called it, a place of judgment. "The essential question is not to take Verdun," Falkenhayn announced to fellow officers, "but to pin down the French, pull them toward the battlefield, and since they will have to defend it shoulder to shoulder, we shall bleed them white by virtue of our superiority in guns."[12]

At 7:15 A.M. on February 21, 1916, that superiority showed when thick fog lifted from the Meuse Valley and German guns opened fire on both banks of the river and on the town of Verdun. Led by the kaiser's son, Crown Prince Wilhelm, German armies concentrated hundreds of heavy guns, light field pieces, and giant mine throwers on the Verdun sector. "Big Berthas" had been moved into place, and with them had come six German infantry divisions. "A veritable fireworks" of high explosives rained down on the region, and under that deluge, French communications posts were leveled and forest groves into which soldiers ran for cover "became an entanglement of broken trunks and branches." Small villages nearby "caved in and disappeared," and as wet snow began to fall, men crawled across a winter landscape transformed into plowed fields by the pounding of two million shells in forty-eight hours. One German aviator, observing the crater-pocked region that conjured up images of the moon, reported: "There won't be anything living out there."[13]

On February 25, while Pierre Dreyfus's unit and others in the immediate area held their ground under fierce attack by cannon, flamethrowers, and machine guns, German troops took the key fort of Douaumont. Moving to a position between Douaumont and the village of Vaux, Pierre directed reconnaissance operations and attempted to co-ordinate the activities of isolated units.[14] Unlike the Champagne region in which Emile Dreyfus had fought and died, Verdun had no network of long trenches connecting French forces and setting them off from the enemy; there was "only an intermingling of separate pieces that soldiers strove to join." Digging into foxholes, forests, burned-out villages, and the remnants of citadels not yet lost, fighting men like Pierre, under attack from all sides and uncertain of the position of German forces, would often cut down their own comrades in the chaos of crossfire.[15]

On the night that Fort Douaumont fell, General Joffre, from his Chantilly headquarters far to the west, named a new commandant at Verdun. Henri Philippe Pétain, the fifty-nine-year-old commander of the Second Army, organized the transport of provisions along the route from Bar-le-Duc and devised a system of troop rotation in and out of the Verdun sector. Of the 330 infantry battalions in the French army, 259 of them would "do time" at Verdun. Pétain realized that no mortal could survive the shock of 100,000 shells falling within an hour, nor could troops tolerate for long the sight of comrades gassed and mutilated. The general's well-publicized concern for his men, along with his celebrated call "Courage . . . we will beat them!" secured his reputation as a humane and effective leader. Like Joffre at the Marne, Pétain emerged as a "savior" of the French fatherland, though in this war, in which the sacrifice of eleven men to the enemy's twelve constituted a victory, "savior" was a relative term.[16]

While most troops in the Verdun sector served an average of eight days at a time, Pierre Dreyfus remained at his post near Douaumont for twenty-one days.[17] Military reports confirmed that he refused to be relieved of duty after the first onslaught in late February; he did not want to "jeopardize the continuity of service during a critical phase." And while the heaviest shelling of the long battle continued through

March, the second lieutenant stayed with his battery and directed the fire of its guns "under continuous enemy bombardment."[18] Like other soldiers in the region, Pierre would have received news at his post of General Joffre's most recent proclamation to his fighting men. "For three weeks," the commander in chief announced in mid-March, "you have been sustaining the most formidable assault that the enemy has ever attempted against us. To this effort, Germany . . . has consecrated its best troops and its most powerful artillery. . . . But it did not reckon with you!" Joffre concluded, "The country has its eyes on you. You will be the ones about whom we shall say: They have barred the Germans from the route to Verdun."[19]

Many days passed before Alfred and Lucie Dreyfus learned their son's fate. "What agony we feel," Pierre's father had said in late February. "We must harden ourselves against anxieties and grief." And when word finally arrived, it contained the quotidian details that soldiers, unable to deal with the cosmic tragedy that surrounded them, so often addressed. Pierre reported that for three weeks in the half-frozen mud of Verdun he had been unable to change his uniform or remove his shoes "one single time."[20] His superiors focused on grander issues, however, and cited the second lieutenant for his "distinguished service . . . in the most perilous conditions . . . since the outbreak of the campaign." Having entered the war as a corporal, Pierre Dreyfus would soon be promoted to lieutenant and given command of his own platoon.[21]

He left Verdun in April for rest and recuperation in the city of Toul, near Nancy, where his father visited him for a day and found him in "excellent physical and moral health." But Alfred Dreyfus's son enjoyed precious little time behind the lines. The carnage of the early spring campaign required the rapid rotation of troops, and in May, Pierre returned to the region that Pétain had dubbed "the Furnace of Verdun."[22] Confronting new French counteroffensives and "disquieted" by reports of Franco-British preparations at the Somme, German military leaders stepped up their attack through the early summer. During Pierre's second tour of duty, enemy troops captured Fort Vaux, a stone citadel built in the wake of the 1870 war and reinforced in concrete in 1911 to insure its "impregnability." German heavy artillery destroyed that fort with ease, but the resistance of French soldiers had been heroic, and to recognize their bravery, Crown Prince Wilhelm used a modern tool to honor an ancient custom. Unable to find a sword to present to the French commander of Vaux, the German prince made him the temporary gift of a pair of infantry wire cutters.[23]

Among the many instruments of war used at Verdun, however, Pierre Dreyfus feared one above all others. He had confided to his father that he would rather be struck by shrapnel or machine-gun fire than be choked to death by poison gas.[24] Introduced by the Germans on the Western Front at the battle of Ypres in 1915, and eventually used by all the major belligerents, chlorine gas gave way to a more deadly phosgene gas at Verdun. French troops near the fort of Souville, south of Vaux, took the worst of it when Germans "inundated" that area with two hundred thousand gas shells, but pockets of noxious smoke covered the entire landscape throughout the fighting of 1916. When Pierre moved forward to direct fire from his observation post between Douaumont and Vaux, he would strap on a practically useless canvas mask and hope for the rains, which kept gas clouds at knee level, or for the winds that shifted them back across enemy lines.[25]

Finally released from the "inferno" of Verdun in the midsummer of 1916, Pierre Dreyfus moved to a relatively calm sector at the foothills of the Vosges. When he left his post near Douaumont, the tide of battle had turned. In August, German casualties would exceed those of the French for the first time since February, and three months later, the region's principal forts, obliterated by heavy artillery and looking like ancient temple ruins, would be retaken by French forces. By December, German armies would be pushed back two miles, "virtually to the line at which the epic, but pointless, battle had begun." Falkenhayn's *Gericht* lived up to its name, though two nations, not one, were bled white at that place of judgment which would gain "the unenviable reputation of being the battlefield with the highest density of dead per square yard." French casualties numbered one half million men and German losses reached four hundred thousand; and all for a stretch of land that had little importance when the campaign began and even less after millions of shells had leveled its villages and destroyed its vegetation.[26]

Having endured the battles of Mulhouse, the Marne, the Oise, and Champagne, Pierre Dreyfus had now survived the worst of them all. In a few weeks, however, he would return to the firing line and to a conflict that rivaled Verdun in its strategic senselessness and the scope of its destruction. Pierre traveled northwest from the Vosges to the Somme.

Designed to be another of Joffre's key contests, the battle had begun in late June with a massive artillery bombardment of German lines. An elaborate trench system marked the Somme landscape, a feature that distinguished it from Verdun, and on the morning of July 1, 1916, one hundred thousand allied troops—thirteen British divisions and five French—went over the top. "The offensive is launched," Alfred Dreyfus wrote from Montmorency on receiving news of the battle, "and for it to succeed we must count not on the gods, but on the fervor of our soldiers and the impact of our guns."[27] With the majority of active French forces still otherwise engaged at Verdun, the British predominated at the Somme, and many of those troops were working-class youngsters from the Midlands recently drafted under the new conscription law. Sharing none of Pierre Dreyfus's long experience on the firing line, they charged toward German trenches, weighed down with sixty-six pounds of equipment, with fixed bayonets, and they believed that the next stop would be Berlin. For too many, however, the last stop was no-man's land, where machine guns leveled them with assembly-line precision and where spirals of barbed wire ensnared the living and the dead alike. The later and more limited French assault, from the river's right bank, succeeded in overrunning a line of German trenches with relatively few losses. But by the end of the first day of battle, the British had suffered sixty thousand casualties, a third of them killed in a matter of hours. There had never been anything like it, even at Verdun; no ground of any consequence had been captured, and as the slaughter continued, no significant territory would ever be secured by either side.[28]

Pierre Dreyfus arrived at the Somme on the eve of two major allied attempts to penetrate the German lines. Those campaigns, however, like subsequent battles along the Ancre River to the north, also met heavy resistance and failed to break the stalemate. Even the dramatic debut of British tanks at the Somme in mid-September, with their bizarre caterpillar tracks and mounted guns, achieved little more than a moment of panic among incredulous German troops. "Armoured they come rolling on in long lines," the young German soldier in Erich Maria Remarque's novel *All Quiet on the Western Front* would describe them. "A fleet of roaring, smoke-belching armour-clads . . . squashing the dead and the wounded—we shrivel up in our thin skin before them."[29] But those machines—slow, unwieldy and, most damning of all, deployed in limited numbers—often sank in the mire of rain-soaked shell holes; and while their armor-plated bodies repelled machine gun fire, troops trapped within were incinerated by the heat of German flamethrowers. Tanks would later help shatter the deadlock on the Western Front, but in 1916 they only helped prolong it.

Near his brother-in-law, Pierre-Paul Lévy, who treated cholera, typhus, and battle wounds in one of the sector's field hospitals, Pierre Dreyfus served for fifty-four days at the Somme. Engaged in "almost constant fighting" and "dangerously exposed" to German attack, he received his second citation for courage under fire. In late November, barely a month after his reassignment to a more "tranquil" post in the Champagne region (where his most pressing worry was how to share his trench with a "society of rats"), the Somme campaign reached its unclear finale. The fighting, which had started in the torrid heat of midsummer, ended six months later under the snowfall of early winter. Allied armies pushed no more than seven miles into the enemy front, at a cost of 420,000 British and 200,000 French troops. Germany lost 500,000 soldiers. The combined casualties of Verdun and the Somme totaled nearly 2 million men. Five centuries had passed since Agincourt and three centuries since Shakespeare had recounted its carnage; but after 1916, contemporary observers, who often used the language of other wars to describe their own, could adapt the words of the English king: Here there was, at Verdun and the Somme, a royal fellowship of death.[30]

In defiance of all logic and against all odds, Pierre Dreyfus had survived the most horrific campaigns of 1914–16. His service had been distinguished, but so, too, had that of Emile Dreyfus, Ado Reinach, Jacques' sons, and countless other men who had died on battlegrounds and in field hospitals. In fact, Pierre's personal history, unlike those of his cousins and friends, had suggested that he would not be able to tolerate the rigors of combat. With its incessant barrage of heavy artillery and machine-gun fire, Verdun had been no place for a young man possessed of delicate "sensibilities." In his early adolescence his parents had often worried about his fragile nature. As a teenager, he had hiked with his father in the Swiss mountains to build his physique, but still he had entered the war cutting a much less impressive figure than the tall, straight-backed Emile, or that well-trained devotee of *la boxe*, Ado Reinach.

Though absent during his son's most formative years, Alfred Dreyfus had worked with Lucie from afar to teach the boy "bravery," "self-lessness," and "the cult of honor"; he should be prepared, said the prisoner on Devil's Island, "for life's battles." Twenty years later Pierre brought those qualities into combat, but as the war continued he would need the blind good fortune that had been denied his cousins and friends. Putting it another way, Alfred Dreyfus compared his son's survival to remaining dry in a deluge. Learning that Pierre had taken charge of his battery after his superior officers had been killed, the commandant said that "up until now, Pierre has had the luck to pass between the rain-drops; I only hope that it continues!"[31]

By 1917 all but four soldiers from the Dreyfus and Reinach families had been killed or listed among the missing. Only Alfred, Pierre, Jacques' son, René, and Rachel's son, Louis, still served, along with their new in-law, Pierre-Paul Lévy. Commandant Alfred Dreyfus, sent to an artillery park in Orléans in April 1916 and then reassigned to Montmorency in December, finally realized his goal of joining a "combat post" in February 1917; he helped direct munitions depots near the Aisne River and, later, in a western sector of Lorraine.[32] If the General Staff worried about anti-Dreyfusard protests when they assigned the commandant to the front, those concerns must have been outweighed by the pressing need for officers—of any age—in the aftermath of Verdun. Going "over the top" and into no-man's-land at the head of their units, officers died, proportionately, in the greatest numbers; and many of them were graduates of *grandes écoles* or young men whose plans for a university education had been interrupted by the war. Of the 293 Ecole Normale Supérieure students sent to the firing line, more than 100 were "killed outright." Commenting on "the enormous losses in the ranks of university students," the Marquise Arconati-Visconti wondered "how much time will be needed for this country to restore itself after such a bloodletting." And she wrote that letter before Verdun.[33]

But Alfred Dreyfus, the fifty-seven-year-old Polytechnicien who had been denied permission to "move forward" so many times, arrived at the front as a fresh and enthusiastic artillery officer. "Despite the mud, the rain, the snow and the absolute lack of comfort," he reported, "I am in splendid health." Sleeping in a "windblown canvas tent on a truss of straw, with no change of clothes and no end in sight," Dreyfus tolerated the "glacial rain" of northern France much as he had tolerated the scorching sun of French Guiana. When the weather cleared, he went on horseback rides (*belles promenades*, he called them) through the sector behind support trenches, and he found one "beautiful spot which would have been perfect for dreaming," he said, "if cannon fire had not called me back to reality." Above all, he appreciated his first opportunity to work with soldiers directly engaged in combat. Having learned from experience about packages from home, he arranged for Lucie's mother to send woolen shirts and socks to his troops, and for Henriette's family to provide tobacco and chocolates. "Our men are admirable," he wrote in late February. "There is never a complaint; and as for me," said the Devil's Island veteran, "I am well accustomed to the routine of savages."[34]

The commandant reported that Pierre was in combat close by, "but it is as if we were miles apart because we see nothing beyond our trench."[35] In fact, vast numbers of French forces had been sent to the Aisne for an offensive that aimed to cripple German armies before a wave of reinforcements arrived from the Eastern Front. With the abdication of Czar Nicholas in mid-March, Germany maneuvered to profit from the revolution in progress and to hasten the political and military collapse of imperial Russia. Aware that Lenin supported the end of Russia's involvement in the war, the German high command provided the Bolshevik leader with a secret train from his place of exile in Switzerland to the Finland station in Petrograd. It was a small gamble for an enormous payoff: If Lenin seized power, German troops could be released from the eastern campaign for a final triumph on the Western Front. Anticipating that enemy offensive, General Robert Nivelle, the officer who had secured Verdun and replaced Joffre as commander in chief in December, called for a mammoth Allied push into the salient where the Aisne and Oise rivers joined. A man of average size and unremarkable features, Nivelle had only one thing in common with the hero of the Marne: Like Joffre, Nivelle promised to break the deadlock and fight a "war to the bitter end" (*guerre à l'outrance*). In an appeal to group commanders, he insisted that "the stamp of *violence*, of *brutality* and *rapidity* must characterize your offensive, and . . . that the first step, which is the *rupture*, must in one blow capture the enemy position and all the zone occupied by his artillery."[36]

Alfred and Pierre Dreyfus survived the "Nivelle offensive," a campaign that led not to rapid victory "within twenty-four to forty-eight hours," as the general had promised, but to the loss of nearly two hundred thousand French troops within a matter of days; one battle along a ridge known as the Chemin des Dames accounted for forty thousand of those casualties. Nivelle's plan, one of the worst-kept secrets of the war, had been thwarted by a strategic retreat of German armies back to secured positions twenty to forty kilometers to the east. The Allies called it the Hindenburg Line, after its chief architect, the general who had succeeded Falkenhayn, while the German high command gave it a Wagnerian twist. Operation Alberich involved the pillaging of French farmsteads and towns and the destruction of fields and woodlands, and by early April, German troops prepared for counterattack along a line they named Siegfried.

In the throes of that catastrophe, the French government shipped Nivelle off to a post in North Africa, leaving Pétain, his successor as commander in chief, to deal with the consequences of defeat. For the first time since the outbreak of the war, French troops had risen in protest. The direct, if delayed, response to the trauma of Verdun and, more immediately, to the "Nivelle system," the mutinies of 1917 involved more than thirty thousand soldiers, many of whom refused to return to the firing line under the conditions that had reigned for nearly three years. Profiting from his reputation as an officer who cared about the welfare of his men, Pétain promised to limit front-line tours of duty and institute other reforms; but he also engineered, as secretly as possible, the removal of rebellious officers and enlisted men. Military courts convicted more than 3,000 soldiers for acts of mutiny, and while 49 men were executed, the majority received prison sentences—in France and in the penal colonies of the Iles du Salut across the narrow channel from Devil's Island.[37]

If thousands rebelled, however, hundreds of thousands followed orders and carried on. Pierre and Alfred, either by choice or under the pressure of military censorship, avoided any mention of the mutinies in their letters home and instead described the ongoing routine of trench life. They focused on the weather in almost obsessive detail; it was a leitmotiv common to every soldier's correspondence. "The heat is torrid and work during the day is hard," the commandant wrote in late July 1917; "I am sunburned and resunburned (*cuit et recuit*), and my face is red and leathery. Happily, the nights are cool enough," he went on, "but they are also shattered by 'fantomas,' which is to say by *boches* airplanes which send us their machine-gun fire."[38]

In that late summer of 1917, father and son met for a few hours in the Champagne town of Epernay, where they dined together before Pierre headed north toward the Verdun sector and Alfred returned to his original post near Paris.[39] Along with exchanging news about the family and the troops they commanded, they must have talked about America. The United States Congress had declared war on Germany in April, but the first soldiers under the command of General John Pershing had not arrived in France until June—and even then the numbers were limited. Still, after the disastrous Nivelle offensive and the recent staggering losses suffered by the British at Passchendaele, the promise of young, healthy "doughboys" from America, remarkable for their tall- ness and their enthusiasm, gave the Allies new confidence. Russia's contribution to the war effort may have been doomed, but once the American Expeditionary Force arrived at the front, the combined armies of France, Britain, Italy, and the United States would finally overwhelm the Central Powers. Addressing a Paris conference on "the intervention of the United States," Joseph Reinach applauded America for remem- bering Lafayette "after nearly a century and a half," and for "repaying its sacred debt to France with joy."[40]

At the same time that thousands of young Americans began to appear on the scene, a septuagenarian French politician also arrived to lead his nation toward victory. In mid-November 1917, the old Drey- fusard Georges Clemenceau became prime minister for the second time in eleven years; and along with the sobriquet the Tiger, he would soon be dubbed Père-la-Victoire by trench soldiers he often visited under heavy shellfire. While a few socialists in the Chamber of Deputies would continue to suspect Clemenceau's dictatorial predilections, nearly ev- erything that Alfred Dreyfus had criticized about his former ally during the labor upheavals of a decade earlier—his intransigence and readiness to use force—now worked to the new prime minister's advantage. French strikers might not have deserved the punishment meted out by "the first cop of France," but German troops certainly did, and Cle- menceau, as a veteran of the Paris Commune, the Dreyfus affair, and the social and political wars that followed, could capitalize on his repu- tation as a fighter and survivor. Rising every morning before dawn, he read official reports, and then, donning exercise clothes, tried to wres- tle his physical fitness instructor to the mat. For a weary population questioning its will to fight on, that image of a seventy-six-year-old brawler, with snow white hair and a walrus mustache, served as the symbol of an ancient nation that had not yet lost its vigor.[41]

Clemenceau adapted his past experience of debating in the cham- ber and dueling in the Bois de Boulogne to the arena of wartime politics and military strategy. He parried with the strong-minded British leader, David Lloyd George, and he tried to fathom the mystical idealism of the American president, Woodrow Wilson. General Pershing's troops had barely begun to fight before Wilson had devised the notion of "Peace without victory"—a goal incomprehensible to Père-la-Victoire, who be- lieved that three and a half years of bloodletting on French soil should end with the total destruction of German armies or their unconditional surrender. "Talk to Wilson!" Clemenceau would later exclaim, "How can I talk to a fellow who thinks himself the first man for two thousand years who has known anything about peace on earth?!" But with "treasonous" Russia now out of the war, Wilson's fighting men provided Clemenceau's main chance to defeat the Central Powers, and the French prime minister showed uncharacteristic patience with the American president's utopianism.[42]

He showed less patience, however, with the high command. As one of his predecessors, Aristide Briand, had done, Clemenceau recoined Talleyrand's maxim "War is much too serious to be left to the military." And it had never been more serious than in March 1918. Not since the first Battle of the Marne had German armies launched an offensive more threatening than their early spring push into Flanders and Picardy. Advancing forty miles in one week (in this war, a dramatic, long-distance journey), they scored a series of victories against Allied forces and then turned, as they had done in the early days of the Schlieffen plan, toward Paris.

In late March, from a point 120 kilometers northeast of the capital, three new German guns, products of the Krupp munitions works, fired 276-pound projectiles toward the city. There could be no hope of accuracy, but that mattered not at all to the German general Ludendorff, whose goal it was to terrorize the civilian population and break its will. The first early-morning bombardment, on March 23, devastated sections of the Quai de la Seine and the neighborhood of the Gare de l'Est: It killed eight citizens, wounded thirteen, and just missed hitting the Saint-Louis Hospital where Lucie Dreyfus worked as a volunteer nurse. On Good Friday, another bomb struck the Church of Saint-Gervais during an afternoon service. Eighty-eight worshippers died under falling stone vaults and pillars, and sixty-eight suffered serious injuries. Most of the victims were women.[43]

Three years earlier, when the technology of aerial bombardment was in a more primitive state, Magui Reinach had given birth to Jean-Pierre in the midst of a zeppelin raid. During subsequent air strikes, frequent in her neighborhood, near the Gare Saint-Lazare, Magui perfected the routine of hurrying her children down to the three beds she kept in the *cave* of their town house on the rue de Liège. That building, constructed by Joseph Reinach's father a half century before, was one of the most solid in the *quartier*, and neighbors in search of shelter joined Magui and her children to wait out the bombardments. For the most part, projectiles from the Germans' new "Paris guns" landed in the city's eastern sections, and the Reinach house, like Lucie Dreyfus's apartment farther west, escaped damage. Through the summer, until the experimental long guns broke down from overuse, a total of 181 shells fell on Paris, resulting in nearly one thousand casualties. General Ludendorff succeded in wreaking havoc, but he also learned, as later generals would forget, that bombardment does more to solidify a civilian population than to destroy it.[44]

The Krupp guns provided clear proof, however, that the enemy had drawn perilously close (the German Eighteenth Army camped barely fifty kilometers from Paris), and shortly after Clemenceau visited the ruins of Saint-Gervais, he called a series of meetings to restructure the high command. One of the most nettlesome problems throughout the war had been the poor coordination of Allied armies and the conflicting strategies (and personalities) of Allied generals. Convinced of the need for a united effort under the direction of a single military leader, Clemenceau proposed sixty-seven-year-old Ferdinand Foch as the first commander in chief of the Allied armies in France. Former head of the Ecole Supérieure de Guerre, veteran of the Marne, and leader of French forces at the Battle of the Somme (one of the few black marks on his résumé), Foch shared none of Pétain's belief in cautious, defensive tactics. Angered by Pétain's gloom—"the Germans will defeat the English in open country," the savior of Verdun reportedly told his prime minister, "after which they will defeat us"[45]—Clemenceau preferred Foch's "aggressive spirit." The restructuring of the Allied command would not put an end to high-level quarrels over strategy, but it would help reverse the course of Germany's most recent offensive.[46]

Unlike prime ministers and commanders in chief, Lieutenant Pierre Dreyfus could not detect the grand patterns of war. The German assault southwest from the Hindenburg Line may have slowed, but the Flanders fields on which Pierre fought at the head of his unit in May 1918 must have seemed no different to him than the forests of Champagne or the plains of Verdun. And when the high command celebrated the American victory at Belleau Wood and felt the first flush of confidence that Germany would be routed, Pierre engaged the enemy in the worst combat he had known since the outbreak of the war. If his letters home did not identify the sector in which he fought (though it seems to have been south of Flanders, between Soissons and Château-Thierry), the outcome was clear. At some point in May or early June, army medics rushed Lieutenant Dreyfus to a hospital in Caen, near the Normandy coast. He had been "seriously stricken by poison gas."[47]

Pierre had finally confronted the one weapon he feared most. But after barely six weeks of recuperation—and a visit from his father, who had recently completed his own tour of duty at Verdun—he returned to the firing line on July 21. Sent back to the Champagne region, he rejoined the Seventh Corps to drive German units east, and in late August, he approached the site of his first major battles in the western hinterlands of Alsace. After directing artillery fire from a forward post and securing crucial reconnaissance information for his group commander, he received his third citation for courage in combat.[48]

Those battles, like others to the north, were part of the Allied counteroffensive that forced the enemy back to the Hindenburg Line. Germany's spring campaign had failed, and by the early fall of 1918 its alliance system had failed as well. Bulgaria fell in September, Turkey in October, and the Austrian army, under attack by Italian, British, French, and American forces, was on the verge of collapse. While some members of the German high command clung to the hope of a new western offensive in the spring of 1919, others looked homeward and realized that revolution in the streets and "mutinous" strikes in naval shipyards would quickly bring an end to the war; food and oil shortages, labor upheavals and violent antiwar protests, combined with the pervasive fear that the Hindenburg Line would break and that German territory would be overrun by enemy troops, led to the disintegration of the Second Reich and to Kaiser Wilhelm's abdication. On November 6, General Foch met German representatives in a railroad car in the Compiègne Forest northeast of Paris, and five days later, at 11:00 A.M. on the eleventh day of the eleventh month of 1918, the armistice was signed.

"What joy there must be in Alsace-Lorraine!" Alfred Dreyfus wrote. "The war is over . . . and Germany has collapsed more completely than I had ever dared hope." Pierre fought with the Tenth Army under the command of General Charles Mangin until the final hours, and on the eve of the armistice he received his fifth promotion since August 1914. Entering the war as a corporal he left it as a captain, wearing the Croix de Guerre with palm, and as part of a regiment awarded a special military commendation. Pierre's father, approaching his sixtieth year, also earned a promotion that was long overdue: "For having fulfilled his duty since the day of mobilization . . . with keen intelligence and fine spirit," the "excellent superior officer" Alfred Dreyfus became a lieutenant colonel. And French officials would soon upgrade—from chevalier to officier—the Legion of Honor he had received in the wake of his affair. Learning of those promotions, Eugène Naville borrowed a line from Virgil and published an article on the captain and the lieutenant colonel in the former Dreyfusard newspaper, the *Journal de Genève*: *Quantum mutatis ab illo*! the title read: "How much things have changed!"[49]

Jeanne's husband had also been decorated for bravery. Following his field hospital service at the Somme, and after a visit with his wife and their first child, Simone, born in 1917, Pierre-Paul Lévy traveled south to the Italian Front. During a battle in which many of his surgeon colleagues were killed or injured, he treated soldiers under intense aerial bombardment on the nights of January 1–2, 1918, and received commendations from the French and Italian armies. Precisely one week after the armistice, on November 18, Jeanne gave birth to her second daughter. Lingering peace celebrations on the streets of Paris provided the backdrop for the birth of Madeleine Lévy.[50]

Alfred and Lucie Dreyfus were now grandparents, but in the late fall of 1918 their expressions of pride focused on their son's four years of "valiant and courageous" service. Hoping that Pierre would reenter Alsace "to liberate Mulhouse . . . at the head of his battery," the lieutenant colonel also hoped that he could leave his post to "embrace" his son on the family's "native soil."[51] In the days leading up to the armistice, French patriots in Mulhouse, anticipating a triumphal march, had worked feverishly to prepare the folkloric costumes of Alsace and to fashion tricolor flags from white sheets and red and blue dyes. Now, with the occupiers pushed east across the Rhine, those flags could fly in public, and citizens could celebrate in the French language that had been prohibited in the German *Reichsland*. They would mount a pageant reminiscent of the Treaty of Union that had brought "the Republic of Mülhausen to rest in the bosom of the Republic of France," and which had set the scene for the Dreÿfuss family's migration to *la ville la plus française de l'Alsace*.

On November 17, 1918, French soldiers, greeted with flowers and the drum rolls of military bands, paraded down the rue du Sauvage and past the Place des Victoires; and a month later, Prime Minister Clemenceau, proud to be "the last survivor of those who had signed the protest against the treaty relinquishing Alsace-Lorraine in 1871,"[52] attended yet another "grand patriotic festival" in Mulhouse. Alfred and Pierre Dreyfus could not leave their units to witness those celebrations, but Mathieu and Suzanne came with Magui and her three children to represent the family and to honor the memory of its men lost in battle.

Suzie, France, and Jean-Pierre Reinach, dressed in Alsatian costumes, complete with velvet bows and tricolor cocardes, watched French troops march into Mulhouse, just as their grandfather and his brothers and sisters had watched them march out in the fall of 1870. The forty-eight-year-old dream of *revanche* had been realized. But "the return of the frontier of the Rhine which will bring peace to France and to the world . . . in two months' time," as Ado Reinach had hoped in August 1914, had taken four years and the sacrifice of more than 1,300,000 French soldiers. The three Reinach children donned playful costumes for the Mulhouse parade, but their mother and grandparents dressed in black.[53]

CHAPTER XXI

Between Times

TWO YEARS before the outbreak of "the war to end all wars," Ado Reinach had urged his brother-in-law Emile to remain on the "front line" of Alsatian industry and to preserve Raphael Dreyfus et Compagnie. Established in the 1860s, that enterprise survived the shock of the Franco-Prussian War and the German occupation of Alsace, and, under the direction of Mathieu and with the hands-on management of Jacques and Léon, it remained productive through the fin de siècle and the early years of the new century, despite the "sluggish growth rate" of the Alsatian cotton industry. Furthermore, the income it generated helped finance, along with the Hadamard fortune, the monumental expenses of the affair. The family never made a final tabulation of legal fees, propaganda costs, travel expenses, and payments to graphologists, private detectives, and free-lance informers (many of them professional swindlers), but the total sum far exceeded one million francs. That Raphael and Jeannette Dreyfus's offspring could support those costs while continuing to live in comfort from the earnings of the Mulhouse and Belfort mills provided the clearest confirmation of the ongoing success of the family enterprise.[1]

Emile Dreyfus and his cousin Charles had been in line to direct a growing industry; a modern three-story annex had been built along the northern periphery of the Mulhouse factory, and Mathieu had drafted plans for another addition on the rue Lavoisier. In August 1914, however, the curious working relationship maintained across four decades by French Alsatian industrialists and *Reichsland* occupiers collapsed, and German authorities seized the Dreyfus mill. After Jacques' death in 1915, Mathieu tried to direct the branch factory across the border in French territory; but when fuel reserves dwindled he rented that enterprise to managers who could secure coal shipments under wartime government contracts. In the summer of 1917, word reached the family that Germans had "pillaged" their Mulhouse buildings, and a year later, in keeping with other desperate measures in the final stages of the war, *Reichsland* officials began liquidating the family's assets by selling off parcels of land to other Alsatian textile businesses—presumably to those with solid credentials of German collaboration. The armistice finally halted the wholesale dismantling of Raphael's "creation," and Mathieu began the bureaucratic process of retrieving his father's first factory. In 1919 the Mulhouse tribunal, now in the hands of French Alsatians, determined that the seizure of Raphael Dreyfus et Compagnie had been an "illegal political and military act"; having "suffered considerable prejudice" at the hands of the Germans, all of its prewar assets must be returned immediately and at no expense to the family.[2]

The victory was bittersweet. Mathieu saved the shell of a once prosperous cotton mill, but lost the two young men—Emile and Charles—who had been groomed to oversee its renaissance. And in the wake of the war, sixty-two-year-old Mathieu learned that French industry had lost more than a generation of leaders: It had lost the concord between capital and labor that manufacturers considered essential to economic progress. The industrial harmony that the Mulhouse "patriciate" tried to secure through housing projects and insurance plans had never been fully realized, and labor unrest marked the decades on either side of 1900 in the eastern provinces as it did throughout industrial Europe.[3] But in the aftermath of 1914–18 the prewar era took on the illusion of stability, and labor problems, in retrospect, seemed less threatening.

"The war is dead," declared members of one French trade union shortly after the November armistice. "Long live the war."[4] The four-year struggle brought on by the nationalist bourgeoisie (labor groups announced) must now give way to the international struggle of the proletariat. In 1914 workers and bosses joined politicians in the nation's "sacred union," and that spirit of cooperation, though threatened by strikes after 1917, held until the German surrender. But with inflation rising and the Russian dream of social revolution gaining strength, membership in the CGT climbed past one million in 1919. And while Clemenceau, Wilson, Lloyd George, and other Allied leaders worked in Paris on a treaty that would make the world safe for democracy, demonstrators made the streets of the French capital safe for no one. The postwar revival of May Day—that annual proletarian march inaugurated in Paris in 1890—brought renewed violence between striking workers and the forces of order; the first day of May 1919 signaled, for those who had not already dated its death from the mutinies of 1917, the demise of the "sacred union."[5]

Alfred Dreyfus noted the early signs of those problems at his fortified "workshop" north of the capital, where soldiers, soon to return to the civilian labor force, dismantled artillery emplacements: "The difficulties of the post-war epoch will be great," he wrote. "Inflation continues and the workers' demands are many. I sometimes hear them talk . . . and it is clear that they will not be easily satisfied." An amateur historian of French syndicalism since the founding of the CGT, Dreyfus now stressed the need for "adapting totally new methods to the conditions of labor." But he dealt in theories of reform, while his older brother, faced with the challenge of reestablishing his family's business, dealt in the daily realities of working-class demands.[6]

Prior to the war, Mathieu, like Joseph Reinach, another longtime critic of the CGT, expressed impatience with trade-union radicalism; but in the wake of the Russian Revolution, the domestic dilemma took on international implications, and the anxieties of the propertied classes intensified. A few weeks before May Day, an ex-anarchist affiliated with the international "Communist Federation" (according to news reports) had shot and wounded Clemenceau on a Paris street, and though police found no proof of conspiracy, popular opinion insisted that "a German or a bolshevik" had done the deed. The Tiger healed quickly (he returned to the peace conference in less than two weeks), but the incident heightened fears of social revolution. "The French bourgeois is determined to defend himself against the Bolshevist wave," went one report in the aftermath of May Day, "which he sees behind the demonstration of the CGT."[7] Mathieu Dreyfus saw it as well: "If a line of defense is not organized against French bolshevists," he wrote on May 5, "we will head toward disaster." With trade-union leaders hoping "to interrupt the life of the nation" through a general strike, Mathieu condemned the "minority of men of bad faith [who] incite poor, credulous people and lead them astray." The clearest lesson could be learned from Russia, he said, "a country on its way to ruin." Attempting to retrieve the prewar promise of solidarism, Mathieu believed that the "worker should not be the enemy of capital, just as the latter is not the worker's enemy. In order to prosper," he said, "those two groups must understand each other, and one should not try to dominate." But it seemed that every concession made by an employer was now followed "by a new demand," and that "nothing would satisfy" the working classes. Turning to his native province, Mathieu warned that its former occupiers, profiting from troubles caused by French syndicalists, would try to convince the local population that it had been "much happier, much more tranquil, under the German regime. . . . Such a future will be brought about by the men of the C.G.T.," Mathieu concluded, "if we do not organize the defense of our society."[8]

Unable or unwilling to shed the habits of the prewar period, Mathieu Dreyfus and other manufacturers spoke an old solidarist language of labor that new trade unionists, in their turn, were unable or unwilling to comprehend. Had Mathieu's son survived the war, he might have brought a different vision to the family enterprise, a new sensitivity to the needs of workers who had fought beside him at the Marne and in the trenches of Champagne. But Emile Dreyfus was gone, and his father's grief had taken its physical toll. Mathieu no longer had the patience to deal with demands that he defined as unreasonable and unpatriotic, and he no longer had the energy to oversee an industry which, for him, lost its raison d'être when it lost its "heir apparent." Consulting Alfred and his sisters, he decided to sell the cotton mill founded by their father sixty years before and the branch factory launched by Jacques in the 1890s.

The Belfort establishment went to in-laws, to Schwob Frères in Héricourt, and in 1920, a group of investors, the Boussac group, took over the original factory on the rue Lavoisier. Three years later, it was sold again, to a textile company in Tourcoing, near the Belgian border. Like so many other enterprises launched in the nineteenth century, Raphael Dreyfus's business had first become a joint stock company, and then, with the concentration of industry that continued in the aftermath of the 1914 war, it had been subsumed by a larger organization based beyond the boundaries of Mulhouse. For a short time, the new owners kept the factory's original name; but when the prosaic title La Cotonnerie de Mulhouse replaced Raphael Dreyfus et Compagnie on the rue Lavoisier facade, and when a Protestant school purchased Mathieu's neo-Gothic mansion on the rue de la Porte du Miroir, the family's last tangible ties to their Alsatian homeland were severed.[9]

* * *

Before resettling in Paris, Mathieu's daughter, Magui Reinach, twenty-seven years old in 1919, traveled with Alsatian friends into villages and small towns along the Rhine Valley—into communities like her ancestors' Rixheim and Ribeauvillé. While the French government prepared reconstruction programs for farms and factories devastated by the war—and while health officials combated the local effects of a murderous worldwide influenza epidemic—volunteers like Magui taught the French language to youngsters raised and educated in the *Reichsland*. By instructing a new generation in a new "mother tongue," the "village school movement" aimed to erase more than four decades of Germanic influence and hasten the reintegration of the eastern provinces into France. Not all Alsatians "who habitually spoke German were disloyal to France, but all who were disloyal habitually spoke German,"[10] and Magui, having grown up in an occupied town divided by the politics of language, knew that the victory of *revanche* must be followed by one of French culture.[11]

Interrupting her volunteer work in the spring of 1919, Magui set out on yet another search, across the Vosges Mountains to the Ardennes Forest and the village of Fossé. Accompanied by a government official, she combed the area where her husband had fought, but, deep in the woods a few hundred yards from the Tyranes farmstead where Ado's troops had been billeted, she uncovered no evidence of the battle that had occurred more than four years earlier. Joseph Reinach urged his daughter-in-law to abandon the search. The family would hold to their last memory of Ado in the weeks before the war, and, at the edge of a field near Fossé, they would construct a large stone monument to that memory—in the classical style that the young archaeologist and Hellenic historian would have wanted.[12] One poet later described the men of August 1914, the men like Ado Reinach, "Leaving the gardens tidy/the thousands of marriages/Lasting a little while longer."[13] Though together for only twenty-seven months, Ado and Magui had been married for seven years, until 1919, when French bureaucrats officially recognized Madame Reinach as a *veuve de guerre*, a "war widow." Her daughters were five and six years old, and her son, Jean-Pierre, born seven months after his father's disappearance, turned four in March 1919.

If Magui confronted no financial worries in the postwar years, she faced the same hard period of adjustment shared by thousands of widowed mothers. Wanting to provide a secure home for her children, she moved into her parents' two-floor apartment on the Avenue Malakoff in the sixteenth arrondissement of western Paris. And Mathieu, with time to spare and his own sadness to overcome, took on the duties of surrogate father to his daughter's three children. On Sunday morning walks through the Bois de Boulogne he recounted the history of their family's affair and described the mysterious psychic powers of the peasant Léonie. Every November 11 he took the children to the Place de l'Etoile, only a few steps from their home, to join the crowd gathered to honor soldiers who had fallen on the battlefield. During the two minutes of silence that marked the ceremony, Suzie, France, and Jean-Pierre prayed for their father Ado and uncle Emile, and then waited with high anticipation for the cannon blasts that roused enormous flocks of pigeons from the Arc de Triomphe.

Mathieu introduced the children to his old Dreyfusard comrades—to Demange, Naville, Clemenceau, and the few other survivors. Rejected in his bid for the presidency of the republic, the Tiger had resigned as prime minister in 1920 and now divided his time between a country house in his native Vendée region and a modest four-room apartment in the sixteenth arrondissement of Paris. It was only a fifteen-minute walk from the Avenue Malakoff to the rue Franklin, and Mathieu visited Clemenceau regularly through the 1920s to share memories of the affair and opinions on contemporary politics. Not surprisingly, the Reinach children were fascinated by the bright-eyed octogenarian with a white walrus mustache and huge head topped off by a curious deerstalker cap. And Père-la-Victoire must have been pleased with Magui Reinach's contribution to the nation's most pressing need: "France must have lots of children," Clemenceau had proclaimed at the time of the Paris Peace Conference. "If not, you can put what you like into the Treaty—France will be done for."[14]

Mathieu's guardianship of his grandchildren had become even more significant after the death of their other grandfather, Joseph Reinach, on April 19, 1921. At the age of sixty-five, he had succumbed to a rare skin disease that massive doses of medication could not arrest. Like his friend of nearly twenty-five years, Reinach had been devastated by the loss of his only son. Until the armistice, he had written daily articles applauding the heroism of trench soldiers and criticizing citizens who threatened the "sacred union," from agitating syndicalists to Jews more committed to Palestine than to France. And at the time of the peace conference, he had tried to renew his involvement in political affairs by inviting dignitaries to his Avenue Van Dyck villa on the edge of the Parc

Monceau; President Wilson's confidant, Colonel House, came, and so
did the British politician Arthur Balfour and the French general Louis-
Hubert-Gonzalve Lyautey, famous for his exploits with the colonial
army in Algeria and Morocco. During one of those visits Reinach
perched his four-year-old grandson, Jean-Pierre, on the knee of yet
another military leader, the "hero of the Marne," and the boy played
with the colorful medals that ornamented Joffre's tunic. But the robust
physical energy and intellectual engagement that had made Joseph Reinach one of the most powerful (and reviled) figures of the Gambettist
era and of the Dreyfus affair had diminished, and one of his closest
friends, the Princess Marthe Bibesco, acknowledged the change. The
survivor of more than a dozen duels, the witty and cultivated salongoer
whose "protruding, laughing eyes" reminded the princess of her "old
French bulldog," had been "reduced" by age, illness, and the personal
tragedy of the "Great War."[15]

Grandson of a horse trader from Mainz and son of a stable boy-
turned-bank clerk who had become one of the principal investors in the
early French railway system (and who believed that "one must live from
the revenue of one's revenue"), Joseph Reinach had inherited an enormous fortune. With his brothers Salomon and Théodore, he owned real
estate in the fashionable western arrondissements of Paris and in Saint-
Germain-en-Laye, and through his contacts with artists, critics, and
connoisseurs, he collected scores of works by academic and avant-
garde painters, engravers, and sculptors. A firm believer in preserving
the national patrimony, Reinach donated part of his collection (which
included works by Monet, Pissarro, Vallotton, Van Gogh, and Gauguin)
to the Louvre; and he contributed to organizations for public assistance.
He also supported Jewish charity work (grandes oeuvres israélites) as his
ancestors had done, but he limited his contacts with the religious community of French Jews to philanthropic gifts. Critic of "Jewish nationalism," he was criticized, in turn, for his "reactionary" anti-Zionist
politics, and, until the end, he remained opposed to modern notions of
cultural pluralism. A republican "freethinker" more at home in the late
nineteenth century than in the early twentieth, Joseph Reinach died
with an undiminished faith in the ideology of assimilation and in the
revolutionary promise of national unity.[16]

Mathieu Dreyfus had been his ideal companion. Virtually the same
age (Mathieu was sixty-four in 1921), they shared the same tastes in
art, music, literature, and politics, and the same religious indifference.
Because of his longtime residence in eastern France and his contacts

with Freemasons in Héricourt and Mulhouse, Mathieu's ties to the Jewish community in Paris were even more tenuous than Reinach's. His philanthropic largesse went not to Jewish charities but to private pension funds he established for the widows of Mulhouse associates and Dreyfusard comrades. And, in concert with the Reinach family, he and his wife aided Russian refugees, victims of the Bolshevik Revolution.

But most of all in the years following 1918, the Dreyfuses and Reinachs shared an exercise in selective memory; they contrasted the contentious society of the postwar period with the triumphant epoch of the affair, when men and women of all classes and backgrounds had rallied to the republic of justice and social solidarity by rallying to the prisoner on Devil's Island. After Reinach's death Mathieu made certain that their grandchildren learned the moral lessons of those Dreyfusard years—lessons that included no religious instruction in Judaism but emphasized a spiritual faith in France. As a result of the war, many grandparents became the informal tutors of their children's children. Clinging to memories of a more heroic era—and unable to imagine that their son might have died in vain—Mathieu and Suzanne Dreyfus helped preserve the nineteenth-century curriculum of duty, deference, and patriotism that had shaped the generation of 1914.[17]

While her father, mother, and a coterie of servants looked after her children, Magui Reinach enjoyed an occasional holiday with friends and relatives. She summered at Hardelot-Plage near Boulogne-sur-Mer, made one trip to Morocco with her cousin Pierre in 1923, and, after a long period of mourning, began to pursue an active social life in Paris.[18] A strikingly handsome woman, with her mother's ash blond hair and large blue eyes, she had many admirers but no steady suitor, and most of her social activities were related to the public service work she had started during the war. As a volunteer nurse, she had compiled a "guide for disabled soldiers" with instructions on prosthetic devices and lists of job opportunities for veterans, and she later contributed to another brochure for war widows. By 1926 she had joined a Paris-based organization that conducted surveys on education, housing, and recreation in the capital and its environs. The Redressement Français (French Renewal) had some methods in common with the postwar "village school movement" in Alsace, but its goal was to counteract the growing influence of communism—of "collectivist solutions"—in poor localities across the nation. In keeping with family custom, Mathieu and Suzanne Dreyfus's daughter devoted her volunteer efforts to paternalist and "neocapitalist" organizations committed to wide-ranging programs of social and economic reform.[19]

Supported by a constellation of large business firms and promising a middle way between old-style laissez-faire capitalism and new-style bolshevism, the Redressement Français set out in the winter of 1925–26 to renovate a nation torn asunder by class conflict and financial chaos. "Enough politics," went one of its slogans, "we want results!"[20] Having paid most of the massive costs of the war through loans rather than tax revenues, the French government had pinned its hopes of recovery on the income from German reparations. But the Weimar Republic suffered staggering inflation rates through the early 1920s, and even the occupation of the industrial Ruhr region by French and Belgian troops (to speed the shipment of wood and coal and to press Germany for cash) could not wring funds from a bankrupt nation. While the French finance minister insisted that "the Boche will pay," his government had to turn to the Morgan Brothers Bank in New York for a $100 million loan, just as an earlier French government had turned to the same bank in the wake of the 1870 war.[21] Responding to the destabilization of the franc and to the social and political consequences of economic distress (the French Communist party had declared its independence from the Socialist party in 1920, and both were gaining strength), the leaders of the Redressement Français launched their appeal: Only a technocratic elite, "disinterested" in politics and inspired by the American model of highly rationalized production, could save French industry, they announced, and only a new age of prosperity, secured by managers with a sense of social duty, could improve the plight of all classes. Rejecting Karl Marx, they revered Henry Ford.[22] But if their rhetoric focused on innovation, their program was, to some extent, a case of old wine in new bottles. Solidarism, born in the fin de siècle, had survived the war, and the founder of the Redressement Français, forty-eight-year-old Ernest Mercier, emerged as its leading advocate.

Magui Reinach met Mercier shortly after joining his organization and quickly learned that he had much in common with the Dreyfus and Reinach families.[23] His French father had made his mark as a reform-minded mayor in Constantine, Algeria, where he also served as the head of the Radical party, the one later dominated by solidarists and Dreyfusards. Ernest Mercier graduated with distinction from the Ecole Polytechnique (where, like Magui's uncle, he learned more about the social responsibilities of the French elite) and became chief engineer and then managing director of the Messine Group, France's largest public utility syndicate. Believing, as Ado Reinach had, that captains of industry, like captains of army units, must work for the "welfare of others," Mercier started to apply his solidarist ideas to the "front line" of his own industrial enterprises. The war interrupted his plans but refined his philosophy.[24] Awarded the Legion of Honor for courage under fire on the coast of Montenegro, and decorated again at Gallipoli, Mercier was sent to the Balkans to fight with Romanian troops against German and Bulgarian armies. Wounded a second time in 1916 and promoted to colonel, he spent the remainder of the war as a chief technical adviser to the minister of armaments and as personal liaison to Generals Foch and Pétain. Dissatisfied with his nation's industrial performance during the war (Ado Reinach had expressed the same concerns as early as August 1914), Mercier planned to redress the balance in peacetime. But, most important, he returned to civilian life imbued with "the spirit of the front," convinced that officers on the firing line had earned the moral authority to reshape the postwar world. While all fighting men, regardless of social class, were ennobled by their heroic sacrifice, the officer corps, said Mercier, set an example by leading cavalry troops into forest clearings and infantry soldiers into no-man's-land. Through its bravery under fire the French elite had redefined the qualities of noblesse oblige for a democratic age.[25]

Returning to his executive position with the Messine Group, Mercier became director of the Union d'Electricité and a key player in the birth of the modern French oil industry. As president of the Compagnie Française des Pétroles in 1923, he developed the oil resources of France, where they were minimal, and of the colonies, where they were abundant.[26] Through those years he amassed a significant private fortune (his average annual income approached 2,500,000 francs by the 1930s), but he continued to insist that material wealth imposed social obligations. Much like members of the old Mulhouse manufacturing "patriciate," he offered his employees a wide range of benefits, from interest-free loans for home construction to special family allowances and recreational facilities. But that, he soon learned, was not enough. With socialists and the newly formed Communist party competing for the allegiance of the working classes, he realized that a national organization, led by "men of goodwill," must "educate the masses." In response to what he perceived as the two corrosive extremes of the postwar epoch—egoistic greed and collectivist ideology—Mercier institutionalized his philosophy of neocapitalism through the Redressement Français. "The misfortune that we suffer is to have lost the sense of solidarity," he would write. "An elite is a community, [and] in order to be a member, one must accept the obligations and the burdens, and not only demand the honors and the benefits."[27]

Neosolidarism, unregenerate anti-Germanism, suspicion of foreign and domestic communism, and a desire to preserve the patriotic "spirit of the generation that fought the war"—all those beliefs animated Mercier's plan for the reconstruction of France.[28] Passionate appeals to the memories of war became a principal leitmotiv of the period, and commentators of every ideological stripe found variations on the same theme. They all spoke of the comradeship of the trenches, but while some focused on the social leveling of the war experience, others, like Mercier, lamented the death blow to hierarchy: "The flower, the ornament, the radiant hope of the French elite had been cut down on the field of battle," he wrote, "and that loss will weigh heavily and for a long time on all of us, even perhaps when we cease to be aware of it."[29]

When Magui Reinach met Mercier, a widower and the father of four teenage children, she found a colleague who shared her commitment to public service and her memories of young fallen officers. She also found, a dozen years after her husband's disappearance and her brother's death, a caring and attractive companion who would raise her children as their father and uncle would have wished. With his "sharp, almost aristocratic features," his salt-and-pepper hair, arched eyebrows, and pencil-thin mustache, Mercier—dapper in his conservative dark blue suits—looked every bit the affluent Parisian businessman. He also looked, as one contemporary put it, just like the Protestant he was.[30]

In 1927 Magui Dreyfus Reinach became the first member of her family to marry a non-Jew. Given her background, the union was not a surprise. Born in an Alsatian city dominated by a Protestant elite, and raised by parents and maternal grandparents who believed in a modern blend of deism and Freemasonry, she had been tutored throughout her life by Dreyfusard "uncles" and "aunts," related and unrelated, for whom science, secularism, and cultural assimilation were all-encompassing faiths.

Other observers, outside the family and always ready to criticize it, were likewise not surprised when a prominent figure of Protestant society married the niece of France's most infamous Jew. Ernest Mercier had pledged his allegiance to the same secular faiths as his bride and her immediate family, and had no significant interest in the religion of his ancestors. But he had emerged in recent years as the Parisian leader of what allies and enemies alike called the HSP, the *haute société protes-tante*. Though barely 1 percent of the French population was Protestant in the 1920s, men like Mercier enjoyed a numerically disproportionate place in the upper reaches of the nation's banking and industrial circles, as they had for many generations; and they had their representatives among the "Two Hundred Families of France" who, their critics insisted, conspired to control the nation's destiny. Muckrakers, of the left and the right, defined Mercier's "plutocratic" programs as part of a "bastardly, pseudomonopoly" which made him "the mortal enemy of the working classes," or (viewed from the right) part of a quasi-socialist conspiracy cloaked in the guise of "public interest." And most of those observers honored Mercier with their highest form of ridicule: He had become, they announced, an "agent of the Rothschilds." Such rumors made up the recipe of social criticism used by parties and individuals for whom stereotypes mattered more than hard facts: What worked for the likes of Edouard Drumont during the affair worked again among those who had inherited Drumont's mantle.[31]

Targets like Mercier, or Alfred Dreyfus before him, proved most useful at times of acute economic and social upheaval. But in the late 1920s, the German economy strengthened (with American aid), and the French government implemented strict monetary policies to control the crisis which had prompted the founding of the Redressement Français. Raymond Poincaré, president of the republic throughout the war and now its prime minister (for a second time), stabilized the French franc in 1926, and the economic situation, if not the fundamental faults of the postwar system, gradually improved.

Those measures had little impact on the plight of the poorer classes, however, and Magui Mercier, serving on the executive committee of her husband's organization, focused her efforts on the condition of working mothers in Paris. She helped create an *artisanat féminin* to encourage seamstresses, former textile laborers, and other craftswomen to work in their homes while tending their children. They brought fabric samples (*echantillons*) to a small boutique on the Avenue Marceau near the Place de l'Etoile and the Redressement Français headquarters. Though the location meant a significant trek for women based in the city's eastern neighborhoods, Magui undoubtedly chose it for its proximity to the affluent clientele that she and her friends found for the materials crafted by their *artisanat*; the directors of other "women's exchanges" in European and American cities had done much the same thing. With one full-time employee and a commission of only 10 percent on each order, the organization never showed a profit, and every year Magui and Ernest Mercier offset its deficit.[32]

Working together, they also traveled together, on business trips throughout France and across Europe for the Messine Group and the Compagnie Française des Pétroles, and on vacations to the coasts of Britanny and the Mediterranean; Mercier, a former naval officer, always opted for a seaside holiday. Magui's three children sometimes accompanied them on summer excursions, but Suzie, France, and Jean-Pierre, now teenagers, spent most of the year at schools in the sixteenth arrondissement near the Bois de Boulogne. According to family custom, the children learned English, German, music, drawing, and dance at an early age, and by the late 1920s, Magui's son and daughters had a firm command of those and other disciplines. They also carried the heavy burden of attempting to repeat the extraordinary achievements of the previous generations of Reinachs and Dreyfuses. While the girls studied at the Villiers school (where their cousin Jeanne had gone nearly thirty years before because of its "Dreyfusard" credentials), Jean-Pierre attended the Lycée Janson de Sailly. In 1928 thirteen-year-old Jean-Pierre transferred to the Lycée Pasteur, even closer to his home, but, like his father and cousin Pierre at Condorcet, he encountered a coterie of young anti-Semites at Pasteur (students who mimicked their elders' battles against mounted police) and returned to Janson de Sailly to prepare for the *baccalauréat*. He hoped to enter the Ecole Libre des Sciences Politiques, and eventually, in the footsteps of Joseph Reinach, earn a "license" in law.[33]

Mathieu Dreyfus's private tutorials with his grandson and granddaughters, conducted on strolls through the Bois de Boulogne, gave way to formal instruction in *lycée* classrooms. The children still visited their grandparents on the occasional Sunday, but increasingly they spent their time in school and with their mother and stepfather. More than ever, they respected the grandfather who had raised them, and more than ever, as children turned teenagers invariably do, they revered him from afar.

Scheurer-Kestner, Zola, Lazare, Jaurès, and most of the other central figures of the affair had died before the war, but a few hearty survivors remained, and through the 1920s Mathieu Dreyfus still enjoyed his conversations with old comrades like Clemenceau. He took a special interest in analyzing the domestic and foreign policies of government leaders who, as young reformers, had cut their political teeth on the affair. Mathieu watched Alexandre Millerand, one of the negotiators for the captain's pardon in 1899, rise to the post of prime minister and then, as the alternative to Clemenceau, to the presidency of the republic; Millerand's socialism had moderated with age (some said it vanished), and Mathieu approved of the hard line that his former ally took with the CGT. Aristide Briand, however, another ex-socialist and Dreyfusard, fared less well with Mathieu. Even before that summer day in 1908 when they stood together at the Panthéon and witnessed Grégori's attack on Alfred Dreyfus, Briand, like other prewar radicals, had been drifting farther toward the center of the political arena, or, more precisely, had remained stationary while French society turned left. But Briand, who would shatter every record by serving as minister of foreign affairs sixteen times and as prime minister eleven, worried Mathieu when he set out on a quest for European harmony through the improvement of Franco-German relations. Reconciliation may be the stuff of which Nobel Peace Prizes are made (and Briand won his in 1926), but for an "ardent patriot" (as one friend described Mathieu Dreyfus in that same year) with a visceral hatred for the Germans who had taken his son, "reconciliation" was another word for weakness. Humane, patriotic, and artfully diplomatic, Aristide Briand led a government that was, according to its critics, impossibly naive. It suffered, Mathieu announced, from a "lack of energy."[34] Long after the armistice, the Dreyfus family, including their new and influential in-law Ernest Mercier, adhered to the maxim, current at the time, that the best way "to treat a Prussian is to stamp on his toes until he apologizes."[35]

By late 1929 Mathieu's audience of old Dreyfusards—the inner circle with whom he could talk politics and share memories—had been reduced to Alfred and Lucie, to his sisters Rachel and Henriette (now well into their seventies and infrequent visitors to family gatherings), and to Eugène Naville, the comrade who had almost single-handedly championed the Dreyfusard cause in Switzerland. All the others were gone. After Léon and Jacques, Mathieu lost his third sibling, his seventy-one-year-old sister, Louise Cahn, in 1922. Rachel had been a more active participant in the fight for Alfred's release—firing off passionate letters to ministers of war and presidents of the republic—and Henriette had turned her Carpentras estate into a Dreyfusard sanctuary; but Mathieu recalled with fondness the school holidays that he and Alfred had spent with the Cahns in Bar-le-Duc, and he remembered Louise rushing to join that unexpected family reunion in Paris in the winter of 1894.[36]

Maître Edgar Demange had spent more hours and faced more disappointments with Mathieu than had any other Dreyfusard, and he had remained a cherished friend. Long after his retirement he still made daily visits to the Palais de Justice, and—appropriately for a devout Catholic—he continued to reside, until his death in 1925 at the age of eighty-four, on the Quai de la Tournelle in the shadow of Notre Dame.[37] In temperament and ideology, however, and in their mutual reverence for the cult of "French justice" over the cult of religion,[38] Mathieu felt closest to Georges Clemenceau. And the Tiger, in his turn, had always preferred the urbane Mathieu to the intensely military Alfred. Ever since the fall of 1915, when Clemenceau made it possible for the family to be with Emile at Mourmelon-le-Grand, Mathieu's fondness for the irascible former Dreyfusard had increased, and though Clemenceau could be condemned for many things, he never lacked the energy and patriotism that Mathieu Dreyfus honored. In his years of retirement, Mathieu relished two activities above all others; the time he spent with his grandchildren and the visits he made to Père-la-Victoire's apartment on the rue Franklin and to his country home in the Vendée. But the grandchildren grew up, and in November 1929, in his eighty-eighth year, Clemenceau died.[39]

"To my loving wife," began Mathieu's private diary, "to you . . . the courageous and intelligent collaborator in our fight for Justice and Right; to you, whose resolute energy always sustained and strengthened my will to establish the truth, whatever the dangers may have been; to you, admirable wife and devoted mother, I dedicate these memories."[40] Mathieu's younger brother had written his own account of the affair and, specifically, of his exile on Devil's Island. But while *Cinq années de ma vie* had been part of the campaign for revision—a book fashioned for public consumption—Mathieu designed his memoirs as a private testament. Charting the course of the affair, he described the negotiations, confrontations, and backroom maneuvers with presidents, prime ministers, private detectives, and foreign correspondents, and he painted, in words, individual portraits of leading Dreyfusards. Like most reminiscences, Mathieu's were selective, but unlike many, they were generous: He recalled Jean Jaurès not as the advocate of radical syndicalism, but as the heroic defender of Dreyfus in the pages of *La Petite République* and on the floor of the Chamber of Deputies. And though Mathieu outlined the conflicts with Picquart and Labori, he applauded the courage of those two difficult men. Across the dozen years that reached from the captain's arrest to his final acquittal, all Dreyfusards, whatever their transgressions, were portrayed by Mathieu as loyal republicans and devoted patriots.

Though it was never explicitly stated, Mathieu's account of his brother's case was a work of explanation rather than a straightforward chronicle. During the affair and in the years that followed, the family had been accused of excessive deference toward the political and military establishment that, at best, had denied Captain Dreyfus due process and, at worst, had framed him. Bernard Lazare was not the only critic of Mathieu's tactics; other, less-patient colleagues had railed against the family's cautious methods and refusal to exploit the political opportunities presented by the affair. Meanwhile, anti-Dreyfusards had defined those same methods as the secret machinations of a "Jewish Syndicate." Through his memoirs, Mathieu wanted his children to understand the decisions he had made, and he wanted them to learn that the affair had exposed the weakness and bigotry of individuals rather than of French institutions. Describing his pursuit of Esterhazy, Henry, du Paty, and the other men who had betrayed the nation by betraying an officer devoted to that nation, Mathieu concluded, as his brother would do, that the outcome of the affair had been much more than a personal triumph. It had been a victory for France.[41]

In the spring of 1930, just short of his seventy-third birthday, Mathieu suffered a minor stroke. He recovered soon after, but his daily walks gave way to daily rides in an open automobile through the fresh air of the countryside environs of Paris. A second stroke followed in the early summer, and a few weeks later, while recuperating in the Mediterranean town of Saint-Raphael, he was struck by a third and massive attack. Suzanne arranged for an ambulance to rush her husband to Paris. Partially paralyzed, he developed pneumonia, and on October 22, 1930—on the same day of the same month as his son's death fifteen years before—Mathieu died in his home on the Avenue Malakoff. Surrounded by family, he was also surrounded by the few simple artifacts of his life that he had prominently displayed: photographic portraits of his mother and father, taken a half century before in Mulhouse; a bust of Voltaire; a picture of Zola; and, with posthumous medals draped over their frames, photographs of Emile Dreyfus and Ado Reinach in full-dress uniform in the summer of 1914.[42]

Mathieu Dreyfus "met death with remarkable philosophical courage," Eugène Naville recorded in his diary. "In my long life, I have never known a man of more noble character, more endowed with integrity and fraternal devotion. Without him," Naville went on, "without his energy, perseverance and selflessness, his brother . . . would have died in prison never having seen the light of justice and reparation."[43] Joseph Reinach's brother, Salomon, called Mathieu a "hero of duty" and said that his death would be a "rude blow for the thin and scattered ranks of the old guard that remain." And the theme of "fraternal devotion" was repeated in the few newspapers that bothered to comment on Mathieu Dreyfus's passing. Jaurès's old paper, *L'Humanité*, the organ of the Communist party since 1920, seized the opportunity to recount the "profound political and economic causes of the affair," and while it applauded Mathieu, it misrepresented Alfred and oversimplified the case: "Much more than his brother, who, though saved by the proletariat never understood its historic role, Mathieu Dreyfus became part of the great social movement of the affair."[44]

Adhering to every wish recorded in her husband's brief, handwritten testament, Suzanne Dreyfus had Mathieu's body taken directly to the small Passy Cemetery near the Trocadéro and the banks of the Seine. A few years earlier, Emile Dreyfus's remains had been brought to Passy from the military graveyard at Mourmelon-le-Grand. No flowers or wreaths draped Mathieu's coffin, and no eulogies were given. Held "in the strictest intimacy," the service included only one participant outside the family: A rabbi gave a "short and simple prayer," and he gave it, following Mathieu's instructions, "in French." In the final lines of his will, Mathieu asked "forgiveness of those whom I have offended," and urged his grandchildren "always to remember the noble qualities of their father, Adolphe Reinach, and their uncle, our beloved son, Emile. It should never be forgotten that they both died for France."

On the night before the burial, family members had gathered for the vigil at the Avenue Malakoff apartment. Close to the coffin, and in a voice barely audible to others in the room, seventy-one-year-old Alfred said good-bye to the brother who had saved his life and restored his honor: "*Je te dois tout,*" he whispered to Mathieu. "I owe you everything."[45]

CHAPTER XXII

Revivals

IN FEBRUARY 1931, less than six months after Mathieu Dreyfus's death, a French writer adapted a German play and staged a revival of the affair at the Théatre de l'Ambigu near the Place de la République. More titillating than enlightening, with its case of drunken General Staff officers and silk-stocking-clad courtesans entertaining a debauched Esterhazy, *L'Affaire Dreyfus* was not the first rendition of the real event. In the years surrounding the captain's retrial and rehabilitation, café-concerts and minor theater companies offered loosely adapted reenactments of the affair, and in 1899 the "father of film art" in France, Georges Méliès, chose the Dreyfus case as the subject for a "long" motion picture. It ran thirteen minutes.[1]

French theater had often intersected with French politics. Molière, Voltaire, and Victor Hugo had known it, and so had less celebrated creators of satirical "boulevard" fare. Politics, royal and democratic, had always provided entertainment. Friendly and hostile witnesses described Dreyfus's trial, degradation, and retrial as dramatic performances; spectators traveled to the Rennes *lycée* as they would to a provincial theater, and they awaited the prisoner's arrival as they would the entrance of a star performer. Modern critics would refine the theory of audience engagement—of penetrating the stage's imaginary wall and confusing the roles of actors and viewers—but the practice had a long and turbulent history in France. And the quality of the material mattered less than the timely political chord it struck. In the wake of the captain's rehabilitation, a Parisian café-concert, the Ba-ta-Clan, staged a revue entitled "The Triumph of Truth," and with every reference to the "traitor's" innocence, demonstrators jumped from their seats to hiss and jeer. Shouts of "Down with Dreyfus! Down with the Jews!" brought down the curtain.[2]

Many of those young demonstrators, weaned on *La Libre Parole* and reared by the Action Française, returned to the subject of the affair as late-middle-aged critics of all that had gone wrong in France since the victory of the Dreyfusard "Syndicate." By the 1930s the café thugs of the turn of the century had graduated from street fights and racetrack brawls to the front offices of militant nationalist organizations, and, serving as the tactical and ideological mentors of a new generation, they prepared a new assault on those whom they held to be France's internal enemies.[3] The old guard's leadership had been decimated by the ravages of time or the war (Drumont was gone and so were Rochefort and Barrès), but sufficient numbers of anti-Dreyfusard veterans remained to revive the strategies and vocabulary of the affair. Charles Maurras, sixty-three years old and half deaf in 1931, still stood at the helm of the neoroyalist, antiparliamentary Action Française, and with him stood his senior partner, sixty-four-year-old Léon Daudet. Their particular memories reached back to the glorious morning of Dreyfus's degradation and to the black day of his rehabilitation; and if they had learned nothing about the truth, they had learned everything about the uses to which lies could be put.

In 1924 a thirty-five-year-old beer-hall tough, serving time in a German prison, wrote that "the magnitude of a lie always contains a certain factor of credibility," and that "the great masses . . . in the primitive simplicity of their minds . . . more easily fall victim to a big lie than to a little one."[4] Adolf Hitler would not have found a partner in Charles Maurras; for now, at least, anti-Semitism could not bridge the differences between the French neoroyalist and the German demagogue. But they had similar ideas about the tactics of modern propaganda, and Maurras knew, as Drumont had known, that for the big lie to work the scene had to be set. Prime Minister's Poincaré's stabilization of the French franc had inaugurated an economic Indian summer that persisted through the collapse of the American stock market in 1929 (one English visitor, noting that the crisis had not yet reached French shores in 1930, suggested that "perhaps God is a Frenchman after all").[5] But immunity from the depression came to an end a year later. Soaring unemployment rates, renewed conflicts between capital and labor, political disarray in the Chamber of Deputies, and waves of immigrants entering France—many of them poor Orthodox Jews from Central and Eastern Europe—raised fears and resuscitated the Action Française.

Putatively Catholic, that organization had suffered a major setback in 1926 when it lost the support of the Holy See. Pope Pius XI may have appreciated the revival of muscular Christianity championed by the Action Française, but he suspected the religious integrity of its leader and the liturgical habits of its followers. In a modern variation on a medieval conflict, Maurras's temporal popularity clashed with the Pope's spiritual authority, and the Vatican weighed in by placing the publications of the Action Française on the Index. Some well-disciplined Catholics followed the orders from Rome, but Maurras's movement, like other forms of pornography, could profit from the publicity surrounding its official condemnation. A crusade that exploited fear and thrived on anger, it enjoyed a resurgence with the upheavals of the 1930s.[6]

Born of the Dreyfus affair, the Action Française came of age with an assault on *L'Affaire Dreyfus* at the Théatre de l'Ambigu. Scores of well-dressed, ill-behaved Camelots du Roi joined free-lance demonstrators and followers of other nationalist groups to protest the "German-Jewish" play. When the actress portraying Lucie Dreyfus read the line, "Our children should be pitied," Camelots shouted back that "the traitor had no pity for France!" Turning on members of the audience whom they suspected of being "Semites," they yelled, "Look at their noses! Down with the Jews!" And violent words gave way to violent deeds, as they had done three decades before. On the night of February 18, police arrested seventy-five members of the Action Française and other organizations for hurling "stink bombs" throughout the theater and for moving the fight onto the Boulevard Saint-Martin. Despite the French playwright's promise that the show would go on (*"Vive la République!"* he shouted back at the hostile audience), the prefect of police suspended the production. Léon Daudet declared victory: "The infamous regime we have vowed to destroy has thrown in the sponge," he wrote. "It has bowed to our force."[7]

But the first affair and the subsequent growth of the Socialist and Communist parties had given birth to other movements, and the theater reopened with actors protected by guards from the Jeunesses Républicaines and the Ligue Contre l'Antisémitisme. Those groups vowed to act against enemies they defined not as the homebred beneficiaries of

Drumont or Maurras but as men out "to transplant into France the morals and methods of Hitler." They may shout anti-German slogans, their opponents said, but their faith was fascist. In late March counter-protests triggered more stink bombs and tear gas, and twelve hundred policemen stood guard in the area surrounding the Théatre de l'Ambigu. "Down with the Germans! Hang the Jews from the lampposts! Spit on Dreyfus!" demonstrators shouted on the night of March 28. Finally, after two more performances, the producers of *L'Affaire Dreyfus*—their actors under siege, the seats and curtains of their theater reeking with the stench of bombs—closed the play for good.[8]

Le Figaro newspaper published a letter summarizing the significance of the "scandalous" production. The letter had been written by members of the Croix de Feu, a movement founded by decorated war veterans committed to the restoration of order in France but aligned with "neither the Right nor the Left"—or so their slogan went. Out to renew discipline and the "spirit of the trenches," the movement appealed to a wide variety of ex-soldiers who wished to reform rather than destroy the republic.[9] But the Croix de Feu also attracted veterans with a sympathy for the extremist tactics of the Action Française, and many of those men had joined the fighting at the Théatre de l'Ambigu. "By recalling the most humiliating hours of our prewar history," their *Figaro* letter announced, the production of *L'Affaire Dreyfus* signaled a new "danger" at a time when "the most profound domestic and foreign problems require national concord."[10]

But that was the point: One group's hour of humiliation was another group's time of triumph, and a working definition of "national concord" proved as elusive in 1931 as it had in 1898—or, for that matter, in 1789, when the birth of the idea gave rise to the first quarrels over its meaning. Like the details of the Revolution, the facts of the affair mattered only to historians in the years after World War I, while as a symbol of national disgrace or national grandeur it attracted legions of interested parties. Maurras and other aging anti-Dreyfusards—who viewed the Revolution and the affair as a duet of national decadence—relished the chance for revenge against old enemies. But most of the demonstrators at the Théatre de l'Ambigu were rooted in the present and anxious about the future. Too young to have participated in, or to have cared about, the affair, they had not been too young to learn its language, and the name Dreyfus, no longer moored to its original context, had become a useful expletive in the lexicon of French protest. As early as 1906, a cattle dealer in the countryside had been forced to pay damages of five hundred francs for using the insult "Dreyfus" against a rival dealer, and two decades later, when a Paris jury accused Léon Daudet of defaming a political opponent, that journalist, always keen to pervert the facts for his own profit, compared his plight to that of the man he detested: "A new Dreyfus affair," Daudet said of his "unjust" conviction, "is now under way."[11] Through the late 1920s and 1930s, newspaper editorialists and the street thugs they subsidized used the epithets of the affair as the lingua franca for a new national crisis.

"I was only an artillery officer, whom a tragic error prevented from following his normal career," Alfred Dreyfus had written a supporter many years before. "Dreyfus the symbol . . . is not me. It is you who created that Dreyfus." Recreated as a "symbol" in the postwar years, he again became a "pretext" (as Maurice Barrès had called him), a "strategic position around which one battles" (as Theodor Herzl had observed). In the quiet study of his Paris apartment, the retired officer, seventy-two years old in 1931, analyzed the new relevance of his name with the same "objective tendency" he had brought to his affair. Montaigne, his companion in exile, described the importance of private conversations in "a back room all our own," and Dreyfus still followed the essayist's lead.[12] Clipping articles from stacks of newspapers, he assembled a scrapbook on the revival of his affair, and next to theater announcements, film reviews, and political editorials, he recorded his private conversations. Above all, he treated the dramatic renditions of his case as "profoundly tactless" invasions of his family's privacy; they may have been entertaining or politically relevant, but they were not, for that man of strict standards, decent. When one journalist commented on Dreyfus's absence from the public scene, he responded again in the margins of his album: "It is not a matter of abstention, because I am passionately interested in all the contemporary publications; but it is too painful to hear the abominable suffering that I experienced come to life again."[13]

Dreyfus retreated from the public role he had never wanted, but did not retire from the status of engaged observer he had always preferred. "Alfred is still well informed about a multitude of issues," his friend Eugène Naville wrote in 1929, "even though he plays no part on the political scene." He had discussed the French occupation of the Ruhr with Edouard Herriot, president of the Radical party and former prime minister of France; and with "clarity, judiciousness and common sense," he offered his opinions (mostly pessimistic) on the devaluation of the French franc. Through Jacques Kayser, a relative of the Hadamard family and a "young Turk" in the Radical party, he kept up-to-date on the policies of center-left groups that traced their finest hour to the affair, and remained interested in the social questions facing France. Curious about the fate of "women factory workers who, having aided the war effort, had grown accustomed to living independently and to earning their own way," he also lamented the wave of "continuous strikes" masterminded by the CGT. Criticizing trade-union ideologues who treated their followers "like common simpletons," he believed that since coal and food shortages hurt working-class families most of all, production must continue "without interruption" so that "supply eclipses demand." His paternalism had not abated, nor had his desire to find a practical solution for the economically disenfranchised. But with "living conditions" deteriorating and "violent anger" rising, he could not help but think that "we are all dancing on a volcano."[14]

Dreyfus's symbol had always cut two ways in France, while abroad, and especially in Britain and the United States, the image had been overwhelmingly positive. As the heroic victim of a corrupt and reactionary system, as a patriotic officer framed by bigoted superiors, Dreyfus had won the support of foreign leaders and citizens' groups. An American "agitation committee" had asked for "a portrait of the hero" that the "Dreyfus Propaganda Society" could enlarge to poster size; and in the aftermath of his pardon an Irish admirer described Dreyfus standing "upon the topmost pinnacle of the 19th century. . . . [In] every civilized country, the honor and earnest sympathy of every right-minded man and woman has rushed out in one great uncontrollable wave. . . . Captain Dreyfus had indeed conquered the world!"[15]

More than a quarter of a century later, new "agitation committees" called on Dreyfus's "moral authority as the living symbol of injured innocence" to help save two Italian immigrants in the United States from the electric chair. In late July 1927, a crowd of twenty thousand gathered in Paris to protest the pending execution of Nicola Sacco and Bartolomeo Vanzetti. Their supporters insisted that the conviction, handed down six years earlier, had not been a rational legal response to a murder conducted during a holdup in a Massachusetts town but an act of state persecution directed against aliens with anarchist sympathies. As the day of execution approached, socialists, communists, and anarchists throughout Europe joined more "peaceful and sensible" citizens (as the always-moderate Eugène Naville observed from Switzerland), and while demonstrators in Geneva invaded cinemas showing American films and attacked shops selling American products, armed guards in Paris protected American news bureaus and the American ambassador. Sacco and Vanzetti on death row—seen as victims of racism, reactionary politics, and a "judicial error"—could not help but conjure up memories of Alfred Dreyfus on Devil's Island. Anatole France, one of the most venerable Dreyfusard survivors, had rallied to Sacco and Vanzetti ("Listen to the appeal of an old man of the old world"), and when political organizers realized that Dreyfus was still alive, they set out to put the old symbol to new use.[16]

Not surprisingly, his response to the case pleased no one. According to the *New York Times*, "Alfred Dreyfus of Devil's Island fame" announced his support for a committee of French notables assembled to make certain that a "miscarriage of justice was not completed" in the Sacco and Vanzetti affair. Interviewed by a correspondent, he asked that his retirement from the public arena be respected ("Dreyfus is living as inconspicuously as possible"), but he also stressed his interest in the American case, "heart and soul." The *New York World* quoted Dreyfus's warning that the execution "would be the greatest moral disaster of many years, fraught with terrible consequences to American justice." Those statements would be enough to convince Dreyfus's enemies that the Jew embraced the cause of anarchists, but they did not satisfy Sacco and Vanzetti's most politically engaged defenders. Dreyfus agreed to sign a petition to the "professors, lawyers and artists" of the United States who should appeal to their government as their French counterparts had done during the affair, but he would go no farther. "Please keep me out of any politics," he asked his interviewer "in appealing tones," and he made it clear that his concerns were "humane," not "political." All that was in keeping for a retired army officer who despised anarchism and who had tried to separate the "political" and "humanitarian" dimensions of his own affair—and all that rekindled accusations of his haughty detachment and rigid militarism. The debate over Dreyfus's engagement in the American affair, like the debate over the guilt or innocence of those two Italian immigrants, came to an end on the morning of August 23, 1927, when the appeals that mattered ran out and Sacco went to his death, followed by Vanzetti.[17]

If Parisians did not react to the news of the execution with massive protests, their silence had more to do with the season than with indifference. Newspaper editors, political leaders, and others who could afford it had fled the capital for vacation homes and seaside hotels.

Always resolute followers of that summer schedule, Alfred and Lucie Dreyfus had gone to the Normandy coast, and when they returned to Paris in the early fall, they moved into a newly constructed apartment in the seventeenth arrondissement on the rue des Renaudes. They had been living with Lucie's widowed mother in the same *quartier* near the Parc Monceau, but after Madame Hadamard's death, they had confronted, along with so many other city dwellers in the 1920s, "the housing crisis which reigns in Paris." To secure a "stable home" for their old age, they decided to purchase rather than rent, and they paid a "formidable sum" for a new penthouse apartment that, with its neoclassical reliefs and art deco designs, was "sun-filled and gay."[18]

The *New York Times* had it right. Alfred and Lucie Dreyfus tried to live as inconspicuously as possible. During their courtship Alfred had written from his garrison at Bourges about his "obstinate refusal to spend time with tiresome men"; surrounded by fellow officers whom he found "sometimes disagreable and often spiteful and envious," he preferred the "sympathetic milieu" of family and close friends.[19] That preference continued forty years later, except that now his oldest comrades—and many members of his family—were dying off.

"One after the other they disappear," Alfred had written after the death of his "excellent friend," Joseph Reinach, in 1921. Two years later he lost the companion who had introduced him to the inner circle of Radical politicians, and who had become, through their frequent correspondence during the war, one of his closest confidants. The Marquise Arconati-Visconti, increasingly "solitary" in her advanced age, had moved from the town house on the rue Barbet-de-Jouy to a smaller apartment close to the Eiffel Tower and the Ecole Militaire. She had lost many of her friends (they had died or fallen from her favor), but she never lost her singular opinions on what had gone wrong in France since the heroic epoch which began with Gambetta's republic and ended with Dreyfus's affair. Until her death at the age of eighty-three, she continued to chastise her old nemesis Clemenceau; for the marquise, Père-la-Victoire ("the father of victory") was "Perd-la-Victoire" ("the loser of victory"), the politician who had bungled the Versailles treaty and who had never been hard enough on Germans abroad or working-class rebels at home. In so many ways that strong-minded woman—fierce republican, fierce nationalist, and Clemenceau's competitor for the title of Tiger—embodied the strange odyssey of radicalism in France.[20]

But no older woman competed for Alfred Dreyfus's affection more successfully than his sister Henriette. His tutor as a child and guardian as a young adult, she had been the first to encourage him to try for the Ecole Polytechnique and to serve the cause of *revanche* not as an industrialist but as an army officer. A widow for nearly three decades, Henriette kept her estate at Villemarie and enjoyed hosting family reunions until 1932, when she died in Carpentras at the age of eighty-four. Alfred seems to have left no record of his response to Henriette's death (there were so few people left to write to), but he had always worshipped his oldest sister, his "second mother." Her departure from Mulhouse in 1870 had been one of his first "sad impressions," and he must have been deeply grieved by her passing. Of Raphael and Jeanette Dreyfus's seven children, now only Alfred and his youngest sister, Rachel, remained.

Following a seven-year absence, Lucie and Alfred had returned to the Navilles' home above Lake Geneva in 1921. "After years of interruption," Lucie wrote in their guest book under her last entry of July 1914, "after the cruel and agonizing world war joyously ended with the return of Alsace-Lorraine to the mother country, I am happy to be with our excellent friends in the profound peace of the countryside."[21] While Lucie and Hélène played the piano *à quatre mains* or knitted and talked in the Navilles' bright, high-ceilinged salon, Alfred and Eugène, now reluctant retirees from horseback riding, took long walks and reminisced. Through the years, Dreyfus's host had learned to shield his famous friend from curiosity seekers, and aside from periodic boat trips on Lake Geneva, they remained within the confines of the Naville estate.[22] At times they discussed the "general political situation," but since "old age puts limits on future projects," as Naville noted during one visit with Dreyfus, the two men mostly looked back to the events that had most marked their lives—the "Great War" and the affair. Supporters and critics who once dominated newspaper headlines now appeared in back-page obituaries, and the transitions triggered memories. It surprised neither man that Esterhazy died in 1923 "in obscurity and shame" in the village of Harpenden north of London. He had taken a pseudonym (Count Jean de Voilemont) that captured the legitimacy he had always wanted, and, depending on the source of the news, he had grown rich as a traveling salesman or had fallen into dissolution as the drug-addicted manager of a brothel. And he had been subsidized, rumor had it, by "hush money" from former French officers. Esterhazy's background suggested that he would earn his living selling something, and profiting from prostitution fit his style.[23]

While old Dreyfusards reacted with "bitterness" and "fury" when they recalled the treachery of Esterhazy and his coconspirators, Dreyfus remained objective and, according to his family, even "serene."[24] He still referred to the "real traitors" as "miserable wretches," but they had been vanquished, and he looked back on their crimes like an archivist cataloging dusty dossiers. As far as recollections of the affair went, he broke his calm demeanor only once, in 1930, on reading the published notebooks of Maximilien von Schwarzkoppen. Those documents confirmed that the German military attaché had been approached on numerous occasions by the French hawker of secrets, Esterhazy, and that Schwarzkoppen, who died in 1917, felt remorse for not having come to Dreyfus's defense. When he drew his last breath (the story went) he thought of the affair and cried out, "Frenchmen, listen to me! Alfred Dreyfus is innocent. . . . All the rest was forgeries and lies." Schwarzkoppen's deathbed words might have been very different, but the published exposé of his relations with Esterhazy mattered more. And when Dreyfus read the account, his anger, expressed so often in prison and suppressed so often since, resurfaced. "Oh, the scoundrel!" he called Esterhazy, shouting loud enough for his family to hear. "The beastly man." A Paris newspaper carried extracts from the attaché's memoirs, and Dreyfus, returning to his public mode of cool objectivity, wrote a letter to the editor: "General von Schwarzkoppen acted as an honest man in revealing all that he knew," Dreyfus observed, "though it is profoundly regrettable that he did not fulfill his duty on the day he realized that a judicial crime may have been committed."[25]

Carefully drafted letters to editors, scrapbook annotations penned in private, and quiet conversations with Naville and, less often, with Pierre served as the only arenas in which Dreyfus broached the subject of his affair. It was otherwise off limits. While his closest brother had looked back on the case as a hard-won victory full of lessons worth teaching his grandchildren, Alfred looked back on the suffering. Many years before, in a letter to a Dreyfusard supporter, Julien Benda, he had maintained that despite his "objective tendency," he was "very capable of enthusiasm for noble ideas, of indignation against vile acts, [and] of a sensitivity to things of the heart." But he could not "analyze" his own feelings or "contemplate" his own person: "I have suffered too much to be able to talk about my case from a sentimental standpoint." The memory of his rehabilitation could not eradicate the tortures of Devil's Island and his nightmares—the sudden "shrieks" that jolted him awake from grotesque dreams of "double buckles," armed guards, and spider-infested cells—persisted three decades after the fact. Lucie, still the strict monitor of her husband's health, made certain that family members visiting the apartment on the rue des Renaudes never introduced the topic of the affair.[26]

Those Sunday gatherings had grown to include eight grandchildren. Shortly after the war, with the Paris Peace Conference under way and the city overrun by American soldiers and foreign diplomats, Captain Pierre Dreyfus, in full-dress uniform with Croix de Guerre, had married Marie Baur, daughter of an investment banker and granddaughter of a rabbi. Their wedding, like that of Pierre's mother and father, took place in two stages and in two locales—at the town hall of their arrondissement, with Joseph Reinach as witness, and in their Paris synagogue. Though tempted by a post with the Armée de l'Orient (which would have made him one of the youngest captains in the colonial forces, his father reported with pride), Pierre returned to civilian life. Trained as an engineer at the Ecole Centrale, he worked as an industrial inspector with the Ministry of Reconstruction and later invested in French textile and rubber companies. He traveled in search of clients to Switzerland, Romania, and the United States, and though not all of his enterprises succeeded (he, too, felt the impact of the international economic crisis), he lived comfortably in the early 1930s with his wife and four children— Françoise, Nicole, Charles, and Aline—on the Square de l'Albioni, just across the Seine from the Ecole Militaire.[27]

His sister Jeanne also had four children. Simone, born in the midst of the war, and Madeleine, born one week after the armistice, were followed by two sons, Jean-Louis and Etienne. Their father had tried to resume his medical career in Paris, but—plagued by physical ailments and stress caused by the trauma of battlefront service—he had moved his family to the "gentler climate and more tranquil life" of Toulouse, his native city in southwestern France. That departure "seriously upset" Alfred and Lucie, who had grown especially attached to their two oldest grandchildren, Simone and Madeleine; it left "a great void" in their lives. But ill-timed investments in a brother's business forced Pierre-Paul Lévy to return to Paris, and as the doctor worked to reestablish his practice, health, and finances, Alfred and Lucie, delighted with the family reunion, if not with the circumstances that prompted it, helped Jeanne care for the children.[28]

Youngsters play favorites and grandparents respond, and while Lucie felt close to Simone, Alfred was devoted to Madeleine. Those sentimental alliances may have dated from the period shortly after Simone's birth, when Jeanne suffered scarlet fever and Lucie took care of mother and child. A few years later Madeleine had also fallen ill, from an ear inflammation, which, given the methods of treatment, proved nearly fatal. Her grandparents waited with "extreme anxiety" while she underwent surgery in a Paris clinic, but the eight-year-old girl took after her mother in more ways than one. Thirty years earlier, Lucie had described Jeanne's strong and "hearty appearance," like "one of those big blond Alsatian babies raised in the open air of the countryside"; with her "fair skin and rosy cheeks," she resembled Alfred's family, while Pierre looked more like the Hadamards. Madeleine, the image of her mother, had the same robust constitution, and though her hearing would be diminished after the operation, she recovered quickly.[29]

On Devil's Island Dreyfus had felt a constant sadness that he would never see his children again. Years passed before he met his son and daughter in Carpentras, as if for the first time, and he always regretted his absence from their early childhood. Through Madeleine, however, he could see Jeanne as she must have been during their long separation; and though constrained by age, illness, and the antiquated habits of his own formal upbringing, he tried to recapture with his favorite granddaughter the years he had been denied with Jeanne.

When the grandchildren came to the rue des Renaudes apartment on Sunday afternoons, they followed a weekly ritual of filing down the corridor to their grandfather's office. Dreyfus appreciated Madeleine's precocious sense of punctuality (she was, the family said, the "best behaved" of the youngsters), and she, in turn, must have understood the meaning of the large pocket watch that her grandfather had constantly at hand. The sweet smell of tobacco filled his room (the strong cigars of Devil's Island had given way to a pipe), and near a cyclamen, his favorite flower, a stamp collection lined the desk that once held military maps and legal briefs. Dreyfus greeted each grandchild with a kiss, recounted the history of a particularly colorful stamp, and then, while Lucie took Simone and the others for an afternoon walk in the Parc Monceau, he "spontaneously sang tunes of the epoch" to Madeleine. Spontaneity had never been his strong suit, nor had a pleasing voice, but his granddaughter represented a safe audience of one, and she most enjoyed his comical rendition of the popular children's song *"Entends-tu le coucou, Malirette?"* ("Do you hear the cuckoo, Malirette?").[30]

As the subject of one of the first motion pictures, Dreyfus had played an indirect role in the history of the French film industry, and

years later he enjoyed taking Madeleine or Pierre's wife, Marie, to the
grand movie houses that lined the Champs-Elysées and other avenues
not far from the rue des Renaudes. But more often he ventured out
alone. A *boulevardier* in his youth, he returned in his old age to the habit
of strolling along Paris streets and observing city life. Now, however,
he walked only a short distance and took buses and metros to more
distant neighborhoods. And the objects of his interest were no longer
racetracks and fashionable restaurants, but stamp collectors' booths off
the Champs-Elysées and card-playing rooms at the Cercle Militaire on
the Place St. Augustin. Bridge had always appealed to him, and he
excelled at the strategy required by that most quiet and precise of card
games. At the Cercle Militaire, Colonel Dreyfus, with his wire-rimmed
glasses and the rosette of the Legion of Honor in the buttonhole of his
three-piece suit, looked more like a distinguished academic who had
done his part in the war than like the most infamous convict of Devil's
Island. The stoop of his shoulders had become pronounced, and he
walked with a cane, and on the streets of Paris or on the boardwalk at
Trouville, he would be recognized only by the occasional old ally or
enemy who had known him personally. One employee at his bank,
another decorated veteran of about the same age, always greeted his
client "with respect." They had first met nearly four decades earlier, as
prisoner and guard on Devil's Island.[31]

In the 1920s and 1930s, as a "lady patroness" with the Comité de
Bienfaisance Israélite, Lucie followed a long family tradition by engaging
in volunteer activities. Her great-grandmother had not only protested
the "cannibalistic" desecration of Jewish cemeteries during the Reign of
Terror; she had also established a "ladies' society" that, in keeping with
"the customs of the oldest Jewish families," made relief work and other
charitable efforts "a fixed and stable rule" in her home. "God created
holy days for the poor as well as for the rich," Rebecca Lambert Hadamard taught her family, and, along with providing clothes to poor
Jewish women, she sent her children out to distribute alms to needy
households. Years later, Lucie's parents continued that regular support
of charity work, though often they helped at arm's length by channeling
donations through the Paris Jewish Consistory. Lucie, however, revived her grandmother's custom when she traveled into city neighborhoods with food and clothes for destitute Jewish families. Entering the
Marais quarter of central Paris, or Belleville to the northeast, she would
recall the many trips she had made to the Colonial Office across the

Seine with other boxes of provisions destined for her husband in exile.[32]

War and revolution in Eastern and Central Europe had driven hundreds of thousands of refugees west, and in the years immediately following 1917, nearly two thousand anti-Jewish riots in eastern regions had prompted the mass emigration of Jewish families. They came for the most part from Poland and Russia, but they were joined by Hungarian, Romanian, Lithuanian, and Latvian Jews and by Jews from Turkey, the Levant, and North Africa. In the early 1930s, with the Weimar Republic near collapse and Hitler near victory, thousands of German Jews began to enter France. Of an immigrant population approaching 3,000,000, Jews would, at first, account for barely 150,000, but as many as 90,000 would settle in Paris (more than the entire Jewish population of France at the time of the Dreyfus affair), and through the 1930s the national total of French and foreign Jews would move toward 300,000, with two-thirds of that number based in the capital and its environs.[33] Hoping to reinvigorate the economy by replenishing the labor force lost in the war, the French government welcomed the early waves of refugees, the Jews and non-Jews, the Polish miners, and the Italian agricultural workers. When Britain and the United States began to close their borders to new immigrants in the early 1920s, France, with its promise of economic opportunity and its revolutionary image as a promised land of equality, became a primary goal of settlement. As the numbers grew, however, along with the realization that new workers could not turn back the oncoming depression, hostility greeted foreigners, who were now seen as competitors, and the cascade of anger that showered down on all refugees fell with particular force on the Jews.[34]

Anti-Semitic demonstrations rocked the Belleville quarter, a neighborhood of recent Jewish settlement with a high concentration of immigrants attracted to communist, socialist, and Zionist movements; and Charles Maurras's cane-wielding Camelots moved their protests into the Marais, the long-established home of the city's most Orthodox Jews. Condemned as Bolsheviks (or as capitalists), as Russian agents (or as German sympathizers), as miserably poor (or as inordinately rich), as outlandishly exotic (or as suspiciously assimilated), they had come in too many numbers and too quickly. For every French Jewish journalist who promised his coreligionists that France would be their "veritable Eldorado," scores of commentators from *Action Française* and less venerable newspapers described Paris as "Canaan-on-the-Seine." And the talents of intruders counted for nothing: Albert Einstein—whose rumored invitation to join a French university raised the hackles of anti-Semites—was judged in the same vein as poor, Yiddish-speaking tailors and the indigent in search of jobs. Precisely one century had passed since Alfred Dreyfus's grandparents had immigrated to a French city in search of a better life; but Mulhouse in the 1830s offered prosperity and tolerance, while Paris in the throes of depression offered only a few islands of employment in a sea of contempt.[35]

Native French Jews of long standing responded in different ways to the immigrants' plight. Lucie Dreyfus's efforts with the Comité de Bienfaisance addressed their most immediate needs in the most traditional manner. Established under the First Empire to aid "in money and in kind indigent members of the Israelite faith," that committee branched out to provide medical care, education, and housing subsidies and services to the elderly. It created a special organization to assist "families and children," and in the 1930s, under the direction of Madame la Baronne Edmond de Rothschild, the group mobilized other affluent Jewish women, including Lucie Dreyfus, who would soon become vice president of the general committee and its highest-ranking woman. Lucie helped conduct surveys on unemployment rates and shortages of heating coal in the "Pletzl" (the Yiddish quarter near the St. Paul metro station, inhabited by many of the poorest immigrants) and in the neighborhoods near the Place de la République (populated by Jewish tailors and artisans). Accompanied by her granddaughter Simone, she visited the "horrible hovels" of Polish Jews and, on hot summer days, witnessed conditions like those described in a novel about Belleville in the 1930s: "Seas of putrescent water, urine heated in the flaming sun, stagnant in the narrow courtyards. Up above, women sew silently in rooms, while tubercular humorists press pants."[36]

Supporting his wife's volunteer work, Alfred Dreyfus responded in his own way to the immigrant crisis. "Charity, which is to say almsgiving, is not sufficient," he had written many years before; "what is needed above all is . . . openness of heart, and the free communication between rich and poor. Material deeds," he noted in his Devil's Island journal, must be accompanied by "moral actions," and that put him in mind of Pascal: "Il faut servir les pauvres pauvrement."[37] Indifferent to the rituals of Judaism ("He believed in God," confirmed one friend in the 1920s, "without practicing"),[38] and opposed to the extremism triggered on the right and left by the swell of refugees, Dreyfus focused on the cultural dimensions of the problem, and appealed, as he had done in his own exile, to the "cult of humanity." Like his friend Salomon Reinach, Joseph's brother, Dreyfus found one overriding ideal in the traditions of his ancestors: "Judaism is the noblest and most considerable moral personality which Humanity has ever known," Reinach had written, "because . . . Judaism represents that which must impose itself one day on all consciences, the ideal of Justice."[39]

The third Reinach brother, Théodore, had taken the occasion of a book on the Dreyfus affair, published in 1924, to make the connections between that ideal and contemporary France. In the concluding pages of his *Histoire Sommaire de l'Affaire Dreyfus,* Reinach described how the Jews' "valiant civic and military duty" during the war had "contributed to the destruction of the evil work of Drumont and his subalterns." But the historian also warned against the illusion that prejudice, with its "deep and multiple roots," had "disappeared from our country." A "sharp revival" of anti-Semitism accompanied the upheavals "born of the war," Reinach wrote, and it was essential that "French Jews, remaining deaf to the temptation of Zionism and loyal to the models of the French Revolution, quickly assimilate their immigrant coreligionists in order to remove all pretext for an offensive recurrence of the spirit of intolerance which has not been disarmed." Forging the links between the Revolution, the affair, and the postwar crisis, Reinach quoted the nineteenth-century historian and Hebraic scholar Ernest Renan: "When the National Assembly declared the emancipation of the Jews in 1791," Renan had written, "it paid little attention to race. It believed that men should be judged not by the blood which runs in their veins, but by their moral and intellectual value. It is the glory of France that these questions take on a human dimension." Overlooking Renan's less enlightened comments on the Jews' collective responsibility for the killing of Christ, Reinach focused instead on his praise of Jewish emancipation. He believed that Renan's "noble statement should remain the motto and rule of conduct of all good Frenchman!" and Alfred Dreyfus, who had studied Renan on Devil's Island, believed that Jewish immigrants in France should learn the motto and follow the rule. Along with shelter and sustenance, they needed instruction in "civic development," the French language, and the history of their new nation.[40]

In 1926 Dreyfus joined the honorary committee of the newly established Accueil Fraternel Israélite. Other members included Grand Rabbi Israël Lévi; Léon Zadoc-Kahn, son of the former grand rabbi; Léon Blum, the Socialist party leader whose early political education dated from the Dreyfus affair; and, as the organization's treasurer, Pierre Dreyfus. A year earlier, *L'Univers israélite,* a publication reflecting the views of the native Jewish community, had called for a special group "charged with the task of facilitating the assimilation of Jewish immigrants into French life." Worried that youngsters would "fall under the bad influence of the street, the café [and] the movie house," *L'Univers israélite* also feared "the worst"—that poor immigrants would be seduced by anarchist and communist "cells." Believing that "Jews in general are endowed with natural abilities of adaptation and assimilation," the paper also insisted that immigrants "disdainfully referred to as 'Polak' will become good Frenchmen while remaining Israelites." And the words mattered: *Juif*, like "Polak," often signified the unassimilated immigrant, while *israélite*, increasingly, though never neatly, stood for French Jews with a religious, rather than a cultural, interest in Judaism. With the founding of the Accueil Fraternel (first given the precise but cumbersome title, "Association for the Instruction of Jewish Foreigners Residing in France"), the native community set out to create libraries, night schools, and information offices to assist immigrants, and they aimed to teach French to those Jews who knew only Yiddish.[41]

The objects of their program, however, did not always cooperate, and the patience of native Jews did not always hold. Alfred Dreyfus's frame of reference was the fin de siècle, and like his brother Mathieu's views of labor relations, Alfred's notions of assimilation were, in the 1920s and 1930s, dated. The Alsatian Jews who had fled to the French interior after the Franco-Prussian War—and the Russian and Polish Jews who had come in their wake following the pogroms of the 1880s—had been relatively few in number and generally eager to adopt the ways of their new homeland. But now, after the deluge, Jewish families long established in Paris were vastly outnumbered by immigrants who brought with them religious customs they had no intention of abandoning and, for some, radical politics, including Zionist politics, they had no intention of compromising. Native Jews, most of them opposed to ideas of cultural pluralism (Yiddish theater, for example, was not rich and enlightening but "pernicious and inferior"), believed that immigrants should learn from the example set by those who had come before; they should be grateful for their sanctuary, and, at a time when their enemies were on the rise, prudent in their actions. "Our foreign brethren are the guests of France," went a warning from the Union Scolaire, an organization that subsumed the Accueil Fraternel Israélite in 1931. "They must not even let it appear that they forget it." A short time later, however, the president of the Paris Consistory, Robert de Rothschild, unleashed his frustration like the short-tempered host of a gathering disrupted by an ill-mannered mob; "If [refugees] are not happy here," he announced, "let them leave. They are guests whom we have warmly received, but they should not go about rocking the boat."[42]

Pierre Dreyfus understood the family traditions that led his mother to the Comité de Bienfaisance and his father to the Accueil Fraternel Israélite. He, too, had volunteered at times of crisis in customary ways—as in the winter of 1910 when the Seine overflowed its banks and Pierre loaded his car with food and clothes for needy families; or in the late 1920s when he organized charitable aid for refugees. He continued to work with committees established by Jewish notables, but as part of a generation unencumbered by the habits of the nineteenth century, he parted company with senior members of the Paris Consistory. Challenging the limited scope of cultural agencies and relief organizations, he turned instead to the defense of Jewish refugees and to the politics, domestic and international, of immigration.[43]

As a director of the Comité pour la Defense des Droits des Israélites en Europe Centrale et Orientale, and as a member of the Comité National de Secours aux Réfugiés Allemands Victimes de l'Antisémitisme, Pierre called for greater government involvement in the refugee crisis and for a more vigorous response to the growing wave of anti-Semitism abroad and in France. The leadership of the Consistory, ready to express its anticommunism but wanting no part of "political activity," rejected proposals submitted by Pierre and his codirector, Boris Gourevitch, a Russian refugee in Paris. Their plans had called for immigrant settlements in the provinces and colonies, and the creation of jobs for French workers in refugee-owned enterprises. But the Dreyfus-Gourevitch Committee continued the fight when the government moved toward anti-immigration measures in 1934, and when some native Jews supported the removal of their foreign coreligionists to America, Africa, or back to Germany. The refugees' "rights of residence and work" should be "boldly defended," Pierre's group announced, and France, long honored as a place of sanctuary, should not "serve as a simple transit country." Wanting "to save the lives and the dignity of refugees," the Dreyfus-Gourevitch Committee confronted hard-liners who wished "to get rid of them all."[44]

Meanwhile, Pierre's father remained aloof from the internecine feuds of the Paris Consistory; he had witnessed similar battles in the late stages of his own affair, when men of goodwill lost sight of their goals in the thicket of politics, and he had little talent for arbitration. Above all, the society in which Dreyfus now lived seemed to have abandoned the qualities of "disinterestedness" he had praised so often. The affair he remembered had been about transcendant moral values, and he believed that the men and women who had rallied to his cause had triumphed by rejecting partisanship for the "cult of humanity," for the ideal of "French justice." In 1927 Julien Benda published a long essay, *La Trahison des clercs,* which captured many of the same concerns. Benda took contemporary intellectuals to task for allowing "political passions" to seduce them from their historic role of remaining outside the "chorus of hatreds among the races and political factions." The true calling of the intellectual—engagement in reasoned objectivity and disengagement from the passions of self-interest—had been threatened, if not destroyed, by the postwar retreat from "disinterest" and by the headlong rush toward party ideologies that were by definition prejudicial and divisive. Dreyfus and the Dreyfusard Benda shared the same sense of regret.[45]

While his son pressed the campaign for Jewish refugees—with an interest in politics but not parties, and with a commitment reminiscent of those who had pressed the campaign for the prisoner in exile—Dreyfus spent an increasing amount of time at home, classifying stamps, reading newspapers, and writing letters—including one to the minister of war. Though long accustomed to rejections from government officials, Dreyfus felt a keen disappointment when the minister denied his request for a *carte de combattant* recognizing his battlefront duty in the war. His service at the Aisne in 1917 and at Verdun in 1918 had lasted less than the required three months (went the official response), and since the colonel had not been wounded during his brief engagements, he was ineligible for special status as a front-line veteran. The only battle for which he would be remembered had taken place in French Guiana, and ex-convicts from Devil's Island received no *cartes de combattant.*[46]

Since the early 1920s Dreyfus had suffered a series of illnesses that his friend Naville—using the vocabulary of another century—had described as "infirmities of an interior type." Treated in Switzerland and, later, in Paris by Pierre-Paul Lévy and another physician, Professor Marion, Dreyfus visited Geneva again and appeared to be in fine health. "The terrible physical and moral ordeal that he endured," Naville wrote in 1933, "no longer seems to weigh on his shoulders; and he does not act old, despite his seventy-four years." But on another summer trip to Switzerland the following year, Dreyfus fell ill and was rushed from a village resort north of Neuchâtel to a clinic in nearby Bienne and then to

Paris. Following emergency prostate surgery, he developed uremic poisoning. Dr. Lévy and Professor Marion consulted a battery of experts, but for "a long year," wrote Dreyfus's son, his "poor body suffered horribly."[47]

On Devil's Island, in a rare moment of black humor, Dreyfus had described himself as "a little like an invalid on a bed of torture . . . who lives because his duty requires it, and who always asks his doctor, 'When will my tortures end?' And since the doctor always responds, 'Soon, soon,' he ends up by asking himself when that 'soon' will come . . . it's been announced for quite a long time."[48] The same dogged strength that kept Dreyfus alive in exile prolonged his life through the early summer of 1935. Bedridden and under Lucie's constant care, he was "sustained" not only by his wife, but by Pierre, Jeanne, and the grandchildren, who made frequent visits to the rue des Renaudes apartment. Still the image of her mother and still her grandfather's favorite companion, Madeleine Lévy was now sixteen, and as the weeks passed she noted the old man's "tender and vulnerable look," his "inward stare," as Madeleine's brother, Jean-Louis, recalled it. Pierre came to visit every day, and on Thursday, July 11, 1935, his seventy-five-year-old father took his hand and held it in silence, as if "passing along his final thought." The next afternoon, at five o'clock, Dreyfus died.[49]

"He lived an intense interior life," his son wrote of Dreyfus's late years and of the legacy of Devil's Island, "but no longer knew how to externalize his feelings. He had lost the habit of expressing himself, and, besides, he found it repugnant to complain, to expose his sufferings in public; he appeared very cold, very distant, to those who hardly knew him."[50] The great majority of those who did know him held memories not of a young officer enjoying the distractions of Paris in the 1880s like a character out of a Maupassant story, but of a General Staff *stagiaire* turned prematurely old by the "martyrdom" of his exile. One of his lawyers during the affair, Henri Mornard, had felt "profound regret" that Dreyfus did not "let himself go, outside of his family circle. . . . One would know him better, and he would only profit by it."[51] On occasion, a journalist who did not know him tried to understand, and Dreyfus, "consoled" by that rare sign of sympathy, noted it down in his diary. "Because the Captain . . . abhorred exposing his wounds," the newspaper *Radical* had reported, "because he suffered with modesty, they judged that he was not sensitive, that he had a cold heart. They wanted more outwardness, more theatre, more of the high-flown; they wanted . . . a bad actor (*"cabotin"*)." Dreyfus knew they wanted an Esterhazy, but they got instead a "philosopher" who talked about "Justice, Law and Truth," as another reporter put it, before he talked about himself. And when pushed to describe the details of his torment on Devil's Island he responded with generalities: "All I wish," he said, "is that no man suffers more than I have suffered."[52]

Dreyfusards had good reason to criticize the "victim's" personality, but their assessments of his faults often missed the mark. He did not stand "abysmally below" his affair (as Clemenceau had said), nor did he remain blind to its "faith" (as the poet Péguy had suggested)—if anything, Dreyfus imbued his case with too much faith and placed himself too high above it.[53] But archetypes and stereotypes (and Dreyfus served as both for allies and enemies alike) make no room for complexity, and only the family knew Dreyfus's true character—the family and the few close friends who had become like family. Gabriel Monod, with his "profound, almost paternal attachment" to Dreyfus, had called him "a grand stoic . . . with an antique soul," and Joseph Reinach, often tempted by florid prose, put it best when he put it most simply in a letter to Mathieu: "Your brother . . . is charming," Reinach had written. "But what a type!"[54]

"Colonel Dreyfus has died," the newspaper *L'Oeuvre* reported on July 13, "at a moment when France seems divided again, as it had been for or against him." His case "remains in the memory of contemporaries," the paper went on, "and only a short time ago a theater production . . . on the Dreyfus Affair provoked a violent demonstration on the *grands boulevards*."[55] Even more recently, in February 1934, and with even more violence, Maurras's Camelots du Roi and other demonstrators shouting "Down with the thieves! Down with the assassins!" had filled the Place de la Concorde across the river from the National Assembly. A coterie of politicians had been implicated in a scandal masterminded by a bond dealer—a naturalized French citizen (he was a Ukrainian Jew) named Serge Stavisky—and the entire government came under attack when Stavisky turned up dead in an Alpine retreat he kept with his mistress. Police officials called it suicide, but Maurras called it murder choreographed by corrupt politicians out to silence their co-conspirator. On the night of February 6, 1934, the forces of order confronted one hundred thousand demonstrators brandishing pistols, canes, bottles, stones, iron pikes, and long sticks tipped with razor blades to slash the tendons of police horses. From the right and left, extremists turned their focus on the parliament they hated with equal intensity, and while some in the crowd waved the tricolor and sang the "Marseillaise," others, carrying red banners, joined in the Communist "Internationale." By midnight fifteen men were dead and more than fifteen hundred wounded, and by the next day, the government had resigned—the first cabinet of the Third French Republic to be forced out by the protests of the crowd.[56]

Twenty-four hours after Alfred Dreyfus's death, on the eve of Bastille Day, 1935, memories of February 6 remained vivid among demonstrators who planned a new round of parades. In the early and unofficial stages of their "Popular Front," Socialists, Communists, and Radicals aimed to show their strength in the friendly neighborhoods east of the Place de la Concorde, between the Place de la Bastille and the Place de la Nation, and included in their Rassemblement Populaire would be many Dreyfusard veterans of the League of the Rights of Man. At the same time members of the Croix de Feu, which now claimed hundreds of thousands of members throughout France, planned their own parade on their own turf, at the Arc de Triomphe, west up the Champs-Elysées. Anticipating Bastille Day, the Communist paper *L'Humanité* took the occasion of its short obituary on Dreyfus to present a longer recapitulation of his affair and to compare the divisions of that time with the crisis facing contemporary France. "The immense gathering for liberty which will form tomorrow," the paper announced on July 13, "will show the reactionaries of today the strength of the people they intend to enslave." And in its turn, the radical right-wing newspaper *Je Suis Partout*—anti-Semitic and antirepublican—promised that "patriots" would hold their ground at the Etoile and that their enemies would "not pass."[57]

Its troops spread thin, the government faced a dual dilemma. Preparing for street demonstrations, police mobilized throughout the city, while, on a more festive note, military authorities planned their Bastille Day review. Since the late 1880s, when General Boulanger used July 14 to thrill his antiparliamentary followers, and since 1906, when rumors spread that Dreyfus would attend the Bastille Day parade and incite demonstrations, government officials had looked on the festival with mixed emotions. And the Place de la Concorde was particularly worrisome: The setting for the execution of a king nearly 150 years before, its symbolic significance as a place of protest had been revived by the events of 1934. In keeping with those memories, a veterans' group announced just prior to Bastille Day that Parliament remained "a collection of old crocks who would never do anything worthwhile except under the pressure of the street."[58]

On Sunday morning, July 14, 1935, with the Rassemblement Populaire lining up to the east and the Croix de Feu gathering to the west, mounted cuirassiers, sporting the high-plumed helmets and armor breastplates of another age, rehearsed the drills they would perform a few hours later on the Place de la Concorde. At the same moment, Alfred Dreyfus's funeral cortege left the rue des Renaudes on its way to the Montparnasse Cemetery across the Seine. Lucie planned a simple religious service, attended only by the immediate family and by Grand Rabbi Julien Weill. At a gravesite close to that of another famous Jewish officer—Captain Armand Mayer, killed in a duel by the Marquis de Morès a half century before—Rabbi Weill would recite the traditional Hebrew prayers and end with the mourner's *kaddish*. En route to Montparnasse, the Dreyfus cortege traveled down the Champs-Elysées, and as it passed through the Place de la Concorde cavalry troops stopped their maneuvers to observe a sacred military ritual. Thirty-six summers before, at Rennes, soldiers had turned their backs in the presence of Alfred Dreyfus, but on Bastille Day 1935 they turned their horses to face the black hearse passing by. Not knowing the identity of the man they honored, the cuirassiers raised their swords in a silent salute of respect for the dead.[59]

CHAPTER XXIII

Generations

"On the night of the day that we brought my father to his final resting place," forty-five-year-old Pierre Dreyfus recalled in 1936, "I took from my library the extraordinary *Cinq années de ma vie* and the admirable *Histoire de l'Affaire* by Joseph Reinach. I reread their long chapters," and if, "controlling my grief . . . I did not shed a tear during my father's last moments . . . I cried like a child on reading the pages that traced his long and frightful martyrdom." Compiling selections from his father's carefully catalogued diaries, scrapbooks, and letters, Pierre published *Souvenirs et correspondance,* a study of "the essential phases of the Affair." He did not aim to debate the case ("the historical truth is established today without question," he said) but "to pay filial homage to the man who will be, for future generations, one of the purest heroes of our dear France."[1]

The book, however, had a purpose beyond hagiography. "The Great War has ended, accumulating ruins," went the opening line of its dedication page, and "among the principal actors of the grand drama of the Dreyfus affair," including those who "fought in opposite camps, how many found each other again on battlefields sharing the same love for the fatherland." Offering a representative roll call of Dreyfusards and anti-Dreyfusards who had died in the war, Pierre listed "Lieutenant Colonel du Paty de Clam; Lieutenant Colonel Henry's only son; Joseph Reinach's only son; the only son of my uncle Mathieu Dreyfus; and still

441

so many others who fell on the field of honor." The work of a veteran of Verdun, *Souvenirs et correspondance* was Pierre Dreyfus's gift to "the admirable men who . . . threw themselves into the fray to defend my father; to my glorious wartime comrades; [and] to the young people who did not know the great battles." Recognizing that the ideological battles of the 1930s recalled earlier divisions ("the passions of the affair are not yet completely extinguished"), and hoping for a new "sacred union," Pierre stressed the harmony among Dreyfusards, rather than the infighting, and told the story of an honorable era. The other dimension of the affair, the schism of the nation, he wanted to lay to rest along with his father.[2]

But Alfred Dreyfus's passing also opened a floodgate of very different memories. While Pierre worked on his book, and while historians, journalists, and filmmakers found new relevance in the subject of the affair, the Socialist leader Léon Blum published seven articles in the weekly *Marianne,* inspired by the "surge of memories that Captain Dreyfus's death brought forth." Offspring of an Alsatian Jewish family (Blum's grandmother came from Ribeauvillé), young legal assistant to Labori at the Zola trial, and successor to Jaurès at the helm of the Socialist party, Blum was among those "admirable men" who had joined "the fray" to defend the prisoner on Devil's Island, though his memoirs made it clear that he had fought more for the symbol than for the man. Acknowledging the "stoic purity" of that "simple and serious" officer, Blum also criticized his "servitude" to the army and accused him of having had "no affinity" with his own affair. "Had he not been Dreyfus," Blum asked, "would he have been a 'dreyfusard?' "[3]

Using his reflections on the case to draw parallels between the 1890s and the 1930s, Blum conjured up the person of Dreyfus only to evoke, like a Proustian *madeleine,* memories of a *"temps retrouvé."* Most important were recollections of Jaurès's heroism, Zola's eloquence, and the revolutionary spirit of the campaign. It was a "profound human crisis," Blum wrote, "less extensive and less prolonged than the French Revolution and the Great War, but as violent." Praising Dreyfusards who challenged the status quo, Blum condemned the caution of Scheurer-Kestner, the Reinachs, and most members of the Dreyfus family. He admired only Mathieu—much as the Communist *L'Humanité* had done at the moment of his death in 1930—and believed that if "the unshakable brother," with his "chivalrous grandeur," had followed his "natural inclination," he would have sided with the "revolutionaries" rather than with the "politicals."[4] But when the family showed too much respect for government institutions—above all, for the military—they made a "fatal error." And those "fainthearted" reactions had been repeated throughout the established Jewish community. "The rich Jews, the middle-class Jews, the Jewish functionaries were afraid to engage the struggle for Dreyfus," Blum maintained, "just as they are afraid to engage the struggle against fascism today. They think only of burrowing themselves in and hiding," and they imagined that "anti-Semitic passion" could be "warded off by . . . cowardly neutrality. They did not understand then any better than they understand today that no precaution, no pretense, fools the enemy and that they remain the victims offered to triumphant antidreyfusism or fascism."[5]

Concerned that the affair's revolutionary lessons were being forgotten when they were needed most, Blum applauded the radical Dreyfusard left that had triumphed against the forces of reaction. But once the "cyclone passed," he wrote, "France refound itself almost identically as it had been. . . . In the final analysis, only the surface had been stirred up by the torment; the heavy depths had remained motionless." The Socialist leader closed his memoirs of the Dreyfus era with questions designed for the present: "Before or after 'the Affair,' before or after the war," he asked, "what had been fundamentally transformed in France? . . . Do we search for the explanation in the materialist philosophy of History?" If little or nothing had changed, "was it because social relations had not been altered?" Those reflections "issue naturally from my subject," Blum concluded, and "bring me back to the present after the . . . evocation of my youth . . . of lost friends."[6]

The greatest loss had been Jaurès, and not only for his pupil Léon Blum. For the Dreyfuses and Reinachs, however, the loss had come a decade before their old ally's assassination in the summer of 1914. When Jaurès abandoned the coalition of Dreyfusard victors for the barricades of class struggle—or when the moderates of the *bloc des gauches* abandoned him—the divisions that had delayed the Socialist's entry into the struggle for a "bourgeois" Jewish officer reappeared. The war postponed the conflict, but with the resurgence of the revolutionary left and radical right the ideological fault line reopened, and for those who rejected extremist parties, or were rejected by them, the political options narrowed.

Through the late 1930s, members of the Dreyfus family intensified their private philanthropy and turned their energies toward national and international organizations: Pierre Dreyfus and his mother worked for Jewish welfare committees; Magui Mercier continued her *artisanat fem-*

inin; Jean-Pierre Reinach launched an enterprise for international students in Paris; and Madeleine and Simone Lévy joined scout movements and schools of social work. Their activities reflected their diverse interests—and not the "cowardly neutrality" of "rich Jews," as Blum would have it—but they also confirmed an estrangement from party politics. Unlike Mathieu Dreyfus, the most politically adept member of the family, the generation of the 1930s found little room to maneuver in the public arena. On the left they faced a shifting coalition of Socialists, Communists, and Radicals which championed revolutionary economic and social change; and those policies threatened the family's class interests, just as the anti-Semitic propaganda of the extreme left—the attacks on "huckstering, capitalist Jews"—threatened their security. On the right they found familiar anti-Dreyfusard enemies, including Maurras and his neoroyalists, being eclipsed by more youthful, action-oriented followers of nationalist and fascist "leagues." Launched to crush the "Judeo-Masonic power which corrupts all regimes," the movements of the far right aimed to manifest their "love for the country" by defending French liberties "imperiled by the conspiratorial action of the Jews."[7]

If members of the Dreyfus family believed they had little or no option on the left or right, and if the political center had virtually disappeared, there was another alternative: Zionism. But to turn to Palestine was to turn away from France, and for now at least the family had too much confidence in its country, if not in its country's party politics, to pledge a new allegiance.[8]

Writing to her old friend Eugène Naville about her charity work with the Paris Consistory, Lucie Dreyfus said she felt "extremely grieved by the persecution of Jews in Germany, Italy and elsewhere." She defined "the cruel and abominable" events of the period as "humanity's disgrace," and she searched for the source of the problem, as she had always done, beyond the Rhine. "It is to Germany," she told Naville, "that we owe this revival of antisemitism."[9] Her son agreed that France's "neighboring country" had shown how "racial hatred could instigate crimes," and he repeated the belief, shared by his mother, that while individual prejudices had played a role in the Dreyfus affair, anti-Semitism was "foreign to the spirit" of liberal France, "a country of generous traditions."[10]

Increasingly Pierre took time away from his small textile enterprise to focus on the fate of refugees in France and of Jews in Germany.

Through the 1930s he stepped up his volunteer work by moving beyond the Paris Consistory to the World Jewish Congress. Calling the task "too heavy for French Jews alone," he urged greater government intervention and approved a resolution to address the problem of German Jewish refugees through international organizations. At meetings in banquet halls from the Hotel Majestic to the Café de la Paix, Pierre expressed his hope that French representatives would go to Geneva "to obtain the reestablishment of civic equality for persecuted Jews." He supported the motion that "Jewish solidarity. . . constitutes the best means of . . . stemming the development of antisemitism," and under the auspices of the Federation of Jewish Societies (yet another group he helped found), he challenged the French government's refusal to recognize refugees as "victims of political persecution." Though he disagreed with those who described assimilation as "a sinking ship in the middle of the sea," he knew that many Jewish refugees would not abandon their religious traditions and linguistic habits in some headlong rush to express their gratitude to France; he knew that assimilation was not a quickly fashioned quid pro quo. And for his sensitivity—for his willingness to work not only with German Jews but with poor, Yiddish-speaking immigrants from Eastern Europe—he continued to feel the wrath of those Jewish notables who wanted no part of "the rejects of society," the "bunch of nonentities of no use to any human agglomeration." Léon Blum's hard assessment of some of his coreligionists carried more than a grain of truth. In a bizarre turn of phrase, Pierre's French Jewish critics called his efforts "pro-Jewish" and condemned the Dreyfus-Gourevitch committee for representing "nothing."[11]

But in the aftermath of the Anschluss, the Nazi takeover of Austria, and in the wake of the Kristallnacht in November 1938, Pierre pressed his appeal. "The Son of Captain Dreyfus Strongly Condemns Nazi Persecution," went the headline to an article in the newspaper *Ordre*. With the parallels to his own family history clear but never stated, Pierre described how he thought constantly of "those fathers torn from their homes, taken to concentration camps, tortured, [and] pushed to suicide"; of "the mothers who could no longer find milk to nourish their children"; and of "youngsters suffering on the street. There is no drama more frightening, more poignant," Pierre went on, and "at a time when the world prides itself for having reached a superior level of civilization. All decent people should have their nights haunted, as mine are haunted, by the abominations . . . inflicted by a government of assassins and sadists." Renewing his call for the international Jewish community to aid their German and Austrian coreligionists, he singled out the generosity of "the American and English people" and the "considerable contributions" of French Jews. "France continues to fulfill its duty to the human confraternity," he added, and the volunteer agencies that he helped direct continued to "exclude" from their activities "all political questions."[12]

At the same time Pierre's niece Madeleine Lévy also moved to help refugee children and other youngsters "suffering on the streets." She made the transition from Girl Scout to social worker. While attending the Lycée Molière in Paris—where she demonstrated her grandfather Alfred's aptitude for mathematics and philosophy—Madeleine, along with her sister, Simone, joined one of the Scouting groups, which were built on the British model and required their members to accomplish a "good deed" (*bonne action*) every day. Catholics dominated the Scouts de France; Protestants had their separate Eclaireurs Unionistes; and many Jewish youngsters joined the Eclaireurs Israélites, established to accomplish the same goals while also providing religious instruction and a platform from which to combat anti-Semitism. Madeleine and Simone, however, served with the fourth of France's Scouting quartet, the Fédération Française des Eclaireuses, a unit of the secular, or laic, Eclaireurs de France. Most of Madeleine's "good deeds" involved children, and in 1936, at the age of seventeen, she decided to pursue a career in child welfare. At the end of a three-year course of study she would become an *assistante sociale*.[13]

Like Madeleine Lévy and Pierre Dreyfus, who excluded "political questions" from their volunteer work, Jean-Pierre Reinach banned "politics" from his activities as well. The young man's grandfathers, Joseph Reinach and Mathieu Dreyfus, had, in their own ways, mastered the art of politics, but Jean-Pierre, like so many other citizens in the 1930s, had lost patience with the "ignoble and imbecilic" travesties of the era. "Enough of politicians," he would write, "of sowers of division and hate[;] we want to understand our neighbors, and we want to help them." Above all, he wanted to help the young. After a conversation with a foreign student who had spent years in Paris without getting to know one French counterpart, Jean-Pierre gathered former classmates from the Ecole Libre des Sciences Politiques (the school from which he graduated in 1936), and launched the Rassemblement International des Jeunes (RIJ). Foreign students would meet friends who shared common academic interests, but, more than a study group, it would be an informal assembly of many nationalities and cultures—and, as its informal rules made clear, it would abide no partisan politics.[14]

Largely at his own expense, twenty-one-year-old Jean-Pierre rented offices for the RIJ in the heart of the Latin Quarter, near the intersection of the boulevards Saint-Germain and Saint-Michel. French and foreign students—mostly of Polish and Yugoslav origin—gathered there every afternoon for informal discussions, and, at times, for a rubber of bridge. Once a month a group of thirty members arranged a conference, followed by dinner at a local restaurant, with guest speakers ranging from the poet Paul Valéry and the novelist André Maurois to a Yugoslavian visitor, Josip Broz, better known as Tito. French members of the RIJ took their foreign colleagues on tours of Paris monuments and the chateau at Versailles, and in 1937 Polish students returned the favor by inviting their new friends to the Polish Pavilion at the Paris World's Fair. The club quickly grew to nearly one thousand members representing thirty-eight nations, and though it received some early funding from the president of the republic and the foreign minister, the amount was never adequate for the job at hand. Jean-Pierre lobbied officials at the Quai d'Orsay, but could not convince those men of another generation that support of the RIJ represented an investment in a future of peace.

Continuing to organize and subsidize his group, he also turned to writing about international affairs, and about the youth of France. His first book, a revision of his "Sciences Po" thesis, had examined a 1905 treaty that attempted to bring Germany into the Franco-Russian alliance. A solid achievement for such a young scholar, that essay said as much about Jean-Pierre's growing commitment to European unity as it did about the ill-fated Treaty of Bjoerkoë.[15] But it was his next book, *Du Gouffre à l'espoir (From the Abyss to Hope)*, published in 1938, that captured his immediate concerns and revealed the influence of his parents and grandparents.

Describing France's "new . . . generation of intelligent, generous . . . young people," Jean-Pierre asked why that generation emerged "only now" and not "immediately after the war." The reason, he said, was not hard to find. "Those born prior to the war had often lost their bearings as a result of the catastrophe; they had returned to their jobs too soon, had been forced to interrupt their studies, or had suffered harsh deprivations. Just after the victory," Jean-Pierre went on, "a crisis of euphoria . . . seized young people. They thought only of their own happiness, and showed little concern for social and moral problems." As for the generation born during the war or just prior to 1914—the generation that included Jean-Pierre and his sisters and cousins—their youth passed in an atmosphere of mourning and reverence. Along with the constant image "of the black veil worn by their mother or aunt," they were "surrounded by photographs of a father and of uncles who had disappeared, of portraits often ornamented with medals"—like the pictures that hung like icons in the Reinach and Dreyfus homes. "The youngster learned the cult of the father," Jean-Pierre wrote, "and said to himself that he had a mission to replace . . . the one who had died so that he could live free." Above all, "the stories told by mothers and grandmothers" taught the new generation "to be proud Frenchmen. France represented for us much more than it did for others," Jean-Pierre concluded. "It evoked the beautiful and noble Fatherland for which our fathers had sacrificed themselves." Marked by "generosity, bravery, intelligence and kindness . . . France was our father." [16]

But Jean-Pierre had three fathers: Ado, whom he had never known but always revered; Mathieu, who raised him; and Ernest Mercier, who, while echoing the family's patriotism, broke with the traditions of Mathieu Dreyfus and Joseph Reinach and helped turn Jean-Pierre against politics. "Throw off the malignant mantle of politics," the young man urged his contemporaries, "and apply yourself to the social problems of your country. . . . Stay young, stay good and generous, and guard yourself against the vices . . . of hatred." In 1938, a year that witnessed the election of Charles Maurras into the august "immortal" body of the French Academy, and a year marked by the collapse of yet another coalition of Socialists, Communists, and Radicals, Jean-Pierre worried with good reason that France was losing sight of its ideals. Quoting a contemporary, he portrayed the right and left as "parallel" roads to dictatorship and ruin; fascism appealed only to "the biceps," he wrote, and communism only to "the belly." And when he described the "shameful scandals" that "humiliated and degraded our country," he repeated his stepfather's beliefs. Referring to the earlier Stavisky affair, he stressed how all that "wretchedness, cowardice, and shame . . . struck us even more intensely, because this was the country for which our fathers had given their lives."[17]

"An ocean of scandal" was how Ernest Mercier described the Stavisky era, and he defined February 1934 as "an explosion of resentment," not against the republic, but against "the disorder of public institutions and public morality." Those same sentiments had led Mercier into a brief alliance with the Croix de Feu. A group that supposedly embraced "neither the right nor the left" was sure to attract a war veteran like Mercier, who hoped to recapture the lost "fraternity of the trenches" and reform France while remaining "above politics." Mercier met the president of the Croix de Feu, François de La Rocque, in 1933, and contributed one thousand francs to the organization. But the mutual attraction was short-lived. Too outspoken about the dangers of "dictatorial parties," Mercier became a liability for de La Rocque, just as the Croix de Feu, transformed into the Parti Social Français, became too "political" for the industrialist.[18]

If he opposed all forms of dictatorship at home, however, Mercier's desire to halt German militarism prompted a series of curious voyages abroad. Driven by a visceral hatred of Germany that his more internationally minded stepson Jean-Pierre did not share, Mercier explored ways to form an economic coalition against the "deceitful" and "arbitrary" Nazi regime—a regime supported by the German people as "a kind of redemption for their misery," and one "which would revolt any other civilized country."[19] Early in 1935 Mercier and his wife joined an official trade mission charged by the French government to investigate the possibility of economic rapprochement with Italy. Like the British statesmen and business leaders who also visited Italy in the mid-1930s, Mercier wanted to drive a wedge between Mussolini and Hitler. After visiting the industrial centers of northern Italy and discussing trade agreements, Mercier met Mussolini on two occasions and reported back to the French foreign minister, Pierre Laval. Some of Italy's recent economic programs appealed to the French industrialist (though he harbored a distrust of the fascist's "dictatorial style"), but little came of those Franco-Italian negotiations, mainly because Mussolini (who would soon call France a nation "ruined by alcohol, syphilis and journalism") cared only about floating a huge loan in Paris, and because the fascist showed his true colors when he prepared for war in Ethiopia. The Bank of France could ignore a client's ideology but not his fiscal reliability, and a volatile Italian dictator was not a good prospect for a loan.[20]

Pressing his search for a partner to contain Hitler, Mercier made another journey with Magui, east into the heartland of bolshevism. Invited by the Soviet ambassador late in 1935, they visited Moscow and Leningrad, and after touring Communist factories and meeting with Red Army officers, they joined Josef Stalin at a formal dinner to celebrate the November revolution. On returning to Paris, Mercier informed Pierre

Laval, now prime minister, of Russia's interest in an economic and military alliance with France. After all, those two powers had joined forces against the Second Reich, and the Third, better armed than its predecessor, menaced them both again. Supporting his government's proposal of a mutual-assistance pact with Russia, Mercier gave a series of lectures to the French business community designed to calm their fears about the Soviet system. Russia could once again become "an ideal French market," he announced, and, most important, it could serve as an ally against Germany.[21]

Unofficial liaison for a divided and ineffective French government, Mercier failed as an economic emissary. And when the left came to power in the summer of 1936 the industrialist stepped down from many of the corporate posts he had held during the past two decades and moved toward a life of retirement. If the far right attacked him as a cryptosocialist and wondered about the allegiance of a Protestant married to the niece of the notorious Dreyfus, the far left portrayed "the king of electricity" as a capitalist leader of the *haute société protestante,* as a member of the detested "Two Hundred Families of France," and as a fascist sympathizer. But as he approached his sixtieth year, Mercier fired one last salvo at the politicians who, in his view, had prevented France's moral and economic renewal. In *Resurrection française, erreurs politiques et vérités humaines,* published in 1937, he criticized the rivalries that split the center, condemned the backwardness of the right, and damned the left for elevating "class struggle" above *fraternité.* "Envy" had become an "endemic sickness" in France, Mercier wrote. "It is a passion that is never satisfied, and once it is loosed it knows no limits; it is public enemy number one." Like elite officers in combat, French leaders should work for "the interests" of the masses rather than for materialist greed or ideological advantage. Two decades after his combat missions in Montenegro, at Gallipoli, and in the Balkans, Mercier still believed that France's salvation lay not in "politics," but in the fraternity and moral strength that had distinguished the fighting men of the Great War and had united the nation. Through the distorted prism of the 1930s, he looked back to four terrible years and saw France at war with its hereditary enemy and at peace with itself.[22]

At the helm of the Socialist party, Léon Blum had adhered to the old doctrine of non-involvement in "bourgeois" governments, and had clung to the promise of France's "revolutionary renovation." But socialists, competing for their constituency with communists and Radicals, could not go it alone. In 1934, the Communist leader, Maurice Thorez, had been the first to call for a "Popular Front of work, liberty and peace," and a year later the Bastille Day parade of the Rassemblement Populaire had announced the conception, if not yet the birth, of that "common front." Finally, in January 1936, it emerged as an official coalition; the parties would campaign separately, but in the end they would rally behind the strongest candidate.[23]

For the right, the leftist "enemies within" had joined forces to destroy the fatherland. Sympathy for bolsheviks who aimed to import a godless revolution; allusions to "class struggle" at a time when Frenchmen needed jobs, not slogans; calls for international harmony rather than for national vigor—all the Popular Front's programs, real and imagined by the right, came under attack in newspaper editorials, campaign manifestos, and street protests. From the old Action Française to the new Solidarité Française (brainchild of the perfume emperor François Coty), Léon Blum's coalition was challenged by countercoalitions, and for an organization like the recently formed National Front—the depository for nearly all the extreme right-wing groups of the 1930s—the Popular Front was nothing but a rogues' gallery of old enemies. If any question remained that Blum's critics saw him as a reincarnation of "Jaurès and Dreyfus combined,"[24] it was answered on February 13, 1936, when Camelots du Roi assaulted the Socialist leader. Driving home from the National Assembly, Blum, along with a fellow socialist, Georges Monnet, and Monnet's wife, turned down the Boulevard Saint-Germain and into the funeral procession of an Action Française notable. Spotting the identification sticker of the Chamber of Deputies on Monnet's Citroën, and then recognizing Blum, the crowd smashed the car's windows and reached in to beat the sixty-four-year-old socialist "with a sharp object torn from the vehicle." While onlookers shouted "Kill him!" two policemen and a group of construction workers pulled Blum from the melee and rushed him into a nearby courtyard, his head bleeding profusely. It took thirty minutes for the director of the municipal police to respond, but Blum's injuries—massive contusions and a severed vein in his temple—were finally treated at the Hotel Dieu.[25]

Prior to the assault on Dreyfus in 1908 and to the murder of Jaurès six years later, the Action Française had filled its newspapers with incitements to violence. Maurras had insisted then, as he would again in 1936, that his freedom of expression should not be jeopardized by the actions of hot-headed followers over whom he had no control. But on the day of the attack on Blum, Maurras had called for "the knife" to be used on traitorous politicians.[26]

Blum's parliamentary colleagues, joined by centrist deputies, condemned "the iniquity of such an act." The situation is "intolerable for the honor of the Republic and the honor of France," announced the Radical Edouard Herriot, and the government pushed for the dissolution of the Action Française, the Camelots du Roi, and the affiliated "Students of the Action Française." Maurras and company argued that the Blum incident had been a frame-up (masterminded by bolsheviks, the British, and the French republican police), but in mid-February 1936, the neo-royalist organization, born of the Dreyfus affair and now outlawed, collapsed (for a time) at the age of thirty-eight. Its newspaper survived, however, and its members found sympathetic homes in other groups that comprised the National Front.[27]

But the leagues' days were numbered. While Léon Blum recovered, his party scored an extraordinary victory at the polls. Socialists, Radicals, and Communists controlled the Chamber of Deputies, and in June 1936 their Popular Front assumed power with Blum as prime minister. Communists refused to take the final step into the bourgeois system, and Blum had to assemble his cabinet from the membership of other parties. But the triumph had been impressive nonetheless, and the successor to Jaurès could now bring about the "revolutionary renovation" for which his mentor had fought and died. The basic goals were already outlined—disarmament, international negotiations for peace, nationalization of industries, collective bargaining, paid vacations, a forty-hour work week, and more—but to that list, which already shocked, the Popular Front added the complete dissolution of all nationalist leagues.[28]

Blum's enemies reacted like a gaggle of adolescents, as they had since the Socialist's first day in office. If it was still possible to shock the parliament, one right-wing deputy, Xavier Vallat, did just that when he announced that "For the first time, this old Gallo-Roman country is going to be governed by a Jew. . . . I dare to say out loud what the country is thinking in its heart," Vallat went on despite the warning of the Chamber's president. "It is better to place at the head of this peasant nation of France someone whose origins, however modest, are rooted in our soil, rather than a subtle Talmudist."[29] Outside the assembly, journalists labeled the Popular Front "the kike's riposte," and while leftist parties celebrated their triumph, their enemies reported that "The Jew Revolution Sings its Victory." One author, in a tract entitled *The Jewish Peril,* proclaimed: "Look what the Revolution has done for Israel. It has made it the king of France!"[30] Many observers expected the leagues to respond to their death notice by threatening civil war, but instead they joined the system they detested and announced their rebirth as legal political parties. The Croix de Feu offered its hybrid nationalism and socialism through the Parti Social Français, while Jacques Doriot, whose totalitarian instincts had taken him from an unrequited affair with communism to a new romance with fascism, launched the Parti Populaire Français. The champagne magnate, Pierre Taittinger, like the perfumer François Coty, had been subsidizing right-wing associations for years, and when Blum's government outlawed Taittinger's Parti National Populaire, the group simply reappeared as the Parti Républicain National et Social. Smaller associations, like the club founded by a former Action Française member, Louis Darquier de Pellepoix, continued the struggle against "the Jewish and alien dictatorship." Soon to be restructured as the Rassemblement Anti-Juif de France, that group would gladly accept all members who could prove that their grandparents were free of Jewish blood.[31]

Anti-Semitism served as only part of the appeal, and for many groups it mattered hardly at all. The specter of Jewish immigrants snatching jobs from Frenchmen clearly worked as a propaganda device for many organizations, but more important to their constituencies was a way out of the depression, out of the threat of another war, and out of the political anarchy that reigned in France. Fed a steady diet of exposés on corrupt politicians who bickered rather than governed, the followers of nationalist organizations had learned to distrust elected officials long before Blum took office. If the old "republic of pals" could not save France, the argument on the right went, there was even less hope for the new "republic of Jews."[32]

Aiming for the annihilation of the Popular Front, the right got its wish within a year—and again a year after that, when another Blum cabinet made a brief appearance only to fall once more. But the failure of the coalition had as much to do with its own inability to cope with the economic crisis at home and with militarism abroad as it did with pressures from its opponents. From the moment it took power, the Popular Front inherited labor upheavals that it could not control; from automobile and aircraft industries to pasta and chocolate factories, strikes spread throughout France, and though Blum initiated programs to improve the lot of the working classes, the conflicts stretched on. Nearly seventeen thousand strikes were reported in 1936, with twelve thousand of them beginning in June. Also, the flight of capital, which had begun in anticipation of a leftist victory, continued after 1936, undermining Blum's efforts to stabilize the economy. Meanwhile, Communists and the Communist-dominated CGT, always unreliable partners in the Socialist-led "common front," steadily defected back into the refuge of "noninvolvement" in bourgeois enterprises. Early in 1937 Blum announced a "pause" to the social programs that the national treasury, long on deficits and short on tax revenues, could not support, but that final effort proved to be the death rattle of an experiment that would succumb in June. The right rejoiced; Blum had always incarnated "all that revolts our blood and makes our flesh creep," said one neoroyalist in 1938. "He is evil. He is death." And for some nationalist critics the efficient Reich beyond the Rhine provided a striking contrast to the anarchy of the Popular Front. "Better Hitler," went one chant of protest in the late 1930s, "than Blum!"[33]

As the first socialist prime minister of France, Léon Blum had hoped to translate Jaurès's generous qualities of humanity and social justice into concrete actions. He had the courage and intelligence to realize those goals, but, in domestic policies and international affairs, he made mistakes, some of them foolish, many of them unavoidable, and the combination of them fatal. His greatest tragedy, however, was to assume power at a moment when the nation—divided along similar lines but even more profoundly than during the Dreyfus era—had become virtually ungovernable. Many of the descendants of Dreyfusards, including members of the Dreyfus family, did not join the man who, in so many ways, was one of their own. He asked them to rally around the memory of the affair, but he did so with new programs and new allies on the far left that they could not support. At the close of the 1930s the dreams of the left failed, the protests of the right persisted, and the ever-diminishing center wondered how the "sacred union" of the war could have so slipped away so quickly and completely.

In his early twenties, Jean-Pierre Reinach had his father's light brown hair, broad forehead, and square jaw—and, it seemed, his same habitual smile. But his straight nose and gentle eyes were more like those of his grandfather Mathieu Dreyfus. And so, too, was his refined, almost delicate, manner; he had inherited much of Joseph Reinach's conviviality but none of his pugnaciousness. At Lincoln College, Oxford, where he studied for a year, he was remembered by an English friend as "a perceptive young French Jew . . . [a] well-mannered, handsome young man who was often to be seen that summer lying in the cushions of a punt on the Cherwell, while some adoring young woman . . . poled him gracefully along."[34] A good horseman, like his father and granduncle Alfred, he often rode with his sisters Suzie and France in the Fontaine-bleau forest or at Chantilly; with his wire-rimmed glasses and angular frame, he had the look of a studious young cavalry officer.

His mother and father had been engaged in 1911, when Ado was in the midst of his military service and when France and Germany were in the midst of the Moroccan crisis. Nearly three decades later, Jean-Pierre's engagement took place against another backdrop of international tension. Naomi de Rothschild, daughter of the English banker and horticulturalist Lionel de Rothschild, lived in London and in southern England on her family's estate at Exbury. In 1938, on her way back from school in Switzerland, she stopped in Paris and met Jean-Pierre through mutual friends. They spent only a brief time together—a few days that included a *bateau mouche* cruise down the Seine and a subsequent visit by Jean-Pierre to Exbury—but their friendship developed through the letters they exchanged. Describing his achievements and frustrations with the RIJ, Jean-Pierre confessed his desire, only partly whimsical, to launch a newspaper filled exclusively with "good news." Given the temper of the times, he thought it would be a unique and worthwhile "challenge." Naomi returned to Paris in the summer of 1939, and the young couple became engaged. But their wedding would have to wait.[35]

The various French governments of the late 1930s—from the Popular Front to the moderate Government of National Defense led by old-line Radicals—had failed to respond to the fascist threat in Germany, Italy, and Spain. Ever since its remilitarization of the Rhineland in 1936, Germany had systematically violated the Versailles Treaty and the peace accords signed at the lakeside town of Locarno. Hitler subsumed his Austrian homeland and the German-speaking Sudetenland in 1938, and in the early months of the following year he moved deeper into the independent republic of Czechoslovakia. Under pressure from his own citizens and from his British counterpart, Neville Chamberlain, French prime minister Edouard Daladier withdrew from Hitler's challenge at Munich in September 1938. "He is so elastic!" said the German Luftwaffe commander, Hermann Göring, of the French leader.[36] But

Daladier was an accomplished politician, and his elasticity had nothing to do with personal cowardice. He faced the array of crises at home that paralyzed all the governments of the late 1930s, and he led a country that, only two decades before, had sacrificed a generation on the altar of "no more war."

If French and British leaders had not chased Hitler from the Rhineland they saw no reason to push him from Prague. And in 1939, they watched him move toward Poland. To ensure success, Hitler joined his archenemy, Josef Stalin, and signed a "nonagression" pact in August. Their goal was simple and the historical precedents were many; they agreed to conquer Poland and divide its spoils. The left in France and elsewhere had clung to one sure thing in that decade of uncertainty: like fundamentalists adhering to a sacred text, they had believed that the Soviet Union would serve as a bulwark against fascism. Even men like Ernest Mercier had hoped to use Russia to contain the Nazi threat. But those hopes died with the Hitler-Stalin pact, and the only certainty that emerged was the prospect of another European war. France and Britain could turn a blind eye to Austria and dance around the wording of commitments to Czechoslovakia ("all the Czechs in the world are not worth the bones of a single little French soldier," announced one journalist),[37] but it would be more difficult to break their alliance with Poland. They were bound by treaty to come to the defense of that country, and France, in particular, was bound by a long tradition of cultural and political ties. On September 3, 1939, two days after the armies of the Third Reich rolled into Poland and Hitler tested the will of the West once more, the parliaments in Paris and London, ill prepared in every way to engage in another international conflict, declared war on Germany.

When twenty-four-year-old Jean-Pierre Reinach joined the French army he expressed little of the zeal and optimism that marked his father's and uncles' accounts of August 1914. It seemed, in France, that the declarations of those two wars had only summertime and Germany in common. The call to arms in 1939 went out to a population that had learned the price of sacred crusades in the trenches of another war and that, through the intervening years, had chewed away at the foundations of its republic like termites at an old wooden beam. Divided by ideologues whose dreams could only be achieved through the destruction of their enemies, who were their countrymen, France had also been "invaded" by thousands of immigrants for whom very few native Frenchmen wished to risk their lives. And the population had aged; the statistics and the profile of the French military high command reflected that obvious fact, but the numbers mattered less than the spirit of the people they quantified.[38]

"When our fathers departed for the front," went Jean-Pierre's reflections on World War I, "leaving their wives, their homes, their jobs, they marched away in the hope that this would be the last war, and that their sacrifice . . . would ensure the beginning of an era of peace for their children. They left and they were killed for peace. . . . Now we, the young generation," he concluded, "want peace with all the force of our filial devotion, with all the energy of the many years we still have to live." With other members of the Dreyfus and Reinach families, Jean-Pierre Reinach would fight to defend France. But he would not, he warned, "be led to the slaughterhouse by an old generation which has forgotten the price of life."[39]

CHAPTER XXIV

Resistance

SCHOOLED IN THE HIGH ART of memorization, officers of the French high command suffered the consequences of their greatest gift. Confident that they had learned from the defeat at Sedan in 1870, they had launched a strike toward Alsace-Lorraine in the summer of 1914, only to find German armies pouring into France by way of Belgium. Fifteen years later, in the chess game of Franco-German military strategy, the memory of Verdun, of a static, sanguinary battle around a series of closely linked citadels, prompted the construction of the Maginot Line. Begun in 1929, that massive string of eastern fortifications—running from Longuyon, south of Sedan, to the Swiss border—was meant, in theory, to block an attack from across the Rhine and enable French armies to deploy troops toward Belgium in concert with British allies. But the broad bunkers and deep tunnels were little more than concrete manifestations of France's moral isolation, reflections of the views of their chief architects: André Maginot, minister of war in the 1920s and an old admirer of Charles Maurras, and Marshal Pétain, "savior" of Verdun and Maginot's septuagenarian military adviser. Through the 1930s, France's "impregnable" line dominated the planning and budget of the high command to the detriment of the second pillar of national defense, the open northeastern frontier, and it lulled soldiers and civilians into a bunker mentality. "If we were short of tanks, aeroplanes, and tractors," wrote Marc Bloch, historian, army officer, and one of the few

458

contemporaries who understood the perils of France's antiquated strategy, "it was because we had put our not inexhaustible supplies of money and labour into *concrete*." Another Frenchman, a member of the National Assembly, captured the prevailing view: "Let us not go into heroics about Austria," he announced when German armies marched through Central Europe, "let us take refuge behind our Maginot Line."[1]

Dividing Poland in three weeks' time, Hitler and Stalin preempted Franco-British involvement in Eastern Europe. Hard winter weather and poor Allied preparation led to a strange and quiet "phony war" across the following months (for the French, a *drôle de guerre*), but in the early spring of 1940, Germany demonstrated that it too had learned a lesson at Verdun; it had learned to forget. "Germany's new tactics" were part of the "quickened rhythm of the times," Marc Bloch observed, and "the metronome at [French] headquarters was always set at too slow a beat."[2] With a vastly superior air force, modern tanks, and well-equipped troops, Hitler turned from an assault on Denmark and Norway in April to a lightning strike through the Low Countries in May. Invading with Stuka dive-bombers and troops parachuted into the region in advance of infantry soldiers, German units secured bridges and principal cities, and then moved through the Ardennes Forest to the Meuse River at Sedan.[3]

Paul Reynaud, a longtime opponent of appeasement, had replaced Daladier as prime minister in March, and the even-more-audacious Winston Churchill had taken over from Chamberlain in early May. But France and Britain needed more than vigorous leadership; they needed time to regroup and rearm, and France especially needed time for its population—and its generals—to decide whether this was a war worth fighting. In late May and early June, Germans blanketed the area north of the Maginot Line and pushed the British Expeditionary Force (BEF) into the dead end of Channel ports. Only a brief and unexpected pause in Hitler's blitzkrieg allowed more than three hundred thousand British soldiers and some French and Belgian troops to escape to England by way of Dunkirk. If the 1914 war had opened with the advancing armies of the Second Reich blocked at the Battle of the Marne, the second war began in France, nine months after its declaration, with the Third Reich shattering all opposition and clearing the way to Paris. In a matter of days, the enemy traversed the same landscape that Pierre and Emile Dreyfus, Ado Reinach, and other family members had defended at the outset of their war, and though brave troops tried to hold at the Somme in June 1940, no modern Joffre emerged as the "hero" of that river battle, and no fleet of Paris taxis rushed reinforcements to the front. Taxis motored in the opposite direction, away from the conflict, along southern roads jammed with refugees.

On June 14, German armies entered Paris with hardly a skirmish, and the French government fled to Tours and, soon after, to Bordeaux, the same port city chosen by earlier governments on the run from the Germans in 1870 and 1914. Paul Reynaud's cabinet voted for an armistice, the prime minister resigned, and into the breech came seventy-four-year-old Pétain. With his snow-white hair and mustache, his gentle blue eyes, and the memory of World War I stamped on his person like the medals on his tunic, the marshal was the embodiment of victory at a moment of defeat. "With a heavy heart," he declared in his June 17 radio address, "I tell you today that it is necessary to stop fighting."[4] Some soldiers had already stopped fighting, while others, waiting in France, North Africa, and England, prepared to defy the marshal's defeatism (défaitisme)—a word that the "immortal members" of the Academy had only recently included in the official French dictionary. French dictionary. But networks of resistance would take time to build, and the summer of 1940 remained a summer of surrender—and of symbols. Hitler played his part when he ordered that the formal capitulation of France be signed in the same railway car in the same Compiègne Forest north of Paris where the great German nation had been humiliated in November 1918. An ebullient Hitler emerged from that meeting to beam with victory for photographers, and a short time later he posed again, in Paris, like any other tourist, in front of the Eiffel Tower.

Following the armistice, Pétain moved his ministers and deputies from Bordeaux to Vichy. With its once-elegant but now slightly tattered hotels and casinos filled with superannuated politicians, that "rococo cure center for liverish bourgeois" soon resembled "a ramshackle copy of an eighteenth-century court."[5] Hitler's terms called for France to be divided into a northern occupied zone (three-fifths of the country) with Paris as its capital and Germans as its masters, and a southern unoccupied sector, with Vichy as its governmental center and Frenchmen in control. Pétain and his men believed that by limiting German domination and by salvaging an autonomous state, they would preserve the honor of the fatherland and construct a new France through a new national revolution. "The old order of things," announced Pétain's commander in chief, General Maxime Weygand, "that is to say, a political regime of Masonic, capitalist . . . and international . . . compromises, has led to our present straits. France wants no more of it." For Weygand—who had helped finance the anti-Semitic monument for Colonel Henry and who, in his seventy-third year, still believed in Alfred Dreyfus's guilt—"capitalists" conjured up Jews, and "international compromises" stood for Bolshevik conspiracies. But the general was right in one respect: Vichy would have no more of it.[6]

The voices of opposition, very few and very soon suppressed, were led by Léon Blum. He traveled to Vichy at great personal risk in early July to rally support for the republic under siege from within. Jacques Doriot's fascist thugs roamed the streets warning politicians that they "would not sleep in their beds" if they voted against Pétain, and the atmosphere within Vichy's hastily improvised halls of government was only slightly less hateful. Finger pointing became the dominant *beau geste* as politicians searched for scapegoats, and nearly all fingers pointed toward Blum and the memory of the Popular Front. "This mad, criminal war," said Pétain's chief supporter, Pierre Laval, had been engineered by "the Frenchmen—fools, criminals—who wanted it"; and now the nation would be saved by Frenchmen who wanted an "authoritarian," "national," and "social" regime. Queried on the problem of personal liberties, Laval shot back, "If you mean by personal liberties rights for all immigrants and all foreigners . . . I will make clear that no one will be eligible to be a Deputy if he has not been a Frenchman for many generations. That is our kind . . . of a race policy."[7]

Of the 666 members of the National Assembly present at Vichy, 569 voted to bury the seventy-year-old republic and give birth to a single-party state led by Marshal Pétain. Not since Napoleon III, whose empire fell with Sedan in 1870, had a French leader assumed such power; and unlike Louis Napoleon in his twilight years, Pétain was a towering popular hero, calm and benevolent in appearance at a time when France needed both peace and kindness. He was almost universally revered. The first phase of the marshal's domestic National Revolution triumphed with ease at Vichy, and in the next phase, the Etat Français would throw off the slogan of anarchy that had divided the nation since 1789 ("Liberty, Equality, Fraternity") and adopt instead the trilogy of order around which, in Vichy's view, all Frenchmen, if not all foreigners, could rally: "Work, Family, Fatherland."[8]

During the debate that culminated in Pétain's investiture, Léon Blum "watched men debasing themselves, becoming corrupt . . . as if they had been plunged into a bath of poison. They were possessed by fear. . . . It was a human swamp in which one saw . . . beneath one's very eyes, the courage and integrity one had known in certain men dissolve, corrode, disappear." Two months later, Pétain's police arrested Blum, and, upon hearing the news, Charles Maurras took his share of the credit; "I know, I see, I have verified, that it is the Judeo-Masonic politicians who have thrown us into the abyss down which we are falling."[9]

In May 1940, when the Nazi invasion of Paris seemed imminent, the Dreyfuses, Lévys, and Reinach-Merciers prepared for their exodus south. It came in stages, but it came quickly. After French forces requisitioned a house rented by the Lévys in the city's environs, the family rushed to arrange an automobile caravan with Lucie, Pierre, and Pierre's wife and four children. Madeleine Lévy, twenty-two years old, left her apprenticeship as a social worker to help with the move, and her older sister, Simone, recently widowed, brought her two-year-old daughter—Lucie's first great-grandchild. While Jean-Pierre Reinach, mobilized months before, waited with other stalled troops at the Maginot Line, his sisters, France and Suzie, drove south from a house they had rented in Brittany (German planes would bomb Rennes in a few days' time) to Biarritz. Caring for her two infant children, France made her way to Bilbao in northern Spain and to a ship bound for Cuba. In Havana she paid the $1,000 fee required on the black market for passage north and chose Canada (engaged in the war) over the United States (still isolationist) as her temporary home. Her sister Suzie, whose husband was serving with the remnants of the French army in the Meuse region, joined her mother and Ernest Mercier in Bordeaux. With a Jewish wife and an international reputation as a militant anti-German, Mercier would be one of the first Parisians visited by the Gestapo, and when asked by the French government to apply his management skills as a liaison with the American Red Cross, he followed what was left of the Third Republic south.[10]

All those family members had been fortunate enough to secure cars and petrol, but in the Pletzl near the Hôtel de Ville, and in neighborhoods farther east, poor Jews rushed toward city gates on foot. "They ran as though spewed from a volcano," reported one witness, "trudging for miles with babies in arms, sacks on their shoulders, afraid to look back to where they had left their homes and possessions."[11] As Nazi dive-bombers strafed roads, they took cover in ditches and forests, and some refugees jumped on trains heading south. Bicycles and motorcycles threaded through long lines of automobiles—old taxis, new limousines, tiny Citroëns topped off with sacks, luggage, and furniture—which carried families from Holland, Belgium, and northern France. Highways became "rivers" of humanity with banks overflowing, but they were more like rivers blocked with ice as cars and trucks crawled along "at no more than a kilometer an hour." By midsummer, nearly eight million people, citizens and immigrants, choked the roads of France. One million Parisians, including tens of thousands of Jews, escaped the capital, and the city to which Madeleine Lévy returned in late June had been transformed from a "maelstrom" into a "mausoleum."[12]

Shortly after Pierre Dreyfus's flight, German troops broke into his apartment on the Square de l'Albioni; having seized the files of Jewish welfare organizations, they aimed to suppress the work of Jewish activists and make a census of their names.[13] Pierre's appeals for the "Jewish victims of Nazi Germany" and his support of the World Jewish Congress attracted the occupiers' interest, as did his notoriety as the son of a renowned French Jew. Paris Consistory documents also confirmed that Madame Alfred Dreyfus, vice president of the Comité de Bienfaisance, worked closely with Jewish immigrants, and her family had been anxious to get her out of town. Street gangs, outfitted in dark paramilitary garb, were railing against the Jewish, Masonic, and Communist traitors who had engineered France's defeat, and Lucie Dreyfus would be a prime target not only for German policy but for her husband's old enemies.[14] Looking back on the exodus, the newspaper *Le Matin* used phone books to quantify the "Dreyfuses," "Lévys," "Blums" and other Jews who had departed; pleased with the plummeting numbers, the paper hoped for "even greater progress" in the future.[15]

On their exodus south, the Dreyfuses and Lévys stopped first in Cholet, beyond Tours, and then in Bordeaux, where they heard Charles de Gaulle's radio appeal from London ("France has lost a battle! But France has not lost the war!" the general announced on June 18. "Our fatherland is in mortal danger. Let us all fight on to save it!"). Pierre took his wife and children southeast to Marseilles, while Lucie and Jeanne's family pushed on to Dr. Lévy's native Toulouse, deep in the unoccupied zone toward the Pyrenees Mountains and the Spanish border. They found a city "overflowing" " with refugees "from every corner of France" and from beyond French borders. Spanish republicans had been trekking across the southern mountains since Franco's fascist victory in 1939; refugees from the Low Countries had come in the wake of Hitler's spring invasion; and Eastern and Central European Jews—

Poles, Russians, Germans—continued to arrive, mostly from Paris, through the summer of 1940. The housing and food shortages that dated from the depression years and the first wave of Spanish immigration quickly became a crisis as hundreds of thousands of homeless people searched for lodging and provisions. They slept on city sidewalks and, often separated from friends and relatives, read the long lists of missing persons posted to building walls. Nearly one hundred thousand children were temporarily lost in the melee of exodus throughout France, and Toulouse had more than its share of broken families.[16]

The Lévys were among them. Given the crush of refugees and the dearth of apartments (Jeanne also commented on the "exorbitant" rents when they did become available), the family could find only a small house outside Toulouse. Madeleine shared apartments with friends in the city center—with former scouts and schoolmates who had fled south—and Simone took her daughter across southern France to the home of in-laws in Grenoble. In the early winter Dr. Lévy finally secured a flat on the rue de la Dalbade in Toulouse, near the eastern bank of the Garonne, but it was damp, cold, and situated down a dark corridor and up four flights of stairs. Lucie, seventy-one years old in 1940 and suffering chronic respiratory problems, opted for a room in a heated boardinghouse a few streets away near the Catholic Church of Saint Etienne.[17]

In the summer, when neither the Germans nor Vichy had sealed the fate of the republic, Lucie began a daily correspondence with family members scattered in temporary homes throughout France. "The news is distressing," she wrote in mid-June. "A change of government now seems assured. . . . [But] I overhear the conversations of railroad workers, and they are certain of our victory . . . the idea of an armistice hardly crosses their minds." At night in Toulouse, Lucie listened to the *radio anglaise,* and though hopeful that "the English will continue the fight," she believed they had "illusions" about French government support and French military strength. After July, her fears realized, she wrote to her granddaughter Simone about her "terribly anguished visions of the future." Anxious for her family, she paced "back and forth, like a lion in a cage." But the dark passages gave way to calls for patience, conciliation, and courage, and to descriptions of her daily routine: "I sit at my writing table, with my letters, my knitting and my books. . . . Despite tired eyes I read a great deal, and English books are a good distraction, perhaps more for overcoming the difficulty of the language than for the amusement of the stories." Lucie never commented on the connection, but her wartime correspondence—and her wartime routine—repeated the themes of her husband's letters from Devil's Island.[18]

Most Parisians who fled the capital in May and June returned north after the armistice to get on with their lives as best they could. The city's population had expected the barbarians, but the German occupying force, with officers comfortably entrenched in Parisian grand hotels, went about its work with quiet efficiency; disciplined troops paid their café bills, gave up metro seats to the elderly and infirm, and conducted most searches in an orderly manner. Those habits—and that reputation—would change, but the early phase of the occupation, surprisingly pacific, was an encouraging sign to those who wished to come home. Magui Mercier came back to manage the *artisanat féminin;* her husband continued his Red Cross work in the capital and began the impossible task of trying to maintain the independence of the French electrical and petroleum industry; and Madeleine Lévy, resuming her apprenticeship as an *assistante sociale,* helped direct an educational and gymnastic program for the children of factory workers in a Paris suburb.[19]

Nearly every member of every branch of the Dreyfus family had escaped south in the summer, but those who did not travel home by early fall missed their chance. On September 27, 1940, a German ordinance closed the entire northern sector to returning Jews and prolonged the family's strange exile as citizen-refugees. "We hope to be able to say 'see you soon,' " Jeanne Dreyfus Lévy wrote a friend, "if Paris reopens its gates to us." But Paris, under German rule, did not.[20]

Concerned about her sisters, grandchildren, and in-laws dispersed in southern villages and towns, and having received little news from Pierre in Marseilles, Lucie set out on an odyssey through what became known as the *zone nono*—the nonoccupied zone.[21] "I would love to be able to split myself between Marseilles and Toulouse," she said in reference to the temporary homes of Pierre and Jeanne, and she attempted to do that and more. Traveling alone—or, at times, with Léon Dreyfus's widow, Alice—she visited family in the environs of Cahors, north of Toulouse; in Montpellier to the east; in Cassis, outside Marseilles; and in Avignon, Carpentras, Grenoble, and Valence. When her sister Marie died in the town of Villeneuve-sur-Lot early in 1941, Lucie arranged for the transfer of her body to Paris. She could not, however, cross into the northern sector with her sister's coffin.

On her travels, Lucie rented small hotel rooms (her letters

stressed both her desire for independence and her fear of becoming a burden), and from afar she helped her grandchildren earn a few francs by knitting sweaters and socks, and by procuring lace for women's hankies. Thinking, perhaps, of leisurely afternoons spent knitting with Hélène Naville in the elegant salon at Hauterive, she smiled, in private, about working for a living for the first time. She knew, however, that family funds were dwindling and that Vichy decrees threatened even harder times to come.

In 1941 Pétain's state created a Commissariat for Jewish Affairs (Commissariat-Général aux Questions Juives) to implement the scores of anti-Jewish measures that had been instituted, with little or no prompting from Germany, since October 1940. First directed by Xavier Vallat, the former Third Republic deputy who had damned Léon Blum's "subtle Talmudism," the commissariat would later be lead by Darquier de Pellepoix, veteran of the Action Française, and then by Charles Mercier du Paty de Clam, descendent of Alfred Dreyfus's most relentless inquisitor. In 1941, under Vallat's direction, the commissariat established a national Jewish council, the Union Générale des Israélites de France, to assume the responsibilities once held by charity organizations and local consistories. By way of reprisal against "terrorist" attacks on its soldiers in the north, Germany demanded that all French Jews pay a fine totaling one billion francs; and the commissariat, eager to please, forced the leaders of the Jewish council to raise money by "taxing" a percentage of their coreligionists' resources. Failure to pay, Nazi officials warned, could lead to "public hangings." The Union Générale followed Vichy's orders, and, along with other raids on Jewish holdings, seized more than twenty thousand francs from the Paris bank account of "the widow Madame Lucie Dreyfus."[22]

In the immediate aftermath of the 150th anniversary of the French Revolution, Vichy's policy of "state anti-Semitism" systematically violated every edict of emancipation. Its Statut des Juifs defined a "Jew" as anyone with "three grandparents of the Jewish race, or with two grandparents of that race if one's spouse is Jewish," and it ordered the exclusion of Jews from key positions in education, the civil service, the armed forces, and the sensitive communications networks (film, theater, press, and radio). A quota system limited the number of Jewish doctors, lawyers, and other professionals. Like the early Nazi Reich, however, the early Vichy regime made exceptions for its "good Jewish citizens"—for the decorated soldiers of World War I and the heroes of the spring of 1940.[23] Lucie's son-in-law, Dr. Lévy, veteran of the

Somme and the Italian campaigns of World War I, confirmed in 1941 that his work had not yet been affected by what he called the "disgraceful Statute." Echoing the sentiments of other Jewish citizens who still had faith in Pétain and who still considered Vichy a barrier against Nazi atrocities, the doctor had "the impression that the government is doing what it must in order to delay and mitigate the measures imposed upon it." He encouraged his family to be optimistic: "The sun continues to shine behind the clouds," he wrote Madeleine, "and all of life's beauty cannot be soiled . . . neither by the civilized nor by the barbarian."[24]

But by early 1942, family members confronted special Jewish "taxes," food and housing shortages, and limited jobs—or no jobs at all. Always a meticulous manager of her household budget, Lucie had left Paris with a significant amount of cash, and she tried to calm her family's anxieties: "Don't worry about the question of money," she wrote Simone more than once. "Tell me what you need and I will send it." In her hotels at Cassis, near Pierre's family, and at Aix-les-Bains, where she took the cure for a respiratory illness, she talked about the surprisingly "good and abundant food" still available in those regions ("though it's not Pantagruelesque"). She considered the obsession with food "exasperating," however, and the life around her increasingly "insipid." Remembering how her husband's allies had confronted the affair, she longed to return to "a milieu where people care about exchanging ideas, especially now, when it is so important." As she traveled, she contrasted the "sun-filled days" spent on terraces overlooking the Mediterranean or the Lac du Bourget at Aix-les-Bains ("there is no impression that a war is going on") with the "despair and anguish deep in us all." "Events are still so sad," she wrote in the summer of 1942. "The world has gone mad. We have lost our way in the midst of all these massacres, of all this universal unconsciousness."[25]

At that moment, and increasingly over subsequent months, Lucie lost touch with relatives and friends who escaped to England, North Africa, and America, and with others who disappeared. After nearly two years in Marseilles and the villages of its coastal hinterlands, Pierre Dreyfus received permission from the United States to emigrate with his immediate family. His wife had relatives there, and authorities were convinced that Pierre's decade-long work with Jewish political groups— as well as his high profile as the son of Alfred Dreyfus—placed him in danger. Given his many contacts with international organizations, he probably received help from the American Joint Distribution Committee, a philanthropic group that aided Jewish immigrants in Paris and moved its offices to Marseilles after the German invasion. In June 1942, with precious exit visas in hand, Pierre, Marie, and their four children boarded a ship bound for New York City by way of Casablanca.[26]

Five months later, Anglo-American forces landed in France's North African colonies, and German armies responded with a massive push, code-named Attila, into the *zone nono* and its key Mediterranean ports. With all of France under Nazi occupation and Vichy now more subservient than ever, Jews who had taken refuge in the south fell victim to the Gestapo and the collaborationist French police. As a notorious black market city supplying weapons to the growing Resistance movement, and as a potential point of Allied invasion, Marseilles and its Old Port (infested with "opposition and crime") became the focus of a "radical and complete solution." In January 1943, German and French authorities staged a "gigantic roundup" (*rafle*) that led to the deportation of thousands of people, of twenty-seven nationalities, including two thousand Jews, foreign and French. The fine "racial" distinctions and special dispensations of the early months of the war slipped away as Germans rushed to occupy all French territory and fill quotas of deportation.[27]

Pierre Dreyfus's World War I record—his three combat citations, Croix de Guerre with palm, and Legion of Honor—would have counted for nothing in Marseilles in January 1943. But by that time he had settled in America, in a rented apartment in New York City, near the intersection of Eighty-first Street and Columbus Avenue. With his two eldest children, Françoise and Charles, he contacted representatives of General de Gaulle's Free French, and, to pay the rent and purchase food and clothes, he lectured to American audiences on an earlier epoch of civil war in his homeland, on the history of his father's affair.[28]

In France, the deportation of Jews from the northern zone had begun long before the Marseilles *rafle*. Nazi officials informed their southern collaborators that Jews were sent to new "homelands" in Eastern Europe; and since the majority of deportees were foreigners, and since Vichy remained committed to the expulsion of "undesirable aliens," Pétain's state facilitated the process of removal. Darquier de Pellepoix, the new chief at the Commissariat for Jewish Affairs, insisted that "cleaning up [the] Jewish scum" was a matter of "public hygiene," of "bringing France back to her true ideals."[29] Interviewed by the newspaper *Le Cri du Peuple* in the late spring of 1942, Darquier recalled with pride how "at the beginning of this century France held the lead in the anti-Jewish struggle, with . . . first-rate men like . . . the polemicist Drumont and the great lord of action, the Marquis de Morès." And others shared Darquier's nostalgia: The "brakes had been put on" anti-Semitism in France by the affair and World War I, reported *La France Européenne,* and Jews "profited" from that calm; but now "anti-Semitism has recovered its inevitable force." In February 1942, the Association of Anti-Jewish Journalists made a pilgrimage to Père Lachaise cemetery to place flowers on the tomb of their "great confrère Drumont, who struck out against the first wave of Jewish power." And a few months later, *Au Pilori* blamed the World War I deaths of 1.3 million Frenchmen on the "race of Christ-killers."[30]

Responding to the arrest of five thousand foreign Jews in Paris, another French newspaper announced that "the solution to the Jewish question is well under way," and the paper hoped that the operation would soon extend to native Jews, to the "old hebraic tribes" of France. It soon did. SS Chief Heinrich Himmler, through his emissary Adolf Eichmann, ordered the deportation of all the Jews of France, and by late 1942, more than forty thousand had been transported east. The time of "exceptions" was passing.[31]

For two years Lucie Dreyfus had traveled across the southern zone with relative freedom. Vichy may have been a masquerade of autonomy from Nazi control, but early on it required no special passports for French Jews, and it policed more foreigners than natives. In the winter of 1942–43, however, Darquier's office ordered that the identification papers and ration cards of all Jews be appropriately stamped (*Juif* or *Juive*); it prohibited travel through certain *départements;* and, on a more minor, but, for Lucie Dreyfus, immediate note, it restricted Jews from the cure centers of the south. Lucie would have to demonstrate that her illness was severe and required treatment. Increasingly, her letters spoke of "curfews," "exorbitant prices," "closed shops," and "threats of evacuation." As living conditions deteriorated, outbreaks of popular anti-Semitism—ignored by Vichy or encouraged by its followers—spread through towns and villages, and Lucie Dreyfus's quotidian problems with identification papers and restricted movement gave way to a search for a hiding place. Jacques Dreyfus's son, Paul, a lieutenant in the French reserve, had been taken prisoner in the spring of 1940, but two other sons—René, a decorated World War I aviator, and Henri, who served as the Radical-Socialist mayor of Carpentras until stripped of that post by Vichy—sheltered Lucie in the Vaucluse region. She soon lost contact with both men, however; arrested and imprisoned in Avignon, they were shipped north. Other in-laws—the only son of Alfred's sister, Rachel Schil, and Lucie's part-time traveling companion, Léon Dreyfus's widow—also disappeared after 1943, one from northern France near Nancy, and the other from the environs of Grenoble.[32]

For the second time in her life, Lucie changed her name for protection. During the affair she had, on occasion, used her brother-in-law's name, Valabrègue. But if that worked in the 1890s, it would not suffice during the Second World War; "Valabrègue" was as obviously Jewish as "Dreyfus." Lucie's third sister, Alice, had married a man named Duteil and had settled in Valence, southwest of Aix-les-Bains. That family had close connections with members of the local Resistance movement, and Alice had friends among a community of retired Catholic nuns. Helped by Alice and using her married name—one which could pass as a non-Jewish name—Lucie found shelter in the retreat house of "the good sisters of Valence."[33]

Seventy-four years old in 1943, "Madame Duteil" spent her time working on English-language exercises, knitting woolen sweaters (which she sold), and reading. Her notebooks listed scores of titles, from Kaplan's *Temoignages sur Israël* and Mauriac's *Vie de Jésus* to Oscar Wilde's prison letters and a recent biography of Adolf Hitler. She studied Spinoza, Renan, Nietzsche, and Gide, and she transcribed quotes and recorded her reflections. "The two most beautiful things in the world," she wrote, paraphrasing Kant, "are the starry sky above my head and the moral law in the depths of my heart." After reading a French translation of Albert Einstein's 1934 book (*Comment je vois le monde*), she selected the passages that most impressed her. "The essential points of the Judaic conception of life seem to be the following: the affirmation of the right to life for all creatures; the idea that an individual's life only has meaning in the service of improving . . . the existence of all living things." Through the "magnificent Psalms" came other "Judaic traditions," Lucie's notes on Einstein continued, "a sort of joyous rapture and wonder in the presence of the beauty and sublimeness of this world." One page of her notebooks closed with thoughts on "memory," that "mysterious instrument," that "echo of all thought and feeling. . . . It is a marvelous creation," she wrote in her Catholic refuge, "because without it all life would melt away."[34]

"I'm happy to hear that you appreciate Kant so much," Lucie's twenty-three-year-old granddaughter, Madeleine Lévy, wrote a friend in 1941. "I do as well, perhaps because of his passage on 'the starry sky above and the moral law within me.' " Madeleine had fled south to Toulouse with her family during the first summer exodus, and before returning to Paris she had joined a friend, another former *éclaireuse*, to hear Pétain's address of capitulation. In response to the marshal, those two young women stood in front of their radio and recited a Kipling poem, "If," they had memorized as Girl Scouts: "If you can meet Triumph and Disaster / And treat those two impostors just the same . . . Or watch the things you gave your life to, broken, / And stoop and build 'em up with worn-out tools . . ." Using quiet verse as a form of protest fitted the reputation that Madeleine enjoyed among schoolmates and Scouts; as a teenager at the Lycée Molière, she and six other Jewish students staged a silent "strike" on the steps of the home of a professor who had slandered the memory of the "Juif" Alfred Dreyfus.[35]

Pretty but not delicate, Madeleine had dark eyes, thick brown hair, a strong, square jaw, and a vivacious smile. Her voice was pleasanter than that of her favorite grandparent, but, like Alfred, she had an air of "natural control and calmness"; one friend described her as sometimes "wreathed in silence." She preferred to express herself in actions rather than words—another trait she shared with the man who helped raise her.[36]

In the spring of 1941, Madeleine returned to her family in Toulouse. Following the lesson of Kipling's poem, she took up the "tools" of her training as an *assistante sociale* and applied them to a new job with the Secours National, the general welfare organization of the French state, which Vichy funded, in part, through the liquidation of Jewish property. "It is interesting work," Madeleine wrote a friend in Paris, "varied and extremely engaging." But the activities were more "engaging" than her censored "interzone" postcard could ever reveal. Though a functionary of Vichy, Madeleine worked clandestinely in the service of its enemies. Throughout France—and nowhere more dramatically than in Toulouse—members of the Secours National created shadow organizations to aid immigrant children, political "criminals" on the run, and Jews searching for an escape route from France.[37]

Madeleine's family—most French families—had clung to the hope that Vichy would limit Nazi persecution rather than ease its administration. But key events in 1941 and, above all, in the summer of the following year turned the reverence that many citizens held for Pétain's "divine surprise" (Maurras's label for the new state)[38] into revulsion, and drew thousands of recruits like Madeleine, her sister Simone, and brothers Jean-Louis and Etienne into networks of resistance. French Communists, many of whom had gone into hibernation after the signing of the Hitler-Stalin pact, renewed their struggle against fascism when the Third Reich invaded the Soviet Union in 1941, and increasing numbers of Frenchmen and -women, though still a minority, mobilized against Vichy when state officials cooperated in the mass roundups of Jewish families.

At daybreak on July 16, 1942, French police in Paris forced thousands of half-dressed men, women, and children from their homes and pushed them onto city buses bound for holding centers, including the huge sports arena, the Vélodrome d'Hiver. In two days, nearly thirteen thousand Jews had been *raflés* by French and German authorities, and one month later, Jews held in camps near Toulouse were shipped north by train. "Men and women pushed into boxcars," wrote one American witness, "thirty to a car, whose only furniture was a bit of straw on the floor, one iron pail for all toilet purposes, and a police guard." In a radio address a few days later, Pétain's Vice-Premier Pierre Laval confirmed, "No one and nothing can deter us from carrying out the policy of purging France of undesirable elements, without nationality." Under pressure to fill Nazi quotas and insisting that immigrant families should be "reunited," Laval approved the deportation of thousands of Jewish children out of France and into the east. More than one thousand were under six years of age, and they were not headed for the family reunion promised by Laval.[39]

"The tears and blood of small children call for us to help," went a Resistance brochure addressed to "Men and Women of Heart" in November 1942. "These Hitlerian monsters have declared a war of extermination on infants, on babies in their cradles. . . . Members of the teaching corps! Do your humanitarian duty as Frenchmen, refuse to turn children over to their executioners. . . . Fathers and Mothers! When you embrace your children remember that little ones like yours are torn away from their parents. Take them in, give them refuge. Form groups for persecuted youth everywhere."[40] As a Girl Scout and social worker, Madeleine Lévy had spent the past decade helping children, and the summer roundup of 1942, more than any other event, spurred her commitment to the Resistance. On November 11 of that year, the day of the World War I armistice, German troops occupied Toulouse and the French prefect issued a warning: "The population must remain absolutely calm. . . . Every act contrary to order will be ruthlessly repressed."[41] At the same moment, still under the cover of the Secours National, Madeleine became a departmental assistant in

Region IV of the "Combat" movement, the premier Resistance organization in the southwest.[42]

"The danger is extreme," went a secret December report from Combat headquarters. "It is absolutely necessary that those of our . . . militants whose names are known to the police change their residence immediately, and after the first search of their quarters that they join underground groups. All meetings in cafés and restaurants must *definitely* end." The orders carried a special warning for men: "Be aware that in every large town there are now dozens, sometimes hundreds of women in the pay of the Gestapo. Do not fool yourself; they are the ones who will arrest you."[43] The school of collaboration, however, was coeducational, and while the Gestapo in Toulouse—with its "interrogation center" on the rue Maignac, the most "feared" address in the city—had fewer than one hundred troops, it called on local men and women known to their victims as the *gestapo français*. Madeleine's job with the Secours National screened her Resistance work, but it also put her in daily contact with potential members of the "French Gestapo," with functionaries loyal to the Vichy regime. Following orders to stay on the move, she spent some nights with her parents on the rue de la Dalbade, others with friends, and still others with her sister, Simone, who had returned to the city with her young daughter and had taken an apartment near the train station. By 1942 the Lévy family had changed their name to "Dupuy," and through contacts known to Madeleine and Simone, they had procured forged identity cards.[44]

Combat, which would merge with other groups in 1943 to form the Mouvements Réunis de la Résistance (MUR), had "political" and "military" sections, and a "general service" unit for which Madeleine worked. Departmental assistants, most of them young women who reported to older female *responsables,* packed boxes of food, clothing, and soap and delivered them (under false identities) to local prisons and internment camps; they washed prison laundry, forged papers, located "safe houses," brought news to the relatives of arrested comrades, and took in, or tried to place, orphaned children. "Yesterday I received a parcel . . . and I suppose it came from you," wrote a friend of Madeleine's who used the code name Nicolas and who was being held in an internment camp near Toulouse. He described the plight of other comrades in neighboring barracks and cells, and he added that "today, they released my neighbor. If I were not of the chosen race, I would hope that for all of us. But, sadly, I have few illusions about our fate. . . .

Morale is good, but I am fatally sad." Madeleine's position with the Secours National, and her work with the Toulouse office of the Red Cross, helped her get provisions to friends like "Nicolas," but her principal task—helping to arrange escape routes across the Pyrenees for those who had few illusions about their fate—placed her in the greatest danger.[45]

Building on the experience of the Spanish Civil War, Resistance groups in the southwest reopened many of the mountain channels (*filières*) used by Franco's enemies crossing into France in the late 1930s. But now the flow was reversed. Toulouse served as a principal city of departure for "clandestine passages" south toward Tarbes, Foix, or Perpignan and on to Spain. Volunteer guides motivated by compassion, and professional smugglers motivated by greed, accompanied a wide range of secret travelers into mountain villages: refugees from the Low Countries and northern France; political prisoners on the run from southwestern camps; soldiers hoping to join the Free French in North Africa (or hoping to disappear); young men about to be conscripted into German factories; and, increasingly, Jews escaping deportation. Fascist at home and neutral abroad, Spain sometimes threatened to close its borders, but international pressure, the greed of individuals who profited from the passages, and, above all, the uncontrollable deluge of refugees kept many routes open; Spanish officials could only hope that the foreigners would pass through their country "as light passes through a glass, leaving no trace."[46] Working from her base in Toulouse, Madeleine Lévy joined other members of Combat's *service social* to arrange the food, counterfeit documents, special identity photographs, and money (usually three thousand francs per person, but often much more) needed for the voyage out.[47]

Combat did not act alone. Madeleine's older sister, Simone, a specialist in forged papers, and her brothers, Jean-Louis, a physician, and Etienne, just out of school, also aided the effort through other organizations. "I pledge to fight on until the total collapse of Nazi Germany," read the small, black-bordered membership card that Simone kept in a secret place. "For honor, liberty, and the right to a Jewish life." The two sisters—one influenced by her grandfather's secularism, the other by her grandmother's religiosity—signed on with separate "laic" and "Jewish" Resistance groups in their common goal to aid the victims of Nazism and the National Revolution.

The Jewish Scout movement, Les Eclaireurs Israélites, contributed so many effective recruits through its camp near Moissac north of

Toulouse that Vichy's Commissariat for Jewish Affairs formally abolished the organization (to no avail) early in 1943. When told that the scouts were "good honest people," France's chief anti-Semite, Darquier de Pellepoix, responded, "Precisely. It is those kinds of Jews who are most dangerous." Among the most dangerous of all were the Lévys' young comrades in "the Sixth," a group associated with "the Jewish Army," founded by Toulouse Zionists in 1941 but most of whose followers pledged their allegiance to France rather than Palestine. In villages near Castres, between Toulouse and the Mediterranean coast, Jean-Louis and Etienne Lévy joined former Scouts engaged in the sabotage of German transport trains; and from her base in Toulouse, Simone assisted Serge Perl, a key figure in the Sixth. A "strong, husky fellow" with dark features and a wide reputation for his "considerable resistance work" (as one report had it), Perl found hiding places and avenues of escape for Jews. He also found a comrade and companion in Simone, a widow for more than five years. Not long after they met, the two *résistants* were engaged to be married.[48]

As roundups multiplied and Jews fled toward the Pyrenees, Perl's organization intensified its rescue efforts. In response, the Gestapo and the local *milice* (paramilitary groups made up of Vichy's citizen collaborators) redoubled their own efforts to destroy the movement they called the "secret" and "sinister" Sixth.[49] But Jews in other Toulouse organizations—Communists in the Francs Tireurs et Partisans Français, and de Gaulle's agents in Combat's Region IV unit—also became targets for the Gestapo and *milice*. Madeleine's group had received a special warning from regional headquarters late in 1942: "It is certain that in a few weeks, perhaps a few days, Jews in the southern zone will suffer the same fate as those in the north. . . . All Jews occupying key positions in the movement should immediately go underground. . . . They must change their place of residence . . . and take on a new identity. . . . One's duty," the Region IV report added, "is not to go to the slaughterhouse, but to escape it."[50]

Promoted to "adjudant" with the French Forces of the Interior (FFI), Madeleine was offered a position with Combat's premier unit in Lyon. Wanting to press on with her work in Toulouse, however, and stay close to family and friends, she refused the transfer.[51]

Suzanne Schwob Dreyfus, Mathieu's widow, remained in Paris after the 1940 armistice and through the early years of the Nazi occupation. In her seventies, she lived alone in an apartment on the rue Litolf between the Trocadéro and the Bois de Boulogne. But at some point after 1942, when Germans forced all Jews to wear the yellow Star of David, and when new *rafles* threatened to include native Jews, Suzanne Dreyfus escaped (through her basement and with the help of her concierge) to the nearby home of her daughter, Magui Mercier. As she had done during the affair, Suzanne used the pseudonym Madame Mathieu.[52]

The Merciers, like many other families who fled south in May and June 1940, had returned to the capital from Bordeaux a few weeks later. As a liaison with the American Red Cross, Ernest Mercier mobilized his contacts at the Société d'Electricité et de Gaz and helped arrange the distribution of milk, grain, children's clothing, and other necessities throughout the unoccupied zone. Along with other Jewish and Protestant families who returned to Paris (though much more than most), the Merciers found enemies on two sides: One band of critics condemned them as leaders of the Judeo-Protestant cabal of high finance that had ruined France, while others, secretly on the scent of collaboration, pointed to the affinity between Mercier's old Redressement Français and Pétain's new National Revolution. The Paris office of the Commissariat-Général aux Questions Juives focused on what it did best: It questioned the ancestry of Marguerite Dreyfus Reinach Mercier and ordered her to prove French citizenship of "long standing." In the midst of an economy ravaged by war, at least one industry flourished in France—genealogy—and Magui engaged a firm with ten busy branches in Paris and the provinces to research her family's background in French Alsace. Traveling to the Haut-Rhin archives, the genealogist produced names reaching back to Abraham Dreÿfuss, born in Rixheim, in French territory, in 1749."You have, therefore, five solid generations," he informed his client, "and your dossier is complete."[53]

The same documentation that satisfied Vichy's rules, however, confirmed Magui's Jewishness for the Gestapo. Like her mother, she was forced to wear the yellow star, and German interest extended to her past involvement in the Redressement Français. Some of its former members may have rushed to embrace the Vichy regime (Pétain himself had attended Redressement meetings), but its founder and his wife were known as much for their anti-Germanism as for their elitist, technocratic philosophy. In one of their first sweeps through Paris, German police had ordered Madame Mercier to provide the names and addresses of other Redressement followers. "I sat at my table," she later wrote, "and thought of the Dreyfus Affair, of my uncle who had also been forced to write." She tried to provide false information, but the names were easy enough for the Gestapo to find. Meanwhile, Magui's *artisanat feminin* remained open throughout the occupation, with some of its women workers secretly distributing clothes to Paris refugee organizations.[54]

While Magui Mercier had to prove that she was a French Jew of long standing, her husband had to prove that, contrary to popular wisdom, he was not a Jew at all. He refused to join old business colleagues who supported Pétain (Mercier called Vichy an "armistice regime" propped up by France's hereditary enemy),[55] and he felt again, as he had in the 1930s, the fallout of rumors spread by the anti-Semitic press. Born in Algeria (true) to the daughter of a rabbi (false), he had counseled a Franco-Soviet alliance in 1935 (true) because of his "flirtation with Communism" (false). Tired stories of links to the Rothschilds reemerged as well. For the weekly paper *Au Pilori,* Mercier had "one foot in the Jewish clan, the other in the Protestant clan," and if he was not a Jew, he was "worthy of being one." Securing his own genealogist, Mercier produced documentation on his "Aryanism" to the Commissariat for Jewish Affairs, and threatened lawsuits against Parisian newspapers. In its turn, Vichy threatened to seize his property. Despite all his enemies, however, Mercier also had friends in Pétain's regime, and in 1943 it was not the French state that moved for his arrest and deportation as a hostage, but the Germans.[56]

Blood poisoning saved him. Hospitalized at the moment that German police rounded up other businessmen and civil servants who refused to collaborate, Mercier, thought to be near death, was passed by. Nor did the Gestapo issue a warrant for Marguerite Mercier's arrest. Less powerful than her industrialist husband, she also fell into the "Group A" category used at internment centers—a category that included French Jewish citizens married to "Aryans" and designated (when the rule was followed) as *"non-déportables."*[57] Nursed by Magui, sixty-five-year-old Ernest Mercier recovered through the late months of 1943 and renewed his contacts with a group of engineers and professional men committed to the defeat of Germany. That coterie of white-collar Resistance, as potentially powerful as it was hard to find in France, had links to General de Gaulle's movement in London. And in Mercier it had the one man who knew more than any other about the vastly complicated system of electrical power in the Paris region; having led the team that installed it, the old "king of electricity" would be a valuable ally if the liberation promised by de Gaulle ever came.[58]

Magui and Ado Reinach's three children also lined up solidly in the

Gaullist camp. The choice fit; they did not share the vision of France's future held by the Communist Resistance or by Jewish movements, Zionist or otherwise. Magui's youngest daughter, France, having reached Montreal from Cuba in the late summer of 1940, worked as a secretary in the naval offices of the French. Her older sister, Suzie, moved from Bordeaux to Aix-les-Bains, in the zone occupied by Italy. Suzie's husband, Emmanuel Amar, a naturalized citizen of Greek birth, had served as a lieutenant and had been taken prisoner by the Germans in the summer of 1940. Released after the armistice, he worked for the French petroleum industry (a job arranged by his father-in-law, Mercier), and then, with his wife (who kept her maiden name), joined the Resistance. On June 4, 1943, only a few hours after Amar left for an assignment in Lyon, two Italian agents in civilian clothes arrested Suzie Reinach in her Aix-les-Bains hotel. Forced to leave her two infant children behind, she was taken to Annecy and then to an old, abandoned prison ward in Grenoble: "The stench was almost unbearable," she wrote, "and the walls were covered with the desperate words" of former inmates. Questioned about her links to an operative named "Maurice" (she had served, in the vocabulary of the Resistance, as Maurice's "letter box"), she was tortured and threatened with death by firing squad. But she led her interrogators "astray" with vague bits of information about a number of acquaintances named "Maurice." On learning of the arrest, Ernest Mercier protested to Italian authorities and came to Grenoble from Paris to secure his stepdaughter's release. But his mission failed, and he could only arrange for the delivery of clothes, bedding, and a Bible. Transported to a women's prison ("an enormous fortress") in the northern Italian city of Turin, Mathieu Dreyfus's granddaughter underwent the same treatment that Mathieu's brother had experienced at the Saint-Martin de Ré citadel a half century before; stripped and searched, she was thrown into a dark cell with an iron cot. But Alfred Dreyfus had been kept in solitary confinement; Suzie Reinach shared her cell—designed for a single prisoner—with six other women. And she would remain in captivity for more than a year.[59]

The youngest of Mathieu Dreyfus's grandchildren, Jean-Pierre Reinach, twenty-five years old in 1940, spent the early months of the war at the sideshow of the Maginot Line. Demobilized after the armistice, he returned to Paris and then, with his stepfather's help, secured an exit visa for a job in French Morocco. The German occupier had not yet decided to round up Jews rather than let them escape, but the job in North Africa had been a ploy for Jean-Pierre to reach England. While in Morocco, he met a nucleus of men who hoped to continue the fight against Germany, and he worked to achieve two goals: to sign up with de Gaulle in London and to rejoin his fiancée, Naomi de Rothschild. His efforts to leave Morocco failed twice, however, and on the second attempt, in early 1941, somewhere on the Atlantic near the port of Tangier, he was arrested and imprisoned. After a short term in jail—and an illness, due to a rat bite that nearly killed him—he went into hiding in the Atlas Mountains. Finally, through the black markets of Casablanca or Rabat, he procured transit papers and sailed to America via Lisbon, "the refugee capital of Europe." Joining the Free French in New York (where his cousins, Pierre Dreyfus's children, would work in the movement's recruitment center in a few months' time), he then visited his sister France in Montreal. He knew that his next assignment would be perilous, and he and his sister spoke only of the present and the past; they sensed that a future reunion would never take place. Days later Jean-Pierre sailed again, east to England.[60]

Engaged since the summer of 1939, Jean-Pierre and Naomi were married in the fall of 1941. They had eight months together in London, with leaves taken at the Rothschild estate at Exbury. Immediately after his arrival in England, Jean-Pierre had enlisted with de Gaulle's army in exile and had been sent by the Bureau Central de Renseignement et d'Action for training with the British. Though more comfortable on a horse, on terra firma, as his father had been, he learned how to parachute—in just a few days' time. By the spring of 1942 he had been promoted to second lieutenant and, after urgent requests for active duty, received an assignment from Colonel Semidei-Servais, his commanding officer. Using the cover name Jean-Pierre Royère, he would parachute from a British Whitley aircraft into the countryside south of Châteauroux, in the Berry region of central France. Traveling alone, he would contact a Resistance unit in charge of collecting economic and military information at their "clandestine radio posts" and then move south to the Mediterranean. His ultimate destination was North Africa, and his orders were to locate the resistance-minded comrades he had met in Morocco. He would be part of the military network helping to prepare for the Allied invasions.[61]

But Second Lieutenant Reinach never made it past the Berry countryside. Bad weather or a pilot's bad judgment forced his plane too low, and when he jumped, his body became entangled in the ropes of his parachute. He was found in a field outside the village of Velles, and when local Pétainist officials refused to bury him ("if he's French he's a traitor, if he's English he's an enemy"), the village Catholic priest provided the coffin and the prayers. Jean-Pierre's father, Ado Reinach, was the same age, twenty-seven years old, when he died in a cavalry charge in the Ardennes Forest in August 1914. And Ado had never known his only son, born seven months later. In October 1942, five months after Jean-Pierre's death, Naomi Reinach gave birth to a daughter who would also never know her father.[62]

"JEWS? . . . NO! JEWESSES!" went the headline of a collaborationist tract in Toulouse in 1943; "The Jewess who dares not speak her name . . . calls herself Miss Madeleine . . . but she is LEVY . . . the grand pontiff of the Secours National. . . . Had you missed that point, good and brave Christians?" the local paper, *The Ironworker (Le Ferro)*, asked its readers. And it ended with an order to "Sweep her out! Sweep her out!"[63]

By 1943, Nazi collaborators and informers riddled the neighborhood surrounding the Lévys' apartment on rue de la Dalbade. And they populated the offices of the Secours National a few streets away on the Croix Baragon. Warnings from Combat headquarters to operatives like "Miss Madeleine"—orders to change domiciles, to beware of double agents, to go underground—intensified through the summer and fall, and it became more important than ever to follow Combat's two cardinal rules: "Everything that is unnecessary to say is dangerous to say," and, "In our metier, a bigmouth [*bavard*] is an assassin." The *milice* stepped up its attacks (for every comrade killed, they promised "ten dead Communists"), and the Gestapo responded to a new wave of explosions and assassinations with a "vast movement of repression." Members of Combat, the Sixth, and other groups in the southwest sabotaged rail lines, train stations, and armament depots, and within Toulouse they blew up German trucks, ambushed police, and lay in wait for collaborators. Following bomb attacks on the Toulouse train station, one hundred German and French agents cordoned off the area and began another "massive operation of roundups, interrogations . . . and internment."[64]

"The actions of the police," reported *La Depêche,* a Toulouse paper that once supported Jaurès but now bowed to Pétain, "will be carried forward in a vigorous way." The actions were, and so were those of the Resistance. On a late summer night in 1943, anti-German militants hurled a hand grenade at soldiers leaving a Toulouse cinema. None were killed, but three men—including one Jew, as *La Depêche* made a point of noting—were apprehended and executed by a firing squad. A short time later, a local *résistant,* armed with a machine gun, hit the most strategic target of all, the Toulouse police intendant. The official was assassinated in front of his home on the night of October 23, and his funeral, in the city's cathedral, attracted a contingent of Vichy dignitaries led by the secretary-general of police. Vowing to crush the "terrorist movement . . . and the foreign forces which give it life," René Bousquet praised the "patriotic faith" of the police of the National Revolution, the men who "render their services to France." On the night after Bousquet's eulogy, Toulouse authorities declared a curfew and ordered the streets cleared by 9:00 P.M.[65]

Informed by Resistance leaders of a pending crackdown, the Lévys fled for the hinterlands. On November 3, two bombs exploded at *milice* headquarters in the city, killing the movement's leader and setting the Gestapo off on another roundup. For nearly a week, since they had seized documents from a regional Combat office, they had been following suspects, including workers attached to the Secours National. On the day of the bombing, or the day before, Madeleine had come back to Toulouse, and, according to her Combat superior and two Red Cross associates, had "worked late into the night."[66] Violating the curfew, she then went to the apartment on the rue de la Dalbade to pack clothes and provisions for her family; she wore only a light summer dress, and that would not do for a winter hiding in the countryside. Nearly deaf in one ear since her operation as a child, she heard neither the concierge who tried to warn her nor the police who entered the building's dark, narrow corridor. Arrested for her work with the Résistance Intérieure Française, she was interrogated with other suspects captured that day. The Gestapo released all the Secours National workers but one. "Because of her name," Madeleine Dreyfus Lévy remained in custody.[67]

She might have been sent to the camp for political prisoners at Compiègne, but in the bureaucracy of deportation "racial" designations eclipsed "resistance" categories, and along with at least three Jewish friends from Toulouse she was transported by train to the Drancy holding center northeast of Paris.[68] A modern five-story, U-shaped apartment project—started before the war to house low-income families but never completed—the Drancy complex had been turned into a prison by the Germans in August 1941. Surrounded by floodlights, observation posts, and barbed wire three meters high, the camp was administered, in late 1943, by SS Hauptsturmführer Alois Brunner. French police stood guard. When Madeleine arrived in the first week of November, Drancy had three thousand prisoners, thousands more having passed through during previous months. Some, like Jacques Dreyfus's son Henri and Joseph Reinach's niece Fanny, were still there, while others, like Jacques's other son, René, had been transported east. No question remained among inmates that the complex, later known as "Drancy-la-Juive," was an "antechamber" of deportation. The question was, deportation to where?[69]

Children populated the camp as well, and Madeleine must have been referring to them when she got word out to a friend in Paris: "Do not concern yourself," she wrote. "I can be useful and help others through my *métier* as a social worker."[70] Convoy Number 62, the fifteenth to leave Drancy in 1943, had 83 children under the age of 12, and Madeleine, along with a friend, Claude Lehmann, born in Mulhouse, helped care for them. Following the normal routine, Adolf Eichmann, lieutenant colonel of the SS, based in Berlin, approved the convoy's departure—using the new and efficient telex system—and sent a "commando of escorts" from Strasbourg. Assisted by French personnel from Darquier de Pellepoix's Commissariat for Jewish Affairs, the commando team loaded 1,200 Jews—634 men, 556 women, and 10 unspecified prisoners—onto freight cars at the Bobigny station near Drancy. The train left at 11:50 A.M. on November 20, 1943, two days after Madeleine Lévy's twenty-fifth birthday.[71]

Crossing the eastern French countryside, past Château-Thierry, Châlons-sur-Marne, and Bar-le-Duc, the train moved south of Verdun through the Moselle region, and then north of Alsace into Germany and then Poland. On the first night, nineteen prisoners escaped at the small town of Lerouville south of Saint-Mihiel, some of them men who had recently tried to dig a tunnel out of Drancy only to be denounced by other prisoners. The voyage took three days and two nights, and Claude Lehmann, in the same freight car with Madeleine, described the "forced gaiety . . . the good camaraderie of old friends who had known each other for so long." Fanny Reinach, related to Madeleine's cousins, and another friend, Nicole Weil, were with them, and so were Resistance colleagues from Toulouse.[72]

Their convoy arrived at Auschwitz at 2 A.M. on November 23. A cold rain fell while 1,181 passengers climbed down and placed their belongings on the train platform; Madeleine still had the suitcase she had brought from Toulouse, but it would be quickly taken from her. An SS captain selected 895 deportees—mostly the old, young, and infirm—and ordered them onto trucks waiting nearby. Madeleine's friend, Nicole Weil, accompanying two children who had been separated from their parents, went with them, and at 3:45 A.M. the trucks drove off. In relatively good health and useful as laborers in the many industries of Auschwitz, the remaining 241 men and 45 women, separated and lined up five by five, were assigned numbers; the group that included Madeleine Lévy and Fanny Reinach, on record as prisoners 69036 though 69080, marched out first. SS troops, holding their dogs on a tight leash, directed the way to quarantine centers at the neighboring camp of Birkenau, where inmates were "disinfected," shorn with scissors and razors, and given uniforms marked with the Star of David.[73]

For six months, Claude Lehmann, assigned to the synthetic rubber plant at Auschwitz, tried to learn the fate of his friends. He knew that most of the women in his convoy—the ones not loaded onto trucks and gassed the first morning, the ones selected as laborers—had worked at an excavation site near the Birkenau woods in late November and December. But not until the following spring did he hear that Madeleine Lévy had been stricken by typhus and taken to one of the barracks that served as the camp's hospital complex, its *Krankenbau*. Patients like Madeleine, too ill to walk to the *Waschraum* showers for compulsory disinfections, were carried on the backs of orderlies; and in the winter of 1943–44, when Madeleine's fever had advanced, hospital workers recorded seventy-four deaths in one day in one block of 250 patients. Disoriented, covered with the eruption of red spots that came with typhus, and deprived of the food and medication needed to fight the infection, Madeleine Lévy weighed less than seventy pounds when she died, in January 1944, at Auschwitz-Birkenau.[74]

Epilogue

LUCIE DREYFUS, still known to her protectors as "Madame Duteil," remained in hiding with the nuns of Valence until the late summer of 1944, when a fire, caused by an explosion at a German armaments depot nearby, destroyed the Catholic retreat house. Uninjured, Lucie was joined by her granddaughter Simone, and after Allied troops liberated the Provence region, and then Paris in August, the two women left for the capital. With the rail lines of Valence also destroyed, Simone helped seventy-five-year-old Lucie walk along the gravel trackbed that led to the next station and the next train north to Paris.[1]

The following year, after the fall of Berlin and the German surrender, Lucie Dreyfus's colleagues at the Comité de Bienfaisance gathered in Paris for the first time since 1940. A third of its members had died or disappeared, two of the Central Consistory's rabbis had been shot, and seventeen had been deported. "There are few Jewish families," the committee announced at that meeting, "rich or poor, French or foreign, who have not been cruelly stricken. . . . To those who have disappeared in the most hideous conditions, for their faith and for their fatherland, we pay our homage." Members of the General Assembly also took a moment to recognize their former vice president, "Madame Lucie Alfred Dreyfus," who could not be with them. Battling tuberculosis and a heart condition, she was treated at the Rothschild hospital in eastern Paris, where the committee's leadership "had the pleasure of

485

visiting her," and where they found her "still interested in the problems of social welfare to which she had devoted all her charitable work in the past." They hoped that she could rejoin their ranks "very soon." But she could not. Survivor of two world wars and the civil war of her husband's affair, Lucie Dreyfus died at home, at the age of seventy-six, on December 14, 1945.[2]

Alfred had died a decade earlier at the same age, in the same apartment, and his son had been by his side. Returning from America after the liberation of France, Pierre also stayed with Lucie until the end. In New York City, Pierre and Marie Dreyfus's son and oldest daughter had worked with French recruiters and, hoping to engage the battle in Europe, had received military training at Fort Meade in Maryland. In 1945, their daughter Françoise served as a second lieutenant, and with her American counterparts she helped repatriate displaced persons in the family's native land of Alsace. Her brother, Charles, remained in the United States to attend university. On December 27, 1946, Pierre boarded a plane for a flight back to New York to visit his son. The Star of Cairo, a Transcontinental and Western Air Constellation, left Paris at midnight with twenty-three persons on board. Scheduled to stop in Ireland before the long Atlantic crossing, the plane hit dense ground fog as it approached Shannon Airport. Instructed to divert to Scotland, the pilot attempted to bank and throttle up, but the port engine caught fire and the plane dived into a riverbank, bounced across muddy water, and came to rest on a deserted island. A "thunderous explosion" killed some passengers immediately, while others succumbed during the two hours it took for rescuers to make their way through shoulder-deep bog in the dark. Eleven people survived, but when young Charles Dreyfus, unaware of the crash, read the New York Times the next day, he learned that his father had been among the victims. "Captain Pierre Dreyfus," as the newspaper listed the veteran of Verdun and the Somme, died at the age of fifty-five.[3]

At home in Paris during her final weeks, Lucie had also been nursed by her daughter Jeanne and granddaughter Simone; and she had been treated by two of the doctors in her family—Pierre-Paul Lévy and his son Jean-Louis. The Lévys had remained in Toulouse through the Allied bombardment of German-controlled aircraft factories in the summer of 1944, and Simone and Jean-Louis had served with Jewish Resistance groups in the mountainous hinterlands until the liberation. Their brother, Etienne, moved with the Free French north to the Vosges, where, as a lieutenant, he led troops against German forces and was wounded by machine-gun fire; yet another member of the family, in yet another war, had fought for French Alsace.

Reunited in Paris a few months later, the entire family took up the search for Madeleine. They had received no word since Drancy. Eventually, her father heard of two men who had traveled with Madeleine's convoy and had returned from deportation. The first had lost contact with his friends after arrival at Auschwitz, but on July 6, 1945, Pierre-Paul Lévy met Claude Lehmann at a small hotel on the rue St. Roch near the Tuileries Garden. And he learned the details of Madeleine's fate. It took more than two years for the official "Act of Disappearance" to make its way through the bureaucracy of the Ministry of Veterans and Victims of War; but by 1950 the French Fourth Republic had awarded the granddaughter of Alfred and Lucie Dreyfus the Military Medal, the Croix de Guerre with palm, and the Medal of the Resistance. Madeleine's remains were never found, but her name, age, and mention of her "deportation by the Germans . . . to Auschwitz" were chiseled on the gravestone with her Dreyfus grandparents in the Montparnasse Cemetery.[4]

A wave of posthumous decorations marked that period, and Mathieu Dreyfus's only grandson, Jean-Pierre Reinach, received his, along with a special citation from his superior officers. "Paying homage" to his "magnificent human and military virtues," they commended that "young officer of high culture and . . . courage" and added, as their predecessors had done for Jean-Pierre's father, that the fatherland had lost "one of its most sublime children." Stamped on his military record, fifteen years after his grandfather's last will and testament had asked him to serve his country as "an honorable man, a brave Frenchman," was the official designation, "Mort pour la France."[5]

Three years before, in 1942, when news of Jean-Pierre's death reached his family, his brother-in-law, Emmanuel Amar, offered a private citation in the form of a poem ("You carried in your heart a surge of hope"). In June 1943 Amar left his wife Suzie Reinach and their two children in Aix-les-Bains and set off to join Resistance comrades in Lyon. The family never gathered again. Arrested by Italian police, Suzie remained for more than a year in a women's prison run by nuns and populated by inmates of all types (from the "highly educated" to "prostitutes"). In damp, lice-infested cells, and on a diet of boiled rice and moldy vegetables, Suzie's condition deteriorated. She suffered bronchitis, and an acute attack of appendicitis. With the help of a local priest and the Swiss consul, she was taken to a clinic where she stayed for months under police surveillance. As Allied forces moved into Italy, and as the antifascist resistance grew, Suzie escaped from the clinic and went into hiding with partisan families in Turin and its environs; the Germans and the remnants of Mussolini's army still made life perilous for a Jew in northern Italy. But since Ernest Mercier's first trip to Turin, the family knew Suzie's whereabouts, and in the spring of 1945 she was rescued by a young British officer—the brother-in-law of Jean-Pierre's widow, Naomi de Rothschild. Officially Anthony Seys had no right to cross the Italian border into France—it was a different theater of operations—but realizing that no one else would help Suzie, he requisitioned a British truck. Crossing the Mont Genèvre pass, which was pockmarked by bomb craters and partially blocked by fallen fir trees, Seys headed for Grenoble via Briançon. He stopped only briefly, at the border, where Suzie Reinach washed her face with snow, embraced her British rescuer, and knelt down to kiss "the soil of France."[6]

But if their arrival at the frontier was joyous, their reception in Grenoble was "dreadful." Local civil authorities, who may have had Pétainist sympathies, offered no help to secure the necessary papers. Late at night, the two travelers found rooms in "a dingy little hotel . . . for refugees," and the next day they were able to get a telephone call through to Paris. Magui Mercier drove all night and arrived in Grenoble with happy news for her daughter: Suzie's two children were safe, and her sister, France, was about to return home from Canada. Anthony Seys, his clandestine mission accomplished, returned to his unit in Turin, no one having noticed his absence.

In Paris, Suzie Reinach searched for news of her husband. In the weeks after the end of the war in Europe, families gathered at the broad, open square near the Sèvres-Babylone metro station to check lists of missing persons, and to post photos in the hope that other passersby, some of them recently liberated from Nazi camps, could share information. Still weak from her long imprisonment, Suzie made the trip many times from her mother's apartment and, eventually, met two witnesses who confirmed that Emmanuel Amar had been arrested and imprisoned in Lyon. A naturalized French Jewish citizen, he had been transported out of the country in February 1944 in convoy number 67, along with the grand rabbi of Strasbourg and 1,212 other men, women, and children. And he had died at Auschwitz.[7]

Ernest Mercier served as a consultant to de Gaulle's provisional government and received the Legion of Honor in 1945. He also faced a new round of attack from the French left. The entire business community had fallen under a shadow of suspicion as handmaidens of fascism, and in the wake of Vichy the few similarities between Mercier's Redressement Français and Pétain's National Revolution mattered more than the many differences. But Mercier, who had never lined up with the collaborationist regime, pressed on with what he did best: He called for economic renewal through technocratic planning; he protested the nationalization of French industries; and he supported the move toward a federated Europe—on the condition that it not include France's "hereditary enemy." A united Germany, warned the old veteran, was "too big for Europe."[8]

Seventy-five years earlier, after another war with Germany, Raphael Dreyfus had asked his oldest son to remain in Alsace so that his family could become French citizens and their industry could be saved. Jacques Dreyfus and his American wife Louise had known a life of sacrifice. Two of their sons had died in World War I, and in World War II, after both Jacques and Louise were gone, two other sons were deported from an internment camp in Avignon. Henri Dreyfus never traveled farther than Drancy; married to an "Aryan" and classified as a "non-déportable," he survived the war and returned to Carpentras. In the spring of 1945, supported by a local coalition of Gaullists and Communists, he scored an overwhelming electoral triumph and served as the town's mayor, as he had done before Vichy.[9]

His younger brother René, however, one of the most decorated members of the family in World War I, the pilot whose stories of dogfights over the Western Front had so fascinated his uncle Alfred, never returned from Auschwitz. Nor did Léon Dreyfus's widow, Alice, Lucie's companion in exile on her visit to the Ile de Ré prison in 1895 and her companion again during the early months of World War II. Nor did Fanny Reinach return from her deportation in Madeleine's convoy. Nor did Rachel Dreyfus Schil's son Julien survive the war. Many years before, during the affair, Rachel's letters to General Mercier and other officials had balanced respect for the French army with a clear accusation that her brother Alfred was being "sacrificed" as a Jew. In her old age Rachel lost none of that courage and none of that faith. But she could not survive the news that her son had been taken by the Gestapo. "This morning at 9:30," went the December 12, 1941, entry in Rachel's diary, "two German soldiers came to arrest Julien as a hostage. It seems that 3,000 Jews have been rounded up today in the sixteenth arrondissement. Where will they take him?" Rachel asked. She soon learned that he had been denounced by the concierge of his apartment on the rue Pierre Demours and that he had been taken to the holding camp at Pithiviers, south of Paris. "Poor Julien," his mother recorded in her diary. "Poor all of us." Four months later, Raphael and Jeannette Dreyfus's last surviving child died of a heart attack, and a few months after that, on September 21, 1942, the Gestapo, assisted by the French police, deported Rachel's sixty-three-year-old son to Auschwitz.[10]

In the immediate aftermath of the liberation of France, the machinery of justice, formal and informal, moved against the leaders and collaborators of Vichy's National Revolution. While personal accounts were settled in back alleys and village squares, the provisional government mounted official trials in Paris and provincial cities. Marshal Pétain and his chief supporter, Pierre Laval, had put the Third Republic on trial in the summer of 1940, and, finding it guilty of treason, they had, with the help of the National Assembly, carried out its death sentence. Now it was Vichy's turn, and to the dock came a long line of men who knew a great deal about the court of the victors. As a point of honor, Pétain had refused to leave French territory when Allied forces moved on Paris, but the Germans, retreating east, had insisted. Held in Belfort through late August 1944, the marshal was then taken by convoy through Mulhouse and across the Rhine. The remnants of his state set up headquarters in the German castle town of Sigmaringen, high above the Danube, and for seven months the marshal and his wife lived in the suite of a Hohenzollern prince. But in 1945, with Allied troops pushing in from Alsace and planes bombing the region, Pétain's entourage joined German soldiers retreating south along crowded roads toward Ravensburg and Lake Constance. One of the marshal's aides compared their flight to the exodus from Paris in the summer of 1940. Only the enemy and the direction had changed.[11]

A few days before the collapse of the Third Reich, Pétain's party made it into Switzerland. The marshal celebrated his eighty-ninth birthday in a Swiss frontier town, where, during a festive one-hour ceremony, he received flowers and chocolates from his officers and aides. Swiss authorities also noted that Pétain traveled with a bankroll of one million francs. On April 26 the marshal got his wish; he returned to his native land, but in the custody of Free French officials. At towns along the way, crowds spit at his train compartment window, hurled firecrackers, and shouted "Death to Pétain!" Held at the fort of Montrouge, south of Paris, he was interrogated over a ten-week period, and he struggled with bouts of confusion and "growing nervousness." At the trial, which began on July 23 in the Paris Palais de Justice—the same building in which Alfred Dreyfus's innocence had been proclaimed thirty-nine years before—Pétain wore his uniform with the single decoration of the Military Medal. Sitting erect in his chair ("looking at nothing and no one"), he remained silent throughout most of the proceedings, though at one point he informed the High Court that if its judgment went against him it would be condemning "an innocent man."[12]

On August 15, 1945, Pétain was convicted of treason and sentenced to death. Two days later, Charles de Gaulle commuted the sentence to life imprisonment. Transferred to the same prison that Vichy had used for Léon Blum, the former marshal was then shipped to an island eleven miles off the coast of Brittany. On the Ile d'Yeu, only a short distance northwest of the Ile de Ré, in the two rooms of the three story house that he shared with prison staff, Pétain read newspapers and biographies (including one of himself), and studied English lessons. He exercised in a courtyard, received visits from his wife, and his memory remained sharp but skewed; he recalled all the details of the "Great War" but could not relive World War II. Pétain died in exile at the age of ninety-five.[13]

His vice premier, Pierre Laval, had never enjoyed a reputation as high as that of the Savior of Verdun, and when brought to trial in October 1945 he enjoyed none of the special dispensations offered the old marshal. Convicted of plotting against the state and of "intelligence with the enemy," Laval was sentenced to "national degradation" and death by firing squad. On October 15, in his prison cell at Fresnes, south of Paris, he tried to kill himself with poison he had hidden in his jacket lining through the late years of the war. But the potion, like the man who tasted it, had lost its power, and a few minutes later, just past noon, Laval was led into a courtyard and shot.[14]

If, in the trials of the postliberation period, some collaborators showed a hint of contrition, real or simulated, seventy-six-year-old Charles Maurras showed nothing but contempt for the tribunal that heard his case. The Action Française, born of the Dreyfus affair and reborn with the collapse of France's "sacred union," had moved its headquarters to Lyon during the war. Its leader was arrested in that city in September 1944 and tried there five months later. Maurras had frequented enough courtrooms in his lifetime to know that the theatricality of the proceedings mattered as much as the evidence—especially when the verdict was a foregone conclusion. Still wearing in his buttonhole the insignia of Pétain's defunct National Revolution—the enameled, tricolored "Order of the Francisque"—Maurras heckled the prosecutor throughout the proceedings and vilified the memory of the Third Republic. Now almost completely deaf, he could hear only himself—but that sufficed, because for him no one else in the room spoke the truth.

On January 27, 1945, the Court of Justice convicted the old Immortal member of the French academy of the crime of "intelligence with the enemy," and sentenced him to "national degradation" and imprisonment for life. Damning his verdict, Maurras cried out the name of a Frenchman ten years dead: "It is," he shouted in that month of the fiftieth anniversary of another degradation, "the revenge of Dreyfus!"[15]

Notes

ABBREVIATIONS USED IN THE NOTES

AA   Archives de l'Armée, Section Historique, Vincennes

AD   Archives Départementales

AMM   Archives Municipales de Mulhouse

AN   Archives Nationales, Paris

APP   Archives de la Préfecture de Police, Paris

BAI   Bibliothèque de l'Alliance Israélite Universelle, Paris

BHVP   Bibliothèque Historique de la Ville de Paris

BN   Bibliothèque Nationale

BSIM   Bibliothèque de la Société Industrielle de Mulhouse

BVC   Bibliothèque Victor Cousin, Sorbonne, Paris—Arconati-Visconti Collection

CA   Alfred Dreyfus, *Cinq années de ma vie* (Paris, 1982; first pub., 1901)

DFPC   Dreyfus Family Private Collection

EN   Eugène Naville, unpublished memoirs, 10 vols. (private collection)

FRB   Author's interviews and correspondence with France Reinach Beck

HAD   Joseph Reinach, *Histoire de l'Affaire Dreyfus* (Paris, 1901–11)

IHTP   Institut d'Histoire du Temps Présent, Paris

LI   Alfred Dreyfus, *Lettres d'un innocent* (Paris, 1898)
MB   Musée de Bretagne, Rennes
MD   Mathieu Dreyfus, *L'Affaire telle que je l'* ai vecue (Paris, 1978)
SC   Alfred Dreyfus, *Souvenirs et correspondance, publiés par son fils* (Paris, 1936)

I PROMISED LANDS

1. For Abraham Dreÿfuss, son of Israel, see AD Haut-Rhin C 1284, Dénombrement des Juifs en Alsace, 1784 (under "Rixheim"), and 4 E, Landser, Feb. 4, 1780. On the village, see AD Haut-Rhin, *Rixheim: Trait d'union*, n.a., Dec. 1971, and 6 M 2, census; *Le Haut-Rhin: Dictionnaire des communes* (Colmar, 1982), t. III, pp. 1196–1213; *Mulhouse et le Sundgau, 1648–1798–1848*, n.a. (Mulhouse, 1948), pp. 111–12; and BSIM, "La Fabrication de papiers peints à Rixheim." To reconstruct the early Dreÿfuss genealogy, public records must be weighed against private accounts. While one family report suggests, for example, that Abraham married twice and that his son, Jacob, and grandson, Raphael, had many siblings, census documents and domicile lists paint slightly different portraits. Here the focus is on family members who can be confirmed through both official contemporary records and family archives, though there may have been other descendants of Abraham and Jacob.

2. Patrick Girard, *Les Juifs de France de 1789 à 1860* (Paris, 1976), pp. 110–11; Bernhard Blumenkranz, ed., *Histoire des Juifs en France* (Toulouse, 1972), p. 14: Solomon Grayzel, *A History of the Jews* (New York, 1968), p. 266; *Le Haut-Rhin*, pp. 1196–1213; and Paul Lévy, *Les Noms des Israélites en France* (Paris, 1960), pp. 124–25.

3. Freddy Raphaël and Robert Weyl, *Les Juifs en Alsace: Culture, société, histoire* (Toulouse, 1977), pp. 6–7, 427–28; François-Georges Dreyfus, *Histoire de l'Alsace* (Paris, 1979), p. 178; Blumenkranz, *Histoire des Juifs*, p. 181; *Mulhouse et le Sundgau*, p. 13; and *Le Haut-Rhin*, pp. 1207 ff.

4. *Mulhouse et le Sundgau*, p. 112. On Jewish butchers, see, for example, Blumenkranz, *Histoire des Juifs*, pp. 171–72; and Arthur Hertzberg, *The French Enlightenment and the Jews* (New York, 1968), pp. 198–99. The *shohet*, the "one empowered to perform the ritual slaughter of cattle and poultry," had to meet rigorous standards; he could not abuse liquor or be a "wanton transgressor of the Law" or ever have "openly desecrated the Sabbath" (see "Shohet," *Encyclopedia Judaica* [Jerusalem, 1971]). On kosher butchers in another region of France, see Marianne Calmann, *The Carrière of Carpentras* (Oxford, 1984), pp. 44–45 and passim.

5. *Le Haut-Rhin*, pp. 1207 ff; Raphaël and Weyl, *Juifs en Alsace*, p. 276 and passim; Blumenkranz, *Histoire des Juifs*, pp. 162, 171; and Daniel Stauben, *Scènes de la vie Juive* (Paris, 1860), pp. 8–11, 20.

6. Stauben, *Scènes*, pp. 50–52, 144, and Raphaël and Weyl, *Juifs en Alsace*, pp. 313–15, 349–54, 404. On the culture of cultivators in general, see Eugen Weber, *Peasants into Frenchmen: The Modernization of Rural France, 1870–1914* (Stanford, 1976).

7. AD Haut-Rhin, 4 E, Landser, 1780, 4, 2, marriages, and C 1284, Dénombrement, 1784. Brändel's name sometimes appears as Brentel or Berthe or Barbe. On local marriage customs, see Stauben, *Scènes de la vie*, p. 122, and Raphaël and Weyl, *Juifs en Alsace*, pp. 249–63.

8. The term is Frédéric Hoffet's in *Psychanalyse de l'Alsace* (Paris, 1954), p. 27, but for a better account, see Dreyfus, *Histoire de l'Alsace*, pp. 153–59 and passim; and Jean-Marie Mayeur, "Une Mémoire-frontière: L'Alsace," in Pierre Nora, ed., *Les Lieux de mémoire*, vol. 2 (Paris, 1986), p. 66.

9. Quoted in Ruth Putnam, *Alsace and Lorraine: From Caesar to Kaiser* (New

York, 1915), p. 19. On Judeo-Alsatian, see Honel Meiss, *A Travers le dialecte Judéo-Alsacien* (Nice, 1929?); Paul Lévy, *Histoire linguistique d'Alsace et de Lorraine* (Paris, 1929), t. 1, p. 357, and his *Les Noms des Israélites*, p. 62; Blumenkranz, *Histoire des Juifs*, p. 172; Raphaël and Weyl, *Juifs en Alsace*, p. 406; Hoffet, *Psychanalyse*, pp. 56–57; and Stauben, *Scènes de la vie*, p. iii.

10. The ambassador, who was Russian, is quoted in Daniel Blumenthal, *Alsace-Lorraine* (New York, 1917), p. 18. See also George Weill, *L'Alsace française* (Paris, 1916), p. 1; Paul Imbs in Jean Schlumberger, ed., *La Bourgeoisie alsacienne: Etudes d'histoire sociale* (Strasbourg, 1954), pp. 307–10; Lévy, *Histoire linguistique*, t. 1, pp. 344–45; and AD Haut Rhin 6 M 2, 1807 census with literacy statistics covering previous decades.

11. AD Haut Rhin, C 1284, Dénombrement, 1784. Given the primitive state of record keeping, Jacob's year of birth would vary from 1781 to 1785, but later documents confirm 1781 as the correct date.

12. Dreyfus, *Histoire de l'Alsace*, pp. 205, 241; Weill, *L'Alsace française*, pp. 96–97; and Blumenkranz, *Histoire des Juifs*, p. 172. For more on the slow penetration of French and French schools, see Weber, *Peasants*, p. 85 and passim.

13. Born in 1782 or 1783, Rösslein appears in the 1784 Dénombrement and then disappears from village records after 1790. On the 1789 fever epidemic, see *Mulhouse et le Sundgau*, p. 117. In 1898, a brief German "biography" of Captain Alfred Dreyfus's family reported that Jacob Dreÿfuss had had brothers, and that one became a rabbi (see Dr. Mayer, "Zwei Brüder [Die Familie des Hauptmann Dreyfus]," *Der Israelit*, vol. 39, 1898, p. 276). But census records, the Alsatian "Denombrement," and family archives indicate that Jacob had only one sibling, Rösslein.

14. Dreyfus, *Histoire de l'Alsace*, p. 169; Raymond Oberlé, *Mulhouse, ou la genèse d'une ville* (Mulhouse, 1985), pp. 197–98; and *Mulhouse et le Sundgau*, p. 112 ff.

15. AD Haut-Rhin, V 612–613, "Inscriptions de créances . . ." See under "Rixheim." Documents cover loans up to 1823, but identify villagers, like Abraham, who had been involved in moneylending over time. See also Blumenkranz, *Histoire des Juifs*, pp. 175–76; and Raphaël and Weyl, *Juifs en Alsace*, p. 374.

16. See Ben Lévi's comments on the *Dictionnaire de l'Académie* in *Les Archives Israélites*, III, 1842, p. 148

17. Deuteronomy 23: 19–20.

18. Raphaël and Weyl, *Juifs en Alsace*, pp. 370–71; and David Cohen, *La Promotion des Juifs en France à l'époque du Second Empire*, v. 1 (Aix-en-Provence, 1980), p. 3. For local reports on "Christian Jews," see AD Haut-Rhin, V 611.

19. On the *cahiers*, see Léon Poliakov, *Histoire de l'antisémitisme*, vol. 2, pp. 105–106; Blumenkranz, *Histoire des Juifs*, p. 275; Dreyfus, *Histoire de l'Alsace*, p. 188; Bernard Blumenkranz and Albert Soboul, eds., *Les Juifs et la révolution française* (Toulouse, 1976), p. 56; and D. Feuerwerker, "Les Juifs en France: Anatomie de 207 cahiers de doléances de 1789," *Annales: Economies, sociétés, civilisations*, XX, 1976, pp. 45–61. There had been a "psychose de l'usure" in southern Alsace since the late 1770s; see Blumenkranz, *Histoire des Juifs*, p. 175, and Béatrice Philippe, *Etre Juif dans la société française du moyen-âge à nos jours* (Paris, 1979), pp. 107–8. On Rixheim and neighboring localities, see *Le Haut-Rhin*, p. 1203 and passim.

20. Philippe, *Etre Juif*, pp. 107–8; Weill, *L'Alsace française*, pp. 14–15; and Georges Lefebvre, *The Great Fear of 1789: Rural Panic in Revolutionary France*, trans. Joan White (New York, 1973), pp. 109–11.

21. Lefebvre, *Great Fear*, passim; and Dreyfus, *Histoire de l'Alsace*, pp. 186–88. Michel Lévy exaggerates when he says that the decades between the 1650s and 1780 were times of peace and prosperity for Alsatian Jews (see *Coup d'oeil historique sur l'état des Israélites en France, et particulièrement en Alsace* [Strasbourg, 1836], p. 12). Poverty was pervasive and incidents like the 1778 "affaire des fausses quittances"— when peasants forged documents showing they had repaid Jewish lenders—increased

tensions. But the evidence suggests that prior to 1788–89, when Abraham Dreÿfuss lived in southern Alsace, there had been no widespread anti-Jewish rebellions.

22. The September 28, 1789, decree is quoted in Philippe, *Etre Juif,* pp. 107–8. On how news arrived in Alsatian Jewish communities, Stauben, *Scènes de la vie,* p. 80; Raphaël and Weyl, *Juifs en Alsace,* p. 363 and passim.

23. François Furet, *Interpreting the French Revolution,* Elborg Forster, trans. (Cambridge, England, 1981), p. 2; Girard, *Les Juifs de France,* p. 50; Eugen Weber, "Reflections on the Jews in France," in Frances Malino and Bernard Wasserstein, eds., *The Jews in Modern France* (Hanover, 1985), p. 16; and Michael Burns, "Emancipation and Reaction: The Rural Exodus of Alsatian Jews, 1791–1848," in Jehuda Reinharz, ed., *Living with Antisemitism: Modern Jewish Responses* (Hanover, 1987), pp. 19–41. For more on the background to the debate, see Frances Malino, "Les Communautés juives et l'Edit de 1787," *Bulletin de la Société de l'Histoire du Protestantisme Français,* t. 134, 1988, pp. 311–28.

24. See, for example, Paul Mendes-Flohr and Jehuda Reinharz, eds., *The Jew in the Modern World* (New York, 1980), pp. 44–46; Hertzberg, *French Enlightenment,* p. 294; and Shmuel Trigano, *La République et les Juifs* (Paris, 1982), p. 66 and passim. Frances Malino explores the contrasts in *The Sephardic Jews of Bordeaux: Assimilation and Emancipation in Revolutionary and Napoleonic France* (University, Ala., 1976).

25. On Clermont-Tonnerre's announcement, see Trigano, *La République,* p. 51, and Mendes-Flohr and Reinharz, *The Jew in the Modern World,* pp. 103–5; and Jay R. Berkovitz, *The Shaping of Jewish Identity in Nineteenth-Century France* (Detroit, 1989), p. 71. See also Trigano, *La République,* p. 47 and passim.

26. Quoted in Hertzberg, *French Enlightenment,* p. 356. The Alsatian deputy's name is sometimes spelled "Reubell."

27. Mendes-Flohr and Reinharz, *The Jew in the Modern World,* p. 108; and Blumenkranz and Soboul, *Les Juifs et la révolution,* p. 10; and Berkovitz, *Shaping of Jewish Identity,* pp. 36, 71–72.

28. Samuel Halevi's 1792 comment on Zion and the Jordan is quoted in Robert Alter, "Emancipation, Enlightenment and All That," *Commentary,* Feb. 1972, p. 62. See also Trigano, *La République,* pp. 30–31, 55; and Philippe, *Etre Juif,* pp. 6, 117.

29. Girard, *Les Juifs de France,* p. 54; Blumenkranz and Soboul, *Les Juifs et la révolution,* p. 59; and Mendes-Flohr and Reinharz, *The Jew in the Modern World,* p. 108.

30. Dreyfus, *Histoire de l'Alsace,* pp. 194–96. On the oath of citizenship, see Robert Anchel, *Napoléon et les Juifs* (Paris, 1928), pp. 4–5.

31. Raphaël and Weyl, *Juifs en Alsace,* p. 361; Lefebvre, *The Great Fear,* p. 22; Robert Anchel, *Les Juifs de France* (Paris, 1946), p. 277; and AD Haut-Rhin, documents on "*juifs étrangers,*" circa 1803.

32. Poliakov, *Histoire de l'antisémitisme,* vol. 2, pp. 111 ff.; Anchel, *Napoléon,* pp. 14–23; and Philippe, *Etre Juif,* p. 5.

33. Blumenkranz and Soboul, *Les Juifs et la révolution,* p. 45; Anchel, *Napoléon,* p. 24; Weill, *L'Alsace française,* pp. 29–30; and Weber, *Peasants,* p. 72.

34. *Mulhouse et le Sundgau,* p. 128; and Anchel, *Napoléon,* p. 17.

35. In general terms, David Cohen discusses this dilemma in *La Promotion,* vol. 2, p. 740, as does Rina Neher-Bernheim in *Documents inédits sur l'entré des Juifs dans la société française, 1750–1850* (Tel Aviv, 1977), vol. 2, p. 337. Jean-Paul Sartre, who was often wrong about the Jews, was right about the following: "If the government is strong, anti-Semitism withers, unless it be a part of the program of the government itself, in which case it changes its nature" (see *Anti-Semite and Jew,* George J. Becker, trans. [New York, 1965], p. 33).

36. *Mulhouse et le Sundgau,* p. 128

37. Dreyfus, *Histoire de l'Alsace,* pp. 194 ff.; and Blumenkranz and Soboul, *Les Juifs et la révolution,* p. 60 and passim.

38. See the excellent account of Schinderhannes in T. C. W. Blanning, *The*

French Revolution in Germany: Occupation and Resistance in the Rhineland, 1792–1802 (Oxford, 1983), pp. 292–97.

39. On Jewish property holding and the royal *lettres patentes* of 1784, see Blumenkranz, *Histoire des Juifs*, p. 157.

40. See the letter to the Jews of Alsace and Thiéry's comments, quoted in Trigano, *La République*, p. 57.

41. Blumenkranz and Soboul, *Les Juifs et la révolution*, p. 49; Philippe, *Etre Juif*, p. 81; Lévy, *Les Noms des Israélites*, p. 61; and Blumenkranz, *Histoire des Juifs*, pp. 140, 162.

42. The date of Brändel's death was confirmed more than a century later. In 1941, in response to state demands that Jews document their French origins, the Dreyfus family hired a genealogist to compile information from the Haut-Rhin archives on previous generations in Rixhiem (see DFPC, M. Coutot to Madame Marguerite Dreyfus Mercier, September 26, 1941). Some family evidence suggests that Abraham remarried after Brändel's death (a common occurrence for village widowers), and that his second wife's name was Jeanne Krimetz. However, there is no documentation in the local archives to confirm this.

43. For Jacob Dreÿfuss (sometimes listed as Jacques Dreyfus) and his profession of *revendeur*, see AD Haut-Rhin, 5 E 416, "Rixheim," and V 612–13, "Inscriptions . . . 1813–23." On the peddler's routine, see Raphaël and Weyl, *Juifs en Alsace*, p. 362; Blumenkranz, *Histoire des Juifs*, p. 177; and Zosa Szajkowski, *Poverty and Social Welfare Among French Jews, 1800–1880* (New York, 1954), pp. 20–30.

44. Raphaël and Weyl, *Juifs en Alsace*, pp. 317, 363, 374; and Ben Lévi, "Memoires d'un colporteur Juif," *Archives Israélites de France*, 1841, II, pp. 686–91; and III, pp. 459–61.

45. AD Haut-Rhin, V 612–13, "Inscriptions," and 3 P 1413, cadastres, Rixheim. Rachel is sometimes listed as "Regin" and Katz is sometimes "Kann." On Rabbi Munius, see Berkovitz, *Shaping of Jewish Identity*, pp. 96–97. See also the various census records in AD Haut-Rhin, 5 E 416.

46. Raphaël and Weyl, *Juifs en Alsace*, p. 364; and Ernest Meininger, *Histoire de Mulhouse* (Mulhouse, 1923), p. 98. On events in Rixheim, see P. R. Zuber, *Rixheim* (Mulhouse, 1947), pp. 11–12; and BSIM, "La Fabrication," p. 7.

47. Anchel, *Les Juifs*, pp. 238–40, 257–59; Cohen, *La Promotion*, vol. 1, p. 4; Malino, *Sephardic Jews*, pp. 69, 95, 100, 108 ff.; Girard, *Les Juifs de France*, p. 75; Weill, *L'Alsace française*, pp. 48–49; Phyllis Cohen Albert, *The Modernization of French Jewry: Consistory and Community in the Nineteenth Century* (Hanover, 1977), p. 46 and passim; and AD Haut-Rhin, V 593 and V 611, "Enquêtes sur les activités usuaires," and the manifesto from a group of Jewish notables. Typically, Napoleon staged a grandiose event and convened, in Paris, an Assembly of Jewish Notables and a Grand Sanhedrin based on the ancient political and religious institutions of Israel. Both groups affirmed the freedom of their religious community within the nation, announced measures to control usury, and proclaimed that Jews would defend France "unto death." It was not, however, enough for the emperor (see, for example, Girard, *Les Juifs de France*, pp. 70–86, and Anchel, *Napoléon*, passim).

48. Quoted in Paul Leuilliot, *L'Alsace au début du XIXe siècle*, vol. 2 (Paris, 1959), p. 180

49. AD Haut-Rhin, V 611, 1823 report on usury between 1806–1808, and 3 P. 1434, Rixheim cadastres. See also Anchel, *Les Juifs*, p. 277; and Mendes-Flohr and Reinharz, *The Jews in the Modern World*, p. 109.

50. AD Haut-Rhin, 5 E 416, Rixheim births; and DFPC, M. Coutot to Marguerite Dreyfus Mercier, September 26, 1941. If Jacob followed local custom, Abraham's last rite of passage would be a testimony to the survival of traditions that had endured in Rixheim through revolution, emancipation, and an emperor's attempt to change it all. Placing a feather on his father's lips to see his last breath, the son would close the father's eyes

and lower the body to the straw-covered floor of the village home—because "dust returns to the earth as it was, and the spirit returns to God who gave it." Earth, a symbol of return to Palestine, was sprinkled on the forehead of the deceased. (The ritual is described in Raphaël and Weyl, *Juifs en Alsace*, pp. 266–86. See also, Stauben, *Scènes de la vie*, p. 87.)

51. Dreyfus, *Histoire de l'Alsace*, pp. 224–25; Neher-Bernheim, *Documents inédits*, vol. 2, p. 101; and Leuilliot, *L'Alsace au début*, vol. 2, pp. 182, 185–93.

52. An 1806 note to the minister of the interior had called the southern Alsatian region that included Rixheim "l'un des plus opprimés par l'usure des Juifs." (See AD Haut-Rhin, V 611, June 10, 1806). See also, Leuilliot, *L'Alsace au début*, vol. 2, p. 192, and p. 191 for statistics on moneylending.

53. Between 1813–23 there were approximately 20,000–25,000 transactions involving Jewish lenders throughout the Haut-Rhin department. The total sum reached 15 million francs, with average transactions, in Rixheim and elsewhere, at 400–500 francs (see AD Haut-Rhin, V 612–13, "Inscriptions," and V 611, unsigned report, probably from the commune of Würtzenheim). The 1818 petition is quoted in Cohen, *La Promotion*, vol. 2, p. 675.

54. AD Haut-Rhin, 4 M 44, September–October, 1819, police reports, and V 611, reports, Jan. 2, 1823, and Oct. 26, 1829. On the background to the "Hep-Hep" riots and their movement through the Rhine Valley, see Eleonore O. Sterling, "Anti-Jewish Riots in Germany in 1819: A Displacement of Social Protest," *Historia Judaica*, vol. 12, 1950, pp. 105–42. See also Moses Ginsburger, "Juifs et Chrétiens à Ribeauvillé en 1819," *Bulletin de la société historique et archéologique de Ribeauvillé*, 1937, pp. 65–66; Leuilliot, *L'Alsace au début*, vol. 3, pp. 243–44; and Poliakov, *Histoire de l'antisémitisme*, vol. 2, pp. 159–60.

55. The incident occurred in Durmenach, near Rixheim. See the report from Jewish spokesmen representing "10,000 citoyens français" to the minister of the interior in AD Haut-Rhin, V 611; and Leuilliot, *L'Alsace au début*, vol. 2, p. 184.

56. AD Haut-Rhin, V 611, prefect reports through 1829–32, and 4 M 44, reports from Wurtzenheim and Ribeauvillé into the 1830s. See also Leuilliot, *L'Alsace au début*, vol. 3, pp. 245 ff.; Neher-Bernheim, *Documents inédits*, vol. 2, p. 339; Szajkowski, *Poverty and Social Welfare*, pp. 8, 23; Cohen, *La Promotion*, vol. 1, p. 24; and Moses Ginsburger, "Les Juifs à Ribeauvillé et à Bergheim," *Bulletin de la société historique et archéologique de Ribeauvillé*, 1938, p. 25.

57. The traveler is quoted in Henry Laufenburger, *Cours d'économie alsacienne*, t. 2 (Paris, 1932), p. 185. On the history of Mulhouse and its name, see Meininger, *Histoire de Mulhouse*, pp. 11–12; Paul Acker, "Une Ville industrielle alsacienne: Mulhouse," *Revue des deux mondes*, t. 8, 1912, p. 423; and Emile Cacheux, *Etude de moyens pratiques de détruire la misère suivie de l'histoire d'une ville industrielle* (Paris, 1876), p. 30. The Germanic name *Mülhausen* was replaced by the Gallic *Mulhouse* in 1848 (see below, chap. 2).

58. Oberlé, *Mulhouse, ou la genèse*, p. 228; *Notice sur le développement des principales industries de Mulhouse*, n.a. (Mulhouse, 1920); *Histoire documentaire de l'industrie de Mulhouse* (Mulhouse, 1902), vol. 1, pp. 219–20, 261 ff.; and Laufenburger, *Cours d'économie*, t. 1, pp. 98, 124, 139, and t. 2, pp. 3–4.

59. Laufenburger, *Cours d'économie*, t. 2, pp. 23 ff.

60. AD Haut-Rhin, 6 M 4, subprefect's comments, 1826. On Zuber's industry, see Zuber, *Rixheim*, pp. 11 ff.; Laufenburger, *Cours d'économie*, t. 2, p. 77; Meininger, *Histoire de Mulhouse*, p. 90; and *Centenaire de la Société Industrielle de Mulhouse*, n.a. (Mulhouse, 1926), pp. 108–9.

61. *Le Haut-Rhin*, pp. 1196–1213; *Mulhouse et le Sundgau*, p. 137; and BSIM, "La Fabrication," p. 4. On customs barriers, see Oberlé, *Mulhouse, ou la genèse*, p. 199.

62. Zuber, *Rixheim*, pp. 13–17.

63. Raphaël and Weyl, *Juifs en Alsace*, p. 381; Szajkowski, *Poverty and Social Welfare*, p. 74; and Albert, *Modernization*, p. 26.

64. AMM, cadastres; and AD Haut-Rhin, 5 E 337, état civil, 1838 under "Jacques Dreyfus." For population statistics, see AMM, "Histoire Municipale," p. 32; *Histoire documentaire*, vol. 1, p. 32; Meininger, *Histoire de Mulhouse*, pp. 100–3; and AD Haut-Rhin, August 25, 1846 mayor's report that describes "plusieurs familles" moving to Mülhausen in years past.

65. Anchel, *Napoléon*, p. 10, note 1; Lévy, *Les Noms des Israélites*, p. 61; Meininger, *Histoire de Mulhouse*, pp. 46, 56, 95; and *Histoire documentaire*, pp. 17–18.

66. Emile G. Léonard, *Histoire générale du Protestantisme* (Paris, 1961), vol. 1, pp. 145–46, 152; Laufenburger, *Cours d'économie*, t. 1, p. 2; Christian Pfister, *Comment et pourquoi la république de Mulhouse est donnée à la France* (Nancy, 1919), p. 15; and on fear of "reversals," see Cohen, *La Promotion*, vol. 2, p. 334.

67. Henri Sée, "Dans quelle mesure Puritains et Juifs ont-ils contribué aux progrès du capitalisme moderne?" *Revue historique*, t. 155, 1927, pp. 61–65; Michael R. Marrus, *The Unwanted: European Refugees in the Twentieth Century* (New York, 1985), p. 8; and Max Weber, *The Protestant Ethic and the Spirit of Capitalism*, trans., Talcott Parsons (New York, 1958), p. 39. For more on French Protestants and Jews, see Poliakov, *Histoire de l'antisémitisme*, vol. 2, p. 186.

68. Luther's early philosemitism gave way to the vitriol seen in "On the Jews and their Lies" (see Franklin Sherman, ed., *Luther's Works* [Philadelphia, 1971], vol. 47).

69. Eugen Weber discusses Protestantism as a "powerful instrument of Frenchification" in many parts of France (see *Peasants*, p. 84). Voltaire is quoted in Jean Schlumberger, *La Bourgeoisie*, p. 309. For more on the French customs of the Mulhouse elite, see Schlumberger, *La Bourgeoisie*, pp. 12, 491; Meininger, *Histoire de Mulhouse*, p. 76; Hoffet, *Psychanalyse*, pp. 142–43; and Theodore Zeldin, *France: 1848–1945* (Oxford, 1977), vol. 2, p. 247.

70. Hoffet, *Psychanalyse*, pp. 73–74; Andre Neher, "La Bourgeoisie Juive," in Schlumberger, *La Bourgeoisie*, p. 439; and Meiss, *A Travers le dialecte Judéo-Alsatian*, p. 40.

II EXODUS

1. AMM, Mülhausen maps; Ernest Meininger, *Histoire de Mulhouse* (Mulhouse, 1923), p. 23; and Raymond Oberlé, *Mulhouse, ou la genèse d'une ville* (Mulhouse, 1985), pp. 218–21.

2. L. G. Werner, *Topographie historique du vieux Mulhouse* (Mulhouse, 1949), pp. 163–64, 184–85.

3. Paul Acker, "Une Ville industrielle alsacienne: Mulhouse," *Revue des deux mondes*, t. 8, 1912, p. 435; Oberlé, *Mulhouse, ou la genèse*, pp. 198–200; *Mulhouse et le Sundgau: 1648–1798–1848*, n.a. (Mulhouse, 1948), p. 5; Meininger, *Histoire de Mulhouse*, pp. 93–94; and Christian Pfister, *Comment et pourquoi la république de Mulhouse s'est donnée à la France* (Nancy, 1919), pp. 44–50.

4. Michel Lévy, *Coup d'oeil historique sur l'état des Israélites en France, et particulièrement en Alsace* (Strasbourg, 1836), p. 18.

5. Patrick Girard, *Les Juifs de France de 1789 à 1860* (Paris, 1976), p. 251; and F. L'Huillier, ed., *L'Alsace en 1870–1871* (Strasbourg, 1971), p. 111.

6. *Histoire documentaire de l'industrie de Mulhouse*, n.a. (Mulhouse, 1920), pp. 117–18; Meininger, *Histoire de Mulhouse*, pp. 100–103; Paul Leuilliot, *L'Alsace au début du XIXe siècle*, vol. 3 (Paris, 1959), pp. 233–43; and Doris Bensimon-Donath, *Sociodémographie des Juifs de France et d'Algérie, 1867–1907* (Paris, 1976), p. 66.

7. AD Haut-Rhin, 5 E 337, 1838, "Jacques Dreyfus." See also Leuilliot, *L'Alsace au début*, vol. 2, p. 191; and Girard, *Les Juifs de France*, pp. 124–25.

8. AD Haut-Rhin, 5 E 337, état civil, 1838.

9. The relation is unclear, as is the curious error in one of Jeannette's death records listing her as "Weil" and not "Libmann." It is not the only confusion experienced

by functionaries trying to sort out the interrelationships—and the similar names—of many Mulhouse Jews. See, for example, Jacob's état civil in AD Haut-Rhin, 5 E 337, 1838, and Jeannette's grave marker in the city cemetery.

10. AD Haut-Rhin, 5 E 405, état civil, Ribeauvillé, 1817, and unclassified documents in Ribeauvillé's Hotel de Ville. For more on Ribeauvillé, see *Le Haut-Rhin: Dictionnaire des communes* (Colmar, 1982), pp. 1156 ff.

11. On young Jewish women working as seamstresses, see David Cohen, *La Promotion des Juifs en France à l'époque du Second Empire*, vol. 2 (Aix-en-Provence, 1980), p. 360.

12. AD Haut-Rhin, 5 E 337, état civil, marriages, 1841.

13. Ibid., births, 1844. See also Robert Anchel, *Les Juifs de France* (Paris, 1946): "Habituellement le premier fils qui naissait après la mort de son grand-père portait le nom de ce dernier comme pour le remplacer sur la terre" (pp. 266–67).

14. AMM, "Histoire municipale de Mulhouse," pp. 13–14; and Meininger, *Histoire de Mulhouse*, pp. 104–9.

15. AD Haut-Rhin, 6 M 8, July 1 and Nov. 11, 1861 notes on urban growth between 1820 and 1860; and Girard, *Les Juifs de France*, p. 111.

16. AMM, "Histoire municipale," p. 118; Leuilliot, *L'Alsace au début*, vol. 3, p. 234; and Zosa Szajkowski, *Poverty and Social Welfare Among French Jews, 1800–1880* (New York, 1954), p. 71, note 161.

17. Georges Livet and Raymond Oberlé, *Histoire de Mulhouse des origines à nos jours* (Strasbourg, 1979), pp. 213–14; AMM, "Histoire municipale," p. 118; *Histoire documentaire*, pp. 117–18; and Meininger, *Histoire de Mulhouse*, p. 124. Samuel Dreyfus would be Mulhouse's rabbi for forty-two years.

18. AMM, J II Hf4, mayor's report, Aug. 19, 1847, and letter from industrialist Adolph Schwartz written while "feux de pélotons" echoed in the background; and *Histoire municipale*, pp. 15–16.

19. Demonstrators looted the premises of one Jewish grain merchant, Isaac Weill, but the majority of targets throughout the city were non-Jewish bakers and shopkeepers. See ANN, J II Hf4; Livet and Oberlé, *Mulhouse des origines*, pp. 220–30; and Henry Laufenburger, *Cours d'économie alsacienne*, t. 1 (Paris, 1932), p. 121.

20. François-Georges Dreyfus, *Histoire de l'Alsace* (Paris, 1979), p. 230; Rina Neher-Bernheim, *Documents inédits sur l'éntrée des Juifs dans la société Française, 1750–1850* (Tel Aviv, 1977), vol. 2, pp. 335–43; Béatrice Philippe, *Etre Juif dans la société Française du moyen age à nos tours* (Paris, 1979), pp. 149–50; Cohen, *La Promotion*, vol. 1, p. 44; Meininger, *Histoire de Mulhouse*, p. 106; Bernhard Blumenkranz, ed., *Histoire des Juifs en France* (Toulouse, 1972), p. 319; and Moses Ginsberger, "Les Troubles contre les Juifs d'Alsace en 1848," *Revue des études Juives*, 64, 1912, pp. 109–17.

21. Livet and Oberlé, *Mulhouse des origines*, pp. 230–31; Meininger, *Histoire de Mulhouse*, pp. 106–7; Georges Weill, *L'Alsace française* (Paris, 1916), pp. 84–90; and *Histoire municipale*, pp. 18–19. Louis Napoléon would make a disastrous trip to Mulhouse in 1850. Greeted with indifference or hostility, he returned to Paris both furious and vexed. Later some industrialists would warm to the good economic climate of the Second Empire, but through the last plebiscite of 1870, Napoléon III was, for the most part, the workers' candidate.

22. AD Haut-Rhin, 5 E 337, état civil, births, 1848, 1851, 1853, 1854, and deaths, 1853, 1854. On the cholera epidemic, see Oberlé, *Mulhouse, ou la genèse*, p. 216, and Meininger, *Histoire de Mulhouse*, p. 108.

23. BSIM, A. L. Walker, "An Alsatian Manchester"; and Oberlé, *Mulhouse, ou la genèse*, p. 207.

24. On the city's textile economy and technological accomplishments, see *Notice sur le développement des principales industries de Mulhouse*, n.a. (Mulhouse, 1920); *Histoire documentaire*, vol. 1, pp. 220–21; Laufenburger, *Cours d'économie*, t. 2, pp. 3–4; and Oberlé, *Mulhouse, ou la genèse*, pp. 208–11. Though his thesis has been

challenged, David Landes discusses the limitations of the French entrepreneurial spirit in "French Entrepreneurship and Industrial Growth in the Nineteenth Century," *Journal of Economic History*, IX, 1949, pp. 45–61. In Mulhouse, it was a period of "complet épanouissement, où l'effort élargi semble avoir devant lui un avenir illimité" (see *Centenaire de la Société de Mulhouse*, n.a. [Mulhouse,1926], p. 13).

25. *Histoire documentaire*, pp. 951–52, 973; Pfister, *Comment et pourquoi*, p. 28; and Laufenburger, *Cours d'économie*, t. 2, pp. 168 ff. Laufenburger quotes a Mulhouse poet who waxed enthusiastic about the city's luxury fabrics: "Sous nos vives couleurs, la nymphe est toujours belle" (p. 170, note 5).

26. On the role of commission agents and wholesale merchants, see Claude Fohlen, *L'Industrie textile au temps du Second Empire* (Paris, 1956), pp. 111–12, 310–11.

27. AMM, N1B 78, Raphael Dreyfus, Feb. 27, 1855; and N1B 103, Oct. 10, 1859. See also AMM, cadastres, 1856, and notices appearing in the *Industriel Alsacien*, March 15, 1855, and Oct. 27, 1959.

28. AMM, N1B 122, Raphael Dreyfus, July 8, 1862.

29. Remy Huber, *Les Progrès de la révolution industrielle en Alsace sous le Second Empire*, n.d. (in BSIM); Laufenburger, *Cours d'économie*, t. 2, p. 302; *Histoire documentaire*, vol. 1, p. 23; and Weill, *L'Alsace française*, p. 109.

30. Quoted in Fohlen, *L'Industrie textile*, pp. 310–11.

31. Ibid., p. 311. Fohlen examines how intermediaries profited at times of crisis.

32. AMM, J II E, cadastres, rue Lavoisier. Fohlen describes Raphael's purchase in *L'Industrie textile*, pp. 100, 113. On the neighboring *cités ouvrières*, see Livet and Oberlé, *Mulhouse des origines*, pp. 223–26. The long, narrow, and symmetrical blocks of workers' houses still stand in the city's northwestern quarter.

33. Raphael's investment, and the importance of Forçat, is described in Michel Hau, *L'Industrialisation de l'Alsace, 1803–1939* (Thèse, Paris X, 1985), t. II, pp. 588–89. See also, Fohlen, *L'Industrie textile*, pp. 113, 310; and for a general discussion of the accumulation of wealth among some French Jews in the nineteenth century, see Phyllis Cohen Albert, *The Modernization of French Jewry: Consistory and Community in the Nineteenth Century* (Hanover, N.H., 1977), pp. 26–33.

34. On the birth certificate of his daughter, Rachel, in 1856, Raphael signed his name "Dreyfus," it seems for the first time (see AD Haut-Rhin, 5 E 337, état civil, 1856). Paul Lévy, who quotes A. Dauzat, believes that "L'assimilation du nom . . . est un des aspects de l'assimilation des minorités ethniques: par la francisation de son patronyme, le naturalisé et ses enfants plus encore se sentiront mieux à l'aise dans leur nouvelle patrie; ce sera une garantie de loyalisme" (*Les Noms des israélites en France* [Paris, 1960], p. 94). It would, of course, take more than a name alone.

35. Engel-Dollfus, quoted in Laufenburger, *Cours d'économie*, t. 2, p. 355. On the personalities of the captains of industry in Mulhouse, see Laufenburger, *Cours d'économie*, t. 2, p. 199, 221, 246, 250–51, 312 ff.; Jean Schlumberger, ed., *La Bourgeoisie alsacienne: Etudes d'histoire sociale* (Strasbourg, 1954), p. 12; and Eric Hobsbawm, *The Age of Capital, 1848–1875* (New York, 1975), p. 241.

36. Fohlen, *L'Industrie textile*, p. 112; Laufenburger, *Cours d'économie*, t. 2, p. 127; Oberlé, *Mulhouse, ou la genèse*, 227; and *Centenaire de la Société Industrielle*. For more on Lantz, see AMM, "Histoire municipale," p. 22.

37. Dreyfus, *Histoire de l'Alsace*, p. 227; AMM, RVI Ac, October 9, 1869; Livet and Oberlé, *Mulhouse des origines*, p. 213; and Dan P. Silverman, *Reluctant Union: Alsace-Lorraine and Imperial Germany, 1871–1918* (University Park, Pa., 1972), p. 20. The Mulhouse municipal council also "placed Jewish teachers on the same footing as those of other religions" (Jay R. Berkovitz, *The Shaping of Jewish Identity in Nineteenth-Century France* [Detroit, 1989], p. 169).

38. AD Haut-Rhin, 6 M 8–9, Dénombrement de la population; L'Huillier, *L'Alsace en 1870–1871*, p. 113; and Livet and Oberlé, *Mulhouse des origines*, pp. 212–13.

39. For a description of Raphael's factory, parts of which still stand in Mulhouse, see the building reports in AD Haut-Rhin, 5 M 78, 1863. On workers and their conditions, see Oberlé, *Mulhouse, ou la genèse*, pp. 215–16, 221, 232; Livet and Oberlé, *Mulhouse des origines*, pp. 225–26; and Laufenburger, *Cours d'économie*, t. 2, pp. 341 ff.

40. AD Haut-Rhin, V 604, Feb. 13, 1821 response to prefect.

41. On poverty, charity, and justice among Alsatian Jews, see Freddy Raphaël and Robert Weyl, *Les Juifs en Alsace: Culture, société, histoire* (Toulouse, p. 1977), pp. 302–3; Blumenkranz, *Histoire des Juifs*, p. 174; and Daniel Stauben, *Scènes de la vie Juive* (Paris, 1860), p. 9. Michael R. Marrus discusses the Hebrew word *tzedakah* in *The Politics of Assimilation: The Jewish Community in France at the Time of the Dreyfus Affair* (Oxford, 1980), p. 77.

42. Quoted in Laufenburger, *Cours d'économie*, t. 2, p. 354.

43. *L'Histoire de l'industrie de Mulhouse*, n.a. (1907), p. 331; Laufenburger, *Cours d'économie*, t. 2, pp. 291–92, 346, 363; *Centenaire de la Société Industrielle*, p. 12; and Emile Cacheux, *Etudes de moyens pratiques de détruire la misère suivie de l'histoire d'une ville industrielle* (Paris, 1876), p. 74. On various benefits, see AMM QV Bc, casier 267. See also, Roger Magraw, *France, 1815–1914: The Bourgeois Century* (New York, 1986), p. 62.

44. The medal is in DFPC.

45. AD Haut-Rhin, 5 E 337, état civil, births, 1856, 1857, 1859; and H. Villemar, *Dreyfus Intime* (Paris, 1898), p. 7. Madame "Villemar," whose real name was Naville, would become a close friend of Alfred Dreyfus's family; her book is the only published account that covers, briefly, the family's early years in Mulhouse.

46. Laufenburger, *Cours d'économie*, t. 2, pp. 243, note 3, and 244.

47. Werner, *Topographie historique*, pp. 214–16, 220–22; Livet and Oberlé, *Mulhouse des origines*, p. 212; Meininger, *Histoire de Mulhouse*, pp. 109–12; and Berkovitz, *Shaping of Jewish Identity*, pp. 107–8.

48. Rabbi Dreyfus is quoted in Livet and Oberlé, *Mulhouse des origines*, p. 213. On Samuel Dreyfus and Solomon Klein, the rabbi in Colmar, see Girard, *Les Juifs de France*, pp. 229–30; Cohen, *La Promotion*, vol. 2, p. 760; Albert, *The Modernization of French Jewry*, pp. 136, 260, 268, 291–92, 301; and Berkovitz, *Shaping of Jewish Identity*, pp. 109, 164, 216–22. For more on Rabbi Klein, see his entry in the *Encyclopedia Judaica*.

49. Schlumberger, *La Bourgeoisie alsacienne*, pp. 311, 491; Weill, *L'Alsace française*, p. 115; and *Centenaire de la Société Industrielle*, p. 14 and passim.

50. See, for example, AD Haut-Rhin, 5 M 78, Raphael Dreyfus building permits, 1863. Alfred Dreyfus would later confirm that his father's first language was German.

51. Livet and Oberlé, *Mulhouse des origines*, pp. 210–12; Weill, *L'Alsace française*, p. 124; and Frederic Hoffet, *Psychanalyse de l'Alsace* (Paris, 1951), pp. 142–43. Allen Mitchell discusses the German influence on French education in *Victors and Vanquished: The German Influence on Army and Church in France After 1870* (Chapel Hill, 1984), pp. 143 ff.

52. Officials quoted in L'Huillier, *L'Alsace en 1870–71*, pp. 52–53. On the *Klapperstein*, or *pierre des bavards*, see Meininger, *Histoire de Mulhouse*, p. 58. See also, R. D. Anderson, *Education in France, 1848–1870* (Oxford, 1975), p. 204; and Theodore Zeldin, *France: 1848–1945*, vol. 2 (Oxford, 1977), p. 247.

53. On Macé and his programs, see Katherine Auspitz, *The Radical Bourgeoisie: The Ligue de l'enseignement and the Origins of the Third Republic* (Cambridge, England, 1982); Livet and Oberlé, *Mulhouse des origines*, pp. 209 ff.; and Mitchell, *Victors*, p. 147.

54. AMM, G III Aa30; and Oberlé, *Mulhouse, ou la genèse*, pp. 217–20, 223.

55. BSIM, "An Alsatian Manchester," pp. 707–8.

56. AMM, house plans cataloged under 45, rue de la Sinne. See also *Histoire documentaire*, p. 498.

57. Villemar, *Dreyfus Intime*, p. 8. Alfred Dreyfus will later describe himself as a "rêveur incorrigible" in a note to his fiancée (see AN, BB 19/101).

III GERMANS AND FRENCH

1. AD Haut-Rhin, 6 M 8, 1866.
2. Georges Livet and Raymond Oberlé, *Histoire de Mulhouse des origines à nos jours* (Strasbourg, 1979), p. 212; and Raymond Oberlé, *Mulhouse, ou la genèse d'une ville* (Mulhouse, 1985), p. 255.
3. Quoted in Livet and Oberlé, *Mulhouse des origines*, p. 231; see also pp. 226–27.
4. F. L'Huillier, *L'Alsace en 1870–1871* (Strasbourg, 1971), p. 111.
5. On the *Volksbote*, see ibid., pp. 116–19; and Vicki Caron and Paula Hyman, "The Failed Alliance: Jewish-Catholic Relations in Alsace-Lorraine, 1871–1914," *Leo Baeck Institute Yearbook*, vol. 26, 1981, p. 4.
6. Quoted in L'Huillier, *L'Alsace*, p. 157; for more on industrialists and Napoleon, see Georges Weill, *L'Alsace française* (Paris, 1916), pp. 84–102.
7. AMM, "Histoire municipale," p. 24; Oberlé, *Mulhouse ou la genèse*, pp. 257–58; and L'Huillier, *L'Alsace*, pp. 175–83. Throughout France the vote was approximately 7.4 million for the Emperor and 1.6 million against. In the greater Mulhouse area it was 26,875 for and 2,653 against; but in Mulhouse *ville* it was a horserace, with 3,397 for, 3,364 against, and 3,842 abstentions.
8. The reports are quoted in Livet and Oberlé, *Mulhouse des origines*, pp. 232–33.
9. *SC*, p. 41; and Dan P. Silverman, *Reluctant Union: Alsace-Lorraine and Imperial Germany, 1871–1918* (University Park, Pa., 1972), p. 21.
10. Michael Howard, *The Franco-Prussian War: The German Invasion of France, 1870–1871* (London, 1981), p. 116; and Livet and Oberlé, *Mulhouse des origines*, p. 233.
11. Quoted in T. C. W. Blanning, *The French Revolution in Germany: Occupation and Resistance in the Rhineland, 1792–1802* (Oxford, 1983), p. 1.
12. Howard, *Franco-Prussian*, pp. 40–76, 221. Howard's is the most thorough account, but see also Thomas J. Adriance, *The Last Gaiter Button: A Study of the Mobilization and Concentration of the French Army in the War of 1870* (Westport, Conn., 1987); and the excellent summary of the war, its origins and outcome, in D. W. Brogan, *The Development of Modern France*, vol. 1 (Gloucester, Mass., 1970), pp. 3–74.
13. Quoted in Howard, *Franco-Prussian*, p. 51.
14. Ibid., pp. 1–39; and Alistair Horne, *The French Army and Politics, 1870–1980* (New York, 1984), p. 7. See also Jasper Ridley, *Napoleon III and Eugénie* (London, 1979), pp. 568–61.
15. Howard, *Franco-Prussian*, p. 55.
16. Ibid., pp. 67–68, 77, 272 ff.; Allan Mitchell, *Victors and Vanquished: The German Influence on the French Army and Church in France after 1870* (Chapel Hill, 1984), p. 15; Horne, *French Army*, p. 7; Paul Appell, *Souvenirs d'un Alsacien, 1858–1922* (Paris, 1923), pp. 71–71, 100–101; and Capt. H. Choppin, *Souvenirs d'un cavalier du Second Empire* (Paris, 1898), pp. 280–81.
17. Quoted in Howard, *Franco-Prussian*, pp. 207–8.
18. Ibid., pp. 209–23; and Ridley, *Napoleon III*, pp. 566–68.
19. Quoted in Howard, *Franco-Prussian*, pp. 228, 380–81. On the consequences of all this, see Allan Mitchell, *The German Influence in France after 1870: The Formation of the French Republic* (Chapel Hill, 1979).
20. *CA*, p. 57.
21. *Histoire municipale*, pp. 24 ff.; Ernest Meininger, *Histoire de Mulhouse* (Mul-

house, 1923), pp. 113 ff.; and *Histoire documentaire de l'industrie de Mulhouse,* n.a. (Mulhouse, 1920), vol. 1, pp. 25–26.

22. Alfred described his memories in a letter to the minister of war in 1897; see BN, N.A.F. 16464, Dec. 25, 1897.

23. L'Huillier, *L'Alsace en 1870–71,* pp. 218, 249–50; Appell, *Souvenirs,* pp. 102–4; J. R. Bloch's novel *Et Cie* quoted in Vicki Caron, "Patriotism or Profit? The Emigration of Alsace-Lorraine Jews to France, 1871–1872," *Leo Baeck Institute Yearbook,* vol. 28, 1983, p. 160; and Guy de Maupassant, "Boule de Suif," in *Selected Short Stories* (Harmondsworth, 1982), p. 36.

24. Meininger, *Histoire de Mulhouse,* pp. 113 ff.; *Histoire municipale,* pp. 24–25; Oberlé, *Mulhouse, ou la genèse,* p. 262; L'Huillier, *L'Alsace,* pp. 229–300; *Histoire documentaire,* vol. 1, pp. 25–26; and BSIM, A. L. Walker, "An Alsatian Manchester," p. 708. Reports on the forced requisitions vary; some say eighty wagons and five thousand shirts, others sixty wagons and six thousand shirts, and so on.

25. As one report put it, "la langue de masse est allemande et son sentiment français" (quoted in L'Huillier, *L'Alsace,* p. 289).

26. Meininger, *Histoire de Mulhouse,* pp. 113 ff.; Silverman, *Reluctant Union,* p. 22; and L'Huillier, *L'Alsace,* pp. 229, 378.

27. On Jacques Dreyfus's service, see DFPC, document signed by the minister of war, Jan. 30, 1912, and a statement notarized by the mayor of Carpentras (Vaucluse). See also *SC,* p. 41.

28. Quoted in Mitchell, *Victors and Vanquished,* p. 16.

29. Howard, *Franco-Prussian,* p. 244; L'Huillier, *L'Alsace,* p. 354; and AMM, "Histoire municipale," pp. 24–25. With Raphael Dreyfus in charge, the mill could function without Jacques, but other families were less fortunate: "So many Jewish sons in Hegenheim went off to fight for their 'beloved Fatherland' that significant numbers of parents were left without means of support" (see Caron, "Patriotism or Profit?" p. 150). Jacques' papers confirm that he was exempted from military service and that he volunteered (see DFPC).

30. See the reports on reprisals in L'Huillier, *L'Alsace,* pp. 242, 246, 354. Bismarck had made it clear (see Howard, *Franco-Prussian,* pp. 380–81).

31. Meininger, *Histoire de Mulhouse,* pp. 113 ff.; L'Huillier, *L'Alsace,* pp. 224–250, 351; and on *francs-tireurs* throughout France, Howard, *Franco-Prussian,* pp. 249–256.

32. L'Huillier, *L'Alsace,* pp. 341–42, 378; and Howard, *Franco-Prussian,* pp. 361, 407–32.

33. Meininger, *Histoire de Mulhouse,* pp. 113 ff. The literature on the Commune is enormous; see, for example, Stewart Edwards, *The Paris Commune of 1871* (New York, 1977), and Louis M. Greenberg, *Sisters of Liberty: Marseille, Lyon, Paris and the Reaction to a Centralized State, 1868–1871* (Cambridge, Mass., 1971).

34. Frederic Seager, "The Alsace-Lorraine Question in France, 1871–1914," in Charles K. Warner, ed., *From the Ancien Regime to the Popular Front* (New York, 1969), pp. 112–13; Meininger, *Histoire de Mulhouse,* pp. 113 ff.; L'Huillier, *L'Alsace,* p. 210; and Howard, *Franco-Prussian,* pp. 446–49.

35. Quoted in Meininger, *Histoire de Mulhouse,* pp. 113 ff.

IV INTERIORS

1. *CA,* p. 57.

2. H. Villemar, *Dreyfus intime* (Paris, 1898), p. 8. On Joseph Valabrègue and his family in Carpentras, see AD Vaucluse, 6 M 103, nominative lists, and 3 M 137, election lists.

3. See Vicki Caron's description of the option in "Patriotism or Profit? The Emigration of Alsace-Lorraine Jews to France, 1871–1872," *Leo Baeck Institute Year-*

book, v. 28, 1983, pp. 141–44. Figures vary, but approximately 21 percent of the Haut Rhin population declared, with as many as fifteen thousand Jews leaving Alsace and Lorraine for France between 1870 and 1900. See, for example, François-Georges Dreyfus, *Histoire de l'Alsace* (Paris, 1979), pp. 251–61; and Béatrice Philippe, *Etre Juif dans la société française du moyen-âge à nos jours* (Paris, 1979), pp. 137–42. On the flight of industrialists, see Raymond Oberlé, *Mulhouse, ou la genèse d'une ville* (Mulhouse, 1985), p. 269.

4. *Mulhouse et le Sundgau: 1648–1798–1848*, n.a. (Mulhouse 1948), p. 6; AMM, "Histoire Municipale," p. 26; Georges Weill, *L'Alsace française* (Paris, 1916), p. 250; Jean Schlumberger, ed., *La Bourgeoisie alsacienne: Etudes d'histoire sociale* (Strasbourg, 1954), p. 491; *Centenaire de la Société Industrielle de Mulhouse*, n.a. (Mulhouse, 1926), p. 14; Dan P. Silverman, *Reluctant Union: Alsace-Lorraine and Imperial Germany, 1871–1918* (University Park, Pa., 1972), pp. 23–24; and Oberlé, *Mulhouse ou la genèse*, p. 278.

5. Quoted in Frederic Seager, "The Alsace-Lorraine Question in France, 1871–1914," in Charles K. Warner, ed., *From the Ancien Regime to the Popular Front* (New York, 1969), pp. 114–15.

6. On the economic situation after 1871, see Silverman, *Reluctant Union*, pp. 165–89; and Allan Mitchell, *The German Influence in France after 1870: The Formation of the French Republic* (Chapel Hill, 1979), pp. 34 ff.

7. Caron, "Patriotism or Profit?," pp. 147–48, 151, 158; Silverman, *Reluctant Union*, pp. 66–70, 174; and Henry Laufenburger, *Cours d'économie alsacienne*, t. 1 (Paris, 1932), pp. 130, 144.

8. BN, N.A.F. 13567, Alfred Dreyfus letter to Joseph Reinach, no date. See also, Mitchell, *German Influence*, p. 44.

9. Quoted in Caron, "Patriotism or Profit?," p. 148; see also p. 145, note 30. For more on families divided by "option," see Joseph Fleurent, "L'Idée de la Patrie en Alsace," *Revue politique et parlementaire*, 51, 1907, pp. 324–45.

10. *SC*, p. 41. See also Jean-Denis Bredin's description of the move in *The Affair: The Case of Alfred Dreyfus*, trans. Jeffrey Mehlman (New York, 1986), pp. 11–12.

11. Jean-Richard Bloch, *Et Compagnie* (Paris, 1947), pp. 74–75.

12. *SC*, p. 42. On *Realschulen*, see Oberlé, *Mulhouse ou la genèse*, p. 225; Laufenburger, *Cours d'économie*, t. 2, p. 243; and Fritz Ringer, *Education and Society in Modern Europe* (Bloomington, 1979), p. 37.

13. "Beaucoup de patrons tenaient à voir leurs fils passer par l'Ecole Polytechnique avant de venir prendre place à la fabrique" (Weill, *L'Alsace française*, p. 112). On the school's "numerous Jewish students," see Jay R. Berkovitz, *The Shaping of Jewish Identity in Nineteenth-Century France* (Detroit, 1989), pp. 112–13.

14. G. Bruno (Mme. Alfred Fouillée), *Le Tour de la France par deux enfants* (Paris, 1877; reprint, Rennes, 1983), pp. 9–10, 25, 34, 300, and Preface. On the book in the context of national acculturation, see Eugen Weber, *Peasants into Frenchmen: The Modernization of Rural France, 1870–1914* (Stanford, 1976), pp. 335–36; and Mona and Jacques Ozouf, "Le Tour de la France par deux enfants: Le petit livre rouge de la République," in Pierre Nora, ed., *Les Lieux de mémoire* (Paris, 1986), vol. 1.

15. Dreyfus, *Histoire de l'Alsace*, p. 252. Robert Gautier also makes the connection with *Le Tour de la France* in "Les Alsaciens et l'affaire Dreyfus," *Saisons d'Alsace*, 17, 1966, p. 58.

16. Gustave Dupont-Ferrier, *Les Ecoles, lycées, bibliothèques: L'Enseignement public à Paris* (Paris, 1913), pp. 30–33; and Theodore Zeldin, *France: 1848–1945*, vol. 2 (Oxford, 1977), pp. 191–92, 278. On Alfred Dreyfus at Chaptal, see registers held at the school concerning "élèves, 1874–75"; see also, Villemar, *Intime*, p. 9, and *SC*, p. 42. It is unclear whether Mathieu Dreyfus attended both Sainte Barbe and Chaptal, or only one of those *collèges*.

17. Zeldin, *France*, vol. 2, pp. 175, 230, 264.

18. Dreyfus's reflections on his education are in BN, N.A.F. 24909, 1898–99 notebook, p. 217.

19. Zeldin, France, vol. 2, pp. 179, 310; and Paul Gerbod, La Vie quotidienne dans les lycées et collèges au XIXe siècle (Paris, 1968), p. 8.

20. Collège Chaptal, "élèves, 1874–75"; Villemar, Intime, p. 9; and Zeldin, France, vol. 2, p. 263. Zeldin also recounts the experience of young Maurice Barrès at a lycée in Nancy, "desperately crying out every night in his dormitory" (p. 277). Barrès had more in common with Dreyfus than he would ever have liked to admit.

21. DFPC, documents concerning Mathieu Dreyfus's military service. On the provision limiting service to one year, see Allan Mitchell, Victors and Vanquished: The German Influence on Army and Church in France after 1870 (Chapel Hill, 1984), p. 30. According to Joseph Reinach, Mathieu Dreyfus had intended to apply to Saint Cyr (see HAD, vol. 1, p. 149).

22. Villemar, Intime, pp. 9–10; and AD Vaucluse, 6 M 103, nominative lists, Carpentras.

23. Ringer, Education, pp. 121, 132, 172; and Zeldin, France, vol. 2, pp. 269–73.

24. AD Isère, T 146, 155–56, Académie de Grenoble, Procès-Verbal, November 9, 1876.

25. SC, p. 42; and Villemar, Intime, pp. 10–11.

26. D. W. Brogan, The Development of Modern France, 1870–1939, vol. 1 (Gloucester, 1970), p. 157. For tuition and fees at private collèges and grandes écoles during these years, see Ringer, Education, p. 172, and Zeldin, France, vol. 2, p. 279. On Raphael's promise to pay, see his letter dated March 10, 1878 in AA, Section historique, 59615.

27. Villemar, Intime, p. 11; and Bredin, Affair, p. 13.

28. For Léon Dreyfus, see Histoire documentaire de l'industrie de Mulhouse, n.a. (Mulhouse, 1902), p. 498. On the changing fortunes of Alsatian industry, see Silverman, Reluctant Union, pp. 165–89; and Mitchell, German Influence, pp. 116–18.

29. Dreyfus recounts this in a Dec. 25, 1897, letter to the minister of war (see BN, N.A.F. 16464).

30. Villemar, Intime, p. 10.

31. On the behavior of occupiers in Alsace, see Mitchell, German Influence, p. 44; and for comments on troops in Mulhouse, see Bloch, Et Compagnie, pp. 55–57.

32. Quoted in Zeldin, France, vol. 2, p. 182.

33. Rabbi Lévy's comments appear in Philippe, Etre Juif, p. 142. See also, Terry Shinn, Ecole Polytechnique, 1871–1914 (Paris, 1980), p. 85.

34. Rina Neher-Bergheim, Documents inédits sur l'entrée des Juifs dans la société française, 1750–1850, vol. 2 (Tel Aviv, 1977), pp. 362, 389.

35. AA, 59615. It is followed by a letter from a doctor saying that Dreyfus, a student at Sainte Barbe, has "aucun vice de conformation, d'aucune infirmité, d'aucune maladie heréditaire ou contagieux."

36. On the crisis, see Fresnette Pisani-Ferry, Le Coup d'état manqué du 16 mai 1877 (Paris, 1965); and Mitchell, German Influence, pp. 144–76.

37. See the essay by Dreyfus's grandson, Dr. Jean-Louis Lévy, in CA, p. 250. Bredin also suggests that young Dreyfus longed for an ordered and secure environment (see The Affair, p. 13).

38. Choppin, Souvenirs d'un cavalier, p. vii.

39. Quoted in William Serman, Les Officiers français dans la nation, 1848–1914 (Paris, 1982), p. 14.

40. Quoted in Mitchell, German Influence, p. 148. Both of Mitchell's volumes provide a convincing account of the French rush to meet the German military challenge (see, for example, Victors and Vanquished, pp. 71–117, 244–48). For more on the attraction of the army, see Serman, Les Officiers: "Le goût d'action, du commandement

et du combat, les rêves de gloire et d'aventure, l'ambition et le patriotisme peuvent, à des degrés divers, justifier l'engagement militaire de ces jeunes gens" (p. 16).

V CAVALIER

1. Terry Shinn, *Ecole Polytechnique, 1871–1914* (Paris, 1980), pp. 8–13, 185; and Fritz K. Ringer, *Education and Society in Modern Europe* (Bloomington, Ind., 1979), pp. 8–9, 114, 124, 171.

2. On Alfred Dreyfus's documents, see AA 59615; despite an "ankylose incomplète congenitale du coude" his "condition et santé" were listed as "moyennes." On the school's buildings, schedules and ethos, see Shinn, *Ecole*, pp. 8, 25–26, 49, 54–56, and 249, note 35.

3. Jean-Pierre Callot, *Histoire de l'Ecole Polytechnique* (Paris, 1958), pp. 189–90; and Shinn, *Ecole*, pp. 58–59. On the politics and religion of French officers, see Ringer, *Education*, pp. 8–9; and William Serman, *Les Officiers français dans la nation, 1848–1914* (Paris, 1982), pp. 45, 87.

4. Shinn, *Ecole*, pp. 45–46, 53, 124; Ringer, *Education*, p. 124; and Allan Mitchell, *Victors and Vanquished: The German Influence on Army and Church in France after 1870* (Chapel Hill, 1984), p. 88.

5. Doris Bensimon-Donath discusses Jews and the cavalry in *Socio-démographie des Juifs de France et d'Algérie, 1867–1907* (Paris, 1976), p. 336; and Callot comments on the equitation program at the Ecole Polytechnique in *Histoire de l'Ecole*, p. 114.

6. AA, 59615 and AN, BB 19/101. On "élèves-officiers," see Shinn, *Ecole*, p. 54.

7. Quoted in Serman, *Officiers*, p. 204; see also, p. 8. On the artillery, see Mitchell, *Victors and Vanquished*, pp. 64–70.

8. AA, 59615; and Jean-Denis Bredin, *The Affair: The Case of Alfred Dreyfus*, Jeffrey Mehlman, trans. (New York, 1986), p. 13.

9. For information on the Dreyfus mill through the 1880s and 90s, see AMM J II E, "rue Lavoisier." On Mulhouse industry in general, see Raymond Oberlé, *Mulhouse ou la genèse d'une ville* (Mulhouse, 1985), pp. 266–67.

10. Marriage contracts, including Mathieu Dreyfus's, along with later investigations of the family's fortune, confirm that each son had access to capital ranging from 290,000 to 500,000 francs, and that by the early 1890s Alfred Dreyfus was receiving an income of 24,000 francs per year (see DFPC, and AN, BB 19/128, Oct.–Nov. 1894 interrogations, p. 406, and DFPC). See also, Serman, *Officiers*, pp. 185–201.

11. AN, BB 19/101, "Feuillet du personnel" and "Etat des services"; and AA, 59615, "Notes," 1883–85.

12. Many of the comments on Dreyfus's habits in Paris and the provinces would come through later interrogations of fellow officers, and many would be full of errors or lies. But a few can be corroborated. Dreyfus himself spoke about his pleasures, from women to books ("J'avais l'imagination très vive et je m'occupais beaucoup de littérature"); see AN, BB 19/101 and 128. On provincial garrison life in the late nineteenth century, see Serman, *Officiers*, pp. 204–14.

13. "Avant mon mariage, j'ai connu, comme tout garçon, beaucoup de femmes," begins Dreyfus's explanation to interrogators in 1894. He admitted that he visited the racetrack (natural for a horse enthusiast), and without volunteering details he spoke of three or four women he had known in the mid-1880s (see AN, BB 19/128, pp. 425–27 and passim; Bredin, *The Affair*, p. 20; and Serman, *Officiers*, pp. 180–83).

14. On Mathieu Dreyfus, see DFPC, marriage contract; *Histoire documentaire de l'industrie de Mulhouse*, n.a. (Mulhouse, 1902), p. 498; and MD. See also his letter to Alfred in AN, BB 19/105, Sept. 19, 1894, and a letter from his Alsatian friend Paul Jeanmaire in BN, N.A.F. 17386.

15. AA 59615 and AN BB 19/101, "Feuillet," 1884–89.

16. On the Ecole de Guerre, see Mitchell, *Victors and Vanquished*, pp. 84–89;

Serman, *Les Officiers*, p. 10; and David Ralston, *The Army of the Republic: The Place of the Military in the Political Evolution of France, 1871–1914* (Cambridge, Mass., 1967), pp. 91–92, 256.

17. On Boulangism, see, for example, William D. Irvine, *The Boulanger Affair Reconsidered: Royalism, Boulangism, and the Origins of the Radical Right in France* (New York, 1989); Frederick Seager, *The Boulanger Affair: Political Crossroad of France, 1886–1889* (Ithaca, N.Y., 1969); Patrick H. Hutton, "Popular Boulangism and the Advent of Mass Politics in France," *Journal of Contemporary History*, 11, 1976; and Michael Burns, *Rural Society and French Politics: Boulangism and the Dreyfus Affair, 1886–1900* (Princeton, 1984).

18. Fustel de Coulanges quoted in F. L'Huillier, *L'Alsace en 1870–1871* (Strasbourg, 1971), pp. 380–81. Some historians believe that Dreyfus's intense patriotism would have made him an admirer of the General (see Theodore Reinach, *Histoire sommaire de l'affaire Dreyfus* [Paris, 1924], p. 22); but later comments confirm his suspicion of adventurers like Boulanger and his respect for the established order (see below, chap. 12). On the disinclination of many soldiers to follow Boulanger, see Alistair Horne, *The French Army and Politics: 1870–1980* (New York, 1984), p. 18.

19. AN, BB 19/101 "Feuillet," 1889.

20. BN, N.A.F. 24909, Dreyfus notebook, p. 327. See also Shinn, *Ecole*, p. 57, and Serman, *Officiers*, pp. 111–23.

21. AN, BB 19/101, Bourges correspondence, 1889–90.

22. The comment is by Lyautey, later to become a celebrated French marshal (quoted in Serman, *Officiers*, p. 216). On Alfred Dreyfus's studies, see AN BB 19/101, Bourges; and on his distractions, AN, BB 19/128, Oct.–Nov. 1894 interrogations, pp. 431–432.

23. AN, BB 19/128, interrogations, pp. 416–17; Shinn, *Ecole*, pp. 86–87, 164–65; and Horne, *French Army*, p. 28. According to David Cohen, "Il semble que les familles bourgeoises juives aient considéré le mariage de leurs filles avec un officier français juif comme un promotion certaine" (*La Promotion des Juifs en France à l'époque du Second Empire*, vol. 2 [Aix-en-Provence,1980], p. 419).

24. *Archives Israélites de France* [1843?], Rebecca Hadamard obituary, pp. 220–23. Author's interviews with Lucie Dreyfus's granddaughter, Simone Perl, July 1983, and niece and nephew, Germaine Franck and Robert Duteil, Dec. 1983.

25. AA, 59615, "Dossier Dreyfus," marriage contract and other documents. According to Serman, less than 10 percent of the dowries of officers' wives in the late nineteenth century were over 120,000 francs, and barely 3 percent surpassed 240,000 francs; a dowry of 120,000 francs made for a "riche mariage." Lucie's was twice that. "L'argent," notes Serman, "attire l'argent." (*Officiers*, pp. 175–78 and passim.)

26. See below, chap. 6.

27. Suzanne Schwob's dowry surpassed 100,000 francs. Mathieu's assets with Raphael Dreyfus et Compagnie were 290,000 francs (see DFPC, marriage contracts).

28. FRB. On Freemasonry and French Jews, see Cohen, *La Promotion*, vol. 2, p. 752; and on its links to the Jewish cabala, see Frances A. Yates, *The Occult Philosophy of the Elizabethan Age* (London, 1979).

29. AN, BB 19/101, Alfred Dreyfus, Bourges correspondence. The letters are undated, but it is possible, through the captain's comments, to determine approximate dates. All quotes below are from those letters.

30. "Mes camarades ont été très heureux d'apprendre que j'étais admissible et leurs félicitations très sincères m'ont fait plaisir. Il paraît que les autres artilleurs candidats à Bourges n'ont pas eu autant de chance; je suis dit-on le seul admissible parmis eux. C'est vous, ma chère Lucie, qui m'avez porté bonheur."

31. "Le partage des peines les amoindrit et en fait facilement supporter les épreuves; la communauté des joies en double au contraire la prix. Tel est l'idéal de la vie à la deux." And regarding their honeymoon plans: "Préparer ainsi jour par jour,

heure par heure, son itinéraire, c'est d'enlever toutes les surprises de l'imprévu, se priver de tous les caprices qui peut suggérer la pensée."

VI FIN DE SIÈCLE

1. AA, 59615, "Bulletin de mariage"; and DFPC, marriage documents.

2. Emmanuel Haymann, *Paris Judaica* (Paris, 1979), pp. 44–46; and Auguste André Coussilan, *Dictionnaire historique des rues de Paris, par Jacques Hillairet* (Paris, 1976), pp. 626–29.

3. Consistoire Israélite de Paris, reg. 6624, Dreyfus-Hadamard *Ketouba;* and DFPC. For a general history of the *ketubbah,* see *Encyclopedia Judaica,* pp. 926ff.

4. Quoted in Michael R. Marrus, *The Politics of Assimilation: The French Jewish Community at the Time of the Dreyfus Affair* (Oxford, 1980), p. 76. See also, Julien Weill, *Zadoc Kahn, 1839–1905* (Paris, 1912).

5. Marrus, *Politics,* p. 98.

6. Quoted in Paula Hyman, *From Dreyfus to Vichy: The Remaking of French Jewry, 1906–1939* (New York, 1979), p. 9.

7. Quoted in Marrus, *Politics,* p. 92 n. 1.

8. Léon Cahun, *La Vie Juive* (Paris, 1886), preface by Zadoc Kahn; and Weill, *Zadoc Kahn,* p. 128.

9. The honeymoon itinerary is discussed in AN, BB 19/101, Bourges correspondence. On Florence, see *SC,* p. 443.

10. AN, BB 19/128, interrogation, p. 418; Ernest Meininger, *Histoire de Mulhouse* (Mulhouse, 1923), p. 129; and Jean Schlumberger, ed., *La Bourgeoisie alsacienne: Etudes d'histoire sociale* (Strasbourg, 1954), p. 324.

11. AN, BB 19/128, interrogation p. 427. On changes in Mulhouse, see AMM, J II E.

12. "These Orthodox Jews . . . were conspicuous. . . . [T]hey tended to remain apart, particularly on the High Holy Days when they could not be seated in the consistorial synagogues. In consequence they founded tiny *shuls* for worship in private apartments, small shops or rooms rented for the purpose" (Marrus, *Politics,* p. 59). On the high cost of seats in consistory synagogues, and other distinctions between rich and poor Parisian Jews, see Phyllis Cohen Albert, *The Modernization of French Jewry: Consistory and Community in the Nineteenth Century* (Hanover, 1977), p. 36; Christian Piette, *Les Juifs de Paris (1808–1840): La Marche vers l'assimilation* (Quebec, 1983), p. 60; and David H. Weinberg, *Les Juifs de Paris de 1933 à 1939* (Paris, 1974), pp. 15–18.

13. On the Marais/St. Paul neighborhood, see Nancy L. Green, *The Pletzl of Paris: Jewish Immigrant Workers in the Belle Epoque* (New York, 1986).

14. On Dreyfus's notebooks, and his interest in mathematics and civil engineering, see below, chap. 12. On the past uses of the Champs de Mars, see, for example, Marc Gaillard, *Les Hippodromes* (Paris, 1984), pp. 34–44.

15. AN, BB 19/128, interrogation, pp. 407, 418. Allan Mitchell discusses offensive and defensive strategies in *Victors and Vanquished: The German Influence on Army and Church in France after 1870* (Chapel Hill, 1984), p. 115. See also Jean-Denis Bredin, *The Affair: The Case of Alfred Dreyfus,* Jeffrey Mehlman, trans. (New York, 1986), p. 15.

16. AN, BB 19/101; and AA 59165, "feuillet du personnel."

17. BN, N.A.F. 17387, letter from Henriette Valabrègue to her children, with a note from Alfred. The long friendship with Joseph Valabrègue is discussed in an undated note in MB.

18. AN, BB 19/128, interrogation, p. 420; and Armand Charpentier, *Les Côtés mystérieux de l'affaire Dreyfus* (Paris, 1937), pp. 292ff.

19. AN, BB 19/101, "Etat des services." On Napoleon's performance, see Jean

Tulard, *Napoleon: The Myth of the Savior,* Teresa Waugh, trans. (London, 1984), p. 25; and for Dreyfus's views on Napoleon, see BN, N.A.F. 13578, Dreyfus to Joseph Reinach, April 16, 1902.

20. AN, BB 19/128, interrogation, pp. 434–35.

21. Ibid., p. 431. This incident is also discussed in *HAD*, vol. 1, p. 168; *SC*, pp. 21–22; Theodore Reinach, *Histoire sommaire de l'affaire Dreyfus* (Paris, 1924), p. 21; and Bredin, *The Affair*, p. 22.

22. See, for example, Edouard Drumont, *La France Juive,* 2 vols. (Paris, 1886); the same author's *La France Juive devant l'opinion* (Paris, 1886); and the spring and summer issues of *La Libre Parole.* See also, Bredin, *The Affair,* pp. 23–32; Frederick Busi, *The Pope of Antisemitism: The Career and Legacy of Edouard-Adolphe Drumont* (Lanham, 1986); Michel Winock, *Edouard Drumont et Cie: Antisémitisme et fascisme en France* (Paris, 1982); Léon Poliakov, *Histoire de l'antisémitisme,* vol. 2 (Paris, 1981), pp. 290–95; and Eugen Weber, "Reflections on the Jews in France," in Frances Malino and Bernard Wasserstein, ed., *The Jews in Modern France* (Hanover, 1985), p. 19.

23. Quoted in David S. Landes, "Two Cheers for Emancipation," in Malino and Wasserstein, *Jews in Modern France,* p. 298. To keep his bigotry consistent, Drumont should have alluded to the "sweet bread" of Passover, not Purim. But consistency was not his concern, and besides, his readership cared little about such distinctions.

24. On Toussenel, see David Cohen, *La Promotion des Juifs en France à l'époque du Second Empire,* vol. 1 (Aix-en-Provence), p. 30.

25. Quoted in Béatrice Philippe, *Etre Juif dans la société française du moyen-âge à nos jours* (Paris, 1979), p. 161.

26. Quoted in Cohen, *La Promotion,* vol. 2, p. 653.

27. Philippe, *Etre Juif,* p. 162. See also, Karl Marx, "On the Jewish Question," in T. B. Bottomore, ed., *Karl Marx: Early Writings* (New York, 1964), pp. 3–40.

28. Drumont, *La France Juive devant l'opinion,* p. 159; and Poliakov, *Histoire de l'antisémitisme,* vol. 2, p. 291.

29. Fore-Fauré, *Face aux Juifs! Essai de psychologie sociale et contemporaine* (Paris, 1891). On the message and impact of *La Croix,* see Pierre Sorlin, *"La Croix" et les Juifs* (Paris, 1967), and Michael Burns, *Rural Society and French Politics: Boulangism and the Dreyfus Affair, 1886–1900* (Princeton, 1984). See also Busi, *Pope of Antisemitism,* p. 47, and Poliakov, *Histoire de l'antisémitisme,* vol. 2, p. 293.

30. Jean Bouvier, *Les Deux scandales de Panama* (Paris, 1964); D. W. Brogan, *The Development of Modern France,* vol. 1 (Gloucester, 1970), pp. 268–85; and Busi, *Pope of Antisemitism,* pp. 111–33. For Drumont's attacks on the army, see William Serman, *Les Officiers français dans la nation, 1848–1914* (Paris, 1982), pp. 101–2.

31. Serman, *Les Officiers,* pp. 101–9; Robert Byrnes, *Antisemitism in Modern France* (New Brunswick, 1950), p. 93 and passim; and Poliakov, *Histoire de l'antisémitisme,* vol. 2, p. 299.

32. Crémieu-Foa quoted in Stephen Wilson, *Ideology and Experience: Antisemitism in France at the Time of the Dreyfus Affair* (Rutherford, 1982), p. 718. See also, Ernest Crémieu-Foa, *La Campagne antisémitique: Les Duels. Les Responsables* (Paris, 1892); and *HAD,* vol. 2, p. 53.

33. Marrus, *Politics,* p. 198. For more on the duel—and on Morès—see *HAD,* vol. 2, p. 59; Bredin, *The Affair,* p. 21; Brogan, *Development,* vol. 1, p. 284; Busi, *Pope of Antisemitism,* pp. 93–95 and passim; and Donald Dresden, *The Marquis de Morès* (Norman, 1970).

34. Quoted in Patrice Boussel, *L'Affaire Dreyfus et la presse* (Paris, 1960), p. 23; see also p. 21.

35. Quoted in Marrus, *Politics,* p. 199. See also Weill, *Zadoc Kahn,* pp. 146–47.

36. Quoted in Boussel, *Presse,* p. 23.

37. See Bredin, *The Affair,* p. 22.

38. Rabbi Kahn's June 26, 1892, sermon in honor of Captain Mayer is quoted in

Weill, *Zadoc Kahn*, p. 147. On the impact of Mayer's death, see Marrus: "Finally, Jewish faith in the ability of France to protect Jewish citizens from insult and injury was strengthened by the *affaire*. Hence their optimism. Jews believed, with some justification, that the death of Mayer had united French opinion against anti-Semitism and had decisively demonstrated the reserve of good feeling upon which the unjustly persecuted could rely. Several years later, when Jews attempted to draw upon this reserve, their mistake became apparent" (*Politics*, p. 201).

39. Dreyfus "ne cherchait point à se faire pardonner sa race" (*HAD*, vol. 1, p. 68). See also Dreyfus's later comments in BVC, Arconati-Visconti correspondence, 1902–3.

40. Mairie, 8e arrondissement, Paris, état civil; and AN, BB 19/109, Nov. 21, 1894.

41. H. Villemar, *Dreyfus intime* (Paris, 1898), p. 14; AN, BB 19/128, interrogation, p. 430; and mairie, 8e arrondissement, Paris, état civil.

42. Serman, *Officiers*, pp. 186–88.

43. The couple's habits and tastes during this period are revealed in letters they exchanged later. See, for example, BN, N.A.F. 16609, Dec. 29, 1894, and 16610, July 12, 1895; AN, BB 19/109, Nov. 21, 1894, and BB, 19/105, letter from Mathieu, Sept. 19, 1894.

44. Dreyfus later described his work routine to Joseph Reinach (see BN, N.A.F. 13567, Feb. 8, 1900). See also Charpentier, *Les Côtés mystérieux*, p. 46. On the Dreyfuses' domestic life, see their reminiscences in BN, N.A.F. 16609–16610, as well as the notebooks in BN, N.A.F. 24909, and the inventory of books in AA, January 8, 1895.

45. BN, N.A.F. 16610, Feb. 1 and June 7, 1895; AN, BB 19/110, Sept. 12, 1896; and MB, Aug. 7, 1898. See also below, chap. 12.

46. *SC*, p. 196; and FRB.

47. Quoted in Bredin, *The Affair*, p. 18.

48. MD, p. 20.

49. Quoted in Serman, *Officiers*, p. 18.

50. BN, N.A.F. 16609, letter to Lucie, May 12, 1895: "Mais tu connais mon tempérament nerveux, mon caractère emporté."

51. *The Complete Works of Montaigne*, Donald M. Frame, trans. (Stanford, 1967), pp. 174–75.

52. AN, BB 19/101, "feuillet du personel," 1893–94; *HAD*, vol. 1, pp. 58–9; and Alistair Horne, *The French Army and Politics, 1870–1976* (New York, 1984), p. 16. On the stereotype of "parvenus," see Leroy-Beaulieu's comments in William E. H. Lecky, *Historical and Political Essays* (London, 1910), p. 115

53. Serman, *Officiers*, p. 225; see also, pp. 221–22.

54. AN, BB 19/128, interrogation, p. 430. See also above, chap. 5.

55. *Le Temps*, Oct. 4, 1890 and Jan. 22–27, 1891; AN, BB 19/128, interrogation, pp. 427–8; *HAD*, vol. 1, pp. 285–87; Bredin, *Affair*, pp. 22–23, 72–73; and Charpentier, *Les Côtés mystérieux*, pp. 36–37. In the 1894 interrogation Dreyfus insisted that he was a friend of Dida's and not her "amant." On *crimes passionnels*, see Ruth Harris, *Murders and Madness: Medicine, Law, and Society in the Fin de Siècle* (Oxford, 1989).

56. AN, BB 19/128, interrogation, p. 434. See also AN, BB 19/78, police reports on Madame Déry, et al., Nov. 1894; and *HAD*, vol. 1, pp. 164–65; 203–4.

57. AN, BB 19/101, Bourges correspondence, 1889–90.

58. "Manifestations de la sottise humaine" is how Pierre Dreyfus describes it in *SC*, p. 22.

59. The friend was Joseph Reinach; see *HAD*, vol. 1, p. 68.

60. AN, BB 19/128, interrogation, p. 413; and BN, N.A.F. 16609, letter to Lucie received Dec. 8, 1894. General Boisdeffre, at the Etat-Major, would say that Dreyfus was "zélé, travailleur, favorablement apprécié partout où il a passé" (see BN, N.A.F. 14311, Dreyfus journal, p. 301).

61. BN, N.A.F. 16609, Dec. 8, 1894.
62. AA, 59615, Dec. 11, 1893; AN, BB 19/128, interrogation, p. 418; and Paul Appell, *Souvenirs d'un alsacienne, 1852–1922* (Paris, 1923): "J'ai connu dans cette période des Alsaciens devenus officiers en France, auxquels avait été refusée l'autorisation de venir en Alsace assister à l'enterrement de leur père" (pp. 181–82).
63. AMM, état civil, Dec. 13, 1893; *Express* (Mulhouse), Dec. 15, 1893, and Jan. 11, 1894. The captain tried to extend his leave, but German authorities ordered him out of Alsace immediately after the funeral. That forced separation from his family and homeland at a moment of crisis would conjure up memories of his first exile, and intensify his hatred of the occupier (see the later interview with Dreyfus in *Gil Blas,* Aug. 10, 1907).
64. For more on this, see Vicki Caron, "Patriotism or Profit? The Emigration of Alsace-Lorraine Jews to France, 1871–1872," *Leo Baeck Institute Yearbook,* vol. 28, 1983, p. 165.
65. AMM, G 111 Aa 28.
66. AN, BB 19/128, interrogation, p. 406; AN, BB 19/105, letter from Mathieu, Sept. 19, 1894; AMM, J 11 E, rue Lavoisier; *Histoire documentaire de l'industrie de Mulhouse* (Mulhouse, 1902), p. 498; Charpentier, *Les Côtes mystérieux,* p. 16; and Louis Garros, *Alfred Dreyfus: "L'Affaire"* (Paris, 1970), p. 41.
67. AN, BB 19/105, letter from Mathieu, Sept. 19, 1894; and Henry Laufenburger, *Cours d'économie alsacienne* (Paris, 1932), t. 1, p. 144.
68. AMM, address registers, 1891–94; DFPC, Paul and Maurice Dreyfus's declarations of French citizenship, Feb. 2, 1893; *Mulhouse et le Sundgau 1648–1798–1848,* n.a. (Mulhouse, 1948), p. 6; *Centenaire de la Société Industrielle de Mulhouse,* n.a. (Mulhouse, 1926), p. 14; Schlumberger, *La Bourgeoisie,* p. 491; Christian Pfister, *Comment et pourquoi la république de Mulhouse s'est donnée à la France* (Nancy, 1919), p. 10; and Robert Gautier, *"Dreyfusards!" Souvenirs de Mathieu Dreyfus et autres inédits* (Paris, 1965), p. 11.
69. *HAD,* vol. 1, pp. 70–71; and Théodore Reinach, *Histoire sommaire de l'affaire Dreyfus* (Paris, 1924), p. 22. On Dreyfus's allegiance to Boisdeffre, see BN, N.A.F. 16609, Jan. 26, 1898.
70. Percy Dearmer, *Highways and Byways of Normandy* (London, 1900), pp. 239 ff; and Francis Miltoun, *Rambles in Normandy* (Boston, 1906), p. 314. On the Dreyfuses' summer outings, see BN, N.A.F. 14307, journal entry, April 14, 1895, and 16610, letter from Lucie, Aug. 15, 1897.

VII　REUNION

1. MD, pp. 19–20; and HAD, vol. 1, p. 240.
2. *HAD,* vol. 1, p. 210; and Jean-Denis Bredin, *The Affair: The Case of Alfred Dreyfus,* Jeffrey Mehlman, trans. (New York, 1986), p. 76.
3. These statements—and the exchange that follows—appear in MD, pp. 19–20.
4. Patrice Boussel, *L'Affaire Dreyfus et la presse* (Paris, 1960), p. 37; and Marcel Thomas, *L'Affaire sans Dreyfus,* vol. 1 (Paris, 1971), pp. 196–97.
5. *CA,* p. 59; and BN, N.A.F. 16610, Lucie to Alfred, Sept. 22, 1895. On why Dreyfus would react to the order to wear "civilian dress," see William Serman, *Les Officiers français dans la nation, 1848–1914* (Paris, 1982), pp. 127–28.
6. *HAD,* vol. 1, pp. 128–31, 137; *SC,* pp. 29–30; AN, BB 19/101, Oct. 17, 1894, inventory; Bredin, *The Affair,* p. 70; and Bruno Weill, *L'Affaire Dreyfus* (Paris, 1930), p. 37. For more on Mercier du Paty de Clam, see Maurice Paléologue, *An Intimate Journal of the Dreyfus Case,* Eric Mosbacher, trans. (New York, 1957), p. 134; and Eugen Weber, *France, Fin-de-Siècle* (Cambridge, Mass., 1986), p. 37.
7. *HAD,* vol. 1, p. 169.

8. AN, BB 19/101, Oct. 16–17, 24, 1894.
9. Quoted in MD, pp. 20–21.
10. BN, N.A.F. 24895, undated note from Lucie; *HAD*, vol. 1, p. 130 n. 1, 167–69; and *CA*, p. 64.
11. MD, p. 21; and Bredin, *The Affair*, p. 77.
12. MD, p. 21. Paul Dreyfus was in Paris preparing for the entrance examinations to the Ecole Polytechnique.
13. Ibid., pp. 22–24. See also, BN, N.A.F. 14379; *HAD*, vol. 1, p. 212; and Bredin, *The Affair*, p. 77.
14. MD, p. 27.
15. DFPC, letters, Nov. 6–9, 1894.
16. Quoted in Louis Garros, *Alfred Dreyfus: "L'Affaire"* (Paris, 1970), p. 78.
17. *SC*, pp. 68–70.
18. See Boussel, *Presse*, pp. 26–30; and Louis L. Snyder, ed., *The Dreyfus Case: A Documentary History* (New Brunswick, N.J., 1973), p. 93.
19. For an excellent summary of these and other news reports, see Bredin, *The Affair*, pp. 78–83. See also *La Libre Parole*, Nov. 3, 1894.
20. MD, pp. 24–26.
21. Boussel, *Presse*, pp. 47, 50.
22. Quoted in Bredin, *The Affair*, p. 79.
23. DFPC, Dec. 26, 1894.
24. MD, pp. 27–28, 30.
25. Ibid., pp. 24ff.: Bredin, *The Affair*, p. 77; and Pierre Sorlin, *Waldeck-Rousseau* (Paris, 1966), p. 392, n. 8.
26. Frederick Busi, *The Pope of Antisemitism: The Career and Legacy of Edouard-Adolphe Drumont* (Lanham, Md., 1986), p. 114. On the Dida case see above, chap. 6.
27. *HAD*, vol. 1, pp. 324–35; and MD, pp. 25–26.
28. MD, p. 31.
29. *CA*, pp. 59–61; *HAD*, vol. 1, pp. 108–14; AN, BB 19/128, du Paty account, 1905; and Bredin, *The Affair*, pp. 54–57.
30. *HAD*, vol. 1, pp. 117–26; and Bredin, *The Affair*, pp. 54–57.
31. *SC*, p. 23; and *HAD*, v. 1, pp. 117–26.
32. AN, BB 19/128, du Paty, 1905; and *CA*, p. 61.
33. See Forzinetti's account in *Le Figaro*, November 21, 1897, and Dreyfus's later account to Joseph Reinach in BN, N.A.F. 24895, May 25, 1900: "A mon arrivé dans la prison, je fus mis au secret le plus absolu. Toute communication avec les miens me fut interdits, je hurlais de douleur à la pensée de ma femme, de mes enfants."
34. Weil, *L'Affaire*, p. 37; and *HAD*, vol. 1, p. 163. Joseph Reinach quotes Dreyfus as saying (during a later interview with du Paty), "Mon malheur est d'être juif!" See also, Theodore Reinach, *Histoire sommaire de l'affaire Dreyfus* (Paris, 1924), p. 21.
35. On Forzinetti's report, see Nicholas Halasz, ed., *Five Years of My Life: The Diary of Captain Dreyfus* (New York, 1977), p. 59. See also, *HAD*, vol. 1, p. 152; and Bredin, *The Affair*, pp. 70–71.
36. Du Paty quoted in Robert Gauthier, "Les Alsaciens et l'Affaire Dreyfus," *Saisons d'Alsace*, 17, 1966, p. 59.
37. *HAD*, vol. 1, pp. 155–62; and SC, p. 28.
38. AN, BB 19/128, interrogation; and *HAD*, vol. 1, pp. 153–66.
39. AN, BB 19/128, interrogation, p. 404. See also, Armand Charpentier, *Les Côtes mystérieux de l'affaire Dreyfus* (Paris, 1937), pp. 292ff.
40. MD, p. 34; and Busi, *Pope of Antisemitism*, p. 37.
41. AN, BB 19/75, Oct. 27, 1985.
42. *HAD*, vol. 1, p. 189.
43. *SC*, p. 29; and AN, BB 19/128, interrogation, p. 407.
44. AN, BB 19/128, interrogation, p. 407.

45. Bredin, *The Affair,* p. 72.
46. AN, BB 19/101, reports, Oct.–Dec., 1894.
47. AN, BB 19/118, reports titled "L'Affaire Dreyfus (de la main de l'agent Guénée)"; *HAD,* vol. 1, pp. 147–48; *CA,* p. 65; and Bredin, *The Affair,* p. 72.
48. AN, BB 19/128, interrogation, pp. 406, 422–32.
49. Ibid., p. 437. Some accounts, through not the published transcript, report that Dreyfus's last statement to d'Ormescheville began, "Ce que j'ai de plus cher au monde, c'est mon honneur; je défie qui que ce soit de me le prendre" (see *SC,* p. 33.)

VIII JUSTICE

1. For Dreyfus's prison letters, see BN, N.A.F. 16609.
2. Ibid., Dec. 6, 1894.
3. Ibid., Dec. 16, 1894. For more on Dreyfus and the "cult of humanity," see his Devil's Island letters below, chap. XII; and Michael Burns, "Majority Faith: Dreyfus Before the Affair," in Frances Malino and David Sorkin, eds., *From East and West: Jewish Experience in a Changing Europe, 1750–1870* (Oxford, 1990). On justice and the "religion" of patriotism, see Michael R. Marrus, *The Politics of Assimilation: The Jewish Community in France at the Time of the Dreyfus Affair* (Oxford, 1980), pp. 106, 273, and passim.
4. BN, N.A.F. 16609, Dec. 6–18, 1894; and *LI,* pp. 23–28. On "Code X," see above, chap. 5.
5. BN, N.A.F. 16609, Dec. 13, 1894; BN, N.A.F. 16610, "Pierrot" letter; MB, Jan. 19, 1895; and LI, p. 28.
6. LI, pp. 24–32, and BN, N.A.F. 17387, Dec. 12, 1894.
7. On Alsatian reactions to the affair, see Vicki Caron and Paula Hyman, "The Failed Alliance: Jewish-Catholic Relations in Alsace-Lorraine, 1871–1914," *Leo Baeck Institute Yearbook,* vol. 26, 1981, pp. 12–16; and Robert Gauthier, "Les Alsaciens et l'affaire Dreyfus," *Saisons d'Alsace,* 17, 1966.
8. BN, N.A.F. 17386, Nov. 4 and Dec. 17 1894; and N.A.F. 16610, Jan. 1, 1895.
9. Gauthier, "Les Alsaciens," p. 64; BN, N.A.F. 16464, "secret dossier"; and *HAD,* vol. 2, p. 510.
10. The quote comes from Commandant Esterhazy (who will surface again); see Bruno Weil, *L'Affaire Dreyfus* (Paris, 1930), p. 28. On the Statistical Section, see Allan Mitchell, "The Xenophobic Style: French Counterespionage and the Emergence of the Dreyfus Affair," *The Journal of Modern History,* 3, Sept. 1980, p. 418; Marcel Thomas, *L'Affaire sans Dreyfus,* vol. 1 (Paris, 1971), pp. 98–108 and passim; and William Serman, *Les Officiers français dans la nation, 1848–1914* (Paris, 1982), p. 103.
11. *HAD,* vol. 1, p. 146; Jean-Denis Bredin, *The Affair: The Case of Alfred Dreyfus,* Jeffrey Mehlman, trans. (New York, 1986), pp. 42–44; and Mitchell, "Xenophobic Style," pp. 420–25. On events in Mulhouse in 1870, see above, chap. 3.
12. *HAD,* vol. 1, p. 146; Weil, *L'Affaire,* pp. 44–45; and AN, BB 19/129, Cour de Cassation, p. 8. For more on Sandherr, see Gauthier, "Les Alsaciens," pp. 61 ff.
13. MD, pp. 37–38; and Bredin, *The Affair,* pp. 90–91.
14. AN, BB 19/73, police note; *HAD,* vol. 1, pp. 428–29; and MD, pp. 35–36. "Jamais nous ne voulions faire de visites," the prisoner wrote his wife, "nous restions cantonnés chez nous, nous contentant d'être heureux" (BN, N.A.F. 16609, letter received Dec. 8, 1894).
15. MD, p. 37.
16. Quoted in Bredin, *The Affair,* p. 74; and Maurice Paléologue, *An Intimate Journal of the Dreyfus Case,* Eric Mosbacher, trans. (New York, 1957), p. 42.
17. *HAD,* vol. 1, pp. 384–86; MD, p. 38; and Bredin, *The Affair,* pp. 92–97. For documentation on the trial, see AN, BB 19/101.

18. *HAD*, vol. 1, p. 388.
19. LI, p. 33.
20. MD, p. 39; *HAD*, vol. 1, pp. 367–68; and Weil, *L'Affaire*, p. 39.
21. *HAD*, vol. 1, p. 400.
22. Ibid., p. 401.
23. AN, BB 19/101, "Feuillet du personnel"; and Bredin, *The Affair*, p. 63. For more on the discovery of Dreyfus as the "traitor," see Thomas, *L'Affaire sans Dreyfus*, vol. 1, p. 163.
24. "La confrontation avec le malheureux qui le croyait son protecteur, le serment peut-être, effrayaient Boisdeffre. Il avait collaboré à la préparation du crime; il ne voulait pas 'faire le coup' " (*HAD*, vol. 1, pp. 403–4).
25. Ibid., pp. 25–26, 411, and passim. On Henry's village background, see Michael Burns, *Rural Society and French Politics: Boulangism and the Dreyfus Affair, 1886–1900* (Princeton, 1984), pp. 144–46.
26. *HAD*, vol. 1, pp. 417–18; Bredin, *The Affair*, p. 94; and *CA*, pp. 68–69.
27. "Je n'attachai aucune importance à la déposition de Bertillon, car elle me parut l'oeuvre d'un fou" (*CA*, p. 69). See also, *HAD*, vol. 1, pp. 422–28.
28. Marrus, *Politics*, pp. 98–99, 111. On Rabbi Dreyfuss and Alfred Dreyfus's family, see APP, BB 19/101, police report, Dec. 5, 1897.
29. On the fire, see Mathieu Dreyfus's letter in AN, BB 19/105, September 1894; and *HAD*, vol. 1, p. 428, note 1. For more on the question of motive, see Armand Charpentier, *Les Côtes mystérieux de l'affaire Dreyfus* (Paris,1937), p. 74.
30. *HAD*, vol. 1, pp. 401–2, 432, 444; and *CA*, p. 69.
31. MD, p. 43.
32. Ibid., p. 44; and H. Villemar, *Dreyfus Intime* (Paris, 1898), p. 30.
33. MD, pp. 44–45; and Bredin, *The Affair*, pp. 96–97.
34. MD, p. 45.
35. AN, BB 19/95 and BB 19/75; and *HAD*, vol. 1, pp. 448–49. On the legal aspects of this and future Dreyfus trials, see Benjamin Martin, "The Dreyfus Affair and the Corruption of the French Legal System," in Norman L. Kleeblatt, ed., *The Dreyfus Affair: Art, Truth and Justice* (Berkeley and Los Angeles, 1987), pp. 37–49.
36. The sum was 1,615 francs (AN, BB 19/95 and BB 19/101).

IX   "FRANCE FOR THE FRENCH!"

1. *HAD*, vol. 1, pp. 449–56; Jean-Denis Bredin, *The Affair: The Case of Alfred Dreyfus*, Jeffrey Mehlman, trans. (New York, 1986), p. 97; and Nichols Halasz, *Five Years of My Life: The Diary of Captain Alfred Dreyfus* (New York, 1977), p. 62.
2. BN, N.A.F. 16610, Dec. 23–28, 1894; and *CA*, p. 74.
3. BN, N.A.F. 17387, Dec. 25[?], 1894; and MB, letter to Léon and Alice Dreyfus, Dec. 1894.
4. DFPC, letter to Grand Rabbi Kahn dated Dec. 23, 1894. Zadoc Kahn's authority flowed "from his moral force, from his extraordinary energy and from his devotion to the Jewish community as a whole, in all of its aspects, both material and religious. . . . In Salomon Reinach's description, he was 'the great chaplain of Judaism' " (Michael R. Marrus, *The Politics of Assimilation: The French Jewish Community at the Time of the Dreyfus Affair* [Oxford, 1980], p. 75).
5. AN, BB 19/75, Zadoc Kahn's letter and Commandant Brisset's response. See also Robert Gauthier, "Les Alsaciens et l'affaire Dreyfus," *Saisons d'Alsace*, 17, 1966, p. 79.
6. BN, N.A.F. 16609, Dec. 24 and Dec. 27, 1894; and MB, Dec. 1894.
7. AN, BB 19/75, Rachel Schil to General Mercier, Dec. 28, 1894.
8. BN, N.A.F. 14382, Mathieu Dreyfus to Pierre Quillard, July 21, 1906.
9. Marrus, *Politics*, p. 213. See also, Bredin, *The Affair*, 79–98.

10. Morès quoted in *Drumont et Dreyfus* (Paris, 1898), n.a. See also, *HAD*, vol. 1, p. 468.

11. *HAD*, vol. 1, p. 469.

12. Ibid., p. 522.

13. DFPC, Henriette and Joseph Valabrègue letters, Dec. 1894–Jan. 1895; DFPC, Marguerite Dreyfus Reinach Mercier (unpublished ms.), p. 12; DFPC, letter from Auguste Lalance, Feb. 19, 1898; and AN F7/12473, police reports, Dec. 27, 1894 and Jan. 7, 1895.

14. BN, N.A.F. 16610, Dec. 26–29, 1894, and BN, N.A.F. 16609, Dec. 27–29, 1894.

15. BN, N.A.F. 16609, Dec. 26–30, 1894; BN, N.A.F. 16610, Dec. 30, 1894; and *SC*, p. 51.

16. *CA*, p. 75.

17. Bredin, *The Affair*, pp. 99–100; and *HAD*, vol. 1, pp. 478–84.

18. *CA*, p. 76; and LI, p. 45.

19. *LI*, pp. 49–51; *CA*, pp. 77–79; and *HAD*, vol. 1, pp. 488–89.

20. *HAD*, vol. 1, p. 488, and *SC*, pp. 54–55.

21. AN, BB 19/75, Lucie Dreyfus to General Saussier.

22. Quoted in Bredin, *The Affair*, p. 100.

23. MD, p. 46.

24. *HAD*, vol. 1, p. 489.

25. DFPC, Dec. 31, 1894.

26. MB, Dreyfus letters to his family before the degradation; and *CA*, p. 79. For the note to Demange, see *HAD*, vol. 1, p. 489.

27. See, for example, the cover of *Le Quotidien Illustré*, Jan. 6, 1895.

28. AN, BB 19/73, Dec. 1896 report recounting events of Jan. 5, 1895; Louis Garros, *Alfred Dreyfus: "L'Affaire"* (Paris, 1970), p. 66; and *HAD*, vol. 1, pp. 494–95.

29. For excellent summaries of the degradation, see *HAD*, vol. 1, pp. 494 ff.; and Bredin, *The Affair*, pp. 3–8. See also, AN BB 19/128 Cour de Cassation, 1905. On the notables in attendance, see Patrice Boussel, *L'Affaire Dreyfus et la presse* (Paris, 1960), pp. 70–75; Léon Poliakov, *Histoire de l'antisémitisme*, vol. 2 (Paris, 1981), p. 299; and Louis Verneuil, *The Fabulous Life of Sarah Bernhardt*, trans., E. Boyd (New York, 1942), p. 207.

30. *HAD*, vol. 1, pp. 496–99. Lebrun-Renault would later spread a rumor—exploited by the press—that Dreyfus had confessed his crime during their wait for the degradation parade.

31. MD, p. 46. Michel de Lombardès estimates that 4000 troops were in the courtyard (see *L'Affaire Dreyfus* [Paris, 1985], p. 65).

32. See *Autorité*, Jan. 7, 1895, and the accounts cited in note 29 above.

33. Quoted in Bredin, *The Affair*, p. 6.

34. *HAD*, vol. 1, p. 512.

35. Daudet quoted in Boussel, *La Presse*, pp. 7–75.

36. Barrès quoted in Bredin, *The Affair*, p. 6. For Viau's reaction, see Jean France, *Autour de l'affaire Dreyfus: Souvenirs de la Sûreté Générale* (Paris, 1936), pp. 41–42; and for Bernhardt, see Verneuil, *Sarah Bernhardt*, p. 207; and for Herzl, see Amos Elon, *Herzl* (New York, 1975), pp. 126–29.

37. *HAD*, vol. 1, pp. 503–05; and France, *Autour l'affaire*, p. 42.

38. *CA*, p. 81.

39. *HAD*, vol. 1, pp. 505–06.

X THE VOYAGE OUT

1. MB, Jan. 5, 1895; and *HAD*, vol. 1, pp. 506, 562.

2. *SC*, pp. 58–59.

3. Ibid., pp. 59–60; *CA*, p. 86; MB, Jan. 13, 1985; and DFPC, letters, Jan. 1895.

4. *LI*, p. 63.

5. BN, N.A.F. 16610, Jan. 12, 1895.

6. *LI*, pp. 60, 69; and BN, N.A.F. 17387, Jan. 12, 1895.

7. *LI*, p. 78.

8. BN, N.A.F. 16609, Jan. 13, 1895. See also above, chap. 5.

9. DFPC, Jan. 20, 1895; and BN, N.A.F. 16609, letter to Lucie, Jan. 14, 1895.

10. *CA*, p. 91–92; and *HAD*, vol. 1, p. 565.

11. On events at La Rochelle, see *CA*, pp. 92–93; HAD, vol. 1, pp. 565–67; Patrice Boussel, *Presse L'Affaire Dreyfus et la* (Paris, 1960), pp. 82–84; and Jean-Denis Bredin, *The Affair: The Case of Alfred Dreyfus*, Jeffrey Mehlman, trans. (New York, 1986), p. 101.

12. *La Libre Parole*, Feb. 20, 1895.

13. *CA*, p. 93; and René James and Louis Suire, *L'Ile de Ré: D'autrefois à l'aujourd'hui* (La Rochelle, 1983), pp. 8–10, 52 and passim.

14. *HAD*, vol. 1, pp. 567–69; *CA*, p. 93; and BN, N.A.F. 16609, Jan. 19, 1895. When the prison director went through the contents of Dreyfus's pockets, he found a summary of the bordereau, which the prisoner had scribbled during his trial. The director immediately sent the document to Paris thinking it was an earlier draft of the incriminating memorandum and additional proof of Dreyfus's guilt.

15. *LI*, p. 101.

16. Ibid., pp. 95–96.

17. *HAD*, vol. 1, pp. 568–69; DFPC, Jan. 23, 1895; and MB, undated letter to Henriette Valabrègue.

18. *CA*, p. 99, and *LI*, p. 84; and MB, undated letter from Joseph Valabrègue to Henriette.

19. BN, N.A.F. 16610, Jan. 27, 1895.

20. MD, p. 69; *CA*, p. 96; BN, N.A.F. 16610, Jan. 22, 1895; DFPC, Jan. 28, 1895; and MB, Jan. 23, 1895. For an account of their journey, see DFPC, Joseph Valabrègue's letters to his wife. The family would later learn that Léon Dreyfus's "lack of energy" was a result of diabetes (see below, chap. 18).

21. James and Suire, *L'Ile de Ré*, pp. 19, 38, 48–59.

22. *HAD*, vol. 1, p. 571, and DFPC, Joseph Valabrègue letters.

23. For Lucie Dreyfus's account of the visit, see BN, N.A.F. 24895. See also *CA*, p. 102; *HAD*, vol. 1, p. 572; and DFPC, Joseph Valabrègue letters.

24. On the Feb. 9, 1895, law regarding the Iles du Salut, see Marie-Antoinette Menier, "La Détention du capitaine Dreyfus à l'ile du Diable, d'après les archives de l'Administration pénitentiaire," *Revue française d'histoire d'Outre-Mer*, t. 44 (1977), no. 237, pp. 460–61; and Bredin, *The Affair*, pp. 113, 124–28. See also, Armand Charpentier, *Les Côtés mystérieux de l'affaire Dreyfus* (Paris, 1937), pp. 82–87; and Michel Devèze, *Cayenne: Deportés et bagnards* (Paris, 1965), p. 104 and passim.

25. DFPC, Dreyfus to Minister of Colonies, Feb. 14, 1895; BN, N.A.F. 16609, Jan. 21, 1895; and *HAD*, vol. 2, p. 129, note 1.

26. BN, N.A.F. 24895, Lucie Dreyfus to Joseph Reinach, n.d.; *CA*, p. 104; and *HAD*, vol. 1, p. 573. See also the account in *Journal*, March 12, 1895.

27. AN, BB 19/101, transfer orders, Minister of Colonies; *HAD*, vol. 1, p. 573; and *CA*, p. 105.

28. *CA*, pp. 106–07; Menier, "La Détention," pp. 461–62; *HAD*, vol. 2, pp. 122–24; Bredin, *The Affair*, pp. 124–25. See also the excellent but unpublished manuscript by A.B. Marbaud, *Dreyfus a l'Ile du Diable* (1960) in DFPC.

29. Marbaud, *Ile du Diable*, pp. 4–5.

30. Devèze, *Cayenne*, p. 12; *CA*, p. 113; and Marbaud, *Ile du Diable*, pp. 6–16. Bouchet is quoted in Menier, "La Detention," p. 464.

31. MB, March 14 and 20, 1895.
32. BN, N.A.F. 16609, March 12, 1895; and *LI*, pp. 107–09. As soon as they learned of the prisoner's transfer from the Ile de Ré, family members started writing to French Guiana in the hope that their letters would be there upon Dreyfus's arrival. Weeks later, however, they were informed that regulations had been changed and that they were required to deposit mail with the colonial minister in Paris. For three months, the prisoner had no word from home (see BN, N.A.F. 14379, Mathieu Dreyfus papers, p. 79).
33. Menier, "La Détention," p. 463; Marbaud, *Ile du Diable*, pp. 18–25; and Devèze, *Cayenne*, p. 104.
34. Bouchet is quoted in Bredin, *The Affair*, p. 125. See also, *HAD*, vol. 2, pp. 125–27. On the leper colony, see Menier, "La Detention," p. 462; and Marbaud, *Ile du Diable*, p. 25.
35. *SC*, pp. 104–05; Marbaud, *Ile du Diable*, p. 21, 26; and *HAD*, vol. 2, p. 129.
36. BN, N.A.F. 14307, journal, April 14, 1895; CA, p. 107; Menier, "La Détention," pp. 464–65; Marbaud, *Ile du Diable*, pp. 21, 49; and Bredin, *The Affair*, p. 126.
37. Menier, "La Detention," pp. 462–63; and *CA*, pp. 113, 116.
38. *SC*, p. 105; *CA*, p. 116; and Marbaud, *Ile du Diable*, pp. 27–28.
39. On the night of April 14, 1895, Dreyfus recorded these thoughts in letters to his wife, and in his journal; see *CA*, pp. 111–16, and BN, N.A.F. 14307.
40. BN, N.A.F. 16610, March 7, 1895.

XI MATHIEU

1. Casimir-Perier quoted in Maurice Paléologue, *An Intimate Journal of the Dreyfus Case*, Eric Mosbacher, trans. (New York, 1957), pp. 26, 62. See also, Jean-Marie Mayeur and Madeleine Rebérioux, *The Third Republic from its Origins to the Great War, 1871–1914*, J. R. Foster, trans. (Cambridge, England, 1984), pp. 161–63; and Jean-Denis Bredin, *The Affair: The Case of Alfred Dreyfus*, Jeffrey Mehlman, trans., (New York, 1986), pp. 110–11.
2. For Drumont's comments, see Stephen Wilson, *Ideology and Experience: Antisemitism in France at the Time of the Dreyfus Affair* (Rutherford, 1982), pp. 320–21. See also, D. W. Brogan, *The Development of Modern France, 1870–1939*, vol. 1 (Gloucester, Mass., 1970), pp. 302–3.
3. Bredin, *The Affair*, pp. 111–12; *HAD*, vol. 1, p. 526; Mayeur and Rebérioux, *Third Republic*, p. 163; and Brogan, *Development*, vol. 1, pp. 303–4.
4. DFPC, Jan. 20, 1895.
5. BN, N.A.F. 16610, Jan. 25, 1895.
6. Ibid., Feb. 26, 1895; BN, N.A.F. 24895, undated letter to Joseph Reinach; and *HAD*, vol. 2, pp. 178–82.
7. MD, p. 47.
8. Patrice Boussel, *L'Affaire Dreyfus et la presse* (Paris, 1960), pp. 67–68. For more on Jaurès, see Harvey Goldberg, *The Life of Jean Jaurès* (Madison, 1962), and the same author's "Jean Jaurès and the Jewish Question: The Evolution of a Position," *Jewish Social Studies*, vol. 20, no. 2 (April 1958), pp. 67–94. Jaurès would later rally to Dreyfus (see below, chaps. 13–14).
9. AN, BB 19/110; and DPFC.
10. MD, pp. 47–52; Bredin, *The Affair*, pp. 116–18; *HAD*, vol. 2, pp. 171–72; and Michel de Lombarès, *L'Affaire Dreyfus* (Paris, 1985), pp. 193–200.
11. AN, F7/12473, police report, Dec. 27, 1894.
12. MD, pp. 56–57; *HAD*, vol. 2, p. 166; and AN, F7/12473, police reports.
13. MB, Joseph Valabrègue letters.
14. MD, pp. 49–51, 64–67; and Bredin, *The Affair*, pp. 117–18.

15. MD, pp. 64–73; and Robert Gauthier, *Dreyfusards!: Souvenirs de Mathieu Dreyfus et autres inédits* (Paris, 1965), p. 58.

16. Quoted in *HAD*, vol. 2, pp. 173–74. See also Bredin, *The Affair*, pp. 117–18.

17. MD, p. 52.

18. Ibid., pp. 52, 68–69.

19. Ibid., p. 74; MB, Dec. 31, 1895; BN, N.A.F. 17387; and BN, N.A.F. 16609. In 1895 "quantités de Dreyfus changent ce patronym qui passe pour celui d'un traître" (Paul Lévy, *Noms des Israélites en France* [Paris, 1960], p. 18).

20. MD, p. 74.

21. MB, July 15, 1895.

22. Ibid.; BN, N.A.F. 17387, Oct. 27,1895; and MB, April 18, June 26, and Nov. 20, 1895. See also, *HAD*, vol. 2, p. 145; and Théodore Reinach, *Histoire sommaire de l'affaire Dreyfus* (Paris, 1924), p. 50.

23. MB, Nov. 20, 1895.

24. MD, p. 75.

25. BN, N.A.F. 16610, April 30, 1895. For more on Lucie Dreyfus's reactions, see the romanticized but interesting essay by Josephine Lazarus, *Madame Dreyfus: An Appreciation* (New York, 1899), p. 43 and passim.

26. The family would spend the summers of 1895 and 1896 in a house rented by Mathieu—in the Valabrègues' name—at St. Cloud. The Hadamards' rue Châteaudun apartment, widely known as the family's base of operations, attracted reporters, police agents, swindlers, and hooligans. Taking a summer house was a long-standing custom for the family and, now, a strategy for protection. "Tout le monde à la maison se porte bien," Lucie wrote Alfred from St. Cloud in May 1896, "tous nos parents, frères et soeurs" (BN, N.A.F. 16610). For Mathieu's appeal to his brother, see BN, N.A.F. 16610, Nov. 25, 1895.

27. MD, pp. 78–80; and Gauthier, *Dreyfusards!* pp. 69ff.

28. *HAD*, vol. 2, p. 305; and Gauthier, *Dreyfusards!*, p. 70.

29. On foreign reactions to the affair, see, for example, Joseph Reinach's comments in *L'Affaire Dreyfus: Vers la justice par la verité*, vol. 1 (Paris, 1898), pp. 132–35, 140–41; and below, chap. XV.

30. MD, pp. 79–83; Gauthier, *Dreyfusards!* pp. 71–72; *L'Eclair*, Sept. 4, 1896; and Marcel Thomas, *L'Affaire sans Dreyfus*, vol. 2 (Paris, 1971), pp. 12–15.

31. T. Reinach, *Histoire sommaire*, pp. 50–51; and Gauthier, *Dreyfusards!* p. 73. See also *L'Intransigeant*, Nov. 23, 1896.

32. BN, N.A.F. 14308, journal, pp. 51ff.; *HAD*, vol. 2, pp. 308–11; *SC*, p. 15; and BN, N.A.F. 23819, Joseph Reinach letter of Sept. 17, 1897, describing a meeting with Lebon. See also, AN, BB 19/110, colonial minister's report, July 7, 1897.

33. DFPC, A. B. Marbaud, *Dreyfus à l'Ile du Diable*, unpub. ms. (1960), p. 73.

34. Ibid.; BN, N.A.F. 14307, journal, Sept. 10, 1896; CA, pp. 8, 163–75; T. Reinach, *Histoire sommaire*, p. 51; *HAD*, vol. 2, pp. 311–22; and Marie-Antoinette Menier, "La Détention du capitaine Dreyfus à l'ile du Diable, d'après les archives de l'Administration pénitentiaire," *Revue française d'histoire d'Outre-Mer*, t. 44 (1977), no. 237, p. 465.

35. Bredin, *The Affair*, pp. 117–18.

36. See Joseph Reinach's comments on the reactions of French Jews in *HAD*, vol. 2, p. 355. On the *L'Eclair* article, see MD, pp. 81–82, and *HAD*, vol. 2, pp. 348–56.

37. The petition is quoted in MD, p. 83. On Lucie Dreyfus as her husband's "tutrice," see AN, BB 19/78, Cour de cassation report.

38. MD, p. 84.

39. *L'Instransigeant*, Sept. 19, 1896.

40. Gauthier, *Dreyfusards!* pp. 77–78; and MD, p. 84. Lucie Dreyfus's letter to the pope would not be made public until the following year (see the translation in *The Sunday Special*, Dec. 5, 1897).

41. AN, BB 19/110, Rachel Schil, n.d.; and BN, N.A.F. 16609, A. Dreyfus, Sept. 7, 1895.

42. AN, BB 19/110, July 8, 1897; and BN, N.A.F. 16464, "secret dossier," July 6, 1897. For a general discussion of "peace and order" as the best guarantors of safety for French Jews, see David Cohen, *La Promotion des Juifs en France à l'époque du Second Empire*, vol. 1 (Aix-en-Provence), p. 61. Mathieu Dreyfus's cautious methods would give rise to heated controversy throughout the affair and across the decades that followed. A particularly negative analysis of his "natural inclination" to avoid political tumult and work with the government is presented by Léon Blum, Dreyfusard and, later, the first Socialist premier of France (see Léon Blum, *Souvenirs sur l'Affaire* [Paris, 1981; first published, 1935], pp. 56–60 and passim). But the most intemperate assessment of the family's "bizarre" methods remains Hannah Arendt's: "In trying to save an innocent man [the family] employed the very methods usually adopted in the case of a guilty one. They stood in mortal terror of publicity and relied exclusively on back-door maneuvers" (*Origins of Totalitarianism* [New York, 1973]), pp. 105–9). Arendt accepted rumors fashioned by Dreyfus's enemies as objective evidence, and relied on an error-ridden article published four decades after the affair. Her conclusions were the product of poor research, a rich imagination, and a desire to fit the Dreyfus story into a general account of Jewish pusillanimity. It would only work, however, by skewing the facts—or by ignoring them. For a more balanced treatment, see Michael R. Marrus, *The Politics of Assimilation: The French Jewish Community at the Time of the Dreyfus Affair* (Oxford, 1980), pp. 6–7, 215, 287. On the varied responses of French Jews to the affair, see Wilson, *Ideology and Experience*, pp. 692–730. See also the interesting comments by Eric Hobsbawm on personal influence as the "classical recourse of the bourgeois in trouble" in *The Age of Capital, 1848–1875* (New York, 1975), p. 244.

43. Rabbi Kahn quoted in Marrus, *Politics*, pp. 98, 145.

44. MD, pp. 60–61; and *HAD*, vol. 2, pp. 164–65. On *shtadlanut*, see Paula Hyman, *From Dreyfus to Vichy: The Remaking of French Jewry, 1906–1939* (New York, 1979), p. 39; Solomon Grayzel, *A History of the Jews* (New York, 1968), p. 439; and *Encyclopedia Judaica* (Jerusalem, 1971), pp. 1462–63.

45. MD, pp. 47–48.

46. See above, chap. 8. See also MD, p. 76; and *HAD*, vol. 2, pp. 186–87.

47. Quoted in Marrus, *Politics*, p. 166. Marrus presents a thorough study of Lazare and the Dreyfus affair (see pp. 164–95, 243–81 and passim). See also, Nelly Wilson, *Bernard Lazare: Antisemitism and the Problem of Jewish Identity in Late Nineteenth Century France* (New York, 1978).

48. Quoted in Marrus, *Politics*, p. 180.

49. MD, p. 77; and *HAD*, vol. 2, 189. On Jewish communities in Carpentras and its environs, see Marianne Calmann, *The Carrière of Carpentras* (London, 1984).

50. Gauthier, *Dreyfusards!* p. 84.

51. Ibid., p. 86. Lazare's pamphlet would eventually appear under the title *Une Erreur judiciaire: La Verité sur l'Affaire Dreyfus* (Brussels, 1896).

52. Marrus, *Politics*, pp. 171, 176, 182.

53. MD, p. 85; *HAD*, vol. 2, p. 427; and Thomas, *L'Affaire sans Dreyfus*, vol. 2, pp. 78–87.

54. T. Reinach, *Histoire sommaire*, p. 73.

55. Ibid.; AN, F 7/12473, police report on *La Libre Parole*, Nov. 11, 1896; AN, F 7/12464, report on Deputy Castelin; and *Paix* and *Radical*, Nov. 20, 1896.

56. Quoted in Marrus, *Politics*, p. 185.

57. Quoted in Gauthier, *Dreyfusards!* p. 87.

58. See Corinne Casset, "Joseph Reinach avant l'Affaire Dreyfus: Un exemple de l'assimilation politique des Juifs de France au début de la Troisième République" (unpublished dissertation, Ecole des Chartres, 1981–82); Henri Rigault, *M. Joseph Reinach*

(Paris, 1889); Mayeur and Reberioux, *Third Republic*, 192; and Marrus, *Politics*, pp. 136–40 and passim.

59. Julien Benda quoted in Wilson, *Ideology and Experience*, p. 404. For more on the history of the Reinach family, see Hélène Abrami, *La Bien-aimée* (unpub. ms., 1935).

60. Daudet quoted in *Wilson, Ideology and Experience*, p. 485.

61. Théodore Reinach quoted in Marrus, *Politics*, p. 142.

62. MD, pp. 87–88. "Si l'on veut bien admettre, un instant encore, que toute cette scandaleuse affaire prit naissance à la suite du bordereau publié par *Le Matin*, on reconnaîtra que le grand coupable, la cause de tout le mal, se trouve être le Papier, le Papier noirci, bien souvent déjà fauteur de désordres et empoisonneur de la paix publique" (John Grand-Carteret, *L'Affaire Dreyfus et l'image* [Paris, n.d.], p. 4). Later, in 1907, Alfred Dreyfus would learn that a former colleague at the Ecole Polytechnique, Philippe Bunau-Varilla, had seen the bordereau in 1896, and, after comparing letters from Dreyfus in his possession, had insisted that *Le Matin* publish the document. Bunau-Varilla's important—and courageous—involvement in the fight for revision is often overlooked (see SC, p. 199; and David McCullough, *The Path Between the Seas: The Creation of the Panama Canal, 1870–1914* [New York, 1977], p. 281). I thank James F. Lewis for bringing additional information on the Bunau-Varilla connection to my attention.

63. DFPC, March 25, 1897; MD, pp. 88–90; and *HAD*, vol. 2, p. 500, note 3, and p. 502, note 1.

64. On Sheurer-Kestner, see *HAD*, vol. 2, pp. 505–8 and passim; SC, p. 200; Gauthier, *Dreyfusards!* pp. 97–100, and the same author's "Les Alsaciens et l'Affaire Dreyfus," *Saisons d'Alsace*, 1966, pp. 66ff. See also, August Scheurer-Kestner, *Souvenirs de jeunesse* (Paris, 1905), and *Mémoires d'un sénateur dreyfusard* (Strasbourg, 1988).

65. Quoted in *HAD*, vol. 2, 539.

66. MD, p. 94; and BN, N.A.F. 23819, Lucie Dreyfus to Scheurer-Kestner, Nov. 15, 1897.

67. BN, N.A.F. 23819, September 18, 1897.

68. MD, p. 299.

69. The *Patrie* article is quoted in *HAD*, vol. 2, p. 633. See also, Frederick Busi, *The Pope of Antisemitism: The Career and Legacy of Edouard-Adolphe Drumont* (Lanham, Md., 1986); and *La Croix de l'Isère*, Nov. 5, 1897.

70. Quoted in Busi, *Pope of Antisemitism*, p. 142.

71. For the letters, postcards, and petitions to Scheurer-Kestner, see BN, N.A.F. 23819, and especially BN, N.A.F. 23821.

72. Quoted in *HAD*, vol. 2, p. 555.

73. Ibid., p. 554. On Scheurer-Kestner's clarity and frankness, see Mathieu Dreyfus's biographical sketch of the Senator in MD, pp. 296–301.

74. MD, p. 95; *HAD*, vol. 2, p. 546; and Gauthier, *Dreyfusards!*, pp. 88–95. Above all, Lazare and Reinach had been making those connections through 1896–97.

75. MD, p. 98; SC, p. 202; and Gauthier, *Dreyfusards!* pp. 106–110

76. "J'appris qu'Esterhazy était un chef de bataillon, en non-activité, qui avait appartenu au 74e régiment d'infanterie en garnison à Rouen. Il avait une détestable réputation. C'était un joueur, toujours à court d'argent, qui avait commis de nombreuses escroqueries" (MD, p. 99).

77. Ibid., p. 99.

XII BANQUO'S GHOST

1. BN, N.A.F. 14307, journal, May 29, 1895. See also, Dec. 5, 1895: "Ah! j'espère que le jour où le veritable coupable sera démasqué; s'il reste un peu de coeur

à ces hommes là, ils trouveront encore une balle de pistolet pour se la loger dans la tête, pour se faire justice eux mêmes, d'avoir fait souffrir un martyr pareil à un homme, à toute une famille."

2. Ibid., Dec. 31, 1895; BN, N.A.F. 16609, Dec. 31, 1895; and BN, N.A.F. 16464, July 6, 1897. On the "terrible heat," see BN, N.A.F. 14307, journal, Dec. 16, 1895.

3. BN, N.A.F. 16609, Dec. 24, 1896 and Feb. 5 and Aug. 10, 1897.

4. BN, N.A.F. 14307, journal, Sept. 29, 1895. Montaigne quoted in Joseph Reinach, *L'Affaire Dreyfus: Vers la justice par la verité*, vol. 1 (Paris, 1898), p. 17.

5. BN, N.A.F. 14307, Sept. 2 and Dec. 13, 1895: "Et pourquoi ne suis-je pas garçon, celibataire? Comme il y a longtemps que je serais là où les déceptions humaines ne peuvent plus vous atteindre" (Dec. 29, 1895).

6. BN, N.A.F. 24909, notebook, Aug. 1898, p. 26; and *The Complete Works of Montaigne*, Donald M. Frame, trans. (Stanford, 1967), p. 57. See also, BN, N.A.F. 16464, letter to Mathieu, July 6, 1897: "Mais si disparaître serait une solution pour moi, elle n'en serait une ni pour Lucie, ni pour mes enfants, ni pour vous tous; ce ne serait qu'ajouter un chagrin nouveau à ma pauvre Lucie, déjà si épouvantablement éprouvée."

7. BN, N.A.F. 24909, notebook, p. 413; and AN, BB/19 101, Bourges correspondence.

8. BN, N.A.F. 14307, journal, April 15–27, 1895; BN, N.A.F. 13567, letter to Joseph Reinach, Oct. 21, 1901; and *HAD*, vol. 2, pp. 161 ff.

9. BN, N.A.F. 16608, May 7, 1896; BN, N.A.F. 16609, April 18, 1895; and BN, N.A.F. 16610, Nov. 10, 1895. See also, BN, N.A.F. 14307, journal, April 25, 1895; *HAD*, vol. 2, p. 161; DFPC, letter from the Minister of Colonies, July 2, 1895; and DFPC, A.B. Marbaud, *Dreyfus à l'Ile du Diable*, unpub. ms. (1960), pp. 30, 46, 84.

10. BN, N.A.F. 14307, journal, April 27, May 9–10, and June 22, 1895; and May 5, 1896. See also, Marbaud, *Ile du Diable*, p. 90.

11. BN, N.A.F. 14307, journal, Sept. 29, 1895, and Jan. 27, 1896; BN, N.A.F. 14213, journal, p. 417; BN, N.A.F. 24909, notebook, pp. 8, 215; and *HAD*, vol. 2, p. 151. "C'étaient en effet, les épouses des Agents en service aux Iles du Salut, qui, cette fois encore, venaient au secours du déporté. . . . Le geste était d'ailleurs symptomatique de la tournure d'esprit qui régnait en faveur de Dreyfus dans l'Archipel. A la verité, les faits reprochés au déporté étaient appréciés ici avec une grande neutralité. . . . On doutait de la culpabilité du deporté" (Marbaud, *Ile du Diable*, pp. 68–70). But if some locals questioned Dreyfus's guilt after 1896, most remained indifferent or hostile. Keeping with the regime of silence, guards were deaf to Dreyfus's appeals, and when they did speak they chided the prisoner and told him, for example, that rumor had it that his wife had remarried and was pregnant.

12. Marbaud, *Ile du Diable*, p. 54; BN, N.A.F. 14307, journal, July 30, 1895; and BN, N.A.F. 23819, clipping from *La Patrie*, Sept. 14, 1897.

13. BN, N.A.F. 14307, journal, June 5, Sept. 27–29, and Dec. 8, 1895. "Je voudrais bien voir à ma place," he wrote Lucie, "philosophes et psychologues qui dissertent tranquillement au coin de leur feu, sur le calme, la sérénité que doit montrer un innocent! Un silence profound règne autour de moi, interrompu seulement par le mugissement de la mer" (BN, N.A.F. 16609, May 8, 1895).

14. BN, N.A.F. 16464, secret dossier. On Dreyfus's voice, see the doctor's report quoted in Louis Garros, *Alfred Dreyfus: "L'Affaire"* (Paris, 1970): " 'Le silence continuel auquel il est soumis a été une grande influence sur sa langue. Il ne répond qu'en faisant des efforts pour articuler. Les phrases ne venant plus directement, il est obligé de reprendre les mots pour exprimer sa pensée' " (pp. 155–56).

15. Dreyfus later referred to this in a 1901 letter to Joseph Reinach; see BN, N.A.F. 13567, and *HAD*, vol. 2, p. 151. On the prisoner's bouts of "nervosité," see BN, N.A.F. 16609, Jan. 3, 1896, Nov. 4, 1897, and March 20, 1898.

16. Carl Nordenfalk, *Celtic and Anglo-Saxon Painting* (New York, 1977), p. 16.

17. BN, N.A.F. 24909, pp. 53, 169, 199, 205; BN, N.A.F. 16610, Mar. 25 and April 25, 1896; DFPC, Minister of Colonies, Feb. 1896, and May 5, 1896. I am grateful to Professor Mark Peterson for his comments on these pages of the prisoner's notebooks.

18. Françoise Henry, *The Book of Kells: Reproductions from the Manuscripts in Trinity College Dublin* (New York, 1977), pp. 149–221; and Charles Rufus Morey, *Medieval Art* (New York, 1942), pp. 181–91.

19. See, for example, SC, pp. 127, 151, 187. "Pense à mon tête-à-tête perpetuel avec moi-même, plus silencieux qu'un trappiste, dans l'isolement le plus profound, en proie à mes tristes pensées, sur un rocher perdu, ne me soutenant que par la force du devoir" (p. 131). "Quel martyr pour un innocent plus grand certainement que celui aucun martyr de la chrétienté [sic]" (BN, N.A.F. 14307, journal, April 21, 1895).

20. Designs similar to Dreyfus's sketches can be found in M. Dupont-Auberville, *L'Ornement des tissus*, 2 vols. (Paris, 1877), and in the collection at the Musée de l'impression sur étoffes, Mulhouse.

21. BN, N.A.F. 14307, journal, July 12, 1895; and Marbaud, *Ile du Diable*, pp. 49–50, 60.

22. Act I, sc. 4.

23. See BN, N.A.F. 24909, p. 268 and passim; AN, BB 19/108, Minister of Colonies, lists of books and documents in the prisoner's possession; and Marie-Antoinnette Menier, "La Détention du capitaine Dreyfus à l'île du Diable, d'après les archives de l'Administration pénitentiaire," *Revue française d'histoire d'Outre-Mer*, t. 44, 1977, p. 467. For more on Dreyfus and Shakespeare, see *HAD*, vol. 2, pp. 151ff.

24. AN, BB/19 101, Bourges correspondence.

25. BN, N.A.F. 16610, Aug. 23, 1895, and March 25, April 25, and July 18, 1896. Worried that clandestine messages might be included in Dreyfus's reading materials—and hoping, perhaps, to fuel his frustration—officials ordered that all volumes be sent with "uncut pages" (see DFPC, Feb. 1896). For more on Dreyfus's book deliveries, see *HAD*, vol. 2, p. 454.

26. *Montaigne*, p. 479.

27. BN, N.A.F. 24909, pp. 208ff. Dreyfus read Loti's *Jerusalem* (1895) and *Ramuntcho* (1897), and probably others (see DFPC, Feb. 1896 and BN, N.A.F. 24909, notebook, p. 4). On Loti's appeal, see Richard Cobb, *People and Places* (Oxford, 1896), pp. 24–27.

28. BN, N.A.F. 24909, pp. 80–81; and BN, N.A.F. 14312, journal, p. 415.

29. *HAD*, vol. 2, p. 151. Joseph Reinach captured Dreyfus's "penetrating observations," but was wrong that the prisoner's journals revealed "no trace of imagination." Alongside theorems and clichéd aphorisms, there are scores of insightful, at times passionate, personal observations.

30. BN, N.A.F. 24909, pp. 82, 333, 365.

31. "Now among the principal benefits of virtue is disdain for death" (*Montaigne*, p. 57).

32. BN, N.A.F. 24909, pp. 4, 106, 257, and passim. "Je regrette profondément, pour le bon renom de notre pays de France devant le monde, de voir se renouveler dans notre siècle l'affligeant spectacle donné avant 1789, où l'on voyait des innocents immolés aux lenteurs de la Justice, aux formes; formes et lenteurs contre lesquelles se sont élévées les protestations de tous les écrivains du XVIIIeme siècle, et avec eux celle de quelques magistrats, comme l'avocat général Sirven, l'honnête Malesherbes, et avant eux, celle du plus illustré de tous, Montesquieu, qui voulait dès cette époque qu'on appartât dans la Justice 'le sentiment de l'humanité' " (BN, N.A.F. 16609, May 23, 1899).

33. BN, N.A.F. 24909, pp. 40, 58, 63, 160, 244.

34. Ibid., pp. 9. See also BN, N.A.F. 16609, April 12, 1898.

35. BN, N.A.F. 24909, pp. 190–91, 198; BN, N.A.F. 24985, undated note from

Dreyfus to Joseph Reinach; and *SC*, pp. 107, 124–25. On Montaigne and Shakespeare, see *Montaigne*, p. vi. No one has described Shakespeare's "grip on the marrow of our speech" more brilliantly than critic George Steiner: "The shapes of life which he created give voice to our inward needs. We catch ourselves crooning desire like street-corner Romeos; we fall to jealousy in the cadence of Othello; we make Hamlets of our enigmas; old men rage and dodder like Lear. Shakespeare is the common house of our feelings" (*Language and Silence: Essays on Language, Literature and the Inhuman* [New York, 1967], p. 198).

36.   BN, N.A.F. 24909, pp. 71, 212.

37.   BN, N.A.F. 16609, Oct. 2, 1897.

38.   Marbaud, *Ile du Diable*, pp. 33, 43; and AN, BB 19/108, note to colonial minister, Oct. 8, 1896. When Dreyfus included the passage from Othello in his letter to Lucie he copied it in French. "I sent it to you translated," he said, "you understand why!" Officials would suspect some sort of "cabalistic" code (see *SC*, p. 125.)

39.   BN, N.A.F. 14307, journal, June 28, 1895; and BN, N.A.F. 24909, pp. 7, 180, 224 and passim.

40.   *Montaigne*, p. 60.

41.   BN, N.A.F. 16610, March 20, 1896.

42.   *SC*, p. 159; and BN, N.A.F. 24895, Aug. 11, 1898.

43.   BN, N.A.F. 24895, July 12, 1895. "Quand je me sens trop triste," Lucie wrote, "et que le fardeau de la vie me semble trop lourd, trop difficile à supporter, je me détourne du présent, j'évoque mes souvenirs et je retrouve des forces pour continuer la lutte" (CA, p. 205).

44.   BN, N.A.F. 23821, Feb. 25, 1898.

45.   BN, N.A.F. 16609, Jan. 10, 12, 1895; BN, N.A.F. 16610, Feb. 4 and July 15, 1895; and BN, N.A.F. 14307, May 19 and Dec. 28, 1895.

46.   EN, vol. 2, p. 540; and *CA*, p. 99.

47.   BN, N.A.F. 16610, Jan. 12, June 7, Oct. 15, and Aug. 14, 1895, June 25, 1896, and June 27, 1897.

48.   Ibid., April 23, 1895. See also June 24, 1897, for the problems of raising the children in Paris.

49.   BN, N.A.F. 16609, July 16, Aug. 7, 1898; BN, N.A.F. 16610, Feb. 1, March 20, June 7, and Aug. 14, 1895; BN, N.A.F. 24909, pp. 28, 134, 375ff; and *Montaigne*, pp. 281–82. "Ne les quitte jamais [the children], vis toujours avec eux de coeur et d'âme, écoute-les toujours, quelques importunes que puissent être parfois leurs questions. Comme je te l'ai dit souvent, élever ses enfants ne consiste pas seulement à leur assurer la vie matérielle et même intellectuelle, mais leur assurer aussi l'appui qu'ils doivent trouver auprès de leurs parents, la confiance que ceux-ci doivent leur inspirer, la certitude qu'ils doivent toujours avoir de savoir où épancher leur coeur, où trouver l'oubli de leurs peines, de leurs déboires, si petits, si naïfs qu'ils paraissent parfois" (BN, N.A.F. 16609, Aug. 10, 1897).

50.   *Montaigne*, pp. 278ff.

51.   *SC*, p. 50; and BN, N.A.F. 24909, pp. 208, 397, 411.

52.   BN, N.A.F. 16610, March 20, 1895. On the form and impact of *images d'Epinal*, see Jean Mistler et al., *Epinal et l'imagerie populaire* (Paris, 1961) and Michael Burns, *Rural Society and French Politics: Boulangism and the Dreyfus Affair 1886–1900* (Princeton, 1984), pp. 65–67 and passim.

53.   BN, N.A.F. 16610, Feb. 28, 1895.

54.   See Michael R. Marrus's discussion of those catechisms in *The Politics of Assimilation: The French Jewish Community at the Time of the Dreyfus Affair* (Oxford, 1980), pp. 117–18.

55.   BN, N.A.F. 24909, journal, p. 411. See also the section of his journal entitled "De la foi religieuse."

56.   BN, N.A.F. 16610, [Mar. 1895?], Nov. 1897, and Jan. 25, 1898. See also the

note from Jeanne (written by her mother) dated Jan. 26, 1896, and another letter from Pierre, July [?] 1897.

57. BN, N.A.F. 16609, May 12 and 18, 1895. See also Dreyfus's letter to his wife dated Feb. 26, 1896: "Le 22 fevrier, c'était l'anniversaire de la naissance de notre chère petite Jeanne . . . combien j'ai pensé à elle. Je ne veux pas insister, car mon coeur éclaterait et j'ai besoin de toutes mes forces."

58. BN, N.A.F. 16610, Mar. 17, Aug. 30, and Nov. 17, 1897; and *HAD*, vol. 2, p. 549. For the note of Sept. 1, see Nicholas Halasz, *Five Years of My Life: The Diary of Captain Alfred Dreyfus* (New York, 1977), p. 217.

59. Marbaud, *Ile du Diable*, pp. 87–93; *HAD*, vol. 2, pp. 533–34; and BN, N.A.F. 14312, journal, pp. 414–15. The tower would not be completed until early in 1898.

60. BN, N.A.F. 16610, May 18, June 16, Aug. 26, Sept. 26, and Nov. 22, 1898; BN, N.A.F. 24909, journal, p. 330; AN, BB 19/108, Commandant's report, Oct. 20, 1898; and Marbaud, *Ile du Diable*, p. 91. For Dreyfus's letter to the President, see AN, BB 19/105, June 7, 1898.

61. *CA*, p. 208; and Halasz, *Five Years*, p. 229.

62. BN, N.A.F. 16609, Nov. 25, 1898; BN, N.A.F. 24909, journal, p. 219; and Marbaud, *Ile du Diable*, p. 97. On Dreyfus's earlier view of the ocean, see BN, N.A.F. 14307, Sept. 1, 1896; and BN, N.A.F. 16609, June 26, 1895.

63. *CA*, pp. 212–14. Though delayed, Lucie's letters were still full of hope: "Cette fois," she wrote on April 1, 1899, "je ne te dis pas adieu, mon chéri, mais à bientôt" (BN, N.A.F. 16610).

64. BN, N.A.F. 24909, p. 261.

65. BN, N.A.F. 16609, June 1, 1899. See also *Montaigne*, pp. 182–83.

66. Quoted in *CA*, p. 215.

67. Ibid., p. 217; and BN, N.A.F. 16609, telegram, June 6, 1899.

68. Dreyfus describes this in a letter to Joseph Reinach (BN, N.A.F. 13567, Oct. 21, 1901).

69. Quoted in *Montaigne*, p. 851.

XIII THE TUTORIAL

1. DFPC, A. B. Marbaud, *Dreyfus à l'Ile du Diable* (unpub. ms., 1960), p. 94; *CA*, p. 218; AN, F7/12465, Cayenne newspaper correspondent, June 7, 1899; AN, F7/12473, telegram to *La Presse*, July 1, 1899; and Michel de Lombarès, "Le Capitaine Dreyfus Revient," *La Revue historique des armées*, 180, Sept. 1990, pp. 66–70. On "les chinoiseries de la jurisprudence" which made the captain a "prévenu," see EN, vol. 2, p. 539.

2. MD, pp. 212–13. On the port of Sfax and the Tunisian campaigns, see D. W. Brogan, *The Development of Modern France, 1870–1939*, vol. 1, pp. 224–27.

3. *CA*, p. 219.

4. Ibid., pp. 219–20. On Dreyfus's arrival, see AN, F7/12464, police reports, June 17 and July 1, 1899; and Lombarès, "Le Capitaine Dreyfus Revient," p. 70.

5. BN, N.A.F. 16610, July 25, 1898, and May 1 and June 22, 1899; AN, F7/12464, police report, June 23, 1899; and *SC*, p. 191.

6. *SC*, p. 192; *CA*, 221; MD, p. 208; Louis Rogès, *Cinq semaines à Rennes* (Paris, n.d.), pp. xi–xii; and AN, F7/12473, telegram to *La Presse*, July 1, 1899.

7. APP, B/A 1052, July 7, 1899.

8. DFPC, July 1, 1899; AN, F7/12464, telegram to Demange, July 1, 1899; and EN, vol. 2, pp. 542–43.

9. DFPC, July 1, 1899; and *CA*, p. 221.

10. MD, p. 213.

11. *CA*, pp. 221–23; and Jean-Denis Bredin, *The Affair: The Case of Alfred Dreyfus*, Jeffrey Mehlman, trans. (New York, 1986), pp. 397–98.

526 * Notes to Pages 222–230

12. AN, BB 19/110, letter to Devil's Island, Nov. 18, 1895.

13. Drumont quoted in Frederick Busi, *The Pope of Antisemitism: The Career and Legacy of Edouard-Adolphe Drumont* (Lanham, Md., 1986), p. 147. For more on the "Jewish syndicate," see AN, BB/19 108, army intelligence reports, July 27–29, 1898; and EN, vol. 2, pp. 516–17.

14. On "Dreyfusard" and "Anti-Dreyfusard" propaganda, see AN, F/7 12463; and Norman L. Kleeblatt, ed., *The Dreyfus Affair: Art, Truth and Justice* (Berkeley, 1987).

15. MD, p. 125.

16. Bredin, *The Affair*, p. 157. See also, HAD, vol. 3, pp. 1ff.; Maurice Paléologue, *An Intimate Journal of the Dreyfus Case*, Eric Mosbacher, trans. (New York, 1957), p. 98; Michel de Lombarès, *L'Affaire Dreyfus* (Paris, 1985), p. 125; Marcel Thomas, *L'Affaire sans Dreyfus*, vol. 1 (Paris, 1971), pp. 51–62 and passim; and the same author's *Esterhazy, ou l'envers de l'affaire Dreyfus* (Paris, 1989).

17. Quoted in Bredin, *The Affair*, p. 380.

18. AN, BB/19 105, Sept. 6, 1898 report on the 1895 degradation. For more on Picquart, see SC, pp. 72–73; Louis Garros, *Alfred Dreyfus: "L'Affaire"* (Paris, 1970), p. 87; and AA, "Dreyfus dossier," May 23, 1898.

19. Quoted in Paléologue, *Intimate Journal*, p. 86.

20. Bredin, *The Affair*, pp. 140–47 and passim.

21. Mathieu Dreyfus's letter is quoted in Bredin, *The Affair*, pp. 210–11. See also MD, p. 135; and Douglas Johnson, *France and the Dreyfus Affair* (London, 1966), pp. 2, 105.

22. MD, p. 191 and passim; and Bredin, *The Affair*, p. 227.

23. MD, pp. 121–23.

24. Bredin, *The Affair*, p. 240.

25. MD, pp. 124–31.

26. See Benjamin Martin's comments on the legal aspects of the affair, in Kleeblatt, *The Dreyfus Affair*, pp. 37–49.

27. Reinach quoted in Johnson, *France and the Dreyfus Affair*, p. 93. See also, Bredin, *The Affair*, p. 229; and BN, N.A.F. 23821, Scheurer-Kestner correspondence, Jan. 22, 1898. On other links with the Calas case, see Nelly Wilson, *Bernard-Lazare: Antisemitism and the Problem of Jewish Identity in Late Nineteenth Century France* (Cambridge, 1978), 152.

28. See Voltaire, *L'Affaire Calas et autres affaires* (Paris, 1975), pp. 34–35, 82; Raoul Allier, "Voltaire et Calas, une erreur judicaire au XVIIIème siècle," *La Revue du Palais*, May 1, 1898, p. 405; Edgar Sanderson, *Historic Parallels to l'Affaire Dreyfus* (London, 1900), pp. 186, 203–5, 223–32; Edna Nixon, *Voltaire and the Calas Case* (New York, 1961), pp. 11–12, 32, 57–58, 98–107, 153, and passim. See also Marc Chassaigne, *The Calas Case*, R. Somerset, trans. (London, n.d. [1931?]); David Bien, *The Calas Affair* (1960); and Peter Gay, *The Enlightenment: An Interpretation*, vol. 2 (New York, 1978), pp. 433–37.

29. On Zola's involvement in the affair, see, for example, Madeleine Rebérioux, "Zola, Jaurès et France: trois intellectuels devant l'Affaire," *Cahiers naturalistes*, 54, 1980; Henri Mitterand, *Zola journaliste* (Paris, 1962); Cécile Delhorbe, *Les Ecrivains français et l'Affaire Dreyfus* (Paris, 1932); and Jean-Claude Le Blond, "Emile Zola et la famille Dreyfus," *Cahiers naturalistes*, 53, 1979, pp. 138–144. Zola's own account, in the spirit of Voltaire's essays on Calas, is found in *L'Affaire Dreyfus: La verité en marche* (Paris, 1969).

30. Zola, *La Verité en marche*, pp. 67–109; Bredin, *The Affair*, pp. 234, 245–46; and *HAD*, vol. 1, p. 367.

31. Abraham Dreyfus's letter is in BN, N.A.F. 24518.

32. Bredin, *The Affair*, p. 247.

33. *L'Aurore*, Jan. 13, 1898. The text also appears in Zola, *La Verité en marche*,

pp. 113–24. Members of the Dreyfus family sent Zola letters of gratitude. See, for example, BN, N.A.F. 24518, Lucie Dreyfus, Feb. 21, 1898, and the following from Jacques Dreyfus on Feb. 26, 1898: "L'aîné des frères du Capitaine Dreyfus se permet de vous apporter l'assurance des sentiments de profonde sympathie, de reconnaissance. . . . Merci est le cri de mon coeur."

34. *Le Procèss Zola devant la Cour d'assises et la Cour de Cassation,* 2 vols. (Paris, 1898); Bredin, *The Affair,* pp. 258–321; and BN, N.A.F. 23821, Scheurer-Kestner correspondence, January 1898. For a unique, fictional account of the intense interest in the Zola trial, see Marcel Proust, *Jean Santeuil* (Paris, 1952).

35. AN, F7/12460–63 and 12467; Stephen Wilson, *Ideology and Experience: Antisemitism in France at the Time of the Dreyfus Affair* (Rutherford, 1982), pp. 106–24; and Bredin, *The Affair,* pp. 285–99. The riots were concentrated in urban centers, while large areas of rural France remained indifferent, or applied the affair's vocabulary to local feuds and rivalries (see Michael Burns, *Rural Society and French Politics: Boulangism and the Dreyfus Affair* [Princeton, 1984], pp. 122–64).

36. MD, p. 107 and passim; DFPC, Auguste Lalance letter to Yves Guyot on Jacques Dreyfus's family, Feb. 19, 1898; AN, F7/12467, police reports, Jan. 1898; AN, F7/12473, police reports, Dec. 27, 1894, Jan. 7, 1895, and Nov. 2, 1897; AN, BB 19/73, police report, Oct. 10, 1897; BN, N.A.F. 16610, March 24 and July 15, 1897; AD Vaucluse, 1 M 809; Wilson, *Ideology and Experience,* pp. 115, 117, 120; *La Croix de la Marne,* March 4, 1898; and EN, vol. 2, pp. 487–88.

37. DFPC, Marguerite Reinach Mercier (unpub. ms.), p. 6, and BN, N.A.F. 16610.

38. Reprinted in John Grand-Carteret, *L'Affaire Dreyfus et l'image* (Paris, n.d. [1898?], pp. 40–42. See also, MD, p. 139.

39. MD, p. 195; and BN, N.A.F. 14382, Mathieu Dreyfus to Pierre Quillard, July 21, 1906.

40. Bredin, *The Affair,* pp. 330–32; Paléologue, *Intimate Journal,* pp. 157–62; and MD, pp. 166–91.

41. EN, vol. 2, p. 482.

42. *La Fronde,* "Appel aux Femmes," March 25–28, 1898; *Le Siècle,* "Réponses à l'Appel aux Femmes," March 25–27, 1898; AN, F7/12465, police report, Dec. 12, 1898; and BN, N.A.F. 17386, letter from Madame de Voisins d'Ambre, Sept. 12, 1899. See also the long letter to Lucie from her Swiss friend Hélène Naville, Feb. 15, 1898 (Naville family private collection).

43. Pierre Quillard, *Le Monument Henry: Listes des souscripteurs classés méthodiquement et selon l'ordre alphabétique* (Paris, 1899); Wilson, *Ideology and Experience,* pp. 125–65; and William Serman, *Les Officiers français dans la nation, 1848–1914* (Paris, 1982), pp. 107–8.

44. MD, pp. 169, 178, 182.

45. Ibid., pp. 186, 206; and Paléologue, *Intimate Journal,* pp. 201–6. Faure lapsed into a coma, his mistress was hurried out of the palace, and the president died five hours later (see Bredin, *The Affair,* p. 372). Anti-Semites, not surprisingly, said that Faure had been poisoned by the Jews (see Wilson, *Ideology and Experience,* p. 187).

46. See Brogan, *Development,* vol. 1, pp. 280, 347.

47. MD, p. 200; and Eugen Weber, *France, Fin de Siècle* (Cambridge, Mass., 1986), pp. 242–43. "Tout commence en mystique et tout finit en politique" (Péguy quoted in Jean Roussel, *Charles Péguy* [Paris, 1963], pp. 71–72).

48. EN, vol. 2, p. 519.

49. Ibid., pp. 419, 512, 527.

50. Quoted in *SC,* p. 237.

51. DFPC, Dreyfus notes, July 1899; and EN, vol. 2, pp. 542–43.

52. See above, chap. 12.

XIV EXTENUATING CIRCUMSTANCES

1. André Siegfried, *Tableau politique de la France de l'ouest sous la Troisième République* (Paris, 1913), pp. 100–101 and passim; Louis Rogès, *L' Affaire Dreyfus: Cinq semaines à Rennes* (Paris, n.d. [1899?]), pp. i, xx; *Le Patriote Breton*, July 12, 1899; and HAD, vol. 5, p. 201, n. 1.

2. AN, F7/12464, police map,; and Rogès, *Cinq semaines*, p. iv.

3. APP, B/A 1052, Rennes photographs; AN, F7/12476, police reports, July 1899; and BN, N.A.F. 24895, Lucie Dreyfus letter to Joseph Reinach, n.d.

4. APP, B/A 1052, police report, July 1, 1899; *Le Figaro*, July 7, 1899; and *HAD*, vol. 5, p. 203.

5. See the photograph of Mathieu Dreyfus and Georges Hadamard accompanied by an inspector in APP, B/A 1052. On Paul Valabrègue, see DFPC.

6. *HAD*, vol. 5, p. 200.

7. AN, F7/12464, reports, July 6–9, 1899.

8. EN, vol. 2, pp. 553–54; Maurice Paléologue, *An Intimate Journal of the Dreyfus Case*, Eric Mosbacher, trans. (New York, 1957), pp. 257–58, 290; and HAD, vol. 5, pp. 202–3, 264–67.

9. APP, B/A 1052, anti-Dreyfus propaganda; and AN, F7/12923, police report, Aug. 24, 1899. Rochefort is quoted in Douglas Johnson, *France and the Dreyfus Affair* (London, 1966), p. 162.

10. *HAD*, vol. 5, p. 200.

11. Jules Soury quoted in Stephen Wilson, *Ideology and Experience: Antisemitism in France at the Time of the Dreyfus Affair* (Rutherford, 1982), p. 458.

12. *Le Patriote Breton*, July 6, 1899; AN, F7/12464, police report, July 11, 1899; and APP, B/A 1052, poster, July 1899. It was not the first time rumors spread of an illegitimate child (see *La Reforme* [Brussels], July 22, 1899).

13. *HAD*, vol. 5, pp. 114–18, 149–54; and Eugen Weber, *France, fin de siècle* (Cambridge, Mass., 1986), p. 207.

14. Consistoire Israélite de Paris, letter from Versailles, July 2, 1899. Loubet is quoted in Jean-Denis Bredin, *The Affair: The Case of Alfred Dreyfus*, Jeffrey Mehlman, trans. (New York, 1986), p. 385.

15. MD, p. 207ff; Rogès, *Cinq semaines*, p. xxi; and Bredin, *The Affair*, p. 402.

16. MD, p. 209; *HAD*, vol. 5, pp. 277–81; and Louis Garros, *Alfred Dreyfus: "L'Affaire"* (Paris, 1970), p. 159.

17. *HAD*, vol. 5, p. 143; *L'Aurore*, Aug. 1899; Paléologue, *Intimate Journal*, p. 224; and Jean Bernard, *Le Procès de Rennes, 1899: Impressions d'un spectateur* (Paris, 1900), p. 395.

18. The Dreyfus Affair was the "prototype de l'evenément moderne, en termes d'histoire de la communication" (Jacques Le Goff and Pierre Nora, eds., *Faire l'histoire*, vol. 1 [Paris, 1974], pp. 210–28).

19. EN, vol. 2, pp. 555–56; MD, pp. 210–11; and Jean France, *Autour de l'Affaire Dreyfus: Souvenirs de la Sûreté Générale* (Paris, 1936), pp. 190ff.

20. Paléologue, *Intimate Journal*, p. 227.

21. Barrès quoted in France, *Autour de l'Affaire*, pp. 190ff; Jaurès quoted in Harvey Goldberg, *The Life of Jean Jaurès* (Madison, 1968), p. 259; and the *Times* correspondent quoted in Johnson, *France and the Dreyfus Affair*, p. 165. See also, *HAD*, vol. 5, p. 282; AN, F7/12465, telegram, July 22, 1899; MD, p. 208; Rogès, *Cinq semaines*, pp. xi–xii; and Maurice Barrès, *Ce que j'ai vu à Rennes* (Paris, 1900).

22. Stewart Edwards, ed., *The Communards of Paris, 1871* (Ithaca, N.Y., 1973), p. 28.

23. Rogès, *Cinq semaines*, p. xi; and Bredin, *The Affair*, p. 405. See also, Bernard, *Le Procès de Rennes*, pp. 12–13.

24. BN, N.A.F. 24895, letter to Joseph Reinach, Aug. 20, 1899; and MD, p. 213.

25. BN, N.A.F. 14310, p. 262; BN, N.A.F. 13569, letter to Joseph Reinach, n.d.; SC, p. 14; and Rogès, Cinq semaines, p. xiii.

26. HAD, vol. 5, p. 234; MD, p. 212; Paléologue, Intimate Journal, p. 226; and L'Aurore, Aug. 8, 1899.

27. AN, BB/19 102, reports to Minister of War, Aug. 16, 1899; MD, pp. 230–31; HAD, vol. 5, p. 264; and Johnson, France and the Dreyfus Affair, p. 174.

28. HAD, vol. 5, pp. 443–44.

29. Mathieu Dreyfus quoted in HAD, vol. 5, p. 286, note 6. See also, L'Aurore, Aug. 8, 1899.

30. MD, p. 212.

31. Bernard, Le Procès de Rennes, pp. 59–61; HAD, vol. 5, pp. 321, n. 3, 335–36; Bredin, The Affair, p. 409; L'Aurore, Aug. 8, 1899; and AN, BB/19 102, reports, Aug. 1899.

32. Bernard, Le Procès de Rennes, p. 61. The actor, Antoine, is quoted in MD, p. 213.

33. L'Aurore, Aug. 8, 1899; and HAD, vol. 5, p. 293.

34. AN, F7/12923, Le Journal clipping, Aug. 18, 1899.

35. CA, pp. 223–24; and AN, F7/12466, telegram, Aug. 10, 1899.

36. Rogès, Cinq semaines, p. xxi; and HAD, vol. 5, p. 268, 479.

37. MD, pp. 216–23; and HAD, vol. 5, p. 348.

38. MD, p. 216.

39. HAD, vol. 5, pp. 457–95.

40. Paléologue, Intimate Journal, pp. 258–60.

41. EN, vol. 3, p. 1201; and Paléologue, Intimate Journal, p. 290. Barrès is quoted in Bredin, The Affair, p. 415.

42. BN, N.A.F. 14308, pp. 65–84; and MD, pp. 219–23.

43. MD, pp. 219–23, 234–36; and HAD, vol. 5, p. 411. See also, Marguerite-Fernand Labori, Labori: Ses notes, sa vie (Paris, 1947).

44. EN, vol. 3, p. 1202; HAD, vol. 5, pp. 209–10, 266–67, 524; and MD, p. 258.

45. EN, vol. 2, p. 557, and vol. 3, pp. 1194–1201; HAD, vol. 5, p. 516; and Bredin, The Affair, pp. 423–25.

46. Bredin, The Affair, p. 399; HAD, vol. 5, pp. 110, 133; BN, N.A.F. 14308, p. 106; AN, BB 19/102, Sept. 6, 1899; and MD, p. 169.

47. Mathieu quoted Demange: "Il ne faut pas qu'ils considèrent que l'aquittement de Dreyfus est la condemnation de leurs chefs" (MD, p. 220). See also, HAD, vol. 5, p. 514.

48. Bernard, Le Procès de Rennes, p. 387.

49. See Bredin, The Affair, pp. 426–27; and HAD, vol. 5, p. 523.

50. HAD, vol. 5, pp. 387–88; and BN, N.A.F. 16609, Jan. 26, 1898.

51. HAD, vol. 5, p. 532; AN, F7/12923, newspaper clippings, Sept. 11, 1899; Bernard, Le Procès de Rennes, p. 391; Rogès, Cinq semaines, p. xxiii; Paléologue, Intimate Journal, pp. 292–93; and Le Petit Journal, Sept. 10, 1899. Dreyfus's statement is quoted in Théodore Reinach, Histoire sommaire de l'affaire Dreyfus (Paris, 1924), p. 181.

52. MD, p. 207; and EN, vol. 2, p. 548.

53. HAD, vol. 5, p. 476.

54. MD, p. 236; HAD, vol. 5, pp. 527–34; and AN, BB/19 102, telegram to minister of war, n.d.

55. L'Intransigeant, Sept. 10, 1899.

56. Emile Zola, L'Affaire Dreyfus: La Verité en marche (Paris, 1969), p. 161; Philip Kolb, ed., Marcel Proust: Selected Letters, 1880–1903, Ralph Mannheim, trans. (Garden City, 1983), p. 197; and L'Aurore and Le Siècle, Sept. 10, 1899.

57. APP, B/A 1047; police report, Sept. 10, 1899; and AN, F7/12465, telegram, Sept. 10, 1899.

58. Paléologue, *Intimate Journal*, p. 217; *HAD*, vol. 5, pp. 533–34.
59. MD, pp. 237–38.
60. Ibid., p. 238; and Rogès, *Cinq semaines*, p. xxiv.
61. *HAD*, vol. 5, pp. 535ff. See also, Pierre Sorlin, *Waldeck-Rousseau* (Paris, 1966), pp. 410–22.
62. Lazare quoted in Michael R. Marrus, *The Politics of Assimilation: The French Jewish Community at the Time of the Dreyfus Affair* (Oxford, 1980), p. 188; see also, pp. 164–95 and passim. For more on Lazare, see Nelly Wilson, *Bernard-Lazare: Antisemitism and the Problem of Jewish Identity in Late Nineteenth Century France* (Cambridge, England, 1978).
63. See Marrus, *Politics of Assimilation*, pp. 179–80, 254–56; and the comments of Alfred Dreyfus's grandson, Jean-Louis Lévy, in *CA*, pp. 255–56. On Lazare and Herzl, see Michel Abitol, *Les Deux Terres promises: Les Juifs de France et le sionisme* (Paris, 1989), pp. 19–29.
64. Quoted in Marrus, *Politics of Assimilation*, pp. 275–76.
65. BN, N.A.F. 14382, June 1, 1901.
66. Quoted in Marrus, *Politics of Assimilation*, pp. 275–76.
67. On Clemenceau's opinions and on the debate surrounding the pardon, see Pierre Vidal-Naquet's introduction to *CA*, pp. 31–43. For more on Clemenceau, see MD, p. 197; *HAD*, vol. 2, pp. 637–38 and passim; Patrice Boussel, *L'Affaire Dreyfus et la presse* (Paris, 1960), pp. 67–69; and David Robin Watson, *Clemenceau: A Political Biography* (New York, 1976).
68. MD, p. 239.
69. Ibid., pp. 197, 239–41. See the excellent description of Jaurès, in Theodore Zeldin, *France, 1848–1945* (Oxford, 1979), pp. 395–96.
70. MD, pp. 241–42; *HAD*, vol. 5, pp. 553–58; Bredin, *The Affair*, pp. 432–33; and Watson, *Clemenceau*, pp. 152–53.
71. *SC*, pp. 266–67; and MD, pp. 243–44.
72. APP, BA 1052, police reports, Aug. 20–22, 1899; and *HAD*, vol. 5, pp. 422–26. The "Fort Chabrol" siege lasted until Sept. 20.
73. *SC*, pp. 265–66; MD, p. 245; and *HAD*, vol. 5, pp. 562–63.
74. *HAD*, vol. 5, pp. 583–84. See also Bredin, *The Affair*, p. 434.
75. The statement is quoted in Bredin, *The Affair*, p. 433.
76. MD, p. 246.

XV HOMECOMING

1. *SC*, p. 268; and BN, N.A.F. 14308, journal, p. 5.
2. AN, F7/12467, telegram, Sept. 20, 1899; MD, pp. 246–49; and EN, vol. 2, pp. 566–67. For more on events at the train station, see AD Gironde, 1 M 431, Sept. 20, 1899. I thank Professor Susanna Barrows for this and other information on Dreyfus's passage through Bordeaux.
3. Stephen Kern, *The Culture of Time and Space, 1880–1918* (Cambridge, Mass., 1983), p. 29; and Eugen Weber, *France, fin de siècle* (Cambridge, Mass., 1986), pp. 4, 71. See also, MD, p. 248.
4. Norman L. Kleeblatt, ed., *The Dreyfus Affair: Art, Truth and Justice* (Berkeley, Calif., 1987), pp. 266–68; and Paul Hammond, *Marvellous Méliès* (New York, 1975), pp. 42, 139. On the telephone, telegraph, and fin-de-siècle journalism, see Kern, *Culture of Time and Space,* passim.
5. Adams quoted in Kern, *Culture of Time and Space,* p. 217 (see also, pp. 111, 214); and Weber, *France, fin de siècle,* pp. 96–104, 195–212.
6. AN, F7/12467, telegram to *Le Temps,* Sept. 21, 1899, and police report, Narbonne, Sept. 26, 1899

7. *Journal du Comtat*, Sept. 17, 1899; and *Le Mont-Ventoux*, Sept. 24, 1899. For population statistics, see *Annuaire de Vaucluse* (Avignon, 1903).

8. *La Croix d'Avignon et du Comtat*, Jan. 30, May 8–15, Nov. 11, 1898; *Le Mont-Ventoux*, March 6, 1898; *Annuaire de Vaucluse*, p. 46; AD Vaucluse, 1 M 809, police report, May 20, 1898; AN, F7/12464, police report, Nov. 11, 1896; and AN, F7/12466, police report, Sept. 7, 1898.

9. AN, F7/12467, telegram, Sept. 23, 1899, and prefect reports, Sept. 24–30, 1899; *Journal du Comtat*, Feb. 27, 1898, and Oct. 8, 1899; MB, Joseph Valabrègue, Sept. 26, 1899; *La Croix d'Avignon et du Comtat*, Oct. 1, 8, 1899; and Jean Bernard, *Le Procès de Rennes, 1899: Impressions d'un spectateur* (Paris, 1990), pp. 404–12.

10. *SC*, p. 268. For more on Dreyfus's health and the choice of Carpentras, see BN, N.A.F. 17387, Dec. 3, 1899.

11. *SC*, pp. 268–69.

12. Ibid., p. 269; and Alfred Bruneau, *A l'Ombre d'un grand coeur* (Paris, 1980), pp. 163–64. For Dreyfus's response to Zola, see BN, N.A.F. 24518, Sept. 30, 1899.

13. *SC*, pp. 12, 269.

14. Ibid., p. 13. The lithograph is reproduced in Kleeblatt, *The Dreyfus Affair: Art, Truth and Justice*, p. 194.

15. *SC*, p. 270; and *HAD*, vol. 6, p. 11.

16. *SC*, p. 269. See also, BHVP, MS 1611, Dreyfus to Forzinetti, Oct. 13, 1899.

17. BN, N.A.F. 14308; and *SC*, pp. 232–33.

18. EN, vol. 1, pp. 433–35, 447, 471–73, and vol. 2, pp. 499, 505–6, 567–68.

19. BN, N.A.F. 17386, n.d. (Reinach's emphasis).

20. *HAD*, vol. 6, pp. 10–11.

21. Quoted in Jean-Denis Bredin, *The Affair: The Case of Alfred Dreyfus*, Jeffrey Mehlman, trans. (New York, 1986), pp. 439–40.

22. *SC*, pp. 270–73; MD, p. 264; and *CA*, p. 17.

23. For the 1898 reports to the Ministère des Affaires Etrangères—and other foreign reactions—see AN, BB/19 103. See also, BN, N.A.F. 17386, letter to Mathieu Dreyfus, Jan. 12, 1898; BN, N.A.F. 23819, letter from the Reform Club, Nov. 1, 1897; BN, N.A.F. 23821, letter from the director of *Le Citoyen Franco-Américain*, March 19, 1898; AN, BB 19/96, letter to General Jamont, May 4, 1898; APP, B/A 1047, letters to Paris police, Sept. 1899; newspaper report from 1899 quoted in *La Quinzaine littéraire*, April 16, 1984, and EN, vol. 1, p. 458. For the affair's impact in the United States, see Egal Feldman, *The Dreyfus Affair and the American Conscience, 1895–1906* (Detroit, 1981).

24. AN, BB/19 103, French embassy reports and news clippings, Jan.–July 1898.

25. DFPC, letter from A. Lundberg, Stockholm, Sept. 6, 1899.

26. APP, B/A 1047, police telegram, Sept. 12, 1899.

27. Quoted in Douglas Johnson, *France and the Dreyfus Affair* (London, 1966), epigram.

28. *The Times*, Sept. 11, 1899, quoted in Edgar Sanderson, *Historic Parallels to l'Affaire Dreyfus* (London, 1900), p. xv.

29. BN, N.A.F. 17386, letter to Mathieu Dreyfus, Sept. 10, 1899; AN, F7/12465, police reports, Sept. 11–19, 1899; and APP, B/A 1047, police report, Sept. 15, 1899.

30. AN, F7/12465 telegram, Sept. 12, 1899.

31. MD, p. 263. See also, Jean Mayeur and Madeleine Rebérioux, *The Third Republic from its Origins to the Great War, 1871–1914*, Jean Foster, trans. (Cambridge, England, 1984), p. 203; D. W. Brogan, *The Development of Modern France*, vol. 2 (Gloucester, Mass., 1970), p. 394; and David L. Lewis, *The Race to Fashoda: European Colonialism and African Resistance in the Scramble for Africa* (New York, 1987).

32. See Charles Rearick, *Pleasures of the Belle Epoque: Entertainment and Festivity in Turn of the Century France* (New Haven, 1985), pp. 117–46; and R. D. Mandell, *Paris 1900: The Great World's Fair* (Toronto, 1967).

33. APP, B/A 1047, police reports, Sept. 11, 16, and 22, 1899; AN, BB/19 103, reports to Ministère des Affaires Etrangères, March 10, 1898; and AN, F7/12465, passim. Mathieu suspected that the family could count only on Waldeck-Rousseau's "sentiments," not on his "actions" (see MD, p. 255).

34. SC, pp. 257–58; and CA, p. 31.

35. BN, N.A.F. 17386, letters, Sept. 11–15, 1899; and SC, p. 13. Twain is quoted in Feldman, *The Dreyfus Affair and the American Conscience*, pp. 69, 94. Much of the correspondence sent to the family during and after Rennes is held in MB.

36. BN, N.A.F. 13567, Dreyfus to Reinach, 1900 (n.d.); and APP, B/A 1047, police report, Dec. 7, 1899. On Dreyfus's response to the *New York Journal*, see AN, F7/12467, May 11, 1900.

37. BN, N.A.F. 17386, Sept. 4 and 10, 1899. On the expenses of the affair, see below, chap.21.

38. BN, N.A.F. 24895, Reinach-Dreyfus correspondence; BN, N.A.F. 13569; and BN, N.A.F. 14309, p. 160. Learning that Emile Zola planned a book that would deal, in part, with civil engineering and with military matters, Dreyfus offered to serve as technical adviser (see BN, N.A.F., 24518, Dreyfus to Zola, Feb. 1, 1900).

39. BN, N.A.F. 24895, Dec. 14, 1899.

40. AN, F7/12467, police report, Cannes, Sept. 23, 1899. On the American invitations, see Feldman, *The Dreyfus Affair and the American Conscience*, pp. 94–95. Dreyfus refers to his doctors' recommendations in SC, p. 274. For Lady Stanley's letter, see SC, p. 254.

41. EN, vol. 1, pp. 424–25, 471, and vol. 3, pp. 997–98.

42. Rearick, *Pleasures*, p. 139; and AN F7/12467, police telegrams and news reports, April–May 1900.

43. SC, p. 274; and EN, vol. 2, p. 595.

44. SC, pp. 274–75, 287; EN, vol. 2, pp. 610–11; and BN, N.A.F. 13567, Dreyfus to Reinach, 1900 (n.d.).

45. HAD, vol. 6, p. 200.

46. MD, pp. 262–63.

47. Ibid., pp. 261–62. For the lawyer's point of view, see Marguerite-Fernand Labori, *Labori: Ses notes, sa vie* (Paris, 1947), pp. 247–77 and passim.

48. MD, pp. 264–74; and HAD, vol. 6, pp. 159–75.

49. SC, p. 278. "Tout ce qu'il [Waldeck-Rousseau] eut eu le droit de dire," Dreyfus wrote after the prime minister's announcement, "c'est que l'Affaire Dreyfus, suivant lui, était terminée en tant qu'affaire politique, mais il eut dû ajouter qu'elle restait, comme toute affaire de ce genre, du domaine judiciaire" (SC, p. 278). The amnesty would finally become law on Dec. 27, 1900.

50. HAD, vol. 6, p. 175.

51. MD, p. 265.

52. SC, pp. 293–94.

XVI LEGIONS OF HONOR

1. R. D. Mandell, *Paris 1900: The Great World's Fair* (Toronto, 1967); and Charles Rearick, *The Pleasures of the Belle Epoque: Entertainment and Festivity in Turn of the Century France* (New Haven, 1985).

2. SC, pp. 302–3.

3. AMM, register, 8, porte du Miroir, 1902–22; *Adressbüch*, 1901; BN, N.A.F. 14382, letter to Reinach, July 17, 1900; and Raymond Oberlé, *Mulhouse: Panorama monumental et architectural des origines à 1914* (Mulhouse[?], 1983). Throughout the affair, and for obvious reasons, all members of the Dreyfus family had difficulty finding living quarters in Paris. They were usually turned away by fearful or bigoted landlords. An exception was Count Frédéric Pillet-Will, who invited Mathieu to take one of

the apartments he owned on the rue Téhéran (DFPC, letter from Pillet-Will family).

4. EN, vol. 2, pp. 626–32; and SC, p. 325.

5. BN, N.A.F. 14308, pp. 96–99; MD, p. 278; and BN, N.A.F. 14309, p. 128 and passim.

6. HAD, vol. 6, p. 175.

7. CA, p. 5; and BN, N.A.F. 13567, Dreyfus to Reinach, 1900, n.d.

8. SC, pp. 314–15; HAD, vol. 6, p. 180; EN, vol. 2, p. 644; Jean-Claude Le Blond, "Emile Zola et la famille Dreyfus," Cahiers naturalistes, 54, 1980, p. 142; and DFPC, letter to Henriette. Even the choice of publishers provoked a minor squabble among Dreyfusards. P.-V. Stock had published most of the books and brochures that supported the captain during the height of the affair, including H. Villemar's (Hélène Naville's) Dreyfus Intime, and the prisoner's own Lettres d'un innocent. Stock assumed that he would publish the memoirs as well. But Dreyfus chose Fasquelle, probably on the advice of Zola and Reinach (see CA, p. 53, and P.-V. Stock, Mémorandum d'un éditeur: L'Affaire Dreyfus anecdotique, vol. 3 [Paris, 1938]). According to Reinach, the captain donated his profits to the League of the Rights of Man (see Liberté, Dec. 2, 1903).

9. BN, N.A.F. 14382, Mathieu to Trarieux, (Aug. ?) 1901.

10. Le Matin, Feb. 8, 1902; La Libre Parole, Feb. 9, 1901; Liberté, Feb. 8, 1902; and BN, N.A.F. 13567, Dreyfus to Reinach, 1901, n.d. The statue was dismantled by the Germans during World War II, and the metal, say local residents, was used for cannon.

11. Jean-Denis Bredin, The Affair: The Case of Alfred Dreyfus, trans. Jeffrey Mehlman (New York, 1986), pp. 454–68; MD, pp. 263–64; Liberté, May 31, 1902; Jean Mayeur and Madeleine Rebérioux, The Third Republic from its Origins to the Great War, 1871–1914, J. R. Foster, trans. (Cambridge, Eng., 1984), pp. 206, 221–22; Roger Magraw, France: The Bourgeois Century, 1815–1914 (New York, 1986), pp. 245–54; and Zeev Sternhell, La Droite révolutionnaire, 1885–1914: Les origines françaises du fascisme (Paris, 1978). For more on the Dreyfus apartment hunt see Bertrand Gold-schmidt, Pionniers de l'atome (Paris, 1987), p. 118.

12. La Libre Parole, June 6, 1902. The paper called Dreyfus a "Grande Im-monde."

13. Gaulois, June [21?], 1902.

14. APP, B/A 1047, police reports, July 1–12, 1902.

15. APP, B/A 1045, police reports, Feb. 25–27, 1904; SC, p. 334; BN, N.A.F. 14309, pp. 143, 147; La Patrie, July 24, 1902, L'Intransigeant, Aug. 7, 1902; and La Libre Parole, Jan. 18, 1903.

16. APP, B/A 1045, police reports; and L'Action Nationale, Feb. 24, 1904.

17. SC, p. 384.

18. DFPC, menus and guest lists, 1902 to 1910; and EN, vol. 2, pp. 640, 660 and passim. The description of Pressensé is in D. W. Brogan, The Development of Modern France, 1870–1939, vol. 1 (Gloucester, Mass., 1970), p. 385.

19. BVC, 1903 (n.d.).

20. SC, pp. 268, 337, 430–31; MD, pp. 296–305; BN, N.A.F. 16460, notice of Scheurer-Kestner's death, Sept. 19, 1899; EN, vol. 2, pp. 687–88; HAD, vol. 6, pp. 279–81.

21. L'Aurore, May 13–14, 1902; APP, B/A 1309, police and medical reports, Sept. 29–Oct. 1, 1902; SC, pp. 328, 335–36; and Alfred Bruneau, A l'Ombre d'un grand coeur (Paris, 1980), pp. 188–90. "Somme toute, Capitaine, sans le procès Zola, vous seriez mort là-bas [on Devil's Island]" (DFPC, Arconati-Visconti to Dreyfus, Jan. 1, 1903).

22. SC, pp. 335–37; Bruneau, A l'Ombre, pp. 191–92; and APP, B/A 1309, police reports and newspaper clippings, Oct. 4, 1902.

23. L'Antijuif, Oct. 5, 1902; L'Intransigeant, Oct. 6, 1902; and La Libre Parole, Sept. 30 and Oct. 5, 1902.

24. APP, B/A 1309, police reports and newspaper clippings, Oct. 6, 1902. For more on the funeral, see Le Blond, "Emile Zola et la famille Dreyfus," pp. 142–43, and HAD, vol. 6, p. 199.

25. *SC*, p. 337; *HAD*, vol. 6, p. 225; and APP, B/A 1047, police report, Oct. 20, 1902.

26. DFPC, Jan. (13?), 1903.

27. Nelly Wilson describes the funeral and the obituaries that followed (see *Bernard-Lazare: Antisemitism and the Problem of Jewish Identity in Late Nineteenth Century France* [Cambridge, England, 1978], pp. 270–71). See also Bredin, *The Affair*, pp. 139, 464. *La Libre Parole* delighted in noting Dreyfus's "ingratitude" toward Lazare and others (see March 7, 1904).

28. Lazare's letter, now in the archives of Hebrew University in Jerusalem, is quoted in *CA*, pp. 251–52.

29. BVC, Sept. 16, 1902. See also Michael R. Marrus, *The Politics of Assimilation: The French Jewish Community at the Time of the Dreyfus Affair* (Oxford, 1980), pp. 275–76; and above, chap. 14.

30. See above, chaps. 7, 19.

31. BN, N.A.F. 14382, Mathieu Dreyfus to Dr. Dumas, March 7, 1904.

32. BN, N.A.F. 13568, Dreyfus to Reinach, Sept. (n.d.), 1903, *SC*, p. 370; and APP, B/A 1309, reports from *Le Figaro* and *Le Matin*, Oct. 6, 1902.

33. Marrus, *Politics*, p. 195. Péguy is quoted in Harvey Goldberg, *The Life of Jean Jaurès* (Madison, 1968), p. 214. In July 1906 Dreyfus wrote to Reinach: "S'est-il formé un comité pour un buste à élever à Bernard Lazare? Je voudrais bien envoyer mes souscriptions" (BN, N.A.F. 13569). Nelly Wilson states that members of the Dreyfus family did not attend the Oct. 1908 dedication of Lazare's monument in Nîmes, and that they were "conspicuous by their absence" (*Bernard-Lazare*, p. 274). But only weeks before, Alfred Dreyfus had been shot and wounded at a memorial for Emile Zola at the Panthéon (see below, chap 17). The debate over Dreyfus's appreciation of Lazare—or lack of it—continues, and the evidence is open to interpretation. Perhaps Dreyfus should have attended Lazare's funeral, but perhaps he should have attended Joseph Valabrègue's as well.

34. MD, pp. 279–87; and *HAD*, vol. 6, pp. 206–14. Mathieu may have contributed funds to Jaurès's (ill-fated) election campaign in the spring of 1898 (see BN, N.A.F. 17386, Dr. Pécaut to Mathieu Dreyfus, March 22, 1898). For more on the "bordereau annoté," see CA, pp. 49–51; and Douglas Johnson, *France and the Dreyfus Affair* (London, 1966), pp. 188.

35. *SC*, pp. 342ff. On Dreyfus's research, see BN, N.A.F. 24208, Dreyfus to Minister of War, April 21, 1903.

36. *SC*, p. 347; MD, p. 287; and Bredin, *The Affair*, pp. 458–59.

37. *SC*, pp. 354–55; and Bredin, *The Affair*, pp. 460–61.

38. BN, N.A.F. 24208, April 21, 1903.

39. *SC*, pp. 373–79; EN, vol. 2, pp. 693–94; and *HAD*, vol. 6, p. 477.

40. EN, vol. 2, pp. 700–701.

41. Dreyfus's 1904 declaration is quoted in Armand Charpentier, *Les Côtés mystérieux de l'affaire Dreyfus* (Paris, 1937), p. 327. On the final verdict, see *Gil Blas*, Aug. 10, 1906. See also *SC*, p. 396; and *HAD*, vol. 6, p. 371.

42. *HAD*, vol. 6, pp. 371–72; and *La Presse*, Sept. 5, 1904.

43. *La Libre Parole*, Oct. 26, 1904.

44. On the "affaire des fiches," see William Serman, *Les Officiers français dans la nation, 1848–1914* (Paris, 1982), pp. 41, 80–81; Mayeur and Rebérioux, *Third Republic*, pp. 233–43; and Brogan, *Development*, vol. 1, pp. 381–86. Mathieu worried that "Les jesuites reviendront maîtres de l'armée et pour longtemps" (BN, N.A.F. 24895, Nov. 2, 1904).

45. *HAD*, vol. 6, p. 437.

46. Bredin, *The Affair*, p. 476; Johnson, *France and the Dreyfus Affair*, p. 196; MD, p. 295; DFPC, Naville notebook; and Théodore Reinach, *Histoire sommaire de l'affaire Dreyfus* (Paris, 1924), pp. 207–12. Joseph Reinach summarized the confrontation between Picquart and Mathieu Dreyfus: "La destinée avait porté Picquart plus haut que sa taille; Mathieu avait l'âme plus haute que sa destinée" (*HAD*, vol. 6, pp. 437–38).

47. Quoted in Bredin, *The Affair*, p. 479. Naville also confirms that Dreyfus did not attend the High Court debates in 1906, but read the transcripts and awaited the verdict at home (EN, vol. 2, 757).

48. T. Reinach, *Histoire sommaire*, pp. 213–16, and Bredin, *The Affair*, p. 478.

49. *SC*, p. 430.

50. On anti-Dreyfusards and the "notorious" Article 445, see Eugen Weber, *Action Française: Royalism and Reaction in Twentieth Century France* (Stanford, 1962), pp. 39–42.

51. The judgment is quoted in Bredin, *The Affair*, p. 480; and in T. Reinach, *Histoire sommaire*, p. 222. See also, *HAD*, vol. 6, pp. 434–77.

52. BN, N.A.F. 14312, pp. 369–89; EN, vol. 2, pp. 760–64; and *SC*, p. 431.

53. BN, N.A.F. 13569, Dreyfus to Joseph Reinach, Aug (?), 1906; BN, N.A.F. 14312, Dreyfus journal, 1906; and DFPC, Minister Etienne's letter to Joseph Reinach, July 19, 1906. See also, T. Reinach, *Histoire sommaire*, pp. 224–25; and *SC*, p. 432.

54. AN, F7/12472, Senate report #387, 1906.

55. BN, N.A.F. 14312, pp. 391–92ff; HAD, vol. 6, pp. 479–84; and Bredin, *The Affair*, p. 482.

56. *SC*, p. 434. In 1890, 80 percent of the captains, 97 percent of the commandants, and nearly all of the lieutenant colonels, colonels, and generals in the French army were members of the Legion of Honor (see Serman, *Les Officiers*, pp. 191–94).

57. HAD, vol. 6, pp. 500–501.

58. Ibid., pp. 502–3; and *SC*, pp. 434–35.

59. *SC*, p. 435; and Bredin, *The Affair*, pp. 481–85.

60. "Mais toutes ces emotions avaient été trop fortes," Dreyfus wrote later. "Des troubles cardiaques me firent subir une crise passagère" (*SC*, p. 436). Mathieu's work kept him in Mulhouse, and he regretted not being able to attend "l'émouvante cérémonie de l'Ecole Militaire." But he added his assessment in a letter to Gabriel Monod: "Notre grand et beau pays enfin ressaisi et guéri de sa passagère folie répare noblement son erreur" (BN, N.A.F. 14382, July 27, 1906).

61. *L'Express* quoted in a retrospective article in the *Journal de l'Alsace*, July 16, 1975.

62. *Archives israélites* and *Univers israélite* quoted in Paula Hyman, *From Dreyfus to Vichy: The Remaking of French Jewry, 1906–1939* (New York, 1979), pp. 34–35.

XVII   GREAT EXPECTATIONS

1. Gérard Baal, "Un Salon Dreyfusard, des lendemains de l'Affaire à la Grande Guerre: La Marquise Arconati-Visconti et ses amis," *Revue d'histoire moderne et contemporaine*, t. 28, July–Sept. 1981, pp. 433–63; and Claude Laforêt, "La Marquise Arconati-Visconti et ses amis politiques," *Mercure de France*, 15, 8, 1939, pp. 45–65. For letters that identify group members and the issues they discussed, see BVC, registers 271–72, "Arconati-Visconti." Dreyfus copied many of his letters to and from the marquise. For an example of Dreyfus's close involvement in legislative issues, see DFPC, Arconati-Visconti to Dreyfus, March 28, 1905; the marquise mentions their lunch with Jaurès and Briand at the time of Briand's proposal regarding the separation of church and state.

2. Baal, "Salon Dreyfusard," pp. 435–36; and DFPC, Arconati-Visconti to Dreyfus, Jan. 1, 1903.

3. Baal, "Salon Dreyfusard," p. 436; DFPC, Arconati-Visconti to Dreyfus, Jan.

25, 1907; BN, N.A.F. 23819, Reinach to Scheurer-Kestner, Oct. 7, 1897. On Madame Straus's *salon*, see Alain Silvera, *Daniel Halévy and His Times: A Gentleman Commoner in the Third Republic* (Ithaca, N.Y., 1966), p. 45. Joseph Reinach describes the Arconati-Visconti chateau in letters to his wife and to Scheurer-Kestner (see DFPC and BN, N.A.F. 23819, Oct. 7, 1897), as does the marquise in a letter to Dreyfus (DFPC, Nov. 4, 1902).

4. DFPC, Nov. 14, 1904.

5. Baal, "Salon Dreyfusard," pp. 436–37.

6. Ibid., p. 437; DFPC, Arconati-Visconti to Dreyfus, (Feb.?), 1903; and BVC, 271, 1904 (n.d.).

7. BVC, 271, n.d. (1903–4?); DFPC, Arconati-Visconti to Dreyfus, Sept. 8, 1902; BN, N.A.F. 14311, p. 346; Jean-Marie Mayeur and Madeleine Rebérioux, *The Third Republic from its Origins to the Great War, 1871–1914*, J. R. Foster, trans. (Cambridge, Eng., 1984), p. 121; and H. W. Paul, "The Debate Over the Bankruptcy of Science in 1895," *French Historical Studies*, 3, 1968, pp. 299–327.

8. BVC, 271–272; and BN, N.A.F. 13570, Dreyfus to Reinach, 1907 (n.d.). "Ma femme est la confidante de toutes mes pensées" (BN, N.A.F. 24493, Dreyfus to Louis Havet, n.d.). For her part, the marquise had a genuine respect for Dreyfus's wife and a special fondness for Pierre and Jeanne (see BVC, 271, June 5, 1902, and passim).

9. Quoted in Mayeur and Rebérioux, *Third Republic*, p. 237; see also p. 222.

10. For statistics and more, see Edward Shorter and Charles Tilly, *Strikes in France, 1830–1968* (London and New York, 1974); and Peter Schöttler, *Naissance des Bourses du travail: Un Appareil idéologique d'état à la fin du XIXeme siècle* (Paris, 1985), p. 12 and passim. See also D. W. Brogan, *The Development of Modern France, 1870–1939*, vol. 2 (Gloucester, Mass., 1970), p. 422.

11. Jean Maîtron, *Histoire du mouvement anarchiste en France, 1880–1914* (Paris, 1955).

12. Sebastien Faure announced in 1903 that "Dreyfus nous indiffére à l'heure actuelle. Il n'est plus pour nous qu'un homme qui jouit paisiblement des revenues d'une grande fortune, ne se souciant nullement des victimes innocentes qui gémissent dans les bagnes, et pour cette raison il est le dernier auquel nous devrons nous intéresser" (APP, B/A 1047, police report, Sept. 13, 1903; see also, police report, May 22, 1900). For more on socialist reactions to Dreyfus after the affair, see *Le Peuple*, April 9, 1903.

13. Hervé quoted in Steven Lukes, *Emile Durkheim: His Life and Work* (New York, 1972), p. 542. See also, Mayeur and Rebérioux, *Third Republic*, pp. 232, 257–59, 266.

14. Baal, "Salon Dreyfusard," pp. 441, 450, 458.

15. Manet's portrait of Clemenceau appears in the exhibition catalog, *Manet: 1832–1883* (New York, 1983), p. 445.

16. David Watson, *Clemenceau: A Political Biography* (New York, 1976), pp. 167–214; Roger Magraw, *France, 1815–1914: The Bourgeois Century* (New York, 1986), p. 311; and Mayeur and Rebérioux, *Third Republic*, p. 264. The most recent biography of the Tiger is Jean-Baptiste Duroselle's *Clemenceau* (Paris, 1988).

17. BN, N.A.F. 14310, p. 243. See also BN, N.A.F. 14311, p. 345. Clemenceau's comment on Jaurès is quoted in Gordon Wright, *France in Modern Times* (New York, 1981), p. 270.

18. DFPC, Arconati-Visconti to Dreyfus, April 20, 1907. See also Baal, "Salon Dreyfusard," pp. 446–47.

19. DFPC, Arconati-Visconti to Dreyfus, Sept. 1907 (n.d.). She said much the same thing directly to Jaurès: "Je me fiche bien, moi, bonne républicaine, jacobine comme feu Maximillien, des libertés du prolétariat. Je donnerais tout pour des canons perfectionnés" (quoted in Baal, "Salon Dreyfusard," p. 144).

20. BN, N.A.F. 13570, Dreyfus to Reinach, March 20, 1909; and BN, N.A.F. 24909, p. 339.

21. BN, N.A.F. 14312, p. 420; and BN, N.A.F. 24909, pp. 339, 408.

22. BN, N.A.F. 14312, pp. 391–92ff.

23. See, for example, Jaurès's letter on Picquart's appointment quoted in Jean-Denis Bredin, *The Affair: The Case of Alfred Dreyfus*, Jeffrey Mehlman, trans. (New York, 1986), p. 496.

24. BN, N.A.F. 14309, p. 119; BVC, 272, 1906 (n.d.); BN, N.A.F. 13570, Dreyfus to Reinach, April 15, 1907; and BN, N.A.F. 14312, pp. 413–15. See also, EN, vol. 2, p. 788.

25. *L'Humanité*, July 16, 1907. Dreyfus said the following about Clemenceau: "Nous verrons, suivant son mot, l'Histoire juger entre lui and moi et je ne crains pas son jugement" (BVC, 272, n.d.).

26. BN, N.A.F. 13570, Dreyfus to Reinach, July 1907; BN, N.A.F. 16609, Dreyfus to Lucie, July 16, 1898; and BN, N.A.F. 14312, p. 434. See also Bredin, *The Affair*, p. 486; and *The Complete Works of Montaigne*, Donald M. Frame, trans. (Stanford, 1967), p. 175.

27. AA, 59615, Dreyfus dossier, June 29, 1907; and DFPC, Dreyfus to Arconati-Visconti, June 27, 1907.

28. BVC, 271, 1904–5 (n.d.); BN, N.A.F. 14308, p. 101; BN, N.A.F. 14382, Mathieu Dreyfus to Louis Leblois, Feb. 10, 1903; and SC, p. 346 and passim. For more on Jaurès and the Dreyfus family, see the recollections of Pierre Dreyfus in *L'Oeuvre*, June 17, 1930.

29. BN, N.A.F. 24909, p. 391.

30. BN, N.A.F. 13570, Dreyfus to Reinach, 1907 (n.d.), and Oct. 30, 1908; and BVC, 271, 1904, 1907–8.

31. BN, N.A.F. 13570, Dreyfus to Reinach, 1907 (n.d.); and Baal, "Salon Dreyfusard," p. 440. See also, BVC, 273, 1905 (n.d.).

32. On "the middle way," see Lukes, *Emile Durkheim*, p. 351. The primary source on Solidarism is Léon Bourgeois, *La Solidarité* (Paris, 1896). See also, J. E. S. Hayward, "The Official Social Philosophy of the Third French Republic: Léon Bourgeois and Solidarism," *International Review of Social History*, 6, 1961, pp. 19–48; Theodore Zeldin, *France, 1848–1945: Politics and Anger* (Oxford, 1979), pp. 276–318; Judith Stone, *The Search for Social Peace: Reform Legislation in France, 1890–1914* (Albany, N.Y., 1985); and Mayeur and Rebérioux, *Third Republic*, p. 283.

33. Lukes, *Durkheim*, pp. 39–43, 58–65, and passim; and Dominick LaCapra, *Emile Durkheim: Sociologist and Philosopher* (Ithaca, N.Y., 1972), pp. 30, 76, and passim.

34. Ernest Wallwork, *Durkheim: Morality and Milieu* (Cambridge, Mass., 1972), pp. 168–69; LaCapra, *Durkheim*, pp. 11, 68, 73–76; and Lukes, *Emile Durkheim*, pp. 332–49.

35. Quoted in Lukes, *Emile Durkheim*, p. 345. Dreyfus put it this way: "Cette affaire n'avait pas été une cause, elle était la conséquence d'un état social préexistant et qui était mauvais. . . . L'affaire, en un mot, a aidé à jeter un peu de lumière dans les ténébres politiques et dans le mal social dont nous souffrions" (BN, N.A.F. 14309, p. 162).

36. Lukes, *Emile Durkheim*, pp. 346–47; see also, 333 n. 49.

37. See SC, p. 437. On Durkheim's break with Judaism, see Lukes, *Emile Durkheim*, p. 44.

38. Emile Durkheim, *Suicide: A Study in Sociology*, J. Spaulding and G. Simpson, trans. (New York, 1966), p. 160. See also Lukes, *Emile Durkheim*, pp. 39–40. This is not to suggest that Durkheim's sociology was primarily influenced by Judaic traditions, but that his family history and his father's teachings must have played a role in his conception of "community." Paula Hyman believes that Durkheim's sociology "is not the product of an intellectual stimulated by marginality and adrift in society but of a figure

rooted in the stability of his own milieu" (see *From Dreyfus to Vichy: The Remaking of French Jewry, 1906–1939* [New York, 1979], p. 22).

39. See AD Haut-Rhin, V 604, response to prefectoral report, Feb. 13, 1821; Bernhard Blumenkranz, ed., *Histoire des juifs en France* (Toulouse, 1972), p. 174; and Rina Neher-Bergheim, *Documents inédits sur l'entrée des Juifs dans la société française, 1750–1850* (Tel Aviv, 1977), vol. 2, p. 367.

40. Quoted in Henry Laufenburger, *Cours d'économie alsacienne*, t. 2 (Paris, 1932), p. 354.

41. Ibid., pp. 291–92, 311; and Mayeur and Rebérioux, *Third Republic*, p. 283. See also above, chap 2.

42. Lukes's description of Durkheim captures Dreyfus as well (see *Emile Durkheim*, p. 546).

43. LaCapra, *Durkheim*, pp. 30, 68; and Lukes, *Emile Durkheim*, p. 347.

44. Quoted in Lukes, *Emile Durkheim*, pp. 542–44.

45. BVC, 272 (n.d. 1905?); and BN, N.A.F. 14311, pp. 342–43. Dreyfus's friend Gabriel Monod would say much the same thing a few years later: "Ah! si Jaurès avait voulu rester le chef des socialistes indépendants, non révolutionnaires, quel rôle il aurait pu jouer!" (quoted in Baal, "Salon Dreyfusard," p. 453).

46. BN, N.A.F. 13570, Dreyfus to Reinach, 1908 (n.d.); and BVC, 272, 1907 (n.d.).

47. For Dreyfus's comments on the La Villette meeting, see BN, N.A.F. 13570, Feb. 15, 1908. On Albert Lévy and the "ultras," see Paul Mazgaj, *The Action Française and Revolutionary Syndicalism* (Chapel Hill, 1979), pp. 7–9, 91–92.

48. BN, N.A.F. 13570, Feb. 15, 1908. Two years later, Dreyfus would repeat his lecture on "The History of Syndicalism in France" at the Bibliothèque Populaire in the eighth arrondissement, and the Solidarist message would be the same (see APP, B/A 1662, clipping from *Le Temps*, [April?] 9, 1910).

49. See Eugen Weber, *Action Française: Royalism and Reaction in Twentieth Century France* (Stanford, 1962), still the definitive work on the organization and its followers.

50. Quoted in ibid., p. 53. See also, Eugen Weber, *The Nationalist Revival in France, 1905–1914* (Berkeley, 1959); and Mayeur and Rebérioux, *Third Republic*, pp. 296–99.

51. APP, B/A 1309, police reports, March 20, April 8, June 3 and June 28, 1908.

52. Ibid., news clipping, *Action Française*, June 3, 1906.

53. APP, B/A 1662, police report, Nov. 26, 1908. See also, Weber, *Action Française*, p. 42.

54. APP, B/A 1309, police reports, June 4, 1908; DFPC, Joseph Reinach to his daughter, June 5, 1908; EN, vol. 2, pp. 800–802; *Le Temps*, June 6, 1908; and *Le Matin*, Sept. 11, 1908. Of the more than two hundred demonstrators arrested, most were in their twenties, and most were medical and other students. The intersection of politics and funerals was not new; see Thomas Kselman, "Funeral Conflicts in Nineteenth Century France," *Comparative Studies in Society and History*, 30, 2, April, 1988, pp. 312–32.

55. *SC*, p. 442; and *Aurore* and *Gil Blas*, June 6, 1908.

56. *Action Française*, June 5, 1908; *Soleil*, June 5, 1908; and *Patrie*, June 6, 1908. See also, APP, B/A 1662, news clippings.

57. On Grégori, see *Gaulois, Patrie*, and *La Libre Parole*, June 5, 1908, and *Le Matin*, Sept. 11, 1908.

58. *Le Matin*, Sept. 11, 1908; APP, B/A 1662, police report, Nov. 26, 1908; and Weber, *Action Française*, p. 42.

59. EN, vol. 2, pp. 810–11. See also, APP, B/A 1662, new clippings.

60. *Gaulois*, Sept. 12, 1908; and *La Libre Parole* and *Patrie*, Sept. 13, 1908. See also, APP, B/A 1662, police report, Nov. 26, 1908.

61. APP, B/A 1662, police reports, Nov. 1908 and Feb. 1909; *Action Française,* Jan. 11 and Dec. 12, 1911; BN, N.A.F. 13570, Dreyfus to Joseph Reinach, 1908 (n.d.); and BN, N.A.F. 24993, Lucie Dreyfus to Louis Havet, June 10, 1908;

62. *Autorité,* Nov. 7, 1908.

63. In 1912, anarchosyndicalists would appeal to Dreyfus to support two of their members accused of murder. Dreyfus, though cautious in his response, insisted that "S'il s'agit de défendre un enfant du peuple contre l'injustice, je serai des vôtres et de toute mon âme" (see APP, B/A 1662, clipping from *Eclair,* Feb. 12, 1912).

64. EN, vol. 2, pp. 808, 925, and vol. 3, pp. 1084–96; BN, N.A.F. 13570, Dreyfus to Reinach, Feb. 1909; and *SC,* p. 443.

XVIII   HEIRS APPARENT

1. DFPC, Marguerite Reinach Mercier (unpub. ms.).

2. Ibid.

3. BHVP, MS 1161, Adolphe Joseph Reinach, 1898.

4. Hélène Abrami, *La Bien-aimée* (unpub. ms., 1935), p. 120.

5. *SC,* p. 13; and *CA,* p. 43.

6. BN, N.A.F. 24493, Lucie Dreyfus to Mme. Louis Havet, Jan. 28, 1900.

7. BVC, 271, Dreyfus to Arconati-Visconti, n.d. [1903?]; and FRB.

8. Private correspondence from the Lycée Condorcet headmaster, March 19, 1984. On the school, see *Dictionnaire de Paris* (Paris, 1964), p. 149; *Dictionnaire historique des rues de Paris, par Jacques Hillairet* (Paris, 1976), pp. 285–86; and Fritz K. Ringer, *Education and Society in Modern Europe* (Bloomington, Ind., 1979), pp. 161–63. See also Joseph N. Moody, *French Education Since Napoleon* (Syracuse, 1978), pp. 104–12.

9. Author's interview with Madame Pierre Dreyfus, March 1984; and FRB.

10. Salomon Reinach, *Adolphe Reinach* (Angers, 1919), pp. 1–2. See also, Adolphe Reinach, *Textes Grecs et Latins Relatifs à l'Histoire de la Peinture Ancienne: Recueil Milliet* (Paris, 1985).

11. Correspondence from the Collège Chaptal headmaster, March 23, 1984; and EN, vol. 2, pp. 923–90. On the Ecole Centrale, see Ringer, *Education and Society,* pp. 125, 173; Moody, *French Education,* p. 228 n. 119; and Felix Ponteil, *Histoire de l'enseignement en France: Les Grandes étapes, 1789–1964* (Tours, 1966), p. 212.

12. DFPC, Marguerite Reinach Mercier (unpub. ms.), p. 18; and EN, vol. 3, pp. 997–98, 1148.

13. Michael R. Marrus, *The Politics of Assimilation: The French Jewish Community at the Time of the Dreyfus Affair* (Oxford, 1980), p. 282.

14. BN, N.A.F. 24909, p. 411 and passim. See also, above Chap. 12.

15. Quoted in *HAD,* vol. 2, p. 160.

16. AMM, J II E, rue Lavoisier, Raphael Dreyfus et Compagnie, 1905–13.

17. BN, N.A.F. 17387, Mme. Paul Jeanmaire to Suzanne Dreyfus, Sept. 10, 1899. See also EN, vol. 2, 953.

18. Joffre quoted in James Joll, *The Origins of the First World War* (London, 1984), p. 69. On Emile Dreyfus's service, see BHVP, MS 1161, letter from Capt. Barrère to Mathieu Dreyfus, Dec. 31, 1912.

19. Joll, *Origins,* p. 74. See also, Geoffrey Barraclough, *From Agadir to Armageddon: Anatomy of a Crisis* (London, 1982); and Laurence Lafore, *The Long Fuse: An Interpretation of the Origins of World War I* (Philadelphia, 1971).

20. See George F. Kennan, *The Fateful Alliance: France, Russia, and the Coming of the First World War* (New York, 1984), pp. 76–77 and passim; and Jean-Marie Mayeur and Madeleine Rebérioux, *The Third Republic from its Origins to the Great War,* J. R. Foster, trans. (Cambridge, England, 1984), p. 273. For the railroad shares held by the Reinachs (annulled by the 1917 Revolution), see DFPC.

21.　BVC 271, 1904 (n.d.). "La Révolution commençait à grandir dans ce pays. Le peuple russe se soulevait enfin contre le régime autocratique et contre une bureaucratie barbare et vénale" (BN, N.A.F. 14311, Dreyfus journal, 1905, pp. 346–47).

22.　André Tardieu, *France and the Alliances: The Struggle for the Balance of Power* (New York, 1908), pp. 1–2.

23.　Eugen Weber, *The Nationalist Revival in France, 1905–1914* (Berkeley, 1959); Alistair Horne, *The French Army and Politics, 1870–1970* (New York, 1984), pp. 21–42; Harvey Goldberg, *The Life of Jean Jaurès* (Madison, 1962), pp. 428–29, 439; and Lafore, *Long Fuse,* pp. 174–75.

24.　BHVP, MS 1161, Mathieu Dreyfus to his son, March 3, 1912; and BN, N.A.F. 24895, Mathieu Dreyfus to Joseph Reinach, Nov. 2, 1904.

25.　DFPC, Ado Reinach to Emile Dreyfus, March 1912. All quotes below are from this source.

26.　Emile thanked his friend for such an "eloquent letter . . . from an officer to a simple soldier," but waited on his decision to join the army (DFPC, March 8, 1912). The metaphor of war and industry was not unique to Ado Reinach's generation: "What a battle!" wrote a French industrialist about economic competition with Britain in the 1850s, "many will die in the struggle, even more will be cruelly wounded" (quoted in Eric Hobsbawm, *The Age of Capital, 1848–1875* [New York, 1975], p. 239).

27.　Roger Martin du Gard, *Jean Barois,* Stuart Gilbert, trans. (Indianapolis, 1969; first published, 1913), pp. 211, 270–72, 309–23, and passim. See also Eugen Weber's introduction, pp. vii–xix.

28.　Barrès quoted in Frederic H. Seager, "The Alsace-Lorraine Question in France, 1871–1914," in Charles K. Warner, ed., *From the Ancien Regime to the Popular Front* (New York, 1969), p. 122.

29.　BVC, 275, June 11, 1911, and Oct. 10, 1913; MD, p. 306; and EN, vol. 3, pp. 1148, 1169.

30.　Quoted in Goldberg, *Life of Jean Jaurès,* pp. 443–44; see also 417–57. On Hervé, see Harold R. Weinstein, *Jean Jaurès: A Study of Patriotism in the French Socialist Movement* (New York, 1936), pp. 173–75.

31.　AA, 59615, report on Dreyfus's reserve activities, Oct. 29, 1911; and BN, N.A.F. 13570, Dreyfus to Joseph Reinach, 1909 (n.d.). On the "three-year law," see Mayeur and Rebérioux, *Third Republic,* p. 345, and Goldberg, *Life of Jean Jaurès,* pp. 440–44.

32.　Goldberg, *Life of Jean Jaurès,* pp. 452–53.

33.　Quoted in Weinstein, *Jaurès,* p. 180. See also, Mayeur and Rebérioux, *Third Republic,* p. 351.

34.　Goldberg, *Life of Jean Jaurès,* p. 462.

35.　MD, p. 307.

36.　Goldberg, *Life of Jean Jaurès,* pp. 464–71; and *L'Humanité,* July 29, 1914.

37.　*L'Humanité,* Aug. 1, 1914; Goldberg, *Life of Jean Jaurès,* p. 472; and Weinstein, *Jaurès,* p. 184. Villain is quoted in Eugen Weber, *Action Française: Royalism and Reaction in Twentieth Century France* (Stanford, 1962), p. 90.

38.　Mayeur and Rebérioux, *Third Republic,* p. 350.

39.　DFPC, Ado Reinach to Magui Reinach, July 31, 1914.

40.　Ibid., Mathieu Dreyfus (unpub. ms.), pp. 28–29.

41.　BVC, 275, Aug. 1, 1914; EN, vol. 3, pp. 1262–67; and Naville guest book, 1903–34 (private collection).

42.　DFPC, Emile Dreyfus to his mother, 1914 (n.d.). On the "Union Sacrée," see Mayeur and Rebérioux, *Third Republic,* p. 350; and Horne, *French Army and Politics,* pp. 34–36. On support for the war among French Jews, see Freddy Raphaël and Robert Weyl, *Les Juifs en Alsace: Culture, société, histoire* (Toulouse, 1977), p. 388.

43. AA, 59165, Dreyfus service record, Aug. 2, 1914–Jan. 25, 1919; and BVC, 275, Aug. 2, 1914.

XIX PRO PATRIA MORI

1. On the battle for Mulhouse, see Capt. P. P., "Le Premier Combat de Mulhouse (du 7 au 10 août 1914)," *Nouvelle Revue*, 37, t. 21, 1916, pp. 8–18; Ernest Meininger, *Histoire de Mulhouse* (Mulhouse, 1923), pp. 142ff; *L'Humanité*, Aug. 9, 1914; and DFPC, documents on the "Entrée des troupes françaises en Alsace" in DFPC. For Pierre's involvement, see BVC, 275, Aug. 10 and 16, 1914; and EN, vol. 3, p. 1301. It is also likely that Jacques Dreyfus's sons, Charles, Maurice and René, mobilized from Belfort, participated in the Mulhouse campaign.

2. DFPC, "Entrée des troupes."

3. DFPC, Emile Dreyfus, Aug. 11 and 14, 1914, and Ado Reinach, Aug. 10 and 12, 1914. Vicki Caron tells us that those exclamations were repeated by many Alsace-Lorraine Jews: "With what joy will I head toward Alsace," wrote a volunteer in 1915, "and with what memories on entering in uniform that country of our dreams!" (see *Between France and Germany: The Jews of Alsace-Lorraine, 1871–1918* [Stanford, 1988], p. 182). See also, Paula Hyman, *From Dreyfus to Vichy: The Remaking of French Jewry, 1906–1939* (New York, 1979): "If France longed for the return of the two lost provinces of Alsace-Lorraine, the longing of the Jews was especially personal and deep, for Alsace-Lorraine was the heartland of their community" (p. 50).

4. BVC, 275, Aug. 10 and 16, 1914; and DFPC, Dreyfus to Arconati-Visconti, Aug. 22, 1914.

5. Capt. P. P., "Premier Combat," and, by the same author, "Le Second Combat de Mulhouse (11 août–25 août)," *Nouvelle Revue*, 37, t. 21, 1916, pp. 81–92; *L'Humanité*, Aug. 17, 1914; and Alistair Horne, *The French Army and Politics, 1870–1970* (New York, 1984), p. 34.

6. Horne, *French Politics*, p. 33; J. M. Winter, *The Experience of World War I* (London, 1988), pp. 70–73; and Robert O. Paxton, *Europe in the Twentieth Century* (San Diego, 1985), p. 79.

7. DFPC, Aug. (n.d.), 1914.

8. Horne, *French Army*, p. 31.

9. DFPC, Aug. 7–10, 1914.

10. Ibid., Aug. 14–17, 1914. See also, Aug. 8, 1914.

11. Ibid., Aug. 25–28, 1914.

12. Ibid., Aug. 24, 28–29, 1914. On the military situation in northeastern France during this period, see Winter, *Experience of World War I*, p. 73.

13. On Ado Reinach's last battle, see BN, N.A.F. 14378, Mathieu Dreyfus ms.; Salomon Reinach, *Adolphe-Joseph Reinach* (Angers, 1919), p. 2; and DFPC, letters to Joseph Reinach from Commandant Guinard, Jan. 15, 1916, and Second Lieutenant A. Gauthier, Feb. 2, 1916. For the citation which accompanied Reinach's "Ordre de l'Armée," see *Les Israélites dans l'armée française: 1914–1918*, n.a. (Angers, 1921): "En toutes circonstances, s'est particulièrement distingué par son sang froid et sa bravoure exceptionels; le 30 août à la ferme des Cyranes [sic] dans un moment difficile, a groupé autour de lui une dizaine d'hommes et, tout en restant à cheval les a entrainé à l'assaut, permettant ainsi à son battalion de se maintenir sur ses positions" (p. 415).

14. Louis Barthou, *The Effort of the French Women* (Paris, 1918), p. 8.

15. EN, vol. 3, pp. 1329–30, 1342; DFPC, Princess Bibesco's unpublished "tribute" to Joseph Reinach; and DFPC, Mathieu Dreyfus (unpub. ms.), pp. 27–29.

16. EN, vol. 3, pp. 1381–86. Mademoiselle Martin (there is no indication of her first name or her nationality) spoke French, German, English, and Russian, and prior to the war she had been living in Russia and teaching English literature. She was described by Naville as a "frail and modest" young woman, and as a "courageous fighter."

17.   Ibid., vol. 4, pp. 1443–45, 1463.

18.   Ibid., pp. 1443–44.

19.   DFPC, Emile Dreyfus, Jan. 3, 1915; see also, March 8, 1915.

20.   Ibid., Marguerite Reinach Mercier (unpub. ms.), p. 35; and EN, vol. 4, 1445. For obvious reasons, the name of the street had been changed from "rue de Berlin" to "rue de Liège."

21.   DFPC, Lucie Dreyfus, March 19, 1915, and Alfred Dreyfus, March 28, 1915. Maurice Dreyfus was killed in combat, while his brother Charles, who also served in the war, died of an undocumented illness (for Maurice, see *Les Israëlites dans l'armée française*, p. 31).

22.   DFPC, Emile Dreyfus, March 19, 1915 (emphasis in letter).

23.   Ibid., Sept. 9, 1914; and Marc Ferro, *The Great War, 1914–1918*, Nicole Stone, trans. (London, 1972), p. 53.

24.   DFPC, Emile Dreyfus, Sept. 9, 1914. See also, BN, N.A.F. 14378 for Mathieu Dreyfus's summary of his son's letters from the Marne. On the battle of the Marne, see Winter, *Experience of World War I*, pp. 70–74; and Ferro, *The Great War*, pp. 52–55.

25.   DFPC, Emile Dreyfus, Oct. 15, Dec. 15 and 19, 1914, and Jan. 11, 1915; DFPC, Mathieu Dreyfus (unpub. ms.), pp. 28–30; BHVP, MS 1161, letter from Armand de Quatrefages describing Lieutenant Dreyfus, Dec. 25, 1914; and BN, N.A.F. 24493, Suzanne Dreyfus, Oct. 27, 1914.

26.   DFPC, Emile Dreyfus, Sept. 10 and Oct. 10, 1914, and Jan. 3 and Feb. 14, 1915.

27.   Ferro, *Great War*, pp. 49–58 and passim.

28.   D. W. Brogan, *The Development of Modern France, 1870–1939*, vol. 2 (Gloucester, Mass., 1970), p. 481.

29.   DFPC, Emile Dreyfus, Oct. 21 and Nov. 8, 1914, and Jan. 10, 1915.

30.   Ibid., Nov. 8 and Dec. 19, 1914, and Feb. 9, 1915.

31.   Quoted in C. E. Carrington, *The Life of Rudyard Kipling* (Garden City, N.Y., 1955), p. 338.

32.   DFPC, Nov. 23, Dec. 15, 1914, and Jan 5., Jan. 17, and April 22, 1915.

33.   Ibid., March 8, 1915, and May 26, 1915.

34.   Emile's letters never reveal his precise position, but they do chart his general movements through northeastern regions. On the military situation in 1915, see Winter, *Experience of World War I*, pp. 80–85, 124–29, and Horne, *French Army and Politics*, p. 37. And for another personal view of "stagnation" on the Western Front, see Robert Graves, *Goodbye to All That* (Harmondsworth, 1973; first published 1929), p. 101 and passim.

35.   DFPC, Emile Dreyfus, July 2 and 28, 1915. On Pierre, see BVC, 275, Alfred Dreyfus to Arconati-Visconti, April 15 and June 14, 1914, and below, chap. XX.

36.   DFPC, Emile Dreyfus, July 2, 1915; see also, April 22, 1915.

37.   On the family's activities through the first year of war, see, for example, EN, vol. 4, p. 1535 and passim; and BVC, 275, letters from Alfred Dreyfus to Arconati-Visconti, 1914–15.

38.   DFPC, Emile Dreyfus, Sept. 19, 1914 and Sept. 4, 1915; and DFPC, Ado Reinach, Aug. (n.d.), 1914.

39.   DFPC, Feb. 14, 1915.

40.   DFPC, Sept. 4, 1915.

41.   BVC, 275, Oct. 7, 1915; and EN, vol. 4, p. 1578.

42.   Ferro, *Great War*, pp. 64–65; Winter, *Experience of World War I*, p. 124; Keith Robbins, *The First World War* (Oxford, 1985), p. 49; and S. L. A. Marshall, *World War I* (Boston, 1987), pp. 224–29.

43.   On Emile's assignment and his injury, see BHVP, MS 1161, Mathieu Dreyfus dossier, and "Certificat d'origine de blessure de guerre," Sept. 29, 1915. "Suddenly I

saw a group bending over a man lying at the bottom of the trench. He was making a snoring noise mixed with animal groans. At my feet lay the cap he had worn, splashed with his brains. I had never seen human brains before; I somehow regarded them as a poetical figment. One can joke with a badly wounded man and congratulate him on being out of it. One can disregard a dead man. But even a miner can't make a joke that sounds like a joke over a man who takes three hours to die, after the top part of his head has been taken off by a bullet fired at twenty yards' range" (Graves, *Goodbye to All That*, p. 98).

44. DFPC, Marguerite Reinach Mercier (unpub. ms.), pp. 45–46; EN, vol. 4, p. 1578; and Mathieu Dreyfus (unpub. ms.), pp. 29–30. The account which follows is taken from Mathieu Dreyfus's ms., pp. 30–36.

45. BHVP, MS 1116, Dreyfus family papers; DFPC, mayor's letter to Mathieu Dreyfus, Dec. 9, 1915; and *Les Israëlites dans l'armée française*, p. 216. Emile Dreyfus was awarded the Croix de Guerre with palm.

46. DFPC, Mathieu Dreyfus (unpub. ms.), pp. 35–36.

XX *REVANCHE*

1. DFPC, Mathieu Dreyfus (unpub. ms.), and BVC, 275, Oct. 28, 1915. On the casualties in Champagne, see Marc Ferro, *The Great War, 1914–1918*, Nicole Stone, trans. (London, 1973), pp. 63–65; and S. L. A. Marshall, *World War I* (Boston, 1987), p. 228.

2. BVC, 275, May–Nov. 1915; EN, vol. 4, p. 1578; and DFPC, Alfred Dreyfus to Henriette Valabrègue, Nov. 2, 1915.

3. EN, vol. 4, p. 1442–55; DFPC, Alfred Dreyfus to Henriette Valabrègue, Dec. 10, 1914 and Jan. 13, 1915; and BVC, 275, letters, 1914–15.

4. Gallieni quoted in Marshall, *World War I*, p. 82. On events in Paris, see *Le Figaro*, Aug. 2, 1914; *L' Humanité*, Aug. 4, 1914; J. M. Winter, *The Experience of World War I* (London, 1988), pp. 170–71; and Anne Lamb and John Offen, *The Thoroughbred Style: Racing Dynasties, the Horse, the Owners, the Stables* (Topsfield, Me., 1987), p. 154. For comparisons with the 1870–71 siege, see Michael Howard, *The Franco-Prussian War* (New York, 1969), pp. 317–31.

5. EN, vol. 3, pp. 1321, 1334–35, and 1434ff.

6. DFPC, Alfred Dreyfus to Henriette Valabrègue, Dec. 10, 1914, Jan. 13 and 31, 1915; BVC, 275, Dec. 27, 1914, and April 25, 1915; BN, N.A.F. 24493, Lucie Dreyfus to Madame Louis Havet, Oct. 21, 1914; and EN, vol. 4, pp. 1442–55, 1499.

7. DFPC, Alfred Dreyfus to Henriette Valabrègue, April 12 and May 8, 1915; BVC 275, letters, 1915; and EN, vol. 4, 1499–1566.

8. DFPC, Alfred Dreyfus to Henriette Valabrègue, Nov. 29, 1915; BVC 275, Dec. 28, 1915; Keith Robbins, *The First World War* (Oxford, 1985), pp. 52–53; and Edward Jablonski, *A Pictorial History of the World War I Years* (Garden City, N.Y., 1979), p. 125.

9. DFPC, Mayor's "Allocution," Jan. 26, 1916; EN, vol. 4, 1638; and BN, N.A.F. 16460, "faire-part de mariage."

10. Marshall, *World War I*, p. 242.

11. On the battle of Verdun, see Alistair Horne, *The Price of Glory: Verdun, 1916* (1962); and *La Bataille de Verdun*, n.a. (Clermont-Ferrand, 1921). The most celebrated fictional account is Jules Romains, *Les Hommes de Bonne Volonté*, vols. 15–16 (Paris, 1938).

12. Quoted in Ferro, *Great War*, p. 76. See also, Marshall, *World War I*, p. 236.

13. *La Bataille*, pp. 14–15; Jablonski, *World War I Years*, p. 126; and Horne, *Price of Glory*.

14. EN, vol. 4, p. 1668; and *La Bataille*, p. 15.

15. Ferro, *Great War*, p. 77.

16. Robbins, *First World War*, p. 54; *La Bataille*, pp. 19–20; Ferro, *Great War*, p. 78; and Winter, *Experience of World War I*, pp. 88–91.

17. On Pierre Dreyfus's service at Verdun, see EN, vol. 4, p. 1668 and passim. On the rotation of troops, see Winter, *Experience of World War I*, p. 131.

18. Alfred Dreyfus quotes the military report on his son in BVC, 275, May 3, 1916.

19. Quoted in *La Bataille*, p. 19.

20. EN, vol. 4, p. 1668; and BVC, 275, Feb. 24, 1916.

21. The citation appeared in the *Journal de Genève* (see EN, vol. 4, p. 1673). See also, BVC, 275, May 3, 1916; and *Les Israélites dans l'armée française: 1914–1918*, n.a. (Angers, 1921), p. 219.

22. BVC, 275, May 3, 1916; EN, vol. 4, 1668; and Jablonski, *World War I Years*, p. 130.

23. *La Bataille*, pp. 55–63; and Jablonski, *World War I Years*, pp. 130–31.

24. "[Pierre] me disait souvent qu'il préférait être blessé qu'être atteint par le gaz" (BVC, 275, Alfred Dreyfus to Arconati-Visconti, June 3, 1918).

25. On "box respirators" and other antigas devices, see Winter, *Experience of World War I*, pp. 142–43.

26. Horne, *Price of Glory*, p. 1; Jablonski, *World War I Years*, p. 131; and Ferro, *Great War*, p. 77. On Pierre's reassignment, see EN, vol. 4, p. 1700.

27. BVC, 275, July 2, 1916.

28. Robbins, *First World War*, p. 56; and Marshall, *World War I*, p. 258.

29. Erich Maria Remarque, *All Quiet on the Western Front* (New York, 1958), p. 244.

30. BVC, 275, Oct. 12, 1916; EN, vol. 4, p. 1739; and *Les Israélites dans l'armée française*, p. 219. On Dr. Lévy, see DFPC, Alfred Dreyfus to Henriette Valabrègue, July 11, 1916.

31. BVC, 275, May 6, 1917. See also above, chap XII.

32. On Alfred Dreyfus's service, see AA, 59615, including Dreyfus's later correspondence with the minister of war in 1930–31. There is some confusion about where and for how long Dreyfus served at the front; but these and other documents confirm his assignments at or near the battlefields of the Aisne and Verdun in 1917 and 1918. See also, BVC, 275, April 14 and 23, 1916; and EN, vol. 4, p. 1823. On Jacques Dreyfus's son, René, an aviator and one of the most decorated members of the family, see *Les Israélites dans l'armée française, 1914–1918*, n.a., p. 220; and Armée de l'air, Service Historique, Vincennes, "Capitaine René Dreyfus."

33. DFPC, Arconati-Visconti to Dreyfus, Oct. 23, 1915. On the mobilization of students from the *grandes écoles*, see, for example, Steven Lukes, *Emile Durkheim: His Life and Work* (New York, 1972), p. 548.

34. BVC, 275, Feb. 27, March 6 and April 2, 1917; and DFPC, Dreyfus to Lucie Valabrègue Bernheim, Feb. 26 and March 6, 1917.

35. BVC, 272, Dreyfus to Arconati-Visconti, May 6, 1917; and EN, vol. 4, 1875.

36. Nivelle quoted in Marshall, *World War I*, p. 288 (Nivelle's emphasis). See also, Winter, *Experience of World War I*, p. 94.

37. Guy Pedrocini, "Indisciplines pendant la Grande Guerre," in Frédéric Bluche and Stéphane Rials, eds., *Les Révolutions françaises* (Paris, 1989), pp. 379–93; Ferro, *Great War*, pp. 181–84; and Winter, *Experience of World War I*, pp. 155–56.

38. BVC, 275, July 28, 1917.

39. Ibid., Aug. 30, 1917.

40. Joseph Reinach, *L'Intervention des Etats Unis* (Paris, 1917), p. 11.

41. David Robin Watson, *Clemenceau: A Political Biography* (New York, 1974), pp. 275–79 and 304 n. 81.

42. Ibid., pp. 293–314.

43. On the bombardment of Paris, see Henri Sellier et al., *Paris pendant la*

guerre (Paris, 1926), pp. 81–84; Winter, *Experience of World War I*, pp. 138, 170–71; Marshall, *World War I*, pp. 361–62; and Jablonski, *World War I Years*, pp. 239–40.

44. On Magui Reinach's family, see EN, vol. 4, 1445; and FRB.

45. Pétain quoted in Watson, *Clemenceau*, p. 303.

46. Ibid., pp. 300–304; Winter, *Experience of World War I*, p. 107; and Ferro, *Great War*, pp. 214–16. The split between Clemenceau and Foch was yet to come; see Georges Clemenceau, *Grandeurs et Misères d'une victoire* (Paris, 1930).

47. BVC, 275, June 3, 1918.

48. The citation is quoted in BVC, 275, Aug. 18, 1918. Alfred Dreyfus's service at Verdun in early 1918 is mentioned in AA, 59615, Dreyfus to Minister of War, July 7, 1930; and *SC*, p. 442.

49. EN, vol. 5, pp. 2207–9, 2299, and vol. 6, pp. 2371–72; and BVC 275, Oct. 15 and Nov. 13, 1918. For more on the promotions of Alfred and Pierre Dreyfus, see AA, 59615, service record; and DFPC, Mathieu Dreyfus (unpub. ms.), p. 27.

50. BVC, 275, Jan. 15, 1918. On Dr. Lévy's citations, see *Les Israëlites dans l'armée française*, p. 348.

51. BHVP, MS 1161, Alfred Dreyfus to Mathieu and Suzanne Dreyfus, Nov. 20, 1918; and BVC 275, Nov. 13, 1918.

52. Ernest Meininger, *Histoire de Mulhouse* (Mulhouse, 1923), pp. 142ff.; and Watson, *Clemenceau*, p. 326.

53. DFPC, Marguerite Reinach Mercier (unpub. ms.), and FRB. For casualty statistics, see Winter, *Experience of World War I*, p. 206.

XXI   BETWEEN TIMES

1. On the Dreyfus family mills and the Alsatian textile economy in general, see AMM, J II E, rue Lavoisier; Dan P. Silverman, *Reluctant Union: Alsace-Lorraine and Imperial Germany, 1871–1918* (University Park, Pa., 1972), pp. 188 and 237 n. 68; and Henry Laufenburger, *Cours d'économie alsacienne*, t. 1 (Paris, 1930), p. 144. The financial cost of the affair is impossible to calculate. Labori's legal fees alone ranged somewhere between forty and sixty thousand francs, and during a four-year period Mathieu Dreyfus paid fees of one thousand francs and more to minor informants. Hotel rooms and rented apartments in Paris and the provinces, and the cost of trips to London, Basel, Brussels, and Rennes, added to the expenses. See, for example, BN, N.A.F. 14309, Dreyfus journal, p. 132; *CA*, p. 254 n. 10; MD, pp. 172ff; and Marguerite-Fernand Labori, *Labori: Ses notes, sa vie* (Paris, 1947), pp. 84–87.

2. EN, vol. 4, pp. 1482, 1878; Laufenburger, *Cours d'économie*, t. 2, pp. 38ff.; and reports from the Tribunal d'instance, Mulhouse, Aug. 3 and 7, 1919.

3. François-Georges Dreyfus, *Histoire de l'Alsace* (Paris, 1979), pp. 269–70.

4. Quoted in D. W. Brogan, *The Development of Modern France, 1870–1939*, vol. 2 (Gloucester, Mass., 1970).

5. Philippe Bernard and Henri Dubief, *The Decline of the Third Republic, 1914–1938*, Anthony Forster, trans. (Cambridge, England, 1985), pp. 87–88; and David Robin Watson, *Georges Clemenceau: A Political Biography* (New York), pp. 380–81. On the origins of May Day, see Susanna Barrows, *Distorting Mirrors: Visions of the Crowd in Late Nineteenth Century France* (New Haven, 1981), pp. 34–35.

6. BVC, 275, Jan. 4, 1919.

7. Watson, *Clemenceau*, pp. 343, 382; *New York Times*, Feb. 20, 1919; and Elisabeth Hauser, *Paris au jour le jour: Les événements vus par la presse, 1900–1919* (Paris, 1968), pp. 715–16.

8. BN, N.A.F. 24895, May 4, 1919.

9. AMM, J II E, rue Lavoisier and rue de la Porte du Miroir, Chambre de Commerce de Mulhouse, Service documentaire, "La Cotonnerie de Mulhouse"; Dreyfus, *Histoire de l'Alsace*, p. 265; Tom Kemp, *The French Economy, 1913–1939* (New

York, 1972), p. 54; and FRB. The evolution of Raphael Dreyfus et Compagnie was typical of many large textile enterprises, but not all: "While [big firms in the post–World War I period] might, for legal convenience, assume the joint stock form, control and finance remained with the heirs of the founders" (Kemp, *French Economy*, p. 92). But the Dreyfus family lost their principal "heirs" in the war, and other possible successors (Pierre Dreyfus or Jacques' youngest sons) were either unprepared to manage the business or, more likely, unwilling to relocate to Mulhouse or Belfort.

10. Brogan, *Development*, vol. 2, p. 621.

11. DFPC, Marguerite Reinach Mercier (unpub. ms.), p. 52; and FRB. For a general view of the postwar period in Alsace, see Dreyfus, *Histoire de l'Alsace*, pp. 288ff.

12. EN, vol. 5, pp. 2294–95; FRB; and DFPC, Marguerite Reinach Mercier (unpub. ms.).

13. Philip Larkin, "MCMXIV," in *The Whitsun Weddings* (London, 1964), pp. 28–29; and Jena Marie Gaines, "The Spectrum of Alsatian Autonomism, 1918–1929" (Ph.D. dissertation, University of Virginia, 1990).

14. Clemenceau is quoted in Bernard and Dubief, *Decline*, p. 146. On the Reinach children in the 1920s, and on Mathieu's contacts with old Dreyfusards, see EN, vol. 6, p. 2774, and vol. 8, pp. 3637ff; and FRB. In 1926, Naville confirmed that Mathieu spoke often of Clemenceau, "avec qu'il est toujours en relations intimes et continues."

15. EN, vol. 6, pp. 2677ff.; and DFPC, Princess Marthe Bibesco, "Tribute to Joseph Reinach" (unpub. ms.). On Reinach's anti-Zionism during the war, see Paula Hyman, *From Dreyfus to Vichy: The Remaking of French Jewry, 1906–1939* (New York, 1979), p. 157.

16. DFPC, Bibesco "Tribute"; Hyman, *From Dreyfus to Vichy*, p. 165; Corinne Casset, "Joseph Reinach avant l'Affaire Dreyfus: Un exemple de l'assimilation politique des Juifs de France au début de la Troisième République" (unpub. dissertation, Ecole des Chartres, 1981–82); and Hélène Abrami, *La Bien-aimée* (unpub. ms., 1935), pp. 58–83 and passim.

17. EN, vol. 8, pp. 3637ff; and FRB. Though he does not explore the intriguing question of grandparents teaching grandchildren in the aftermath of 1918, Robert Wohl provides an excellent analysis of the prewar, war, and postwar generations in *The Generation of 1914* (Cambridge, Mass., 1979).

18. EN, vol. 7, p. 3057.

19. Magui Reinach's guides for war widows and disabled soldiers are in DFPC. On the Redressement Français, see Richard F. Kuisel, *Ernest Mercier: French Technocrat* (Berkeley, 1967), p. 65 and passim; and Robert Soucy, *French Fascism: The First Wave, 1924–1933* (New Haven, 1986), p. 240.

20. Kuisel, *Mercier*, p. viii.

21. Bernard and Dubief, *Decline*, pp. 94–97, 111–15; Kemp, *French Economy*, pp. 46–74 and passim; Eugen Weber, *Action Française: Royalism and Reaction in Twentieth Century France* (Stanford, 1962), p. 116 and passim; and Ron Chernow, *The House of Morgan: An American Banking Dynasty and the Rise of Modern Finance* (New York, 1990), p. 26.

22. Kuisel, *Mercier*, pp. 48, 69.

23. The introduction may have come through Maréchal Lyautey, a friend of Magui's late father-in-law and an idol of Mercier's since the publication of Lyautey's influential article on the "social role" of the French military elite. On Joseph Reinach and Lyautey, see DFPC, Princess Bibesco "Tribute." Lyautey's article, "Du rôle social de l'officier," appeared in the *Revue des deux mondes*, vol. 104, 1891, pp. 443–59. See also, Kuisel, *Mercier*, pp., 46–47.

24. *Ernest Mercier, 1878–1955: Une Grande Destinée*, n.a. (Paris, 1958), pp. 11–41; and Kuisel, *Mercier*, pp. xii–5.

25. Kuisel, *Mercier*, pp. 6–7, 46, 104, and passim.

26. Ibid., pp. 24–31. See also, Daniel Yergin, *The Prize: The Epic Quest for Oil, Money and Power* (New York, 1990), pp. 190, 197.

27. Ernest Mercier, "Réflexions sur l'élite," *Revue des deux mondes*, t. 43, 1928, p. 884; and Kuisel, *Mercier*, pp. 49, 54, 78, 119. When it came to capital and labor, Mercier shared much in common with that earlier Polytechnicien and solidarist, Alfred Dreyfus, who believed that all "humanity" has a right to "happiness," and that it is "our responsibility to give it to them." Dreyfus, again like Mercier, also worried about two "perils" facing France: socialist extremism and the fright of the propertied classes (see above, chap. XVII).

28. Kuisel, *Mercier*, p. 106.

29. Mercier, "Réflexions," p. 890.

30. Kuisel, *Mercier*, pp. 89–90.

31. Ibid., pp. 2, 14, 41, 75–78, 90, 120. For more on French Protestants during the interwar period, see Bernard and Dubief, *Decline*, p. 257; and Stuart R. Shram, *Protestantism and Politics in France* (Alençon, 1954). Mercier, like some other Protestants, would shift toward a "new conservatism [and a] nationalism in which the disillusions of the war years may have been of some significance" (Weber, *Action Française*, p. 195); but he would not, for reasons which will be discussed below, migrate as far to the right as those Protestants, few in number, who embraced Maurras's integral nationalism or the varieties of French fascism.

32. FRB; Kuisel, *Mercier*, p. 64; and Kemp, *French Economy*, pp. 5, 79–82.

33. Kuisel, *Mercier*, pp. 89–90; FRB; and Weber, *Action Française*, p. 347.

34. EN, vol. 8, pp. 3637ff. On the policies of Millerand, Briand, and other interwar leaders, see Bernard and Dubief, *Decline*, pp. 93–170. For the most detailed account of Briand's career, see G. Suarez, *Briand, sa vie, son oeuvre avec son journal et de nombreux documents inédits*, 6 vols. (Paris, 1938–52).

35. Quoted in Brogan, *Development*, vol. 2, p. 612.

36. On Louise Dreyfus Cahn's final illness, see EN, vol. 6, pp. 2773–74.

37. Ibid., vol. 8, pp. 3435–36; and Jean-Denis Bredin, *The Affair: The Case of Alfred Dreyfus*, Jeffrey Mehlman, trans. (New York, 1986), pp. 497–98. See also the obituary on Demange in the *Journal de Genève*, Feb. 16, 1925.

38. The description is Eugène Naville's (see EN, vol. 9, pp. 4220ff.).

39. On Clemenceau's death, see Watson, *Clemenceau*, p. 393. Alfred Dreyfus wrote to Clemenceau's family on Nov. 24, 1929: "Je garderai jusqu'à mon dernier jour le souvenir reconnaissant de celui qui en des jours tragiques fût le défenseur heroïque de la justice" (Musée Clemenceau, Paris).

40. BN, N.A.F. 14378, Mathieu Dreyfus, n.d. Mathieu's account of the affair abridged from his memoirs, was published posthumously under the title *L'Affaire telle que je l'ai vécue* (Paris, 1978).

41. For later critiques of the family's tactics during the Affair, see Léon Blum, *Souvenirs sur l'affaire* (Paris, 1936), and Hannah Arendt, *The Origins of Totalitarianism* (New York, 1973), pp. 89–120.

42. EN, vol. 9, p. 4165; and FRB.

43. EN, vol. 9, pp. 4330–31.

44. Ibid.; DFPC, Salomon Reinach, Oct. 23, 1930; and *L'Humanité*, Oct. 24, 1930. See also, *Journal de Genève*, Oct. 24, 1930, and *Le Temps* and *Le Figaro*, Oct. 25, 1930.

45. DFPC, Mathieu Dreyfus testament, May 9, 1924; and FRB. Family records do not specify the date of the transference of Emile Dreyfus's remains from grave number 109 at Mourmelon-le-Grand to Passy, but it occurred, as had so many similar rituals, sometime in the 1920s.

XXII REVIVALS

1. AN, F7/13951, police reports, February 1931. See also, Paul Hammond, *Marvellous Méliès* (New York, 1975), p. 42; and Norman L. Kleeblatt, ed., *The Dreyfus Affair: Art, Truth and Justice* (Berkeley, 1987), pp. 266–68.

2. APP, BA 1662, newspaper reports, April 1907. On the Rennes retrial as "theater," see above, chap. 14. For more on the intersection of entertainment and politics during the "belle époque," see Roger Shattuck, *The Banquet Years* (New York, 1968); Charles Rearick, *The Pleasures of the Belle Epoque: Entertainment and Festivity in Turn-of-the-Century France* (New Haven, 1985); and Eugen Weber, *France, Fin de Siècle* (Cambridge, Mass., 1986), pp. 159–76. In 1933, the Comédie Française production of Shakespeare's *Coriolanus* would cause an uproar—and a cut in the theater's state-controlled budget—because it touched on issues "of the most burning actuality" (see Eugen Weber, *Action Française: Royalism and Reaction in Twentieth Century France* [Stanford, 1962], pp. 313–14).

3. The "alumni of the Action Française became the backbone of the staffs of the most rabidly anti-Semitic publications of the 'thirties and 'forties" (Weber, *Action Française*, p. 201). See also, Paula Hyman, *From Dreyfus to Vichy: The Remaking of French Jewry, 1906–1939* (New York, 1979), pp. 200–202.

4. Adolf Hitler, *Mein Kampf*, Ralph Mannheim, trans. (Boston, 1971), p. 231.

5. Quoted in Tom Kemp, *The French Economy, 1913–1939: The History of a Decline* (New York), p. 99, n. 1.

6. "But, as always in a time of insecurity and fear, the state of the Action Française was getting better" (Weber, *Action Française*, p. 306; see also, pp. 219–55, 299). For more on the economic crisis of the early 1930s, see Philippe Bernard and Henri Dubief, *The Decline of the Third Republic, 1914–1938* (Cambridge, England, 1985), pp. 179–80.

7. Quoted in Weber, *Action Française*, p. 298.

8. Ibid., pp. 298–99; AN, F7/13951, police reports, Feb.–March, 1931; *Action Française*, Feb. 19–24 and March 30, *Peuple*, Feb. 24, 1931, 1931; *L' Humanité*, March 28–29, 1931; and *Figaro*, March 30, 1931. For a discussion of the theatre protest, placed in the broad context of collective violence in France, see Charles Tilly, *The Contentious French: Four Centuries of Popular Struggle* (Cambridge, Mass., 1986), pp. 321–22.

9. "Ni à droite, ni à gauche" was the movement's slogan. See Zeev Sternhell, *Ni droite ni gauche: L'Idéologie fasciste en France* (Paris, 1983); Antoine Prost, *Les Anciens Combattants et la société française* (Paris, 1977); William D. Irvine, "French Conservatives and the 'New Right' during the 1930s," *French Historical Studies*, vol. 8, 4, Fall 1974, pp. 534–63; and Weber, *Action Française*, p. 311 and passim. On Mercier's controversial support of the Croix de Feu, see below, chap. XXIII.

10. AN, F7/13951, clipping from *Figaro*, March 30, 1931.

11. The Feb. 11, 1906, ruling of the Château-Thierry tribunal (Aisne) is described in Weber, *France, Fin de siècle*, p. 124. Daudet is quoted in *Univers israélite*, Nov. 27, 1925, p. 256.

12. *The Complete Works of Montaigne*, Donald M. Frame, trans. (Stanford, 1967), p. 177. Dreyfus's comment to Victor Basch is quoted in Stephen Wilson, *Ideology and Experience: Antisemitism in France at the Time of the Dreyfus Affair* (Rutherford, 1982), p. 1. Barrès is quoted in *La Liberté*, Dec. 1, 1903, and Herzl in *CA*, p. 257.

13. DFPC, annotated scrapbook in the possession of Dreyfus's grandson, Dr. Jean-Louis Lévy. Dreyfus had made similar comments in his Devil's Island journal: "Les hommes sont vulgaires dans la proportion où ils manquent de tact" (BN, N.A.F. 24909, pp. 375ff.)

14. BVC, 275, Dreyfus to Arconati-Visconti, Oct. 15, 1918, and 1923 (n.d.); and EN, vol. 7, p. 3074, vol. 8, pp. 3764–65, and vol. 9, p. 4165.

15. BN, N.A.F. 17386 and DFPC, letters to Mathieu Dreyfus, 1898–1899.

16. Anatole France quoted in *The Nation,* Nov. 23, 1921; Pierre van Paassen, *Days of Our Years* (New York, 1939), p. 171; and EN, vol. 9, pp. 3931ff.

17. *New York Times,* July 28, 1927; and the *New York World,* Aug. 21, 1927. The few accounts of Dreyfus's involvement in the Sacco and Vanzetti case are either romanticized or hostile. For example, Johnston D. Kerkhoff, in *Traitor! Traitor! The Tragedy of Alfred Dreyfus* (New York, 1930), applauds Dreyfus's plea for justice (pp. 289–90), while van Paassen, in *Days of Our Years,* condemns the "arrogant militarist" for his indifference (pp. 171–73). Van Paassen's report is suspect; he describes visiting Dreyfus's home "on the Avenue Friedland" (Dreyfus lived on the rue Desrenaudes), and complains that the captain refused to see him at his, Dreyfus's, Deauville villa. But across three decades, the family and their servants had learned to turn away unknown, unannounced visitors, and for good reason. The *New York Times* report, on the other hand, appears reliable. See also Robert Strauss Feuerlicht, *Justice Crucified: The Story of Sacco and Vanzetti* (New York, 1977), p. 393; and G. Louis Joughin and Edmund M. Morgan, *The Legacy of Sacco and Vanzetti* (New York, 1948), p. 296.

18. Eugène Naville visited the apartment and discussed its construction costs with his friend (see EN, vol. 8, pp. 3708–19, and vol. 9, pp. 3871–72, 3961). The building, at 7, rue Desrenaudes, still stands, but unlike so many other apartments and townhouses in Paris, it has no plaque commemorating its most celebrated resident. On Madame David Hadamard's death, see *Le Temps,* April 17, 1926.

19. See above, chap. VIII.

20. BVC, 275, Dreyfus to Arconati-Visconti, 1921 (n.d.); Gerard Baal, "Un Salon Dreyfusard, des lendemains de l'affaire à la grande guerre: La Marquise Arconati-Visconti et ses amis," *Revue d'histoire moderne et contemporaine,* t. 28, July–Sept. 1981, p. 438; and Claude Laforêt, "La Marquise Arconati-Visconti et ses amis politiques," *Mercure de France,* 15, 8, 1939, pp. 64–65.

21. Guest book, 1903–1934, Naville family private collection. By 1921 the Navilles had moved from the Hauterive estate to another villa, also near Lake Geneva.

22. EN, vol. 6, pp. 2721ff.; vol. 7, pp. 2933–34; vol. 8, p. 3356; and vol. 9, pp. 4301ff.

23. Ibid., vol. 7, pp. 2933–34, 3151–52. For more on Esterhazy's death (in 1923) and on the fate of other anti-Dreyfusards and Dreyfusards, see Jean-Denis Bredin, *The Affair: The Case of Alfred Dreyfus,* Jeffrey Mehlman, trans. (New York, 1986), pp. 496–501.

24. See the interview with Pierre Dreyfus in *L'Oeuvre,* June 17, 1930.

25. Ibid.; and APP, B/A 1662, news clippings, *L'Oeuvre,* July 2, 1930. Schwarz-koppen is quoted in Michel de Lombarès, *L'Affaire Dreyfus* (Paris, 1985), p. 192. Naville learned about the notebooks through a German contact in the early 1920s, and campaigned, unsuccessfully, to have them published (see EN, vol. 7, pp. 3228–39, and vol. 9, 3911). See also *SC,* pp. 444–45.

26. Interviews with Madame Pierre Dreyfus, March 13, 1984, and Lucie Drey-fus's niece, Germaine Franck, and nephew, Robert Duteil, Dec. 1984. Alfred Dreyfus's Aug. 20, 1901, letter to Benda is quoted in Jacques Kayser, *L'Affaire Dreyfus* (Paris, 1946), p. 273.

27. BN, N.A.F. 13570, Alfred Dreyfus to Joseph Reinach, Feb. 3, 1919; BVC, 275, April 15, 1919; EN, vol. 5, pp. 2299, 2323, vol. 6, p. 2730, vol. 7, pp. 3161, 3264, and vol. 8, p. 3421; and interview with Madame Pierre Dreyfus, March 1984.

28. EN, vol. 6, p. 2497, vol. 7, p. 3300, vol. 9, pp. 4001, 4098, and vol. 10, p. 4438.

29. Ibid., vol. 5, p. 1917, and vol. 9, p. 3872; and FRB. See also above, chap. XII.

30. Information on Dreyfus and his children and grandchildren comes from: in-terviews with Dr. Jean-Louis Lévy, July 1983, Simone Perl, July 1983 and March 15, 1984, and Charles Dreyfus, June 1983; *CA,* p. 252; *SC,* p. 123; EN, vol. 9, p. 4059;

BVC, 275, July 20, 1920; and Jean Toulat, *Juifs mes frères* (Paris, 1963), p. 206. I also thank Mavis Gallant for her comments on Jeanne and Madeleine Lévy.

31. DFPC, clipping from *Le Quotidien*, Feb. 10, 1932; and interviews with Simone Perl, July 1983, and Madame Pierre Dreyfus, March 1984. On the cinemas near the Dreyfus quartier, see Bernard and Dubief, *Decline*, pp. 267–69.

32. BAI, Comité de Bienfaisance Israélite, reports, 1904–1906, and *Univers israélite*, June 4, 1926, p. 299, and June 16, 1933, pp. 291–92. Interview with Simone Perl, July 1983. See also, Toulat, *Juifs mes frères*, p. 200. On Rebecca Hadamard, see the "nécrologie" in the *Archives Israélites de France* (1843?), pp. 220–23.

33. By 1939 the Parisian Jewish population would reach two hundred thousand. Given the mass of Europeans made refugees by the wars, revolutions and pogroms of the early twentieth century, precise figures are impossible to calculate. The best recent overview is Michael R. Marrus, *The Unwanted: European Refugees in the Twentieth Century* (New York, 1985), pp. 63, 114, and passim. See also, Hyman, *From Dreyfus to Vichy*, pp. 31, 62, 68; Bernard and Dubief, *Decline*, p. 233; David H. Weinberg, *A Community on Trial: The Jews of Paris in the 1930s* (Chicago, 1977), pp. 3–4; and Jacques Adler, *The Jews of Paris and the Final Solution: Communal Response and Internal Conflicts, 1940–1944* (New York, 1987), pp. 5–6.

34. On this point, see Eugen Weber, "Reflections on the Jews in France," in Frances Malino and Bernard Wasserstein, eds., *The Jews in Modern France* (Hanover, N.H., 1985), pp. 26–27.

35. Hyman, *From Dreyfus to Vichy*, p. 134; Vicki Caron, "Loyalties in Conflict: French Jewry and the Refugee Crisis, 1933–1935," *Leo Baeck Institute Yearbook* (forthcoming); and Michael R. Marrus and Robert O. Paxton, *Vichy France and the Jews* (New York, 1981), pp. 35–37.

36. Arnold Mandel's novel, *Les Temps incertains*, is quoted in Weinberg, *Community*, p. 9, n. 21. On the Jewish quarters of the city center during an earlier period, see Nancy L. Green, *The Pletzl of Paris: Jewish Immigrant Workers in the Belle Epoque* (New York, 1986). On the Comité de Bienfaisance and Lucie Dreyfus's work with that organization, see BAI, report of the General Assembly, 1936; *L'Univers israélite*, June 16, 1933, pp. 291–92; Weinberg, *Community*, pp. 23, 38 n. 9; and interview with Simone Perl, July 1983.

37. BN, N.A.F. 24909, Dreyfus journal, p. 303.

38. "Il croyait en Dieu sans être pratiquant" (quoted in Toulat, *Juifs mes frères*, p. 207). See also the interview with the *femme de chambre* who had spent many years with Alfred and Lucie Dreyfus: "Ils n'étaient pas pratiquants; ils allaient seulement à la synagogue pour les mariages. Mais ils se montraient très respecteux de la religion. On nous facilitait l'assistance à la messe du dimanche. . . . Madame Dreyfus m'a donné comme souvenir la Bible que son mari avait à l'île du Diable" (p. 201). It is unlikely that Lucie would have given away "the Bible" that her husband had on Devil's Island; but inventories from the colonial ministry confirm that he had more than one (see above, chap. 12).

39. Salomon Reinach quoted in Hyman, *From Dreyfus to Vichy*, p. 46.

40. Théodore Reinach, *Histoire sommaire de l'Affaire Dreyfus* (Paris, 1924), pp. 235–36. See also Jay R. Berkovitz, *The Shaping of Jewish Identity in Nineteenth-Century France* (Detroit, 1989), p. 241. Dreyfus, alluding to the historical works and contemporary essays of Théodore and Salomon Reinach, had said that "la race n'a rien à voir avec le caractère; et l'on trouve des présompteux dans toutes les races" (BVC 271, Jan. 22 [1903?]).

41. *L'Univers israélite*, May 29, 1925, March 26 and June 11, 1936; and Hyman, *From Dreyfus to Vichy*, pp. 138–39.

42. Rothschild is quoted in Caron, "Loyalties," p. 9. For more on that much-publicized remark, see Weinberg, *Community*, pp. 76, 95 n. 15; and Hyman, *From Dreyfus to Vichy*, pp. 203–204, 207, 295 (see also pp. 47, 62–63, 89, 138–39, 147–49).

43. BVC, 274, Alfred Dreyfus to Arconati-Visconti, Feb. 11 (n.d.). "Mon fils a rempli Dimanche une auto avec du pain and des vêtements et a été faire une distribution à Clichy." On French Jews and the "fraternity of the trenches," see T. Reinach, *Histoire sommaire*, p. 235.

44. Madeleine Coulon, General Secretary of the Dreyfus-Gourevitch Committee, is quoted in Caron, "Loyalties," pp. 15–16 (see also, pp. 4, 18–19, 49). For more on Pierre Dreyfus's various committees—and their critics—see, Hyman, *From Dreyfus to Vichy*, pp. 221–22; *Archives israélites*, June 22, 1933; and Michel Abitol, *Les Deux Terres promises: Les Juifs de France et le sionisme, 1897–1945* (Paris, 1989), p. 162.

45. See Julien Benda, *The Treason of the Intellectuals* (*La Trahison des clercs*) Richard Aldington, trans. (New York, 1969).

46. AA, 59615, Dreyfus to the minister of war, July 7, 1930, and the minister's response, Feb. 14, 1931.

47. EN, vol. 7, pp. 2935–36, vol. 10, pp. 4597, 4705, 4784–85; SC, p. 446; and interviews with Madame Pierre Dreyfus, March 1984, Dr. Jean-Louis Lévy, Jan. 1990, and Dr. Etienne Lévy, Jan. 1990. Some accounts report that Dreyfus was operated on in Switzerland, but Eugène Naville, who would have known, confirms that he was sent to Paris for surgery (see EN, vol. 10, p. 4784).

48. BN, N.A.F. 16609, March 26, 1896.

49. SC, pp. 445–46; and interview with Pierre Dreyfus's son, Charles, June 1983. Jean-Louis Lévy describes his grandfather's final days in *CA*, pp. 252–53. Also drawing on family memoirs, Bredin presents a moving account of Dreyfus's death in *The Affair*, pp. 488–89.

50. *SC*, p. 13.

51. Quoted in ibid., p. 14.

52. AN, F7/12469, clipping from *L'Action*, April 8, 1903; and BN, N.A.F. 14310, Dreyfus journal, p. 255.

53. Charles Péguy, *Oeuvres en prose, 1909–1914* (Paris, 1961), p. 543. Clemenceau quoted in Betty Schecter, *The Dreyfus Case: A National Scandal* (Boston, 1965), p. 243. One friend from the years of the affair described how Dreyfus "comprenait à merveille que son 'affaire' dépassait sa propre personalité" (Alfred Bruneau, *A l'Ombre d'un grand coeur* [Paris, 1980], pp. 164–66).

54. Monod had shared those insights with Péguy, who was surprised to learn of a private side of Dreyfus he had never imagined (*Cahiers de la Quinzaine*, July 16, 1910). For Reinach's letter to Mathieu Dreyfus, see BN, N.A.F. 14381, Nov. 22, 1901.

55. APP, BA 1662, clipping from *L'Oeuvre*, July 13, 1935.

56. On the events of February 6, see Weber, *Action Française*, pp. 319–40; Brogan, *Development*, vol. 2, pp. 652–61; and Bernard and Dubief, *Decline*, pp. 225–28. One of the more insightful—and detailed—contemporary accounts is Janet Flanner's, in *Paris Was Yesterday, 1925–1939* (Harmondsworth, 1979), pp. 109–16.

57. APP, BA 1662, clipping from *L'Humanité*, July 13, 1935. See also Bernard and Dubief, *Decline*, pp. 296–97; and Weber, *Action Française*, p. 361.

58. Quoted in Weber, *Action Française*, p. 357. Not one to disrupt a national *fête*, Dreyfus had stayed away from the 1906 revue (see APP, BA 1045, police report, July 13, 1906).

59. On the Dreyfus funeral, see *L'Univers israélite*, July 19, 1935. Family members confirm the incident on the Place de la Concorde (interviews with Charles Dreyfus, June 1983; Simone Perl, Jan. 1990; and Germaine Franck and Robert Duteil, Dec. 1983). Dreyfus died late on Friday afternoon. The funeral service, with the Grand Rabbi officiating, could not take place on the Sabbath, and had to wait until Sunday, July 14. Dreyfus's modest flat marker in the Montparnasse cemetery carries the simple inscription "Here lies," chiseled in Hebrew letters, but, unlike the tombstones of his parents and grandparents in Mulhouse, the years of his birth and death are not those of the

Jewish calendar. The marker reads "Lieutenant Colonel Alfred Dreyfus; Officier de la Légion d'Honneur; 9 Octobre 1859–12 Juillet 1935."

XXIII GENERATIONS

1. *SC*, pp. 11–18, 222. See also Eugène Naville's comments on Pierre Dreyfus's project in EN, vol. 10, p. 4886.

2. *SC*, "Dédicace."

3. Léon Blum, *Souvenirs sur l'affaire* (Paris, 1981; first published, 1935), pp. 11, 33–34. On Blum's life and career, see Jean Lacouture, *Léon Blum*, George Holoch, trans. (New York, 1982); and Joel Colton, *Léon Blum: Humanist in Politics* (New York, 1966).

4. Blum, *Souvenirs*, pp. 57–60, 132.

5. Ibid., pp. 44, 68. See also, Paula Hyman, *From Dreyfus to Vichy: The Remaking of French Jewry* (New York, 1979), p. 227.

6. Blum, *Souvenirs*, pp. 150–53.

7. See, for example, Paul J. Kingston, *Anti-Semitism in France During the 1930s: Organisations, Personalities and Propaganda* (Hull, England, 1983), pp. 8–15, 44–46, 73.

8. On the general topic, see Michel Abitol, *Les Deux Terres promises: Les Juifs de France et le sionisme* (Paris, 1989); and Hyman, *From Dreyfus to Vichy*.

9. EN, vol. 10, pp. 4877, 4970, 5073, and passim.

10. *SC*, p. 222.

11. Hyman, *From Dreyfus to Vichy*, pp. 208, 216, 225, 231; and *L'Univers Israélite*, May 19, June 9, June 23, and Aug. 18, 1933, and July 19, 1935. See also, Vicki Caron, "Loyalties in Conflict: French Jewry and the Refugee Crisis, 1933–1935," *Leo Baeck Institute Year Book* (forthcoming), p. 13; and David H. Weinberg, *A Community on Trial: The Jews of Paris in the 1930s* (Chicago, 1977), pp. 103–47.

12. *Ordre*, Nov. 24, 1938.

13. Alain Michel, *Les Eclaireurs Israélites de France pendant la Seconde Guerre Mondiale* (Paris, 1984), pp. 17–25, 36–38; Hyman, *From Dreyfus to Vichy*, pp. 179–81, 191–8; Abitol, *Les Deux Terres*, pp. 118–23; and author's interviews with Simone Perl, July 1983 and Jan. 1990; Madame Jacques Kayser, Dec. 1983; and Yvette Baumann Farnoux, March 1984.

14. Author's correspondence regarding the RIJ with Madame Bertrand Goldschmidt, April 21, 1990. The comments on politics are in Jean-Pierre Reinach, *Du Gouffre à l'espoir: Essai social et politique* (Paris, 1938), pp. 123–26, 159.

15. Jean-Pierre Reinach, *Le Traité de Bjoerkoë, 1905: Un essai d'alliance de l'Allemagne, la Russie et la France* (Paris, 1935).

16. Reinach, *Du Gouffre à l'espoir*, pp. 123–26, 181–83. On this general subject, see Robert Wohl, *The Generation of 1914* (Cambridge, Mass., 1979), pp. 5–41, and passim.

17. See Reinach, *Du Gouffre*, pp. 123–28, 159, 201–6, and his third and last book, *Produire: Essai sur la multiplication des richesses* (Paris, 1938), pp. 47, 105–109, which he dedicated to his stepfather, Ernest Mercier, "en témoignage de respect, d'admiration, d'affection."

18. Richard F. Kuisel, *Ernest Mercier: French Technocrat* (Berkeley, Calif., 1967), pp. 102–13. For other assessments of Mercier's attraction to the right, see Robert Soucy, *French Fascism: The First Wave, 1924–1933* (New Haven, 1986), pp. 238–41; and Philippe Bernard and Henri Dubief, *The Decline of the Third Republic, 1914–1938*, Anthony Forster, trans. (Cambridge, England, 1985), pp. 290–91. See also Zeev Sternhell, *Ni droite ni gauche: L'Idéologie fasciste en France* (Paris, 1983). Mercier had fired members of the Redressement Français who had wanted to align with reactionary political parties, and he had felt the wrath of François Coty, owner not only

of a perfume company but of a leading right-wing newspaper, *Le Figaro* (Kuisel, *Mercier*, pp. 75–77).

19. Quoted in Kuisel, *Mercier*, pp. 99–100.

20. Ibid., pp. 124–25.

21. Ibid., pp. 127–35.

22. *Resurrection française, erreurs politiques et vérités humaines* (Paris, 1937). The book was published anonymously "in order to focus attention," Mercier's biographer suggests, "on the ideas rather than on the author" (see Kuisel, *Mercier*, pp. 135–39).

23. Colton, *Léon Blum*, pp. 105–12.

24. Bernard and Dubief, *Decline*, p. 310.

25. Lacouture, *Léon Blum*, p. 225; and Colton, *Léon Blum*, pp. 115–16.

26. Colton, *Léon Blum*, p. 116.

27. Eugen Weber, *Action Française: Royalism and Reaction in Twentieth Century France* (Stanford, 1962), pp. 363–64.

28. Ibid., p. 376; Colton, *Léon Blum*, pp. 125–34; and Bernard and Dubief, *Decline*, p. 323.

29. Quoted in Pierre Birnbaum, *Un Mythe politique: La "Republique Juive"* (Paris, 1988), pp. 327–28; see also, Lacouture, *Léon Blum*, p. 271.

30. Quoted in Kingston, *Antisemitism*, p. 101. See also Weber, *Action Française*, p. 374.

31. William D. Irvine, "French Conservatives and the 'New Right' During the 1930s," *French Historical Studies*, vol. 8, 4, Fall 1974, pp. 534–62; and Kingston, *Antisemitism*, pp. 15–22.

32. On this, see Birnbaum, *Un Mythe politique*, passim.

33. The royalist Pierre Gaxotte is quoted in Weber, *Action Française*, p. 411. On the economic and social problems faced by the Popular Front, see, for example, Tom Kemp, *The French Economy, 1913–1939: The History of a Decline* (New York, p. 1972), pp. 6, 112–76; Bernard and Dubief, *Decline*, p. 327; and Charles Tilly and Edward Shorter, *Strikes in France, 1830–1968* (New York, 1974).

34. Michael Wharton, *The Missing Will: An Autobiography* (London, 1984), pp. 60–61. Wharton adds the following: "A dark thought sounds like a harsh-toned bell through this trivial chronicle—what became of young Reinach when, six years later, the Germans conquered France."

35. Author's correspondence with Madame Bertrand Goldschmidt (Naomi de Rothschild), Jan. 1990.

36. Quoted in Herbert Tint, *France Since 1918* (New York, 1980), p. 71.

37. Quoted in Weber, *Action Française*, p. 425.

38. The most eloquent account of France on the eve of the Second World War is Marc Bloch's *Strange Defeat: A Statement of Evidence Written in 1940*, Gerard Hopkins, trans. (New York, 1968). Bloch, distinguished historian and co-founder of the "Annales school" in France, considered himself part of "the last of the generation of the Dreyfus Affair." He joined the Resistance during the Second World War, and, a few days short of his fifty-eighth birthday, was executed by the Gestapo (see Carol Fink, *Marc Bloch: A Life in History* [Cambridge, 1989]).

39. Reinach, *Du Gouffre à l'espoir*, pp. 181–86.

XXIV   RESISTANCE

1. Marc Bloch, *Strange Defeat: A Statement of Evidence Written in 1940*, Gerard Hopkins, trans. (New York, 1968), p. 52 (Bloch's emphasis); Eugen Weber, *Action Française: Royalism and Reaction in Twentieth Century France* (Stanford, 1962), pp. 149, 301, 422; John Campbell, ed., *The Experience of World War II* (New York, 1989),

pp. 30, 33; and Judith M. Hughes, *To the Maginot Line: The Politics of French Military Preparation in the 1920s* (Cambridge, Mass., 1971).

2. Bloch, *Strange Defeat*, pp. 37, 43.

3. Alistair Horne, *The French Army and Politics, 1870–1970* (New York, 1984), pp. 62ff; and Campbell, *Experience*, pp. 30–34.

4. Quoted in Robert O. Paxton, *Vichy France: Old Guard and New Order, 1940–1944* (New York, 1975), p. 8.

5. Ibid., p. 18; and Alfred Cobban quoted in Gordon Wright, *France in Modern Times* (New York, 1987), p. 393.

6. Horne, *French Army*, p. 65; William Serman, *Les Officiers français dans la nation, 1848–1914* (Paris, 1982), p. 104; and Philip C. F. Bankwitz, *Maxime Weygand and Civil-Military Relations in Modern France* (Cambridge, Mass., 1967), pp. 9–10 and passim.

7. Laval quoted in Joel Colton, *Léon Blum: Humanist in Politics* (New York, 1966), p. 380 (see also pp. 368–81).

8. Paxton, *Vichy*, pp. 32, 37, and passim. See also, Marc Ferro, *Pétain* (Paris, 1987), p. 132 and passim.

9. Blum is quoted in Herbert Tint, *France Since 1918* (New York, 1980), p. 95, and Maurras in Jean Lacouture, *Léon Blum*, George Holoch, trans. (New York, 1982), p. 418.

10. FRB; and Richard F. Kuisel, *Ernest Mercier: French Technocrat* (Berkeley, 1967), p. 143.

11. See the June 27, 1940, report reprinted in the *Jewish Telegraphic Agency*, June 15, 1990.

12. Charles Tilly, *The Contentious French* (Cambridge, Mass., 1986), p. 331; Michael R. Marrus, *The Unwanted: European Refugees in the Twentieth Century* (New York, 1985), pp. 200–201; Colton, *Léon Blum*, p. 354; and Doris Bensimon, *Les Grandes Rafles: Juifs en France, 1940–1944* (Toulouse, 1987), pp. 54–55. See also the eyewitness accounts of the exodus in AN, 72 AJ 46, "Combat."

13. Author's interviews with Madame Pierre Dreyfus, March 1984, and Charles Dreyfus, Jan. 1991. See also Anny Latour, *The Jewish Resistance in France, 1940–1944*, Irene R. Ilton, trans. (New York, 1981), p. 13.

14. On the street protests, see Tilly, *Contentious French*, p. 331.

15. *Le Matin*, Nov. 1, 1941.

16. Philippe Wolff, ed., *Histoire de Toulouse* (Toulouse, 1974), pp. 506–8; AN, 72 AJ 46, "Combat"; Marris, *Unwanted*, p. 201; and author's interviews with Madame Pierre Dreyfus and Simone Perl, March 1984.

17. For the family's wartime correspondence—with many letters undated—see DFPC.

18. Ibid.

19. Ibid.; and Kuisel, *Mercier*, p. 144.

20. DFPC, Nov. 15, 1940; and Michael R. Marrus and Robert O. Paxton, *Vichy France and the Jews* (New York, 1981), pp. 6–7.

21. Michel Goubet and Paul Debauges, *Histoire de la Résistance dans la Haute-Garonne* (Cahors, 1986), p. 6.

22. DFPC, notary's document, Feb. 15, 1945; Marrus and Paxton, *Vichy France and the Jews*, pp. 109–11, 334; Bensimon, *Les Grandes Rafles*, p. 59; and Jacques Adler, *The Jews of Paris and the Final Solution: Communal Response and Internal Conflicts, 1940–1944* (New York, 1987), pp. 25–26, 86, 110–11.

23. Marrus and Paxton, *Vichy France and the Jews*, pp. 3–21; and Bensimon, *Les Grandes Rafles*, pp. 57–59.

24. DFPC, June 16, 1941. A few observers were less sanguine, and one French Jew expressed his disquiet in a letter to the "savior" of Verdun. "Would you be so kind as to inform me," the lawyer Pierre Masse asked Pétain, "whether I should rip the

stripes from the sleeves of my brother, Second Lieutenant in the 36th Infantry Regiment, killed at Douaumont in April 1916; of my son-in-law, Second Lieutenant in the 14th Cavalry Regiment, killed in Belgium in May of 1940; of my nephew . . . Lieutenant in the 23rd Colonial, killed in May of 1940" (Quoted in Latour, *Jewish Resistance*, p. 19). To such accusations, Pétain and Vice Premier Laval would continue to insist that the "national revolution" aimed to purge the country of "undesirable elements" while saving French citizens from Nazi persecution.

25. DFPC, June 8 and Aug. 18, 1942 (see also undated letters from Cassis and Aix-les-Bains).

26. Author's interviews with Madame Pierre Dreyfus, March 1984, and Charles Dreyfus, Jan. 1991; Latour, *Jewish Resistance*, pp. 124–25; Adler, *The Jews of Paris*, p. 143; and Bensimon, *Les Grandes Rafles*, p. 111.

27. Marrus and Paxton, *Vichy France and the Jews*, pp. 302–07; Bensimon, *Les Grandes Rafles*, p. 82; Latour, *The Jewish Resistance*, p. 185; and Yerachmiel (Richard) Cohen, "The Jewish Community in France in the Face of Vichy-German Persecution, 1940–44," in Frances Malino and Bernard Wasserstein, eds., *The Jews in Modern France* (Hanover, 1985), p. 199.

28. Author's interviews with Charles Dreyfus, June 1983, and Madame Pierre Dreyfus, March 1984. See also Pierre Birnbaum, *Un Mythe Politique: La 'République Juive'* (Paris, 1988): "Pendant la guerre, Pierre Mendès France rencontre à l'étranger le fils du capitaine [Dreyfus] et, de suite, l'invite instamment à rejoindre les Forces libres qui combattent le régime de Vichy et ses partisans, les survivants du camp antidreyfusard" (pp. 235–36).

29. Quoted in Marrus and Paxton, *Vichy France and the Jews*, p. 298.

30. *Au Pilori*, Aug. 13, 1942; *Le Cri du Peuple*, May 18, 1942; *La France Européene*, Aug. 5, 1942; and *L'Oeuvre*, Feb. 3, 1942.

31. "Gone was the confidence of the French, the former servicemen, or the decorated soldiers" (Adler, *The Jews of Paris*, p. 150). See also, AN, 72 AJ 1837, clippings from *La France au Travail* and *Paris-Midi:* and Marrus and Paxton, *Vichy France and the Jews*, pp. 220, 256, and passim.

32. DFPC, Lucie Dreyfus, May 5, 1943; FRB; *Le Petit Parisien*, Feb. 10, 1942; *Aujourd'hui*, Jan. 21, 1943; and Marrus and Paxton, *Vichy France and the Jews*, pp. 182–87, 304. On Henri Dreyfus, see AD Vaucluse, 3 M 361, and *Le Ventoux*, Nov. 29 and Dec. 1 and 6, 1940. As a prominent assimilated Jew, Carpentras's mayor was applauded by local newspapers as an "honorable exception"; it would be "unjust" not to recognize his achievements (*Le Ventoux*, Oct. 25, 1940). After 1942, however, local praise could not save Henri Dreyfus from internment.

33. Author's interviews with Germaine Franck and Robert Duteil, Dec. 1983, Simone Perl, March 1984, and Jean-Louis Lévy, July 1983 and Jan. 1991. For more on the protection of Jews throughout France during World War II, see Marrus and Paxton, *Vichy France and the Jews*, pp. 203–6; and Philip Hallie, *Lest Innocent Blood Be Shed* (New York, 1979).

34. DFPC, Lucie Dreyfus notebook, Valence, 1943–44.

35. DFPC, Madeleine Lévy, Aug. 17 [1941–2?]; and author's interviews with Simone Perl and Yvette Baumann Farnoux (Madeleine's schoolmate at the Lycée Molière), March 1984. See also, Ania Francos, *Il était des femmes dans la Résistance* (Paris, 1978), p. 149.

36. See the description by a former teacher of Madeleine's in Paris, Anne Bairard, in DFPC, Jan. 11, 1949.

37. On the Secours National, see Marrus and Paxton, *Vichy France and the Jews*, p. 102; Bensimon, *Les Grandes Rafles*, p. 116; and Latour, *Jewish Resistance*, p. 65. For Madeleine Lévy's involvement, see DFPC, March 17, 1941 and Aug. 17 [1941–42?], and DFPC, "In Memoriam," *Bulletin de l'association des anciens élèves du lycée Molière* (n.d.), p. 127.

38. Quoted in Goubet and Debauges, *Haute-Garonne*, p. 13.

39. Ibid., 30; Adler, *The Jews of Paris*, pp. 123, 196; Bensimon, *Les Grandes Rafles*, pp. 11–19; and Marrus and Paxton, *Vichy France and the Jews*, pp. 250–69.

40. Quoted in Bensimon, *Les Grandes Rafles*, p. 107. See also, Cohen, "The Jewish Community": "Resistance and rescue activity . . . became a central force within the organized community, overcoming the differences between Eastern European Jews and native French Jews. A common purpose was reached, and nowhere was this more apparent than in the area of rescuing children" (p. 203).

41. Quoted in Goubet and Debauges, *Haute-Garonne*, p. 45.

42. DFPC, testimonies of Henriette Léon (Madame Léon Lamy), local director of the "Service Social" branch of Combat, dated June 18 and July 21, 1950. On the movement in Toulouse, see AD Haute-Garonne, Daniel Latapie, "La Résistance à Toulouse et dans la Haute-Garonne," WMS 378, p. 6 and passim; AN 72 AJ 46, "Combat"; and Goubet and Debauges, *Haute-Garonne*, pp. 41–42, 72–73 and passim.

43. Archives Latapie (private collection, Toulouse), t. 1, p. 24.

44. DFPC, "Cartes d'identité"; and author's interviews with Simone Perl, June 1984 and Jan. 1990. On the "gestapo français," see AD Haute-Garonne, WMS 378, p. 8.

45. DFPC, letter from "Nicolas," June 6, 1943. On the work of the "Service Social," see the "temoignages" in AN, 72 AJ 46, "Combat"; and Jean-Louis Cuvelliez, "Historique du Mouvement 'Combat' en Haute-Garonne, Juillet 1940–Janvier 1944," (Université de Toulouse le Mirail, maîtrise, June 1987): "Jamais le Service Social n'aurait pu fonctionner sans ces admirables femmes qui risquaient leur liberté" (p. 37). See also, Archives Latapie, t. 1, p. 56; and Margaret L. Rossiter, *Women in the Resistance* (New York, 1986).

46. Marrus, *The Unwanted*, pp. 258–65; Wolff, *Toulouse*, p. 509; Goubet and Debauges, *Haute-Garonne*, pp. 133–38; and Emilienne Eychenne, "Les Evasions en Espagne pendant la deuxième guerre mondiale dans les vallées d'Aure et de Louron," *Fédération des sociétés académiques et savantes Languedoc-Pyrénées-Gascogne*, June 1980, pp. 331–39.

47. DFPC, "In Memoriam," p. 27; Archives Latapie, t. 1, p. 121; and Cuvelliez, "Historique du Mouvement 'Combat,' " pp. 51–54.

48. Latour, *Jewish Resistance*, pp. 11, 24–39, 72–86, 103–4, 166–67, 242–45; Michel Abitol, *Les Deux Terres Promises: Les Juifs de France et le sionisme* (Paris, 1989), pp. 223–24; and author's interviews with Simone Perl, March 1984, and Jean-Louis Lévy and Etienne Lévy, Jan. 1990.

49. Latour, *Jewish Resistance*, p. 73; and Archives Latapie, t. 1, p. 242.

50. Archives Latapie, t. 1, p. 20.

51. DFPC, testimonies of Henriette Léon (Madame Léon Lamy), June 18 and July 21, 1950; and "In Memoriam," p. 27.

52. FRB. On the yellow star, see Bensimon, *Les Grandes Rafles*, p. 66.

53. DFPC, letters from Maurice Coutot, genealogist, to Madame Ernest Mercier, Sept. 9 and 26, 1941. For more on the key role played by genealogists during the war, see Karl Schleunes, *The Twisted Road to Auschwitz: Nazi Policy Toward German Jews, 1933–1939* (Chicago, 1970), p. 130. On Mercier's activities with the Red Cross, see *Ernest Mercier, 1878–1955: Une Grande Déstinée* (Paris, 1958), p. 97.

54. DFPC, Marguerite Reinach Mercier (unpub. ms.), pp. 55–64 and passim.

55. Kuisel, *Mercier*, p. 147.

56. Ibid., pp. 148–50.

57. Ibid. On "non-déportables," see Adler, *The Jews of Paris*, p. 150, and Bensimon, *Les Grandes Rafles*, p. 75. Bensimon provides examples of Parisian Jews who, like Magui Mercier, escaped deportation (see pp. 108–9).

58. Kuisel, *Mercier*, pp. 150–51.

59. DFPC, Suzanne Reinach, unpub. memoir; and FRB. On French Jews held in

Italy, see Michael R. Marrus and Robert O. Paxton, "The Nazis and the Jews in Occupied Western Europe, 1940–1944," *Journal of Modern History*, 54 (Dec. 1982), pp. 708–9; and Bensimon, *Les Grandes Rafles*, p. 81.

60. I thank Jean-Pierre Reinach's widow, Madame Bertrand Goldschmidt, for the information concerning these years. On Lisbon, see Marrus, *The Unwanted*, p. 263.

61. DFPC, signed testimony by Colonel Semidei-Servais ("Jean-Pierre Reinach était sous mes ordres"); and Archives, Secrétariat d'Etat des Anciens Combattants, Jean-Pierre Reinach, military dossier.

62. DFPC, Semidei-Servais report; DFPC, Marguerite Reinach Mercier (unpub. ms.); FRB; and author's conversation with Madame Bertrand Goldschmidt, Jan. 1990.

63. DFPC, *Le Ferro*, n.d.

64. Archives Latapie, t. 1, pp. 63, 87–91, 157, 186–210, 309–22; AD Haute-Garonne, WMS 378, p. 9; IHTP, 72 AJ 125, Haute-Garonne; *La Dépêche*, Oct. 11–13, 1943; Goubet and Debauges, *Haute-Garonne*, p. 50.

65. *La Dépêche*, Oct. 12–28 and Nov. 3–6, 1943.

66. DFPC, signed testimonies of Henriette Léon, July 21, 1950, and Juliette Lasvignes and Jean Baudot, July 18, 1950; and DFPC, "In Memoriam," p. 27. On the events of early November, see *La Dépêche*, Nov. 4, 1943; IHTP, 72 AJ 125, Haute-Garonne, reports, Nov. 1943. On Jewish families "abandoning their apartments" in Toulouse in 1943, see Marcelle Rumeau, "Les Femmes dans la Résistance Toulousaine," *Résistance R4*, 7, 1979, p. 21.

67. DFPC, "In Memoriam," p. 27; DFPC, letter from Anne Bairard, Jan. 11, 1949; and author's interviews with Simone Perl, March 1984, and Madame Jacques Kayser, Dec. 1983.

68. IHTP, 72 AJ 125, "Liste des deportés, internés et fusillés de la Haute-Garonne," Nov. 1943; Archives Latapie, "Madeleine Lévy"; DFPC, "Acte de Disparition," Ministère des Anciens Combattants et Victimes de Guerre, Aug. 26, 1947; and DFPC, testimony, Claude Lehmann, July 6, 1945.

69. Bensimon, *Les Grandes Rafles*, pp. 74–82, 108; Adler, *The Jews of Paris*, pp. 117, 198; Latour, *Jewish Resistance*, pp. 49–50; Marrus and Paxton, *Vichy France and the Jews*, pp. 252–55; Georges Wellers, *De Drancy à Auschwitz* (Paris, 1946); DFPC, letter from Paul Cerf, July 12, 1945; FRB; and author's interviews with Simone Perl and Yvette Baumann Farnoux, March 1984.

70. DFPC, Anne Bairard, Jan. 11, 1949.

71. DFPC, Claude Lehmann, July 6, 1945; Serge Klarsfeld, *Le Mémorial de la Déportation des Juifs de France* (Paris, 1978), "Convoi No. 62 en date du 20 Novembre 1943"; Archives du Centre de Documentation Juive Contemporarine, "Abtransport," Nov. 20, 1943; and Adam Rutkowski, "Les Déportations des Juifs de France vers Auschwitz-Birkenau et Sobibor," *Le Monde Juif*, 57–58, Jan.–June 1970, p. 70. On Bobigny, see IHTP 72 AJ 126, Haute-Garonne, "Temoignage," Madame Elina-Gruffy; Latour, *Jewish Resistance*, pp. 214–15; and Marrus and Paxton, *Vichy France and the Jews*, p. 294.

72. DFPC, Claude Lehmann, July 6, 1945; and Klarsfeld, *Le Mémorial*, "Convoi No. 62."

73. Klarsfeld, *Le Mémorial*, "Convoi No. 62"; and DFPC, Claude Lehmann, July 6, 1945. The first editions of Klarsfeld's work stated that 941 deportees had been "gassed immediately," but subsequent editions revised the figure to 895. The most thorough study of the deportation and selection process is Raul Hilberg, *The Destruction of the European Jews* (New York, 1961). For accounts by survivors, see, for example, Olga Wormser and Henri Michel, eds., *Tragédie de la Déportation, 1940–1945* (Paris, 1954); and Marco Nahon, *Birkenau: The Camp of Death*, Jacqueline Havaux Bowers, trans. (Tuscaloosa and London, 1989), pp. 36–39.

74. DFPC, Claude Lehmann, July 6, 1945. See also letter to author from the Auschwitz-Birkenau museum director, 1984; and below, Epilogue. One report had it

that Madeleine Lévy, holding the hands of the children she had cared for in her convoy, was gassed immediately on arrival at Auschwitz (see Francos, *Il était des femmes*, pp. 149–50). But Claude Lehmann, who had been deported with Madeleine, learned of her death from a number of sources—nurses and inmates—at Birkenau. See also, Nahon, p. 87.

EPILOGUE

1. Author's interviews with Simone Perl, March 1984 and Jan. 1991; Madame Jacques Kayser, Dec. 1983; Germaine Franck and Robert Duteil, Dec. 1983.

2. BAI, Comité de Bienfaisance, General Assembly, July 8, 1945; and author's interviews with Drs. Jean-Louis Lévy and Etienne Lévy, Jan. 1990. See also David H. Weinburg, *A Community on Trial: The Jews of Paris in the 1930s* (Chicago, 1977), p. 213.

3. *New York Times*, Dec. 29, 1946, and author's interviews with Charles Dreyfus, June 1983 and Jan. 1991; Françoise Kullmann, Jan. 1991; and Madame Pierre Dreyfus, March 1984.

4. DFPC, "In Memoriam," *Bulletin de l'association des anciens élèves du lycée Molière*, n.d., p. 27; "Acte de Disparition," Ministère des Anciens Combattants et Victimes de Guerre, Aug. 26, 1947; Claude Lehmann, July 6, 1945; letter from Paul Cerf to Dr. Lévy, July 12, 1945; and author's interviews with Simone Perl, March 1984 and Jan. 1991. In 1946, the memory of Alfred Dreyfus and his granddaughter, and of the wars in which they fought, came together in a new book on the affair by Jacques Kayser, one of the "Young Turks" of the Radical party in the 1930s, and a relative of the family through marriage. His dedication, which got only Madeleine's age wrong, read: "A la mémoire de Madeleine Lévy, petite fille d'Alfred Dreyfus qui, ayant accompli, elle aussi, comme son grand-père son devoir de patriote français, et ayant été, comme lui, martyrisée, a été assassinée à Auschwitz, en 1944, à l'age de vingt-deux ans" (Jacques Kayser, *L'Affaire Dreyfus* [Paris, 1946]).

5. Archives, Secrétariat d'Etat des Anciens Combattants, Jean-Pierre Reinach, military dossier, letter from Colonel Servais, Feb. 22, 1945.

6. DFPC, Emmanuel Amar, "Aux Combattants de la Résistance Clandestine, Morts pour la France"; Suzanne Reinach, unpub. memoir; and letter from Anthony Seys, May 19, 1945.

7. FRB; and DFPC, Suzanne Reinach; and Serge Klarsfeld, *Le Mémorial de la Déportation des Juifs de la France* (Paris, 1978).

8. Quoted in Richard F. Kuisel, *Ernest Mercier: French Technocrat* (Berkeley, Calif., 1967), p. 152 (see also pp. 153–56).

9. *Le Comtadin*, April 29, 1945; DFPC, genealogy, "Jacques Dreyfus family," April 5, 1989; and FRB. The "Group A" category is described in Jacques Adler, *The Jews of Paris and the Final Solution: Communal Response and Internal Conflict, 1940–1944* (New York, 1987), pp. 150–53. The last of Jacques and Louise Dreyfus's five sons, Paul, served as a lieutenant in the reserve and was taken prisoner by the Germans in May 1940. He was held in an officers' camp and released in April 1945.

10. DFPC, genealogy, Jacques Dreyfus family; Rachel Schil diary, 1941; and Klarsfeld, *Le Mémorial*, convoy number 35.

11. Marc Ferro, *Pétain* (Paris, 1987), 591–614; Herbert R. Lottman, *Pétain: Hero or Traitor, the Untold Story* (New York, 1985), pp. 332–55; and Robert O. Paxton, *Vichy France: Old Guard and New Order, 1940–1944* (New York, 1975), p. 329, and passim.

12. Ferro, *Pétain*, pp. 614, 621–56; and Lottman, *Pétain: Hero or Traitor*, pp. 353–63.

13. Lottman, *Pétain: Hero or Traitor*, pp. 368–81.

14. Geoffrey Warner, *Pierre Laval and the Eclipse of France* (New York, 1968),

pp. 409–16; and René de Chambrun, *Pierre Laval: Traitor or Patriot?* trans. Elly Stein (New York, 1984), pp. 133–34.

15. *Le Procès de Charles Maurras* (Paris, 1946), p. 371; Paxton, *Vichy France,* p. 243; and Eugen Weber, *Action Française: Royalism and Reaction in Twentieth Century France* (Stanford, Calif., 1962), pp. 474–75.

Bibliography

ARCHIVES, LIBRARIES, AND MUSEUMS

Archives de l'Armée, Service Historique, Vincennes
Archives Départmentales de la Haute-Garonne, Toulouse
Archives Départmentales du Haut-Rhin, Colmar
Archives Départmentales de Vaucluse, Avignon
Archives Municipales de Mulhouse
Archives Nationales, Paris
Archives de la Préfecture de Police, Paris
Archives, Secrétariat d'Etat des Anciens Combattants, Fontenay-sous-Bois
Bibliothèque de l'Alliance Israélite Universelle, Paris
Bibliothèque Historique de la Ville de Paris
Bibliothèque Municipale de Mulhouse
Bibliothèque Nationale, Paris
Bibliothèque de la Société Industrielle de Mulhouse
Bibliothèque Victor Cousin, Paris
British Museum Library, London
Centre de Documentation Juive Contemporaine, Paris
Institut d'Histoire du Temps Présent, Paris
Jewish Museum, New York
Musée de Bretagne, Rennes
Musée Clemenceau, Paris
All private collections consulted, as well as the author's interviews and correspondence, are given in the notes.

SELECTED BOOKS AND ARTICLES

PART 1: OUT OF ALSACE

Albert, Phyllis Cohen. *The Modernization of French Jewry: Consistory and Community in the Nineteenth Century.* Hanover, N.H., 1977.
Anchel, Robert. *Les Juifs en France.* Paris, 1946.
———. *Napoléon et les Juifs.* Paris, 1928.
Appell, Paul. *Souvenirs d'un Alsacien, 1858–1922.* Paris, 1923.
Berkovitz, Jay R. *The Shaping of Jewish Identity in Nineteenth-Century France.* Detroit, 1989.
Blanning, T. C. W. *The French Revolution in Germany: Occupation and Resistance in the Rhineland, 1792–1802.* Oxford, 1983.
Blumenkranz, Bernhard, ed. *Histoire des Juifs en France.* Toulouse, 1972.
Blumenkranz, Bernhard, and Albert Soboul, eds., *Les Juifs et la révolution française.* Toulouse, 1976.
Burns, Michael. "The Rural Exodus of Alsatian Jews, 1791–1848." In Jehuda Reinharz, ed., *Living with Antisemitism: Modern Jewish Responses.* Hanover, N.H., 1987.
———. "Majority Faith: Dreyfus Before the Affair." In Frances Malino and David Sorkin, eds., *From East and West: Jews in a Changing Europe, 1750–1870.* Oxford, 1990.
Cohen, David. *La Promotion des Juifs en France à l'époque du Second Empire, 1852–1870.* 2 vols. Aix-en-Provence, 1980.
Dreyfus, François-Georges. *Histoire de l'Alsace.* Paris, 1979.
Fohlen, Claude. *L'Industrie textile au temps du Second Empire.* Paris, 1956.
Furet, François. *Interpreting the French Revolution.* Translated by Elborg Forster. Cambridge, England, 1981.
Girard, Patrick. *Les Juifs de France de 1789 à 1860.* Paris, 1976.
Hertzberg, Arthur. *The French Enlightenment and the Jews.* New York, 1968.
Hobsbawm, Eric. *The Age of Capital, 1848–1875.* New York, 1975.
Howard, Michael. *The Franco-Prussian War: The German Invasion of France, 1870–1871.* London, 1981.
Laufenburger, Henry. *Cours d'économie alsacienne.* Paris, 1932.
Lefebvre, Georges. *The French Revolution.* Translated by Elizabeth Moss Evanson, John Hall Stewart, and James Friguglietti. 2 vols. New York, 1962, 1964.
———. *The Great Fear of 1789: Rural Panic in Revolutionary France.* Translated by Joan White. New York, 1973.
Leuilliot, Paul. *L'Alsace au début du XIXème siècle.* 3 vols. Paris, 1959.
Lévy, Michel. *Coup d'oeil historique sur l'état des Israélites en France, et particulièrement en Alsace.* Strasbourg, 1836.
Lévy, Paul, *Histoire linguistique d'Alsace et de Lorraine.* 2 vols. Paris, 1929.
———. *Les Noms des Israélites en France.* Paris, 1960.
L'Huillier, F. *L'Alsace en 1870–1871.* Strasbourg, 1971.
Livet, Georges, and Raymond Oberle. *Histoire de Mulhouse des origines à nos jours.* Strasbourg, 1979.
Meininger, Ernest. *Histoire de Mulhouse.* Mulhouse, 1923.
Meiss, Honel. *A Travers le dialecte Judeo-Alsacien.* Nice, [1929?].
Mendes-Flohr, Paul, and Jehuda Reinharz, eds. *The Jew in the Modern World.* New York, 1980.
Nora, Pierre, ed. *Les Lieux de mémoire.* Vol. 2. Paris, 1986.
Oberle, Raymond. *Mulhouse, ou la genèse d'une ville.* Mulhouse, 1985.
Philippe, Béatrice. *Etre Juif dans la société française du moyen-age à nos jours.* Paris, 1979.

Poliakov, Léon. *Histoire de l'antisémitisme.* Vol. 2, Paris, 1981.
Raphaël, Freddy, and Robert Weyl. *Les Juifs en Alsace: Culture, société, histoire.* Toulouse, 1977.
Schama, Simon. *Citizens: A Chronicle of the French Revolution.* New York, 1989.
Schlumberger, Jean, ed. *La Bourgeoisie alsacienne: Etudes d'histoire sociale.* Strasbourg, 1954.
Stauben, Daniel. *Scènes de la vie Juive.* Paris, 1860.
Szajkowski, Zosa. *Poverty and Social Welfare Among French Jews, 1800–1880.* New York, 1954.
Weber, Eugen. *Peasants into Frenchmen: The Modernization of Rural France, 1870–1914.* Stanford, 1976.
Weber, Max. *The Protestant Ethic and the Spirit of Capitalism.* Translated by Talcott Parsons. New York, 1958.
Weill, Georges. *L'Alsace française.* Paris, 1916.

PART 2: SENTIMENTAL EDUCATION

Anderson, R. D. *Education in France, 1848–1870.* Oxford, 1975.
Auspitz, Katherine. *The Radical Bourgeoisie: The Ligue de l'enseignement and the Origins of the Third Republic.* Cambridge, England, 1982.
Bensimon-Donath, Doris. *Socio-démographie des Juifs de France et d'Algérie, 1867–1907.* Paris, 1976.
Bruno, G. (Mme. Alfred Fouillée). *Le Tour de la France par deux enfants.* Paris, 1877; Reprint. Rennes, 1983.
Busi, Frederick. *The Pope of Antisemitism: The Career and Legacy of Edouard-Adolphe Drumont.* Lanham, Md., 1986.
Byrnes, Robert. *Antisemitism in Modern France.* New Brunswick, N.J., 1950.
Callot, Jean-Pierre. *Histoire de l'Ecole Polytechnique.* Paris, 1958.
Caron, Vicki. *Between France and Germany: The Jews of Alsace-Lorraine, 1871–1918.* Stanford, Calif., 1988.
———. "Patriotism or Profit?: The Emigration of Alsace-Lorraine Jews to France, 1871–1872," *Leo Baeck Institute Yearbook* 28 (1983), pp. 139–68.
Caron, Vicki, and Paula Hyman. "The Failed Alliance: Jewish-Catholic Relations in Alsace-Lorraine, 1871–1914," *Leo Baeck Institute Yearbook* 26 (1981), pp. 3–21.
Drumont, Edouard. *La France Juive.* 2 vols. Paris, 1886.
———. *La France Juive devant l'opinion.* Paris, 1886.
Gerbod, Paul. *La Vie quotidienne dans les lycées et collèges au XIXème siècle.* Paris, 1968.
Mitchell, Allen. *The German Influence in France after 1870: The Formation of the French Republic.* Chapel Hill, N.C., 1979.
———. *Victors and Vanquished: The German Influence on Army and Church in France after 1870.* Chapel Hill, N.C., 1984.
Ponteil, Felix. *Histoire de l'enseignement en France: Les Grandes étapes, 1789–1964.* Paris, 1966.
Prost, Antoine. *Histoire de l'enseignement en France, 1800–1967.* Paris, 1968.
Ringer, Fritz. *Education and Society in Modern Europe.* Bloomington, Ind., 1979.
Ralston, David. *The Army of the Republic: The Place of the Military in the Political Evolution of France, 1871–1914.* Cambridge, Mass., 1967.
Seager, Frederic. "The Alsace-Lorraine Question in France, 1871–1914." In Charles K. Warner, ed., *From the Ancien Regime to the Popular Front.* New York, 1969.
Serman, William. *Les Officiers français dans la nation, 1848–1914.* Paris, 1982.
Shinn, Terry. *Ecole Polytechnique, 1871–1914.* Paris, 1980.

Silverman, Dan P. *Reluctant Union: Alsace-Lorraine and Imperial Germany, 1871–1918.* University Park, Pa., 1972.

Sorlin, Pierre. *"La Croix" et les Juifs.* Paris, 1967.

Villemar, H. (Hélène Naville). *Dreyfus intime.* Paris, 1898.

Weber, Eugen. *France, Fin-de-Siècle.* Cambridge, Mass., 1986.

Weill, Julien. *Zadoc Kahn, 1839–1905.* Paris, 1912.

Winock, Michel. *Edouard Drumont et Cie: Antisémitisme et fascisme en France.* Paris, 1982.

Zeldin, Theodore. *France: 1848–1945.* 2 vols. Oxford, 1973, 1977.

PART 3: THE AFFAIR

Arendt, Hannah. *The Origins of Totalitarianism.* New York, 1973.

Baal, Gérard. "Un Salon dreyfusard, des lendemains de l'affaire à la Grande Guerre: La Marquise Arconati-Visconti et ses amis," *Revue d'histoire moderne et contemporaine* 28 (1981), pp. 433–63.

Bernard, Jean. *Le Procès de Rennes, 1899: Impressions d'un spectateur.* Paris, 1900.

Bredin, Jean-Denis. *L'Affaire.* Paris, 1983. (*The Affair: The Case of Alfred Dreyfus.* Translated by Jeffrey Mehlman. New York, 1986.)

Boussel, Patrice. *L'Affaire Dreyfus et la presse.* Paris, 1960.

Bruneau, Alfred. *A l'Ombre d'un grand coeur.* Paris, 1980.

Burns, Michael. *Rural Society and French Politics: Boulangism and the Dreyfus Affair.* Princeton, N.J., 1984.

Chapman, Guy. *The Dreyfus Case: A Reassessment.* London, 1955.

Charpentier, Armand. *Les Côtés mystérieux de l'affaire Dreyfus.* Paris, 1936.

Dreyfus, Alfred. *Cinq années de ma vie.* Paris, 1901; reprint, Paris, 1982.

———. *Lettres d'un innocent.* Paris, 1898.

———. *Souvenirs et correspondance, publiés par son fils.* Paris, 1936.

Dreyfus, Mathieu. *L'Affaire telle que je l'ai vecue.* Paris, 1978.

Feldman, Egal. *The Dreyfus Affair and the American Conscience, 1895–1906.* Detroit, 1981.

France, Jean. *Autour de l'affaire Dreyfus: Souvenirs de la Sûreté Générale.* Paris, 1936.

Garros, Louis. *Alfred Dreyfus: "L'Affaire."* Paris, 1970.

Gauthier, Robert. "Les Alsaciens et l'affaire Dreyfus," *Saisons d'Alsace* 17, 1966.

———. *"Dreyfusards!": Souvenirs de Mathieu Dreyfus et autres inédits.* Paris, 1965.

Goldberg, Harvey. *The Life of Jean Jaurès.* Madison, Wis., 1962.

Grand-Carteret, John. *L'Affaire Dreyfus et l'image.* Paris, 1898.

Green, Nancy L. *The Pletzl of Paris: Jewish Immigrant Workers in the Belle Epoque.* New York, 1986.

Jaurès, Jean. *Les Preuves: L'Affaire Dreyfus.* Paris, 1898; 1981.

Johnson, Douglas. *France and the Dreyfus Affair.* London, 1966.

Kayser, Jacques. *L'Affaire Dreyfus.* Paris, 1946.

Kleeblatt, Norman L., ed. *The Dreyfus Affair: Art, Truth and Justice.* Berkeley, Calif., 1987.

Labori, Marguerite-Fernand. *Labori: Ses notes, sa vie.* Paris, 1947.

Lazare, Bernard. *Une Erreur judiciaire: La Verité sur l'affaire Dreyfus.* Brussels, 1896.

Lipschutz, Leon. *Une Bibliographie dreyfusienne: Essai de bibliographie thématique et analytique de l'Affaire Dreyfus.* Paris, 1970.

Lombarès, Michel de. *L'Affaire Dreyfus: La Clef du mystère.* Paris, 1972.

Marrus, Michael R. *The Politics of Assimilation: The Jewish Community in France at the Time of the Dreyfus Affair.* Oxford, 1980.

Martin, Benjamin I. *Crime and Criminal Justice under the Third Republic: The Shame of Marianne.* Baton Rouge, 1990.

Menier, Marie-Antoinette. "La Détention du Capitaine Dreyfus à l'île du Diable, d'après les archives de l'administration pénitentiaire," *Revue française d'histoire d'Outre-Mer* 44 (1977).

Paléologue, Maurice. *An Intimate Journal of the Dreyfus Case.* Translated by Eric Mosbacher. New York, 1957.

Péguy, Charles. *Notre Jeunesse.* Paris, 1913.

Quillard, Pierre. *Le Monument Henry: Listes des souscripteurs classés méthodiquement et selon l'ordre alphabétique.* Paris, 1899.

Rebérioux, Madeleine. *La République radicale?: 1898–1914.* Paris, 1975.

Reinach, Joseph. *Histoire de l'Affaire Dreyfus.* 7 vols. Paris, 1901–11.

Reinach, Theodore. *Histoire sommaire de l'Affaire Dreyfus.* Paris, 1924.

Révision du procès de Rennes: Débats de la Cour de Cassation. Paris, 1904.

Scheurer-Kestner, Auguste. *Mémoires d'un sénateur dreyfusard.* Strasbourg, 1988.

Sorel, Georges. *La Révolution dreyfusienne.* Paris, 1909.

Sternhell, Zeev. *La Droite révolutionnaire, 1885–1914: Les Origines françaises du fascisme.* Paris, 1978.

Stock, P. V. *Memorandum d'un éditeur: L'Affaire Dreyfus anecdotique.* Paris, 1938.

Thomas, Marcel. *L'Affaire sans Dreyfus.* Paris, 1961.

————. *Esterhazy, ou l'envers de l'affaire Dreyfus.* Paris, 1989.

Weber, Eugen. *Action Française: Royalism and Reaction in Twentieth-Century France.* Stanford, Calif., 1962.

Weil, Bruno. *L'Affaire Dreyfus.* Paris, 1930.

Wilson, Nelly. *Bernard Lazare: Antisemitism and the Problem of Jewish Identity in Late Nineteenth Century France.* Cambridge, England, 1978.

Wilson, Stephen. *Ideology and Experience: Antisemitism in France at the Time of the Dreyfus Affair.* Rutherford, N.J., 1982.

Zola, Emile. *L'Affaire Dreyfus: La Verité en marche.* Paris, 1901. Reprint. Paris, 1969.

PART 4: THE THIRTY YEARS' WAR

Abitol, Michel. *Les Deux Terres promises: Les Juifs de France et le sionisme, 1897–1945.* Paris, 1989.

Adler, Jacques. *The Jews of Paris and the Final Solution: Communal Response and Internal Conflicts, 1940–1944.* New York, 1987.

Barrès, Maurice. *Scènes et doctrines du nationalisme.* 2 vols. Paris, 1925.

Benda, Julien. *The Treason of the Intellectuals (La Trahison des clercs).* Translated by Richard Aldington. New York, 1969.

Bensimon, Doris. *Les Grandes Rafles: Juifs en France, 1940–1944.* Toulouse, 1987.

Birnbaum, Pierre. *Un Mythe politique: La "République Juive": De Léon Blum à Pierre Mendès France.* Paris, 1988.

Bloch, Marc. *Strange Defeat: A Statement of Evidence Written in 1940,* trans. Gerard Hopkins. New York, 1968.

Blum, Léon. *Souvenirs sur l'affaire.* Paris, 1935; 1981.

Campbell, John, ed. *The Experience of World War II.* New York, 1989.

Clemenceau, Georges. *Grandeurs et misères d'une victoire.* Paris, 1930.

Colton, Joel. *Léon Blum: Humanist in Politics.* New York, 1966.

Duroselle, Jean-Baptiste. *Clemenceau.* Paris, 1988.

Ferro, Marc. *The Great War, 1914–1918.* Translated by Nicole Stone. London, 1973.

Fink, Carol. *Marc Bloch: A Life in History.* Cambridge, England, 1989.

Goubet, Michel, and Paul Debauges. *Histoire de la Résistance dans la Haute-Garonne.* Cahors, France, 1986.

Hilberg, Raul. *The Destruction of the European Jews.* 3 vols. New York, 1985.

Horne, Alistair. *The French Army and Politics, 1870–1970.* New York, 1984.

———. *The Price of Glory: Verdun, 1916.* New York, 1963.
Hyman, Paula. *From Dreyfus to Vichy: The Remaking of French Jewry, 1906–1939.* New York, 1979.
Joll, James. *The Origins of the First World War.* London, 1984.
Kemp, Tom. *The French Economy, 1913–1939: The History of a Decline.* New York, 1972.
Kennan, George F. *The Fateful Alliance: France, Russia, and the Coming of the First World War.* New York, 1984.
Klarsfeld, Serge. *Le Mémorial de la déportation des Juifs de France.* Paris, 1978.
———. *Vichy-Auschwitz: Le Rôle de Vichy dans la solution finale de la question Juive en France, 1942.* Paris, 1983.
Kuisel, Richard F. *Ernest Mercier: French Technocrat.* Berkeley, Calif., 1967.
Lacouture, Jean. *Léon Blum.* Paris, 1977.
Latour, Anny. *The Jewish Resistance in France, 1940–1944.* Translated by Irene R. Ilton. New York, 1981.
Marrus, Michael R. *The Holocaust in History.* Hanover, N.H., 1987.
———. *The Unwanted: European Refugees in the Twentieth Century.* New York, 1985.
Marrus, Michael R., and Robert O. Paxton. *Vichy France and the Jews.* New York, 1981.
Miquel, Pierre. *La Grande Guerre.* Paris, 1983.
Noguères, Henri. *Histoire de la Résistance en France, de 1940 à 1945.* 5 vols. Paris, 1967–1981.
Paxton, Robert O. *Vichy France: Old Guard and New Order, 1940–1944.* New York, 1975.
Prost, Antoine. *Les Anciens Combattants et la société française.* Paris, 1977.
Sternhell, Zeev. *Ni Droite ni gauche: L'Idéologie fasciste en France.* Paris, 1983.
Watson, David Robin. *Clemenceau: A Political Biography.* New York, 1974.
Weber, Eugen. *The Nationalist Revival in France, 1905–1914.* Berkeley, Calif., 1959.
———. *Varieties of Fascism: Doctrines of Revolution in the Twentieth Century.* New York, 1964.
Weinberg, David H. *A Community on Trial: The Jews of Paris in the 1930s.* Chicago, 1977.
Wellers, Georges. *De Drancy à Auschwitz.* Paris, 1946.
Winter, J. M. *The Experience of World War I.* London, 1988.
Wohl, Robert. *The Generation of 1914.* Cambridge, Mass., 1979.

Index

The following abbreviations are used in this index: AD for Alfred Dreyfus; MD for Mathieu Dreyfus.

567

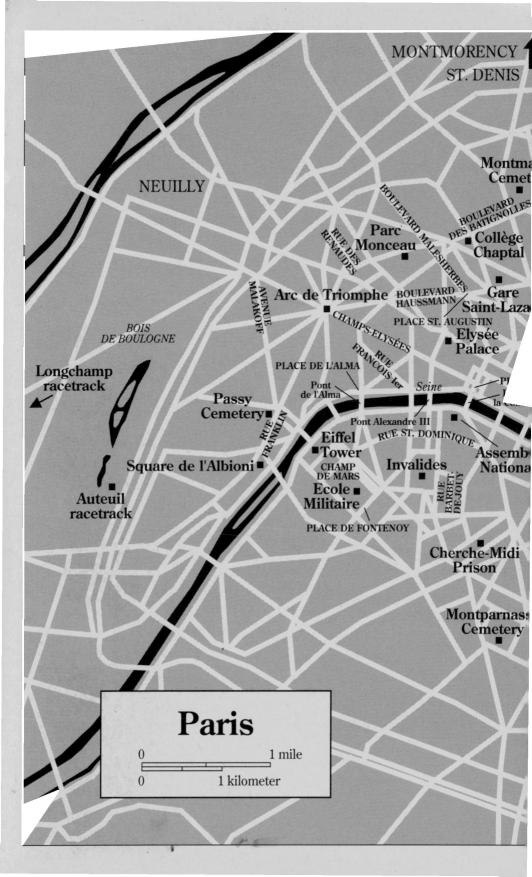